A Good Southerner

The Fred W. Morrison
Series in Southern Studies

A Good Southerner

The Life of Henry A. Wise of Virginia

by Craig M. Simpson

The University of North Carolina Press
Chapel Hill and London

Manufactured in the United States of America

Library of Congress Cataloging in Publication Data

Simpson, Craig, 1942–
A good southerner.

(The Fred W. Morrison series in Southern studies)
Bibliography: p.
Includes index.
1. Wise, Henry A. (Henry Alexander), 1806–1876.
2. Legislators—United States—Biography. 3. United States. Congress. House—Biography. 4. Virginia—Governors—Biography. 5. Diplomats—United States—Biography. 6. United States—Politics and government—1815–1861. 7. Virginia—Politics and government—1775–1865. I. Title. II. Series.
E415.9.W8S57 1985 328.73′092′4 [B] 84-7384
ISBN 0-8078-1623-X

Designed by Patrick G. O'Sullivan

For my father, Robert Gordon Simpson, and
my mother, Virginia L. Simpson

Contents

Illustrations

Maps

Preface

I call Wise a good Southerner because he would have wanted it that way. He took pride in efforts to sustain the best traditions of Southern masterhood while acknowledging the influence of world opinion and respecting the powerful forces opposed to the South. He never stood with those in his state or region who counseled resistance to change. Indeed, he embraced to some extent the ethic of his eventual enemies on the battlefield. Systematic, industrious, and always with an eye to the main chance, he believed that he might defeat the Yankees at their own game. He regarded himself as flexible, resilient, and well-informed. The dull men around him inspired only his contempt, which of course they cordially reciprocated. Reversing Virginia's decline from her Revolutionary glory created challenges enough to fill a lifetime. Innovation and modernization—whether in the form of improved education, political rights for the white masses, or internal improvements on a grand scale—would allow his troubled state to ride out the storm. If enough could change while enough remained the same, Virginia might even reclaim her entitlement. The Wises, more prescient than most, would thus stand ever deserving of their state's and the Union's honors.

Wise's vision allowed him to project a sense of hopefulness and energy that focused popular aspirations. Although many found him incomprehensible and bewildering, and others despised his arrogance, most accorded him a grudging respect—if for no other reason than that his presence automatically jacked up the emotional ante. He never bored anyone. Disgusting and loathsome some felt he was—as they inspected his shabby clothes, grew more than vaguely uncomfortable at having their conversations dominated, stood clear of his spewing tobacco juice, and tried to overcome their embarrassment at his foul language. Fascinating and incredible, others exclaimed. Perhaps only Virginia could have produced such a paradoxical man. His later portraits suggest a man of no half measures. Thin and intense, hard-eyed and coiled, he seems ready to assault anyone who might dare to stand before him and utter a trifling remark or suffer such a thought to pass.

Wise's politics looked to the transcending of many of the choices he finally made. Deflected from his hopes by national crises, he gave ground bitterly. He wavered and vacillated under the pressure of attempting to hold together fragmenting loyalties. Moreover, he read of his own contributions to the crisis. Here, many claimed, was a master Southern ideologue—a dueling slave driver for whom violence was always an option. Or was he, as many Southerners believed, an opportunist totally devoid of principle, ever ready to sell out his state and region? Attempting to straddle the diverse interests of several constituencies, he became his own political machine, constantly turning out letters, addresses, and occasional tracts. Trusting few, he longed to operate independently on the electorate. He best obtained this lonely rapport in the oratory that made him famous. Speechmaking also permitted him to mask or dissolve his uncertainties.

Among the many paradoxes he found difficult to resolve was the impossibility, in his view, of behaving like a decent man while succeeding at politics. Good Southerners and good men were allegedly possessed of both vision and conscience. Honor had palpable meaning. So did Christian duty. Even the slaves deserved kindness and justice. But what Wise wanted to believe of himself reflected the fantasy and romance of what should have been. The retreat from some of his best intuitions, the lies, deceptions, and silences, the hunger for recognition and assurance, left a series of spiritual abrasions that manifested themselves in anger, frustration, and fury. Like his state and his region, Wise was more troubled than some historians have recognized. His fabled eccentricities of conduct and policy resulted from constant effort to harmonize and integrate objectives increasingly at variance with one another and to live in accord with different ethics that also clashed.

From the early 1830s until his death in 1876, no Virginian other than Robert E. Lee lived a more important public life. As a congressman from 1833 until 1844, Wise broke fatefully with Andrew Jackson and lent powerful support to the emerging Whig opposition. He also acquired considerable notoriety as a result of his idiosyncratic contributions to Southern extremism during the "gag rule" debates. Eventually he joined the so-called Virginia Cabal, that small group of Whigs who bolted the party to support President John Tyler in the early 1840s. After an acrimonious tour as United States minister to Brazil in the mid-1840s, he returned to dominate Virginia's Constitutional Convention of 1851. He won election as governor in 1855 and thus encountered John Brown at Harpers Ferry. Ambitious to redeem the nation as a presidential candidate in 1860, Wise thereafter led Virginia out of the Union in April 1861. He served four years as a Confederate brigadier and was never again able to assert his customary political influence, although friends and enemies alike persisted in thinking him too dangerous to discount.

The traditional tests of biographical relevance—representativeness and significance—imply both a focus on externalities and on a subject's achievements. I want to meet those criteria, but in such a way that I show Wise's feelings and attitudes resonating with his environment. Complex as he was, he could never be explained by a facile approach. I wish to follow a mode that seeks to integrate what we can know of his private and intimate life with his public action. How this integration took place at various times illuminates Wise's motives. Certain predispositions from childhood, for example, along with his upbringing and his need for assurance influenced his career. Similarly, Wise's posturing, scheming, and above all his falsehoods and self-deception offer a commentary on his character. Few public figures have published more and longer vindications of their own conduct. It is thus difficult for me to place any more credence in a concept of Political Man than most sensible people place in a concept of Economic Man.

Much of Wise's eccentricity stemmed from ambivalence about authority, slaveholding, the fate of Virginia, and the value of the Union. In somewhat exaggerated form, I suspect that his attitudes reflected those of most Virginians. That Wise was repeatedly elected to office and never suffered defeat at the polls suggests that in some measure he represented the attitudes and aspirations of his countrymen. I think that Wise was unsure, particularly in early manhood, about the morality of owning slaves. He was decidedly uncertain in later life about the propriety of secession. Ambivalence not only channels the decisions that people make, it regularly prevents them from making decisions and can inhibit and paralyze them altogether, placing their fates ultimately in other hands. Wise frequently made a show of doing nothing. This is one of the reasons why many regarded him as an eccentric mediocrity, unable ultimately to claim the entitlement that he believed Virginia's representative man deserved.

In going beyond representativeness to meet the test of significance, I wish to show that Wise made a difference. Certainties are also forbidden to us here, for no one can confidently predict what would have occurred without him; but the probabilities are great that the world would have been different. It would certainly have been far duller. I read the historical record as affirming the power and decisiveness of individuals.

My dissent from the formalism of traditional biography is thus a respectful one. So are my reservations about the prevailing myths and methods of the social sciences which emphasize rationality and structure, typically dismissing such subjects as paradox and ambivalence. One once took an equivalency between biography and history for granted, but no longer. The popularity of the more rigorous methods of the social sciences, and the skill of their practitioners in manipulating aggregate data with apparent success, has undermined the confidence scholars once had in the ability of individual actors to influence history. I wish to defend both the connection between biography and history and the power of individual agents, but I also want to acknowledge the commendable efforts of many systematically oriented scholars who have called on historians to present their findings more rigorously and to state their biases more directly—precisely as I am doing here. In accord with much modern historical writing, as David Hackett Fischer judges it, my work is cast in the form of a "braided narrative."[1] I want to render both a life and an argument—indeed, a series of arguments. Implicit upon me, then, is the responsibility to discriminate among other explanations of the phenomena I have encountered. Such care is particularly important in the chapter on Harpers Ferry—arguably the most renowned public affair in which Wise acted. In order to make history more cumulative, as Lee Benson and others have advocated, I have tried to mark out what is new in my findings with regard to the personalities whom Wise encountered, such as John Brown, as well as the important events, decisions, and movements in which he participated.

In the last eighty years, two other men have tried to comprehend Wise. From each I have learned much. Wise's grandson, Barton H. Wise, published an admirable biography in 1899. The distinguished historian of the South, Clement Eaton, published three articles between 1935 and 1942 on aspects of Wise's career in the 1850s. Because he evinced a critical attitude, Barton Wise's book is a model nineteenth-century biography. It is no mere "life and letters." Barton knew about Henry's uncertainties and forthrightly portrayed him as the eccentric character that he was. He had special concerns, of course, such as his preoccupations with the Civil War and with providing explanations for Henry's checkered military career. Barton also made assiduous but not especially successful efforts to collect his grandfather's papers, which had been dispersed during the war. Eaton had access to far more material and appreciated how Wise, in his own way, attempted to mediate between conservative national politicians dedicated to preserving the Union and Southern extremists anxious to destroy it. Perhaps Eaton never attempted a biography because he found it impossible to reconcile the twin themes of liberalism and fire-eating defiance of Yankee aggression that dominate his writing on Wise.

A major problem for both these scholars was the dispersal of Wise's papers. After seizing Norfolk early in 1862, federal troops raided Wise's nearby farm and ransacked his library. Most of his letters and correspondence ended up in Boston, where according to family tradition they were inspected to detect the identities of any Northerners expressing sympathies for the South or passing on intelligence to Wise.[2] Following the war, the noted bibliophile and collector Benjamin Perley Poore acquired control of much Wise material. Most of Poore's holdings were auctioned in 1888. After that, Wise's papers circulated among private collectors, gradually found their way into repositories across the country, and returned in driblets to the Wises in Virginia.

By the early 1970s, the late John Sergeant Wise of Charlottesville, great-grandson of my subject, had accumulated a sizable collection of letters, books, pamphlets, and photographs relating to all the Wises. Most of this material is now in the Virginia Historical Society in Richmond. John Sergeant Wise was unfailingly generous to me. He permitted unrestricted access to his entire collection. He and Mrs. Wise drove me across the state to the farm on the Eastern Shore where Henry had grown up. Their son, E. Tayloe Wise, maintains the family's tradition of unerring courtesy and hospitality.

Acknowledgments

Of the many obligations I have incurred over the years, none are now more cheerfully acknowledged than to the five men who taught me: Frank O'Malley and Marshall Smelser at Notre Dame, both now deceased, the late David M. Potter, and Don E. Fehrenbacher and Carl N. Degler at Stanford. I would also like to recognize special debts to Mr. and Mrs. Gordon Wright and to Barton J. Bernstein of Stanford University. William W. Freehling of The Johns Hopkins University has been a constant source of encouragement and inspiration over the years. I have profited much from the support and counsel of Eugene D. Genovese of the University of Rochester, Bertram Wyatt-Brown of the University of Florida, and Michael F. Holt of the University of Virginia. At crucial moments I received important aid from Whitman Ridgway of the University of Maryland, Willie Lee Rose of The Johns Hopkins University, Wythe Holt of the University of Alabama Law School, Thomas Belser of Auburn University, John O'Brien of Dalhousie University, Nettie Lee Benson of the University of Texas, John Craig of the University of Chicago, Stanley Engerman of the University of Rochester, Tom Dillard of Little Rock, Arkansas, and Curtis Carroll Davis of Baltimore.

I also wish to express my deep appreciation to the staffs of the following libraries and archives, in particular: National Archives, Washington, D.C. (especially Michael P. Musick of the Military Archives Division); Manuscripts Division, Library of Congress, Washington, D.C. (especially Chuck Cooney, a former employee); Virginia Historical Society, Richmond (especially John M. Jennings, Howson W. Cole, Waverly K. Winfree, Virginius C. Hall, Jr., and the late James A. Fleming—and most especially to a loyal friend and counselor, the late William M. E. Rachal); Virginia State Library, Richmond (especially William G. Ray, Paul I. Chestnut, and a dear friend, Gwynne Tayloe); Alderman Library, University of Virginia, Charlottesville; Southern Historical Collection, Wilson Library, University of North Carolina at Chapel Hill (especially Carolyn Wallace and a dear friend and former employee, Ellen Garrison); the William R. Perkins Library, Duke University, Durham, North Carolina (especially Mattie Russell); the D. B. Weldon Library, University of Western Ontario, London, Canada (especially George Robinson, Jerry

Mulcahy, and Walter Zimmerman). I also thank Brig. Gen. John Letcher (USMC, Ret.) of Lexington, Virginia, and Lucas Phillips of Leesburg, Virginia, who permitted access to privately held manuscript collections. Finally, I would like to express my fond regard for the dedication and skill of the Interlibrary Loan Department of the D. B. Weldon Library, University of Western Ontario.

My colleagues, current and former, at the University of Western Ontario must also join this litany. I thank David H. Flaherty, Richard S. Alcorn, A.M.J. Hyatt, Carl Swanson, Jean Matthews, George Emery, José Igartua, Fred Armstrong, George Metcalf, I. K. Steele, Thomas N. Guinsburg, Lewis R. Fischer, Robert A. Hohner, Jim Freedman, and Antonio Santosuosso. I also acknowledge my friend Richard P. Fuke of Wilfrid Laurier University. And I owe a special debt of gratitude to Jack Snead Blocker, Jr., and Gary L. Owens of Huron College, London, Ontario.

It is also most important that I acknowledge the advice and support of the remarkable men and women who, over the years, have taken History 344 at the University of Western Ontario. I hope that my students will find in this work some effort to resolve the questions we grappled with. If they are satisfied, it will be my greatest tribute to them.

At one important point, the Canada Council provided me with a grant for travel and research, which I now gratefully acknowledge. I also recognize the important financial assistance I have received from the Faculty of Social Science and the J. B. Smallman Memorial Fund, University of Western Ontario.

Ruth Lemon, Chris Speed, Jeanette Berry, and Rita Mabbs typed portions of the manuscript. Fay Stirling typed the final version with unyielding courtesy, skill, and dedication. Trudie Calvert's copyediting enhanced the manuscript's quality. Chris Dennis prepared the index.

My friend Peggy, a woman with a life of her own, was my final inspiration. She and our children, Annie and Nora, have over the years enhanced my interest in men and women in the nineteenth century. Such insights as I have gained took time to acquire, seldom came without cost, and seem in the end terribly fragile.

This book has been published with the help of a grant from the Social Science Federation of Canada using funds provided by the Social Sciences and Humanities Research Council of Canada.

London, Ontario
Fall 1984

A Good Southerner

Chapter 1
The Character and Politics of a Young Virginian

The time and place of Henry Alexander Wise's birth are reminders that people lived in Virginia long before the United States had a history. When young Henry arrived in 1806, the American republic was younger than one person's lifetime, but the Wises had already lived for nearly two centuries in Accomac County on Virginia's Eastern Shore. An isolated and clannish community, across Chesapeake Bay from the Virginia mainland, Accomac occupied the narrow peninsula between the bay and the Atlantic Ocean. Though the land was too flat to be picturesque, the soil was rich and well watered by small creeks that often formed the boundaries between the estates that developed there. The squires planted trees near the creek beds, and these in time enclosed their property and afforded them considerable privacy, while further limiting their already circumscribed vision. Like many of his countrymen, Henry A. Wise deeply loved his birthplace. He regularly recouped his energies near it and, in a sense, never lost the special perspective on national affairs—with all its strengths and weaknesses—that the highly insular and unchanging Eastern Shore furnished him.[1]

Of Wise's immediate ancestors, relatively little is known. His father, Major John Wise, held a commission in the Virginia militia following the American Revolution. He later served ten terms in the Virginia House of Delegates, from 1790 to 1800, and acted as Federalist elector in the presidential campaign of 1800.[2] After retiring from politics, Major Wise served briefly as Commonwealth attorney and then held the clerkship of the county court until his death in 1812. His numerous farms made him one of the wealthiest men in Accomac. He married twice and sired ten children, though only five reached maturity.

In his later correspondence, Wise seldom mentioned his father or mother. His mother died in 1813, making orphans of Henry, his brothers, and a sister. But if no clear physical memory of his parents persisted, or if Wise chose to say little about his recollections, this did not mean that he lacked impressions and feelings about them. One can speculate on how these memories might have influenced his attitudes and behavior as an adult. The few statements he made about his parents, such as those in a long letter written to James Hambleton in 1855, were usually warm and positive. Unquestionably, Wise suffered deeply because of his loss.

He seems to have regarded his father as a strong personality, a leader, and a man worth emulating—except politically. Though "pure and patriotic," Wise asserted many years later, his father was not a man for "popular sovereignty." Instead he "preached the doctrine . . . that *the people were not to be trusted with their own power.*" This legacy, along with at least one other, Wise lived to transcend. "I never heard of a whisper against his name," Wise wrote in 1855. "He was a major of the militia and had he lived would, I have no doubt, have supported the measures of the war [of 1812]."[3] Then he went on to clarify the context of that statement. In 1799 Thomas Jefferson had accused Major Wise of harboring Tory sympathies during the Revolution and thus raised suspicions about his trustworthiness and patriotism. The major's family, perhaps including Henry, felt that charge's sting ever afterward. Actually, when Major Wise challenged Jefferson to substantiate his charge, the great Virginian graciously backed down and all but admitted that he had confused Wise's Federalist politics with Revolutionary Toryism.[4]

Toryism never tarnished the major—or did it? Although he was enrolled in the Accomac militia, his birth date in the early 1760s may have prevented him from serving actively in the Revolution. If this were so, however, it would seem difficult to explain how a Revolutionary pension claim, processed in 1832, affirms that he enlisted in the Ninth Virginia Regiment and served more than three years in the North. The claim was rejected. Major Wise came from one of the few counties in Virginia where Toryism flourished. Jennings Cropper Wise, who completed the family genealogy in 1917, defends his ancestor's patriotism at length. He asks, reasonably enough, how the major could have acquired so much prestige after the Revolution if there had been the slightest hint of disloyalty in his past. Cropper Wise is probably right, but his defensiveness and use of circumstantial evidence suggest that though the issue was important, he could not precisely specify Major Wise's Revolutionary loyalties.[5] Ironically, similar uncertainties about Henry's allegiances dogged him perennially as enemies flailed him repeatedly with charges of disloyalty and treason—a bitter though unintended legacy from his father. But other, more tangible legacies were to have a greater influence on Henry's career.

John Wise bestowed his lands unevenly among his descendants. His principal estate of nearly eight hundred acres passed to his eldest son, George, then to his second son, John, and to John's eldest son. This property remained in the family until after the Civil War. The major provided less handsomely for Henry, his sister Margaret, and younger brother, John Cropper Wise. Each received a small parcel, but Henry's was a particularly meager bequest of fewer than one hundred acres.[6] He gained title to several slaves upon the death of his mother and also shared an interest in two more with one of his brothers. Even so, John Wise's long and carefully drafted will clearly reveals discrimination against his youngest children, with Henry, though not the youngest of all, probably receiving the least valuable portion. Henry never seems to have forgotten this inequity. It later allowed him to reflect self-righteously on how far he had advanced from humble beginnings.[7] At about the time that Henry's mother died, one of his younger brothers also passed away. Their deaths more than doubled his inherited holdings.[8]

Henry spent most of his adolescence with two paternal aunts, Elizabeth Wise and Mary Wise Outten, and his maternal grandfather, John Cropper. Cropper had served with conspicuous gallantry in the Revolution, having raised the first company from Accomac when but nineteen years old. Young Henry was not the only one to regard him as a hero; Washington himself had testified to his bravery. As with many who enrolled in the Revolutionary armies, Cropper's military service became the formative experience of his life and was something he talked about repeatedly during his later years, especially when among his descendants. The bitterness he felt for the mother country had not abated before his death, and with good reason: at one point while Cropper was away fighting in Pennsylvania, a small British expedition had attacked and terrorized his neighborhood, badly damaged his farm, and carried away about thirty of his slaves. It appears that he never obtained compensation, which must have caused him great anguish in his declining years, when he was heavily in debt.[9]

A personal acquaintance and occasional correspondent of George Washington, Cropper remained an ardent Federalist until his death in 1821. He frequently read to family and servants from John Marshall's *Life of Washington* and declaimed for them the entire Farewell Address each 22 February. Cropper retained his commission in the Virginia militia and died a brigadier general. Of impetuous temperament, he was a stickler for etiquette and insisted upon his prerogatives as an officer. Wise took special pride in his grandfather's patriotic achievements and referred to them regularly during his adult life. Indeed, he commemorated his grandfather's life more frequently than his father's.[10]

Although Henry spent considerable time at Bowman's Folly, the Cropper family residence on the Atlantic side of Accomac County, he lived at Clifton, his father's principal farm, on the Chesapeake side during most of the years before he left for college in 1822. Not much is known of the two paternal aunts who raised young Henry, but an indication of their influence is that in their honor Henry gave his first and favorite daughter their two first names—Mary Elizabeth.

Problems persist in documenting Wise's early life because of a fire in 1837 that destroyed his correspondence and records. From scraps of information available in biographical sketches of Wise, which he either prepared or encouraged, it appears that the elder of his aunts, Mary Wise Outten, had considerable impact in raising him and fixing his early values.[11] She seems to have been an unusually self-reliant woman, perhaps as a response to her husband's early death and her own poverty amid a proud and relatively wealthy family. In her benevolent but austere fashion, she taught Henry to read and strove to bridle his spirit. Mary Outten had, moreover, lost a son, her only child, so that she came to feel for her nephew all the affection and concern of a parent.[12] Indeed, the care and guidance he received from his aunt, though it won his undying gratitude, might have been detrimental in its long-term effects had not Henry learned how to protect his independence. No one will ever know the exact nature of the interplay between this middle-aged widow and her nephew, but years later Henry emphasized his aunt's responsibility for his sense of self-respect. This trait likely grew out of the conflict of wills that developed between a high-spirited boy and his father's severe sister. Always inclined to self-assertion, Wise in early life may have confronted a person whose strength made it positively necessary. Later he would often find himself torn between the priorities of following those whose authority he respected and the almost compulsive need to assert his own independence.

"He was a pale and puny boy in body," Wise later wrote of himself, "of large eyes and mouth and ugly, and so odd and oldish he wouldn't mate with the children, but sought the old folks and learned their sayings, and was fond of sweethearts older than himself, and spent his pocket money for red ribbons and climbed after nuts and fruit for their favors." The web of family relationships that surrounded him contributed to the loneliness he remembered from these years. The excesses of expression habitually conceded to young members of the master class further influenced the peculiar urgency of this orphan's search for identity. He was "called by hard nick-names, but especially by the name of Prince Hal, because of a high-strung nervous temperament; and, fondled by black nurses, he was wilful in his humors and sharp and quick and imperious in temper."[13]

It has been commonly understood at least since Jefferson that the slaveholding regime bred "wilful" and "imperious" temperaments. The great Virginian maintained that exercising full dominion at an early age over the lives of others inevitably and irrevocably corrupted the human spirit.[14] It was, after all, the damage that slavery did to white people that convinced Jefferson of its scandal and shame. In Wise's case, "fondled" and humored as he was by black servants, it is almost too obvious to argue that he fitted into a classic pattern and suffered the predictable moodiness, irritability, and intolerance. And yet most later descriptions of Wise emphasize either his erratic and high-strung temperament or his whole-souled congeniality, kindness, and charismatic attractiveness. These traits, of course, accord with what many believed was the other half of the Jekyll-and-Hyde creature slavery produced—the benevolent Southern master confident of his identity and matured by the early and constant exercise of his responsibilities. Wise's behavior conformed at least superficially to that predicted by the classic model. As he later put it: "There was a strange admixture of hardy recklessness and extreme caution in his nature; he was a great mimic and game maker, often offended by his broad humor, but was frank and genial, and so warm in his affections, and generous in his disposition, that he was generally popular, though he could when he tried make some hate him with a bitter hate."[15] The peculiarities of Wise's upbringing, along with his position as a younger and comparatively disadvantaged son, probably contributed to his exceptional ambition and assertiveness, as well as to his fondness for being appreciated. He was in a sense an exaggerated personification of a type common enough in Virginia and the Old South.

Two other influences help explain his well-known "erratic behavior." One was Wise's marginal financial position, which deprived him of the self-assurance that great wealth can provide and perhaps encouraged his desire to seek notoriety. The other was his ambivalence about holding slaves. For most Southern politicians, including Wise, slaveholding served as a source of pride. Moreover, their impulsiveness and eccentricities served them well in a society that valued a particular style of leadership. Still, Wise maintained a peculiar ambivalence toward authority, including his own authority as master, husband, and father. In any crowd of Southern politicians, he always stood out.[16]

Young Henry received the rudiments of a secondary education at Margaret Academy, located near his home. It was a miserable place, Wise recalled years later, "a curse to every youth whom it endangered by its vicious training," but during the six years he spent there, the school provided welcome release from Mary Outten's harsh regime. "I could kill chickens, rob hen roosts, steal from water melon patches, climb lightening rods to third story windows, and murder Latin and Greek with any of the lawyers who were taught nothing but mischief there." He benefited from having as one of his teachers a graduate of Washington College of Pennsylvania (now Washington and Jefferson College), who interested him in enrolling there. Tradition and location would normally have persuaded Wise to enroll at William and Mary, but the bracing climate of southwestern Pennsylvania probably appealed to him more. Wise never enjoyed good health and would have been especially wary of Williamsburg's swampy climate. His inheritance, though meager, was sufficient to finance a college education, so Henry traveled north for the first time in the autumn of 1822.[17]

Despite the college's limited resources, Wise found his education highly stimulating, principally because President Andrew Wylie took a personal interest in him. The president dominated proceedings at Washington College and did much of the teaching as well. He favored a "paternal" system of discipline and aimed at retaining firm control over the students without exercising a rigid "espionage." Henry responded enthusiastically to this treatment, sharing the first honors of his graduating class. Years later, he claimed that much of his success sprang from his desire to gratify Andrew Wylie. Always loyal to Wylie, he later sent his eldest son and several of his nephews to Indiana University, where Wylie then served as president.[18]

Wise first developed his talents as one of America's foremost orators during his college years. As it was at many other colleges during this period, public speaking was Washington's foremost extracurricular activity. The college possessed so few resources that its students probably gave more allegiance to their literary societies than to the institution itself. The Union and Washington societies divided almost the entire student body between them. At their Friday evening sessions every member present either debated or contributed a declamation, an original composition, or an extemporaneous speech. Assignments rotated, so that each member of the fifteen- to twenty-man organization acquired experience in all four modes during the academic year. An admirable custom required that student censors criticize all compositions, and Wise acted as censor regularly. As a member of the Union Society, he won numerous prizes in various competitions during his three years at Washington. Among them was one he earned in his graduating year for debating the proposition: Should the policy of a nation be governed by justice or expediency? It would have surprised few of his later political enemies that Henry defended the latter part of the proposition. So tenacious and competitive was he that even though his opponent broke into his desk and stole his argument before the debate, Henry still managed to tie the jurors.[19]

A more revealing incident took place when the marquis de Lafayette visited Washington, Pennsylvania, in 1824 during his national tour commemorating the Revolution. Wise literally embodied his heroic fantasies before Lafayette's arrival. After crowds had gathered on the streets, he rode into the country, donned a disguise that included a large sash, and raced into town proclaiming the general's imminent arrival to cheering crowds. After a time, as Henry's grandson quaintly put it many years later, "the people realized that they had been made the victims of a hoax, and had not the perpetrator kept well out of sight, he would have fared badly on the occasion."[20]

Following his graduation, Henry returned to the South and completed his education by attending the law lectures of Chancellor Henry St. George Tucker in Winchester, Virginia. Wise had already read Blackstone before his arrival during the summer of 1826. Tucker supplemented Blackstone with his own commentaries on Virginia law, which he published several years later.[21] Wise regarded himself as deeply indebted to the judge and once praised him as "a father to his class."[22] Admitted to the Virginia Bar in 1828, Wise had received one of the best educations available. Throughout life he read widely and dabbled in scholarly research. His investigations into the Virginia banking and internal improvements systems during the 1850s, for example, dazzled many of the Commonwealth's less learned legislators.

Though the law provided an effective way of earning a living, Wise never saw it as a way of life until after the Civil War. It gave him visibility, access to important contacts, and intellectual stimulation. His own career ambitions were probably fuzzy at this time, and it was more or less accidental that he came to hold public office a few years later. Politics eventually provided him with the status and recognition that he craved. Politics also furnished him with as much financial security as he could have expected from the law, though he was never completely satisfied on this point.

While at Washington College, Wise fell in love with Anne Jennings, daughter of a local Presbyterian minister. In 1828 her family moved to Nashville, Tennessee. After completing his legal education, Wise pursued Anne to Nashville and, following their marriage, stayed in the area for about two years. He was initially excited about his prospects in what appeared to him "a rich, trading, commercial and litigating metropolis, offering an arena upon which the most vaulting ambition might find 'game worthy of the hunt,' and be covered . . . with the dust of forensick contention in the temple of Justice."[23]

The Jennings family's friendship with Andrew Jackson permitted Wise to spend considerable time at Jackson's plantation near Nashville. For a while he became another of Jackson's many surrogate sons—though he remained very much on the periphery of affairs at The Hermitage. Perhaps reacting against the strict Federalism of his father and grandfather, during his college years Wise had favored the presidential claims of the Georgia states'-rights politician William Crawford, but he took to Jackson "owing to the Coalition against him" in 1824 and favored him for the presidency in 1828. At Washington College in 1824, Wise had watched Jackson pass through town on his way to Washington, D.C. Enthralled, he remained envious and enamored of the future president, who served as the symbol of American strength and patriotism for two generations. An orphan too, Jackson had long searched for a secure and confirmed authority, much as Wise would.[24] Even after they divided over removal of federal deposits from the United States Bank, Wise never lost his love for Jackson. Late in life, after the sorrow of defeat and the acrimony of partisan conflict had eased, he still referred to him as "the greatest man, take him all in all, that we have ever known."[25]

Increasingly drawn to The Hermitage, Wise found the luster wearing off his law practice back in Nashville. He perceived the bar as clannish and quickly noticed the limits to what a stranger could accomplish. Moreover, he lost his first case in the state supreme court, after preparing an elaborate defense for Tennessee's attorney general, who was involved in a dispute with the legislature.[26] At one point, he considered forsaking the law altogether to take up planting. He scouted the cotton country near Memphis, picked out 650 acres, and schemed to get rich quick. Because he owned so few slaves, the entire project depended on persuading his brother-in-law Tully R. Wise to sell his estate in Accomac, purchase more bondsmen, and enter a partnership in Tennessee.[27] Tully refused. Restless and frustrated, Wise returned to the Eastern Shore in 1830.

His earnings immediately improved, as did his spirits. With all the advantages of name and reputation, he quickly built a solid law practice. At ease among his own people, he actively and energetically pursued their friendship and managed to convince himself that homesickness alone had driven him back to them. Wise found contentment and a sense of place on the Eastern Shore. Here he probably hoped to equal or surpass the prestige of his father—"a good man," as he put it, "whose memory the old people still cherish as a friend of the poor, and of the widow and the orphan."[28] Indeed, his extraordinary political career during the next decade demonstrates his ability to vitalize the world view of his native region.

Wise never sought to enter politics, but the timing of his invitation suggests an inevitability about his entry into public life. Early in 1833 the Jacksonian leadership on the western side of the Chesapeake in Wise's district lacked a candidate to challenge Congressman Richard Coke, who had turned nullifier. They appealed to the party's ruling elders on the Eastern Shore, who nominated Wise despite his youth.[29]

The young lawyer's first act as a candidate was to announce his opposition to both nullification and the Force Bill, which Jackson had obtained from the United States Congress to overawe the South Carolinians. At the same time, he sanctioned secession as the final remedy for states whose grievances could not be redressed within the Union.[30] Wise's willingness to admit the possible legitimacy of secession, hedged with numerous qualifications, grew out of his opposition to nullification, and he did not regard it as a probable or even remote course of action. His position suggests how far John C. Calhoun's opponents went to oppose his doctrines. Thomas Ritchie, the influential editor of the *Richmond Enquirer*, employed the same tactics and looked upon Wise as a kindred spirit. Even James Madison, whose Unionist sympathies Wise shared, developed a similar line of argument.[31] If one remained a consistent Madisonian, however, secession rather than nullification would seem a proper way of resolving constitutional conflict in the American system.[32]

The campaign was rancorous, to put it mildly. Wise eked out a narrow victory but not before Coke challenged him to a duel after Wise insinuated that his opponent had softened his commitment to nullification on the Eastern Shore, where it was unpopular, while defending it elsewhere in the district. Late in January 1835, the two principals and their retinues met just outside the District of Columbia. On first fire, Wise shot Coke through the shoulder. Coke survived but never recovered the full use of his arm. It was the only time in his life that Wise actually fought a duel, though he became deeply embroiled in several of them during the next decade.[33]

Like many other Virginians, Wise considered himself an expert in constitutional doctrine and its subtleties. At Tucker's law school he had mastered Madison's writings and thereafter referred to the former president as his guide on all questions involving the fate of the Union.[34] This discipleship was significant because it meant that during his years in Congress Wise had relatively little sympathy for the states'-rights constitutional tradition of such Old Republicans as John Randolph, Spencer Roane, and John Taylor of Caroline. These Virginians referred to themselves as strict constructionists, as Wise later did. The young Virginian was as much opposed to an extortionate protective tariff and to internal improvements financed by federal monies as were the Old Republicans, but they probably valued the Union far less than either he or Madison, and they also suspected the legality of a national bank.[35] Wise's Madisonian faith not only separated him from them but, at least until John Tyler's administration, created a psychic distance between himself and men such as Nathaniel Beverley Tucker and Abel P. Upshur, who acted as intellectual heirs of Virginia's Old Republicans.

Madison's endorsement of a national bank in 1816 legitimized that institution in Wise's view, although his residence in a backward area, which possessed something of a Tory and Hamiltonian political heritage,[36] probably confirmed his sympathies. He publicly criticized the bank's opponents as early as 1828. Yet given the political climate of the early 1830s, how could a Jacksonian be elected to Congress who endorsed the "constitutionality and expediency" of the United States Bank, as Wise did in 1833?[37] Moreover, Wise had published a manifesto several months earlier praising Jackson's veto of the bill to recharter the bank as the most "illustrious" act of his administration.[38] How can these contradictions be explained?

In Wise's district the bank was a secondary issue. Thoughtful people worried more about nullification. The fate of the Union, which their ancestors had done so much to create, and of slavery, which Nat Turner had recently shaken to its foundations, preoccupied Tidewater Virginians. It was, after all, in lower Virginia that Calhoun's doctrines achieved their greatest popularity outside of South Carolina. The Wise family's Federalist leanings, along with his own extensive travels and devotion to Madison's writings, helped to determine Henry's support for the Union. The material dependence of the two Eastern Shore counties on markets in Baltimore and Philadelphia also influenced him. In 1832 the preservation of the Union required Jackson's reelection, for Wise feared that a victory by Henry Clay might provoke the more fanatical South Carolinians to Civil War.[39] He therefore felt justified in praising an action which, under other circumstances, he would have deemed unwise. In the end, however, no creditable explanation exists for a bank sympathizer's endorsement of the veto as "illustrious." The phrase suggests that Wise knew the advantages of lying.

Because the election in his area had focused on the fate of the Union and not the bank, Wise failed to appreciate how intransigent Jackson became on the bank issue following the 1832 election. Wise therefore supported the bank in his 1833 election address.[40] Along with many other Jacksonians, he later suggested that the president's earlier equivocations about the fate of the institution had led him to think that a modified and reformed bank might prove acceptable.[41] Certainly this attitude was a rationalization, but Wise probably made an honest mistake in overestimating the resiliency of the Jacksonian coalition. He evidently did not realize before arriving in Washington that opposing the administration on a fundamental issue automatically threw him into the arms of the opposition. In Wise's district, and among the nullifiers generally, the United States Bank was the least objectionable mechanism of Henry Clay's American system. Wise made certain that his election address condemned a protective tariff and federally sponsored internal improvements. In doing so, he probably wanted as much to appease potential opponents as to suggest enthusiasm for Jacksonian principles.

At the same time Wise's loyalty to Jackson had definite limits. For example, Wise cherished only contempt for Martin Van Buren, Jackson's closest confidant. As delegate to the Democratic National Convention in 1832, he had refused to support Van Buren for the vice-presidential nomination, favoring instead a Virginia strict constructionist, Philip P. Barbour.[42] Van Buren's political organization, the celebrated Albany Regency, had met the challenge of mass politics in New York.[43] Its leaders hoped to build a political movement that they could allegedly use to elect Democratic candidates regardless of principle. Innumerable politicians protested self-righteously that the Regency "machine" compromised the "manly independence" of the electorate, but they continued shamelessly to copy its most effective tactics. Because Wise later did his utmost to involve the Virginia masses in politics, it is tempting to attribute his loathing of Van Buren to suppressed envy. But it would be incorrect to do so: Virginia's narrowly restricted and deferential electorate in the 1830s made politics in the Old Dominion markedly different from New York's. This divergence, moreover, was probably greater in the Chesapeake area than in the rest of Virginia. Too, Van Buren's brand of institutional loyalty alienated Wise, whose notions of political allegiance were firmly rooted in the pride and self-confidence he possessed from his family's tradition, his region, and his role as a master. Indeed, Virginia politicians seemed generally more individualistic and independent than their New York counterparts because of the hierarchical character of society in the Old Dominion and the more informal way in which her squirearchy governed. Their behavior tended to reflect neighborhood views rather than those of a larger, more diverse constituency.[44] Wise and others habitually mistook Van Buren's grace and wit as evidence of "fawning servility." The significance of this perception lay in the way Wise, who respected and feared autonomy, thought himself threatened by Van Buren's willingness to embrace an "effeminate" dependence in relations with Jackson and his party.[45] The New Yorker's support for a revenue tariff provided Wise and most others in Tidewater Virginia with an objective rationale for repudiating him as Jackson's successor, despite the failure of the emerging Whig opposition to furnish a genuine alternative. Finally, Wise later maintained (though he said nothing on the matter in the early 1830s) that Van Buren had always been dangerously cautious about annexing Texas to the Union. Wise had first grown interested in Texas in 1828 during his stay in Nashville, and he remained actively involved with the annexation movement until its consummation.[46]

On the eve of his arrival in Washington, the young Virginia congressman personified many traits that contemporaries associated with his state and its Tidewater region. He was intensely ambitious, confident and even pompous in exercising the prerogatives that his family's position had provided him, and quick to take offense. It would be wrong to classify him among the Virginia gentry, however, because in 1833 he owned no land,[47] nor did he possess personal property as did the famous "first families" on the western shore of the Chesapeake to whose status he aspired. Upon taking his seat in Congress, he owned six taxable slaves (only those aged twelve and older were taxed, so he conceivably could have possessed some young blacks) and two horses.[48] If not wealthy, neither was he desperately poor. He therefore depended upon his law practice to support his wife and two children. Common sense must have told him that opportunities for growth were limited in an economically and demographically stagnant area. Accordingly, it is fair to say that having entered Congress, he valued the salary and additional economic benefits that elective office conveyed at least as much as the opportunity to influence public affairs.[49] Along with many others from his area, he grounded his pride and identity in things other than material possessions because he could not afford to do otherwise.

He bore the lean and nervous look that his status implied. Nearly six feet tall, he was so thin as to suggest someone from whom ambition had taken its toll. Worry, toil, and regular bouts of serious illness contributed to his pale and bloodless complexion. But Wise never wished to detract from the sympathies that his appearance might elicit; indeed, he highlighted the contrast between himself and other apparently healthier and more vigorous men by constantly wearing a white cravat. Animation instantly enlivened him, however, when challenged or called upon to speak of his vision and hopes. Blood flushed and darkened his complexion. Nervous gestures suddenly acquired a pattern, beating out the rhythm of his argument and differentiating him from friends and enemies. Impassioned outbursts alternated with barely audible delivery that reporters and listeners alike strained to hear. His very fluency and passion gave him an altered appearance, which is recorded in the dashingly virile and darkened features of at least one notable contemporary portrait; his eyes were in fact gray and his hair flaxen.[50] Wise only saw the amplitude of his expressions and emotions expand under the impact of the great crises ahead.

Chapter 2
A Long Farewell to Jackson

When Wise arrived at the bar of the House to be sworn, he looked so youthful that the Speaker mistook him for a page. To see him fidgeting impatiently in his seat, one might have doubted his commitment to the fray, but he never acted the part of a stripling. When he bolted up, gray eyes flashed and scanned, language spat out from a core of scarcely containable energy. This transfiguration took place almost daily; in Wise's ten years in the House only the venerable John Quincy Adams spoke as frequently. Although controversy dogged Wise everywhere, reticence and regret never seemed to trouble him. In his first full-dress speech, Wise embarrassed John Randolph's successor in the House by noting the absence to date of any remarks properly commemorative of the recently deceased Virginian. When this congressman rose to defend himself the next day, he collapsed, and expired shortly afterward.[1]

Undeterred by this omen, Wise plunged ahead. He assailed Jackson's removal of the federal deposits from the United States Bank. Arguing that this decision had "deranged the money market" and "convulsed and stunned business of every description," he demanded "an atonement from the man whom I supported for the presidency for such acts of misrule." It mattered not that near the close of his remarks Wise retreated from further indictment of Jackson and pointedly blamed his advisers for attempting to "gull, deceive, and enslave the people."[2] As one who never permitted qualified loyalties, Jackson instantly repudiated another wayward surrogate son, although their farewells lasted for several years afterward.

Increasingly, it seemed a foolish wager to gamble a career on the prospects of the United States Bank. A sharp economic downturn in the spring of 1834, for which its officers hoped, failed to materialize. Arguments for the bank's indispensability thus collapsed. Alone, however, among the "awkward squad" of former Jacksonians in the House now at war with their leader, Wise never retreated. Far from it. Even the most jaded politicians snapped out of their reveries when a young and inexperienced congressman called the Speaker of the House "a cancer on the body politic." The fireworks continued when Wise insulted the "puppies" and "pimps" among the Jacksonians and "literally *rasped* the flesh" from their leaders.[3] The young Virginian quickly emerged as a folk hero among Whig loyalists. But John Quincy Adams, the most incisive of them, vented his loathing of Virginia by caricaturing Wise "as a successor of John Randolph, with his tartness, his bitterness, his malignity, and his inconsistencies."[4] Wise would return this favor in due course.

Meantime, membership in the Whig opposition conferred only marginal advantages. An irrevocable break with Jackson bordered on personal humiliation, for Wise had probably relied on the president's friendship for support among his constituents. The return of vibrant prosperity later in 1834 further undercut the credibility of the bank's advocates. The Whig battle cry of "executive usurpation" was potentially exploitable, particularly among the nullifiers in Wise's district, should he risk stirring that caldron. A campaign whose touchstone was resistance to domineering authority resonated compellingly with Wise's personal experience.

Above all else, however, Southern Whigs like Wise found slavery an irresistibly attractive issue, as William J. Cooper has recently pointed out. Even before the onslaught of antislavery pamphlets and petitions later in 1835, Wise was proclaiming the unity of Southern unionists and nullifiers—"ready ripe for revolution, if the worst must come"—should abolitionism triumph in the District of Columbia or anywhere else. For Wise, the gag rule debate began early.[5]

His first antiabolition speech, in February 1835, yielded an unusual and eccentric message, however, as if to herald Wise's decidedly ambivalent commitment to the later debate. He spoke calmly and dispassionately: no forefinger jabbed into the air or pointed directly at an antagonist, nor did he mumble, thereby allowing reporters to record his remarks with uncharacteristic ease. The speech was actually a balanced, nonpartisan effort that permitted a confident and unfragmented delivery. The less well-noticed sections deplored the erosion of moderation that abolitionism signaled. A brief allusion to those Southerners who seized "upon every pretext to inflame the public mind on . . . slavery" suggested his antipathy toward the nullifiers.[6]

Such holidays from partisanship were luxuries indeed for Wise. He also was wary of antagonizing the cocksure South Carolinians, whose constituents shared an outlook similar to his. The final element in Wise's revised political identity, and one common to most Southern opponents of Jackson, was his repeatedly proclaimed enmity for the Old Hero's chosen successor, Martin Van Buren. He hammered at the New Yorker's personification of "unscrupulous Regency politics" and the Empire State's profit-taking from the immoral treatment of the bank. Because the young abolitionist movement also had roots in New York, there was a tendency to associate opportunism and unreliability on slavery with Van Burenism.[7] Gregarious, unmarried, and without formal education, Van Buren never seemed a gentleman to his detractors.

These were the issues on which Wise staked his political future. Despite frequent shifts in partisan allegiance, from Jacksonian to Whig to Tylerite, he won election to the House of Representatives six times between 1833 and 1844 and easily survived reapportionment of his district in 1840. The Tidewater's political culture dictated resistance to most forces of progress or improvement, as mid-nineteenth-century Americans understood those terms. This ethos suited Wise's variety of manly and colorful politics perfectly, except for one factor that substantially distanced his district from one similarly constituted in South Carolina. This was the Eastern Shore, whose political heritage was Federalist, probank, and perhaps mildly liberal on slavery. Wise was also probank, but it seemed unlikely that any of his other views cost him much support on the Shore, where his friends and kinsmen dominated and the population almost equaled that of the district's other counties. When Wise maligned Van Buren's manliness, harassed the abolitionists, and blasted Jackson's tyranny, it did little to shake his solid support in his neighborhood. Across Chesapeake Bay in the pro–South Carolina lowland counties, moreover, such stances only enhanced his reputation and rendered his position impregnable. When former congressional incumbent Richard Coke challenged Wise in 1835, he met such resistance that midway into the canvass he resigned and announced himself a supporter of the man who had crippled him for life.[8]

Not that Wise took anything for granted. Besides day-to-day participation in House debates, he delivered dozens of set speeches during his congressional career and then revised many of them for publication. Beyond his regular correspondence, he prepared various polemical productions for the press, along with an occasional vindication of his honor or impugning of someone else's. Because his constituents depended on untrammeled use of Chesapeake Bay, he secured membership on the Naval Affairs Committee, rising to its chairmanship early in the 1840s. He encountered his heaviest burdens when serving on select committees raised by the House to investigate particular problems. Amid these responsibilities, he kept contact with his patrons at home. Virginia's *viva voce* voting system and property qualifications restricting suffrage to perhaps two-thirds of the adult males confirmed the power of rich men and socially prominent families who typically exercised power through the self-perpetuating county courts.[9] After it had turned hostile toward Wise in the early 1840s, the *Richmond Whig* alleged that he held "most of the prominent men" of his district "under an anomalous and little creditable species of personal awe to himself."[10] To control the commoners, Wise relied on oratorical skill aided by the visibility acquired from his law practice. Monopolizing attention was easier in a district where no newspapers existed and between one-quarter and one-half of the adult males were illiterate.[11]

One thing that no one expected was legislative achievement. During his years in Congress, Wise introduced thirteen bills or resolutions; only one was ever approved.[12] Aggressive defensiveness, not advocacy of positive legislation, met the needs of lower Virginians, whose traditionalism was under assault from the abolitionists—as if their lengthy and grievous suffering needed further compounding.

A deepening agricultural depression had by the early 1830s affected commerce in the region, restricting capital formation and preventing development of an efficient internal improvement system. "Faced with a declining white population," as James R. Sharp puts it, "depleted soils that would no longer profitably grow tobacco, and a growing slave population that many felt could no longer be efficiently used, [Tidewater] planters . . . were desperately looking for a way out of their genteel poverty." According to another historian, "nostalgia, pessimism, and malaise" often afflicted sensitive and articulate witnesses to Virginia's decline.[13]

Wise was a living antidote to these traumas. Thin, wiry, with a single hand uplifted and long hair shaking in the breeze as he admonished his countrymen, Wise became his own phenomenon. His perseverance and fearlessness stimulated pride and hope in lower Virginia. What really distinguished him from numerous other Tidewater Virginians, however, was his air of brash confidence and optimism. There was some affectation in this attitude, for he recognized and publicly acknowledged Virginia's material decline. Both in speeches and conversations, Wise's brisk, spasmodic style conveyed energy and intensity. He concentrated on the important positive theme that his friends should be up and doing. Vigorous and diversified economic development always attracted him. "We in the South," he once said, "claim to be high-minded, gentlemanly, lordly fellows, who think nothing of money; and, therefore, we are poor." With an eye to the potential effectiveness of naval appropriations in promoting his region's development, Wise implored his friends to action and enterprise after the fashion of Yankees, who typically monopolized these funds. Older Virginians, such as John Randolph and Judge Nathaniel Beverley Tucker, feared the future and spent much of their lives fondly endeavoring to recapture a lost commonwealth. Wise mightily admired the life of the Tidewater gentry and aspired to it, but he remained critical. Although he was emaciated in appearance, his boldness and visions transformed him into a "corpse galvanized" whenever he spoke—precisely the appropriate metaphor for someone who craved the chance to energize the Old Dominion. Wise's oratorical abilities, republican values, and skill in the practice of law probably encouraged him to look forward to the future nationalization of commercial capital.[14]

What produced these attitudes? Wise's relatively cosmopolitan education and experience in early manhood had some influence. Unlike many in the Old Dominion, he knew that Virginia risked continued decline by relying only on her moral authority. Moreover, the Eastern Shore as distinct from counties Wise represented on the western side of the Chesapeake exerted an influence. An odd amalgam of insularity, clannishness, love of place, and the intolerance typically associated with an isolated community seems to have constituted the special perspective on affairs which the shore suggested to Wise. But more progressive forces were also at work, many of them forced upon Eastern Shore men as they marketed their small surpluses or cropped the waters around them. An important transition had occurred even before the American Revolution, when tobacco was abandoned in favor of cereal grains. Farms and slaveholdings were smaller on the Eastern Shore than across the bay. The presence of a large free Negro community probably created a less rigid social hierarchy than elsewhere in the Tidewater. In 1830 slaves made up less than 28 percent of the population in Accomac—the lowest proportion of any Tidewater county. The grain crop, fruit and vegetable gardening for the Baltimore and Philadelphia markets, and oyster fishery seem to have enhanced commercial values above the repute in which they were held across the Chesapeake. When debating slavery's merits, Wise never alluded to the leisure and culture it allegedly encouraged.

As late as the eve of the Civil War, no banks existed on the Eastern Shore. None of the South's traditional staples grew there. The area probably avoided the full impact of the agricultural depression that devastated the rest of the Tidewater. By 1840

Accomac ranked either first or second among counties in the Old Dominion in bushels of oats and potatoes produced and in value of its poultry. There was thus a materialist dimension influencing Wise's animated hopefulness.[15]

Barely thirty years old at the time he acquired a national reputation, Wise was an active, virile, and increasingly conspicuous politician with a highly cultivated sense of self-esteem. Gossipers linked him regularly with beautiful women. His first two wives were very pretty. From them, he demanded—and usually obtained—the same respect for which he fought when among peers.

Culture dictated revulsion at female dominance, though Wise's adolescent experience probably intensified his fears. "My wife," he wrote Anne a few months before her death in 1837, "is not competent to advise the statesman or the politician—her knowledge, her advice, her ministry is in a kindlier sphere. Though she cannot advise, cannot direct, cannot extricate me from difficulties, dangers or snares . . . yet she can hear my griefs, know of my troubles, understand the cause of my perplexities, be the confidant of my secret feelings and sympathize with me in them all. Blessed is she to me in that alone." More than most of his Southern colleagues, he noted and resented the presence of independent and resourceful women in the abolitionist movement. "Devils incarnate," he once called them. On another occasion, he presented a petition from several citizens of Halifax County, Virginia, "praying Congress to furnish husbands at public expense to all female petitioners upon subjects relating to slavery, thereby giving a direction to their minds calculated to make them good matrons, and averting the evils with which the fanaticism of the Eastern States threatens the people of the South." Anne Wise thought these tactics unfair and ungentlemanly, and she dared to reprove him: "Don't again say that one Priest or half a dozen, can persuade all the women in a parish to be anything that is wrong or opposed to good sense and good judgment, for I know that in general they have as much sense and good judgment as you lords of creation."[16]

Anne feared the violence of politics, dreaded the immobilizing loneliness of winters on the Eastern Shore, and regretted Henry's failure to hear her admonitions. "I feel half disposed to quarrel with you," she wrote in January 1835, "for chewing that new kind of tobacco, 'which makes you very nervous from being strong and stimulating' do take the old kind, or I fear you will lose all your boasted flesh, before we meet." She was also jealous of her husband's freedom and opportunities to encounter attractive young women.[17]

Presumably she encouraged Wise's active commitment to temperance. Among Southerners of equal political notoriety, perhaps only Robert Barnwell Rhett of South Carolina matched Wise's zeal in publicly condemning alcohol. He took a special pride from this commitment, particularly when critics hinted that rum and whiskey inspired his verbal pyrotechnics and reforming zeal in Congress. But he also cherished an aristocratic taste for fine wines throughout his life. Moreover, on at least one occasion during his congressional career, and while apparently under the influence, he and some friends acted the part of young rowdies and broke up a theater performance.[18]

Anne triumphed unequivocally on one issue. As the daughter of a preacher, she insisted on a religious atmosphere at home. Wise accommodated her preferences, although he did no more than profess a belief in Divine Providence. Until midlife, he made no serious religious commitment. Even then, he never acknowledged a conversion experience. Although born an Episcopalian, he periodically followed the Methodist and Presbyterian rituals. As on most issues, he expressed himself unabashedly. "*I stand where I was*," he wrote to a minister friend. "I believe God through his Son will save *me—even me* yet. My heart is exceedingly hard—my life desperately wicked—my love not warm—my fears not alarmed—but, thanks be to God in whom I would trust and never be confounded, I have evidences to my soul that it is not deserted & *will* not be deserted by His Grace! . . . I hope. I am not deceived. Pray for me. I am a vile sinner!"[19]

That he remained among the fallen surprised none of his enemies, although it brought his wife near despair, particularly after the duel with Richard Coke. Anne feared that Henry's pride and recklessness would make him either a corpse or a murderer. She implored him to repent and "turn now from the service of the world to the service of God to devote your life which He had made his care to Him hereafter."[20] Neither Henry nor his close friends heeded such advice. How could they? As Wise's political activities intensified, he inspired such reprehension among opponents that he carried arms in Washington for self-protection. Anne recognized that more than the code of honor's requirements prevented Henry from heeding her admonitions. She also complained of his heedless anxiety to get rich.[21]

Finances were a further source of Wise's edginess. No comparative advantage accrued to grain-growing Eastern Shore farmers, and large fortunes scarcely existed there. By March 1837, the time of Martin Van Buren's inaugural, Wise had three children and his wife was expecting a fourth. With tastes that evidently exceeded his means, he remained chronically in debt for much of his life and frequently depended on his brother-in-law as financial surety. Financial constraints probably prompted his interference in domestic spheres typically left to the management of wives and mothers. "I do not admit," Anne once wrote him, " 'that you always know best how to advise': instances too tedious to enumerate I could give to prove the contrary."[22] Just after Wise had purchased a farm and accumulated sufficient reserves to permit investment in United States Treasury land warrants, tragedy struck. Under mysterious circumstances, as we shall see, fires twice destroyed his residences, ultimately prompting Anne's death after childbirth. Wise then liquidated his assets, including several slaves, and presumably used portions of these funds to compensate the friends and kinfolk who cared for his children.

Wise also depended for help on Anne's mother, who moved from Nashville to Philadelphia following her husband's death. Perhaps during a trip to Philadelphia he met Sarah Sergeant, daughter of a distinguished Whig congressman, advocate of the United States Bank, and secretary of the Pennsylvania Colonization Society. With Henry passionately anxious to "bless" and "kiss" his "chosen one," Sarah desperately assured her parents that she "never cared for but one person in the world." "I would rather live in the country," she added, "and listen to his sweet voice as I have heard it read a chapter in the Bible than have any gratification in the world." The wealthy and prominent Sergeants apparently worried about Henry's situation and prospects. "As to his being poor," Sarah wrote, "I am not afraid of being poor, and I am not afraid I could not do my duty by those children, if I undertake it."[23] But her parents' suspicions proved correct. Following the marriage in 1840, their personal fortune, credit, and connections helped stabilize Wise's own chaotic finances.

Despite occasional protestations, Sarah was perhaps more deferential than Anne. Thus she transfixed him. In less than nineteen years with his first two wives, Wise fathered fourteen children, only seven of whom survived. At least one of Sarah's pregnancies was unwanted.[24] She later died in childbirth. Of Sarah, Henry might have written, as he did of Anne: "If she had a besetting sin, it was this—that she loved me too well."[25]

Large egos also predominated among Wise's spirited and temperamental friends in Congress, Sergeant S. Prentiss of Mississippi and Balie Peyton of Tennessee. Peyton was probably Wise's link with Senator Hugh Lawson White, the prime hope of anti-Jacksonian Southerners in 1836. Wise knew Peyton and his uncle,

John Bell, another important wheelhorse in the White movement, from Nashville. By the time his second term in Congress commenced in December 1835, Wise boarded with several people sympathetic to White's presidential aspirations.[26]

A dour though kindly man, Judge White exuded republican simplicity. To an orphan congressman from a backwater area of Virginia with no kinship connections to sustain him, the fatherly advice and counsel of such a dignified political veteran meant a great deal. White joined General Cropper, President Wylie, and Andrew Jackson among Wise's idols and patrons. He compared the Tennessean to James Madison, "the perfect model of a statesman," and venerated him as "one of the living few worthy of the illustrious dead of his country and mine."[27] White raged when Jackson slighted him for Van Buren and longed to capitalize on the New Yorker's unpopularity in the South. Thus White's alienation from Jackson had been as humiliating as Wise's; both carried persecution complexes, which required bold and vainglorious posturing. Two other important factors cemented their alliance. One was the rumor circulated during that canvass that White would not have opposed reestablishment of a bank, albeit one of limited powers. The other was their impeccable proslavery credentials, which permitted Wise no halfhearted loyalties when vindicating White's candidacy.[28]

The heterogeneous Whig opposition could agree upon no single nominee with sufficient appeal in all sections to rival Jackson's chosen successor. With Daniel Webster running in Massachusetts, William Henry Harrison heading the ticket elsewhere in New England and the Midwest, and White standing in the South, Whigs confronted charges that they aimed to frustrate popular will (as supposedly occurred in 1824) by throwing the election into the House of Representatives, where the United States Bank would presumably wield a controlling influence.[29] Although there were no compelling economic issues because of prevailing prosperity, the united opposition candidates polled 49 percent of the popular vote nationally. It was thus an enduring tribute to the Jacksonian coalition that Van Buren succeeded, particularly in view of his immense unpopularity in some areas of the South.

White gained the satisfaction of carrying Tennessee, but only Georgia, among the other Southern states, broke ranks with the Democracy to join him. Four years later, the judge was dead, mourned by Wise "as a father."[30] He was neither the first nor the last of the older politicians of usually benign disposition and even temperament who both aided and manipulated Wise effectively. Insecure about his own authority, Wise typically separated from the more aggressive and domineering of this class such as Jackson and John Quincy Adams with often fierce repudiations that revealed the scars his former patrons had left on him.

A Long Farewell to Jackson

The painful frustrations Wise experienced in the winter of 1836–37 stemmed partly from his consciousness of a tactically mishandled campaign. His long-winded effort earlier in 1836 demonstrating how the Jacksonians had contrived to defeat one of their own fortification bills faltered upon the inescapable fact that White had approved the conduct Wise censured. Although Calhoun called it "the most effective speech ever delivered against the Administration," the Jacksonians easily riddled its inconsistencies.[31] Nor did White himself do better. His supporters had made much of alleged maladministration of the executive departments, especially when contrasted with the "purity and integrity" of the judge's character. Some insight into the lameness of this effort comes from White's subsequent statement that he knew not "of any frauds actually practised either as to the sale of public lands, or in the purchase of Indian reservations," although he believed "great frauds have been practised, and are going on as to both."[32] Notwithstanding these evidentiary failures, the sizable Treasury surplus that Congress finally distributed to the states in the summer of 1836 had tempted the morals of numerous public servants. Land frauds were a way of life, especially in the old Southwest, and this infusion of federal funds encouraged them. Wise voted proudly against the distribution scheme, which Jackson had supported only lukewarmly. Until distribution, the federal funds withdrawn from the United States Bank had been held in a small number of deposit or "pet" banks, presenting to their managers the most obvious temptations to corruption. But Wise's attempts in the House to investigate the uses to which public servants and the "pet" bankers had put these monies demonstrated such luminous partisanship that even many Whigs refused to sustain him.

Delighting in the travail of his enemies, Jackson tormented them further with his last annual message. Never self-effacing, he outdid himself in a document that glowingly reviewed American affairs, happily anticipated his successor, and unabashedly praised the fashion in which his appointees had administered the government. Most Whigs simply endured the arrogance, but not Wise, who repelled this "worst" as well as "last annual message" in language ripe with fury and renunciation: "Its vanity and egotism . . . its impudent boast of the intelligence and patriotism of the successor, whom executive patronage and dictation have succeeded in electing—its shallow political economy . . . its miserable rhetoric . . . its grovelling moral sentiment—its total want of all sage counsel or advice, and of all pathos and feeling—all are equalled only by its false *certificate in chief* 'to the prosperous condition of all the various executive departments.' "[33]

After an acrimonious debate lasting several weeks, Wise finally obtained his investigatory committee. Congressman James Garland of Virginia secured a similar committee. Garland intended to examine the relationship between Reuben Whitney, a shadowy man of all work who acted in several capacities for the Jacksonians during the 1830s and the deposit or pet banks that had existed prior to the previous July. Both Wise and Peyton also served on Garland's committee. Perceiving Whitney as a spineless surrogate for the president, they charged him with the entire catalog of human rascality, from thievery to perjury to treason. Whitney then shocked them by firing back an immediate attack branding them "Siamese" companions guilty of "falsehood and slander." Despite the bankruptcies and transparent lack of principle that made him notorious even among his Jacksonian associates, Whitney further accused his enemies of defaming him in Congress, where they could not be held accountable. The former bank agent risked survival with this language, but perhaps he relied implicitly on outside support. If so, he certainly received it. The *Washington Globe* responded to Wise's "sublime effervescence" by commending Whitney as an honest and capable agent for about twenty deposit banks. And Speaker of the House James K. Polk evened up old scores and took a long step toward neutralizing Peyton and Wise by appointing Jacksonian majorities to both the investigating committees.[34]

The president himself also stood between the executive departments and any random, freewheeling investigation. The previous summer, during one of his slow processions home, Jackson had denounced Wise as a liar. He also directed a letter to Wise protesting his investigation and insisting that specific charges be presented in advance. Jackson complained of a "spanish inquisition" and derisively directed members of his cabinet to "answer . . . request[s] as they please, provided they do not withdraw their own time . . . from the public business." The administration press dutifully asserted the absurdity that to charge wrongdoing in the executive departments required Wise to seek Jackson's impeachment. These tactics outraged Wise, principally because they confronted him with Old Hickory's irresistible power. Call him what they would, the Virginian and most other Whigs found Jackson's popularity, decisiveness, and success intolerable. The president regularly reduced the opposition to an impotent rage.[35]

During neither congressional inquiry were Wise and Peyton

permitted freely to question such administration spokesmen as Treasury Secretary Levi Woodbury. Wise was thus left with the weak alternative within his own committee of calling such obviously biased witnesses as John Bell and Judge White to support allegations that executive patronage controlled federal elections.[36] Maddened by these frustrations, Peyton and Wise determined to lacerate Whitney when he appeared before Garland's committee. Expecting humility, they were amazed by his air of superiority and studied recalcitrance. The tension mounted until Peyton came within a hair's breath of exterminating him one evening early in February.

Wise later declared that he had expected Whitney "to draw a deadly weapon on my friend"—upon which action he would have suffered retaliation in kind: "I watched the motion of that right arm, the elbow of which could be seen by me; and, had it moved one inch, he had died."[37] Understandably, Whitney had no stomach for any further testimony. When called before Wise's committee, he refused to appear.

When Whitney was later hauled before the bar of the House on charges of contempt for failing to testify, the situation assumed the character of a comic opera. As Charles Sellers writes, Wise and Peyton both realized too late that the Jacksonians had indulged this proceeding only to make their enemies appear ludicrous before the country. With tables turned, both of them stood trial rather than their antagonist. While Peyton and Wise sputtered about their own innocence and peaceful intentions, the Jacksonians smugly released Whitney within a few days and disposed of the entire affair.[38]

Whitney's release was unfortunate. Serious corruption existed among the Jacksonians, especially involving Indian affairs, land transactions, and customs duties, demonstrated in particular by the fabulous defalcation of Samuel Swartout. While serving as collector of the port of New York Swartout absconded to Europe with more than a million dollars. When this affair was fully ventilated during the next Congress, Wise claimed a full vindication. What "other course could I [have pursued]," he asked, "but fearless boldness—ay, apparent recklessness?" After a few condescending comments to those who damned him with faint praise, despite his "faults" and "indiscretions," he prepared for the next presidential campaign by suggesting that when Senator Thomas Hart Benton succeeded Martin Van Buren, the former president would follow Swartout's example and slink away to England. As if to convince himself, he insisted that it was only the frauds and abuses afflicting the country that drove him to a frenzy and allowed his opponents to think him "mad." This outburst helped obtain for Wise a place on the House committee that examined the Swartout affair. He played an efficient role in generating political propaganda that assisted the Whigs through the presidential canvass of 1840.[39]

Wise sought revenge, liberation, clarity, and decisiveness from his struggle with Jackson. He got a bit of each, though only after absorbing repeated thrashings. Van Buren was a much easier mark, of course, because an economic depression wracked both the country and his administration within months of his inauguration. But Jackson stood proud and unscathed. That meant much to Wise, who found himself unable to endorse the Old Hero's policies but never failed to observe and emulate his personal style. Decisiveness and a penchant for the dramatic gesture ever afterward characterized Wise. He followed "a policy in rashness," he frequently remarked, repeating Jackson's words. He turned this designed impulsiveness on the Jacksonians themselves. The results seemed clear enough in most areas, except when it came to slavery. On that issue especially Wise sought the sense of righteous conviction that frequently eluded him during the protracted and embittered struggle with Jackson.

Chapter 3
Defending Shaky Outposts

Of the many important issues potentially bedeviling Whig unity, none was more menacing than slavery, as manifested during the gag rule debate. No Southerner in the House of Representatives equaled Wise's prominence in this struggle. But here, contrary to his unyielding efforts against Van Buren, Wise eventually acknowledged defeat amid circumstances suggesting that perhaps he believed himself undeserving of victory.

In the spring of 1836, after abolitionists had flooded Congress with petitions whose principal demand was emancipation in the District of Columbia, the Jacksonian leadership apparently persuaded Congressman Henry L. Pinckney of South Carolina to move establishment of a select committee to which all memorials would be referred.[1] The committee reported the first of several gag rules that operated until antislavery forces eliminated them in 1844. But because Pinckney's resolves permitted the tabling of petitions and failed to require their rejection, Wise branded him a "Judas Iscariot" and "a deserter from the principles of the South."[2] Perhaps mere residence in an area where Nat Turner was a living memory accounted for Wise's extremism, but neither of Virginia's senators and none of her other representatives in Congress—Whig or Jacksonian, from either slaveholding or yeomen-dominated regions—matched him in boldness or determination. Even admirers could only guess at Wise's intentions. Throughout the early stages of the debate, he remained a loner and consulted with no one.[3]

Although Wise seemed technically in violation of the Constitution by advocating nonreception of petitions, he was not, as even most antislavery strategists admitted. The Constitution guarantees the right of petition, not the right to be heard.[4] There is, however, the inescapable language of that instrument, which extends Congress's jurisdiction over the District of Columbia to "all cases whatsoever." To counter the obvious conclusion that Congress possessed authority to abolish slavery there if it chose, Wise contended that as local legislature for the district it could not enact any law that superseded its position as national legislature. To suggest, he said, that Congress might expropriate property without compensation, or to argue that it could violate any of the numerous restrictions placed upon it by the Constitution, would be absurd. His speeches consisted of more than legalisms, however. The supercharged sections of them held up the specter of slave revolt as a consequence of abolition in the district. They predicted conspiracies resulting from the symbiotic relationship between English and American abolitionists and dolefully reflected on a British army one day descending upon the South, leaving emancipation in its wake. Even without further palpable violations of the Constitution, the "spirit of fanaticism" abroad in the land already encouraged "amalgamation" and prevented his constituents from reclaiming fugitive slaves in the free states. What sort of government, he asked, "are we to have if women and priests are to influence our legislation?"[5] Had anyone risen to defend the female "devils" among the emancipationists or the Christian ministers whom he accurately depicted as leaders of the movement, Wise would instantly have challenged him to a duel. But when he went further and asked rhetorically whether Congress was permitted to do in the district things forbidden the states (such as abolishing the fugitive slave clause in the Constitution), his enemies had the opening they desired.

Congressman William Slade of Vermont, the South's most determined critic in the House during this period, seized on the obvious fact that states possessed full power to abolish slavery. Several had already done so. The petitioners desired of Congress only what many states had already approved. For the sake of argument, Slade accepted Wise's statement that emancipation in the Northern states had occurred either *post nati* (a principle that required years of service from slaves before their liberation) or following the payment of compensation to their owners. But according to Slade, *post nati* abolition interfered with property rights by depriving masters of their slaves' progeny. Wise's implied endorsement of this highly compromised form of emancipation set him directly against Virginia's slavery conservatives, who demanded unequivocal protection for their property rights.[6]

But in response to that portion of Wise's argument stressing limitations on Congress's power over the district, Slade did some fudging of his own. He argued incorrectly that neither Virginia nor Maryland had placed any conditions or restraints upon their cessions of territory. But he strengthened his position by referring to an 1828 abolition petition emanating from the district and signed by more than eleven hundred people.[7] He then infuriated Wise by citing the 1832 debate in the Virginia General Assembly and the *Richmond Enquirer's* condemnations of the institution.

Defending Shaky Outposts

Wise never replied to Slade, though he blustered about petitioning in behalf of Northern "white slaves."[8] Instead, he insisted on the truth of his dubious assertion that abolitionists were converting Congress's "exclusive" jurisdiction into absolute power over the district. The South wanted "peace and safety," he said, which could be obtained by "faithful observance" of the federal compact. Unlike South Carolina's representatives, Wise never dwelt on slavery's grandeur and antiquity or its healthy influence on Western civilizations.[9] But neither did he, like some Virginians, compare it to a "cancer" or assure abolitionists that the right price would purchase his bondsmen.[10] Eventually he admitted the strength of Slade's position by demanding the retrocession of Virginia's portion of the district, which took place in 1846.[11]

No one seemed more determined to silence the discussion of slavery. More than anyone in the House, including such Southern radicals as Robert Barnwell Rhett of South Carolina, Wise fought for tougher gag rules. House approval of the notorious Twenty-first Rule in 1840, forbidding reception of all antislavery petitions, was an impressive personal victory. Never was he willing to discuss slavery except as applied to the District of Columbia, because he avowed that the Constitution had already settled all other ramifications of the issue. Wise openly acknowledged that Southern Whig partisanship influenced his motives, but success in 1840 did not prompt him to retract his proposed retrocession of the district, because he could devise no constitutional argument adequate to protect slavery there.[12] He may therefore have supposed other parts of his position weak or unsound. In 1844 he gave up and urged slavery's congressional opponents to lay their designs before the country.

It was once possible to encompass Wise's motives exclusively within the framework of a Southern Whig offensive against the Northern, antislavery wing of the party led by such men as Slade and John Quincy Adams. With the Jacksonians determined to avoid the issue at all costs, Southern Whigs were tempted irresistibly to differentiate themselves as unqualified defenders of slavery. This interpretation correctly predicts the strategy of the White candidacy in 1836.[13] It is also consistent with the view that Van Buren's presidency stimulated so much unity among Whigs that disagreements over the gag rule were politically affordable. Moreover, antislavery Whig politicians were never numerous in Washington.

But the persuasiveness of this older interpretation is reduced by

Wise's decision to open full fire on the abolitionists before the gag rule debates began. He also, as noted, experienced difficulty in producing a thorough and consistent defense. Finally, scholars have not yet fully appreciated the weaknesses, which Wise correctly identified, in gag rules moved and carried during the 1830s by such Jacksonian sympathizers as Pinckney and Charles Atherton of New Hampshire. None was rigorous enough. They failed to silence Adams and Slade, both of whom managed frequently to stall the House's business, particularly when opposing annexation of Texas.[14] The Jacksonians had buried too many bodies to afford anything but equivocation. But often as not, Wise, the most eccentric of the Southern Whigs, retreated just when victory seemed assured. His vacillations and inconsistencies forfeited the trust of even those otherwise inclined to indulge him.

When the first session of the Twenty-fifth Congress opened in December 1837, Slade immediately began an assault on slavery in the Old Dominion, made possible because Pinckney's resolutions of the previous Congress had lapsed. Wise responded by leading the entire Virginia delegation out of the House. Other Southerners followed. In the ensuing caucus, Calhoun and Rhett advocated a Southern convention. Instead, the majority agreed to a resolve interdicting a greater variety of petitions than had Pinckney's but renewing the tabling proviso. Wise later claimed that he wrote the caucus recommendations, but oddly enough he refused to vote for them. He subsequently explained that their weakness compelled this decision, even though they were alledgedly his own and no one denied that they went further than Pinckney's resolves.[15]

Some other factor may well have influenced him. Wise, after all, did not come from a context that sanctioned or legitimated slavery, despite its material importance. Virginia's grand debate of 1832 revealed a society deeply critical of the peculiar institution. Indeed, even those opposed to emancipation expected Virginians to abandon slavery.[16] Educated in the North, Wise served as secretary of the Tennessee Colonization Society in Nashville, acted as a vice-president for many years of its Virginia counterpart, and revered his law professor, Chancellor Henry St. George Tucker, whose antislavery sympathies were unconcealed.[17] Although his own views on the 1832 debate are lamentably unrecorded, Wise frequently heard arguments that presumed slavery a curse instead of a blessing. Nor was it unusual for Virginians as late as a half-century after the American Revolution boldly to proclaim the humanity of slaves and its precedence over any vested rights claimed by their masters.[18] Most informed Virginians believed that black bondage would persist only until some unforeseen and magical inspiration should end it. Meanwhile, colonization seemed the most socially acceptable approach. Great care, shrewdness, and circumspection were necessary, however, because the Old Dominion retained far more slaves than any other Southern state. Perhaps we can get closer to Wise's motives if we hypothesize that he feared an extended discussion of slavery as tending to weaken and corrupt Virginia's commitment and maybe even his own.

Certainly Virginia had seen corruption enough, most of it attributable to slavery. At one point, for example, Wise rose in the House to denounce Northern shipping interests for fastening slavery on the South during the colonial period.[19] Such statements suggest a degree of shame at the institution's influence in Virginia, particularly in view of the continuing economic depression, and they echoed current informed opinion in the Old Dominion. Even those incisively critical of Virginia's emancipationists, such as Wise's constituent, Professor Thomas R. Dew of the College of William and Mary, acknowledged slavery's economic liabilities and expected its eventual disappearance from Virginia. The Old Dominion's climate and geography made large-scale plantation agriculture an impossibility, Dew believed. As internal improvements strengthened the state and permitted her to tap the wealth of her western hinterland, slaves would gradually find their way further south. White immigrant labor would occupy small farms specializing in fruit and vegetables. Dew's was not a voice in the wilderness; most influential Virginians during the 1830s agreed with his prognosis. In their view, Virginia would one day resemble an urbanized version of Accomac. Twenty years later, as governor, Wise advocated such a program, though changed intellectual and political circumstances inhibited him from fully articulating it.[20]

Dew, of course, acquired most of his notoriety from his critique of Virginia's 1832 emancipationists, who typically endorsed colonization. At the same time as radical abolitionists flailed the colonizationists, Dew concentrated on demonstrating the enormous expense and utter impracticality of their schemes. Despite Dew's persuasiveness, Wise maintained his connection with Virginia's Colonization Society, allegedly because of its avowed determination to concentrate on removing free blacks, not slaves. Yet he also believed that the destiny of all blacks lay providentially in Africa. Southern masters would school them for a time in the distant future when they would return to their native land, he remarked early in 1838. A great and noble hope inspired slaveholders like himself: "*to make light shine of darkness and to colonize a Nation of free men in a fatherland out of our kitchens of slaves* . . . Africa gave to Virginia a *savage* and a *slave*, Virginia gives back to Africa a *citizen* and a Christian. Against which does the balance lie?"[21]

A Good Southerner

Thus Wise belonged in the grand Jeffersonian tradition, which dissolved ever so gradually in antebellum America. His inconsistencies and doubts about the efficacy of his own constitutional arguments suggest an ensnarement in the great Virginia paradox of maintaining a social system collectively judged as rightfully doomed. In earlier years, no one better symbolized this dilemma than John Randolph—famous alike for fiery defenses of Southern rights and the testamentary emancipation of his slaves. Later, many Virginians who contributed to the proslavery argument, such as Judge Nathaniel Beverley Tucker, Reverend Thornton Stringfellow, and Dr. William A. Smith, shared this outlook.[22] But had Wise—a fledgling lawyer with no land, few slaves, and little money—gone no further and never acted on his antislavery convictions, there would be less reason for taking them seriously.

Instead, Wise emancipated a slave, as he publicly admitted in 1854.[23] He also insisted on treating blacks with dignity and respect despite their possible complicity in the death of his first wife, and he maintained throughout the 1830s a remarkable relationship with a young mulatto boy, William Henry Grey. When and why did Wise emancipate? No one will ever know for certain, though Grey perhaps knew more than anybody.

Although Accomac sustained a significant emancipationist tradition and the county order books show that people distantly related to Wise had freed slaves since the year of his birth, no one in his immediate family did so. Nor did he ever acknowledge sending a slave to Liberia, although as a colonizationist he had innumerable opportunities. His act, then, is an exceptional gesture, made in behalf of a nonemigrating black, which presumably took place early in his life; and was confessionally acknowledged in the altered climate of the 1850s partly in order to repudiate it.

Grey seemed to be an exceptional person. The youngster escorted Wise into the House almost every day, folded documents at his desk, and heard the speeches. After serving Wise for several years, Grey left for Pittsburgh and later as a clergyman emerged as the most eloquent and influential black leader in Arkansas after the Civil War.[24] Because an intimate relationship remains unprovable, it may be only that Wise saw in him a body servant along with a convenient outlet for his own parental impulses. But why Grey in particular?

There were some noteworthy coincidences. Grey's tombstone in Helena, Arkansas, indicates that he was born free in Washington, D.C., on 22 December 1829. On at least one occasion, however, Grey stated publicly that he came from Virginia.[25] Educated in Methodist schools (a faith Wise frequently practiced, though born an Episcopalian), he later served as a minister of the African Methodist Episcopal church. Even opponents testified to his oratorical talents. Like Wise, Grey was a Mason. Furthermore, the 1870 federal census designated him as a mulatto. In this connection, of course, one wonders about the significance of his middle name. One also wonders about the attention Grey gave to the issue of miscegenation in the Arkansas Constitutional Convention of 1868. At one point in the debates he commented that whites and blacks had the same blood running in their veins.[26] Wise frequently condemned "amalgamation" both before and after the war. Could the intensity of his convictions have been rooted in personal experience?

If the date of Grey's birth given on his tombstone is correct (and no corroborating records exist), there is no issue of Wise's paternity. He had lived in Nashville for an extended period before Grey's birth. Grey's descendants are no longer traceable, either in the Helena area or elsewhere. Although Grey's career was distinguished,[27] he never attained wealth, and his family seems to have scattered from eastern Arkansas after 1900. Court records revealed nothing; the black community in Helena chose silence.

No evidence exists of any communication between Wise and Grey in later years. More important, among the legion of Wise's political foes, none ever suggested any illicit personal relationship. Unsparing and unforgiving, Wise's enemies charged him with almost every political crime known to the human family, but they never assailed the purity of his domestic life. There is, however, a curious and decidedly ambiguous reference in the voluminous correspondence addressed to Wise during the Harpers Ferry crisis. Although many Northerners reflected unfavorably on his treatment of John Brown, one Republican laboring man from Wisconsin gave his comments a special twist: "We think [Brown's] object was good because liberty is dear to us, then why not dear to those you are depriving of its blessings. Don't you think liberty dear to that nearly white mulatto who perhaps is endebted to you for life. We believe your Bondsmen are now panting for liberty and we shall try and give it to them in every constitutional way."[28]

Whatever the import of this allusion, the substance of which it is perhaps a reflection will in all likelihood never be known. Beyond the curious relationship between Wise and Grey, the only other concrete justification for pressing an investigation into these matters remains Wise's emancipation of a single slave. Because many regarded the District of Columbia as a safe haven for newly freed blacks, I examined the Manumission and Emancipation Record for the district. An oath sworn before a justice of the peace and dated 19 October 1827, at the time when Wise was studying law in Winchester, affirms that a Negro woman, Elizabeth Gray, and her two children, Mary Jane and William Henry, are free.[29] Could this be the same William Henry Grey? Was his mother the single slave emancipated by Wise?

Although Wise occasionally described blacks as "woolly headed," "splay footed," and "odiferous," he never thought them subhuman or impervious to progress. Anxious to improve the world for whites and blacks alike, he regarded them as maimed by circumstances, not inherently inferior. Decent and respectable free blacks in the Washington area, particularly those from the Eastern Shore, found him a patron.[30] Wise would, of course, have derived a condescending satisfaction from his interventions, but with only a few slaves and much debt, he dared not put on many airs. Wise learned benevolence as his slaveholdings expanded during the 1840s and after he had observed firsthand the horrors of the Brazilian slave trade.

Meantime, while retaining an honest acceptance of black humanity, he reached for the most convenient defense available to a man with little leisure and not many slaves. "Wherever black slavery existed," he remarked in 1842, "there was found at least equality among the white population. . . . The principle of slavery was a leveling principle. . . . Break down slavery, and you would with the same blow destroy the great democratic principle of equality among men." This outburst was provoked by his and Virginia's chief tormentor, John Quincy Adams. Wise knew that his rhetoric failed to describe Virginia's reality, and his passionate efforts years later to reduce the alienation of her nonslaveholders proved it.[31] As well, his own experience showed that a racialist defense worked neither for whites nor blacks. Fancied notions of black inferiority would have accounted neither for his pleasure in Grey's company nor the utterly unspeakable fears that slaves on a rampage evoked in a community where nightmares turned easily into daydreams.

Early in February 1837, Wise's rented home in Accomac burned down. The fire consumed most of his personal papers and much of his law library. "Conjecture couldn't account for it," he wrote in retrospect, "until years after death had put in the prison house of the grave the probable incendiary." Three months later another home occupied by Wise's pregnant wife and children also burned. This second incident apparently induced a premature delivery. The child survived, but Anne failed to recover and died in June.[32]

A comparison of Wise's statements with those of his grandson and biographer indicates that arsonists set both fires. According to family tradition, a slave set the second fire. It is impossible to tell from the sketchy information provided in the principal collection of Wise Family Papers whether the slave belonged to Henry. No evidence remains to identify the first incendiary. The Accomac County Personal Property Books show, however, that between 1837 and 1838 Wise's holdings declined from five to one (adult) slave. Perhaps these four blacks died suddenly. It is more likely that Wise sold them, for his wife's death and the need to provide for his family may have constituted compelling economic reasons.[33]

Six months after Anne's death, Wise and most other Southern congressmen withdrew from the House of Representatives. There followed the confusing episode in which the Virginian disavowed his own anti-gag-rule resolutions and criticized their insufficient radicalism. Whatever the impact of family tragedy on his action, slavery—whether manifested in the gag rule debate or turned privately like a dark jewel at moontide simultaneously inspiring the hopefulness of opportunity or the edginess of fear—commanded passions engaged equally only in his most intimate relationships. To touch it was to strike at the root of his ambivalence and eccentricity. Indirectly, it was about to produce the "greatest difficulty" of his life.[34]

In February 1838, Wise served as second for a protégé of Henry Clay's, Representative William Graves of Kentucky, in one of the most notorious duels of the period. On third fire, Graves mortally wounded his opponent, Jacksonian Congressman Jonathan Cilley of Maine. The issue between them seemed shockingly insignificant, but it was not and neither were its effects.

No one doubted Wise's loyalty to the Southern code of honor. Even Preston Brooks, whose assault on Massachusetts Senator Charles Sumner in 1856 confirmed his impeccable credentials as a devotee of the code, once sought his advice. Amid tedious rhetorical flourishes and skirmishing in the House, Wise always announced himself personally responsible. Acceptance of this responsibility ensured civilized debate, he believed. The code of honor standardized conflict resolution and helped prevent both character assassination and undignified violence. In addition to peculiarly Southern and intimate influences that assisted in implanting his attitudes, Wise's grandfather probably had a role. Furthermore, it was and remains an important part of the family's heritage that in 1799 Henry's father, Major John Wise, called for "explanations" from Thomas Jefferson when the latter equated Wise's Federalist politics with Revolutionary Toryism and urged his defeat for reelection as Speaker of the House of Delegates. Jefferson responded urbanely, denying any personal allusions, and no challenge resulted. Henry doubtless was told of this incident; it necessarily legitimized the code.[35]

After his 1835 duel with Richard Coke had presumably proved his courage, Wise suggested to his wife that opponents would steer clear. Weak-wristed ones did so. Wise never fought another duel, although he physically assaulted his enemies and then typically accepted the intervention of friends. As one who followed the code to the letter, Wise always placed full power in the hands of his seconds—usually Peyton or Prentiss—who deserve credit for preserving him from a murder indictment, for rumor acknowledged him a dead shot. "My protection," he once advised his constituents, "has depended upon my own trusty weapon, and a trusty friend, upon whom I have been daily liable to call."[36] Despite a reputation for hotheadedness, Wise compiled a superb record as an adjudicator. During his congressional career, he probably resolved at least a half-dozen potentially deadly quarrels.[37] But the one he failed to adjust earned him lifelong opprobrium as a cruel and reckless duelist. It also scarred him with remorse, created an explosively antagonistic relationship between himself and the leader of his party, and provided a devilishly perverse old enemy with an almost irresistible weapon. Insults directed at his aspiring but uncertain claims to masterhood inclined him to participate, perhaps against his better judgment.

Early in February 1838, several weeks after Wise's ambiguous, temporary secession from the House, the Washington correspondent of the *New York Courier and Enquirer* charged an unnamed member of Congress (probably Democratic Senator John Ruggles of Maine) with corruption. Wise instantly called for an investigation. Cilley ridiculed his suggestion, implying that the allegations emanated from a corrupt and partisan newspaper editor. Few men would have dared such bold words. Wise concluded their sharp exchange with a sneer: "But what is the use of bandying words with a man who won't hold himself personally accountable?"[38]

Wise later referred to this incident as "a slight misunderstanding between us in debate," but his mood was serious, and he had reason to resent the slightest provocation. Several days before this exchange with Cilley, Wise made a stinging denunciation of the war against the Seminole Indians of Florida, which he termed a "disgraceful, wicked, fatal contest." At this point the territorial delegate from Florida, noting the alliance of fugitive slaves and Seminoles against his constituents, all but accused Wise of abolitionist sympathies and inquired of his policy should another Nat Turner ever lurk in Virginia's swamps. Cilley then lambasted his effort to cut the Seminole War appropriation from $1 million to $500,000. Cilley favored carrying on the war "with vigor, on the old New England plan, where the Indians had been wholly exterminated." He also ridiculed "this sympathy for the dark red man which seemed to be akin to that expressed in some quarters for the man of yet a darker hue." Unlikely to forget these fighting words, the Virginian determined to intimidate Cilley when he again defied him.[39]

Wise mistook his man. Like himself, Cilley was proud and ambitious. His recent slashing attacks on the opposition had stirred the admiration of enfeebled Democrats. Southerners seemed surprised, if not affronted, that someone from Maine could be an expert rifleman. Francis Pickens of South Carolina said after his death, "Cilley was the most gallant man I ever saw from the North. He was the first northern man who openly denounced the abolitionists and spoke as a Southern man." Pickens called Cilley "an open nullifier" and added that he even "looked like a Southern man."[40]

Cilley's star was rising. His increased visibility emboldened him to repel charges of corruption against his party. What thoroughly provoked Cilley about the allegations was their source, James Watson Webb, editor of the *Courier and Enquirer*, a Jackson supporter before switching to the Whigs in 1832. Most Jacksonians believed, as Cilley indicated, that the United States Bank obtained Webb's conversion by extending a sizable loan to him. A few days after the Cilley-Wise exchange, Webb prevailed upon Graves to deliver a note to the Maine congressman demanding an explanation. Webb subsequently maintained that as an editor he had grown tired of seeing himself and his family maligned while his enemies refused him recourse to the code of honor.[41]

Cilley, however, rejected Webb's note and told Graves his reasons. Among them, according to the Kentuckian, was an unwillingness "to get . . . into personal difficulties with conductors of public journals for what [he] might think proper to say in debate." Graves also believed that Cilley had disclaimed any personal antagonism to Webb as a gentleman.[42] Graves's interpretation of this conversation created the "question of veracity" which Wise later insisted had produced the duel.

Confused by Cilley's reply, Graves consulted several of his associates, including Wise. Graves then asked Cilley for a written explanation. But the high-spirited Cilley had taken enough from Webb and his Whig friends. He repudiated Graves's version of their interview and curtly stated that he had refused Webb's note because he "chose to be drawn into no controversy with him," adding that he "neither affirmed nor denied anything in regard to his character."[43] Graves was incensed. To vindicate his friend's honor and his own reputation for truthfulness, he pressed Wise into service as second and drew a challenge.

On Saturday, 24 February 1838, all parties met at the Bladensburg, Maryland, dueling grounds, a short distance from the District of Columbia. On third fire, Cilley fell. Moments earlier, Wise admitted to Cilley's second that both men "have met here without animosity towards each other; they are fighting merely upon a point of honor."[44] Cilley's anguished friend Nathaniel Hawthorne caught the significance of this unfortunate remark in a memoir that summarizes much of the public reaction: "A challenge was never given on a more shadowy pretext; a duel was never pressed to a fatal close, in the face of such open kindness as was expressed by Mr. Cilley; and the conclusion is inevitable, that Mr. Graves, and his principal second, Mr. Wise, have gone farther than their own dreadful Code will warrant them, and overstepped the imaginary distinction which on their own principles, separates Manslaughter from Murder."[45]

It was not so much Cilley's death as the manner of it that outraged public opinion. Dueling deaths occurred infrequently, because social convention made it a mark of dishonor to kill. The point was to repay a moral wound with a physical one. Thus a Boston newspaper vilified Wise as "a disgrace to humanity" and hoped "that the penitentiary or gallows will soon relieve society of his baneful presence."[46] Wise survived the congressional investigation that followed, but even in Virginia the duel's effects threatened him for several years.

Deadly issues prevailed between Graves and Cilley, however. Wise's comment on the field misrepresented the gravity of the situation; he was inclined to seek a peaceful solution if possible. Certain of Cilley's friends acknowledged that veracity was at issue and admitted that he would never have certified Webb's standing as a gentleman, as required by the code. Furthermore, the Jacksonian-controlled investigation into Cilley's death later missed or ignored the significance of the New Englander's note to Graves. Cilley never asserted his constitutional privileges as a member of the House; it was not for defending them that he fell. Indeed, he pointedly refused to mention them.[47]

It was most unusual, however, that the parties fired three times. As the challenger's second, Wise had full power to terminate the affair earlier. Because he did not, Hawthorne, Horace Greeley, and others argued that he had made a barbarous mockery out of his own code. Moreover, he had proposed "to shorten the distance" if the third shot proved ineffectual. He later maintained in a statement to his constituents that he acted at Grave's behest because the Kentuckian "had no confidence in his own shooting." But knowing Wise's fiery temperament and reputation, and noting the inconsistency of his statement with the responsibility accorded to seconds under the code, few believed him.[48] Had not he submitted quarrels of his own to the discretion of his friends? But as Wise later explained with some delicacy and reticence to John L. O'Sullivan, the editor of the *Democratic Review*, the real reason for the three shots had never been revealed. Cilley had misfired his weapon during the first exchange, and Graves had done likewise during the second. Neither Wise nor George W. Jones, who served as Cilley's second, could have divulged this fact at the time because it would have slurred the courage of their respective principals. "The truth was," as Wise wrote, "that there was but one deliberate and satisfactory *exchange* of shots—and that was the third and the fatal time."[49]

Wise's apologias were not only brilliant but accurate. The only problem was their incompleteness. No mere "slight misunderstanding" divided him from Cilley. Here was an enemy who had called directly into question his loyalties to slavery. Indeed, the South Carolinians might well have chosen Cilley before Wise in a contest over purity of allegiance to the peculiar institution. Thus an ambivalence about the propriety of his own motives in this incident—an inability to find assurance—dogged him until his dying day. Despite his expertise, Wise experienced the misery of his inner conviction that dueling was wrong, unchristian, and against the spirit of the age. When Virginia's high priest, Bishop R. K. Meade of the Episcopal church, preached a sermon criticizing his participation in the duel, Wise exploded:

> Should not the blow be the harder, the harder the mark? Yes, most truly most materially. But against what? the *sinner*? no—the *sin*. I can curse the *sin* with that pious prelate who can weep in charity alone over me a *sinner*; but humbleness and contrition are not the fruits of his preaching who usurps the high prerogatives of Heaven in hurling its anathemas against

even the "front offender." Christ came to save *sinners* and his ministers should not drive them from his sanctuary. An unchanged heart may never be changed if it be *excommunicated*. How near my dear Sir, did you come to putting me out of the reach of Mercy even to-day?[50]

Eternity aside, along with the ramifying effects of Graves-Cilley over the years, Wise encountered the duel's effects in daily life. They carried overtly political overtones of national significance because of Henry Clay's participation. Clay had publicly renounced the code of honor some years earlier. In anticipation of a presidential run against Van Buren in 1840, the Kentucky senator was systematically wooing Southern Whigs such as Wise. None of this group, Wise least of all, wanted Clay's part disclosed. Dashing and imperial, Clay himself simply brushed off the threat posed by an investigation. "Sir, it is a nine day's bubble!" he told Wise. "If they want to know what I did in the matter, tell them to call *me* before them, and I will tell them."[51] Flattered by such gallantry, Wise shielded Clay, though he always prided himself on this trump. In the early days of Tyler's administration, when Wise learned that Clay had little respect for such an implied obligation of honor, it signaled that the Whigs would soon begin to devour one another.

It was, however, Wise's great antagonist in the House who brought before him the terror of the Graves-Cilley affair. John Quincy Adams understood that Virginians wanted to be better men than they were. He knew about their peculiar pretensions to high-mindedness. He understood how maddened they were to remember the abolitionists among their Revolutionary forebears. He mercilessly exposed the Old Dominion's stagnant economy and ramshackle school system.[52] When they counterattacked, Adams turned on them with such fury that they were swept almost beyond their moorings.

All this came to a head early in 1842. Adams had defended Wise four years earlier. Now, smarting from yet another defeat in his ongoing campaign to defeat the gag rule, Adams cunningly maneuvered the House into considering a Georgia petition that sought his removal from the chairmanship of the Foreign Relations Committee. Mortified by the failure of additional Northern congressmen to support him over the gag rule, Adams tried to show that this latest petition represented yet another example of the slave power's conspiracy to smother its critics. In support of this position, Adams read a passage from one of Wise's recent letters to his constituents expressing apprehensions that the Foreign Relations Committee would seek diplomatic recognition of Haiti. The racially amalgamationist implications of such a policy, which Adams favored, appalled Wise.[53] He thereupon exhausted himself with a windy and vituperative discourse against the former president, emphasizing his supposed jealousy of Virginia and associations with the English influence allegedly dominating American abolitionism.[54] Never flinching, Adams brought forward the celebrated petition from Haverhill, Massachusetts, that prayed for a dissolution of the American Union. In the din that followed, Wise suggested in the House that Adams be censured. He cleverly stepped aside to permit a friend to offer the resolution and then announced with false magnanimity that he would refrain from voting on it. Failing to grasp Adams's tactics, which were to provoke his Southern enemies so as to promote extended commentaries on the otherwise taboo question of slavery, Wise was shocked by what followed. Adams electrified everyone by immediately claiming the right to be heard in his own defense and then singling out as unfit to judge him one slaveholder who had years earlier entered the House "with his hands and face dripping with the blood of murder, the blotches of which were yet hanging upon him."[55]

Unnerved by this oracular reference and rendered hors de combat during the remainder of the Haverhill petition controversy, Wise rushed into a newspaper controversy designed to affix a portion of the responsibility for the duel to Henry Clay. He succeeded in proving that Clay had composed Graves's challenge; Clay acknowledged that, despite his disclaimers, he had refused "to arrest the progress of the affair."[56] Wise was freed from much odium, though at great cost. Part of it he paid every time he recollected how the duel highlighted his own ambivalence about an unforgettable protagonist.

Wise never wanted the enmity of the "hissing serpent of Braintree," as he later described Adams.[57] Rather, he craved the old man's friendship and respect. He sought Adams's advice on issues unconnected with slavery and seemed anxious to preserve civilities between them. With Adams immune to censure following presentation of the Haverhill petition, the House retaliated by censuring one of his more vulnerable friends, Congressman Joshua Giddings of Ohio. After Giddings secured reelection, Wise publicly congratulated him on "the greatest triumph ever achieved" by any congressman.[58]

But Adams's principles were more important to him that the adulation or even respect of his peers. His age and prestige also immunized him (along with Andrew Jackson) from challenges of violence, which the frustrated Wise must have regularly contemplated. His knowledge of Wise's inner doubts allowed him to implant his mark indelibly on the young Virginian. In particular, the suggestion initially made by Adams on 25 May 1836, during his first extended speech against annexation of Texas, that a massive slave uprising could provoke federal intervention leading to abolition forever worried Wise. To prevent such debate, Wise affirmed the gag rule. Schooled well, he properly acknowledged a debt to his instructor. "I have had a very severe training . . . with the acutest, the astutest, the archest enemy of Southern slavery that ever existed," he remarked during his 1855 gubernatorial canvass in Virginia. "Again and again, he said he would not abolish slavery in the District of Columbia if he could, for he would retain it as . . . a lever for agitation . . . until slavery in the states was shaken from its base. And his prophesies have been fulfilled—fulfilled far faster, and more fearfully, certainly, than he ever anticipated before he died."[59]

Chapter 4

Supporting Tyler and Escaping the Consequences

Despite their hostility to one another, the presence of men such as Wise, Adams, and Clay in the same political formation offers compelling proof of the dominating power of party over section twenty years before the Civil War. The vitriolic gag rule debate bent but never broke party loyalties. Simultaneously, Martin Van Buren's presidency further solidified the Whig opposition down to the time of its grand triumph in 1840. "We are all now necessary to each other and must concede something from every quarter," Wise remarked to a strong Clay backer early in 1838.[1]

Every American Whig benefited politically from Van Buren's mistakes and misfortunes. But the president's description of Wise as a "notorious scamp" underestimated his effectiveness, visibility, and skill in profiting from the errors of an old adversary. Wise's slashing attacks on executive power and malfeasance, along with his call for the impeachment of Treasury Secretary Levi Woodbury, aided materially in wrecking the New Yorker's presidency.[2] Much more important, of course, was the economic depression that struck several months after Van Buren's inauguration. The president's cold-hearted devotion to the standards of Jeffersonian asceticism in government while massive unemployment persisted encouraged even his most conservative opponents to concentrate on the alleged humanitarianism of their positive state theories. Thus a new bank was said to serve the people, not merely the capitalists. Conversely, Van Buren's Sub-Treasury ranked as an autocratic scheme that distanced popular control and legitimized management by unresponsive bureaucrats. The president's ill-fated proposal to embody a national militia put him in the untenable political position of presumptively threatening liberty by uniting "the purse and the sword."[3] Van Buren's hard-money, antibanking, antitariff, and laissez-faire prescriptions for the crisis singlehandedly rehabilitated Henry Clay's American system, even among Southern states'-rightists of relatively strict observance. It also set the great Kentuckian's heart to palpitating with his perennial hope for elevation to the presidency.

Subsuming the antagonism the Graves-Cilley duel engendered, Wise led the way in trumpeting Clay's claims in Virginia. Despite strong backing, the Kentuckian suffered a humiliating reverse when, in December 1839, the Whig national convention conferred its presidential nomination on William Henry Harrison. After Harrison's death, John Tyler's accession splintered the Whigs. Clay's imperiousness reopened the issue of the duel. Grievously resentful, Wise encouraged Tyler's effort to veto the Kentuckian's program out of existence. Ostracized thereafter, Tyler never recovered. But Wise tenaciously created a future for himself, even as he worked mightily to sustain a stillborn administration. Eventually he fled the country to repair both his reputation and his finances as American minister to Brazil.

So much of American history before 1850 was influenced by Andrew Jackson that we often forget how deeply Henry Clay was loved and admired. With that superb combination of aristocratic panache and democratic collegiality common to many native Virginians, he captivated thousands. Wise's suggestion in 1840 that the presidency "could not add a cubit" to Clay's stature reflected the appeal of Clay's magnetism and friendship, for which Wise was admittedly prepared to sacrifice his principles.[4] In a career marked by painful embarrassments and inconsistencies, this comment became one of those he most regretted.

More than a personal alliance, cooperation between Wise and Clay reflected agreement on the prerequisites for economic recovery and political reform. Each espoused the Madisonian variant of American federalism, in which a moderately dynamic central government would aid in the creation of a national market while respecting state and local interests such as slavery. The filtered and frequently edited debates in the *Congressional Globe* and other sources, though often fiery and marked by violence, fail to convey the scorn and invective heaped by men such as Wise and Clay upon their enemies for leaving the country without a reliable currency and threatening, with the Sub-Treasury, to promote further deflation in an economy that required an expansion of credit. Wise repeatedly sustained the expediency and constitutionality of a national bank. He also remarked that Virginians currently in vassalage to New York bankers might be no worse off with higher tariffs, which would encourage the growth of Southern manufacturing. Even though Wise's legal education and immersion in Virginia's political culture equipped him with appropriately reverential postures toward strict doctrines of states' rights, he embraced the Whig program more naturally. In his most candid moments, he acknowledged that positive government in New York and elsewhere made the difference between Northern prosperity and Virginia's genteel decline.[5] Years later, as governor, he proposed unprecedented initiatives to reverse this trend. And, of course, whenever Wise smelled out Democratic corruption or misappropriations threatening the republican values of purity and economy in government, he heralded them from his seat in the House and thus satisfied many potential critics back home that he was indeed a good Virginian. Finally, Wise and Clay shared the conviction that American slavery should not last indefinitely. In the meantime, Clay's stepped-up offensive against the abolitionists, encapsulated in a February 1839 speech, confirmed and increased his strength across the South.

But there were limits to what Clay could achieve in Virginia, which aid in making the later Whig rupture comprehensible. In a widely circulated speech in November 1839, Wise carefully avoided sanctioning Clay's latitudinarian doctrines on their own merits. Instead, he put them in context. He asked how a bank or a higher tariff could possibly damage Virginia more than Van Buren's policies. He made much of Clay's public hedging on the bank issue—of his declared preference to "be guided wholly by the sense of the nation." Not daring to defend Clay's views on slavery in the abstract, he contrasted them with Van Buren's so as to point up the Kentuckian's greater reliability.[6]

Although the evidence yields no certain confirmation, it suggests that in 1840 most Whigs probably wanted a bank and the rest of Clay's system, but they dared not pronounce unequivocally for them. In other words, the prize more than the program probably controlled the Whigs the closer they came to achieving a goal they had never won before. They never adopted a national platform. A mixed record on the bank prevailed in the states, though Delphic ambiguity often triumphed. Clay himself paid homage to Virginia's tender sensibilities by coining a marvelous and noncommittal euphemism avowing his respect for "enlightened public opinion" during a speech at Taylorsville in June.

Harrison was Virginia-born, of course, but of his sentiments respecting the American system no one knew or cared. Not so, however, with his strict constructionist running mate, John Tyler. An acquaintance and constituent of Wise's, former Senator Tyler had repeatedly rejected a national bank. Because he had run with Hugh Lawson White in 1836, Tyler's very presence on the ticket in 1840 seemed reassuring to states'-rights Whigs, especially those who took seriously Virginia's celebrated "abstractionism." Years later, Wise wrote that acting in behalf of White, he interviewed Clay in 1839 and secured from him a series of pledges to soften or moderate his program. This story finds only limited support from contemporary evidence and may well have been self-serving fabrication. But the fact remains that despite the economic depression and his renewed popularity in the South, and even in the midst of a glorious campaign against an unpopular incumbent president, Clay's partisans seldom dared articulate their master's fondest and fullest hopes.[7]

Anxious to forget the constraints of program, Wise spent all of 1840 smashing every Jacksonian idol and pretension. When his health cracked, he took minimal breaks before launching fresh assaults. He undertook an ambitious speaking tour through Pennsylvania and New York, culminating in a Fourth of July rally at Poughkeepsie. Never again would he travel north of Philadelphia. Commencing his address "under excitement evidently too deep for words," Wise proved, at least to the *Albany Evening Standard*, that "Virginia has no worthier son." But such hyperbole typically neglected the substance of his remarks. Historians therefore can only surmise what "truths" could possibly have rested "like a burning coal on the brow of tyranny" and "haunted the sleep of thousands."[8]

Months earlier Wise had revealed to an old college friend his more serious motives for spending himself in this canvass. They had nothing to do with a final struggle against a great Goliath. "The only apprehension I have is that Harrison, if elected, will be elected too much by *one section alone*—the North, & East & West—the non-slaveholding section, thus leaving the friends of the Union who belong to the opposition chiefly in the South in a minority and at the mercy of a merciless majority of renegades there. There is nothing more inimical to the Country, more odious to me, than this *sectional* danger."[9] These sentiments, privately expressed, were summarized in Wise's public battle cry across the nation during the campaign: "The Union of the Whigs for the sake of the Union!"

Wise grew up around a hero of the American Revolution. With most of his generation, he never knew war firsthand. Politics was his surrogate for war; the use of warlike and militaristic metaphors in politics also conveyed his sense of its significance. The 1840 canvass climaxed a long crusade, full of battles and skirmishes, which Wise believed would culminate in a triumph of righteousness. No other struggle, except his own successful gubernatorial campaign in Virginia fifteen years later, ever provided him with greater satisfaction, and for good reason. Accomac's five-hundred-vote majority for Harrison and Tyler was among the three largest in the state. The Whigs carried his congressional bailiwick by nearly fifteen hundred votes, making it the banner Whig district in Virginia and perhaps in the Union. Though the Old Dominion remained Jacksonian, it did so by only the narrowest margin. Recognizing Wise's role, in a shrewd letter, John Tyler took measure of his accomplishments and stimulated his hopes for the future: "Let me say, I scorn to flatter, that I regard you as having been as much instrumental in bringing about the present state of things as any man who lives, and your views of the future should be as much sought after as your opinions in the past."[10] So they would, and in predictable fashion.

Supporting Tyler

The advantages of hindsight were not required to sense that sooner or later discord among Whigs would shatter their party irreparably. Interested observers, such as Thomas Ritchie of the *Richmond Enquirer*, confidently predicted it shortly after the election.[11] Both Wise and Tyler anticipated their later difficulties as early as December 1840.[12] Upon returning to Washington for the Congressional session, Wise cordially saluted Clay, who responded icily: "Ah! we are strong enough without the Whigs of Virginia, and are rejoiced that she voted against us and that we are not to be embarrassed by her peculiar opinions."[13] If any portion of this exchange is recorded accurately, it makes the subsequent alienation between the two men more intelligible. Wise was appalled. Clay scorned what the Virginian regarded as his own exhausting efforts. Had the ticket not done brilliantly in his district? Virginia, after all, had never gone Whig. To have come close and earned the plaudits of Tyler made Clay's ingratitude and insensitivity doubly difficult to bear. The memory of the Graves-Cilley affair created a further presumption of debt owed the Virginian. The Kentuckian's lack of graciousness repulsed Wise and affronted his honor. He probably had never seen this side of Clay's domineering character directed at anyone but their common political enemies. Dealing with Clay thereafer was like reliving some of his experiences with Andrew Jackson.

Some weeks later, Wise consumed three days of the House's time with a speech designed to squelch rumors of his opposition to the incoming administration and to silence those who ridiculed his erratic behavior. But the address's timing and Wise's manner of delivery suggest the limits of his loyalty to Whiggery. He deplored the "premature agitation of the National Bank question" and argued against a special session of Congress until the people had been further consulted about the bank and other issues. He devoted most of his address to a vigorous and learned exposition of the nation's financial crisis. With the federal debt so large, it would be foolish to distribute the proceeds from the sales of the public lands to the states because there was no surplus. Most Southerners, including Wise, had reason enough to fear an additional assault on the federal Treasury, for it would endanger the tariff compromise of 1833 by increasing the pressure (already strong among Northern Whigs) for higher duties.[14]

Despite this sensible argument, Wise's tone was typically high-handed. John Quincy Adams accused him of lecturing the House and pretending to the Speakership. Adams was right; Wise craved the honor, as rumor had already hinted.[15] The industrious Ritchie quickly seized upon the speech. He headlined and italicized Wise's declaration of loyalty to the "Republican portion of the Whig party" as evidence of prophecy fulfilled. Meanwhile, the *Richmond Whig*, which had been carrying on guerrilla warfare against Wise, now nervously reaffirmed his Whig orthodoxy.[16]

Before Harrison's inaugural, as Wise wrote many years later, "the *disjecta membra* of the Whig party rushed pell-mell to Washington, every man with a raccoon's tail in his hat, and tugged at the string of the latch, out at the White House door, as if sure enough it was a log cabin."[17] Among those trampled underfoot was the old president himself. Overwhelmed and exhausted by office-seekers, Harrison caught pneumonia and expired on 4 April.

It took Wise almost two weeks to reach Washington for an interview with Tyler. Recalling this encounter, he claimed to have advised his friend to veto the United States Bank and annex Texas. Having first developed an interest in Texas when he lived in Nashville, Wise might well have recommended annexation, particularly because it would differentiate Tyler's administration and confer upon it a glory that had eluded Jackson. Wise's advice perhaps influenced Tyler a few months later when he wrote out his famous "hint" to Secretary of State Daniel Webster that both of them might consider "the possibility of acquiring Texas by treaty."[18] This letter, however, came after the resignation of Tyler's cabinet, at the nadir of his presidency, and suggested how important the Texas issue would become in the effort to foil Clay by securing his own reelection in 1844.

Wise embroidered on his conversation with Tyler for both literary and political effect. In fact, he expected that Tyler would approve a national bank in some form and was surprised to learn of the president's undiminished hostility. Indeed, after reading his initial presidential message, although before meeting him personally, Wise had gone so far as to advise one of the leading lights of Kentucky Whiggery that Tyler might be willing to accommodate the bank wing of the party. His correspondent later saw to it that this private communication enjoyed a wide readership. Much to Wise's chagrin, it became a minor classic amid the acrimony that divided Tyler's friends from Clay's.[19]

Supporting Tyler

Finally, Wise boldly told Tyler that he should dismiss Harrison's entire cabinet, including Webster (though he later denied it). Events proved the soundness of this advice, although Tyler kept his own counsel and retained them until all but Webster had resigned in September 1841. Indeed, the new president seems to have followed his own best lights most of the time. This supposition runs counter both to Wise's modest assertions that he was the moving spirit of the administration and the architect of its leading measures, and to the contemporary notion that the Virginia congressman was Tyler's *eminence grise*.[20] Wise's mercurial temperament, his rashness, and his capacity to hate made him slightly suspect to Tyler and his other advisers. In the tense Washington atmosphere of the summer of 1841, Wise and Tyler both oscillated between seeking compromise with the Whig majority and endeavoring to steel themselves for resistance. In fact, Wise probably worried about the strength of his ability to resist Clay. He had gone through it all with Jackson before.

In no mood for patience or subtlety, and having already engineered a special congressional session, Clay wanted to confront Tyler with an integrated set of proposals so popular with Whig majorities in the House and Senate as to force his compliance. Among them were the repeal of the Sub-Treasury, establishment of a United States Bank, and passage of tariff, bankruptcy, and distribution bills, along with necessary appropriations.

More cautious than his advisers, Tyler seems to have hoped for compromise. He contemplated supporting most of the Whig program, including a tariff that offered some measure of protection for domestic industry. Wise wanted to go even further because the economic depression had depleted federal resources.[21] Tyler first asked Clay to postpone the bank issue. When the Old Dictator refused, he sensibly declined to accept responsibility for any measure that won approval from Congress. Tyler wanted a bank chartered in the District of Columbia, with drastically limited powers of discount and deposit, on the model proposed by Hugh Lawson White.[22] When Secretary of the Treasury Thomas Ewing drew up a bill satisfying most of Tyler's reservations, Clay opposed the requirement that states grant their approval before the new bank could establish branches within their borders. After Clay had amended the legislation to presume a state's assent (unless positively refused), Tyler's veto was inevitable. For a time, Wise believed that Jacksonians and renegade Whigs would defeat the bill in Congress. But he accurately perceived Clay's intention to provoke at least one veto from Tyler, thereby killing his chances for the succession four years hence.[23]

Tyler was more culpable the second time around. Evidently he saw and approved the second bank bill before its submission to Congress. After its approval, shouting mobs insulting him from the White House porch and scurrilous letters assailing his manhood took their toll. The more Tyler and his friends absorbed such a shellacking, the more their highly developed senses of personal honor seemed to dominate. As Oliver P. Chitwood suggests, Wise probably wrote Tyler's second veto message, a technical argument that never obtained much circulation or sympathy. Its tone, however, was remarkably conciliatory. The message reflected Wise's nationalistic biases, describing the Constitution as the "embodied and written will of the whole people of the United States." With this concession, one modern historian writes, Tyler "granted the first premise of consolidationists and made his high-principled vetoes look somewhat ridiculous."[24]

Even in the denouement of a hot and venomous summer, Wise stood at no great distance ideologically from Clay. That he loathed the Kentuckian nonetheless says much about the importance of personal relations and face-to-face encounters in nineteenth-century political culture. Clay compounded his arrogance of December 1840 in another interview with Wise late in May. "I told him we differed in toto," Wise reported to one of his constituents. He replied, "I never give up." "I know it," said I. "Wise, I have defended you." "Mr. Clay, I have defended you to an extent that I shall never need defense. You were paid in advance, and we must join issue."[25] Graves-Cilley remained just beyond the vocal range of this exchange, but Wise alluded to it only because of Clay's imperiousness. Clay no longer wished to pay deference to the queer theorists who inhabited Wise's congressional district, including John Tyler. Instead of honoring or acknowledging his debts to Wise, he decided to repudiate. Soon the Whig press was hinting at Wise's culpability in the duel. The Virginian reciprocated by inserting in the *New York Herald* a warning to Clay's partisans that they risked an exposé of their favorite's responsibility.[26]

He then took what vengeance he could. Edgy and violent, he

assumed the role of Tyler's dark angel in the House of Representatives. John Forney went too far in identifying him as "the undoubted dictator of the Tyler Administration," but there was much truth in his description of Wise "standing between the two great parties in the House," delighting "in his isolation," and rioting "in the eccentricities of his genius."[27] Defeated for the Speakership, he presided instead over the president's small band of supporters. As captain of "the Corporal's Guard"—Clay's denigrating nickname for the Tylerite minority that Wise proudly embraced—the young Virginian toiled incessantly over the next two years. He bore principal responsibility for introducing Tyler's measures in the House and then deflecting the hail of invective from all sides which they invariably inspired after the summer of 1841. In a classic example of psychological projection, Wise wrote of Clay that "to make him admired and his great qualities shine, he must ever be kept down in a minority, for the moment the weights are taken off the swings of his vaulting ambition, his head flies into the clouds."[28]

Supporting Tyler

Though he denied that the Tyler presidency was a "third force" in American politics (an updated version of Randolph's earlier *tertium quid* movement), for a time Wise thought of it as a providential opportunity to reorder American politics and protect the South. "Let the factions devour one another," he wrote, when it seemed apparent that Tyler would command the sympathy of neither Whigs nor Democrats, "and let the Republicanism left among us thrive by the contest." Virginia might stand again at the head of an alliance of true Whigs and others, particularly Northern conservatives, willing to take orders. But as the chorus rose identifying his own erratic conduct with Randolph's memory, Wise divined the limitations of this particular vision and within a year was maneuvering for favor among both Calhounites and Jacksonians.[29]

An independent presidency might also successfully reform the corrupt practices exposed by his investigations during the 1830s. Wise professed that the administration, because Virginian in its orientation, would guarantee a purer conduct of public affairs. Relishing the political leverage he possessed within the executive branch of government, he monitored patronage appointments carefully and fought hard to obtain positions for his friends, many of them impecunious Virginians with large families to support.

Certain of Wise's sensitivities were shared by his friends and neighbors in the so-called Virginia Cabal—principally Professor Nathaniel Beverley Tucker of the College of William and Mary, Congressmen Francis Mallory and Thomas Walker Gilmer, and

Judge Abel P. Upshur. Although Tyler made his own decisions, this group of unofficial counselors had easiest access to him and frequently filtered Virginia public opinion, about which he was zealously sensitive. The Old Dominion's fading glory illuminated the schemes of these designing men. What they wanted, as Edmund Ruffin wrote Tyler, was an affirmation, "in their integrity and purity," of "state-rights and republican principles & policy."[30] What they meant was a rejuvenation of the Virginia principles of 1798, formulated by James Madison and emphasizing state sovereignty, although interpreted by themselves. As a Tidewater Virginia representative, Wise appreciated the concerns of these men, but he had seen more of the world than any of them and, with the exception of Tyler himself, had spent longer in public life. He was, in other words, more cosmopolitan and less ideological in outlook than they.

Within this group, both Tucker and Upshur flirted with Southern independence; Tucker systematically exhorted South Carolina extremists through the mails. But Tyler's Virginians were principally Unionists. Along with Wise, they feared the loss of Virginia's prestige to South Carolina and to the more prosperous Northern states. They also found it difficult to admit that slavery might have influenced their state's decline. Under siege, Wise and his associates abandoned more honest explanations of Virginia's decline, which he had advanced earlier, and focused instead on the alleged inequitable distribution of the national domain that increasingly favored the free states.[31] These Virginia ideologues, along with their predecessor John Randolph, resolved to firm up the Old Dominion's sagging reputation. For their troubles, they earned from contemporaries and historians alike a reputation for ludicrous abstractionism.

Despite their unwillingness to acknowledge it publicly, all of them now believed that a reaffirmation of Virginia's principles was vitally necessary to protect the Old Dominion's chief vested interest—slavery. They wanted to avoid a choice between slavery and the Union, in part because they regarded themselves as representatives of the weaker section. Wise's own speeches regularly portrayed the South as overwhelmed by the federal census, in danger of losing parity in the Senate, and conspired against by an international crusade aimed at promotion of servile insurrection. He monitored antislavery activity, quoted extensively from English and Northern abolitionists during his remarks in the House, and always remained mindful of Adams's call for emancipation by martial law. Safety and security were precious commodities, available nowhere in any great quantity, although perhaps awaiting discovery in Texas.[32]

The example set by Andrew Jackson provided an additional inspiration to Tyler and his associates. Along with the liberal use of the veto, one of the ways that Jackson created a new presidency was by establishing useful parallel institutions such as his famous Kitchen Cabinet. The Tylerites emulated this practice, although it could be argued that they had little choice because their congressional support was so thin. Most important, Jackson demonstrated the immense political advantages in bypassing the other branches of government and acting directly on the "passions and prejudices" of the people—and, indeed, in creating popular attitudes. Jackson's example probably gave Wise confidence, neutralized his fear of isolation, and strengthened his extremism. Jackson took unpopular positions but survived. A large number of Tyler's advisers, including almost the entire cabinet he appointed in September 1841, had formerly supported the Old Hero. As the president's man in the House, Wise had a sense of the power that the new presidency would confer. It helped steel his opposition to the Whig majority, particularly as party structures polarized and grew far more rigid.

But instead of an independent republican administration influencing the political process, it had become much easier for the major political parties to reject or absorb anomalous formations such as Tyler's.[33] Nonetheless, as Wise aggressively maintained ever afterward, the Tyler presidency eliminated the possibility of ever enacting Clay's centralizing economic program. The results, particularly in the South, crippled efforts to displace perennial sensitivities to slavery with a national politics grounded on conflicting theories of economic development. The focus of national politics remained on slavery and thus consistently exposed the peculiar vulnerability of the Whig intersectional coalition. "We are *done*," remarked John Bell, who resigned from Tyler's cabinet at Clay's request.[34]

Wise narrowly escaped the same fate. As criticism mounted among his constituents, he responded with a fascinating though indiscreet speech on Texas in mid-April 1842. Previewing later Tylerite arguments favoring annexation, he correctly noted that both Adams and Clay had negotiated for Texas in the mid-1820s. Thus they would have added slave territory to the Union because Mexican emancipation did not technically take effect until 1829 and even then exempted Texas. He also defended annexation as a means of preserving America's cotton monopoly, which Tyler later maintained was the crucial influence on his own motives. He dared the English to fight and offered, if war came, to lead an assault on Mexico, rob all the gold from a "lazy besotted priesthood," and extend slavery to the Pacific. Not anticipating the skill and flexibility of those who converted abolitionism during these years into a militant assault on the slave power, Wise predicted that war would subject the abolitionists "to the law of tar and feathers."[35]

This rhetoric was predictable from a Virginia congressman, but Wise astonished the House by also promoting annexation as a great antislavery measure. The abolitionists had no direct influence on the Texas slave system. Annexation represented the only way "to mitigate its severity or restrain its abuse." Besides eliminating "the evils of slavery" over which certain "philanthropic gentlemen" had "made such doleful lamentation," annexation could lead to emancipation by bringing "it within our reach and jurisdiction." If the antislavery forces "were really sincere in their professed desire to see slavery abolished, their true and only course was to annex Texas to the United States." Laughter and catcalls instantly followed these remarks. Wise had managed to convince a sizable percentage of his audience of his own dishonesty. He had not, of course, associated himself with the abolitionists. But significantly, he did not dissociate himself from them either.

In justifying annexation as an abolitionist measure, Wise's thinking might be compared with the celebrated argument of Mississippi Senator Robert J. Walker, published in January 1844. Both men correctly sensed that slavery's center of gravity was drifting to the Southwest; Wise speculated that insurrectionary violence would be a consequence of being "damned up" with slaves. Walker speculated confidently that annexation would create a "safety valve" for the South's slaves, who would gradually congregate in the Southwest before being funneled out of the Union and into Central America. Wise's views were less detailed, although both he and Walker believed in and desired slavery's eventual disappearance. Each man condemned the abolitionists and yet confirmed their growing power by disputing the notion that annexation would reinvigorate American slavery. Wise claimed to have originated these arguments. He reacted indignantly when Walker obtained most of the credit.[36]

Nonplussed at this revelation of his strategy, and disturbed by its potentially adverse impact on negotiations leading to the Webster-Ashburton Treaty, Tyler probably intervened personally to suppress publication of the speech.[37] Under no similar obligations, John Quincy Adams broadcast its message far and wide in circulars advertising the sinister objectives of the annexation conspiracy.[38]

Supporting Tyler

Adams, however, seriously underestimated the later efforts of Sir Robert Peel and Lord Aberdeen to preserve Texas's independence and promote emancipation. Contrary to the views of many historians, British agents encouraged Texans and others who sought both these objectives. When these developments came to light in 1843, Tyler and his friends justifiably called attention to an English conspiracy. Prescient, though increasingly isolated, Wise complained about how his alleged "impetuosity" undercut his ability to influence policy.[39]

To protect himself, he angled toward readmission to the Democratic party. John L. O'Sullivan, editor of the *Democratic Review*, apparently initiated contact with Wise. In May 1842 the *Review* retracted its earlier condemnation of his role in the Graves-Cilley duel. At about this time, one of the more acerbic Whig congressmen described Wise as "a gentleman who was able to transfer himself, as if by a wand of magic, from one party, and a most virulent state of hostility to his opponents, to the lead of the other."[40] Leadership, however, offered little security for Wise and no satisfaction for his leader. Thus Tyler planned an honorable and lucrative exit for him. Three times in the spring of 1843 the Senate rejected his nomination as American minister to France.

Wise might have grounded arms, but with the pride of one denied an entitlement properly earned, he prepared a furious counterattack that was only narrowly successful. To preserve his future, he required reelection to Congress. For the first time in eight years opposition surfaced in the form of the distinguished and wealthy Hill Carter of Shirley, one of the showplace estates of the lower Tidewater. Wise expected a thousand-vote victory and excused his four-hundred vote margin by theorizing that "farming operations" had distracted the electorate. His recently reestablished links with the Democracy aided him indispensably. Arriving in Washington after this victory, Wise encountered a president and Senate anxious to find a place for him outside the country.[41] Three months later, though only after several remarkable developments, he left for Brazil to take up his appointment as American minister.

In February 1844, just at the time Wise was resigning from Congress, an explosion aboard a warship in the Potomac River killed Secretary of State Abel P. Upshur and several of Tyler's other intimates. Knowing of John C. Calhoun's anxiety to recruit him for the upcoming presidential race, and counting on the Carolinian's trust and goodwill, Wise took an extraordinary initiative.

He conferred with one of Calhoun's close friends, Senator George McDuffie, who in turn saw Tyler and then urged the great Southern oracle to accept appointment as secretary of state. Tyler had previously offered cabinet positions to the Carolinian, but Wise, as he later claimed, probably persuaded McDuffie to write Calhoun on the understanding that Tyler had already approved the nomination. Then he presented the president with a fait accompli that compelled him either to yield to Calhoun's nomination and forward his name or disavow Wise and his characteristic "policy of rashness."[42]

The Carolinian never forgot. Impressed with Wise's services, he intervened decisively in 1845, after James K. Polk's election to the presidency, to convince Polk to retain in Rio de Janeiro an old and bitter enemy.[43]

Before departing for Brazil, Wise published the last of his many addresses to his constituents. Having recently established himself on a salary of $9,000 per year, he took pains to advise his friends that "economy and taxation" governed sound public morals. He then recommended that all surplus public revenues be directed to the assistance of his district's educational system. "I felt no blows which were ever stricken at me—never," he wrote, "but the blows which they struck at you, every one of them reached home to my heart. There was one—the unkindest cut of all—which I felt more deeply because there was too much truth in the approach. They said—Yes! they will always elect him, but then *many of them cannot read and write*!" Improvements in public instruction, he advised, would confirm the loyalties of the white poor. Eventually, nonslaveholders would become the focus of his attention.[44]

This "farewell address" represented yet another concession to the slashing attacks of John Quincy Adams. Only two years earlier Wise had gloated over the absence of newspapers in his congressional district, maintaining that without them his constituents were happier and less inclined to indulge reforming schemes. But these remarks betrayed his uneasiness over Virginia's backward condition. In his published address, Wise produced a table, based on calculations from the federal census of 1840, which showed more illiterates than voters living in his congressional district. The primary constituency of Virginia's miserable and ineffective system of common schools, he wrote, was impoverished children stigmatized by the charity of free instruction provided by the state. Charity must end, Wise argued. Education should be free and compulsory, rich and poor deserved equal treatment, and the wealthy should happily bear the burdens of increased taxation because they had the most to lose should an ignorant and uncivilized rabble ever seize power. If taxes raised locally could supply the costs of instruction, state funds would be released for teacher training and construction of badly needed school buildings.[45]

No record exists of Adams exulting over this concession, although he made the most of another triumph granted him by the departing Virginian. When the first session of the Twenty-eighth Congress convened in December 1843 (a few months before Wise's departure for Brazil), Adams again prepared his assault on the gag rule and Southern sensibilities generally. Calling reporters to his side to avoid errors in transcription, Wise announced his unwillingness to continue the struggle. He proposed that Adams organize a select committee of his own, in order to receive all petitions and report thereon, so that the South might know the petitioners' designs. He conceded the uselessness of further resistance. A beaten man, he acknowledged his defeat and the ineffectiveness of his arguments. The South "had been wholly worsted in the fight," he remarked. He would "cease the war in this House and oppose nothing." Southern spokesmen in the House of Representatives, such as Isaac F. Holmes of South Carolina, expressed shock and surprise at the Virginian's decision. They predictably fought on until the abrogation of the gag rule one year later, in December 1844.[46]

Six weeks later, everything had changed. As a member of the Rules Committee chaired by Adams, he filed a scathing minority report that summarized all his old constitutional arguments, reviewed the recent enormities of the abolitionists, proclaimed the dangers to the South, and urged maintenance of the gag rule. Should the rule be abrogated—as many now confidently predicted—he called in Madisonian fashion for a national convention to harmonize relations among the states. Some likely particulars were missing from Wise's defiant farewell to this remarkable debate, however. At no point did he retract his proposal for retroceding the District of Columbia. Nor did he threaten secession and violence, as did Congressman Holmes. Wise's language reflected the charges he was most anxious to avoid: "Late events, and a series of instances lately, prove that a minority section . . . weakens in power faster than it weakens in numbers. Renegades will take the bounty, at the very moment when their birthplaces need their best nerves, and their best thoughts, for defense. They will sell out the hearths and the graves of their fathers, to those who alone any longer can give them the hopes and the honor of power and place and political preferment."[47]

What had happened? Perhaps Wise's willingness to abandon

the struggle early in the congressional session reflected an effort to curry favor among Northern senators whose votes would shortly aid in confirming him as minister to Brazil. He might also have wanted to deflect Northern antagonism away from such projects as the annexation of Texas, which meant far more to the South than maintenance of the gag rule. But the tone of his remarks in December suggests a sense of relief from a burden lifted. Wise carefully staged an affirmation of his own decency and best intentions. The composition of the minority report followed what must have been intense criticism, mostly in private and addressed to the legitimacy of his credentials as a true Southerner. When an inoffensive Pennsylvania representative touched on Southern disunity early in January, Wise bristled and inquired instantly about the identities of those allegedly promoting it.[48] Shortly afterward, having taken his "place and political preferment," he left the House and the country.

Chapter 5
The Good Slaveholder

Wise arrived in Rio de Janeiro on 2 August 1844. He read French and understood a smattering of Spanish, but no Portuguese. Aided by an efficient secretary of legation, he returned nearly twelve thousand pages of manuscript to Washington in about three and one-half years. Wise worked conscientiously to expedite the growing trade in Brazilian coffee and American wheat. Curious about Brazilian flora and fauna, he regularly sent specimens home to interested parties and his neighbors to test their viability in North America. In conformity with Secretary of State Calhoun's instructions, he also labored to settle the claims of American citizens against the imperial government. As his correspondence shows, however, Wise spent at least two-thirds of his time in a sustained, passionate, and ultimately unsuccessful effort to suppress American involvement in the African slave trade.[1]

Calhoun's instructions set forth two primary objectives for Wise's mission but ignored the slave trade controversy, into which the Virginian plunged on his own responsibility. Calhoun wanted Wise to negotiate a new commercial treaty, but it proved impossible because of the antagonism he provoked among the Brazilian authorities. His successor obtained the desired treaty. The secretary of state also requested Wise to explain and justify United States policy toward Texas. Annexation, Calhoun wrote, was necessary to prevent abolition. If Great Britain's emancipationist policy should succeed, he continued, it would "destroy the peace and prosperity of both [Brazil and the United States] and transfer the production of tobacco, rice, cotton, sugar and coffee from [them] to her possessions beyond the Cape of Good Hope." Calhoun added his congratulations to the Brazilians for not abolishing slavery in order to get their sugar into the British market duty free. Wise complied enthusiastically with these instructions, although his mission failed to promote the cooperation that Calhoun thought should exist between the hemisphere's two great slaveholding nations.[2] His greatest enthusiasm, however, was reserved for the bold and uncompromising effort he made to end illicit American participation in the international slave trade.

Since 1820 American citizens engaging in the trade risked conviction for a capital offense. Although American law thus imposed a harsher penalty than that of any other nation, it proved impossible to enforce. The American navy was too small to patrol the Caribbean region and the Brazilian and African coasts efficiently. The British wanted to use their formidable navy to police American shipping. As part of their long campaign against slavery and the slave trade, they gradually coerced the other Atlantic powers into allowing the British navy to search all suspected slavers flying any flag but the American. Keenly recalling the evils of impressment, Americans defended the doctrine of freedom of the seas. By 1839 the system of British bribery and alliances had reached the point (according to one historian) that "immunity from search by the British squadron was now only to be obtained under the flag of the United States."[3]

Neither the Brazilian nor Portuguese ensigns, for example, offered sure protection. Both countries had conceded to the British the right to search their vessels, although the treaty stipulating Brazil's agreement to this measure would expire in 1845. Moreover, Brazilian law since 1831 had made the slave trade a crime and automatically emancipated all Africans henceforth victimized by it. Large numbers of slave-trading vessels, of course, continued to fly the Brazilian or Portuguese flag. Some trusted to their speed. Others took their chances on evading punishment, if captured, from one of the various mixed commissions charged with trying slavers.

In the mid-1840s, when Wise arrived, slave imports averaged around thirty thousand per year, evidently about 20 percent of them protected by the American flag.[4] Between 1842 and 1851, more than three hundred thousand African slaves entered Brazil. Given the power of the wealthy traders and their corrupt political associates, and the immense popularity of the trade among aspiring Brazilians, it proved impossible to stop. The demand for labor in the expanding sugar and coffee regions made the slave trade well worth the risks of capture. "Nothing is lost," Wise calculated, "if two out of five trips succeed."[5] The magnitude of this traffic was too great even for the proud British to control; they therefore directed a good deal of their frustration toward the United States for refusing to cooperate wholeheartedly in its suppression.

British insistence during the negotiation of the Webster-Ashburton Treaty of 1842 forced Americans to station a fleet of not less than eighty guns on the African coast. The fleet's ostensible purpose was to arrest American slavers, but it was also obligated to prevent British interference with any United States shipping. An onerous duty in an unhealthy area, it was indifferently performed.[6] A heavy responsibility therefore fell upon the equally weak but more efficient United States Brazilian squadron. But here again, the navy's primary obligation was the protection and encouragement of legitimate American commerce. As Wise quickly perceived, relatively little legitimate commerce made its way to Africa in the mid-nineteenth century. Short of interdicting all American trade to Africa, he acknowledged, American authorities could hope only "to snatch the flag" periodically from its "pollution" by slave traders.[7] Previous ministers had reached the same conclusion.

American shipowners and crews ran the risk of heavy penalties, of course, but typically disguised their movements to allow them to evade both detection and prosecution. No shipowner could lawfully claim the protection of the American flag if his vessel was owned "either in whole or in part by a foreigner" or by an American citizen "not usually resident in the United States." American participants in the slave trade secured their profits by renting vessels in Rio or elsewhere in Brazil at prices often far in excess of their value and dealing with agents of the great slave traders, such as Manoel Pinto da Fonseca. The notorious Captain Joshua Clapp of New York, for example, who acted for the Rio traders, "acquired" former United States merchantmen, which were converted to slavers. Nothing but perjury on a grand and systematic scale, wholly sustained by American consuls, could explain the ease with which foreigners passed themselves off as Americans while genuine Americans claimed ownership of vessels they did not possess.

The ships were not chartered but instead secretly sold for delivery on the African coast. This procedure allowed them to fly the American flag on their outbound voyages from Brazil. They were thus protected against British naval patrols, whose treaty authority permitted them to confiscate a vessel flying any other ensign merely if the ordinary implements of the slave trade were located on board. After loading a cargo of Africans, the slavers often disposed of the American flag. Given the dreaded American law, they seldom took chances even with the inefficient United States African squadron and preferred capture while flying either another flag or none at all. After painting over the names of the vessels, Brazilian or other foreign nationals ran the slavers back across the Atlantic. The Americans among their crews (who had shipped in order to preserve an ostensibly American nationality on the eastward voyage) left them on the African coast and returned to Rio aboard an auxiliary vessel of American registry supposedly engaged in legitimate trade.[8]

No general interdiction of American trade with Africa was possible without congressional assent. Neither Congress nor the State Department responded to Wise's requests for additional naval patrols in Brazilian waters. The powerlessness he experienced proved both dominating and corroding. At one point, he nearly provoked an international incident by threatening arrest and detention of suspected American slave traders on board a vessel safely at anchor in the harbor at Rio. The commander of the American naval squadron had already seized the ship, but Wise feared the escape of the passengers because no extradition treaty existed between Brazil and the United States. Satisfied with the ship alone, the commander refused to act on Wise's rash and illegal recommendations. The passengers departed, and the Virginian thereafter endured a mild reprimand from Secretary of State James Buchanan. Reaction from the State Department was less ambiguous, however, after Wise persuaded one consul to prohibit the sale of American vessels to other American citizens at Rio. Following protests from American merchants, the department ordered this policy reversed. Thus Wise's extreme and heroic measures proved unavailing in either scotching the slave trade or restricting American participation in it. It was only the massive shift of British naval power to Brazilian waters late in 1849, a result of complex forces operating on the Whig government, that eventually terminated the Brazilian slave trade.[9]

Wise had "no conception of the extent, the universality, and the notoriety" of this traffic until he attempted to suppress it.[10] Nonetheless, he remained unyielding. He refused to concentrate on the objectives Calhoun had outlined in his instructions. During his years in Rio, he personally investigated between twenty and thirty cases of suspected American involvement in the slave trade. He sent several vessels home for condemnation, along with about a dozen American citizens, although only one appears to have been convicted. He grilled every American consul in Brazil about each rumor or suspicion, however implausible, that came to his attention. He revoked the credentials of several American consuls whom he suspected of conniving in the slave trade. His domineering attitude and monopolization of duties belonging ordinarily to consuls led to an explosive collision with George W. Gordon, the consul in Rio until mid-1845. The quarrel surfaced when the Virginian accused Gordon, a Northerner, of insufficient vigilance in policing American participants in the slave trade.[11]

Secretary of State Buchanan eventually intervened and recalled Gordon, although he was frequently hard-pressed to defend Wise. The Virginian's abrasiveness and his interference in what they regarded as Brazil's internal affairs irritated both President Polk and George Bancroft, the secretary of the navy. The American mercantile community and the Brazilian minister in Washington exerted considerable pressure to secure Wise's recall.[12] Moreover, his zealousness lost him the favor of Calhoun, who wrote, "I fear . . . that Wise is pursuing an injudicious course in reference to the Slave trade. My instructions to him were full and pointed on the necessity of preserving the most friendly relations with Brazil. . . . It would be greatly to be regretted, if he has taken any step calculated to have a contrary effect."[13]

Wise turned to the only member of Tyler's cabinet retained by Polk, John Y. Mason of Virginia. Too proud to beg but desperate to retain the Brazilian mission, he requested Mason's intervention with both Polk and Buchanan. Despite having mercilessly assailed the president, he claimed in retrospect that no one did "*more* perhaps . . . to restore or regain power for the Republican party. . . . I alone upheld 'the weary arm with the rod in it' whilst the battle waxed warm at the called session [of 1841]—and Thos. W. Gilmer and I alone for a long while brought on the decisive issue of the Texas question, and I finally, before I left the country, at New York, arranged with others the withdrawal of Mr. Tyler." He highlighted his suspicions of Northern Whigs who owned vessels engaged in the slave trade and also alluded to his muddled finances. Mason and Buchanan protected him for a time, but Wise's determination to enforce American law wrecked his mission.[14]

Wise's actions are incomprehensible without appreciating both the moral reprehension the slave trade elicited in him and his doubts about the efficacy of slavery as a social system. Adams and the abolitionists, he must have thought, had a point. The trade was barbarous and cruel. He would show his enemies that a Southerner and a slaveholder was decent enough to respect human dignity and to reprobate kidnapping and man-stealing. As he wrote shortly after taking up his mission: "The fact of my being a slaveholder, is itself a pledge & guarantee that I am no *fanatic*, foolishly & wickedly bent on running amuck against any lawful property or trade; and that I find the same old interest at work here & now, to fasten American slavery on Brazil, which in our early history fastened its condition of a slave state on Virginia."[15]

Wise thus acknowledged his conviction that Brazil's principal problem was the likelihood that the slave trade would make it more like Virginia—or, at least, the corrupt and economically backward Old Dominion that he hoped to modernize. It was neither safe nor necessary for him to elaborate this justification for his campaign against the slave trade. Once his investigations had established that Northerners owned the vast majority of American vessels chartered for the trade, he reveled in throwing the moralism of the Yankees back in their faces. "Out of twenty-two vessels of our merchant marine engaged in the African trade between 'The Coast' & Brazil since June 1845," he advised a Virginia correspondent, "but four hail South of Philada. & they were from Balt[imore]." He charged that Delaware Quakers and Maine abolitionists, among others, owned vessels committed to the trade.

> Such are mere samples of tens & twenties of cases going to show that the navigation int[erest] of the North is now doing for Brazil what it did for Virginia and the other Southern States in N. America—carrying the slave cargoes from Africa under the protection of the U. States flag; with the additional evil to us at this day that they are thus affording the only good cause upon earth to the English to search our vessels, at the very moment they would plunge us into a war with Gt. Britain under the expectation of compelling emancipation in the Southern States by the treaty-making power, & by the black regiments of Jamaica.[16]

The furtive and illegal slave trade, conducted mainly by hypocritical Yankees, represented the greatest threat to the lawful trade then existing in both Brazil and the United States. Wise noted in particular how few females arrived, thus sharply retarding natural increase and the potential for family life within the Brazilian slave community. Moreover, he correctly blamed Northern shipping interests for harassing him and attempting to obtain his recall.[17]

Unknown to Wise, his enemy and antagonist George W. Gordon vindicated many of his charges in the last despatch he wrote from Rio de Janeiro before another American consul replaced him. His lengthy description of American involvement in the trade duplicated Wise's. He also attached a detailed tabular statement estimating that from January 1840 until September 1845 at least thirty-four (and probably the vast majority) of the sixty-four American vessels sold in Rio engaged in slave trading. Of these, a number hailed from Baltimore, but the great majority were registered in Northern ports, principally New York City.[18]

Not content with disputing Yankee humanitarianism, Wise also questioned British sincerity about suppressing the trade. American participation in it provided opportunities for British interference that rankled him. He wanted to end this threat and whenever possible to deflate the effrontery and self-righteousness of the English. In correspondence with the British minister in Rio and with his own government, Wise repeatedly alluded to the materialist basis of English policy. He suggested that if they were serious about abolition, the English would compel their own merchants to cease selling the articles to Portuguese and Brazilian merchants that later were exchanged for slaves on the African coast. He also asserted that British cruisers seldom prevented "the *shipping* of slaves in *Africa*," so that they could collect the per capita bounty for seizing them on the high seas and later send them as apprentices to various British possessions. Tyler communicated these charges to Congress.[19]

The British appreciated Wise's "zeal and activity" but rejected his arguments. Lord Aberdeen responded indignantly. The contention that English sailors coveted merely the bounty on captured Africans was absurd, he wrote, because from 1838 to 1844 the navy had seized four times as many unladen vessels as those carrying slaves. The number of captures demonstrated the navy's insensitivity about offending English commercial interests.

Aberdeen felt doubly vexed at Wise's charges because they surfaced precisely at the time when, most British leaders believed, Brazilian recalcitrance had provoked a crisis in relations between the two countries. They feared that Wise might further encourage the already balky Brazilians to resist extension of the treaty permitting the British navy to visit and search Brazilian vessels. Peel and Aberdeen saw to it that Parliament enacted in 1845 a new measure sanctioning the navy's power. Popularly known as the Aberdeen Act, it drew on the first article of the still effective Anglo-Brazilian Treaty of 1826 to reaffirm (despite opposing Brazilian interpretations) both parties' condemnation of the slave trade as piracy. Because nations generally agreed that their warships possessed the right to search and detain suspected pirates, British politicians looked no further for justification. Between 1845 and the end of the slave trade to Brazil in 1851, the British navy seized nearly four hundred ships carrying slaves to Brazil.[20] Wise's charges were therefore made to look unfounded and reflective of his own frustrations, anxieties, and unreasoning nationalism. It bears noting, however, that one reason for the British navy's success in the late 1840s was the tremendous flowering of the trade shortly before. British political pressure compelled in 1850 both the enactment and vigorous enforcement of new prohibitory legislation by the Brazilians.

Aberdeen further denied that any Africans had been apprenticed in the West Indies since emancipation. He admitted, however, that exceptions were occasionally made "for very young children" and added that the Africans—along with all immigrants —were "asked" to sign labor contracts of twelve months duration. Whatever the evasions of Peel and Aberdeen, tens of thousands of blacks "liberated" on the open seas by the British navy found themselves a short time later in a system approximating slavery. British policy during this period forced many of these Africans to take up residence in the West Indies.[21]

Although the evidence in Wise's rebuttal was a bit thin, he found no difficulty showing from British sources that government policy favored continuation of a system of quasi slavery in the West Indies, disguised by the euphemism "contract labor." He also cited an advertisement from London newspapers for "goods for the coast" to emphasize that British goods seldom appeared coincidentally in West Africa. Indeed, Peel's speech of 19 March 1845, which Wise wanted to refute because it denied the existence of apprenticeship in the West Indies, all but conceded the large-scale involvement of British capital in the slave trade. In recapitulating at length the cases of the most notorious slave ships captured during his time as minister, Wise demonstrated conclusively that British goods, bankers, and credit were all indispensable to the slave trade economy. He conceded that in recent years the British had captured more unladen than laden slave ships in Africa. But the relative number of unladen vessels captured should have been even greater, he argued, because at any point on the African coast they outnumbered ships filled with slaves in the ratio of twenty to one. Moreover, he correctly pointed out that the system of bounties operating in the Royal Navy recognized the necessity of providing incentives to encourage the capture of empty slavers.[22]

These arguments seemed increasingly hollow and irrelevant as the slave trade metastasized beyond all efforts to control it in the mid-1840s. Disillusioned by the uselessness of his labors and possibly fearing recall by the president, Wise determined in the summer of 1846 to return home. It took more than a year to make the necessary arrangements. During that time his relations with the Brazilians deteriorated further. After his intervention in one particularly ugly incident, his status declined to nearly that of a quarantined alien.

Late in October 1846, the Brazilian authorities arrested a group of American sailors on liberty in Rio, charged them with rowdiness, and kept them in close confinement for a short time. Urged on by the American naval commandant on the Brazilian station, Wise decided to play "old Hickory on them" by demanding both the immediate release of the prisoners and a street-scraping *amende* from the Brazilians. He wanted "to make these Spanish and Portugese mongrells in South America understand that *the U. States must be respected*." When the proper satisfaction was not forthcoming, he snubbed the imperial family at an important public function. Thereafter, the Brazilians refused him official contact.

Polk and Buchanan stood by him, although all seemed relieved when he returned home in the fall of 1847. Before leaving he attempted to prevent his successor, "a decent man on the order of an *Ohio* farmer or *coal digger*," from presenting his credentials until a proper *amende* had been offered. This worthy refused, whereupon Wise wrote that for disgracing his mission his successor would eventually wish himself thrown into the sea with a millstone around his neck.[23] Deeply concerned about the damage his efforts in behalf of the sailors might do to his reputation, Wise caused the publication of his State Department correspondence relating to the incident.[24] He relied on his patriotic enthusiasm to guarantee a vindication. Following his return to the United States, he expressed his gratitude to Polk and Buchanan personally and used these conversations to affirm his Democratic orthodoxy.

To protect himself further, Wise presumably alluded to the recent death of his cousin Tully, which significantly increased his private obligations. Tully's wife Margaret, who was Henry's sister, derived little support from a heavily encumbered estate and barely managed as operator of a boarding house in Washington, D.C. Her eight children, as she plaintively expressed it, could in the end look only to Henry for guidance and protection.[25] It thus seemed sensible for Wise gravely to avow a dedication to private life, although Polk and the other Democratic elders never dared trust him beyond the doors of their own offices.

Nearly forty-one years old when he returned to Accomac, Wise seemed genuinely anxious to take up his rightful place among his kin and the farming gentry of the Eastern Shore. At midlife, with most of those who raised him long since dead, Henry assumed the power and responsibility of family patriarch. John Cropper Wise, his invalid brother and only potential rival for authority, suffered from chronic rheumatism. Henry supervised John Cropper's affairs and ensured that two of his sons, along with his own eldest boy, enrolled at Indiana University in the late 1840s.[26] They studied under Henry's old mentor, Andrew Wylie, now president of the university. He was also responsible for Margaret's children, two of whom soon emigrated to San Francisco, where they and their descendants enjoyed material success. Finally, six of Henry's own children remained at home, imposing a significant continuing financial burden.

A Good Southerner

Wise thrived during this period on the reciprocity of duty and reward. He spent "the labor of his life on some of the poorest [land] a bird ever flew over. But I am resusitating it!" he advised an old friend.[27] Between times he refurbished his law practice, which required considerable traveling in the Tidewater area. He secured an appointment from the county court in 1849 as surveyor of the highway, probably because he needed the small stipend the post carried. Hustling for every extra dollar, he contemplated turning entrepreneur and investing in a proposed "Ocean Bathing Place" on the coast of Virginia. Planters could presumably bring themselves and their servants to such an establishment without risking either the loss of their blacks to kidnappers or any embarrassing harassment from Yankees. But the idea fell through.[28]

Intimately familiar with death, illness, and suffering, Wise seemed to take pleasure from the moment. Contemporaries thought him calm, happy, and introspective. With his wife Sarah, he oversaw the education of his children and planned for their future. Lacking funds to pay a tutor, Wise heard their lessons and corrected their English compositions. He left instruction in the foreign languages to Sarah, whose facility extended to Greek, Latin, Spanish, and French. She also loved Shakespeare and, until her death in childbirth in the fall of 1850, inspired her family to read extensively. Wise took his turn at cleaning, cooking, and nursing the sick. The result of this deepened warmth and compassion was a family fanatically loyal to him. Unlike certain other Virginians (Edmund Ruffin comes immediately to mind), Wise experienced no great family rifts or blood feuds among his closest kin. He took his parental obligations seriously and believed that strength, security, and companionship were the best gifts he could provide. In return, he demanded obedience and flew into rages when occasionally his youngsters defied him. He also expected them to accept his counsel as they matured. In a sense, he never ceased regarding them as children. Profoundly in need of assurance, he was never certain that his family—let alone his peers—could satisfy his demands.[29]

Wise dealt decisively with the first serious challenge presented to him by his eldest son and favorite, Obadiah Jennings. Shortly after arriving at the university in Bloomington, Indiana, "Obie" joined a literary society. After a night of carousing which disrupted a faculty party, two members of the society withdrew from school under pressure from Dr. Wylie. The society, with Obie as one of the leaders, censured the faculty and Board of Trustees and all but accused Wylie of misrepresenting the facts of the case. When the faculty instituted disciplinary proceedings against the society, Wise's son threatened to withdraw from the university rather than submit. To this threat Henry responded:

> I am, to my mortification, *constrained* to say that your tone and language are those *of a rebel* against *a father* and *a father's friend*. . . . You say to your mother and sister that you wish them to "repose more confidence in" you, and you add that "if there is one thing that you hate above all others, it is to be treated like a poor, miserable being without judgment or decision." This is a proper feeling and one to be much admired and respected, but whilst you live and retain a filial regard for me, you must remember that *I your father* claim to have some confidence reposed in me too and that my judgment and decision is not to be set a nought and despised by my first born son who is to set the example of implicit obedience and submission to parental authority to all the rest of my sons.

Wise demanded that Obie resign from the offending society. In the same letter, he ordered his nephews to cease fighting with one another. He also acknowledged embarrassment at having been informed by Dr. Wylie that the "*Wises have never attended*" chapel service on Sunday "*but once*." He ordered them all "*regularly* [to] *attend the service by Dr. Wylie in the chapel every sabbath*."[30]

Wise never wished to humble Obie's "just manly pride," but so great were his own needs that his intimates risked utter dependence unless they contrived to assert their autonomy. Wise's adult life thus found him replicating the experience of his own austere regimen under Mary Wise Outten. Most members of his family found a way through the emotional thicket he created for them, but few of his peers took the trouble, with the result that Wise retained scarcely any close friends as he grew older. Obie found it a sufficient defense of his manhood to remain a member of the Philomathean Society, although his rebelliousness ceased.[31] Still, there always remained the possibility of questioning his father by taking his injunctions to manhood seriously when Wise himself appeared unwilling to act on them. This may have occurred at a supremely important moment ten years later.

Before leaving Bloomington, however, Obie confessed filial subordination and avowed his determination never to displease his father. Leaving behind habits of "blasphemy" and "occasional dissipation," Obie gradually commenced a "deep study of divine things," thereby convincing himself "of the existence of a God, of the truth of divine revelation, and of the immortality of the soul."

He neglected his other studies to concentrate on instruction provided by his father's professor. "Grant me your forgiveness," he asked his father, "and I promise you shall never again be robbed of my entire confidence." A few months later young Wise graduated from Indiana University. Before leaving, he composed a public oration and delivered it on 4 July 1850. It argued for the centrality of a love of home and family in the development of any virtuous republic.[32]

Assurances of respect for both domestic serenity and Christianity implied an acknowledgment of two of Wise's most important priorities during this period. In common with most contemporaries of his station, Wise had regularly evinced a private code of Christian piety—far too private, in the eyes of those who regarded him as shamelessly unprincipled and given ever to seeking his own gain. Both of Wise's wives and their mothers regularly urged him to focus on matters eternal. Following Wise's return from Brazil, John Tyler reported a rumor that he was "studious of the Scriptures, and deeply engaged in theological subjects. Nay, I have heard it said that he is studying for the ministry." The speculation that Wise had "grown pious and would finally adorn and illustrate the pulpit" had also circulated in 1842 during the renewal of the Graves-Cilley controversy. Perhaps some deeper concern with the proprieties, consistent with his efforts during these years to bevel down the hard edges, led him to procure for his children a white nurse. No longer would they be fondled (as he was) by old black Charlotte, who remained among his possessions.[33]

Wise's moratorium on public life permitted him to consider his values and attempt to integrate those potentially in conflict. Slavery, for example, seemed vaguely unsettling, yet he wanted and obtained more bondsmen. By 1850 he had more than doubled his slave force. Of his nineteen slaves, several had presumably been purchased with the income from his diplomatic appointment.[34] Perhaps because of slavery's immoral origins, as he noted in Brazil, Wise wanted masterhood to represent a set of obligations, a special calling that no principled man dared disavow. A humane and caring master, as he by all accounts became, could point to the increasingly popular Christian doctrine of stewardship as conferring both justification and entitlement. It meshed nicely with the role Wise had recently assumed in his white family. The dutiful kindness on which he prided himself would be extended from free born to bond, who would reciprocate by affirming his masterhood. "I cherish a fond regard for the race," he remarked some years later, "and those of them who are my slaves love me."[35] Most of Wise's blacks lived in stable family settings.[36] Though he remained capable of uttering the most scurrilous crudities, his public defenses of slavery during the 1850s sharply deemphasized the racial issue and increasingly acknowledged the common humanity and spirituality of whites and blacks. Fewer problems would have arisen in living out this deformed ideal had not Wise regularly felt the compulsion to defend himself.

Encouraging people to claim their dignity by praising their capacities risks the chance of being taken seriously. Instead of dehumanizing their slaves, masters such as Wise, who preferred intimacy and transparently advertised their need for assurance, may well have nurtured a potentially combustible longing for freedom. Three of his (evidently unmarried) male slaves, including his most trusted body servant, expressed their judgment on Wise's benevolent posturing by seizing their freedom at the first good opportunity a decade later. Like Wise, masters who viewed themselves as sole bestowers of worth upon their bondsmen were most appalled by developments such as these. Perhaps they should not have been. Paternalism did not so much create slave consciousness as it evolved in response to that consciousness, but masters could not accept this without recognizing the slaves' humanity.[37]

The clue to the lack of naturalness in Wise's benevolence—his adaptation of a persona—comes from the hard-eyed and two-fisted outlook he manifested when contemplating his tasks in the years ahead. He often sounded like a good though orphaned Yankee. "It is the glory of the American name," he told the Virginia state convention early in 1851, "it is my pride that I am not dependent upon my father or my grandfather for my standing in the world, and that I am armed with all the attributes that God has given me to carve out my own fortune in the world and lay the foundation for myself and my children." Because of his law practice, whose earnings far exceeded the income supplied by his slaves, Wise was less dependent on his bondsmen than he would be in another decade. Wise's paternalism thus grew more sincere as time passed and prospects of retirement and old age suggested closer bondings with his slaves. Whether the slaves reciprocated by accommodating him more than superficially no one can know, although Wise and his family believed they did.[38]

Espousing paternalism, however, meant renouncing important fragments of his own biography. He had once freed a slave. Following the requirements of Southern politics in the 1850s, he later recanted. For both his critics and himself, his assaults on the slave trade represented an indirect condemnation of slavery. His record in Brazil made him vulnerable. He eventually repudiated his diplomatic mission, even to the point of calling Brazil a "negro heaven" and flirting with explosive Southern proposals to renew the African slave trade. His best instincts withered at precisely the time when he most desired others to believe in him. The restlessness, inconsistency, and propensity to violence remained. Whenever Southern enemies questioned his loyalty by allusions to the Brazilian mission, they provoked an incandescent fury.[39] Not even the efforts necessary to defend himself ever removed certain of Wise's doubts about slavery as a social system. These bore heavily on his inability to embrace the cause of the Southern radicals, despite the fears his posings often inspired in the Yankees.

Wise alleged that his respite from public life was necessary and enjoyable, though political maneuvering had become a compulsion for him. "I am," he wrote Professor Nathaniel Beverley Tucker in Williamsburg early in 1848, "*happy where I am*—that's the main thing in life—politics to me are a burning & consuming fire, *truth* has too much power over you & me for the publick arena."[40] But even this sentence, identifying politics with lying and misrepresentation, contained a kernel of untruth. Although Wise wrote such letters to Tucker, he also traveled to Washington, D.C., to maintain his contacts among national politicians. And he schemed, as a member of the Board of Visitors of Tucker's own College of William and Mary, to influence Tidewater politics by manipulating the board's composition.[41] His temporary retirement inspired no epitaphs.

Contemporary politicians thought him too dangerous to leave unattached. As the 1848 presidential contest heated up, old enemies remembered him. Tennessee Congressman Meredith P. Gentry, once his critic, invited him to "come home again" to the Whigs. He refused but accepted a Democratic invitation to address the voters of his old congressional district in behalf of Lewis Cass. An extended speaking tour followed, despite Wise's misgivings about the Democratic nominee. Having once accused Cass of crooked and unsavory deeds by the score, Wise found it necessary to retract all these old charges dating from his investigations of the Jacksonians in the 1830s.[42] Repelled by having prostituted himself, he then tried to mind his own business for the next year and a half. "I care nothing about your politics, very little about my own," he wrote an old college classmate from whom he desired a visit in the spring of 1850. "Politics of any kind are the last thing I wish to think or talk about. Not that I am disappointed nor disgusted so as to make me unhappy or sardonic or sentimental; for, in fact, though no better than I ever was I am far more contented and happy now than I ever was in public life with all its trappings."[43]

Only two weeks earlier, however, Wise had acknowledged an interest in returning to public life, even if it required financial sacrifice. If called upon "*by anything like a general and strong invitation*" from the people of his county, he would consent to serve in the state legislature. But he had already decided independently of any solicitation to seek office again. "Whenever a state Convention is ordered I shall, I now think, be a candidate to serve in it."[44]

The "burning and consuming fire" held a relentless attraction for him. Perhaps he also craved stimulus and a challenge after enduring a full dose of family life, child care, and the timeless monotony of the Eastern Shore. Having taken much, including financial solvency, from public life, he now behaved generously. Despite his widely known interest in the pecuniary rewards associated with high office, Wise wanted to serve the Old Dominion, which commanded his primary political loyalty. Popular education, internal improvements by the state, and reform of Virginia's antiquated constitution all attracted his interest. With a national crisis over slavery brewing and compromise perhaps unreachable, it was time for an enduring Virginia compromise. The ease and gentility of Wise's new status notwithstanding, his hair-trigger temper manifested itself dramatically during the canvass preceding the election of delegates to the state convention. During a debate held in Temperanceville on the Eastern Shore, Wise commented contemptuously on the motives of one of his opponents. When called a liar, Wise knocked his man down and jumped him, only to be hauled away by members of the audience.[45]

While debating a reentry into public life, he simultaneously played out an elaborate charade to escape the taint of Southern radicalism. In the winter of 1849–50, several Mississippians led by Governor John A. Quitman planned a Southern rights convention at Nashville for the following summer. Originally a fond notion of Calhoun's, the convention would presumably prepare ultimatums designed to counter the Wilmot Proviso and other forms of Northern aggression, while planning for disunion should the necessity arise. The *Enquirer* offered support and asked Virginia to send a full delegation. Wise endorsed the Nashville gathering but shrewdly announced that unless the General Assembly clothed Virginia's delegation "with the full authority of the state," he would not attend. The assembly refused. It determined that delegates would be selected by meetings held in each congressional district. This decision suggested that no delegates would attend as official representatives of the Old Dominion and that about half the state would go unrepresented because opposition and apathy would prevent the organization of meetings in many districts.

In May a nonpartisan caucus in his old congressional district selected Wise as delegate. The thought of participating in a treasonous conspiracy nearly unnerved him. He used the excuse of canvassing for the forthcoming Constitutional Convention to avoid this dubious honor. Then he manipulated Tucker, the designated alternate, to attend instead. The professor, a fiery advocate of secession, probably needed no impetus and presumably anticipated this evasion from Wise, whom he intensely disliked despite their recent correspondence about "truth."[46]

Stung memorably by John Quincy Adams on the absence of a statewide network of common schools in Virginia, Wise tended to some unfinished business several weeks before taking a seat in the Virginia Constitutional Convention. On 4 July 1850 he delivered a speech at the free school celebration in Northampton County on the Eastern Shore. Although his views fitted into an established context that legitimated sweeping critiques of Virginia's ramshackle school system, Wise's highly progressive and controversial proposals set him apart from most other Virginia reformers, which may explain why his address never appeared in any of the metropolitan newspapers along the Atlantic seaboard.

Returning to a principle he first advocated in his farewell address of 1844, he termed education a universal right. It must therefore be free. Parents possessed no more authority to bar their children from instruction than they would have to starve them. Elementary education serves both a moral and a political purpose. Decency, industry, and steady habits follow from schooling. Good schools would aid in eliminating caste divisions, he suggested, thus emphasizing both his optimistic and hopeful stance toward the ameliorative powers of reform and his fears of an untutored yeoman class. He even proposed the Maine scheme of district schools for the Old Dominion, although their administration might threaten Virginia's venerable system of county government. He also made an eloquent plea for female education, including physical education, so that mothers might be better prepared to nurture their children. "Oh! a mother's love, who can describe it that has realized it," he said, "who can realize it that has never known it!" He called aggressively for increased taxes on the wealthy. But tempted by the humor of an eccentric indulgence, he then weakened the force of his proposal by suggesting that bachelors should bear the highest taxes of all because they evaded a good citizen's duty to maintain a wife and family.

Like Wise, a number of other Virginians found inspiration in the work of Northern educational reformers such as Horace Mann and Henry Barnard. By 1850 illiteracy in Virginia had become scandalous. Even the most rudimentary forms of industrial development required a minimally educated work force. It was more typical during this period for informed Virginians to reflect fondly on improved schools as the guarantors of republican virtue and the social order than to fear the polluting encroachment of Northern schemes for educational improvement. Wise's ideas stood out, yet the priorities governing his advocacy of reform had shifted subtly, even as his more personal objectives moved from the getting to the keeping.[47]

If Wise hoped for establishment of an egalitarian and universal system of common schools, he also expected to impose his reforms from above. "Pure democracy levels upward, false democracy downwards," he remarked, signaling conservatives that he really was one of them. No such language had appeared in his 1844 address. His version of liberty, equality, and fraternity derived from Christian sources, not the French. Moreover, Wise dared not advocate the establishment of free schools by the state. In his scheme, localities would retain the option of initiating them, which was merely the power they already possessed. His proposals therefore remained dependent on the will of local communities to tax themselves. Since 1846 Virginia law had permitted counties and towns to organize free schools financed by local taxes in addition to state appropriations. At the time Wise spoke, however, only about a dozen had done so.[48] Very little changed during the next decade, despite the success of Wise and others in the Constitutional Convention in securing additional funding for primary schools. As might have been expected from a conservative politician who often masqueraded as something else, Wise's enthusiasm for educational reform gradually dissipated. The changes he later contemplated would enhance the advantages of Virginia's rising middle class as well as preserve the privileges of her aristocracy.

Chapter 6
Political Compromise and the Protection of Slavery

To many it probably ranked as the antebellum period's most memorable celebration of florid and utterly stultifying oratory. In the eight and one-half months of its sessions, more than three million words were recorded, as time and again various delegates "sank back exhausted" only to be hauled away while colleagues finished reading their remarks. The *Register of Debates* ended abruptly when the official reporter unsuccessfully requested higher wages. Such was Virginia's Constitutional Convention of 1850–51. Through it all, with tedium threatening to become a way of life, Wise energized the proceedings and accounted for much of the worth and interest they achieved for participants and observers alike.

He amazed everyone with his stamina. Well rested and in better health than for years past, he occupied the floor more than anyone else. His major speech of late April 1851 consumed nearly five days but was heard by unprecedented crowds. His commitment and attractiveness were compelling. Jabbing a forefinger into the air, Wise imparted the urgency of his conviction that the "crisis of our fate has come." His voice had a lyrical quality, so that he was able to vary the cadence of his remarks and at times lighten their impact. He possessed a perceptive and quick wit and retained the attention of his audience better than most delegates.

Even outside the daily sessions, he drove himself with remarkable tenacity to effect a renewal of the Commonwealth. He importuned fellow delegates when he found them in their rooms or in hotel lobbies to recognize with him that the existing constitution was a "miserable wreck of ideas and the curse of Virginia."[1] He spent long hours in these conversations, preferring to encounter his colleagues one at a time and, after the manner of Calhoun, mesmerize them with an hour or more of intensive monologue.

It was partly a compulsion to fill the void left by the death of his second wife late in 1850 that thrust him into the work of the convention. But he also had a vision reminiscent of the optimism that had appealed so effectively to constituents during his congressional career. Wise transcended the political maneuvering leading to the effort to reform Virginia's antique constitution. He took for granted, as did most other informed observers, the belated acceptance of universal manhood suffrage that some still regard as the convention's major achievement.[2] Instead, he forcefully delineated two priorities. The threat to the Union manifest in debates over the Compromise of 1850, Wise told a Richmond political meeting some months before the convention met, made it imperative that Virginians effect a compromise of their own. First, an enlightened policy of political reform and economic renewal would neutralize the alienation of western Virginians. Improved canals and railroads would funnel western resources into the ports and markets of eastern Virginia. Westerners would then purchase slaves with their new-found wealth, thereby assuring the Commonwealth's integrity and safely diffusing the slaves. Second, Wise boldly argued for the controlling influence of class rather than sectional antagonisms in Virginia. The primary western objective was more equitable representation in the General Assembly. Wise argued that without this concession by the slave-dominated regions of Virginia it would be impossible to quarantine abolitionism to those few peripheral pockets where it persisted.[3] "Let it ever be whispered in the Western country," he said, "let it be . . . sent back to the lowlands . . . that black slaves are proposed here as the foundation of power in your government, and . . . you array the free men, the white man of this state against your property, and there can be no security for it."[4]

Political Compromise

The convention addressed many abuses. It moderately reformed Virginia's judiciary, for example. Wise thought this drone work and evaded it by abandoning Richmond. In the end, however, he so controlled the convention's deliberations that his agenda became its agenda. The crucial decisions taken had little to do with the perfection of democratic institutions, which remained primitive and underdeveloped. The convention's success depended on the tense but ultimately irresistible effort to grant important political concessions in return for western consent to a series of intricate provisions for protecting slavery. Wise wrought this Virginia compromise, a local version of its federal analogue and equally doomed to disappoint those who hoped fondly that it heralded perpetual peace and stability.

The system Wise repudiated governed election of the delegates to the convention, just as it had for decades biased representation in the General Assembly—the "mixed" basis of population and taxes paid. Western revulsion with this arrangement increased when returns from the 1850 census demonstrated that white population east of the Blue Ridge had fallen further and substantially behind that to the west.[5] Nonetheless, the 135 delegates to the convention were divided so that each represented either $7,000.24 in taxes or 13,151 whites. Or, as Wise later put it, for purposes of representation each white person equaled about fifty-three cents.[6] The election criteria yielded a seventeen-vote majority for eastern Virginia, the narrow reversal of which resulted ultimately from threats of western secession and hard political bargaining in which Wise was the pivotal figure.

From the distance of more than a century Wise appears as a brilliant conservative, shrewdly permitting and even promoting necessary change in order to preserve fundamental values and institutions. But in his time, with the proof coming from enemies he almost seemed to cherish, no one mistook his genuinely progressive instincts. A grand historian of the South, Clement Eaton, realized this long ago.[7] No one better articulated pure Jacksonian republicanism than Wise. His ideas on public education also placed him far in advance of Virginia's run-of-the-mill statesmen, though some victories in this area came so easily during the convention that they cost him no effort. In scorn for reactionaries of the past and present no one matched him. He threatened them with revolution if their ignorance and folly prevented reformers from gaining justice and equity. Anything less than full popular representation would reduce Virginia whites to slavery. When conservatives such as the gifted Richmond lawyer James Lyons rose to defend themselves, Wise intimidated them into returning to their seats. Lyons, whose sister later married Wise, proved forgiving in time, but the moody and irascible Muscoe R. H. Garnett, nephew of Senator Robert M. T. Hunter, reacted furiously to such treatment and never forgave him. Realizing the democratic implications of what Wise achieved in 1851, Virginia's genuine conservatives waited until the Civil War began before launching a reactionary counteroffensive against the new constitution, which came within a few hundred votes of success.[8]

Final proof of his proper place among the convention's progressives came in his five-day marathon speech on government and slavery delivered in late April 1851. Countering the narrow legalism and pragmatism of most delegates, Wise unburdened himself in the discursive and romantic style that suited him best. For his constitutional theories, he produced a lengthy philosophical justification based ultimately on Christian benevolence. As those closest to him realized, much more than farming and the law had attracted his attention during the moratorium on the Eastern Shore. In Jacksonian style, Wise proclaimed that he would either crush his task or be crushed by it. Very nearly the only subjects he ignored in this extravaganza were federal political issues. The convention collectively appears to have agreed to their suppression.[9]

On the issue of constitutional reform, Wise's villain was his former associate in Tyler's administration and neighbor from the Eastern Shore, Abel P. Upshur. In the Constitutional Convention of 1829, Upshur had mounted a classic defense of Virginia's oligarchy. In candidly practical style, he denied the existence of any elaborate natural law of original principles of government, endorsed the use of power whenever necessary by those whose vested interests required it, and maintained that taxpayers should control the state. He also pointed out that egalitarians who opposed him in the name of justice for white men, if not unfaithful to their own principles, would extend freedom to slaves and grant the elective franchise to "women, and children, and paupers." Wise had no intention of falling into this trap, although he loathed the temptation to ground his politics in the menace of naked power. He accused his mixed-basis opponents of preferring this policy, which he blasted as atheistical, barbaric, and incorporating the worst features of modern Continental philosophy. He cited approvingly the views of Alphonse Lamartine, the French Catholic politician, poet, mystic, and opponent of slavery, on the coincidence of republican and Christian principles. No longer, he announced, could we rely on the principle of "an all-absorbing selfishness in government." The Scriptures contained suitable safeguards. They justified dominion over slaves and established the subordination of women and children. They therefore permitted reform in behalf of only white men, who might thereby remain in Virginia, in order "to restore our dominion in this Union." We all look expectantly to reform, he continued, to obliterate a collective "sense of humiliation and degradation, if not despair."[10] "Thank God," Wise added, when grasping the most fundamental of his self-appointed tasks, it is unnecessary "to prove that slavery is justified in the state of Virginia." Yet he consumed himself in the attempt and nowhere else shone forth as so conspicuous a liberal.

Freighting his argument with the language of Christian benevolence, Wise justified slaveholding "by the natural as well as divine law, the prescribed law in the book of books . . . and by all the dispensations of Jesus Christ on earth." In short, he meant that society and property proceeded from God's grant of dominion, as expressed in Genesis. But nowhere did he call slaves property. Instead, he consistently identified them as persons and suggested that as children of God they were in some sense the equals of whites.

He declared, for example, that slaves possessed reason and conscience. By what right, therefore, were they held in bondage? Wise asserted that they lacked free will and thus were unable to control the state. But did not bondage alone incapacitate their wills? Wise also suggested that slavery conformed to natural law—itself "the will of God, natural and revealed." Wise's speech contained no Old Testament exegesis, however—no references to the curse of Ham or to a people bereft of culture and benighted throughout history. Instead, he grounded both his politics and his masterhood in the kindliness and generosity of spirit preached in the New Testament. "Do unto others as you would that others should do unto you," he remarked, just as an abolitionist might have. But having once placed blacks on a scale of racial development and acknowledged their capacity for sustained improvement, how could he deny them its highest levels? Would they not one day be free? He thus trapped himself in a classically circular argument; the slavish characteristics, by which we might identify Africans as properly held in bondage, are in a very considerable measure the result of slavery itself.[11]

Another side of his dilemma appeared when he cited various sources to buttress his argument. "If I had not the consent of Almighty God to hold my slaves," he declared, "if I had not the justification of His revealed will as it appears in the bible, I would not hold any human being by your title or the title of your government." The inspiration for this statement came from two pamphlets. One was an 1850 commentary on St. Paul's Epistle to Philemon—a prized portion of the Scriptures among defenders of slavery—from Dr. N. S. Wheaton, a Connecticut minister. The other, a scriptural defense of slavery dating from the early 1840s, came from a Baltimore Whig, Joseph J. Speed. Each of these authorities, however, insisted on slavery's transitory character, sustained the colonization movement, and criticized abolitionists for disrupting God's foreordained plans. One could remain a Christian and a slaveholder, they suggested, but not perpetually. Despite Speed's claims for "the high origin of the Institution of Slavery," he called it a "political evil" and associated himself with conservative Northerners and Easterners who sought to eliminate it. Wise termed Speed's argument the ablest he had ever read.

If slavery were thus a mutable condition, how could Wise justify an appeal to natural law? Neither of his authorities blamed abolitionists for challenging natural law, nor, one supposes, did Wise; he and they were more practical than that. Both Speed and Wheaton condemned abolitionists as traitors and fools who ignored the slaves' true interests. Descended from Northerners originally responsible for foisting slavery on the South, the abolitionists—far from promoting emancipation—now risked dissolution of the Union and racial war leading to the extermination of slaves.[12]

Political Compromise

The qualified nature of Wise's argument and his failure to mount a more extreme defense of slavery drew fire from William O. Goode, a young southside Virginia planter and lawyer who later served in Congress. Goode disdained the credentials of Wise's authorities. Instead, he pointedly announced his partiality to the more hardheaded scriptural defense of slavery composed some years earlier by Reverend Thornton Stringfellow of Culpeper County, Virginia. There was no nonsense in Stringfellow's aggressive calls for slaveholders to meet their responsibilities to heathen Africans and to defend their interests. Abolitionists quarreled not with the South but with the Divinity who sanctioned slavery, as the Scriptures demonstrated. "Even the words of our Lord Jesus Christ," Stringfellow argued, in perhaps his most original and controversial contribution, "sanctioned bondage." In his only acknowledgment of ignorance, Wise admitted no familiarity with Stringfellow.[13]

Wise exhausted the convention and himself. Two days after he finished, speeches were limited to one hour and balloting on the basis of representation commenced. For almost two weeks early in May, it appeared that the conservatives, led by Robert E. Scott of Fauquier, would achieve a narrow victory. But the westerners convinced enough eastern representatives to block irreversible action by threatening secession. Caucuses proceeded day and night and evidently lasted the entire second weekend in May. The following Monday a relatively obscure representative from the southern Piedmont, who had joined neither of the principal caucuses, moved to charge a committee of eastern and western members with responsibility for preparing a compromise. This movement, which surprised and mortified mixed-basis spokesmen such as Scott and Muscoe Garnett, resulted from a concert among "a portion of Eastern Gentlemen" supporting an adjustment.[14] Wise had evidently struck this arrangement by personally buttonholing several wavering easterners. When the convention established the committee, westerners admittedly concentrated on electing four easterners presumptively favoring compromise. They got three out of four. Wise mistakenly fingered his own Eastern Shore colleague, Louis Finney, who not only rejected compromise but broadcast his quondam friend's manipulations on the convention floor. Victory eclipsed Wise's momentary embarrassment. The three eastern delegates on the committee, along with Thomas Jefferson Randolph and a crony of Wise's from Williamsburg, plus the easterners already pledged to reform, narrowly obtained the west's nonnegotiable demands.[15]

The new House of Delegates, apportioned on the suffrage basis, yielded a western majority of fourteen. The east retained three-fifths of the Senate. Here the apportionment was arbitrary; easterners gave up four seats otherwise theirs on the mixed basis in return for a postponement of reapportionment until 1865, by which time everyone anticipated a full conversion to the suffrage basis. Meanwhile, westerners would hold a four-seat advantage on a joint ballot, thereby obtaining possible leverage in the election of United States senators.

Eastern extremists issued poignant lamentations and jeremiads. Muscoe Garnett wrote his mother that the settlement signified "the first step in revolutionizing the whole structure of Virginia society . . . and converting her into a humble imitation of New York and Ohio in all their Socialist propensities." Publicly, he argued that the Compromise of 1850 "was in some measure the father of this now before us. . . . A lesson was there and then taught not easily to be forgotten: that in the name of peace Virginia may be induced blindly to surrender her rights and the means of self-protection."[16]

Garnett had every reason to fear Wise's propensities, as the decade ahead proved, but here he had not calculated sufficiently on his foe's determination and adroitness. Following an extended absence from Richmond, Wise returned in early July to engineer ironclad protection for slaves. In a series of insufferable homilies, Wise told westerners that they should not "halloo before reaching the end of the woods" because a reconsideration of the basic settlement was then pending and the convention could conceivably reject it.[17]

Wise originally favored a capitation tax applied equally to white men and slaves. Such an arrangement would permit slaveholders all the constitutional security they would ever need. Critics quickly pointed out the results if whites were formally degraded to this level. The restiveness of certain nonslaveholders already appeared provocative. One representative from an Ohio River constituency infuriated Wise by referring to a memorial from white mechanics in Portsmouth praying for relief from Negro competition in their trades. The convention suppressed the memorial, and Wise altered his tactics.[18]

Political Compromise

On 5 July, while searching for the right formula, Wise suggested applying a capitation tax on white males not to exceed taxes assessed on $400 worth of land (48¢). Revision of this proposal provided the settlement. The eastern delegation brushed aside western demands for uniform ad valorem taxation, exempted slaves below age twelve from all assessments, and fixed the assessment on older slaves at that applicable to $300 worth of land (36¢). Because masters formerly paid a yearly levy of 38¢ on each slave, the new constitution actually lowered the assessment on older bondsmen in addition to undervaluing them for the purpose of future taxation. It was openly admitted in 1851 that older slaves were worth more on average than $300.[19] During the next decade, slave values more than doubled, and westerners came to regard slaveholders' special advantage as the most obnoxious feature of the constitution, even though the ad valorem taxes that now applied to all property except slaves (as a result of Wise's suggestion) actually represented an incentive to purchase them. Slaves had become a kind of tax shelter.

Wise then completed the Virginia compromise by carrying an annual capitation on white males equivalent to taxes paid on $200 worth of land.[20] Henceforth, taxes computed on land, slaves, and white men would be intricately related, making it impossible to increase one without raising the other two. Unlike the settlement reached on representation, which promised an adjustment in 1865, the guarantees furnished to slavery were regarded as permanent.

Long before the convention, Wise had told his friends on the Eastern Shore that under favorable conditions, slavery could be diffused throughout Virginia within twenty-five years. The Tidewater would emerge from economic decay, especially the area around Norfolk, which he predicted would become a great port and distributing point. Some enemies wrote that he seemed "wild as a March hare" and had "a screw loose somewhere about his head or heart or both." Others found repulsive the arrogance with which he proclaimed his vision. But he scorned them all and, reveling in his powers, dominated the convention. When challenged by trusted friends to account for his motives, he fondly repeated Andrew Jackson's reply to a question from Wise about his impulsive nature. "Young man," Jackson said, "I am called rash, but depend upon it, there is a policy in rashness."[21]

Everyone knew what a triumph it had been for Wise, including such westerners of decided ambivalence toward him as future Governor John Letcher, who should have known better. Letcher had signed the celebrated Ruffner *Address* of 1847, which was the work of a neighbor of his in Lexington. He presumably favored gradual emancipation via colonization. The *Address* also anticipated Wise's scenario by predicting that low slave prices then obtaining in the Deep South would prompt efforts by eastern Virginians to market more slaves in the Shenandoah Valley and beyond. Henry Ruffner, a Presbyterian minister, and Letcher fiercely opposed this prospect on economic grounds. But Letcher, although condemning Wise as a turncoat, caved in and supported his scheme for enshrining slave protection in the new constitution. Out of a perverse sense of gratitude, or caught in the optimism that a coming economic boom would somehow eliminate the need to think about slavery, or for motives unfathomable, Letcher acquiesced.[22]

Wise never believed that political rights or improved educational opportunities alone would confirm the loyalty of westerners and nonslaveholders. Rather, he maintained a more, though not exclusively, materialist outlook. That is, he gambled on the infusion of political democracy demanded by western elites to produce the harmony necessary to complete an ambitious program of railroad and canal construction. These projects would promote development sufficient to assure the Commonwealth's unity and to render her independent of Northern economic domination. The loyalties of westerners such as Letcher to old Virginia increased dramatically during the 1850s, vindicating his foresight. But insufficient resources, political haggling, the distracting intensity of the national crisis, and the steady slave and cotton prices in the Deep South had all fragmented the grand design by mid-decade. Wise insisted on prescribing for nonslaveholders, despite his ignorance of them. When he actually visited West Virginia in 1855, he realized that slavery had no future there. His subsequent gubernatorial administration—and he along with it—nearly collapsed from the pressures of threatened financial disaster and fiery partisan recriminations. Thus it always seemed appropriate for him—amid the difficulties involved in unifying Virginia and in diffusing slavery to the west—to retain and occasionally to refer concretely to a different hope. This was the other part of the bifurcated vision of Virginia Wise always maintained: perhaps one day a great slaveholding Commonwealth—though maybe, as he again suggested in 1856, an unburdened Commonwealth eventually emancipated altogether.

Chapter 7
Political Entitlements

Wise was not tempted to snatch too quickly the fruits of a brilliant success, and for good reason. He remained a renegade. Old Tom Ritchie, though screened away in Washington with the editorial control of a major Democratic organ, still dominated the *Enquirer* and thus Virginia's Democracy. His long memory hobbled Wise, who predictably was soon pronouncing consistency "the worst enemy to the public service that I know of."[1] When Ritchie finally died in 1854, many old Jacksonian apostates, including Senators Hunter and Mason, must have rejoiced. The way now seemed open for a confirmation of new political entitlements. There would, of course, be a fight for supremacy, with slavery increasingly the test of every aspirant's credentials.

Wise was more comfortable as a slavery politician than as a slavery advocate, though even here, his inconsistency undermined trust among those disciplined enough to remember. For example, Wise proudly recalled his centrality in the gag rule debates, though never acknowledging his ambivalences. He claimed as much credit as he dared for the annexation of Texas but indulged no further allusions about abolition as a crowning result. Along with many Southerners, he anathematized the Compromise of 1850, charging that the "military arm" had legislated "free soilism" into California.[2] Surely such fierce and valiant defenses of Southern rights guaranteed him more plaudits than the waffling Whigs could ever earn. Yet whenever Wise posed as a Southern extremist; difficulties followed. As we shall see, Wise believed that the loss of California cost the South a last, golden opportunity to emancipate itself at a profit.

Thus Wise had his problems as both a partisan and an ideologue. No group looked more fondly to restricting his maneuverability than the small coterie of young Virginians who preferred loyalty to South Carolina. Elder statesman and in many cases mentor of the group was Professor Nathaniel Beverley Tucker, though to his dying day in 1851 he remained a far more dedicated disunionist than most of his pupils. Because he suffered from a severe speech impediment that impaired his public effectiveness, Tucker relied on his teaching and prolific pen to advance the cause. "Oh, that I had the voice of John Randolph," he remarked early in 1850 in a letter to James H. Hammond.

> What an enviable thing is that power of speech which draws men in crowds to hear for the sake of hearing! What a pity to see it thrown away on a man like Wise . . . who drew the people together . . . a month ago to listen to his crude notions, among which it was hard to say whether devotion to the Union or impatience of its evils predominated. He is truly, as you say, a petted child: a man incapable of great ideas, but with the faculty of putting forth conceptions of a cannon ball by dint of velocity. After all, his best speech is but "the tale of a madman, full of sound and fury, signifying nothing." You listen with pleasure and interest, and go away in a state of collapse. You have swallowed the east wind, and were blown up for the time like a bladder, and are left equally empty and flawed by its escape. Such men serve no end but to derange the plans and operations of others. I hope you will not be troubled with him at Nashville.[3]

Tucker found it distasteful enough to observe Wise's Nashville Convention charade, but the transparent hypocrisy of someone who judged the Compromise of 1850 a disaster for the South yet failed to act on his convictions may have hurried him to his grave. Tucker's group, termed the "Young Chivalry" by Wise, had no power, however, and were regarded as faintly disreputable in Virginia. It would be their task throughout the decade to aim at a triumphant vindication, largely by advancing the claims of Wise's greatest rival, Senator Robert M. T. Hunter, whom they felt was entitled to Calhoun's estate in the South.

Indeed, Southern extremists throughout the decade often doubted whether their homeland would ever claim its proper destiny, prostituted as it was by opportunists questing only after political rewards. The letters and diaries of Tucker, Hammond, Edmund Ruffin, and Muscoe Garnett show them embittered and frustrated, speculating morbidly about vanished opportunities and their own unpopularity. Hammond's close encounters with the daughters of a powerful South Carolina family had compelled him to accept political semiretirement. Cynical humor used to ridicule most anything—not merely the Union—came easily to Hammond. He seemed bemused by the bloated letters he received from Professor Tucker, whose isolation approached his own.[4] Ruffin, at least, had his reputation as an agricultural reformer—along with whatever consolation he took from efforts to influence the few politicians, such as John Tyler, whom he regarded as congenial, pliable, and sympathetic to his designs. But not so for a much younger man like Garnett. After publishing an incisive pamphlet entitled *The Union: How It Works, and How to Save It* following his graduation from the University of Virginia in 1850, Garnett spent much of the decade worrying about both his declining political credibility and his receding hairline.[5]

Meantime, the Young Chivalry only vexed Wise. Through good fortune, his most powerful and dangerous enemies guaranteed his political indispensability. Wise's old masters of 1840, despite many recent disappointments, remained unbeaten and absorbed. Virginia's Whiggery made a difference, but not enough to win, as Michael Holt has recently shown. Unlike their conquered brethren in the Deep South, border state Whigs retained an independent organization throughout the 1850s.[6] Indeed, Virginia's Whigs calculated in 1851 on executing a reversal on their enemies by presenting themselves as the party of compromise and union.[7] Thus, Wise believed, the stupidity of Southern radicals rivaled their arrogance. Both attitudes disclosed a profound insensitivity to the Virginia masses. With a Whig revival threatening, it was essential for Wise to endorse publicly the Compromise of 1850, despite his private reservations about its odiousness. Rejecting the efficacy of secession, he proclaimed in the classically mainstream fashion of Southern politicians that the Democratic party was "pre-eminently best constituted to save the country in this crisis of danger."[8] Of course, he needed the Democracy. Just as important, the Democracy needed him—though not yet.

At the same public meeting in which he enunciated Compromise strategy, held concurrently in early 1851 with the Constitutional Convention, Wise inquired after Virginia's best chance for preserving the Union. Insightfully he observed the obsolescence of Ritchie's preferred alliance with New York. Abolition-infested, its reliability was gone. Among the large Northern states of sufficient electoral strength to serve the South only Pennsylvania remained. Virginia should now latch herself to the Keystone State, Wise believed, as he busily cultivated one of her favorite sons.[9]

Wise remarked that the next campaign would demand a Jackson or a Napoleon, but the man he had in mind was merely James Buchanan, to whom he owed much for refusing to recall him from Brazil. Buchanan, like John Tyler, was a skillful flatterer, and Wise, more than most, enjoyed hearing his political talents praised. This was especially true by 1851, when many of his associates from earlier years were either dead or estranged. Because Wise seldom confided in anyone, Buchanan's friendly letters gratified him all the more. Understanding his restless character, Buchanan admonished him in fatherly fashion to beware the dangers of an impulsive temperament. But Wise typically responded that "*movement, bold* movement" was necessary to advance the cause of his friend.[10] This mutual recognition of shrewd pragmatism may have been a powerful source of respect and admiration. Yet amid the bantering and affection neither knew nor trusted the other.

In June 1851, Wise pledged himself to procure Buchanan's nomination. "To make you successful," he declared, "the South in some way must be united upon you. Quo modo? You must reconcile or crush factions of your own party at home—the Fraziers, Porters, Camerons, Dallases in Pennsylvania." Wise promised a full quota of "county demonstrations" in Virginia, which would "strengthen you *at home* and strength *there* is all you want to insure the nomination and success in the election." He looked confidently to support from across the Commonwealth because Buchanan had won support from Virginia in both the Democratic national conventions of 1844 and 1848.[11] And, of course, while Wise bided his time, it did no harm to wield a controlling influence over one of the Union's prime presidential candidates.

He was four years too early. Franklin Pierce of New Hampshire secured the Democratic nomination and also an anticlimactic victory when the Whigs fractured North and South over their collective inability to endorse the compromise. Wise loafed his way through the canvass. Even before hearing the result, he had already calculated the extractable benefits from the forthcoming patronage circus. Working primarily through his old Tylerite colleague, Caleb Cushing, now Pierce's attorney general, Wise obtained a host of consulates and other offices for various cavaliers, impoverished and otherwise. He also secured a prize appointment for his eldest son, Obadiah Jennings. In the summer of 1853, Obie assumed the secretaryship of the American legation in Berlin.[12] Surveying these successes, Wise wrote confidently to Buchanan that his own time had "not yet come," but he added, in June 1853, "I will be in position by next campaign."[13]

These triumphs also added confidence to his suspicions of the Young Chivalry. This group was led by such men as Muscoe Garnett and Congressmen William O. Goode and James Seddon. Almost without exception, they were descendants of distinguished families, well educated, and proprietors of large Tidewater estates. Wise repeatedly tried to make them irrelevant. At about the time that Garnett encouraged his friends in South Carolina to secede and vowed Virginia's support if coercion followed, Wise compared the difficulties of the Carolinians to the "Jesus-mania in the French hospitals." "Let her alone," he advised Buchanan. The French had taught that "if the patient really affected to be Christ, the best treatment was *total neglect*."[14] Such a policy required reciprocity, which the restless Young Chivalry refused. Affronted by the popularity of opportunists like Wise and wary of his alliance with Buchanan, they feared preemption of their own favorite's claims and collapse of their fond hope for a Virginia–South Carolina alliance. Their time would also come.

Wise measured his distance from the Young Chivalry by more than political tactics. Senator Hunter, the abiding though reluctant hero of Virginia's extremists, ranked as one of the wealthier slaveholders in the American Congress. Wise owned a farm, appropriately called Only (after an earlier proprietor). His property lay along Onancock Creek near where it empties into Chesapeake Bay's eastern shore; his home, still standing, commands a fine view of the bay. His farm included more than four hundred acres, half of which were productive. Together with nineteen slaves, his holdings ranked him among the dozen wealthiest men in Accomac. Across the Chesapeake, however, old and aristocratic families maintained lands and slaves more than sufficient to justify the condescension with which they typically beheld men from the Eastern Shore.

Wise's operation was superbly diversified. He grew corn and oats on his best ground. Later in the decade he added wheat, which probably suggests successful efforts at agricultural improvement. He also raised livestock, grew sweet potatoes, and maintained orchards of peaches and pears. To maximize output, he employed an overseer and also relied on a white man from his neighborhood who helped out occasionally and shipped his cash crops to market—usually in Baltimore. Altogether, however, he probably grossed less than $500 per year from his farm during this period.[15]

Such financial stability as he obtained came from another source. Wise may have loathed his law practice from time to time because of the sacrifices it required, but he also thrived on it. Court days for each of the Tidewater counties were staggered, so that by determined effort lawyers might attend several in a single month. Thus Wise crossed Chesapeake Bay regularly to seek clients in roughly the same area that for eleven years he had represented in Congress.

His practice allowed Wise to continue educating himself. No newspapers existed on the Eastern Shore. Mail boats from Philadelphia, Baltimore, and the Virginia mainland arrived only twice a week; they seldom brought anything animate. Few immigrants had arrived since the seventeenth century. This is not to say, of course, that the tempo was much different elsewhere on Wise's professional circuit. Court days were exceptional, however, attracting hundreds to dilapidated villages strewn along Chesapeake Bay. These people loved political discussions, but trials for high stakes transfixed them. Increasingly, they fancied the "posturing, florid oratory, and impromptu persuasion" deemed essential for victory.[16]

No systematic records of Wise's legal practice remain, but at the height of his powers he anesthetized all challengers. His courtroom skills and reputation took time to refurbish, however. After returning from Brazil, he acted principally in cases of assault and battery, contested wills, and recovery of debt. He formed a temporary partnership with a lawyer of only local reputation in Accomac. Then, beginning in 1849, with his confidence and visibility reestablished, he sought and obtained the more lucrative cases he craved. These typically involved capital crimes that gave counsel as much notoriety as accused. At the 1849 spring term of the Worcester County Court in Maryland (just north of Accomac), for example, he consumed three days addressing the jury and secured an acquittal for his client charged with murder in the first degree. By all accounts, his man had shot down an antagonist in cold blood and broad daylight. In 1854 he cleared a murderer in Norfolk, shortly before winning the Democratic gubernatorial nomination. Two other cases involved a man accused of shooting another to death and a boat captain gone berserk, who stabbed several blacks with a sword knife. The first of these characters skipped bail. Wise helped obtain an acquittal of the boat captain on a murder charge, although he died before trial could begin on indictment for stabbing with intent to kill.[17] Thus Wise made money and occasionally a lot of it, though some may have thought him guilty of unforgivable pandering.

It is difficult to imagine Wise's primary Virginia rival or any of his close associates adapting easily to this lifestyle or respecting it in anyone else. It discouraged reflection, it frustrated statesmanship, and it disqualified Wise from assuming Calhoun's mantle, which the Young Chivalry was anxious to drape over the sizable shoulders of Senator Robert Mercer Taliaferro Hunter. Not fully appreciating his friends' expectations, Hunter evidently reflected on rejecting his destiny. But his friends violently opposed these notions and held up his earlier relationship with Calhoun as proof of his proper lineage. As a younger man, Hunter had indeed loved the Carolinian and suffered on that account. With Tom Ritchie despising Calhoun almost as much as Clay, the wounds went deep. Far from disliking Wise, Hunter probably recognized him as a brother rebel against Jackson, whom the times were only now making respectable. When Hunter, at the importuning of his advisers, consented to support Stephen A. Douglas for the presidency in 1852 against Wise's choice, their rivalry flashed into the open. But a fight was probably fated in any case.

Corpulent and lumbering, Hunter had a metabolism that precluded quick changes of pace or direction. His mother died early, and Robert endured a rigorous upbringing by his father, a merchant who amassed a fortune by the sweat of a lifetime. An insomniac, James Hunter called Robert to his bedside at all hours of the night to read to him. His father's hopes rested on Robert, if only because his two older brothers had died young. Robert's companions in adolescence were mainly his older sisters. Before long, people noticed his "lonesome ways." Although possessed of financial talents, he disliked details and the responsibility of keeping accounts. At the University of Virginia's law school, he met his lifelong friend and political adviser, Lewis Harvie. Hunter derived little satisfaction from the law. Though capable of sustained effort, he sometimes disdained his work entirely.[18]

Throughout his career, the letters Hunter wrote to his wife reveal him as abysmally depressed by enforced absences from his family and the demands of politics. Such an attitude would have been incomprehensible to Wise, who thrived on public life and took sustenance from personal conflict, despite the grievous physical tolls. No one ever wrote Wise advising him to forego "masterly inactivity" and deny himself "reveries of thought." Seldom did Wise's friends complain of his laggardness in correspondence, but Hunter's advisers protested regularly. They urged him to speak more frequently in the Senate and held out the prospect of greatness if he did.[19] Toward the end of his senatorial career, Hunter obliged by speaking more regularly, forcefully, and even eloquently. But in oratory, too, Hunter and Wise exhibited completely different styles. "I should myself willingly travel several hundred miles," commented Henry S. Foote, "to hear . . . Wise respond to one of Mr. Hunter's drowsy, phlegmatic and overcrammed discourses."[20]

While laying plans to master Virginia's politics and thereby wield the Old Dominion's prestige nationally, Wise was irritated to contend with someone he refused to take seriously. During the 1852 Democratic National Convention in Baltimore, for example, Wise probably influenced a number of the Virginia delegates to remain loyal first to Buchanan and then to Pierce by taking it upon himself to inform them unabashedly that Senator Hunter was not "*at heart*" a supporter of Douglas. Confused and unnerved, Hunter later admitted that he never preferred Douglas "to all the world." But "of those who were considered the prominent candidates," he added, "I preferred him." He intimated that Wise's "impulsive nature" influenced his action at the convention. Wise sarcastically reminded the senator of those who had "evidently calculated upon an advantage to be gained out of my 'impulsive nature,' a mistake that has been more than once made by calculating people." Professing to know Hunter's mind better than the senator himself, Wise conceded that Hunter "*sincerely preferred* Douglas." But, Wise told the senator, "You were not, as I said, *at heart* for Mr. Douglas."[21] Wise probably estimated Hunter's views accurately, but his action was nonetheless inexcusable, as the bewildered senator attempted to tell him. After Pierce's victory, Wise also artlessly suggested that Hunter might enjoy administering the Treasury Department, thereby creating a convenient vacancy in the Senate for "some other Virginian."[22] George Booker, a mutual friend, feared the consequences of a rupture and asked Wise about its likelihood. "George Booker," he answered, "I would crawl on my hands and knees to make Hunter President." This statement was, purely and simply, a lie.[23]

Why did Wise find Hunter so provoking? They had differed over presidential aspirants, and Wise coveted his erstwhile friend's Senate seat, as Hunter's advisers had suspected for some time.[24] A further explanation might be that Wise knew as much about Hunter's somnolence as the senator's friends did. To have behaved toward him in such patronizing fashion, however, is evidence of a calculated disrespect exceeding the ordinary limits of political ambition and rivalry. It must have galled him that Virginia lacked a man of greater energy to represent her in the Senate just when she needed to reclaim her former glory. Finally, and crucially, Wise's most abrasive frustrations sprang from the necessity to respect appearances. Disliking Hunter intensely, he remained obligated to conciliate him, as we shall see. On Hunter's part, the real fear was the likelihood that the future belonged to men such as Wise.

The deference accorded to Hunter and his friends in their communities never exceeded that which Wise received in his. It was one of the anomalies of Wise's life that though his family ranked among the most prominent in Virginia, it resided in one of the state's least prestigious districts. His rivalry with Hunter was enmeshed with the elusive elements of class, family, and regional pride. In challenging Hunter, Wise also advanced the claims of his community, of his class of middling farmers, and of his ancestors, who were as prominent in settling the country as those of his rivals. Wise had studied Virginia history, and he knew how to emphasize the antiquity of his family's roots in the Commonwealth. Throughout much of his adult life he wore his hair down close to his shoulders. With his lean frame and high cheekbones, he looked remarkably like an Indian.

His appearance suggested his pride and, indeed, his passion. Wise's own needs always exercised an independent authority with him, although his family's requirements presumably affected his decision to marry for a third time. In October 1853, he summoned Attorney General Cushing to serve as his chief groomsman. "In all my life," he wrote shortly afterward, "woman has been my stay and solace. Without her attraction I would have been careless how the world went. Wife and children have nerved & stimulated me. Woman kept me from the gross & ordinary vices, and I adore her above all earthly blessings." He remarried on 1 November, about three years after the death of his second wife, Sarah.[25]

Wise's bride was Mary Lyons of Richmond, sister of the prominent lawyer, James Lyons. It was the second successive marriage Wise had made with a member of a wealthy family. A gentle but sickly maiden of nearly forty, Mary seemed entirely devoted to Wise and his children. Little is known of their courtship, which took place in the spring and summer of 1853. By September, Wise was writing, "You have made me *wild*! Bless you! . . . Think not I misspent the whole of yesterday's Sabbath. *I prayed for you*! I pray for you again, forever! I looked out upon the moon last night and I'll look out again and think of you."[26]

Wise loved Mary Lyons deeply though he also pitied her and took strength from her dependence on him. Judging from available evidence, Mary regarded herself at first as utterly inferior to her husband. Also an orphan, she had spent much of her life caring for motherless children. "But I feel my insufficiency nonetheless," she wrote Henry, "and can only trust that God will guide me aright. Even now, if your happiness and that of your children require it, don't hesitate to give me up, and take to your heart and home, one more worthy to fill *her* place, than myself." Henry wrote to her while sitting at the bedside of one of his sick children: "Please always be 'childish' with me as you are in this last and sweetest letter. Always tell me like a little child, like this little child I am watching tells me: 'how *very*, very dear I am to you.' "[27]

After the ceremony, Wise asked Cushing not to accompany him to Accomac. Sufficient tension would result from Mary's encounter with his family without the obligation to preserve perfect decorum for the sake of a third party. Three young children from his two marriages still remained at home in 1853 under the tutelage of an older daughter and his widowed sister, Margaret. Another daughter, with his "consent and approbation," had married Dr. Alexander Y. P. Garnett of Washington, later one of Wise's best informants on affairs in the capital.[28] The domestic stability formerly contributed by his eldest son was now missing. Before departing for Berlin, Obie had tutored several of Wise's younger children and intermittently supervised his father's farming operations, besides serving as county lieutenant of militia and obtaining a law license.

One senses that although Wise demonstrated considerable patience with young children and touching devotion at times of sickness, he preferred the bantering and more egalitarian exchanges possible with older youngsters, especially his sons. Mary's primary preoccupation would thus be relationships with his daughters. Obie's absence and Mary's presence would allow further reflection on the fate and future of Wise's primary domestic distraction, his second son and namesake.

Henry, Jr., got along so badly with his older brother that their father refused to enroll them simultaneously at Indiana University. At age seventeen, young Henry administered a caning to his schoolmaster. Thereafter, he matriculated at the Virginia Military Institute. In September 1851, he was court-martialed and dismissed for dueling. After assuring himself that the boy's action was honorable and "high-minded," though imprudent, Wise at some financial sacrifice sent him to the College of William and Mary. Within a few months young Henry experienced a change of heart and renounced violence. Shortly afterward, he commenced theological studies and eventually was ordained an Episcopal priest.

Although Obie's letters from Europe reflected the standards of hard work, useful activity, and close attention to finance that his father inculcated, something about his second son harassed Wise unendingly. Was it his weakness for women, as Wise once suggested? His sickliness? Or his oscillations, less predictable than those of Wise's older children, between obedience and defiance? Ever a partisan in the distribution of favors, Wise once plaintively inquired of Obie whether Henry would "give me the least pleasure in him as a son?" Such rejections are often reciprocated. "He is so much like me I sometimes hate him," Wise later confided to an Alabama friend.[29]

Wise wanted to control his personal environment and demanded power over the emotional context of his most intimate relationships. As he wrote Mary two years after their marriage: "I would give anything if you will only cease to think and say anything to me about such matters as changing your habits and character so as better to conform to my wishes. Why mar your letters, or your conversation or your looks even with what reminds me of my weakness? Why appeal to God to attest your innocence of an intention to offend me, when you know that annoys me itself? I implore you to drive away such thoughts and feelings and never to express them to me."[30] This admonition proved too much for Mary. After a time, irritants predictably appeared. "Can't you let my 'anger' alone, my sweet, gentle wife?" Wise wrote her in 1855. "Can't you understand me enough to know that I never want it alluded to?" Though acknowledging Wise "an honest truthful man," she found his "peculiar temper" and many "faults" frustrating. His coercions raised even an underdeveloped consciousness to a higher level. Mary relied on her brother James for support. At one point, during a brief tiff between Henry and James, she urged him to "agree to disagree" with Henry, "as he & I do."[31]

Relations between Wise and James Lyons remained close, however, because Henry agreed to press Cushing and Secretary of War Jefferson Davis to settle James's outstanding claim on the federal government for legal services rendered. Lyons never got his money, but it was not for lack of effort on Wise's part. He pestered appropriate officials with requests and importunities and made Lyons part of that large group of friends and retainers whose interests he attempted to promote.

Wise worked no less hard for himself. He seldom came up empty, but Pierce's officials balked at endorsing his most lucrative professional opportunity of the decade. Along with a Richmond friend, he acted in behalf of heirs of a former Spanish subject to secure damages with interest for injuries suffered from American military operations leading to the annexation of East Florida in 1819. Wise's share, had the claim been paid, was $37,500. All he could obtain from the Treasury Department, however, was a recommendation for congressional consideration, which amounted to rejection. Wise wrote later of his previous determination to seek the gubernatorial nomination in Virginia, but the loss of this case in the summer of 1854 removed any mild temptations to remain in political semiretirement.[32] A new and proscriptive political movement, vulnerable for both its illiberal and antislavery tendencies, provided a perfect foil. But before Wise secured the Democracy's permission to unleash himself against the Know-Nothings, he first found it necessary to justify an eccentric opposition to his party's principal legislative achievement of the decade.

A Good Southerner

Wise's frequent trips to Washington in the winter and spring of 1854 kept him informed on the status of the Kansas-Nebraska Bill. Virginians applauded its repudiation of the Missouri Compromise of 1820; it amply vindicated the judgment of Thomas Ritchie and others who had condemned the compromise from its inception. "Instead of joy," Ritchie had remarked, when news of the settlement reached Richmond, "we scarcely ever recollect to have tasted of a bitterer cup." He called ever after for Texas as compensation to Virginia—a call Wise echoed during his indiscreet 1842 speech on annexation, which noted the perils consequent on failing to diffuse slavery.[33] Now, a generation later, the newspaper Ritchie founded continued to regard the compromise as dangerous and degrading. "While the restriction of 1820 remains to attest the jurisdiction of Congress over slavery," wrote the *Enquirer*'s editors, "there remains no security for the rights of the South. The South then should be content with nothing less than a surrender of the usurped power and a repeal of the odious statute."[34]

The *Enquirer*, however, turned noticeably lukewarm in its support for the bill after its amendment by Senator George Badger of North Carolina, a leader of the Southern Whigs. The Badger amendment prevented the revival of the French law protecting slavery within the Louisiana Purchase, which the Missouri Compromise had repealed. The *Enquirer* suggested that the presumptive operation of the French law might have given Southerners an advantage before the territorial legislature was organized. The editors, who contended for the Calhounist dictum that slavery legally existed in all American territories unless prohibited by positive enactment, also suspected the bill of squinting at "squatter sovereignty." They admitted that it might be interpreted as giving to territorial legislatures the power to exclude slavery.[35] But the *Enquirer* located this power exclusively in a state constitutional convention.

Throughout the debates on the bill and down to the time President Pierce signed it on 30 May 1854, Wise had regularly consulted his own congressman, John Millson of Norfolk, as well as Senator Hunter. Millson was the only Virginian elected to federal office and one of only two Southern Democrats in the House of Representatives who voted against the measure. Wise defended Millson's course throughout the summer and thus risked incurring the displeasure of the rest of Virginia's congressional delegation. It was a dangerous position for a man who now aspired to the gubernatorial nomination. On 1 August 1854 he published an explanation in the *Enquirer*, in the form of a letter addressed to western Virginia Congressman Zedekiah Kidwell. Wise acknowledged that rumors of his opposition to the Kansas-Nebraska Act threatened his chances for the nomination. He avowed that had he been in the House of Representatives, he would have voted for the bill, despite certain "unanswerable" though not "insuperable" objections. In particular, both he and Millson opposed the Badger amendment, just as the *Enquirer* had done. Both men argued that this proviso once again singled out Southern institutions for special and degrading treatment. They maintained that but for Badger's action the repeal of the Missouri Compromise would have revived the French law sanctioning slavery throughout the extent of the Louisiana Purchase. Now, in the crucial interval between passage of the act and convening of the territorial legislature, Southerners, unlike Northern immigrants, would be inhibited from taking their property into Kansas and Nebraska.[36]

Unlike Millson and the *Enquirer*, Wise seemed undisturbed by the legislation's studied ambiguity, which permitted commentators to argue that it both sanctioned and repudiated "squatter sovereignty." Public reservations about the territorial settlements of 1850 and 1854 left it open for Wise to argue Congress's obligation to protect slavery in all the federal territories. But the elaboration of that dubious and extreme proposition remained far from his mind in the summer of 1854. The *Enquirer*'s eventual endorsement of the act gave him problems; so did its general popularity among Virginia Democrats. To them, it both affirmed the support of their Northern colleagues in Congress and removed a gross insult to Southern honor. By failing to sustain the act unequivocally, Wise again risked charges of "renegadism" and political treason. As an unpublished section of his public letter proves, he was especially anxious to conciliate Senator Hunter.[37]

Wise, Millson, and Hunter all believed that Kansas did not represent a substantive issue because slavery could never exist there. But southside Virginia Congressman William O. Goode pointed out that Kansas occupied the same latitude as Virginia. Hemp, cereal grains, and even tobacco might profitably be cultivated with slave labor. This striking position, taken by one of Senator Hunter's principal lieutenants, implicitly questioned the loyalty to slavery of those opposing the Kansas-Nebraska Act. Perhaps with Hunter's interests in mind, Goode soft-pedaled these sections of his speech. Instead, he and others in Virginia's congressional delegation concentrated on pulverizing Millson. To oppose the act on the absurd grounds that it incorporated the Badger amendment, Goode declared, was to leave Southerners with the prohibitive Missouri Compromise when they wished to settle the prairies. The only positive direction in which Millson's views implicitly led made it incumbent on Congress to implant and protect slavery in the territories. But no one dared go that far, Goode pointed out, because it was impossible to attain and would "condemn ourselves to our present unjust restriction and exclusion forever." Moreover, Goode asked how reviving an "antique" French law in Kansas could ever confer a practical, substantive benefit on slaveholders. Objections to the Badger amendment, he argued, rested on the common law doctrine of *revivor*. This abstract rule of construction lacked any express authority in America or France. British authorities contested it, and many American jurisdictions, including Virginia, had emphatically rejected it.[38]

Wise's eccentric opposition to the Kansas-Nebraska Act, although not altogether pointless, may well have indicated serious doubts about the efficacy and propriety of repealing the Missouri Compromise. Millson probably agreed.[39] Was not the Kansas-Nebraska Act a foolish gamble? The South's hope for another slave state seemed ridiculous and self-defeating. Kansas's climate made slavery's rootedness tenuous in any case. Along with Southern Whigs such as John Minor Botts of Virginia, Wise envisioned the act as troubling the waters to the minority section's disadvantage. Once repeal of the Missouri Compromise was settled, however, he quickly shifted to extreme ground to defend himself, before turning to reestablish his credibility with Hunter and others whom he might have offended. Little wonder, then, that people suspected his honesty, loyalty, and occasionally his sanity.[40]

After this strange performance, what Wise needed by midsummer 1854—if he wanted to make good his claims to the gubernatorial nomination—was another chance to prove himself a good Southerner. It came unexpectedly, bestowed by an unlikely Yankee, the Reverend Nehemiah Adams of Boston. Adams had visited Richmond, Columbia, and Charleston earlier in 1854, collecting materials for his book, *A South-Side View of Slavery*. On 15 August, with his volume in press, Adams wrote Wise asking several questions about slavery's destiny in America. Adams had written similar letters to various Southerners and regarded them as private inquiries. In response, Wise composed a vigorous defense of slavery and then resourcefully contrived to have it published along with Adams's queries in the *Washington Union*. The *New*

York Times, *Richmond Enquirer*, and *New York Citizen* all reprinted it. The letter provoked a furious reaction.[41]

Allegedly a Northerner of antislavery sympathies before his trip South, Adams underwent a sudden conversion. Slaves looked comfortable and happy. As a result, he wrote one of the more favorable and compassionate accounts of Southern life to come from any Northerner during the 1850s. Any pro-Southern assault on his views would thus appear extreme. Adams and his would-be antagonist agreed so thoroughly that the contrived character of Wise's performance stands out boldly. According to Adams's flattering estimate, for example, most slaves counted themselves Christians, thanks to kindly masters. A black, enslaved lower class eliminated paupers and discouraged propagation of "delusions and fanaticisms." A good Providence had thus inspired a rewarding system for blacks and whites alike. Those who tampered with slavery were not only irresponsible but un-American. As did so many others, including Wise, Adams described abolitionism as a foreign ideology, rooted in Great Britain. Instead of treacherously attacking slavery, Yankees should patiently abide the counsels of toleration. Good Southerners could then eliminate grosser abuses in their system, such as the sale of young slaves and the nonsanctification of slave marriages.

Political Entitlements

In fact, Adams typically either agreed with Wise—as in his statements acknowledging slavery's economic liabilities and reporting the collective Southern judgment of slavery as a "curse"—or he nearly outdid the Virginian in his defense of the South. For example, he suggested that blacks would return to Africa, just as Wise had predicted. But he also speculated openly that a permanent caste system might evolve in the United States—albeit out of some near-cosmic inspiration. With the perpetual dependence of the blacks settled, Northerners might sustain missionary work among them. Territorial struggles would cease with establishment of a zone in the Southwest where uncontested Southern migration might take place. But Wise had all along conceived of the Southwest as a corridor through which slaves might be funneled *out* of the Union. He said so in 1842, repeated it now, and would reaffirm this conviction again in the mid-1850s. Adams also refused to condemn "the revival of the trade in African negroes" and speculated about "voluntary immigration of Africans to our southern regions."[42]

Despite the Northerner's aggressive support, Wise criticized Adams for meddling. Southerners lived in "a house *full of combustible materials*." Forget about diverting "Northern antagonism to slavery into a mutual effort with the South to plan for the good of the African race," he advised the dismayed reverend. "Let our property alone, and make your people obey the laws." Dismissed as a harmful encumbrance, Adams read on to find a role for himself only a few paragraphs later. Wise enjoined him to communicate more effectively to Northern audiences the tasks and dilemmas faced by masters—precisely one of Adams's objectives. Wise defied Adams so as to erect a convenient straw man before whom he might dance happily to the tune of the Southern extremists. The Virginian confessed to emancipating a slave, as we have seen, but vowed never to do so again. Difficulties intervened, however, when Wise posed as a tough and hardhearted Southerner.

He could argue the ethical appropriateness of slavery only while positing the eventual return of blacks to Africa. This prospect, along with their conversion to Christianity and improved civility, more than compensated for cruelties they had experienced. Repatriating them to Africa would redeem their degradations. Men of conscience rested uneasily with acknowledgments of their own coercions, which is one reason why they speculated about ending slavery someday. Christ's example, Wise added boldly, showed the redemptive power of suffering. His critics responded by charging the slaveholders with scourging their bondsmen as did the Jews to Jesus. "If the cases are parallel," one commentator put it, "then you are the Egyptians and the Assyrians; the Pharaohs and the Sennacheribs. And what does God himself say of such wicked instruments of his purposes, except that they are 'vessels of wrath fitted for destruction'?" Was it necessary to enslave Africans in order to Christianize them? Were they now kept in bondage to improve their piety?[43]

To show that history, slow and inexorable, nonetheless favored him, Wise pointed to the Union's 430,000 free blacks. More than half resided in the South. The time approached, he added ominously (and uncharacteristically, for he never uttered this view again), when they must accept colonization, even against their wills. Sending them north merely provided the abolitionists with recruits.[44] But it seemed morally risky to excise an emblem of the South's good intentions. If the glacially slow progress Southerners made in meeting their obligations tempted Yankee interference, men such as Adams must teach "them that they are not responsible for *our sin*, if slavery be a moral crime." "And will you," Wise added, "permit me to say that, if slavery be the curse of the South . . . Babel-building is more emphatically the curse of the North." What had happened to the traditional Virginia preference for affixing responsibility to the Yankees, which he had repeated a few years earlier in Brazil? Concessions of this sort required instant qualification.

He scrambled quickly to the highest ground that "*the descendants of Africa now here in bondage* in the United States, *are, en masse, as a whole wealth of people, in bodily comfort, morality, enlightenment, Christianity, and actual personal freedom, worth more than their mother country entire, not excepting the Europeans there combined with the natives*!" Just in case anyone missed the point, he continued:

Political Entitlements

> The slaves are universally fed and clothed well, and they are happy and contented. Look at the tables of their increase and their ages of longevity. Look at their religious privileges; come and listen to them preach and pray, and see them dance and *'eat fat meat and lie by de fire*!' see their masters' love for them and their love for their masters. With white officers, I would fight a regiment of them against any foreign troops which could land on our shores. . . . They have no occasion to buy anything but fine clothes. They have their rations weekly of molasses, coffee and tobacco. They are not allowed to work, and carefully nursed, when sick, and when well don't average ten hours of labor per day. They have their feast days and holidays, and enjoy them more than whites do. . . . Besides this, they have crops of their own, which they sell for their own use.

Through labeling the slaves "property," Wise inescapably emphasized their humanity when justifying himself. What happened if these men and women rejected his benevolence and attempted to escape? By what right might he reclaim them, Adams asked. In response, Wise made no assertion of a natural right to own other persons. Instead, he described African society as naturally heathenish and barbaric: "He, the slave, has no natural right to escape; for his social are his natural rights, and the law of his social being forbids his choice to escape." But Wise's prime justification for enslavement rested on the progress worked in the slaves' "social state" by the master class. The plasticity of black nature, molded by good masters such as himself, made it logically impossible to deny the ultimate improvement—freedom. The same problem appeared when Wise simultaneously attempted to hold the slaves responsible as moral agents for their actions while postulating their obligation to conform to their masters' commands.[45] The source of Wise's difficulty was his effort to find, as he admitted, a middle position between egalitarians, who derived inspiration from a literal reading of the Declaration of Independence, and those who dismissed the Declaration as rubbish and asserted such vast differences among peoples that some deserved to rule because of obvious and verifiable superiority. His effort failing, it proved impossible for him to move beyond the ephemeral legal and constitutional arrangements current in the United States. In a sensible effort to cut his losses, he concluded that the subject of fugitive slaves "requires much more elaboration than I can now bestow on it."

A painless and heaven-sent emancipation would have avoided the necessity to construct such vulnerable arguments. The Compromise of 1850, he wrote, foreclosed one such priceless opportunity. True, California's admission to the Union with a free-soil constitution threatened Southern interests and sensibilities. But in a fashion similar to his advocacy of Texas annexation years earlier, Wise argued that in Southern hands California gold mines would have siphoned off most of the Union's slaves. "Every cornfield in Virginia, and North Carolina, in Maryland, Missouri, Tennessee and Kentucky, would have been emptied of black labourers, and I doubt whether many slaves would have been left to work the cotton and sugar estates of the other Southern plantations." In five years time, masters could have afforded colonization in Polynesia. As one road not taken, this prospect fascinated Wise. Two years later, albeit in more equivocal language, he mentioned it in the midst of a celebrated endorsement of James Buchanan's nomination for the presidency. Finally, as evidence of his doubts about the efficacy of the Kansas-Nebraska Act, he denied the profitability of slavery beyond certain midcontinental "isothermal lines."

The editors of the *Richmond Examiner* smelled a sellout. They wasted little time before flailing Wise: "True philanthropy to the negro begins, like charity, at home; and if Southern men would act as if the canopy of heaven were inscribed with a covenant, in letters of fire, that *the Negro is here, and here forever; is our property, and ours forever*; . . . they would accomplish more good for the race in five years than they boast the institution itself to have accomplished in two centuries."[46]

Possibly anticipating such criticism, Wise thought it necessary to disavow immediate emancipation. He wasted no subtleties. The slaves "can never amalgamate with the whites in this country. The cross is hybrid and against nature. Nature loathes a mulatto as much nearly as she does a mule. It is wicked to encourage a mixture of the races. Contrast with the whites and free negroes demoralizes both." Wicked it was to encourage a mixture, though impossible to avoid—as well he knew.

For several reasons, he felt compelled to provide a Southern constituency with additional proof of his credibility. "I would recommend the repeal of every act to suppress the slave trade," he wrote, in perhaps the most startling sentence of his letter. "The philosophy of Thiers was true. The contraband increases the horror of the trade, and don't in the least diminish the number of victims." Such a reckless recommendation, particularly from a Virginian conversant with his state's dependence on high slave prices, risked identification with South Carolina extremists such as Leonidas Spratt, who had initiated in 1853 the movement to revive the African slave trade.[47] Why did Wise do it?

Wise finished the letter to Adams within days of drafting the preliminary document announcing his candidacy for the Democratic gubernatorial nomination. At about the same time he wrote Senator Hunter and struck a bargain which improved his prospects considerably. He also wished to placate the Young Chivalry, who identified with Hunter and presented themselves as Virginia's most radical Southerners. Among the many reasons they might assign for mistrusting Wise, the record of his Brazilian mission stood out. Enraged by any reference to it from those who professed a greater commitment to Southern rights, Wise turned into a bully of near-violent inclinations.[48] But this record, like others, required expunging. An even more stunning passage in the Adams letter found him describing Brazil as a "negro heaven." Only the most corrosive effects—with consequences perhaps for both his public and intimate life—could have followed such a direct renunciation of his experience.

Later in the 1850s, with a presidential nomination in view, he returned to a dance of death with the slave trade issue—alternately embracing, rejecting, burying, and resurrecting it. He never called outright for more Africans. Instead, he advocated divorcing the federal government from the slave trade in the same fashion that Republicans demanded withdrawal of all federal support for slavery. These cynical flirtations ceased in 1859, when Wise's conscience and good sense prompted him to condemn as immoral all Southern efforts to reopen the trade.[49] With good reason, few of those he most wanted to trust him ever did.

Chapter 8
Saving Virginia, Preserving the Union

Despite the grand success of the Kansas-Nebraska Act, though perhaps partly because of it, Virginia's fabled Democracy seemed unusually fragmented in 1854. Its cohesion and discipline were undermined by a disorganized and momentarily stunned Whig opposition. Moreover, Tom Ritchie's death implied the collapse of the powerful central committee known as the Richmond Junto that he and close friends had dominated for years. These events suggested a waning of partisanship, further evidenced by constitutional reform and economic prosperity that blurred party lines in many states, not just in the Old Dominion. Patronage quarrels involving prominent Virginia Democrats highlighted the ineptness and venality of Pierce's administration. Finally, a major intrastate struggle followed the introduction by Senator Hunter of a homestead bill in the Senate, which one Richmond newspaper branded an "iniquity" for allegedly discriminating against older states and favoring railroads, immigrants, and newer states. With Hunter grasping at Calhoun's mantle, and striving simultaneously for transsectional statesmanship and preeminence within Virginia, a Richmond repudiation embarrassed him more than the eventual defeat of his bill.[1] Added to these difficulties, a new and ominous political movement, far more fearsome because of its allegedly nonpartisan character, threatened further to distract the Democracy and vitalize its traditional enemies.

Know-Nothingism, or the American movement as it was formally known, grew out of nativist responses to the influx of immigrants during the early 1850s. Know-Nothings not only intended to cleanse American institutions of alien influences, they were also a secret and fraternal organization. The ritual and constitution of the American party, drawn up at New York in June 1854, required members to vote only for native-born American Protestants. All initiates agreed to comply in social and political affairs with the will of the party majority. They also promised that when they became public officials, they would, if legally possible, prevent all foreigners and Roman Catholics from holding office. These oaths were binding, and anyone who betrayed the secrets of the order risked expulsion and ostracism. Moreover, everyone who progressed beyond Know-Nothingism's first degree agreed to support only members of the order for public office.[2]

In several states the American movement united antislavery Whig middle classes, whose party had collapsed, with traditionally Democratic Protestant workingmen, who feared the growing presence of immigrants in their communities. In July it carried city elections in Norfolk, an area of traditionally Whig sympathies and also the only place in Virginia, outside of Richmond, with any concentration of foreigners.[3] By November, Know-Nothings controlled the legislatures of Massachusetts and Delaware and had joined with fusion groups to carry Pennsylvania, Indiana, and Ohio.

With that special prescience that characterized his singular political skill, Wise identified earlier and more clearly than any of his potential competitors the necessary step to stir a sluggish party while simultaneously advancing his own interest. A political dinner in Norfolk in mid-September was obviously contrived to request comments on the new political movement from several Democratic luminaries. With the exception of one fascinatingly weak and evasive reply, most were perfunctory repudiations. Wise, however, delivered a twelve-thousand-word manifesto, which ranked as the most scathing indictment of Know-Nothingism yet written anywhere in the Union.

He concentrated on exposing the new order's illiberal and proscriptive tendencies by showing how its ritual and charter contravened all accepted foundations of civil and religious toleration. Its secrecy violated the Reformation's best traditions. Although Catholics were a distinct minority in America, the politicization of Protestant sects would open them to all the corruptions of Jesuitry, he predicted. Having aided indispensably in the triumph of the American Revolution, foreigners and Catholics deserved the protection of its great principle, freedom of conscience. Nowhere did Wise denounce the new order as abolitionist. It was not until later in the fall that the antislavery proclivities of Northern Know-Nothings became clear.[4]

But Wise needed more than his own eloquence and incisiveness to obtain the gubernatorial nomination. At about the same time that he composed both the letter to Adams and the discourse on Know-Nothingism, Wise wrote Senator Hunter and endorsed his land bill. He may also have promised support if the Senator's friends sought to enshrine him as Virginia's favorite son for the presidency in 1856.[5] Soon afterward, anonymous communications defending Wise's consistent devotion to Virginia's interests began to appear in the *Enquirer*. A minority of the Democratic Central Committee met secretly in mid-October and set an early date for the state convention. This important coup, designed to head off the organizing efforts of Wise's opponents, evoked hostile reaction across Virginia. Then, in the Staunton convention, Wise's supporters overturned the traditional proviso requiring successful nominees to secure a two-thirds vote. Wise enjoyed substantial backing in his own right from western delegates. But only the aid of Senator Hunter's associates and kinsmen, along with the editors of the *Enquirer* who voted proxies from at least twenty counties, secured a slim victory on the second ballot. One of the most incongruous political developments of the age found Muscoe Garnett, who despised Wise, serving as his floor leader.[6] But with a new and volatile political movement threatening further to fracture Southern unity and even endangering the Kansas-Nebraska and the Fugitive Slave acts, Hunter's resourceful advisers risked defections to put forward the only man who could win.

In a state where the foreign-born constituted less than 3 percent of the population, the nativists obviously counted on more than nativism. The expected secessions from Democratic ranks promptly materialized. In the subsequent campaign, they became the principal but by no means the only significant element in Know-Nothing efforts to stage an upset. Several of Wise's chief competitors simply sat out the race, while a number of Democratic legislators and congressmen accepted the new order's aid in securing their own reelection.[7] By far the most important defector, however, was former Governor William Smith, who now represented a northern Virginia congressional district. Author of a notably equivocal letter to the Norfolk dinner, Smith openly embraced Know-Nothingism. Nativism made sense for the South, he argued, because discouraging immigration would aid in restoring population parity among the sections. But Smith also detested Wise, who had once described his election to the state senate as "a *degradation* to Virginia," over which he "mourned in sack cloth and ashes." In response to accusations of apostasy, Smith disdained such renegade Whigs as Hunter and Wise, who now dominated the Democracy at the expense of loyal regulars like himself.[8]

Surely the long political memory of Virginians was Wise's second imposing liability. The *Richmond Whig* reprinted his earlier letters and speeches characterizing "the entire Democratic party as spoilsmen, rogues, and swindlers." In probably their finest moment, *Whig* editors unearthed Roger Pryor's comments on Wise's five-day speech during the Constitutional Convention. Then editing the Petersburg *Southside Democrat*, Pryor had denounced the effort as "socialistic," "mischievous," and "revolutionary." Now, however, the embarrassed Pryor found himself the *Enquirer*'s principal editorialist, charged with manufacturing the propaganda necessary to prompt collective amnesia.[9]

Know-Nothingism in Virginia was practically a Whig movement, which meant that its strength came from urban areas, northern counties bordering on the Potomac River, and several counties in the upper Shenandoah Valley conspicuously lacking railroads and turnpikes. Considerable Whig strength also existed in the lower Tidewater counties. Whig leaders such as John Minor Botts, Alexander H. H. Stuart, John D. Imboden, and William C. Rives eventually endorsed the new order in the winter of 1854–55. None of these men had previously been known as nativists or religious bigots. In part, their eventual embrace of Know-Nothingism resulted from superb strategy by leaders of the movement's Southern wing. Late in the fall of 1854, Kenneth Rayner, a former Whig congressman from North Carolina, amended the order's ritual to require an oath of allegiance to the Union from all members. Virginia's Whigs enthusiastically embraced their immemorial tactic of branding Democrats as disunionists. With victory seemingly in its grasp, the Whiggery also renewed its bold claim that Virginia's decadence followed from decades of Democratic rule and fanatical devotion to the anti-improvement abstractions in the Virginia and Kentucky Resolutions of 1798–99.[10]

Still, considerable tension and disorganization inevitably prevailed during efforts to engraft Virginia's traditional opposition on the new movement. Although the *Richmond Whig*'s editor eventually endorsed its gubernatorial ticket, for example, he denied membership.[11] The Whiggery experienced considerable soul-searching before eventually rejecting an independent state convention. This action lent credence to the foolish view, increasingly popular throughout the South, that Know-Nothings had fully absorbed the Whigs and thus rendered Wise's situation desperate.[12] Actually, Wise obtained impressive support from historically Whig rural areas. He also benefited enormously from the lateness of the nativists' nominations and from their vulnerability.

Fittingly, the Know-Nothings gathered secretly in Winchester on 13 March and nominated a states'-rights Whig, Thomas S. Flournoy, for governor. In his letter of acceptance, Flournoy scarcely mentioned the future of the Union. He compressed into two paragraphs a scathing attack on Roman Catholics, whom he wanted to see "excluded from the offices of the Government in all its departments." His affirmation of a religious test for public office went much further than the convention's mild platform. Flournoy also warned the South, in language resembling former Governor Smith's, that the Northwest and the Mississippi Valley were filling up with immigrants hostile to her interests. Unless Southerners resisted this movement, an increasingly adverse balance of power would result. In response to those who maintained that only small numbers of foreigners and Catholics lived in Virginia, Flournoy urged the Old Dominion to assert once again a moral leadership over the Union—this time in behalf of nativism.[13] Wise thus had the opportunity he craved to appeal to Virginians' nobler and more generous instincts.

Compounding Flournoy's intolerance was a public antislavery record. Some years earlier, while addressing a railroad promotion meeting in Charlotte County, Flournoy had traced Virginia's degeneracy to slavery—"*asserting that no country can be prosperous with a slave population*."[14] Instead of arguing as Wise did that internal improvements would bring peripheral areas into the market economy and diffuse slavery, Flournoy blamed the Old Dominion's fixation on slavery for the failure of numerous canals and railroads. The Know-Nothing candidate for lieutenant governor, a former Democratic congressman from northwestern Virginia, espoused the same doctrine.[15] In the Deep South, these nominations provoked suggestions of Virginia's sufficiently abolitionized status to present easy pickings for the Know-Nothings. But with Wise uniquely capable of smelling out antislavery sympathies, Flournoy took such a hammering that to preserve his good name he recanted shortly after his defeat.[16]

Opportunities thus existed for Wise though he preferred, understandably, to regard his situation as desperate. To improve the odds, he decided on an unprecedented personal canvass of Virginia. Beginning at Norfolk in early January 1855, more than two months before the opposition had fielded any candidates, and continuing for nearly four months he shuttled across the state, preaching destruction of the Know-Nothings. Never apologizing for his political antecedents, he took and retained the offensive, traveled more than three thousand miles, and exhausted himself. Know-Nothings were unable to secure orators daring enough to challenge him. Despite numerous entreaties, some almost pathetic, Flournoy refused debate and made not a single speech during the canvass. Wise thus spoke without contradiction to perhaps one hundred thousand people—many of whom never saw a newspaper and could not read anyway.[17]

The man they saw and heard cut a striking figure. Wise stood an inch below six feet but was so thin that many commentators thought him taller. At age forty-nine, he still looked frail, with angular features, steel-gray eyes, and a sallow complexion. "Cadaverous" is how John Fourney described him, and even Wise's admirers acknowledged his homeliness. Despite his sensitivity on matters of honor, he dressed carelessly and often looked downright disheveled. He probably cultivated the nondescript appearance of a commoner, to which his habit of incessantly chewing tobacco undoubtedly contributed.

Once he began the canvass, however, his oratory was of an eloquence and decisiveness unmatched in Virginia and scarcely equaled in the Union. Moreover, he offered practical proposals and, as we shall see, spoke to what he and his people regarded as real issues. Building on his candid assessment of Virginia's dilemmas during the Constitutional Convention of 1850–51, he offered solutions. Always a superb conversationalist though never much of a listener, he finally had an opportunity to persuade a mass of men. The drama of a nonchalant soul springing to life—the thundering calls to battle and renewal, the long pauses while gathering his flagging energy for yet another outburst—all drew their vitality from Wise's conviction that he spoke as a fearless progressive. The times had changed from the 1830s, when his oratory drew its power from his defense of traditionalism. Speaking in public had always tended to mask his uncertainties, but the more so in 1855 because his cause was so good.[18]

Wise dedicated his remarkable powers to the annihilation of the "lousy, godless, Christless" Know-Nothings.[19] They evoked this intemperance because they appeared simultaneously illiberal and antislavery. Wise pilloried them from one end of Virginia to the other for their alleged efforts to enslave white consciences while they freed the blacks. All this would be achieved secretly, dishonorably, by way of edicts issued from culverts. They were perfect enemies for a man of his ambitions and convictions. They allowed him to advance his claims as both a Southern progressive and an ultimately unshakable defender of slavery.

Like most of his associates, Wise equated Democratic hegemony with preserving both slavery and the Union. He had little difficulty demonstrating the antislavery sympathies of Northern Know-Nothings. The legislature of Massachusetts, for example, which the new order dominated, had recently sent the free-soiler Henry Wilson to the Senate and had nearly elected Theodore Parker as its chaplain—"a man anti-Christ, so much devil incarnate that he can hide neither tail nor hoofs."[20] Wise repeated these themes in each of his fifty speeches across the state in language as colorful and penetrating as he could muster. He even intimated that Virginia's Know-Nothings might rise up to support an abolitionist invasion, in case their powerful Northern allies attempted to overwhelm the South. In one prophetic passage, Wise assured his audiences that if, as governor, he ever drew the sword of Virginia, he would use it either against the enemies of the Old Dominion, foreign and domestic, or himself.[21]

Because Wise had a more favorable view of slave capacity than some of his contemporaries, he feared the consequences of slaves somehow creating an organization of their own that, like the Know-Nothings, stressed anonymity of membership and covert, unsupervised gatherings. The *Richmond Enquirer* mentioned this potential enormity only once during the canvass, but the circumspect treatment it received in the Southern press probably belied the apprehensions it induced. Wise never discussed the issue publicly in Virginia but alluded in his private correspondence to the threat of "Sam with a dark lantern among the negroes!!"[22]

Not only had a Virginia gubernatorial candidate never before canvassed extensively, few had ever commented candidly on the state's long-term crisis and declining prestige. To promote renewal, Wise returned to the themes of the 1850–51 convention and pleaded for completion of Virginia's principal lines of internal improvement. "Your canals and your railroads," he told a large audience in Alexandria, "are like ditches dug in the middle of a plantation, without outlet at either end." In particular, he urged construction of the Covington and Ohio Railroad to funnel the trade of the Ohio Valley into Richmond and Norfolk. "You have said," he told his audiences, " 'let us have capital—let us have population, and then we will have a city.' But you never will have capital—you never will have population, until you have the internal improvements to build up a city." And, he added, it behooved Southerners and Virginians to welcome instead of discouraging immigrants when overcrowding among the Yankees drove them away.[23]

Wise called Virginia's agriculture a disgrace and promised "an institute of applied science" as a remedy. The scandalous absence of free elementary education for the poor must also cease. Finally, Wise grasped the issue of nonslaveholder loyalty and suggested that unless improvements took place, working-class whites might fall prey to Northern heresies other than Know-Nothingism.

About one Virginia voter in 5 is a slaveholder, I say it boldly and no man will dispute it who has been to Norfolk and Portsmouth, that the last and

> worst element that is appealed to by the Know-Nothings is the agrarian element. . . . The very men who, for ten years have been petitioning the secretary of the navy to forbid the employment of slave labor in Gosport navy yard—the very men who petitioned the last convention to frame a new constitution for Virginia, to make it a part of the organic law of the state that slaveholders should not allow their slaves to be taught the mechanic arts—these are the men who are the very hot-bed of Know-Nothingism.

Following these remarks, Wise rejected suggestions from Senator Hunter that he keep silent. Indirectly, however, the Democratic press muzzled him by refusing to publish lengthy and specific summaries of his speeches. Instead, it wrote emptily of his smashing the "Goths and Vandals" and "covering himself with glory" as he perambulated around the state.[24]

There was, however, a quantum of sounding brass amid Wise's refreshing candor, particularly in western Virginia. While soliciting support, promising reform, and assuring them of their allegiance to the Old Dominion, Wise complained privately that "these Western people are *not Virginians* in their social or political sympathies." He was more specific when writing from Point Pleasant, on the banks of the Ohio River, in mid-March. It was "one of the most beautiful spots I ever saw, looking down the Ohio and up the Kanawha rivers, over bottom lands as fat and fertile as land can be, from hills full of building rock and coal and other mineral wealth and high with seats for homesteads . . . that I would like to lord it over if I could only 'hold my niggers here!' But they can't and are a coarse and menial and ill-mannered people . . . covered with coal dust, and you touch coal dust and taste coal dust in everything you handle and eat, and a *white* slave has to clean your boots of the stiffest mud of the muddiest streets and roads that ever did bespatter breeches legs of a wayfarer."[25]

When the end finally came in May, Wise lay prostrate in Washington, hardly able to talk, having suffered especially from the "scourging effects" of limestone drinking water in the Shenandoah Valley. Despite the difficulties, indeed perhaps because of them, he took tremendous satisfaction in fighting for both principle and his own political life. Never reticent about his feelings, he wrote revealingly to one of his western supporters: "I am as willing to die a martyr in this cause as in any other, if I am to be defeated; and if I am to be successful I would as leave win the victory alone, without any other aid than that of my friends among the people and of the people themselves. Our members of Congress are all, except two or three inactive for me and kept still by their fear of Know-Nothingism. Let them die the death which they select, I can paddle my own canoe."[26]

Far from the smashing victory predicted by Wise, he defeated Flournoy by a margin smaller than Franklin Pierce's 15,000-vote majority in 1852. Final totals gave Wise 83,424 votes; Flournoy received 73,244. Still, Wise obtained more votes than any other Virginia politician in any election held during the nineteenth century.

It is probably indicative of Know-Nothingism's antislavery appeal that only seven counties along Virginia's northern and western borders voted Democratic. On the other hand, Wise gained considerable ground in the southern tier of counties along the North Carolina border, where Whigs had heretofore dominated. He did extremely well in southwestern Virginia along the route of the projected Virginia and Tennessee Railroad, where both the white and black slave populations were growing faster than in any other area of the state. Wise campaigned extensively in the northwest and southwest and in both regions emphasized his contributions during the Constitutional Convention of 1850–51. But his appeals were presumably more attractive in those areas in which slavery was dynamic and expanding—not stagnant, as in the Tidewater, or almost nonexistent, as in the northwest. Wise also received a good part of his winning margin, as was customary with Democratic gubernatorial candidates, from the so-called Tenth Legion districts in the lower Shenandoah.[27]

Thus Wise's constant calls for organization, vigilance, and committees of correspondence among Democrats must have had some effect, reinforced as they were by the clamor of the party's press. There were some new and decidedly unsubtle twists to these traditional tactics, however. Because the Know-Nothings could win only with Democratic support, Wise and his associates launched a concentrated effort early in May to identify "traitors" and compel them to abandon the new order. Wise boasted that many Democrats had infiltrated the Know-Nothing lodges. They might thus threaten the turncoats with exposure and social proscription. This strategy proved effective; informed observers reported numerous withdrawals from the lodges during the final month of the campaign.[28] These tactics coincided with successful efforts to recruit such Democratic wheelhorses as Senators Mason and Hunter, and even Stephen A. Douglas, for appearances on the stump during the campaign.[29] Finally, Wise and his associates were absolutely unscrupulous in their manipulation of the federal patronage.

The triumph of 1855 was Wise's most memorable. It also broke the momentum of the nativist movement nationally. As victory's euphoria slowly left him, a sharp sense of his achievement came into focus. Henceforth he would speak not merely with his own voice but with Virginia's. For Virginia, Wise had been bred to believe, was not simply another state but the greatest of the states—an old and noble commonwealth in fact as well as in name. One of the reasons why Virginia politicians struggled so hard for control of her destiny was their conviction that with her support a sense of entitlement descended on them, conferring a presumptive right to rule the nation. No amount of ridicule could dissuade Henry A. Wise from believing that other men might do as they would, but Virginians were born and destined to govern.

Wise knew that what the country needed above all was bold and decisive leadership capable of denouncing fanatics in both sections. It required someone who resembled the most powerful and effective politician of them all. Though they had quarreled and forsaken one another, Wise never ceased believing that Andrew Jackson was the greatest man of his time. Now, more than a generation after their first encounter, he fondly recalled Jackson's strength, vitality, and decisiveness. He permitted himself to reflect on how many of these qualities he shared with the immortal Old Hero. Were not both of them rash and impulsive, often by design? Had they not survived persecutions before emerging victorious? Did not each scorn the support of hucksters to carry their appeals directly to the masses? Throughout this period, Jackson's name studded Wise's correspondence, as gradually he began to conceive it as his personal mission to rebuke elements of discord and calm troubled waters. America "never needed a Jackson so much as in these times," he wrote. But to gain the presidency, "a man must be, like him, *persecuted into the place*." Had he not already experienced the requisite suffering? "No man, I may say," he wrote an old friend, "ever more made his own position, and no man shall take it away from me. The most appalling part of my canvass was its literal loneliness—the politicians of our state left me much alone. They are not willing I should occupy it, alone now."[30]

Wise had little money, few personal friends, and no organization outside Virginia. Moreover, he thought far less about these things after his momentous victory in 1855. To some it seemed absurd to speculate about a national candidacy without laying organizational groundwork, but such absurdities appealed to Wise. Characterizations of his approach to politics as ridiculous and anachronistic never deflected him. The people and not the

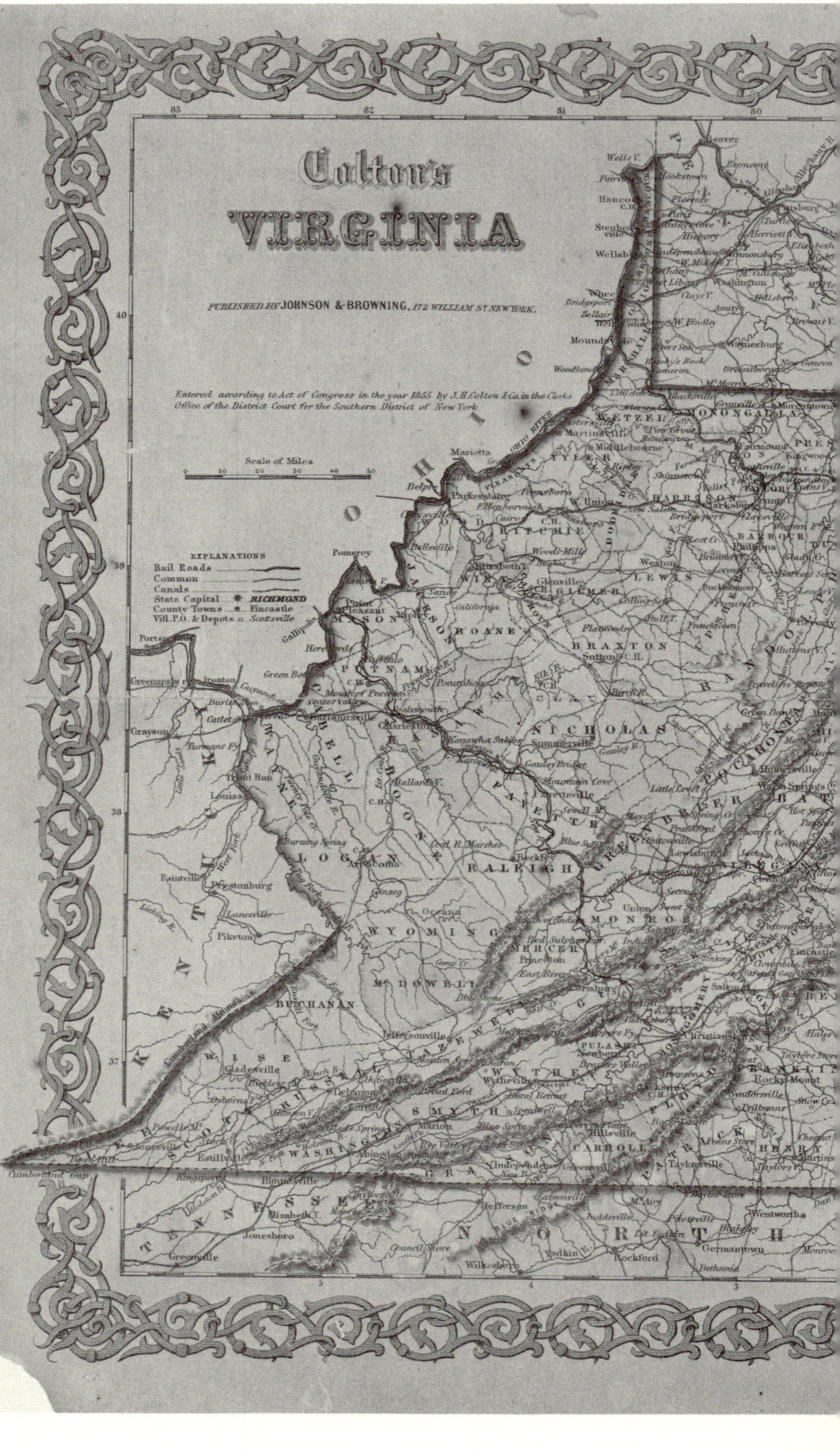
Colton's
VIRGINIA
PUBLISHED BY JOHNSON & BROWNING, 172 WILLIAM ST. NEW YORK.
Entered according to Act of Congress in the year 1855 by J. H. Colton & Co. in the Clerks Office of the District Court for the Southern District of New York
Scale of Miles
EXPLANATIONS
Rail Roads
Common
Canals
State Capital RICHMOND
County Towns Fincastle
Vill. P.O. & Depots Scottsville
OHIO
KENTUCKY
TENNESSEE
NORTH
MASON
JACKSON
ROANE
BRAXTON
LEWIS
NICHOLAS
PUTNAM
CABELL
WAYNE
BOONE
LOGAN
RALEIGH
WYOMING
MERCER
MONROE
BUCHANAN
WISE
SMYTH
WASHINGTON
CARROLL
Marietta
Parkersburg
Charleston
Pomeroy
Greenup
Grayson
Louisa
Prestonburg
Piketon
Cumberland Gap
Blountsville
Jonesboro
Greenville
Jefferson
Wilkesboro
Rockford
Germantown
Wentworth
Weston
Lewisburg
Princeton
Abingdon
Marion
Jeffersonville
Summerville
Fayetteville
Hillsville
Taylorsville
Rocky Mount
Wheeling
Washington
Waynesburg

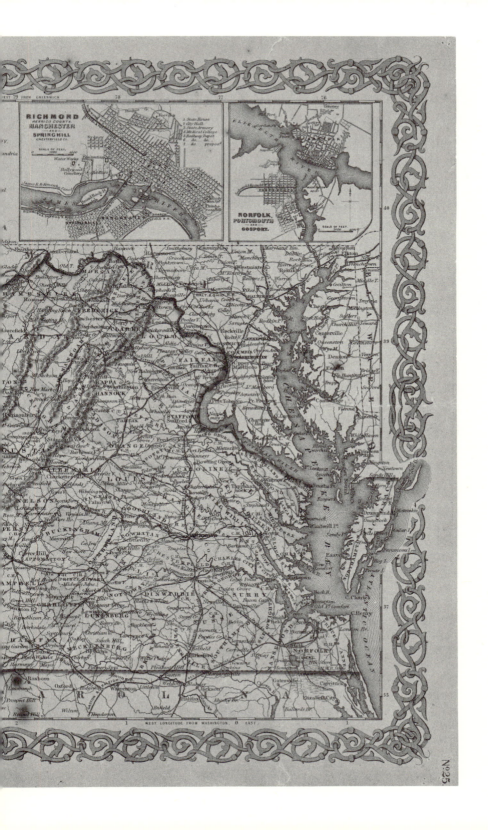

WEST 79 FROM GREENWICH
78
77
76
RICHMOND
HENRICO COUNTY,
MANCHESTER
AND
SPRINGHILL
CHESTERFIELD Co.
SCALE OF FEET.
1. State House
2. City Hall
3. State Armory
4. Medical College
5. Railway Depot
James R. & Kanawha Canal
Hollywood Cemetery
Water Works
Penitentiary
Sydney
JAMES RIVER
NORFOLK,
PORTSMOUTH
AND
GOSPORT.
SCALE OF FEET.
ELIZABETH RIVER
Cemetery
40
39
37
WEST LONGITUDE FROM WASHINGTON 0 EAST
Cumberland
Hancock
Hagerstown
Smithsburg
Emmitsburg
Union M.
Westminster
Manchester
Maryland Tin.
Havre de Grace
Elkton
Frenchtown
Middle T.
Cecilton
Georgetown
Chester
Centerville
Church Hill
Queenston
Easton
Denton
Cambridge
Vienna
White Haven
Princess Ann
Newtown
Snow Hill
Frederick
Middletown
Westminster
BALTIMORE
Ellicotts M.
Rockville
ANNAPOLIS
WASHINGTON
Upper Marlboro
Pt. Tobacco
Alexandria
FAIRFAX
LOUDOUN
Leesburg
Charlestown
Martinsburg
Winchester
Romney
FREDERICK
CLARKE
Warrenton
Brentsville
Dumfries
Fredericksburg
Falmouth
STAFFORD
ORANGE
Gordonsville
Charlottesville
ALBEMARLE
LOUISA
CAROLINE
Bowling Green
Tappahannock
HANOVER
GOOCHLAND
RICHMOND
BUCKINGHAM
CUMBERLAND
POWHATAN
CHESTERFIELD
Petersburg
DINWIDDIE
NOTTOWAY
PRINCE EDWARD
APPOMATTOX
CHARLOTTE
LUNENBURG
MECKLENBURG
HALIFAX
BRUNSWICK
GREENSVILLE
SOUTHAMPTON
SUSSEX
SURRY
Williamsburg
Yorktown
Hampton
Old Pt. Comfort
C. Charles
C. Henry
NORFOLK
Portsmouth
Suffolk
Eastville
NORTHAMPTON
Drummondtown
Onancock
CHESAPEAKE BAY
ATLANTIC OCEAN
POTOMAC RIVER
NELSON
Lovingston
Harrisonburg
Staunton
New Market
Woodstock
Front Royal
Washington
Culpeper
Madison
Hillsborough
Roxboro
Oxford
Warrenton
Halifax
Weldon
Gaston
Jackson
Gatesville
Elizabeth City
Currituck
Enfield
Henderson
Littleton
Hicksford
Belfield
C A R O L I N A

N°25.

politicians would vindicate him, if only he could speak to them—all of them.[31] The people had sustained him in Virginia, where he had suffered and nearly died to redeem the Commonwealth. They would do so again, providing he could cast out the wireworkers, bureaucrats, and managers who controlled national politics and also sponsored a branch office in Virginia devoted to Senator Hunter's claims.

Wise's defeat of the Know-Nothings did much to sectionalize their power and create an audience across the Union prepared to acknowledge the self-serving manifestos he published in subsequent months. Younger men found him an attractive and fascinating personality. A solitary figure, frustrating a conspiracy against republican liberty, proved captivating. But did Americans dare trust him, particularly when he manifested the perverse talents of those confidence men whose pretensions he ridiculed so persuasively? As had Jackson, Wise matured his own style of manipulation—including even the legendary public rages. Desiring to appear above the battle, he nonetheless maintained contact with a number of New York's shadiest politicians. Like Jackson's, Wise's antispoils rhetoric came from a man who seldom shied away from a piece of the action.

The boundlessness and perfectionism of an earlier American generation had given way by the mid-1850s to an enervating sense of the possible. As always, fatalism bred nostalgia, which in turn masked and legitimated contempt for politics. Reactionaries such as Edmund Ruffin gained in notoriety; hopeful experiments such as British emancipation in the Caribbean seemed increasingly naive and foolhardy; the apparent intractability of the sectional crisis prompted reveries of violence. In a time of fear and uncertainty, Wise recalled Jackson's ability to invoke the Revolutionary legacy of a community threatened by conspiracies against individual liberties. But Jackson, despite his usefulness, was inevitably a partisan and recognized as such. More appropriate under the circumstances were appeals to the example, legacy, and bipartisanship of Washington, whose life integrated almost perfectly the themes of pure and generous manhood (threatened now by the Yankee women's movement) and the judicious but decisive use of power. Wise identified himself directly with Washington in his inaugural address as governor of Virginia, as we shall see. He thus appealed to thousands of Americans in the mid-1850s who looked expectantly for strong leadership, a determination to eliminate mediocrity in politics, and the capacity to rebuke irresponsible extremists in both sections.[32]

Anxious to recruit a national audience, Wise reached regularly for his "inexhaustible inkstand," as Horace Greeley put it. Throughout 1855 he wrote a series of patriotic letters to various Democratic meetings across the country, many of them called to celebrate his victory. For the edification of participants in an Alabama festival, he affirmed the doctrine that "Cotton is king" but called for the defense of the Union, with slavery, so as not "to destroy the hopes of mankind for the light, and love and charity of human freedom."[33] Letter writing followed consistently from Wise's intention to transcend ordinary political organizations, but it carried risks. Not fathoming the impassable thickets of New York's politics, for example, he penned a friendly letter in June 1855 to a meeting of the "soft-shell" faction. Southerners reacted critically and accused him of meddling in Yankee affairs on the side of the abolitionists. He quickly attempted to recover lost capital in the South by telling a group in Boston, which had invited him to lecture on slavery in Tremont Temple, that the building could not hold money enough to pay him. He would, however, happily suppress an insurrection or repel an invasion free of charge.[34] These tactics drew a piece of fraternal advice from Mayor Fernando Wood of New York City, whose Machiavellianism exceeded even Wise's. An old friend from their days together on the Naval Affairs Committee during the early 1840s, Wood was now extracting whatever he could from an alliance of convenience with the leaders of New York's notorious Democratic club, Tammany Hall. In a kindly remonstrance, Wood advised epistolary caution.[35]

Americans expected pretentiousness from Virginians, though they grew less patient as the Old Dominion's material decline appeared to deepen. Wise argued for the reversibility of those economic and political processes that had undermined Virginia's influence. The Old Dominion remained a genuine political prize, despite the national consensus on her decrepitude and imbecility. In electoral strength, Virginia ranked fourth in the Union and first among the slave states. Nor could anyone ignore her moral authority, upon which Wise and others forever descanted. The press referred to it constantly. Moreover, one of the state's most serious crises—the long-term exodus of her white population—could be transformed from a weakness to a strength in the event of a national crusade conducted by her most brilliant politician, thus resurrecting the state's greatness and confirming the Union's permanence. Almost four hundred thousand whites had left Virginia by 1850—far more than had vacated any other state. A Virginia candidacy would energize these expatriates. It would also silence those critics who wondered aloud about Virginia's current inability to produce great men. Wise dreamed that the long wait was over. He read the Scriptures and knew all about redeemers, the promises they fulfilled, and the hard of heart forever impervious to inspired doctrine.[36]

Most of the state's powerful politicians, however, were reluctant to confer even a portion of Virginia's dignity on Wise. They acquiesced only out of desperation. Senator Hunter's nervous friends had feared all along that Wise's success would animate his ambition and derail their own candidate. Directed by the wily Lewis E. Harvie, the senator's supporters marshaled their energies, prepared for the inevitable moment when Wise would disavow his earlier commitments, and saw to it that Hunter did little and said less. They got what they expected in August 1855, when Wise repeated to Hunter his promise to "use every influence in my power, to give you a nomination for the Presidency." He squirmed out of this commitment in his very next sentence: "For myself I never dreamt of it; but if it cannot be given to you and is forced upon me all I can say is—'if they will have me to rule, I will rule 'em!' "[37] To control the governor, Harvie and associates trusted to the press, their influence on the Democratic Central Committee of Virginia, and suspicions of Wise among members of the congressional delegation. They presumed that, given time, his vanity and eccentricities would burst his own bubble.

Trusting neither to chance nor to friends he lacked, Wise secretly engineered the publication of two books in the spring of 1856 designed to promote his national prospects. In March *A Biographical Sketch of Henry A. Wise, with A History of the Political Campaign in Virginia, in 1855* appeared, edited by Dr. James P. Hambleton of Danville, Virginia. This five-hundred-page documentary included all the principal speeches and newspaper editorials on both sides, a number of Wise's published letters, and a biographical sketch. It also memorialized Wise's victory by reprinting proceedings of celebrations that followed the election. Hambleton took special pains to assuage Senator Douglas's ego by including his Senate speech on the Kansas-Nebraska Act. Though perhaps solicited at first, the governor-elect enthusiastically offered his encouragement and supplied Hambleton with a series of autobiographical letters. When the *Richmond Whig* announced publication of this volume, it wryly challenged Senator Hunter's forces to rouse themselves.[38]

Even less subtlety suffused an anonymously written, book-length melodrama that appeared shortly afterward. *The Life and Death of Sam, in Virginia* is so shamelessly self-laudatory that Wise could never have acknowledged authorship, if indeed he wrote it. The book is a thinly veiled memorial to his "fitness, power, genius, patriotism and chivalrous spirit." The story centers on the temptations faced by a young Virginian, Maurice Meredith, whom the Know-Nothings seduce away from maiden Fannie Bell. Her Catholicism only buttresses her claims to be "a true Virginia woman." It follows predictably that she remains loyal to her principles. Meredith eventually departs—ticketed for the lower regions, one supposes. Fannie then meets the man she deserves. He forthrightly condemns culvert politics and devotes life and fortune to pure and ever-victorious Democracy. The 1855 campaign's enduring effects on personal relations thus dramatize further the achievements of Virginia's master intellect and intrepid leader.

The text personalizes its rehash of nativist strategy by caricaturing several of Wise's opponents. John Minor Botts, the former Whig congressman from the Richmond district, appears as John James Gustavus Adolphus Fox. Another mouthful of a name, Americus Winks, betrays Wise's revenge on Vespasian Ellis, an old enemy from the Eastern Shore who edited the *American Organ* in Washington. These villains fomented both racial unrest and class conflict. They endeavored, that is, to use the nativist issue to divide white laborers and mechanics. Old Scip, a prototype of the faithful slave, confirms Wise's privately expressed fears during the 1855 canvass that Know-Nothings might abolitionize the slaves. Having demonstrated his intelligence, Old Scip then proclaims Harriet Beecher Stowe's ignorance of the South. Another character responds to *Uncle Tom's Cabin* by citing the humanitarianism of Virginia's masters as a principal impediment to emancipation.

In Wise's view, Stowe maligned both masters and slaves. By painting too many slaveholders as brutal reprobates, she ignorantly rejected patriarchy. She also never understood slaves and thus intentionally romanticized them. Wise again acknowledged, as in 1855, that slaves knew more and did more than whites gave them credit for, despite the allegedly derivative character of their culture. The gravamen of these criticisms, however, was Wise's conviction that slavery must one day disappear—and his affirmation that no national candidacy could succeed without disavowing it. If the Know-Nothings sinned once by embracing abolitionism, *The Life and Death of Sam* finds them doubly sinful in their refusal to accept the "slow process of obliterating slavery from the South."

References to "Christian politics"—a nineteenth-century legacy of Puritan fanaticism frequently rebuked by Wise during the 1850s—and to lessons learned from John Quincy Adams prove the governor's close association with the book. If not the author himself, then Wise employed a ghostwriter. It evidently fooled nobody, for even the *Enquirer* acknowledged "criticisms this work has solicited." No mention of it exists in any extant writings by Wise, which might charitably suggest an effort to distance himself from one of the more notable testaments to his vanity.[39]

Wise never relinquished his presidential aspirations. But his long-standing and widely known attachment to James Buchanan restricted his maneuverability and limited accessions of support. Buchanan's plans were fuzzy and undeveloped in the fall of 1855. Wise advised Robert Tyler, a mutual friend and an important figure in Buchanan's Philadelphia machine, that the Pennsylvanian would run poorly in the South because he had previously supported the extension of the Missouri Compromise line to the Pacific as the best solution for the territorial problem. He added that Buchanan "could insure my nomination if he would." When Tyler informed him that Buchanan at long last had mastered his local enemies and claimed the united strength of Pennsylvania, Wise backtracked. On 5 March 1856, the governor wrote a widely circulated letter to a Buchanan meeting in New York, offering a personal endorsement, though again affirming his own availability. If the Pennsylvanian's candidacy somehow miscarried, he expected the Keystone State's support in nominating Senator Hunter or "some other" Virginian.[40]

Graceless as it may have been, Wise's support proved effective if not crucial to Buchanan. By mid-May Buchanan's supporters controlled Virginia, which always voted at national conventions under the unit rule. "Outstripped by other states in material development," she required this device to preserve her moral prestige, the *Enquirer* admitted.[41]

Though Wise concentrated on infighting among Democrats, he never lost an opportunity to abuse the Know-Nothings. Following Millard Fillmore's nomination for the presidency by both the Whigs and the Southern branch of the American party, he devised one of the most vulgar and demagogic letters to appear in print during the 1850s. If the Democracy stood as the white man's party and the Republicans as the black man's party, then the Know-Nothings constituted the mulatto party—a term of perhaps more than merely political significance for him. "All nature abhors vacuums and mongrels," he remarked, "so do conscientious, conservative, and constitution-loving Whigs of Virginia. They can put up better with pure Africans—wool, flatnose, odor, ebo-shin and gizzard-foot and all—better than they can bear that cross of the

Caucasian and cuffey which you call a—mulatto."[42] The enormity of this insult so riled Richmond Know-Nothings that they held an indignation meeting and denounced Wise's indecency in violent language. Young James Lawson Kemper feared a duel and offered to fight it for Wise. But the governor advised him to forget the "cowardly, vulgar, drunken wretches" among his opponents and predicted that his letter would only endear him to the Democratic masses.[43]

Virginia's firm support aided Buchanan indispensably at the Democracy's Cincinnati convention, although Stephen A. Douglas's decision to bow out after the sixteenth ballot guaranteed the Pennsylvanian's nomination by the required two-thirds vote. Even more satisfactory was the convention's resolution on the status of slavery, which exemplified the increasing Southern domination of the Democratic party during the 1850s. With Senator Hunter's friend, James Seddon, and his associates pressing for congressional protection of slavery in the territories,[44] the convention moved close to the prevailing Southern view that only a state constitutional convention—not territorial legislatures—might exclude slavery. Its language was far less equivocal than the Kansas-Nebraska Act and appeared to foreclose squatter sovereignty—the attempt of Kansans or others while still under territorial government to eliminate slavery. Southern national Democrats used the Cincinnati platform against regional extremists and secessionists.

One may thus understand the momentary consternation in Virginia and the South which greeted Buchanan's letter of acceptance. Desperately in need of votes from Douglas's Northwest, Buchanan affirmed that "the people of a territory, like those of a state, shall decide for themselves whether slavery shall or shall not exist within its limits." When the Southern Whig press assailed Buchanan for advocating squatter sovereignty, Wise sped off two letters to Wheatland warning his friend that support for that doctrine would doom him in the South.[45] In a "private and confidential" reply, the Pennsylvanian reflected angrily on those Southerners who would now betray him after he had spent nearly a lifetime defending their interests. Then, proving that his letter of acceptance had been a ploy, he assured Wise that nothing in it contradicted the platform or favored squatter sovereignty.[46]

The governor presumably expected such assurances from Buchanan because at all times he reckoned on wielding power over the nominee. As he had recently remarked in a letter to George W. Munford, Virginia's secretary of state, "Most Northern politicians are men of *expediency*, and you have them with you just as soon as you make them believe it to be their interest or make them apprehend some necessity for union. As long as the Union is for us to rule, let them . . . come in and be counted as of the party."[47]

It was characteristic of Wise to await no one's praise. He claimed a great triumph for Virginia and himself at Cincinnati—one they deserved following the victory over Know-Nothingism. In a remarkably frank, semiextemporaneous speech before a raucous meeting called in Richmond to ratify the presidential nomination, Wise refused to endorse unequivocally his friend of convenience. Even *his* talents could not induce amnesia among auditors determined to reflect thoughtfully on the Pennsylvanian's nondescript political career. What good could Buchanan do? He would buy time and prevent matters from getting worse, Wise argued. Virginia Democrats required the electoral strength of at least one large Northern state to perpetuate their power. Buchanan's conciliatory and evenhanded temperament ensured his reliability in both foreign and domestic affairs. Wise mentioned his diplomatic experience and knowledge of English affairs in the context of deploring current American relations with Great Britain. He singled out, in particular, the vexatious Clayton-Bulwer Treaty of 1850 that prevented a unilateral American effort to construct a canal across Central America. War was unthinkable, however, because of the inevitability of an American defeat and the certainty of a successful abolitionist crusade. He recounted, once again, John Quincy Adams's old threat to emancipate the slaves by means of the war power in the Constitution. What happened to all the bravado with which he had contemplated a war with the English fifteen years earlier?

Abolitionists in old and New England relished an opportunity to assail Virginia's institutions, which were weak and unstable, he conceded inferentially. Buchanan's election would preclude the need to defend them. Countering earlier and private statements to the contrary, Wise reversed himself and suggested that Buchanan's commitment to the extension of the Missouri Compromise line to the Pacific to resolve the nation's domestic crisis deserved commendation. In one sense, this allusion was gratuitous because both Wise and Buchanan now accepted the Kansas-Nebraska Act. But the Virginia governor wanted to improve his candidate's credibility among the Young Chivalry in his own state. He therefore contrasted the effects of implementing Buchanan's policy with the Compromise of 1850, which cost the South all of California: "The cost of not running that line to the Pacific may be valued thus to Virginia: We now get a thousand dollars for a sound slave; we would have gotten from 3 to $5,000 for an operative in the gold mines of California—400,000 multiplied by 5,000, or even 3000 will show our immense loss. One billion of dollars wouldn't compensate Virginia for her loss in not running the line on to the Pacific."[48]

This frequently quoted projection yielded no clear meaning, however, which compelled Wise afterward to attempt a clarification of his intent. Northern critics could have read him as pleading for slavery's diffusion across the Southwest so as to increase the South's political power. But in making a similar analysis of the compromise two years earlier, in the Adams letter, Wise had specifically rejected any intent to maximize the South's advantage. Throughout most of the 1850s, he reacted with equanimity to the depopulation of Virginia's slaves and the vitiation of Southern political power consequent on that process. Thus he again acknowledged his conviction that shortsighted agreements on the national level had cost Virginia a superb and potentially profitable chance to eliminate slavery. Recognizing an opening, the editors of the *Richmond Whig* censured his "stupid" California infatuation and ranked him as an emancipationist "side by side with Garrison and Wendell Phillips." His subsequent explanation repeated that Southern acquisition of a portion of California "would have enabled the slave owners to free their slaves at a larger profit than they can now sell them." Northern Democrats, he added unabashedly, should agree to disagree about slavery with men like himself, just so long as they voted for Buchanan and preserved the Union's integrity and their own power.[49]

The urgency and cynicism with which he advocated Buchanan's claims highlighted Wise's conviction that Virginia herself was uncertain about slavery's future, just as he was. A Republican victory would mean the end of slavery in the north and west of the Commonwealth, if indeed it had not already collapsed. "You might as well own a thousand dollars floating on a chip on the Ohio River," he remarked in September, recalling the hitherto private impressions from his gubernatorial canvass, "as to own a slave worth a thousand dollars on the banks of that stream in Virginia." Why worry about the status of slavery in such a faraway place as Kansas, he asked, when abolitionism threatened Virginia directly?[50]

A new day had dawned in Virginia. The Republicans held a state convention in Wheeling, nominated an electoral ticket, and raised a Frémont pole as far south as Portsmouth, near Norfolk. At least twenty thousand Virginians, Wise wrote early in the fall, who planned to vote for Millard Fillmore "would hurra over the election of Fremont." Not only that; Wise predicted that "man after man" among the Whigs would take office under the Republicans and thus destroy the South's ability to resist.[51]

Wise refused to acknowledge that moral imperatives had molded Republican antislavery convictions. Instead, Senator William H. Seward's speeches demonstrated their intention to foster "*agrarianism*" and "to summon class against class." The Black Republicans, Wise wrote, "wouldn't abolish 'cotton and sugar' slavery tomorrow or the next day. They will be masters of masters and slaves and so *they dominate* that is all their philanthropy. They would laugh at the honest, earnest Abolition fanatics, and themselves turn slavetraders as soon as the plantations are made tributary to the factories."[52]

Seward, in fact, talked as much about power as about humanitarianism. In speeches Wise studied carefully, he found that Seward consistently arraigned the authority and accomplishments of the "privileged class" of only 350,000 slaveholders whose "barbarous and tyrannical" behavior everywhere stifled freedom and enterprise. As did many other Republican commentators, some of whom cited Wise's remarks during his gubernatorial canvass, Seward emphasized Virginia's retarded and unenlightened condition as a sufficient response to the Southern boast that slavery produced cultivated statesmen whose achievements were unparalleled. Slavery would either disappear peacefully, he predicted, or the masses would end it by whatever means necessary.[53]

Seward's candor and manliness at least entitled him to respect not owed to some of the other, effeminate Republican leaders. Charles Sumner's allegedly feigned illness following the assault on him by Preston Brooks disgusted Wise. "Such skulking poltroonery," he wrote, "would hurt a man sure enough anywhere that the institution of slavery exalts masters to a pride of genteel manhood." No treatment could be too severe for Frémont, whose nomination Wise seemed at times to regard as a personal insult and a degradation of all values he held dear. He wrote to his nephew some details for a newspaper article that would expose Frémont's family history: "His mother was a strumpet of a Richmond brothel. Old Col. Pryor married her. Frémont [father of the nominee] was a French teacher . . . and ran off with her first to Norfolk, afterwards to Charlestown. Fry him up to cracklings!"[54] Thus the personal objections to the Republicans melded together with a denial of their interest in benevolence. This evaluation of Republican objectives permitted Wise to identify defiance of Frémont and his hordes with the preservation of private property, morality, religion, and the family.[55] Jealous of Republican claims to fame, Wise regarded himself as one of America's great though very frightened humanitarians.

When Wise wished to embody his fears, he simply conjured up the oversized visage of John Minor Botts. Three times the rotund Botts, nicknamed "Bison," had represented the Richmond district in Washington. He owned slaves and bred fast horses at his estate in Henrico County, north of the city. But he also retained a devoted following in the working-class neighborhoods on Richmond's northside. With prophetic accuracy, Wise fingered Botts as one Southerner likely to turn Republican.[56]

In regular letters to the Richmond press and speeches whose eloquence even his opponents acknowledged, Botts assailed the Democrats for keeping Southerners in bondage. What indeed had prevented the completion of Virginia's internal improvements? he asked. What had retarded her industry? A slavish adherence to states'-rights doctrine and a parochial attitude toward the tariff, he answered, in true Whiggish fashion.[57] Intrepidly, he condemned the Kansas-Nebraska Act as dooming all territories in the United States along with any subsequently acquired to Republicanism and free soil. Led on by the "little Giant, Douglas, and the Great Dwarf, Pierce," and ably assisted by various "pigmies," "butterflies," and "grasshoppers," the Democratic party had plunged the country into civil war over Kansas. In speeches widely praised and circulated in the North, Botts ridiculed the idea that the South would secede if Frémont were elected. Not slavery but the Democrats stood as the South's and the nation's principal affliction. To make way for sensible economic development slavery would eventually disappear from Virginia, he predicted.[58] Though he actually preferred Fillmore, Botts announced his willingness to vote for "Fremont or the devil" in preference to Buchanan. Botts helped convince Northerners that under no circumstances would Southerners countenance secession, despite the fulminations of Wise, Jefferson Davis, and the Southern press. Before large and enthusiastic crowds, Botts referred to Wise as "general Quattlebum," called him a "madcap," and suggested that he would have to use Virginia oysters for powder and shell if ever he fought the Yankees.[59] No other man east of the Blue Ridge spoke as Botts did in the 1850s, and he paid a price. Even leaders of his own party frequently found his presence and influence distasteful. Perhaps it was only his impeccable Virginia pedigree that allowed him to survive the withering abuse of nearly all the newspapers and politicians in the state. Wise dared take no chances, however, because Botts continued to draw large crowds across Virginia down to the eve of secession.[60]

Fearful of the aid and comfort Botts's remarks provided Republicans, Wise responded in mid-September during a notable address at Corinthian Hall in Richmond. He accused Botts of treason to Virginia, threatened his arrest, and nearly incited mob action against him. There was a curious hyperbole in these assaults, however. Botts commanded no massive following, despite his success in unraveling Wise. Centered in the enmity between them may have been a consciousness of their agreement on issues such as the folly of the Kansas-Nebraska Act, which Wise had no desire to confront. Both were Whigs, after all. Each had always believed that territorial policy in the mid-nineteenth century proceeded at the expense of the Union and the South. Finally, each was on record as expecting slavery's demise.[61]

Botts therefore required special attention. To undermine him among his "rowdy" constituents of "Butchertown," Wise worked prodigiously to complete an address for delivery in mid-October at the Mechanics Institute in Richmond. He duly praised the dignity of manual labor but also called for development of a Mechanics and Farmers Institute at the University of Virginia. He calculated that an appropriation of $300,000 could establish such a facility and, more important, recommended that one-half of the five hundred students receive scholarships. Virginia's independence required a school for mechanics, he affirmed. "In ten years we can make a revolution," he told an audience which he feared might make a revolution of its own.[62] Following the election, he expressed to a visiting Northerner his anxieties over a possible insurrection of nonslaveholders and suggested as evidence of their tenuous loyalty to the Old Dominion that an attempt would be made during the next session of the General Assembly to restrict slaves from learning the mechanical arts and to restore these trades exclusively to whites.[63]

Despite the specter of a slave uprising, which he could still conjure up, complete with Jamaican regiments commanded by pale-faced and round-headed abolitionists, Wise's fears focused more intensively on Virginia's yeomen. As a slaveholder of substance, he reacted calmly during the insurrectionary scare of late December 1856. To suppress an alleged slave uprising, he frequently supplied fewer muskets than panic-stricken Virginians requested. He also successfully resisted demands to mobilize the state militia and place it on patrol duty.[64] But his sensitivity to the nonslaveholders increased in proportion to his political power and responsibility. This concern would frame his reaction to John Brown, as we shall see.

Radicalism came easily for Wise in the fall of 1856—or did it? Declaring that he would await no "overt act" should Frémont secure election, he ordered the commandants of militia regiments in Virginia to fill all vacancies in company and field offices. He attempted to exchange a number of old flintlock muskets for percussion muskets, but Secretary of War Jefferson Davis refused. He even ordered a custom-made carbine and a brace of new pistols for himself.[65] Not wanting to forfeit the symbols and emblems of national power, he reflected on a preemptive strike against the Capitol in Washington or the federal arsenal at Harpers Ferry and the navy yard at Portsmouth. He spoke openly about such a movement, rumor circulated his remarks, and a number of Republicans called him a traitor ever afterward.[66]

Given his temperament and penchant for grabbing headlines, however, Wise inspired critics closer to home to expect him to take foolish and self-serving action. If forced to fight, he told cheering crowds at Corinthian Hall on 20 September, he intended to save both the United States Constitution and the Commonwealth. Ever the venturesome leader, he vowed to accomplish whatever Virginians would back him at doing. This would be precious little, if his state were as divided and disabled as he suggested. The Republicans might have "fifty or sixty thousand supporters in Virginia," he openly confessed. But the South might rely "in every Northern state" on the "hundreds of thousands of arms that are with us." Secessionists, grown weary by Wise's nationalism and disgusted by his judgment that war would necessarily follow from the severing of the Union, prepared for another elaborate charade. So did the Whigs, though they always remained less certain about his lack of seriousness.[67]

Against this background, Wise mounted one of the strangest initiatives of his career. Little can be known about it for certain. Evidently moved by Republican victories in New England, Wise wrote the governors of eleven slaveholding states on or about 15 September, summoning them to meet him in Raleigh, North Carolina, on 13 October. This was the day preceding the state balloting in Pennsylvania, on which the decision in the national election would turn. He excluded the Whig or Know-Nothing chief executives of Delaware, Kentucky, and Missouri for "obvious reasons."[68]

Several executives telegraphed acceptances to Wise only to back out shortly thereafter. Governor Charles A. Wickliffe of

Louisiana protested the exclusion of American party governors from Missouri and Kentucky. This point carried little validity because the Know-Nothings would have given no aid or comfort to extreme action, no matter what the provocation. More sensibly, Wickliffe suggested that the meeting would be interpreted as a barefaced attempt to pressure Northerners into supporting Buchanan and would inevitably backfire.[69] Like most Southern politicians, Wickliffe probably felt confident of Buchanan's victory by early October and wished to do nothing that might jeopardize it. A number of genuine extremists in the South also discountenanced Wise's call. They had probably given up on the idea of a national or sectional convention after their failure at Nashville in 1850. The radicals, moreover, feared taking any public role in a movement to defeat Buchanan because they would then bear the responsibility and witness their program deprecated accordingly.

A Southern movement designed in any sense to influence a Northern election required visibility. Wise's movement proceeded in mock secrecy—though any loud stage whispers heard across the Union conformed entirely with his purposes. The *National Era*, an antislavery weekly published in Washington, D.C., got wind of the conference in early October and denounced it as a treasonous conspiracy. There is no mention of it, however, in the *New York Times*, *Herald*, or *Tribune*. Four of Pennsylvania's principal newspapers made no allusion to it whatever.[70] Yet their ignorance seems inconceivable. Perhaps the meeting seemed so comical and inane that they chose to ignore it.

Only the governors of North and South Carolina met Wise at Raleigh. No record survives of the three days they spent together during the North Carolina state fair. Rumors and suspicions abounded, however, with the ever-friendly reflections of the *Richmond Whig* setting the standard: "Does a solitary citizen of Virginia or the South know what these men are after? Will they publish the *whole* or any *part* of the proceedings of this conference? We predict not. But we wait for '*Gizzard Foot*' to return. We have faith in the fact that, being the prime mover in the getting up of this traitorous and ridiculous little convention of Southern governors, his intolerable vanity will impel him to blab out most of what was said and done."[71]

On the contrary, Wise remained defensive though never close-mouthed about his designs at Raleigh. Interrogated by a Whig organ, the *Raleigh Register*, he refused comment on the substance of his "consultations." Instead he defended his right to travel across state lines. How could he contemplate radicalism in the heart of sturdy old North Carolina, he asked. He dwelt on the dangers confronting the South unless, he implied, Northern Union-lovers were sufficiently roused to action: "Slavery dwarfed in the Union, Federalism, Blue Federalism of the Essex-Junto stripe will rear its horrid front, and you will again have Banks and Tariffs and Internal Improvements by the Federal Government, all that Jefferson and Macon, North Carolina and Virginia, ever contended against."[72]

Perhaps the best clue to Wise's purposes in Raleigh comes from the last extant letter he wrote before departing from Richmond. "The difficulty," he advised Robert Tyler, "is in holding thousands back, and the spirit is almost too irresistable." Not only Republicans but irresponsible hotheads in his own section threatened the stable and Virginia-dominated Union for which he fought. Wise grew morbid at the thought of Southern extremists promoting Frémont's candidacy so that they might successfully provoke disunion.[73] Should Frémont secure election, Wise expected the radicals to act quickly; therefore, he must act even more quickly. One man who allegedly encountered him in a Raleigh hotel said Wise talked of a prompt declaration of martial law followed by the calling up of 150,000 militiamen. Governor James H. Adams of South Carolina supposedly agreed to supply an additional 75,000.[74] No Southern revolution, Wise believed, could dare take place without his influence and leadership.

Had Frémont secured election, the events of 1861 might well have arrived five years earlier. With the prestige of his recent victory and Virginia in his grasp, it would have been inconceivable for Wise to permit others an unchallenged influence. To be sure, it conformed with his image of self to act rashly in defense of conservatism. On the day he returned to Richmond from Raleigh and before results from Pennsylvania were confidently known, he cautioned one of President Tyler's sons: "I hope that our friends will not precipitate movements which will be certain to fail. They may understand each other and know their men, and be prepared to act when called or compelled—not before."[75] "I am more deliberate and guarded than some of my friends know of and give me credit for," he reminded an associate. "My conscience is not disturbed about slavery and I mean to defend our rights," he had advised Virginia's Episcopal Bishop William Meade in the summer of 1856, "but I will act only under the law and to keep the peace and preserve good government."[76] Wise both nominated and withheld himself from a traitor's halter in the fall of 1856. He would do so again four years later.

Whenever he contemplated irrevocable measures against the Union, the governor encountered supreme difficulties. Only traitors rebelled against governments consecrated by the affirmation of their own allegiance. The charge of treason had tracked and tainted his father. Enemies vilified Wise himself as a supreme political traitor. The charge immobilized him, but if the crisis were grave enough its effects might dilute his own fears. Despite the bravado, he would doubtless have done something in 1856 had Frémont been successful. In late October, with the crisis past, he sketched a theory for an old South Carolina enemy whose good opinion he now valued: "I have an irresistible *minority* to back me. A consentaneous *majority* never was obtained for revolution in human history, and *therein was Calhoun's failure*. He speculated upon moving masses, well fed, well clothed, standing at the 'flesh pots.' Masses, nor representative bodies of masses, never made a revolution. It is essentially and necessarily an Executive Act. The Declaration of Am. Independence was stolen from the masses, a large majority of whom were Loyalists, the day the paper was read from Carpenters Hall."[77]

Four years later, after the Republicans took power, he hesitated and again inflamed the passions of the Southerners who despised him. Jaded and cynical from the disappointments of his own time in power, he had less confidence in either his own or Virginia's revolutionary potential. Finally, a mere suggestion from a friend on an April afternoon in Richmond snapped his loyalties, focused his rage on revolutionary violence, and authorized the displacement of others formally entitled to command by himself.

"The signs . . . all indicate," Governor Thomas Bragg of North Carolina wrote Wise ten days after the Raleigh conference, "that we will be spared the trial of meeting the crisis so much dreaded." Buchanan's forces triumphed in Pennsylvania, thus sealing his success in the Union. With the Raleigh movement vindicated, Wise left his critics impotent, though not speechless. While Wise and his surrogates took credit for frightening Northern conservatives sufficiently to preserve the Union, Robert Ridgway of the *Whig* recommended the governor's confinement for life in the state penitentiary and pronounced him the "most outrageous and unapproachable ass the winds of heaven ever blew upon." Nonetheless, Ridgway confirmed Wise's power over Virginia by reprinting his effusive campaign letters and attributing to these "ravings" Buchanan's victory in several Northern states.[78]

But Wise now had nothing more outlandish on his mind than

the usual business of grabbing offices and policing a pliant national administration. He traveled quickly to Wheatland, declined Buchanan's offer of a cabinet position, and repudiated the president-elect's ruminations about constructing a railroad to the Pacific, whose constitutionality would rest on the war power. He was buttressed by a private letter from Buchanan in 1853 discountenancing any interest in such a project.[79]

The governor exercised considerable authority over the distribution of minor patronage, and he had a prime nominee for the seat in the cabinet to which Virginia would be entitled. At a secret dinner in Richmond Wise promoted the candidacy of former Governor John Floyd, who recently had forsaken the Hunter wing of the party. Shortly after the Democratic National Convention, as Wise put it, "Floyd had seen that he had been playing bad cards, that he was a partner with hands who held braggers and aces and were beaten by deuces and tres. Sagaciously and adroitly he came to me, I didn't go to him, not one step. He played his part faithfully and fairly the campaign through."[80]

News of the meeting leaked, however. The *New York Herald* instantly derided the spoilsmanship of politicians in the Old Dominion and contrasted Wise and his friends with the "honest fanatics" of South Carolina. "Our state has been burlesqued, ridiculed and sneered at North and South, by all classes of people," Congressman John Letcher advised a Lexington correspondent.[81] Deeply embarrassed, Wise attempted to allay some of the commotion by writing a third-person account denying that the governor had schemed to promote Floyd. He then "raged and bullied for an hour and a half" to secure its insertion into the *Enquirer* of 13 December. Roger Pryor quickly wrote the full particulars to Senator Hunter, denouncing the governor for his "indecent and undignified exhibition" and calling him a "vulgar fool." He also reported that Wise had "declared war against us all with the comprehensive curses of a Bull of Excommunication." Not the least of Wise's sins was his endorsement of Beverley Tucker for the editorship of Buchanan's projected Washington organ, a position coveted by Pryor.[82]

No warmth or understanding existed between Wise and Floyd, whom Buchanan duly appointed his secretary of war. Wise had once compared Floyd with his despised cousin, Thomas H. Bayly, and other "such cattle." The former governor was no stranger to political conniving. His kinsmen had monopolized most of the high offices allotted to southwestern Virginia for the past thirty years. Later, at a crucial moment, he broke completely with Wise.

Their antagonism would have decisive consequences for the early history of the Confederate States of America. With the nation for the present under Buchanan's good and malleable management, however, Wise turned full attention to effecting a much-heralded renewal of the Old Dominion.

Chapter 9

A Futile Effort to Revive the Old Dominion

Wise took office during a time of rising optimism that his own confident predictions helped sustain. Steady tobacco and wheat prices meant widespread prosperity. Economic diversification strengthened Virginia's position relative to other Southern states and encouraged hopes that she would reclaim her fabled grandeur. Slavery had proven more versatile than its critics believed, chiefly because slave-hiring and rental mechanisms appealed to eastern Virginians and encouraged those who argued for the system's indispensability.[1] But Virginia's economic growth depended on her ability to keep and attract labor and capital. Slave sales to the Deep South literally embodied the continuing departure of both, although helping to finance economic diversification. This result vexed some obsessed Yankee abolitionists.[2] Virginians admitted its significance—at least in their more candid moments. Wise, however, remained silent. He worried instead about the continuing exodus of whites, Virginia's capital requirements, and the intolerable and undeniable decline of Virginia's influence in national affairs.

Wise believed that a coordinated and energetic renewal program could produce sufficient political democracy and economic growth in Virginia to preserve slavery until the time when it might be eliminated painlessly. These objectives led him to support what I call the "Virginia consensus." This policy, reflecting the mandate of the Constitutional Convention of 1850–51, would integrate slavery with modernization. No one during the 1850s wrestled more intensively with Virginia's classic dilemma: how to take on the trappings of modernity, as Maryland was doing, while simultaneously remaining a slave state until it became safe to exile the blacks. But the lateness of the hour, the vastness of the endeavor, and the crippling effects of national politics on his gubernatorial administration fragmented Wise in the end. Adding to his problems were his difficulties in trusting people.

Although most Virginia politicians sustained the consensus, none confused Wise with his lackadaisical, platitudinous predecessor, Governor Joseph Johnston, or with anyone else. Wise was "no straw effigy," according to Horace Greeley, "but a real force—a real personality," whose election would benefit Virginia more than the annexation of many Cubas.[3] Wise proposed to enlarge the state government's prerogatives—exactly in the style of a Southern Yankee, certain critics believed.[4] He worked, read, and reflected more intensively about Virginia's problems than most other leaders and devised imaginative proposals to improve the Commonwealth's disordered finances and promote internal unity. He planned, for example, a reformed system of public education, albeit one whose primary appeal was to the rising middle class. He proposed a tax on Virginia's oyster beds, partly to discourage Yankee fishermen. He also advocated a system of state insurance on lives and property.

The times, Wise declared, required and encouraged bold measures. He had grown up among Virginians who bewailed the pawning of their heritage. Starting out with a meager personal inheritance, he had prospered—and so again would his state. The boom of the 1850s created the opportunity, but it might be lost without the most dedicated and self-sacrificing effort, he told his countrymen. Extremists South and North were intent on narrowing Virginia's options, although the Yankee fanatics seemed more dangerous in 1856. Republican spokesmen such as Hinton R. Helper and Frederick Law Olmsted smugly exposed Virginia's backwardness. Once wealthy and powerful, wrote Senator Henry Wilson of Massachusetts, Virginia now ranked as "a poor and driveling commonwealth, with a broken-down and proud aristocracy . . . and a helpless and dissipated people."[5] To make their case, Republicans frequently quoted from the indictments featured prominently in Wise's speeches during the 1855 gubernatorial canvass. Cassius M. Clay, a Kentuckian who aspired to leadership among Southern nonslaveholders, encapsulated these charges in an October 1856 address in New York City. After summarizing Wise's descriptions of Virginia's "desolation," Clay blasted him for refusing to admit that slavery was "the root of all our woe."[6]

Following these attacks, Wise stopped commenting on Virginia as a provincial state. Instead, he made a virtue out of her underdevelopment and shopped unabashedly for capital from anyone ready to deal. But such generalized disrespect and indignity as the Old Dominion had endured must cease. Virginia's moral authority needed reconfirming, as he suggested in one of the first public papers he wrote after taking office. When a group of Philadelphians invited him to participate in the unveiling of monuments on Independence Square, he responded:

At a time when the fires of revolution seem to be dying out, when there is growing irreverence for Washington himself, when there is a wicked disposition to pervert the work of Jefferson, a treasonable tendency to destroy the limitations of law laid down by Madison, a fanatical purpose to dissolve the Union, let us hasten to co-operate in laying the foundations of a monument at Independence Hall, which shall rear its grandeur above the degeneracy of the times, which shall point to heaven its moral elevation, and draw down anew the inspiration of sainted patriots who have gone to repose in the bosom of God.[7]

Along with many other conservatives, Wise specialized in nostalgic evocations of the Union and its heroes. One of his more notable performances occurred on 4 July 1856 at the Virginia Military Institute in Lexington. The occasion was the dedication of a copy of Jean-Antoine Houdon's statue of George Washington. It was a situation ready-made for a stem-winder from Wise on the character of Washington. Its subsequent publication in the *Southern Literary Messenger* ensured a wide circulation. Wise conferred additional prestige on the address by calling it his inaugural message, although Virginia's governors had not so indulged themselves previously.

America owed its founding, Wise reminded his audience, to a Christian slaveholder—precisely like himself. Even the pious must have pricked up their ears an instant later when Wise admonished everyone "never [to] permit an irreverent allusion" to Washington. About which Virginian, one wonders, were irreverent allusions most likely to be made? Raised according to the canons of the "magic word—'*Domesticity*,' " Washington knew the meaning of keeping a trust. The "frugal, self-denying, sagacious, industrious, systematic mistresses of *homes*" taught him the meaning of duty and responsibility. In dark days of defeat he never faltered but instead bided his time until at an unsuspected moment he invoked the "policy of rashness" and seized the initiative from his enemies.

This reference opened what Wise regarded as his most original contribution to the abounding literature of the 1850s on Washington and the Founding Fathers. Most other commentators mistakenly canonized Washington, the governor suggested. He was "but a good and great *man*. He was no demi-god," as proved by his passionate outbursts. Though "systematic" and "exact" in business and never tempted to sport "away his time amidst horses and fox hounds," Washington had too often been described as forbidding and distant—like a monument cast in stone. "No such idea is true of him," Wise proclaimed. "He was no Northern Iceberg which repelled by coldness. He was the very opposite rather, a Mt.

Sinai of a man who glowed with the fervent heat and was guarded by the thunders and lightning of the Deity." Though the product of a special providence, Washington's very ordinariness—the plain dress, simple manner, and disingenuous honesty—must inspire young men with the confident expectation that they might emulate him. Only rootless fanatics, whose shallow sense of history matched the irresponsibility of their politics, failed to nurture the hope for a revival of patriotism and statesmanship.[8]

Along with Washington, the governor continued, all who serve "must expect persecution and ingratitude, and must not be deterred by malice and uncharitableness." Against long odds, Washington had saved Massachusetts, whose current generation of effeminate leaders repaid his efforts by spouting a perverted version of "Christian politics" and failing to enforce the fugitive slave law. Scouting all obstacles, Washington rendered his finest service to his own state by projecting her principal system of internal improvements and promoting education. If his vision were now realized, Virginia would stand renewed and ready to resume her proper place in the Union. "He now presides over us," Wise concluded, "more potent than ever to prevail with Providence, the Guardian Genius of the United States of North America! He guards Virginia, and Virginia guards the Union."[9]

Subtlety always escaped Wise. He wanted more than a metaphoric revival of patriotic enthusiasm for Washington; he anticipated a full-blown reincarnation and left no doubt about who best resembled the great man. He appended to his speech a long and friendly letter from Washington to his grandfather, John Cropper, the hero of the American Revolution. Predictably, this document convinced no one that Wise was a modern-day Washington. Ridgway, his old enemy at the *Richmond Whig*, flailed him for degrading Washington "to the level of his own passionate and brutal nature."[10]

Instead of replying, Wise acted. Like Andrew Jackson, he knew the value of symbolic gestures, which usually succeeded better than did his efforts to promote substantive change. He campaigned aggressively in behalf of the successful national effort to make a shrine out of Washington's plantation, Mount Vernon. He secured the return of President James Monroe's remains from New York. He attempted to transfer Jefferson's body from Monticello to Richmond, so that it might lie next to Monroe's in Hollywood Cemetery. As part of his campaign to refurbish Virginia's reputation, Wise arranged for commissions to resurvey the Old Dominion's boundaries; he also supervised efforts to draw an accurate state map. Privately, he bemoaned the absence of elegant public buildings and well-appointed committee rooms that might lend increased dignity and significance to politics.[11] When the massive equestrian statue of Washington was dedicated on the grounds of the state capitol early in 1858, he officiated proudly. But reflecting the pessimism induced by two harried years in office, he spoke briefly and pointedly suggested that "the kindred heirship of one Patriot Father" might draw the country together if "none other under heaven" could.[12]

Wise's efforts won him considerable praise from men as disparate in their sensibilities as Horace Greeley and George Fitzhugh. A Tidewater Virginia farmer of middling means whose family had seen much better days, Fitzhugh earned a reputation during the 1850s for his skillful critiques of Northern "wage slavery" and his assaults on the chaos, violence, and selfishness generally enshrined by the cult of capitalist individualism. Like Wise, Fitzhugh regarded himself as a reformer. He believed, as Eugene D. Genovese writes, that "the South . . . must diversify her economy, increase her population, raise cities and towns, promote industry, and decentralize her economic and political life."[13] Wise was less confident than Fitzhugh of slavery's resilience and malleability in a modernizing economy, though he espoused the patriarchal persona that powered Fitzhugh's apologia. Both men suspected that states'-rights metaphysics had impoverished Virginia. Vigorous leadership and government participation in the economy would revitalize her. Fitzhugh therefore dedicated to Wise the book he published in 1856, entitled *Cannibals All! or, Slaves without Masters*: "I dedicate this work to you, because I am acquainted with no one who has so zealously, laboriously, and successfully endeavored to Virginianize Virginia, by encouraging, through State legislation, her intellectual and physical growth and development; no one who has seen so clearly the evils of centralization from without, and worked so earnestly to cure or avert those evils, by building up centralization within."

The common perspective of middling lowland Virginia slaveholders informed the outlook of both Fitzhugh and Wise. In his preface Fitzhugh also praised Wise's devotion to the Union. Secessionism filled him with foreboding. Compelling extremist Yankees to leave the Union seemed more sensible to both than taking revolutionary risks. Despite Fitzhugh's efforts to construct a rigorous and consistent defense of slavery, he confessed in 1856 to seeing great evils in it; a year before he described himself as "no friend of slavery or the slave trade." His own self-preservation required him to seek a patronage appointment from Buchanan's administration in 1857. With an eye for contractual reciprocity, he sought Wise's aid, but it did no good because the job never materialized.[14]

As a politician required to seek votes, Wise never dared indulge Fitzhugh's speculations that poor whites and Northern workingmen might be better off as slaves. As his 1855 letters from western Virginia suggest, however, he loathed many of his constituents and thought some little better than slaves. Fitzhugh's easy conversion to racism during the war and after, along with Wise's attempts to ignore the blacks and eliminate them entirely from his world, prompts some doubts about the seriousness of their commitment to paternalism. Whether founded on substance or fantasy, the optimistic outlook they shared contrasted sharply with that espoused by the despairing though far wealthier crowd associated with Senator Hunter.

Despite an auspicious beginning, Wise's most innovative proposals scarcely received a hearing from the Virginia General Assembly. Unable to promote sufficient political unity or economic vitality to preserve Virginia's integrity, he grew distracted and absorbed himself in administrative detail. As several historians have suspected, Wise's increasing frustrations as governor deflected his energies into national politics, which in 1855 he had called the "curse" of Virginia statesmen.[15] Slaves and land acquired greater value for him as his optimism receded. Powerlessness and the repudiation of his hopes made him grimmer, tougher, and resigned to the campaign of violence launched in 1858 against his enemies by his eldest son.

Wise raised expectations beyond his power to realize. His abrasiveness also deflated the hopes inspired by the settlement of 1850–51 although limitations on his power undoubtedly contributed. By making the governorship an elected position, the new constitution increased the office's prestige while preserving significant checks on executive authority that stemmed from the Revolutionary heritage. Virginia's chief executives, for example, possessed no veto, nor could they succeed themselves, a provision Wise had condemned in the 1850–51 convention. The General Assembly met biennially, with sessions limited to ninety days, unless three-fifths of the members agreed to a thirty-day extension. Wise successfully recommended extensions in 1856 and 1858 but refused to challenge public opinion by calling a special session.[16] Virginia's governors dispensed patronage—principally militia commissions, bank directorships, and visitors' appointments at the University of Virginia and Virginia Military Institute. But Wise's penchant for operating in isolation caused him to make poor choices for several of these appointments.[17] No evidence suggests that Wise—"wondrously hospitable and condescending" on occasion—extended himself in behalf of obtaining a legislative consensus. His social schedule may have been restricted by his wife's semi-invalidism. Much of his program was in any case lost irretrievably by the midpoint of his administration. Wise's repudiation of the proslavery Lecompton Constitution for Kansas cost him favor and votes in the General Assembly. Senator Hunter's partisans happily bottled up most of his proposals in committee.[18]

Futile Effort to Revive the Old Dominion

Despite the acrimony prevailing in the General Assembly, most Virginians reflected fondly on the Old Dominion's unequaled potential for industrial, commercial, and agricultural development. The new-found prosperity of the 1850s stimulated efforts to realize the dreams of Washington and others that Virginia might once again rule by completing her major internal improvements and thereby profiting from the commerce of the interior. But insuperable difficulties abounded, over which Virginia's governors had relatively little control. The Old Dominion's long-standing commitment to Washington's policy had nearly outrun her resources. At the time of Wise's inauguration, the state had invested more than $24 million in various railroads and canals, which yielded an annual return of only 1.5 percent. Virginia's per capita debt would soon nearly equal New York's and approach Pennsylvania's, which ranked first in the Union. The uneasiness prompted by these economic facts had compelled Wise to denounce repudiation both during his gubernatorial canvass and after his inauguration.[19] At no time since the adoption of the new constitution had the state government completed a fiscal year without either securing a loan or issuing treasury notes.

With Virginia's bonds selling at several points below par, Wise bluntly told the legislators to double the taxes. They more than complied. Within a few weeks of his inauguration, land taxes were increased from twenty to forty cents per hundred dollars of assessed valuation. Following from the Virginia compromise of 1850–51, this meant doubling the capitation tax, as well as the levy on a sizable proportion of Virginia's slaves. The assembly also provided for a land reassessment that produced additional revenue.[20] These concessions—the last granted during the antebellum period by the planter-dominated legislature—guaranteed completion of the Virginia and Tennessee Railroad. They also permitted work to proceed on that grand sinkhole of Virginia's fortune, the extravagant central canal and railroad link to the Ohio Valley, first conceived by Washington and now almost as much an official article of faith as the Resolutions of 1798.[21]

Raids on the treasury continued, however. With Democrats dominating both houses of the assembly, little discipline existed among the legislators. Trade-offs and pork barreling encouraged localist-oriented improvement appropriations, bitter urban rivalries, and a patchwork of unconnected or rival canals and railroads.[22] The expanded railway network and other improvements, however, aided tens of thousands of Virginians to escape subsistence farming, particularly in the southwestern portion of the state. But these completed improvements did not guarantee Virginia's solvency during the late 1850s. Only the most ingenious and skillful manipulations of her governor and first auditor prevented the Old Dominion from going bankrupt immediately after the panic of 1857.[23] Much of the fixation on maintaining Virginia's credit following the Civil War evidently sprang from the tremendous difficulties experienced in attempting to manage the state's debt during the antebellum period.[24]

In search of capital, the governor and his agents endlessly trumpeted Virginia's claims. The *Richmond Enquirer* printed reams of material touting Virginia's attractiveness for investors, particularly after Wise's eldest son took over primary editorial responsibilities in 1858. Wise himself advertised the Old Dominion as "an empire in herself, *in the anomalous condition of an old state with all the underdeveloped resources of a new state, and of a new state with all the ameliorations of an old state*." These widely circulated remarks appeared in a letter to Monsieur E. Lacouture, whose French consortium had expressed interest in purchasing Virginia's grand improvement—the James River and Kanawha Company. Beyond an understandable interest in marketing the largest white elephant in the Union, Wise's comments betrayed his candid fears of Virginia's inability to complete her canal and rail lines alone and unaided.[25]

The *Enquirer* dismissed the objections of those who resisted opening Virginia to all comers. Economic diversification, it argued, would increase the value of slave property. It also rebuked the South Carolinians for endeavoring to dissociate slavery from the entire nineteenth century—for maintaining its incompatibility, that is, "with universal suffrage, foreign trade, commercial development, and popular education."[26] The governor, however, never went quite that far. Instead, he attributed Virginia's backwardness to slave-based plantation agriculture that now happily might be disappearing altogether.

The source of Virginia's problems, Wise advised the French capitalists, was the historic dependence on the "*plantation inter-*

est," which required "slave operatives," whom Virginians "were encouraged by Great Britain to import from Africa."[27] Wise made this same charge and affixed more directly to slavery the responsibility for Virginia's enthrallment in instructions he prepared in 1857 for William Ballard Preston's commercial mission, which failed to establish direct shipping connections between Europe and Virginia.[28] The Old Dominion's economic legacy ensured "a class of *masters* who have leisure for the cultivation of morals, manners, philosophy and politics" but evidently lacked the talent for good farming. To one of his audiences, Wise irreverently claimed to have "derived more information on agricultural subjects from 'old negroes' than all the farmers of the state put together."[29] Far less politely than at Lexington in 1856, he reproached Virginia's planters for their laziness, lack of systematic learning, and unyielding fondness for "brandy, foxhounds, and horse racing."[30]

Futile Effort to Revive the Old Dominion

Never fear, Virginia's noble governor counseled, history may be reversible. For Lacouture's benefit, he reinvoked the vision of Thomas R. Dew. Prosperity in eastern Virginia during the 1850s "has changed the large *plantation* system of culture into a *smaller horticultural and arboricultureal farming*, and the immense fields once scourged by tobacco are brought under a rotation of cereal and garden products, or made green again by manures and grazing."[31] In other words, the governor wanted to transpose Accomac's relatively healthy economy to the Old Dominion as a whole.

To make this vision a reality required all the human capital Wise could obtain, especially of the light-skinned variety. "We are wanting in a body of laboring white yeomanry," he counseled the French capitalists. The defeat of the Know-Nothings would help. "We are now about to get the benefit of emigration, let us have it," he privately advised. "It will help us to overtake the north as fast as any one cause can." The *Enquirer* speculated openly about eliminating slavery and attracting Yankee immigrants and investors should nefarious Deep Southerners succeed in dissolving the Union in order to reopen the African slave trade. The paper steadfastly sustained the colonization movement and ran sympathetic assessments of Liberia's progress. As usual, Edmund Ruffin smelled out the loyalties of the Wises and properly lambasted them. In view of the "known family" and "partisan relations of the chief editor," he dismissed the *Enquirer*'s "non-essential contingencies." It advocated, he charged, the sale of all Virginia's slaves and their replacement by white immigrants.[32]

Neither Wise nor the authorities who influenced him ever doubted that white labor far outstripped slave labor in value and efficiency—exactly as the Republicans believed.[33] Like Dew,

Wise sensed that Virginia was in the wrong latitude for slavery. After all, Dew had rooted his support for state-sponsored internal improvements in the conviction that slaves would ride the rails out of Virginia and into the Deep South.[34] Wise said nothing about this scenario, although a number of his proslavery critics resisted internal improvements appropriations during the 1850s on precisely these grounds. Perhaps he recognized that beyond proving its resiliency and adaptability in industry, slavery in Virginia during the 1850s was fueling a genuine wheat and tobacco boom. Much of what Wise *did* say, however, suggested a vision of Virginia dominated increasingly by whites, populating growing cities and deriving advantage from improved educational facilities, while simultaneously fostering an aggressive development of the Old Dominion's resources so as to outdo the Yankees. Slavery in this context was a phenomenon forever transitory—a sideshow, enormous perhaps, but never destined to secure top billing.

Only safe ways might be chosen to manifest this conviction, however. Wise welcomed Northern capital and immigrants because they seemed so conservative. He also observed his closest political associates in western Virginia openly selling land to Yankee free-soilers such as Eli Thayer and John C. Underwood.[35] He said nothing and maintained confidence in his western political lieutenants—at least until early 1860, when their own distractions and incompetence inexcusably cost him Virginia's support in the Democratic National Convention in Charleston. Wise also maintained a vice-presidency in the Virginia Colonization Society. When the Reverend Phillip Slaughter published his muted anthem to the Virginia colonization movement in 1855, he featured Wise's old 1838 address and quoted extensively from his 1854 letter to Nehemiah Adams. Slaughter was nothing if not respectful of planters' sensibilities—which is why his organization remained so threatening to critics who distrusted the actions of ambivalent Virginians with the option of emancipation still open to them. What fond and forbidding feelings must have possessed Wise as he read an old and noble sentiment of his own embossed on the cover of Slaughter's text: "Africa gave to Virginia, a Savage and a Slave; Virginia gives back to Africa a Citizen and a Christian."[36]

Virginia held a healthy percentage of its white population during the 1850s. Whites numbered slightly more than one million in 1860 and had increased at the rate of 17 percent during the previous decade—4 percent lower than the growth rate during the 1840s. Slave population increased by less than 4 percent during the 1850s to a figure of roughly half a million. Such backhanded achievements failed to keep pace with the prerequisites of economic and political power, as Eugene D. Genovese writes. But the agricultural prosperity of the 1850s boosted slave prices and hiring fees and thus suggested to Virginians that there was a labor shortage. The expanding urban and industrial sectors required many more workers.[37] Wise wanted whites in these positions. He never complained about the slave drain to the South and Southwest. Consistent with his commitment to white immigrants, he condemned the freedom necessarily available to the thousands of blacks in Richmond, whose masters had contracted for them to work in the city tobacco factories.[38]

In broad measure, however, the idea of a labor shortage anticipates the more rapid modernization that Wise predicted and worked for but never witnessed. This notion was rooted as much in perception as in reality. Continuing slave exile and white migration suggested an overpopulation within the agricultural sector of the economy, which in turn implied that Virginia suffered from a labor surplus, not a shortage. Virginia's slave population was aging during the 1850s. The long-term movement of younger blacks and whites out of Virginia continued to feed the humiliation consequent on the loss of political power.[39]

Evidence of a half-modern, half-colonial economy appears in Virginia's urban and manufacturing sectors. Impressive growth notwithstanding, Richmond and her sister cities remained Yankee-dominated. One knowledgeable observer estimated at the end of Wise's gubernatorial term that Virginians paid the Yankees an annual tribute of $3 million for the privilege of marketing their wheat and tobacco. As late as 1860, Virginia's railroads exported about $1 million a year to purchase railroad iron. The extent to which this continued "vassalage," as Wise called it, affected day-to-day life and economic decision making may well be disputed. But it is indisputable that Virginia's position relative to the industrial centers of the Yankee juggernaut changed scarcely at all in the 1850s. Under these circumstances, it proved impossible to generate by private or public means the revenues Wise thought Virginia required.[40]

Nor could he touch the state's most important interest in order to obtain them. Virginia's prosperity rested massively on agriculture, which in turn rested on slavery—an interest constitutionally protected by a compromise of Wise's own devising and thus impervious to ad valorem taxation. The growth and export of predominantly young slaves represented a valuable addition to Virginia's income during the 1850s. Though not of a magnitude approaching in value the income derived from the wheat or tobacco crops, sales from slave exports averaged in the millions of dollars per year throughout the decade. In their campaign to convict the slave power of every iniquity, abolitionists frequently touched this sensitive nerve. But it was untouchable and even unmentionable for Wise.[41]

To gain badly needed revenue for Virginia's internal improvements, he proposed two initiatives. The first envisioned a regulatory code governing the oyster fishery in Chesapeake Bay. A licensing procedure would eliminate Northerners and raise an annual revenue of thousands. So unpopular was this proposal that for a time Wise could convince no one in the General Assembly to introduce it. Nearly every legislator from Tidewater Virginia attacked it. "The Gubernatorial thunder bolt fell still-born," trumpeted the *Richmond Whig*. Wise's state insurance scheme fared no better. Private insurance companies reacted furiously. During his entire term, it obtained only a few hours' consideration from the General Assembly.[42]

With Wise's initiatives blunted, power gravitated to his enemies at the extremes of the political spectrum. Spokesmen for both free soil and slavery began a double-barreled assault on the traditional priorities of the Virginia consensus. They challenged and sometimes defeated internal improvements appropriations. This ominous coalition of northwestern and Tidewater legislators might have dominated the General Assembly had not secession intervened.[43]

John C. Underwood led the free-soil movement in Virginia. A New Yorker by birth, Underwood came to northern Virginia as a young man and organized a dairy farm. There he matured his scheme for redeeming the Old Dominion. Unlike most others who cherished visions of Virginia's renewal, however, Underwood eliminated slavery from his plans. In a series of letters to Republican papers in New York, written principally in the spring of 1857, he blamed slavery for Virginia's undiversified economy, its lack of internal markets, and the poverty and illiteracy of its nonslaveholders. He suggested that the degrading influence of slave labor had driven away much of the state's white population. He also noticed the thousands of slaves annually departing for the lower South, thereby aggravating the state's population drain. Underwood believed that in the current financial crisis, "our only alternative is freedom and free labor, or insolvency and repudiation." He scored Wise, "our brilliant but superficial governor," for thinking that railroads created the differences between the North and South. Rather, it was the numbers of people who rode them. Slaves and poor whites, Underwood noted, seldom if ever patronized Virginia's railroads.[44] White immigrants represented the state's only possible salvation. Slavery discouraged their settlement, hence the necessity for emancipation.

Futile Effort to Revive the Old Dominion

A highly visible and active member of the Republican party, Underwood frequently found his neighborhood unsafe. He therefore spent much of his time out of state and away from his Clarke County farm. The American Emigrant Aid and Homestead Company, which he founded in 1857 with the cooperation of Massachusetts Congressman Eli Thayer, manifested his seriousness. It aided free-soilers who wished to settle in slave states. Underwood believed that compelling slaveholders to defend themselves at home would eliminate their ability to cause trouble in such places as Kansas. Thayer, of course, enjoyed considerable notoriety from his success in organizing and transporting companies of Northern immigrants to Kansas. He believed that colonizing free labor in Virginia "would soon so increase the value of lands that the slaveholders themselves would recognize the benefit, and be ready to send away their darkies, who as Gov. Wise says, are skinned by the planters and in turn skin the land, and leave only ignorance and poverty where there should be fertility and enterprise."[45]

Underwood's colony at Ceredo, near the confluence of the Kanawha and Ohio rivers, never succeeded, partly because of financial difficulties exacerbated by the national fiscal crisis late in 1857. Nonetheless, Underwood popularized his views incessantly, recruited dozens of sympathizers, and urged Republican leaders such as Senator Seward to bombard them with speeches and documents. Predictably, the irrepressible John Minor Botts all but nominated himself for the leadership of Virginia's free labor party.[46]

In August 1857 Wise pronounced judgment on the Ceredo scheme in a strange public letter to western Virginia Congressman Albert G. Jenkins. The governor gratuitously pointed out that Thayer's plans had "never been submitted in any manner whatever to my approval or disapproval." He then denied, almost incredibly, any knowledge of Thayer's objects, which by that time had been ventilated for months in both the Northern and Southern press. He duly repudiated reports in a Cincinnati journal that he favored establishment of a free-soil colony, which of course implied his approval of gradual abolition in Virginia. Wise's letter advised Jenkins to relax. The Old Dominion desperately needed immigrants; he declared himself confident that they represented no serious threat to slavery and could easily be disciplined if they violated the law. "Why not calmly wait, then," he wrote, "for the *fact*, as it may arise?"[47] The colony at Ceredo, which owned slaves and maintained that profits meant more than emancipation, scarcely qualified as abolitionist.[48]

Jenkins, who later fought bravely and effectively as a Confederate cavalry commander, never became a friend of Wise, but Wise and Underwood enjoyed a public reconciliation in the late 1860s. With Wise welcoming his own emancipation from slaveholding, both fleshed out their vision of a yeoman-dominated Virginia and pressed vigorously for immigrant settlers. Most of the governor's direct descendants learned the same lesson. They remain Republicans to this day.

Despite the withering assaults from the Richmond press and the failure of the Ceredo project, Underwood's movement provoked further fears that abolitionist pressures would overwhelm the border states and render them easy prey even if the Republicans never took power in Washington.[49] Underwood's correspondence confirmed these fears. Early in 1858, Jonathan M. Bennett, perhaps Wise's most powerful political friend in the trans-Allegheny region, offered Underwood some of the extensive properties he owned in Lewis County. John F. Hoffman of Clarksburg, formerly a member of the House of Delegates and also a strong Wise backer, established a consortium that planned to sell land either to Underwood or to immigrants he pledged to settle in Virginia. The New York–born entrepreneur also contacted Gideon D. Camden, a state judge in northwestern Virginia, and Colonel Benjamin Wilson, an important local politician and another of the governor's devoted followers.[50] It was the same story in eastern Virginia. Alexander Dudley, president of the financially troubled Richmond and York River Railroad, attempted in 1857 to sell a controlling interest in his enterprise to Northerners. Underwood endeavored to facilitate this transaction. He also reported an offer from the Fredericksburg city council to sell the town's waterworks. Both the principal newspapers in Norfolk virtually begged for Yankee capital and expertise at a time (before the panic of 1857) when by most accounts Virginians prospered as never before. One of them—the *Herald*, a Whig sheet that had long advocated replacing Virginia's slaves with white immigrants—specifically compared Thayer's scheme with Virginia's grand internal improvements plan and declared its willingness to accept either.[51]

As land values rose, more people seemed ready to sell out. The popularity of Underwood's projects highlights a tradition of Northern settlement in the northern and eastern Tidewater. For years the *New York Tribune* had argued that Yankee immigrants and labor aided indispensably in Virginia's agricultural recovery; on the eve of secession, it maintained that Northern farmers had purchased more than one million acres of land in the Old Dominion during the 1850s.[52]

Futile Effort to Revive the Old Dominion

Penetration on such a large scale, matched with potential disaffection of native Virginians, suggested a community that had already distanced itself from slavery and might easily succumb to further temptations.[53] Wise had this situation in mind when he repeatedly reminded audiences in the late 1850s of slavery's weakness in Virginia and specified that its condition at home was influencing him to deemphasize Southern access to Kansas—precisely the reaction Underwood had hoped for. In 1857 the editors of the *Southern Planter*, published in Richmond, put on a brave face and asked what harm could come from a handful of Northern immigrants. But their optimism quickly turned to foreboding as they speculated at the close of the same article on the inundation of Virginia with white laborers in order "to fill up the vacuum created by the exportation of our negroes to the South."[54]

The continuing dispersal of Virginia's slaves—at an increased rate over that of the previous decade—could scarcely fail to disturb more thoughtful and prescient states'-rights politicians such as James Seddon. A close adviser of Senator Hunter's and an owner of plantations in both Virginia and Louisiana, Seddon was obsessed with the Old Dominion's loss of slaves. He distrusted the "western trash's" loyalty to slavery, refused to think the construction of more railroads would command their allegiance, and reflected on advantages to be gained by eliminating westerners from the Commonwealth. Like many other slaveholders, Seddon suspected immigrant labor and believed that Virginia's resources could not be developed without slaves. But as they disappeared, and immigrants stayed away, the natural tendency was to convert Virginia into a free state—unless men such as himself dissolved the Union. Seddon thought that a decision must come quickly on Virginia's destiny, or slavery might soon be confined to its last stronghold along the rich river valleys. He further advocated the reintroduction of Africans as apprentices. Their enslavement would follow—a status to which all free Negroes should be reduced.[55]

By Virginia's standards Seddon was an extremist, but his views, which implicitly repudiated Wise's leadership and the traditional Virginia consensus, became more widely shared as time passed. Interestingly enough, his analysis resembled in some particulars the views advanced by free-soilers. Seddon suspected, for example, that railroads alone did not produce centers of trade, as Wise had asserted. With Underwood and the Republicans, he argued that only people could build cities and make them profitable and that without cities Virginia's improvements would simply make her more of a tributary to the North. Important eastern Virginia state legislators, such as Seddon's brother John, his close friend John Coles Rutherfoord, and Senator James K. Bruce of Charlotte County turned vigorously against expansion of the internal improvements system. They and their associates maintained a lukewarm interest in the James River and Ohio line but fought and sometimes blocked or reduced appropriations for other improvements. An owner of several hundred slaves, Bruce had worried for years that more railroads would, as in Maryland, simply facilitate the black exodus. Rutherfoord worried about the effects of Virginia's huge debt on her ability to secure further credit in case of war. In the spring of 1857, the editors of the *Richmond South* joined this chorus by openly acknowledging that only the presence of the tobacco culture retained slavery in Virginia. No comparative economic advantage existed in the cultivation of the "cereal crops," which might be "too light and occasional for the employment of slave labor."[56] Should the logrolling and unrestrained appropriations continue, ever higher taxes would be required, which eventually would reach the most outrageously undertaxed property in the state—the slaves. Prominent westerners called repeatedly for such a measure.[57]

Achieving Virginia's political unity, for which Wise had fondly hoped, thus seemed increasingly problematic. Nervousness, bad health, and irritability afflicted the governor, particularly after the General Assembly's session of 1857–58. "Obstinacy and caprice," manifested by an unwillingness to accept advice or to provide credit where it was due, cost him the support and respect of two loyal friends—delegate James Lawson Kemper of Madison County and William H. Richardson, Virginia's attorney general.[58] He dwelled increasingly on relatively insignificant, trivial matters and focused on quickly resolvable problems. He engaged, for example, in passionate campaigns to reform the Eastern State Hospital at Williamsburg and the Richmond public guard, who served as the city's police force. Wise also labored intensively at two duties common to all chief executives: he regularly reviewed prison administration and responded to appeals for executive clemency. Here the results imply compassionate motives, for which he was scorned, and a callousness perhaps attributable to Virginia's general crisis.

Hard times awaited those convicted and sentenced during Wise's administration. The Executive Papers of the late 1850s are filled with requests for black prisoners, principally from internal improvement companies, whose straitened finances made it difficult for them to procure other laborers. Free blacks figured disproportionately among the prisoners. Alarmed by their maneuverability, Wise simultaneously acknowledged that "the moral sense of our people would revolt" at legislated reenslavement. No such protest, however, would follow the leasing of free and slave convict blacks. Many suffered outrageous brutalities, especially when deployed along the James River canal, on which private contractors did much of the work.[59]

Futile Effort to Revive the Old Dominion

The origins of this policy may well lie in a forced alteration of the methods Virginia authorities traditionally favored in dealing with certain types of slave criminals. For slaves convicted of capital crimes, whose punishment was commuted, the law required their transportation "beyond the limits of the United States." In practice, this meant sale to the lower South. In September 1857, Wise received a vigorous denunciation of this policy from Governor John A. Winston of Alabama, who protested that Virginia's "vicious and criminal" slaves threatened to turn his state into another Botany Bay. Wise promised reform, the General Assembly granted him the necessary authority in 1858, and thereafter he began assigning black convicts to labor on the public works.[60]

The delicacy Wise often lacked in dealing with black prisoners he sometimes reserved for whites—at least until late in his administration. Wise pardoned or released about eighty whites during his four years, many of them Irish immigrants. Edmund Ruffin was not alone in condemning the pardons as a by-product of Wise's "general and systematic pursuit of popular favor, and votes, to aid the ambitions of this greatest of demagogues." Predictably, the *Enquirer* defended him, but the economic crisis, pointed public criticism, and his own dissipating optimism deflected his sympathies. As time passed, pardons came less frequently for whites. In his final message to the General Assembly, he recommended that white as well as black inmates of the state penitentiary labor on the public works.[61]

Wise had always believed in reform from the top down, but as governor his reforming enthusiasm waned. "Virginia won't bear common schools," he wrote his cousin shortly before his inauguration. "She appropriates almost entirely to her University and really I am beginning to half believe it is the true policy in this age of 'isms.'" Branded again as an educational radical during his gubernatorial canvass, once in power he refused to advocate free, universal, and compulsory education. Never again would he argue, as in 1850, that democratic schooling eliminated distinctions formerly attributed to environmental or inherent inferiority.[62]

Evidently in view of the resources required for canals and railroads, Wise abandoned recommendations for increased local taxation. He no longer argued the justice of wealthy Virginians absorbing increased educational costs so as to free state revenues for other purposes such as the construction of school buildings. Thus no assault on the traditional system of subsidizing paupers took place. Their stigmatization persisted, and so did high rates of illiteracy, to which this system contributed inordinately.[63]

Acknowledging that his approach "was not such as would be preferred, if the means were ample or not limited," Wise aggressively promoted administrative reforms in order to squeeze out additional funds. He hoped to provide a longer school year and at least some advanced education for the poor. That he succeeded marginally testifies to the corruption afflicting Virginia's state and local government. In one of his typical investigative tours de force, he demonstrated that between 1851 and 1857 more than $150,000 from the literary fund had been illegally appropriated to serve the state debt. He also revealed that considerable fractions of the capitation tax, one-half of whose revenues the constitution of 1851 directed to the support of primary education, never left those who collected it. With Jefferson as his inspiration, Wise trusted that properly managed revenues might guarantee a college or university education for a few poor people, who then would repay the state by teaching in the common schools.[64]

Wise also began to worship at the traditional shrines. "Having regard to old prejudices and habits," he now favored extending "more patronage to the University, Military Institute, our colleges and higher schools in order to raise the standard of instruction, and to elevate the grade of teachers for the lower schools." By 1860 the General Assembly had increased appropriations for both the institute and the university—both beyond the means of the poor. Wise never proposed a mechanics institute, as he had promised in 1856.[65]

In fairness to the governor, however, little evidence exists that white working folk wanted or expected change. Demands for improved education came principally from the middle class. Wise adjusted his priorities to account for middle-class aspirations, particularly for college education.[66] His proposal to educate middle-class teachers, who would in turn civilize the masses, obtained impressive support at two Richmond educational conventions in 1856 and 1857. Faculty members from the denominational colleges that stood to benefit dominated both conclaves.

From the 1857–58 General Assembly he secured grants of $3,000 to each of Virginia's ten colleges. The assembly never acted, however, on his proposal to build three additional colleges in the northwest and at least one agricultural institute. It also had the good sense to ignore the rigidly hierarchical and unworkable implications of his general plan for educational renewal. Once a democratic reformer, Wise now advocated a system in which the rector of the university supervised the colleges, and they in turn superintended the high schools and academies.[67]

Wise initiated one other substantive effort to promote elementary education among the working class. He commissioned Dr. William A. Smith, current president of Randolph-Macon College and former architect of the Southern secession from the Methodist Episcopal church, to investigate Virginia's educational needs at the local level. Early in 1857 Smith began a speaking tour in eastern Virginia. He defended the governor's program, particularly its emphasis on teacher training. He advocated broader educational opportunity, but he wanted to strengthen slavery simultaneously. He recommended, for example, removing all abolitionist sentiments from textbooks used in Virginia schools. Unable to lecture and complete the required research at the same time, Smith suspended his tour after only eleven appearances. Most audiences received him politely, but some were reportedly so hostile that it was useless, if not dangerous, to address them. Nine-tenths of the white laborers in Norfolk and Portsmouth "are . . . abolitionists, and would vote the slaves out of the state tomorrow if they could," he advised the governor. "I can fill the churches," he added, "but not with that class of people who most need what I have to say."[68]

Smith obtained this appointment because of his skilled lobbying on behalf of Virginia's denominational colleges. His recently published *Lectures on the Philosophy and Practice of Slavery* testified further to his impeccable credentials. A copy of it, which arrived on the governor's desk in the midst of their negotiations, helped convince Wise to recruit Smith more vigorously. Yet Smith and anyone who agreed with him must stand, on the basis of this book, as highly eccentric and curious defenders of slavery. So humane was Smith's justification that Wise promised to send the book to Lamartine, the celebrated French poet, political liberal, and opponent of slavery.[69]

Smith began his lectures by acknowledging "a private but painful impression that there must be something wrong in the principle of domestic slavery," which had pervaded "a portion even of the Southern mind."[70] As a good slaveholder, he insisted that masters owed an elaborate series of duties to slaves, including the responsibility to keep slave marriage inviolate. Preserving the dignity of their servants would presumably allow masters to transcend the evils Smith saw as necessarily following from slaveholding. He also rejected the idea of innate Negro inferiority and ascribed the slave's condition exclusively to environmental influences, just as Wise did in his lengthy speech before the Virginia Constitutional Convention. He predicted that under God's Providence and aided by the colonizationists, most slaves would eventually return to Africa. Others would remain and integrate themselves, at least politically, into white society. Wise had never taken seriously the view that the Scriptures sanctioned property in man; Smith denied it outright. Along with the governor, he saw prospective "racial pollution" as the principal impediment to black survival in America. He expected to emancipate one of his own slaves and help him emigrate to Liberia. Finally, Smith noted apologetically that it was not possible to educate the slaves along with the whites because slaves worked so inefficiently that their masters lacked the capital necessary to supply them with schooling. He predicted (and one can only wonder at Wise's reaction to these passages) that despite its problems, the South, through slavery's conservative influence, would save the country from the deluge of Roman Catholic immigrants who threatened it.[71]

Ideas such as those of William Smith and Henry Wise ran increasingly across the grain of Southern purposes during the late 1850s. Despite the governor's wariness and altered educational priorities, emboldened reactionaries suspicious of reforms even remotely smacking of Yankee influences repudiated his proposals. Some of them, as Edmund Ruffin, never supported the grand designs Wise had recommended for Virginia's internal improvements. One of Ruffin's few Virginia friends and the only one he consistently praised for agreeing with him, Willoughby Newton of Westmoreland County, debated the governor's educational scheme with him in 1857. Newton considered himself both an agricultural and an educational reformer. He had served one term in Congress as a Whig back in the early 1840s. Following their public exchange, Newton published a searching indictment of Wise's views in the *Richmond South*.

Newton rejected a district system of education, such as existed in New England, because Virginia's white population density equaled only eighteen per square mile. The state could never support the more than fourteen hundred primary schools envisioned by Wise. How could the commonwealth expect religious or educational peace, he wrote, if officials of denominational colleges supervised instruction and approved textbooks in the academies and high schools? Newton recognized that the governor had abandoned his effort to eliminate barriers between rich and poor. Still, he feared that Wise's repeated criticism of "charity" education would foster "a spirit of discontent and a morbid sensibility" among the poor. Virginians had heard enough from their leaders about illiteracy, ignorance, and degradation. Newton pointed out that a higher percentage of Virginians enrolled in colleges and the university than in the New England states. On the other hand, the idea of free public education at the elementary level soured him. The principle justifying it, he argued, granted to the state a greater interest in the education of children than did their parents. This notion smacked of despotism and "northern socialism" and enjoyed the unenviable endorsement of the governor of New York. What disturbed Newton most was Wise's consuming desire to accumulate all the advantages of Yankeedom in a commonwealth whose primary interest was slavery.[72]

Futile Effort to Revive the Old Dominion

Newton and other conservatives shed no tears when the General Assembly dismissed most of Wise's proposals. Sensing his opportunity in the spring of 1858, Newton accepted an invitation to address the literary societies of the Virginia Military Institute. His oration, *Virginia and the Union*, a direct assault on consensus thinking in the Old Dominion and on Wise as its advocate, was delivered in the same place where the governor had pronounced his inaugural address two years earlier. Virginia's very existence, according to Newton, was the result of slavery, whose triumphs as a system of political economy deserved praise, not deprecation. "No event in the history of modern times, save the discovery of America itself," could equal in importance "the landing in Virginia from a Dutch ship in the month of August, 1620, of twenty African slaves." Newton paid scant attention to the Founding Fathers as individuals but argued that slavery had "no little influence in forming that race of great men." We "are continually taunted with our decline and our inferiority," he continued, "and these assertions of our assailants are too often inconsiderately re-echoed among ourselves by patriotic gentlemen who are overzealous in the cause of improvement." If Virginia lacked commerce and manufacturing, if direct trade with Europe had proved a delusion, it was no fault of her own. The fault was with the Union, whose oppression no longer made it worth preserving. "Disguise it as we may," he concluded, "the time is in fact approaching when there will be no alternative but separation from the north, or tame submission to uncontrolled despotism." Wise wanted to avoid this choice, although developments in the Old Dominion and the crisis of national politics made it impossible. He had hoped that economic renewal and his political skill and influence might allow Virginia to weather the storm. But men such as Newton repudiated his leadership with arguments that gained in persuasiveness as time passed. Newton, too, wanted renewed grandeur for his proud state. Return it would—but only when Virginia became "the leading star of a great Southern constellation."[73]

Chapter 10

Kansas

If the sectional controversy of the 1850s had existed in a static environment, it might have evoked less militancy. But because the nation was so rapidly absorbing virgin territory, statesmen North and South had come to identify expansion with perpetuation of their institutions. To a certain extent, then, Southern demands for slavery in the territories represented a normal response to the times, which found Americans anxious to capitalize on opportunities offered by the West. Another element, however, underlay this race. A deep-seated fear that equated loss of the territories with encirclement and proscription of their institutions and differing ways of life had seized upon much of the public mind in both sections. In abrogating congressional authority to prevent slave labor from migrating to the territories, the Supreme Court, in the *Dred Scott* decision, exacerbated Northern apprehensions. Many Northerners, including Abraham Lincoln, now professed belief in a conspiracy to hand over the unsettled national domain to the retarding effects of slavery. Lincoln even speculated that after conquering the territories, the South might attempt to overthrow free labor in Illinois and elsewhere in the North, just as Calhoun had believed that the abolitionists would use leverage gained from control of the West to destroy slavery in the Southern states. The amalgam of historical rivalry, pride and prestige, fear and interest all blended to intensify the struggle for control of the national domain. In the 1850s this struggle focused on Kansas.

But should it have? Was anything substantive at stake in Kansas, in view of rapid Northern settlement and prospective control? Wise never believed that the fate of the Union, the South, or slavery depended upon what happened in Kansas. Blizzards, dust storms, and tumbleweeds meant as much to him as the Kansas issue when balanced against the need to preserve Virginia's integrity and the Democracy's stability. Along with other moderates, he feared not only radicals North and South but also the established politicians who had staked their identities and reputations on success in Kansas. When Senator Hunter and his associates preempted an extreme position in defense of slavery in Kansas, it was predictable that Wise would take an opposing stance. In the end, however, Wise's sense of urgency and his conviction that Kansas was a manufactured crisis manifestly in need of defusing transcended his rivalry with Hunter. The governor was probably right, even though the consequences of his stand never permitted him a comfortable certainty about its correctness.

With the exception of his encounter with John Brown in 1859, Wise's public career intersected most significantly with national politics in connection with the Kansas crisis. His eventual decision to stand with Stephen A. Douglas in opposition to the proslavery Lecompton Constitution separated him from James Buchanan and probably forfeited any slim chance he had for the presidency. To understand Wise's motives, it is important both to clarify the Kansas issue and to know more about how he viewed the political landscape in the late 1850s.

Few of the governor's public acts were unaffected by his feud with Senator Hunter. As Wise's popularity increased, along with his apparent influence over Buchanan's administration, the senator's friends grew anxious. To frustrate Wise's ambition and dilute his strength, Lewis E. Harvie, Hunter's most trusted adviser, arranged publication of a new states'-rights paper in Richmond. It was called, rather pretentiously, the *South*. Roger Pryor agreed to serve as editor.[1]

From its inception, the *South* suspected Buchanan's southern loyalties and endeavored to align itself with "fire-eating" organs like the *New Orleans Delta* and the *Charleston Mercury*. It demanded the admission of Kansas to the Union as a slave state. In an early issue, it reminded its readers that Buchanan had denounced slavery during the congressional debates on the annexation of Texas. It remarked that like all presidents, he craved tranquillity, which meant that he knew a free-soil constitution in Kansas would win more favor throughout the Union that a proslavery instrument. It also accused a number of Buchanan's associates of abolitionist sympathies.[2]

Wise was infuriated by the "selfish, false and furtive" tactics of Senator Hunter's supporters.[3] Had he not himself procured Buchanan's nomination and election? How could the president be disloyal to the South when he owed nearly all the honors of his public life to Southerners? What was the meaning of this opposition that had sprung up against the president and himself? Wise determined to resist it and readied his friends to support Buchanan. Following his return from Europe, Obadiah Jennings

Wise contributed editorials to the *Enquirer* that reprobated Pryor's efforts to discredit an administration of the South's choice.[4]

Wise believed that Hunter and his friends had never obtained the confidence of the Virginia masses and hence lacked proper credentials to speak for the Old Dominion. Moreover, these wealthy planters and slaveholders, whose incomes were richly augmented by public service, talked virtuously of the South's and Virginia's rights but retreated when it came time to defend them. As he put it in early 1857, with obvious reference to the Raleigh conference: "Some men's state rights are so abstract that they can't be applied . . . or brought into action."[5] Wise calculated that he had borne the brunt of the battle in both 1855 and 1856, when Virginia and the South were nearly overrun by Know-Nothing and Black Republican infidels and fanatics.

Hunter's disgusted partisans fully reciprocated the governor's animosity. Most of them viewed Wise as an ambitious demagogue, especially dangerous because of his impulsive nature. His obvious political talents commanded some respect, but he was not a man who deserved a place in Virginia's ruling class. His appearance and manners appalled Hunter's supporters. None of them chewed tobacco, for example, a habit Wise persisted in even during the speeches he substituted for conversation. He also had a terrible temper and more than once flew into undignified, semipublic rages. These distasteful outbursts confirmed to the senator and his allies their judgment of Wise as an unrefined and vulgar man, to whom the destinies of the commonwealth had most unfortunately been entrusted. "I would as soon have a baboon for my leader," wrote John Seddon, an important state legislator from the Fredericksburg area.[6]

What made Wise angry? The fastest pull on his hair-trigger temper and the most spectacular outbursts always followed even the most remote suggestion of his disloyalty to the South or slavery. In particular, any mention of his Brazilian mission infuriated him. Then, after calming himself, he normally reminded his listeners of Calhoun's intervention with Polk in his behalf. Whether he knew of the South Carolinian's reservations about his conduct in Brazil is unclear. Wise claimed an extensive correspondence before Calhoun's death in 1850.[7] The loathing for Wise among Hunter's counselors must have been intensified by his seeming to want to claim as much of Calhoun's prestige as possible.

The rivalry reached explosive proportions in 1857, when Hunter's friends sought in the midst of the Kansas crisis to reelect him to the Senate. As he had in 1852, Wise probably wanted the Senate seat, particularly if he could get it by provoking Hunter into a major error that might alienate him from a Democratic administration of the South's choosing. William W. Crump of Richmond epitomized the view of Hunter's friends in assailing the governor's "unscrupulous," "sedulous," and "envious" tactics. "No man can approach him and believe him fit to fill a statesman's place," concluded Crump, who presided many years later at the memorial service of the Richmond Bar preceding Wise's funeral.[8]

If Virginia politics seemed envenomed, by mid-1857 Kansan conflicts had turned positively lethal. A large majority of Kansas's settlers were free-soilers, but the territory's fate remained undecided. The partisan warfare of the previous year had abated somewhat, although each side retained separate "capitals." Proslavery forces, headquartered at Lecompton, aware that they stood in far greater favor with Buchanan's administration than their free-soil counterparts, wanted to press for immediate statehood. If successful, they intended that Kansas should enter the Union as the sixteenth slave state. Such a settlement would in all likelihood have inaugurated yet another civil war on the chilly and windswept Kansas plains, for the free-soil majority was ably led and well supplied with Massachusetts weapons.

To avoid further bloodshed and placate the Topeka "government," Buchanan appointed Robert J. Walker the new territorial governor of Kansas. Pennsylvania-born and Mississippi-bred, Walker was one of the most talented and versatile Democrats of the antebellum period. A former senator and secretary of the treasury under Polk, he was as responsible as any man in the Union for the annexation of Texas and then duly saw to it that the ensuing war with Mexico was properly financed.[9]

Walker preferred to see Kansas a slave state, as he later admitted, but at the time of his appointment he realized it was already too late.[10] He and Buchanan also knew that the territorial legislature at Lecompton, anathematized throughout the North, had provided for a constitutional convention to meet under its auspices in September 1857. Such a gathering might conceivably frame a proslavery instrument, but ensuing difficulties and objections could be obviated if it were then submitted to all the residents of the territory and freely voted upon. Without assurance that the administration supported such a submission, Walker would have refused his appointment.[11]

This guarantee reflected Walker's understanding of the Kansas-Nebraska Act, which he sought to enforce so as to preserve the integrity of the Democratic party. His future in Kansas did not augur well, however, because the Lecompton legislature, in providing for the upcoming convention, had said nothing whatever about submitting its work to the people. Rumors circulated that its leaders advocated any measure of electoral corruption necessary to obtain favorable results. Nonetheless, in his inaugural address, which evidently had been read and approved by both Buchanan and Senator Douglas,[12] Walker reaffirmed his commitment to a plebiscite. He also alleged that an "Isothermal line" made Kansas' climate unsuitable for slavery.[13] Wise had used the same phrase three years earlier when publicly expressing his reservations about the Kansas-Nebraska Act. Indeed, many years earlier both Walker and Wise had proclaimed the irresistible influences of climate and geography on slavery's future when they advocated the annexation of Texas.

When news of Walker's inaugural and his projected policy, which aimed at adding Kansas to the Union as a free but Democratic state, began to circulate, Southerners reacted immediately. Many in the lower South felt themselves cheated out of an additional slave state. When the Whig and American opposition sought higher ground by accusing Democrats of betrayal, Democratic state conventions in Georgia and Mississippi promptly demonstrated that their loyalties to slavery exceeded their commitment to the party. They condemned the Kansas governor and insisted on his removal.[14] Walker was charged with usurping the powers of the Lecompton legislature. By advising Congress to reject the new constitution unless submitted for ratification, he had intervened in territorial affairs and thus defied the Kansas-Nebraska Act.

Well might Southerners have felt betrayed by both Walker and the administration that seemed to sustain him. Had not their own leaders assured them that the legislation of 1850 and 1854 guaranteed the expansion of their institutions within the Union? Now that the South received shadow for substance, no group of Southerners grieved more than Unionists such as Alexander H. Stephens and Howell Cobb, who had sold the earlier compromises to their section. The brilliant but irascible Stephens was beside himself with rage at Walker's course. With honor and perhaps political future at stake, Stephens wanted Kansas a slave state by whatever means necessary.[15]

Other men in the South, however, saw no need to vindicate their devotion to the doctrine of congressional nonintervention in the territories and seemed unperturbed at the potential loss of Kansas. Edmund Ruffin, for example, cared little about slavery's fate there. The Virginia agricultural reformer and proslavery publicist thought the territory lost to free-soil. He probably regarded this development with equanimity because without Kansas his section would think more seriously about fulfilling its destiny by withdrawing from the Union.[16] Ruffin was one of the very few secessionists in the South at this time. His position helps indicate that many who wanted a slave Kansas sought to preserve the Union, albeit on their own terms.

Henry A. Wise subscribed to the views of neither Stephens nor Ruffin. He had not influenced the course of national legislation for many years and thus had no particular stake in sustaining any part of it. While Congress debated the compromise measures of 1850, he was working in Virginia on a compromise of his own. In 1854, he remarked, the South had "poked its finger in its own eye and it is not for those who blinded us to say now we can't see!" For the benefit of an Alabama friend Wise repeated his position on the Kansas-Nebraska Act, with characteristic emphasis on the false step taken in approving the Badger amendment:

> I happened unfortunately to agree with my friend Mr. Millson in opposition. . . . The Dred Scott decision proves too late our sagacity. The law of slavery was the law of the La. territory, N. and S. of 36°30', prior to 1820. It was unrepealed, up to the Kansas act, by any law other than that of the law and line of the Missouri Compromise. That compromise was constitutional or unconstitutional. If constitutional it affected only the territory n. of 36°30'—that S. of it was left unaffected. In other words slavery was the status south of 36°30' in Kansas. But for the Kansas bill, the Dred Scott decision would have established that the compromise law of 1820 was void and that the old Spanish law of slavery was untouched, unrepealed north of 36°30' in all the La. territory. . . . There was no law prior to '20 *prohibiting* or abolishing, but there was a law establishing and protecting slavery in Kansas, and *that law this proviso* [Badger] repealed. How can they who repealed slavery in Kansas abuse Walker for saying it is or will be a free state![17]

By mid-1857 Wise estimated that the more mobile free-soil population outnumbered Southern-born settlers by upward of ten to one. Under such circumstances, Southern resistance appeared foolhardy and stupid. The Virginia governor also believed that it would be impossible to grow the profitable staples usually cultivated by slave labor on cold Kansas prairies. He therefore doubted that the attempt to make Kansas a slave state would be worth the risk of disrupting the Democratic party and the Union. The party, he thought, had for years ruled the Union in the interests of the South. Besides, the fracture of either party or Union would shatter his own hopes for political advancement.

Wise sought to influence the editorial course of the *Enquirer* and thereby exact from Hunter an endorsement of the administration in return for his official withdrawal from the senatorial race.[18] Despite the advantages of incumbency, Hunter was vulnerable. Ruffled by the catechizing efforts of his enemies, he responded with two public letters in October, affirming his loyalty to Buchanan and declaring his hope to support the administration "in the main." But lest Wise's friends think they had humiliated him, the senator coupled his affirmations with a strong censure of Governor Walker's conduct in Kansas. He suggested that the governor had violated the Kansas-Nebraska Act by illegally intervening in territorial affairs. He also insisted that the Lecompton convention was under no obligation to submit its work to the people, provided that it "was legally constituted and elected."[19]

Wise now struck a magnanimous pose. In yet another public letter reviewing his recent career and vindicating himself, the governor pronounced Hunter's epistles satisfactory and bowed out of the senatorial contest. He again deprecated those Southern extremists who had hoped for revolution in 1856, adding sarcastically that they probably would not have followed him out of the Union if the tug had come. He countered Hunter by praising Walker's past services to the South. He suggested that if the Lecompton convention prepared a proslavery instrument, it would be perfectly acceptable to him, but he recommended a popular ratification of the constitution. His conciliatory temper manifested itself in a declared willingness to accept the constitution without submission (a position grossly inconsistent with the one he thereafter assumed, as his enemies delighted in pointing out[20]), although the cause of popular sovereignty would best be served by a ratification vote. He argued, rather weakly, that because the Lecompton legislature had not expressly authorized the constitutional convention "to make and adopt" an instrument for Kansas, the people had reserved the right to approve its action. Wise admitted that there were many contrary precedents, but these he termed "exceptional" and "anti-democratic." He closed with a characteristic appeal to the honor of the South, which he said must never be tarnished, even at the cost of a free-state Kansas. If elections were fraudulently conducted in the territory, Governor Walker was right to have invalidated them. The slaveholding population, according to Wise, had too high a "moral tone" and had too long stood heroically on the defensive against those who wished to abrogate the federal Constitution to forsake its position in order to further "falsehood and injustice."[21]

Shortly before the governor's letter was published, news of the

Lecompton convention's deliberations reached the East. It opted to provide Kansas voters with a choice of accepting the new constitution with or without slavery. Wise was probably aware of this development and aimed at criticizing it in his *Enquirer* letter of 17 November.[22] He wanted the Kansans to have the opportunity of accepting or rejecting the entire document. Buchanan, of course, had earlier assured Walker of this choice, but Wise knew of the president's weak-wristedness, especially when confronted by Southerners in his cabinet and among his friends who seemed prepared to take any risks to gain an additional slave state. He desperately wanted to bolster Buchanan's commitment to his word, and so, even before Senator Douglas, he had attacked the Lecompton settlement.

For reasons unclear and ever afterward subject to dispute, Buchanan chose to endorse the Lecompton Constitution. Perhaps he genuinely wished a resolution of the crisis, although many historians believe that deep emotional attachment to the South and fears of secession led him to a gesture of appeasement. The most impressive recent review of these matters suggests that "in addition" Buchanan may have chosen "to take a calculated risk, tempted by the apparent opportunity to remove forever from national politics the dangerous problem of Kansas."[23] Senator Douglas, whose public career could not have sustained the imputation that his legislative talents had wrought a slave Kansas, defied Buchanan and condemned Lecompton. In a celebrated interview, he allegedly reminded the president that he should not confuse himself with Andrew Jackson. Wise had been aware of this problem for some time.

By mid-December, following Buchanan's pro-Lecompton message to Congress, the Virginia governor had to make a choice. As a slaveholder, he could understand the position of Southerners who argued that the Democratic party was worthless if it refused to sanction expansion of their institutions. But, to paraphrase from another day, he believed that Kansas represented the wrong fight, in the wrong place, with the wrong weapons. More serious dangers to slavery existed in Virginia itself, where he had always thought it difficult enough to preserve the institution. In 1856 he had pointedly observed that a slave Kansas would have no effect on the price of bondsmen in Virginia.[24] A careful observer might have predicted his opposition to the Lecompton Constitution, although his 30 December 1857 letter to the New York Tammany Society was a veritable "bombshell" that astonished politicians and editors across the country.[25] With more evidence at his command than in November, Wise accused the Lecompton convention of "unveiled trickery and shameless fraud" in preventing Kansans from voting on their constitution. His argument contained many of the elements appearing in his November letter, but now he recommended that Congress not admit Kansas until her voters ratified their organic law. Instantly, he opened himself to the accusation that he advocated antirepublican intervention in territorial affairs inasmuch as the legislation governing the election of delegates to the Lecompton convention made no provision for submission of the convention's work to the people of Kansas.

Without a strong argument, he plunged ahead anyway. He suspected, as later appeared, that members of Buchanan's cabinet had directly influenced the deliberations of the Lecompton convention.[26] "I know that a conspiracy exists," he remarked in a letter to Douglas, "to drive the northern Democracy from the Administration on the Kansas and the Southern from it on the filibustering Walker affair." The primary threat came from Southern extremists who thought only abolitionists lived north of the Mason-Dixon line. "I want to cure the egregious blunders of proslavery blind leaders," he wrote Robert Tyler.[27]

Wise knew that a sizable number of Douglas's constituents in the Northwest were expatriate Virginians who despised blacks and might well assist the South in the event of war. Moreover, the governor feared alienation of conservative Northerners who might someday aid in suppressing the influence of New England and even in forcing that recalcitrant and fanatical section out of the Union altogether. Wise had family and close friends in Philadelphia and New York, including the Tylers and Mayor Fernando Wood, who were committed to slavery. Another associate originally from Accomac County, John Beauchamp Jones, who later acquired considerable fame as a diarist writing from inside the Confederate capital, edited the *Southern Monitor* in Philadelphia. Their friendships with sympathetic Northerners may later have led Southerners such as Wise to misjudge probable Northern response to secession, prompting them to increase their demands for such concessions as a congressional slave code. Wise seems to have had the same faith in the strength of Northern conservatism that Lincoln, according to David M. Potter, had in Southern conservatism.[28]

Beyond these feelings and attitudes, Wise may also , if I am correct, have had a fatalistic sense of what was possible for the South. It was difficult to fight merely for slavery, particularly when dishonorable means (with which he was familiar) were required. It was as if slavery was such a burden that only the most high-minded tactics could be employed in its defense. How could the weaker party stand on anything less than honor? "Esop taught his cock to be wise enough when he entered the stall of the steed—to say to the iron-shod animal: 'if you wont tread on my toes I wont upon yours.' But it seems our leaders had'nt the sagacity of the cock in the fable, but attempted to set up the . . . game of grab—to catch as catch can with an overwhelming and unscrupulous majority."[29] This thinking, however, which ran counter to the optimism, arrogance, and self-assurance more characteristic of public figures from the Deep South, could promote indecision and paralysis. At the same time, it could tempt Wise to strike out violently in an effort to resolve the ambiguities in his life and thought.

The uproar following Wise's explicit denunciation of the Lecompton Constitution won him more national recognition than he had enjoyed since the canvass of 1856. Republican papers and also the *New York Herald* immediately suggested that the Virginia governor had set a snare to trap Northern votes.[30] The *Herald* and the *New York Times*, reputedly the organ of William H. Seward, asserted that Wise meant to seize from Douglas the inside track leading toward the presidential nomination in 1860. James Gordon Bennett, who edited the *Herald*, felt that Wise had nothing to lose by opposing Lecompton because if Kansas entered the Union as a slave state the credit would go to his rivals among the so-called Southern ultras.[31] Bennett's legendary cynicism equipped him to calculate Wise's worst motives, and the Virginia governor knew it. He despised Bennett, the most widely read Northern editor in the South, yet feared him and worried constantly about the thrashing he took in the *Herald*.[32]

If the Tammany letter signaled the opening gambit of Wise's active drive for the presidency, he had miscalculated. No one, not even as iconoclastic a politician as Wise, could have craved the fury it produced. In a tremendous blow to his prestige, the Virginia General Assembly with near unanimity adopted resolutions sustaining Buchanan and endorsing the prompt admission of Kansas to the Union. Old enemies with scores to settle, such as Democratic Congressman William Smith, read these resolves on the floor of the House of Representatives, ridiculed the governor, and pronounced him excommunicated.[33] Not a single member of Virginia's congressional delegation supported him. Even Congressman John Millson of Norfolk, whose criticisms of the Kansas-Nebraska Act Wise had sustained in 1854, later voted for the admission of Kansas under the Lecompton Constitution.[34] Whig editors rejoiced, while much of the Democratic press across Virginia challenged him and even the *Enquirer*, in a carefully phrased editorial on 30 January, endorsed Lecompton. Critics such as Edmund Ruffin and Senator Robert Toombs of Georgia traced Wise's behavior exclusively to his "inordinate vanity" and "crazy" desire for the presidency. Robert Barnwell Rhett, writing some time later, suggested that Wise's rejection of Lecompton defied a nearly united South and thus nearly destroyed his political credibility in the region.[35]

Wise's Tammany letter was the first full-scale attack on Lecompton to come from the South. Throughout the controversy, he remained the only prominent Southern Democratic politician to oppose Lecompton unequivocally. Observers quickly pointed out that the "Southern Achilles" of the administration had dealt the constitution a body blow. Recalling Wise's role in the 1856 campaign, Republican papers emphasized that because of his letter Northerners who supported Lecompton would now be denounced as more extreme in their devotion to the South than even the Southern fire-eaters.[36] Wise's Tammany letter and his succeeding communications went far to dispel any notions that the South would secede if the Lecompton Constitution was not approved by Congress, just as Botts's speeches in 1856 had aided Northerners in thinking that Frémont's election presented no danger to the Union.[37]

The alliance of Douglas, Wise, and former Governor Walker boded ill for the administration. Robert Tyler, a son of the former president and a Buchanan lieutenant in Philadelphia, seemed baffled at first by Wise's course but then turned increasingly fearful and angry. He warned Buchanan to beware of the governor because "opposition is his natural element."[38] Alexander H. Stephens, the most skilled parliamentarian in the House of Representatives, was confident in mid-December that despite Douglas's defection Kansas would enter the Union as a slave state—though he admitted that Wise's opposition had made that objective considerably more difficult to obtain.[39] "If Kansas is lost," the *Charleston Mercury* added, "this letter will have had its effect in producing that result." As William Dennison Porter, one of South Carolina's most important state senators, put it: "the defection of Douglas was bad enough—but that of Wise is infinitely worse."[40] When it is remembered that the Senate approved Lecompton and it failed by only eight votes in the House of Representatives, these comments take on considerable significance.

The Virginia governor and the Illinois senator justified their objections to Lecompton on different grounds. They agreed that fraud had corrupted the Lecompton convention. Douglas believed, however, that the territorial legislature was not empowered to call a constitutional convention without a congressional enabling act; hence the convention was "an unauthorized and illegal body."[41] He argued that territorial legislatures had every right to inhibit the expansion of slavery, whereas Wise defended the Calhounist doctrine that no positive injunctions against slavery could legally exist until prescribed by a constitutional convention called preparatory to seeking statehood. Wise also asserted that the Kansas-Nebraska Act was an enabling statute, which forced him to concede the legitimacy of the Lecompton convention despite the frauds that had accompanied its election.[42] For a time, Wise's only constitutional objection was that the power to approve or reject the constitution was reserved to the people of Kansas. But this argument, made from inference and unsustained by precedent, seemed extremely weak because state constitutions had often gone into effect without popular ratification.[43]

Early in February, with his views under heavier fire, Wise strengthened his position with another long letter on Lecompton, this time addressed to a Philadelphia meeting. Characteristically, he scorned retreat and boldly assaulted his enemies. In a brilliant effort, he exposed the inconsistency of the Lecompton convention by quoting the eleventh section of the schedule attached to the constitution:

> Before *this Constitution* shall be sent to Congress for admission into the Union as a State, *it* shall be submitted to all the white male inhabitants of this territory, for *approval* or *disapproval*, as follows. . . . The president of this Convention shall appoint three commissioners in each county in the Territory, whose duty it shall be to appoint three judges of election in the several precincts of their respective counties, at which election *the Constitution framed by this Convention* shall be submitted to all the white male inhabitants . . . for *ratification* or *rejection*.[44]

Wise thus demonstrated that the convention had provided for the submission of its work to the voters. It had stultified its proceedings by deciding in the end that the ballots should be marked "Constitution with Slavery" and "Constitution with no Slavery." This was not the choice its own decisions had guaranteed.

Wise added several other objections, each of which estranged him further from Buchanan and his associates. He bristled at the oath that required any voter, if challenged in the ratification election, to support the prospective constitution, "if adopted." This, he said, smacked of odious Know-Nothing test oaths, which Democrats had recently repudiated.[45]

Wise wanted the constitution, as it stood, returned to Kansas for a fair vote. He knew Buchanan's position—that if Lecompton were speedily accepted by Congress, the free-soilers of Kansas might soon abolish slavery—but he quickly turned this argument on its head and asked whether in fact that procedure "commends itself to pro-slavery gentlemen." "Some of them," he remarked, with reference to the Badger amendment, "once repealed laws protecting and establishing slavery in Kansas. They had better not make it too apparent in the South that 'prompt admission' would most speedily unmake the slavery there which was restored by the Dred Scott decision." This latter point was self-serving and stated altogether for political effect. As his letter showed, Wise knew of and vigorously opposed the proviso in the Lecompton Constitution that slave property then in Kansas could not be interfered with before 1864. Buchanan may have as well. Perhaps unfairly, Wise refused to acknowledge Buchanan's proposal to eliminate this problem by advocating "congressional modification" of the Lecompton Constitution "to guarantee after statehood [the] immediate right of constitutional amendment." But this point was relatively minor. Not even Buchanan's most skillful defenders can absolve him of the inconsistencies that Wise and many others pointed out. The most charitable thing that can be said about the president during this crisis is that he blundered terribly.[46]

Wise believed that if Lecompton were rammed through Congress, Kansan free-soilers and their Northern allies would fight to overthrow it. They would succeed, and then flushed with success they would look South, just as they had in 1856. In his view, Lecompton could produce only a free-state Kansas and the destruction of the Democratic party.[47] "If the Congress adopts that Lecompton schedule," Wise wrote Robert Tyler, "Democracy is dead."[48]

On 28 May 1858, Wise composed a remarkably prophetic letter to his second wife's brother in Philadelphia. Lecompton, he wrote, had not produced the crisis in the Democracy; rather, the crisis resulted from "an organized, active and dangerous faction, embracing most of the Federal politicians, who are bent upon bringing about causes" of a destruction of the Union. This Southern-dominated group hoped to pack the Charleston Convention in 1860, secure an extremist candidate, and then provoke a defeat "by a line of sections." The Lecomptonites in the North and the administration's minions, their allies, were not numerous but would be heavily represented in the convention. Several Northern delegations at Charleston might be split and therefore neutralized. Lecomptonites would therefore make the nomination, leaving anti-Lecomptonites with the option of returning to their respective states and making "their own nominations." "This may save the North from absorption by Black Republicanism, may throw the election in the House of Representatives and save the Union. I see no other course." Quiet and efficient organization was the only option available, he concluded. But for what? He did not say, probably because he could not. He discerned no way through the portending calamities, although he perhaps reflected that only the candidacy of an independent politician such as himself might resolve the crisis. In the meantime, his exposed position required great efforts to conciliate the sheep and oxen of the Democratic establishment, including the president himself.[49]

It was Wise's tragedy that he seldom managed to act on the courage of his convictions. After mounting a penetrating critique of Buchanan's policy, he drew back in order to protect his share of the federal patronage. This tactic inevitably weakened his indictment of the South's federal politicians, whose commitments to secession were halfhearted at best. But Wise had rightly arraigned their ridiculous endorsements of Lecompton. The governor's fascination with the presidency influenced his conduct, set limits on his freedom, and thus may have fed his erratic temperament, even to the point of provoking doubts and self-hatred. Certainly he hated his enemies, as his son's dueling campaign against them soon proved. He lived to enlist again the combination of passion and morality that inspired his gubernatorial canvass in 1855. All too often, however, as happened at Harpers Ferry in 1859, political structures and the requisites of expediency thwarted his best instincts and led him to ponder roads not taken.

With presses in the Deep South pouring hot shot into Douglas for his treason, Wise sniffed the wind and took a long holiday in western Virginia during the summer of 1858. The Southern congressional delegation in Washington, led by Alexander H. Stephens, had arranged a compromise with the president's consent and kept Kansas out of the Union, thus preventing the Republicans from gaining two additional senators. The resubmission of the Lecompton Constitution virtually unchanged, which Kansas voters promptly rejected, satisfied Wise, while the end result (maintenance of territorial status) and the terms devised by Stephens and others assuaged Southern honor.[50] For both high-minded and selfish purposes, Wise promoted party harmony. In a card published in the *Richmond Enquirer* on the day he and an associate acquired an interest in the paper, Obadiah Jennings Wise made the same plea, pointedly complimenting Buchanan's ability and patriotism.

Later on, the *Enquirer* called the Lecompton crisis "a temporary division of opinion among [the] party."[51]

Even amid disagreements with the administration, Wise continued seeking patronage from it for his friends. Occasional potshots from Buchanan's organ, the *Union*, annoyed him because they strengthened the Hunter wing of the party in Virginia. But his craftiness allowed him for the moment to escape some of the attention focused on Douglas by the president's editors.[52]

When Buchanan's passion for vengeance inspired him to intrigue against Douglas while the senator battled Abraham Lincoln for reelection, Wise traveled to Washington and rebuked him directly. Such a renunciatory encounter never took place between Wise and Andrew Jackson. Shortly afterward, and even while he requested a foreign mission for William Ritchie, a part-owner of the *Richmond Enquirer*, the governor minced no words: "Douglas's *success* in Illinois, *without* the aid of the Administration, will be its rebuke, his *defeat, with its opposition*, will be the death of the Administration; and *his success with the aid of the Administration* may save it and the Democratic party."[53] Wise further advised Buchanan that a free-soil Kansas would enter the Union eventually, though his supposed Southern friends would find one pretext or another—such as the Pacific railroad or the protective tariff issue—upon which to oppose him. Buchanan nevertheless rejected all appeals and stripped Wise of influence over the federal patronage. The enraged governor reacted bitterly. In January 1859 he condemned the president's annual message, saying that after his "mad" efforts to defeat Douglas in Illinois, Buchanan now proposed a series of Federalist schemes exceeding any "which a Hamilton or Adams . . . ever dared to project or propose." He offered Cuba, the Isthmus of Panama, and northern Mexico to the Southern filibusterers, a federally financed Pacific railroad to the West, and tariffs on iron and coarse woolens to the North. The only possible explanation, according to Wise, was that Buchanan craved another presidential term—a charge with little basis in fact that revealed as much about the Virginia governor's objectives as it did about the president's.[54]

Despite their different reasons for opposing Lecompton and Douglas's opposition to the congressional settlement enacted months earlier, Wise rallied to the senator's defense in the fall of 1858 by sending spirited letters to Illinois for use in the campaign against Lincoln.[55] Although anxious to appear gallant and generous in aiding Douglas, Wise privately advised his friends that he was playing for higher stakes, precisely the tactics he was soon to find Buchanan so loathsome for adopting. "Douglas wd'nt consent to be *Vice*. He wd regard the offer as an insult. Let him run his line out & he will then be obliged to come to me. I have every evidence of more strength in the North than he has."[56] This strength came principally from conservative politicians of generally unreliable loyalty. Far more important from his point of view, as long as Wise cherished any visions of the presidency, was support in the Deep South. For some time, the governor had charged Senator Hunter's friends with efforts "to ostracize me in the cotton states."[57]

Following the Lecompton apostasy, Hunter's criticism proved redundant. The *New Orleans Crescent* pronounced Wise "the most tremendous fool in all Christendum or Heathendum."[58] The *New York Herald* reported in July 1858 "an entire and complete abandonment of Wise in all quarters South."[59] Moreover, Wise's personal popularity in slave-dominated eastern Virginia had waned. Almost all local politicians in Tidewater Virginia, for example, excoriated him for twice proposing the Oyster Fundum, as it was derisively called, punctuating their objections with charges that Wise had shown himself fixated, unbending, and despotic. An ill wind, threatening a tempest, billowed around him powerfully enough to dissolve his dreams of Virginia's renewal and a heroic national canvass. A desolate and wilted political landscape, devoid of hope and inviting carnage, would then be laid bare, particularly if some cataclysm should inspire the nonslaveholders to defend their true interests.

Many prominent Southerners who shared Wise's fears and some of his hopes probably fantasized about the presidency during the 1850s. Few of them carried his proven record of electrifying the masses. Despite the national reputations of men such as Hunter, Robert Toombs, Jefferson Davis, and Wise, something forlorn and ludicrous colored all their ambitions. The Democratic party in the late 1850s had but one serious candidate: Stephen A. Douglas. In service and achievement, command of a national following, and resourcefulness in argument and political maneuvering—indeed, in everything but physical stature—Douglas dwarfed the dozen Southerners who aspired to his place. Beyond their agreements on Kansas policy, Wise respected Douglas, though he never trusted him. In particular, Wise remembered a crucial intervention on his behalf by the Illinois senator. When during the 1855 gubernatorial campaign Wise badly needed friends Douglas had contributed a stirring speech in Richmond.[60] After Douglas's victory over Abraham Lincoln, Wise wrote Senator George Jones of Iowa (a Buchanan Democrat and one of Douglas's bitterest enemies) that he did not think the Illinois senator could secure the presidential nomination, "but I shall not oppose his nomination if made."[61] Several of Wise's supporters in Virginia looked to Douglas as their second choice for the presidency.[62] Moreover, the strategy Wise pursued throughout the Kansas crisis found him vindicating the principles of popular sovereignty. Under these circumstances, it required the most remarkable self-assurance even to think of differentiating his candidacy. And given Wise's need to protect his Southern flank, an extreme declaration would seem necessary. Certainly, it came—first in the pages of the *Enquirer* and then in a book-length pamphlet published in March 1859. Everything that Wise wrote and said in appearing to advocate congressional protection for slavery in the territories followed from Douglas's difficulties in appeasing the Deep South after his own apostasy during the Lecompton dispute and in harmonizing his doctrine of popular sovereignty with the *Dred Scott* decision. Douglas's problems gave Wise the opening he needed, but his response seemed puzzling, surreal, and contrived. In the end, it made about as much sense as the hatred for Douglas that he professed and then manipulated his eldest son into emulating.

Douglas's common-sense approach to the territories, never justified successfully by an appeal to the Constitution, suggested local option as a way of determining slavery's fate in them. This approach appealed more to experience than to legalism, which bored Douglas. And, like the violence it inspired, popular sovereignty could be defended as a favored and patriotic mode of solving America's problems. Unlike Virginia politicians, Douglas professed no special reverence for either the Constitution or the Founding Fathers. Advertising himself as a practical man and a problem-solver interested in national improvement, which in concrete terms meant expansionism and economic development, he preferred to leave slavery to its fate in the territories.[63] Douglas's ambiguous formula, which neglected to specify when citizens of a territory could properly pronounce on slavery, served the national Democracy admirably until the *Dred Scott* decision.

Few observers could have expected to read the capstone of the entire proslavery argument in a judgment from the Supreme Court, yet that was precisely what Chief Justice Roger B. Taney produced. Taney's opinion is now authoritatively regarded as the consensus of the Court's majority. He held that Congress had no power to inhibit the spread of slavery to the territories; hence he ruled unconstitutional the Missouri Compromise of 1820. This position presented no problems to Douglas, for the Kansas-Nebraska Act had already voided the compromise. But Taney additionally declared that because the principal could not threaten slave property, its creature, a territorial legislature, was similarly inhibited. Even though many commentators viewed this extension of the Court's holding as obiter dictum because *Dred Scott* had nothing to do with the acts of a territorial legislature, it nonetheless augured ominously for Douglas. Under pressure from the Deep South and Abraham Lincoln, the Illinois senator found himself compelled to disavow the implications of *Dred Scott* in order to save his doctrine of popular sovereignty. He declared eventually that whatever the courts might decide, slavery could never exist in any territory without a framework of legislation to enforce *Dred Scott*.[64] When Douglas's position became clear in the fall of 1858, the *Richmond Enquirer* boldly suggested that he had demonstrated to Southerners the need for federal legislation protecting slavery in the territories. This doctrine and the interventionist strategy it implied were anathema to Douglas. The calculated misreading of Douglas's position (which is suggested by the *Enquirer*'s failure to acknowledge the Illinois senator's subsequent repudiation of a slave code for the territories) sprang from the editor's determination to assist Douglas's bid for reelection.[65] Nonetheless the *Enquirer*'s misreading foreshadowed the position Wise would take publicly in April 1859, in an effort to satisfy his Southern constituency and particularly the slaveholding and slave-exporting regions of his own state.

Sensing Douglas's vulnerability both in Illinois and the South, Wise had sent him a ringing endorsement near the end of his contest with Lincoln. Buried toward the end of a lengthy catalog of causes that united them, Wise listed "Protection in the Territories and everywhere to all rights of persons and property, in accordance with the rights of the States, and with the Constitution and laws of the Union."[66] Shortly afterward, Wise appeared to acknowledge the carefully contrived nature of this letter.[67] From a position favoring nonintervention by Congress in territorial affairs, he seemed poised to advocate precisely the opposite policy in order to protect slavery and himself.

Isolated by his Lecompton stance and perhaps tempted to cynicism by the response to one of the most intelligent and principled decisions of his career, Wise gravitated toward the orbit of that prince of Deep South fire-eaters, William Lowndes Yancey. With Yancey's benediction what Southerner could doubt the governor's reliability? Wise approached the radicals, particularly in Alabama, through a trusted intermediary. But here care was needed. The *Enquirer*, for example, carried on a peculiarly inconsistent flirtation with the African slave trade issue during which Wise avoided making any direct statements. It was now late October 1858—the time chosen by Seward to sound the anthem of an "Irrepressible Conflict."

Wise's principal correspondent in the Deep South was William F. Samford of Auburn, Alabama, a prolific newspaper editor of extreme sympathies. The two men met only once, but Wise's gubernatorial canvass of 1855 electrified Samford and ever after he trumpeted Wise for the presidency. What seemed so different about Wise was precisely what the Virginia governor wanted everyone to notice about him: his appeal potentially transcended the ordinary political structures that so many, including Wise himself, had come to despise. This capacity made him unpredictable and dangerous—but not to Samford, who advised Senator Clement C. Clay, of Alabama, that

> Wise is our *only* hope—Davis' *cottoning* to N. England is perfidious—Hunter is too cold, selfish, aristocratic, politic. . . . Let him roll on his cushions, pronounce his ivory orations and keep his Senatorial dignity—it becomes him!
>
> [To] Wise we owe a great debt. The popular heart will leap toward him like flames of fire to their native heavens. He will come surrounded by the memories of all that is grand in the best days of Va. & the Republic. . . . For Heaven's sake, let's do a fitting thing! Lift the crown to the head that *Justice* awards its due, vindicate great souls by one decisive election. Save the Republic![68]

Clay seems to have ignored this appeal, but not so Yancey, who was another intimate of Samford's. The last thing that their careers and values could have predicted was a relatively close association between Yancey and Wise. To my knowledge they never met, nor did they ever directly exchange letters, but the Virginia governor's efforts to legitimize himself in the Deep South and undercut rivals such as Jefferson Davis led him to treat Yancey's radicalism with increasing respect. He even paid tribute, although *very* privately, to Yancey's efforts to organize a league of united Southerners, whose purpose was preparation for disunion and possible war. He never joined, of course.[69] Perhaps the association with Yancey confirmed Wise's determination to argue for congressional protection of slave property in the territories. In any case, Yancey and several other fire-eaters remained convinced of Wise's availability as a presidential nominee all the way into the Charleston Convention.[70]

The views of Wise, Yancey, and Samford all converged on

perhaps the most explosive issue to affect Southern politics in the late 1850s—the agitation to reopen the African slave trade. From the spring of 1858, when Yancey seized the subject during the Southern Commercial Convention in Montgomery, Alabama, politicians of all stripes scurried to state their views. Everyone wanted to extract temporary advantage from this issue, while warily observing the threat it represented to Southern unity. Even Yancey had his problems with more dogmatic advocates such as Leonidas Spratt, the nonslaveholding editor of the *Charleston Standard*, who originally broached the issue in 1853 and remained its most ardent devotee. Yancey later repudiated the charge that he endorsed outright renewal and advanced the lesser notion that all laws prohibiting the slave trade were unconstitutional and insulting to the South.[71]

Yancey's argument largely coincided with Wise's in the Adams letter of 1854, which had recommended the repeal of all federal laws suppressing the slave trade. The *Enquirer* printed manifestos from both Samford and Yancey but nothing from Wise. It merely affirmed that he stood by the Adams letter and accompanied its authoritative statement of his views with denials that he held any influence over editorial policy. If the slave trade were no longer piracy and treaties forbidding it were abrogated, the *Enquirer* suggested, the issue would effectively be left to the states.[72] Yancey openly advocated this position, although Wise merely left it as an implied conclusion. But if one was willing to go halfway, why no further? The *Enquirer* had no good answer to those who asked why it should be more correct to purchase slaves in Virginia than in Africa. After Yancey had originally ventilated the idea at Montgomery, the *Enquirer* in a celebrated editorial had wondered whether "the South of a Northern Confederacy would not be more preferable for [Virginia], than the north of a Southern Confederacy" in the event of a dissolution. It thereafter conceded that matters of economy divided the South on this issue and implied that hordes of African savages overrunning the South would disturb patriarchal sensibilities. It then oscillated over the next several months between gingerly endorsing Yancey's radicalism and repudiating everything, including Yancey's league of united Southerners, that even faintly squinted at disunion. The *Enquirer* also confessed that because slaves did work of less value in the border states than in the Deep South their worth was not the same in both sections. Acknowledging this differential constituted the principal liability of the debate over renewing the trade because it undercut other salutary efforts to promote unity among Southerners.[73] By December 1858, the *Enquirer* was featuring a classic critique of the slave traders by R. G. Harper, whose lengthy essay summarized the various arguments on his side of the debate and also charged that the positions assumed by Wise, Samford, and Yancey were tantamount to sanctioning immediate renewal of the trade. Seward and other Republican notables made exactly the same charge.[74]

Wise happily read of his lack of control over the *Enquirer* so long as it engaged in these miserable charades. It was inconceivable that a Virginia politician could speculate about reopening the trade under any auspices. Wise's earlier stance in the Adams letter created an opening that he exploited to solidify support among certain Southern extremists, who themselves were pressed by others yet more rigid and demanding than they. Besides the opportunism he displayed, the confused and incomplete proposals he advanced implied a defensive posture in a time of darkening prospects. It was "immoral and disgraceful" to import more slaves, he finally said—it would make us "obnoxious to ourselves."[75] After the summer of 1859 he never touched the issue again. Most established politicians, many of the South Carolina radicals, and even Yancey soon found the African slave trade a dangerous distraction, which fortunately for them lapsed into insignificance as the presidential contest of 1860 approached.

In the space of twenty-six months, Wise had endorsed at least three different solutions to the territorial crisis: an extension of the line 36°30' to the Pacific, popular sovereignty as ambiguously written into the Kansas-Nebraska Act, and congressional protection for slavery in the territories. Having acquired a reputation as one of the shiftiest politicians in the South, Wise found himself the regular subject of caustic and malevolent reflections in the press, to say nothing of the private furies he inspired. Robert Ridgway of the *Richmond Whig* led the way in flailing "the Emperor of all the Virginias" for typifying everything odious and reprehensible in public life.[76]

Wise's high position prevented him from responding directly, but no such constraints inhibited his eldest son, Obie. Edmund Ruffin referred to young Wise as "a professional duellist, and a bravo, bully, and designed murderer upon system, and calculation . . . I hope that the son may yet meet the bloody doom, which he so well deserved long ago," added Ruffin, "and the father suffer the remorse that will follow the using his son as his partisan and bravo, and by both precept and example, to make him a professional bully for political gain, and a murderer in intention, if not yet in deed."[77] Only a few years later, Obie was dead—the victim of a Yankee bullet as he substituted for his sick father on the battlefield.

In January 1858, young Wise barged into Ridgway's office, denounced his "insolence," and beat him over the head with a cane. Obie later took satisfaction in noting that Ridgway "seemed much frightened, and made no effort, except to seize and hold my stick and call for assistance." Ridgway denied these aspersions on his manhood and proposed a duel, but not according to the usual canons, which he said Wise had already violated by assaulting him. Instead, he suggested that friends blindfold both and lock them in a room, each with a pistol presented to the breast of the other. A single bullet would be in one of the guns, put there by lots. Wise contemptuously declined on grounds, among others, that such an arrangement would leave everything to chance and nothing to skill.[78] Ridgway's challenge was absurd and reflected his fears and unwillingness to hazard his life against a man thoroughly exposed to the European dueling traditions and acknowledged as a crack shot. But Ridgway's trepidation did not extend to his conduct of the *Whig*. Before long he was again reviewing the governor's "mad eccentricities," "consuming ambition," and "stupendous follies," and, with vengeance in mind, calling him "a melancholy object of pity and scorn."[79]

The most dangerous and only near fatal duel in which O. J. Wise participated resulted from the complicated political maneuvering attendant on the choice of a Democratic gubernatorial nominee and presumptive successor to his father. In early summer 1858, a united Virginia congressional delegation nominated Congressman John Letcher. Senator Hunter's support was crucial and freely given, in large measure because Hunter had genuinely feared Wise's efforts to overthrow him the previous winter and appreciated Letcher's loyalty. But in the carnival of opportunism that Virginia politics had become, loyalties were only ephemerally maintained. Letcher had once urged Wise to challenge Hunter's Senate seat. When this news broke later in the summer, Hunter reacted with characteristic equanimity, as if nothing untoward had ever occurred, advising Letcher that "they can't sow tares between you and me." In 1855, moreover, Letcher had refused to canvass for Wise during the gubernatorial contest.[80] His nomination, by a congressional delegation sharply at odds with Wise over Kansas, threatened the governor directly.

Scratching for an alternative, the *Enquirer* fell back on a westerner, Judge John Brockenbrough. At this juncture, and after revealing certain of his intentions in advance to Letcher, northwestern Virginia Congressman Sherrard Clemens schemed to derail Brockenbrough's candidacy. He visited the judge on his circuit in Clarksburg and secured from him an equivocal denial of interest in the nomination and then, without Brockenbrough's permission, published it to the world.[81] O. J. Wise deliberately insulted Clemens in the *Enquirer*, forcing him into a challenge. The duelists and their friends met early on a September morning at the Fairfield race track and fair grounds in Henrico County, north of Richmond. Three exchanges of fire only steeled their hatred and goaded their anger. On the fourth fire O. J. severely wounded Clemens. In April 1861, still smarting from young Wise's victory, Clemens on crutches led some of his friends out of the Virginia secession convention and later proclaimed his resistance to the Confederacy.[82]

The encounter at Fairfield must have reminded Henry of his own painful experience during and after the Graves-Cilley duel twenty years earlier. "I AM TRYING TO GUARD MY SON," he wrote a friend, "if they don't kill him he will take care of himself and me too."[83] Henry's fears were actually misplaced because his son's skill and reputation made it unlikely that the field of honor would ever claim him. What probably gnawed at Obie was the obvious political fact that no matter how many enemies of his father he assaulted, he was never able to silence unremitting criticism.

Public life thus took on the smell of a supremely dirty and dissatisfying business, particularly in view of Letcher's triumph some months later, that had to be transcended periodically, at least in fantasy, if it was to be endured. With his enemies triumphant and hunting his son's blood and with his own deceptions subject to public scrutiny, Wise tried to comprehend his suffering. Persecution and defeat were maddening and may well have threatened his mental stability. When reflecting, for example, on the unpredictability and inconsistencies of his politics, an abnormally large number of people described him as "mad," "crazy," or "insane."[84] Perhaps he might have appropriated the Christian example of suffering and sacrifice and allowed it to confer meaning on his own struggle, but it would be a perverted Christianity that informed his thoughts and ambitions and in the end denied their legitimacy, as he came close to acknowledging in a remarkable passage on suffering, written to William F. Samford at the height of his troubles in the fall of 1858: "*Suffering is part of God*! I take it then as a part of the Divinity which stirs within me, and then I may set my nerves *to bearing all*, and chloroform and electricity can't ease pain, like the worship of *suffering*. Is this sinful madness? Christianity run mad? Is it not rather 'balm in Gilead?' . . . It is good—it is good to say '*Weary and worn me*!' Suffer on, bear on, then, your old disorder, watch at the bedside of your child, and take on every care and labor. Every suffering is a precious gift of Heaven, if you will but recognize the angels." The Christian message emphasized self-sacrifice and a generosity of spirit that Henry A. Wise aspired to but typically failed to attain. Wise craved justification, transcendence, and freedom, but his ambitions were too deeply rooted in the love of fame, applause, and adulation. "What has this letter run to?" he added, "I sat down to write *politics*, full of worldly and it may be wicked thoughts, and here am I, a poor, unprofessing, sick and sore sinner, pouring out some drops of piety." They were only drops, however. The "wicked thoughts," the lies he knew politics required, the "caucuses" and "cliques" he condemned in this letter to Samford—all spun out their webs further to trap and tangle him. In the end, it cost him less than it did his state. When he closed the circle by advocating congressional protection for slavery in the territories, that act marked a remarkable hardening of his own attitudes. It also signaled, in some measure, the abandonment of liberal orthodoxy and the final collapse of Jeffersonian Virginia.[85]

The centerpiece of Wise's effort to return to the good graces of those Southerners repelled by his course over Lecompton was a book-length pamphlet entitled *Territorial Government and the Admission of New States into the Union*, which originally filled nearly thirty columns in an extra edition of the Richmond *Enquirer* of 30 April 1859. As a further indication of Wise's contempt for Letcher, its publication preceded the close of the gubernatorial canvass. Wise later had two thousand copies of the book printed at his own expense. Most of these he circulated among supporters and newspaper editors during the summer and fall of 1859. The book was addressed, in letter form, to William F. Samford, which immediately suggests the constituency Wise most wanted to reach. It remains, to this day, perhaps the most neglected (and most trenchant) major production by a principal Southern politician during the late 1850s.[86]

Wise described his book as a "treatise," which suggests that he meant it as a final and authoritative statement on the subject of constitutional power in the federal territories. The legal term also implies a thoroughly researched and carefully reasoned piece, in which Wise's skills as advocate would dominate. Like much of the other literature on these subjects, *Territorial Government* is a didactic effort to demonstrate the historicity of a set of abstract and controversial principles.

It is unclear whether Wise began the book at about the time of the debate in the Senate on 23 February 1859 in which both Jefferson Davis and Albert Gallatin Brown of Mississippi attacked Stephen A. Douglas and called for congressional protection of slavery in the territories. But early in March, and with a touch of sorrow, Wise advised a friend privately that he had no desire to assail Douglas, although to protect his position in the South he must assert Congress's power in the territories to protect slave property. By his stand on Lecompton, the governor admitted, "I was injured deeply in the prejudices of the South, whilst my true ally Mr. Douglas allowed the enemy to put him upon the opposite extreme error of *sovereignty* in Territorial Gov't."[87]

Between the Mississippians, who advocated positive presettlement protection, and Douglas, who favored nonintervention, the governor groped for middle ground. Even though his loyal Northern friend Fernando Wood implored him to refrain from taking a position on the issues dividing the Democratic party, he did so anyway. In advancing the doctrine of congressional obligation to intervene in territorial affairs whenever territorial laws or regulations threatened the viability of slavery, he thus came up with a variety of "pale" and negativistic slave code. To protect his consistency, the *Enquirer* pointed to the relevant passages in his carefully crafted letter of the previous fall to the Illinois Democracy. "I would not seem even to assail Judge Douglas," Wise remarked, suggesting that, in the end, he regarded his views as much closer to Douglas's than to those of his Mississippi critics.[88] The *Enquirer* also maintained its own two-faced reputation by rejecting a federal slave code, which it had previously advocated, and by embracing Wise's doctrine of insisting on a policy that would institute one in practice.

The primary argument in Wise's book was that territorial history from the commencement of the Constitution revealed the repeated intervention by Congress to protect personal rights and property, including slave property. As for contrary precedents, he dismissed the Northwest Ordinance of 1787 because its enactment antedated the Constitution. The Missouri Compromise presented no problems because of the *Dred Scott* decision. Wise's difficulty was that, for all his ability to detail the massive power Congress wielded over the territories historically (such as appointing officials and granting various entitlements), he never showed that Congress had intervened directly (in the Old Southwest, for example) to protect slavery. To be sure, settlement in the West proceeded during much of the century on the assumption that if predictable patterns of migration were maintained, a more or less equal division of the national domain between freedom and slavery would take place. In the territories settled by Southerners, however, Congress had permitted local custom to operate, precisely as Douglas continued to urge. Because Wise and other Southerners argued for a radical departure in national policy, it was essential for them to produce either an unanswerable case constitutionally or an unassailable set of precedents, or both. They produced neither. The most that Wise could show was that Congress had never prohibited slavery in the territories informally allotted to Southerners. This was a paltry achievement in what purported to be a legal treatise and not an essay on customary influences determining the settlement of the territories.[89]

Territorial Government proved the impossibility, for Wise, of constructing a constitutional argument that would solve the South's crisis. He may well have recognized this toward the end of his treatise, as we shall see. Certainly the politicians had failed the South. They had established a tradition of intervention, but one favoring the restriction of slavery, not its protection. He repeated a familiar litany about the usurpations leading to California's admission to the Union in 1850. He criticized the 1850 abolition of the slave trade in Washington, D.C. Indeed, he specified the compromise measures of 1850 as "in many respects, more obnoxious to constitutional objections, and to the rights and interests of slavery, than was the Missouri prohibition itself."[90] Again, he singled out the Badger amendment as having deprived the South of much of the presumptive advantage it would have gained from the Kansas-Nebraska Act and the *Dred Scott* decision. *Dred Scott*'s apparent assertion of a Southern right to the territories underlaid Wise's treatise throughout. But he could not surpass *Dred Scott* by establishing an independent constitutional tradition favoring the protection of slavery throughout all phases of territorial settlement. Indeed, the best sections of his book demonstrate, with a perverse brilliance, that many advantages of worth to the South had already been conceded. Ultimately, slavery appears as such a weak and rickety concern that extraordinary measures discriminatory in its favor are necessary to sustain it in the national domain.

"No positive code," according to Wise, "is required to establish" Congress's "power and duty to protect persons and property. The constitution itself dictates and enjoins both." But this assertion rested on the assumption that the Constitution recognized slaves as property. They are invariably acknowledged in that instrument as persons—precisely as Wise himself continued to describe them. Thus Wise's treatise, very much like Taney's *Dred Scott* opinion, assumed what it was necessary for him to prove. Perhaps *Territorial Government* is an indication of how impervious to rational analysis some matters had become by the late 1850s. But Wise himself could not avoid conceding that the Constitution recognized slaves as special sorts of persons, not simply as "*property in persons*."[91]

A final difficulty suggested that much of Wise's energy and scholarship had been wasted, although not all of it, because a remarkable degree of support developed for his candidacy after the publication of *Territorial Government*. Wise never pointed specifically to any territories, foreign or domestic, where slavery might require protection if his proposals were adopted. A year and a half later, he acknowledged the good press he had obtained in the North and admitted that much of the Southern press had dismissed his treatise as hopelessly abstract. He and the *Enquirer* occasionally alluded to the promise of slavery in a place like New Mexico, but it was far more typical of the governor's personal organ to trivialize the practical significance of his own doctrine. The *Enquirer*, for example, later repudiated the *Charleston Mercury*'s suggestion that the South held surplus population sufficient to engage in a race for the territories. The greater mobility of the Yankees also doomed all such efforts. Yet in the hope of some unforeseen eventuality and to maintain honor, Southerners must demand protection.[92]

A grim and defiant mood pervades the concluding passages of Wise's treatise. Perhaps no argument could abate the unholy ambitions of "mere numbers" and "brute force." Yet he had made his best case. With its aid, those who agreed with him could now rest confident in never having "yielded the claim of right." Here he may well have desired to appropriate Calhoun's legacy. Southerners "must put in continued claim for justice and equality; and, then, when they have been denied both, and been oppressed and insulted beyond sufferance, they may appeal with effect to the moral sense of mankind to justify revolution." Foolish Southern extremists were now an intolerable luxury because they weakened the moral resolve that alone would permit the South to affirm and achieve its destiny in a hostile world.

What was this destiny? Here Wise struggled more intensively than ever to justify his region and himself. The problem of origins bothered him less, although it still seemed elusive in the end. "Our holding and governing our slaves in the United States now, don't depend upon the right or wrong of their original acquisition, but upon existing relations—upon the lapse of time, upon the laws of centuries, upon the habitudes of society, upon every thing which can perfect a title to anything." He excluded, of course, the consent of those to whom title was claimed.[93]

Tradition commanded his personal loyalty, he stated as unequivocally as possible. "I am north of 36 deg. 30 min. north latitude, and am a slaveholder myself, by inheritance and by purchase; and I would gladly own a great many more than I do if I were able." But Wise remained, as always, an environmentalist in predicting slavery's future, though for the first time publicly he now seemed to accept it north of the Missouri Compromise line—even in Virginia, as he and so many other Virginians had always denied. Then, also for the first time, he sketched a vision of a national economy in which slavery remained a permanent and beneficent presence—one that aided in the perpetual preservation of the Union.

> Frost and sun say how near boreas the Africans, and how near the tropics the white men may labor in the fields of the respective northern and southern climes; and all nature says that . . . wheat, and corn, and tobacco, and cotton, and rice, and sugar, in a plantation interest of the sunny fields of the South shall have, and must have, the African operatives fitted for the climate, and . . . a superior race must master and govern and guide and provide for them; and . . . wheat, and corn, and grass, and potatoes, and cattle, in a farming interest adjacent to commerce and manufactures and mechanics art, must in the regions of cold have the superior race to be operatives and artizans there, to be masters of themselves, and the equals of masters anywhere, and to be benefitted by the labors of the slaves, in the exchange of products, as the masters of slaves are in the productions themselves. This is all as harmonious as heat and cold, if God alone be acknowledged the supreme providence, and if his work and law be not obstructed and opposed by the folly of man.[94]

Where did Virginia fit into this scheme? Wise did not say. Having affirmed his personal commitment to slavery north of the Missouri Compromise line only three paragraphs earlier, he now refused to confirm it. All his life he had believed that one day Virginia would be free. Now he did not know.

"This nation wants reverence more than anything else to preserve its peace and prosperity," Wise wrote in the concluding section of *Territorial Government*. His personal offensive in behalf of decency, slavery, and the presidency embraced several components. Not every enemy was a Republican. The presence and potential influence of the Mormon experiment in Utah offered further evidence of the nation's degeneracy. By establishing "polygamy and the prostitution of women," these "Satyrs of lust" would "destroy the sacredness of Christian marriage, so necessary to identify offspring in a Republic founded on private virtue and the holy family relations and ties." In Wise's thinking, similar influences had somehow spawned both the Mormon and Republican enterprises.[95]

When he shifted his attention from tendency to fact, Wise often focused, as did many other Southern politicians, on Republican successes in enacting personal liberty statutes that nullified the Fugitive Slave Act of 1850. He complained bitterly about escaping slaves and rejected financial indemnities for masters as a solution. "The *states* are not answerable for the runaways," he wrote. "But retaliation for 'unfriendly legislation,' for which states are responsible, would be just, but how to enact it would be the rub, without putting yourself in the wrong."[96]

Probably it was Wise's sensitivity to the threats represented by Northern personal liberty laws that inspired his interest in the doctrine of interstate comity. Southern rights might everywhere appear in jeopardy, Wise suggested, but the tremendous victory gained in *Dred Scott* opened the way for a powerful counterattack. Masters historically had sojourned in the North, accompanied by their personal chattels. They had, in other words, lived for brief periods outside the South precisely as they lived within it—and Northern authorities had thus granted comity, or temporary recognition, to the law of slavery. But in recent years hostile Northern legislation, adverse court decisions, and threats of violence had compromised masters' right to travel with slaves north of the Mason-Dixon line. A splendid opportunity, however, now presented itself for the reassertion of what Wise and others regarded as a constitutional right.

In 1852 the Lemmon family of Virginia visited New York City with eight slaves. Before they could embark for New Orleans, their final destination, the Lemmons were served with a writ of habeas corpus. Within a week New York courts had freed the slaves on grounds that an 1841 state law automatically liberated all bondsmen, except fugitives, who touched New York soil.[97] Virginia authorities, Wise foremost among them, sponsored an appeal of this decision that gradually worked its way through the New York court system during the 1850s. After the rendering of *Dred Scott* in 1857, Wise wrote Reverdy Johnson of Maryland—one of the victorious counsels in the case—and offered to make him counsel, along with James Lyons and Virginia's attorney general should the Lemmon case reach the Supreme Court. In April 1860, after John Letcher had succeeded Wise as governor, the New York Supreme Court predictably rendered judgment against the Lemmons and in favor of the slaves. Although Johnson and the New York attorney who acted for the Lemmons both advised Letcher of their interest in appealing the decision to the Supreme Court, Virginia's governor mysteriously refused to act.[98]

Had he retained power, Wise might well have acted differently. But at no point—and particularly in *Territorial Government*, his most extreme pro-Southern statement of the decade—did Wise contemplate turning masters' traditional right of transit into a scheme to nationalize slavery judicially. "To defend our slave property at home, on the borders of the free states," he wrote, "requires all the aid we can obtain by sympathy from within and without; and we need especially that our friends in the south shall do nothing to prejudice the cause of African bondage, and of its defenses as it exists in the United States, in the minds of any."[99] As their messages to the General Assembly suggest, Virginia governors during the 1850s were far more concerned about recapturing fugitives or preventing their departure than about assuring visiting privileges in the North for themselves and their bondsmen. Wise wanted protection for transient rights but not at the expense of destroying whatever credibility the Northern wing of the Democratic party still possessed. Misbegotten extremism in this area would cost the South as much—he had belatedly realized—as the stupid and dangerous movement to reopen the African slave trade.[100]

Despite Wise's pro-Southern reading of the Constitution, it seems remarkable that so many endorsements from the Northern press followed the publication of *Territorial Government*. Strong support appeared in the Philadelphia and New York City newspapers, as well as a scattering of endorsements from New Hampshire west to Indiana. The *New York Times*, for example, suggested that *Territorial Government* might make Wise president.[101] These endorsements indicate that significant elements of the Northern Democracy retained only a skeleton organization dependent entirely on federal patronage. The victims and sometimes willing accomplices in the demise of their own party may have looked upon Wise as their only hope. This may well have been true despite the campaign Wise launched—in a style reminiscent of Calhoun's—to discredit the current scheme of representation in the Democratic National Convention because it left too much power in the hands of Republican-dominated Northern states. Of all the Southern candidates, he alone sparked enthusiasm among the predominantly Catholic immigrants who made up the bulk of the Democracy's remaining urban strength in the North. In addressing their leaders, he claimed an equal priority for the protection of slave property and for the rights of naturalized citizens. Such was their conservatism that, he may well have suspected, little chance existed of their ever fighting the South. That they—or anyone else in the North—could have taken his candidacy seriously suggests how deep the national mood of sentimentalism and nostalgia had reached, how fondly people hoped for a settlement of the crisis, and how real were the possibilities of a national reconciliation at the expense of the lower orders.[102]

William F. Samford trumpeted Wise's candidacy in the pages of his *Auburn Signal*. Elsewhere in the Deep South, and even in Virginia, reaction was decidedly mixed. The *Enquirer* gave scant attention to the adverse reaction in western Virginia, where Whig and Republican minorities had for some time rejected anything that smacked of protectionism for slavery. Even the Democratic press there reacted adversely to *Territorial Government*. These editors did not so much fear the protection of slavery in the territories as efforts to strengthen and sustain the institution in their own region. Another open fissure thus appeared in the Virginia consensus to which Wise had dedicated so much of his public life.[103]

Locally, *Territorial Government* inspired accusations of inconsistency and bitingly hostile reviews of Wise's career. Having already chastised Ridgway of the *Richmond Whig*, Obadiah Jennings Wise concentrated on the staff of Hunter's organ, the *Examiner*. This journal pronounced Wise's doctrine of intervention in territorial affairs in order to protect slavery a "barren abstraction"—conveniently neglecting to recall that Senator Hunter's friends had supported a nearly identical policy at the Democratic National Convention in 1856.[104] Obie exposed Patrick Henry Aylett—a Richmond lawyer and now one of the *Examiner*'s coeditors—as the author of several offensive articles and convincingly demonstrated that his treachery to Governor Wise dated from 1854. A challenge followed. The principals and their associates headed for North Carolina, evaded two policemen lurking in women's clothing near Danville, Virginia, and used assumed names. After all this effort, young Wise fired both his shots into the air, Aylett proved himself a miserable marksman, and everyone went home. Obie declined a reconciliation and announced himself satisfied if henceforth they should meet as "perfect strangers." In response to this latest crisis, the governor wrote mournfully to Mayor Wood in New York City, acknowledging how depressed and mystified he was by all the personal strife around him and affirming his desire only to "love and serve" mankind.[105]

Wise could never leave well enough alone. No politician in America wrote more for public consumption in the late 1850s. He tinkered unendingly with his arguments—itself an indication of his uncertainty about them. He defied the traditions that had mythologized the manipulative and horse-trading skills of Yankee politicos and continued his meddling in New York politics until humiliatingly exposed in the summer of 1859. Far from promising a redemption, his antics fulfilled the prophecies of his enemies that he must inevitably victimize himself. They also confirmed the prejudices of those then and since who affirmed Virginia's decline, as evidenced by her failure to produce great men.

In mid-July 1859, Wise wrote a private letter to Bernard Donnelly of Staten Island, New York. Its purpose was to convince Mayor Wood's opponents in the state's Democratic organization that Wise was independent of his influence and potentially an appropriate candidate around whom conservatives might rally at the Charleston Convention some nine months in the future. Either a fool or a knave, Donnelly showed the letter to a few cunning politicians in Albany, then coyly left the room while they took copies. A few days later the *New York Herald* bought one for twenty dollars and gave all the world the chance to inspect the governor's confidential correspondence. People read his gratuitous advice that if unable to control the state, New York's conservatives should "organize by districts, and either whip the enemy or send two delegations" to Charleston. He then wrote of Buchanan's shadow candidacy and the impossibility of the South's accepting Douglas's platform of nonintervention. Who, then, was left? "If [Douglas] runs as an independent candidate, and Seward runs, and I am nominated at Charleston, I can beat them both! Or, if squatter sovereignty is a plank of the platform at Charleston, and Douglas is nominated, the South will run an independent candidate on protection principles, and run the election into the House. Where, then, would Mr. Douglas be? The lowest candidate on the list. If I have the popular strength you suppose, it will itself fix the nomination. Get that and I am confident of success."[106]

The publication produced a festival of self-righteousness, although many people were truly dumbfounded. At first, Mayor Wood thought the letter a forgery; he reportedly telegraphed Wise begging him to deny authorship.[107] Nothing appeared in the columns of the *Richmond Examiner* for several days. Then an unsigned communication reviewed the letter in terms less harsh than might have been expected. A challenge quickly ensued, however, when Obadiah Jennings Wise accused one of the coeditors of the *Examiner* of cowardice for refusing editorial comment. Wise and

William Old, along with their retinues, left Richmond a few days later under assumed names. The duel took place in Maryland near the District of Columbia. Old's eyesight was notoriously poor. Despite obtaining a position with the sun at his back, he failed in two attempts to hit Obie. Young Wise, by this time wary of adverse political fallout, missed twice before permitting an adjudication.[108]

If Wise felt any of the vilification and abuse heaped upon him and Virginia politicians generally after the publication of the Donnelly letter, he never showed it. "For myself," he wrote Wood, "I have treated the publication and all its incidents with sovereign contempt and loathing." "Their own dark lantern revealed the assassins," he advised another correspondent, "and the Donnelly letter will prove a sharp dagger to the demons themselves who intended to use it upon their intended sleeping victim."[109] Although the letter took strong Southern ground before a Northern audience, and despite the continuing fascination Wise evoked from the public, the momentum of his candidacy dissipated. The *Enquirer* grew defensive; fewer endorsements of Wise appeared in its pages. When Douglas's long article in vindication of his territorial doctrines appeared in the September 1859 issue of *Harper's Magazine*, Obadiah Jennings—largely unaided by the usual corps of guest columnists—exhausted his every epithet in replying to it. He failed to secure space in *Harper's* for a response and then unabashedly branded Douglas's candidacy shameless because he now propagated his views in book form![110] The governor had recently proclaimed an interest in loving and serving mankind, but his anger and frustration increasingly controlled him. Just when he had wrenched himself into believing them, his values would be shivered to their foundations by the appearance at Harpers Ferry of another violent man.

Henry A. Wise (c. 1830), attributed to John Gadsby Chapman, by permission of the Executive Mansion of Virginia, gift of Mrs. James Garnett

Portrait of Henry A. Wise (c. 1840), by Sarah Miriam Peale, courtesy of the Virginia Museum

Henry A. Wise (c. 1855), courtesy of the Virginia Historical Society

Henry A. Wise (c. 1865), by John A. Elder, courtesy of the Virginia State Library

Henry A. Wise (c. 1867), photograph courtesy of the South Carolina Historical Society

Andrew Jackson (1870), engraving by Johnson, Wilson, and Co., after a painting by Alonzo Chappell, courtesy of the Virginia State Library

John Tyler (1841), portrait by William Hart, courtesy of the Virginia State Library

James Buchanan (1892), by Eliphalet Frazier Andrews, after a portrait by G. P. A. Healy

Muscoe R. H. Garnett (c. 1858), photograph courtesy of the Virginia Historical Society

John Minor Botts (1847), engraving by Thomas Doney, courtesy of the Virginia Historical Society

Robert M. T. Hunter (c. 1860), portrait by G. P. A. Nealy, courtesy of the Virginia Historical Society

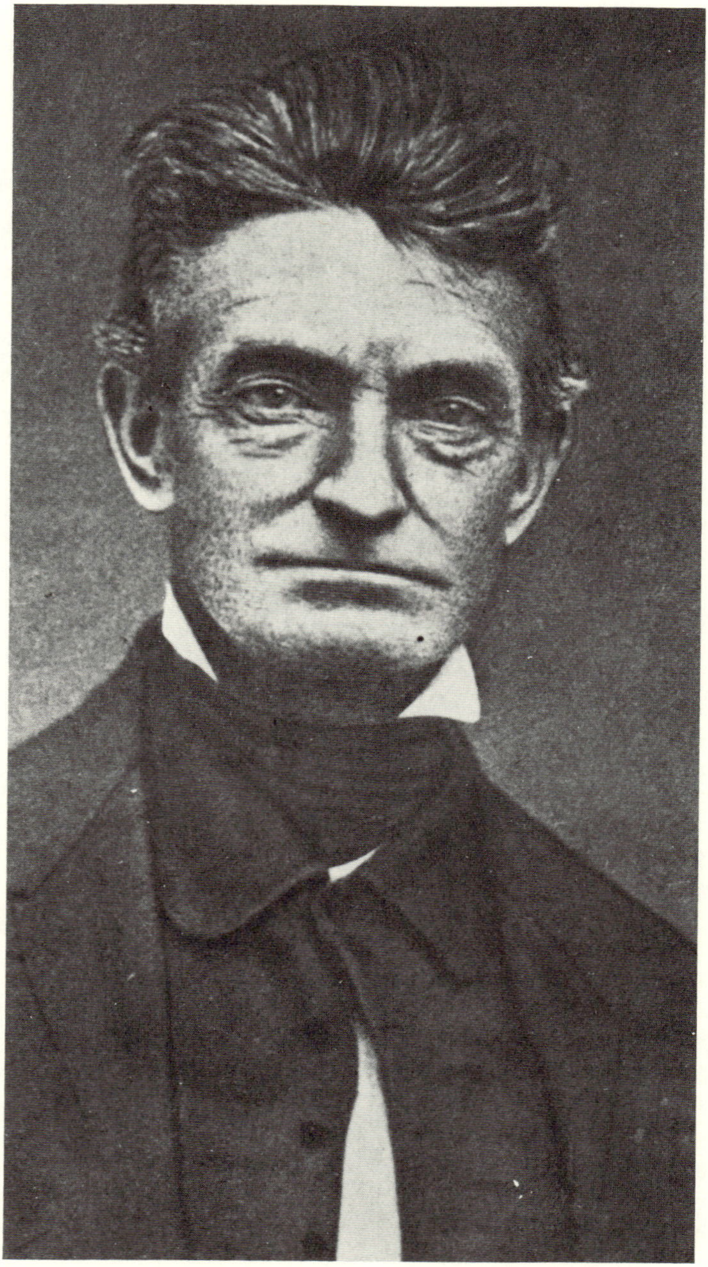

John Brown (c. 1857), photograph courtesy of the Kansas State Historical Society

Chapter 11

Two Men at Harpers Ferry

No event in Henry A. Wise's life commands the significance of Harpers Ferry. With the exception of Andrew Jackson, no one he ever met exercised greater influence or illuminated his own fond hopes and desires more clearly than John Brown. For many historians, Wise's name and reputation intersect with the historical record and take on meaning exclusively from his encounter with Brown. Allegedly irreconcilable enemies met at Harpers Ferry—peerless representatives, as many believed, of civilizations fated to claw away mercilessly at one another.

One of the most remarkable aspects of the Harpers Ferry incident, however, is that neither Brown nor Wise was altogether comfortable with his role, which may explain why they admired and respected each other, even though in the end one man hanged the other. Instead of behaving like a fully committed revolutionary, confident in his righteousness and impervious to the sufferings his actions produced, Brown at Harpers Ferry experienced anxieties about the morality of his action. His ambivalences fatally inhibited him from extricating himself and his followers from the Ferry before their position grew untenable. The Virginia governor, though regarded by many as a fiery proslavery extremist, harbored real doubts about the propriety of owning slaves, had acted on these feelings in the past, and genuinely admired Brown's moral courage. Wise's encounter with Brown called his own values into question, forced him however briefly to reconsider them, and gave him a perspective on Harpers Ferry that historians have largely ignored. Wise's perspective is valuable in addressing the issues of Brown's rationality and the very real though slim chance his movement had for success. It may also aid in focusing on a number of issues obscured to date by the contrasting political and ethical sensibilities of historians, who seem unable to resist judgments about the rightness or wrongness of Brown's actions.

The spectacle of a seemingly self-possessed revolutionary who avowed the destruction of an entire social system as the only rational choice available to America riveted Wise's attention and accounts for the inability of contemporaries and historians to avoid or forget him. But perhaps it is time to transcend the accusatory historiography of conservatives, the heroic literature of radicals, and the vague, lukewarm pieties of liberals who seek a vicarious identification with Brown but generally abhor the use of violence for any purpose. If one figuratively breaks these molds, a reexamination of the Harpers Ferry incident might disclose several interesting issues, such as the preoccupations of both Brown and Wise with the nonslaveholding whites. Moreover, an elimination of narrow political bias would allow an effort to address directly questions about the motivations influencing both Wise and Brown. One wonders, for example, what connection there is between Brown as an irresponsible Kansas fanatic and as an apparently selfless Virginia revolutionary. One of the crucial problems in the biographical literature on Brown, though ignored by most historians, is what if any effect the Kansas murders at Pottowatomie Creek in 1856 may have had on his idealistic but bungled effort at Harpers Ferry in 1859.[1] Should the discussion prove persuasive enough on these contested points, it might be appropriate to hazard a comment on the risks undertaken by anyone dedicating his life to revolutionary violence.

The governor acted in no self-serving or vengeful spirit during his interviews with Brown. In fact, Wise rather liked and admired him. Ralph Waldo Emerson noticed this and wrote: "High courage, or a perfect will superior to all events, makes a bond of union between two enemies. Inasmuch as Governor Wise is a superior man, he distinguished John Brown. As they confer, they understood each other swiftly, each respects the other; if opportunity allowed, they would prefer each other's society and desert the rest; enemies would become affectionate."[2] Following their first encounter after Brown's capture on 18 October 1859, they expressed respect for each other. In the true cockfighting style of the gentry class, Wise pronounced Brown "the gamest man I ever saw."[3] He went further: "He is a bundle of the best nerves I ever saw cut and thrust and bleeding and in bonds. . . . He is cool, collected and indomitable . . . and he inspired me with great trust in his integrity as a man of truth. He is a fanatic, vain and garrulous, but firm, truthful and intelligent."[4]

Both men were of the same generation (Brown was three years Wise's senior but preferred to think of himself as much older, in conformity with the patriarchal and prophetic identity he had established in the 1850s), and the two even looked vaguely alike, except for Brown's recently grown beard. Each was slightly above medium height, wiry and angular in feature, and wore his hair long. Both spoke well, exhibited nervous dispositions, and dressed shabbily (or rustically, in Brown's case) for effect. Both were extraordinarily vain, cranky at times, and accustomed to command. What Wise recognized of himself in Brown (and probably vice versa) and what he saw in Brown's qualities that he desired to emulate help to account for his considerable respect for his foe (which the latter reciprocated in an interview shortly before his death).[5]

More concretely, however, Wise respected Brown because he believed him a reasonable man whose attempted insurrection made some sense. Brown planned to use the arms captured from the federal arsenal to supply recruits as he advanced southward to the Appalachians. He expected to "place the slaves in a condition to defend their liberties" within the slave states. His goal, in other words, was freedom for the slaves obtainable by any means he and they should deem necessary; white Southerners, as Willie Lee Rose suggests, properly regarded his schemes as direct (though not indiscriminate because Brown's orders made it plain that he intended to spare the cooperative) encouragement of insurrectionary violence. He denied before his death any intentions of merely running off with some fugitives, although he admitted conveying that impression in his celebrated courtroom speech, shortly before Judge Richard Parker pronounced sentence. But "taken wholly by surprise" and "in the hurry of the moment," he forgot much of what "I had before intended to say, and did not consider the full bearing of what I then said."[6]

The potential of a full-scale insurrection was never far from the minds of thoughtful Southerners, even though they suppressed the notion and constantly reassured themselves of its impossibility. The rise of the free-soil movement and the growth of the Republican party again thrust the issue close to the center of Southern consciousness. Insurrections were not fairy tales for Wise. In his youth, and not very far from his home in Accomac County, the slave Nat Turner had inspired a bloody uprising in 1831. So threatened was Virginia by a heritage of economic decay, abolitionists within her borders, and the intensity of antislavery criticism that during his gubernatorial campaign several years earlier Wise had experienced premonitions of a Northern assault on the Old Dominion, which he promised to repel.[7]

Nor could Wise have thought Brown a fool for making his move where he did. Brown chose to assault a portion of Virginia where slavery was in retreat. Besides the loyal Virginians in these areas, scattered communities of Northern free-soil colonists and a few antislavery Quakers also lived there. The slave population increased in only five counties along Virginia's northern and western borders during the 1850s. The seven-county area surrounding Harpers Ferry reflected this trend. Between 1850 and 1860, the slave population declined by 10 percent while that of whites increased by 6 percent. Wise knew of this situation and may have believed that an alleged fanatic and his twenty-one followers had come reasonably close to threatening a social system in jeopardy. In a remarkable confession, he suggested that the slaves rejected Brown because they were held by their own sufferance in the Harpers Ferry area and could run off to Pennsylvania "easier than liberators can come to their emancipation."[8]

One wonders, however, about Brown's decision to begin his insurrection in an area of low slave density. Although extraordinarily egotistical, he was not given to random behavior. He had reflected on and discussed an attack on slavery for many years. He had carefully examined population statistics in the slave states on a county-by-county basis and had read the Republican and abolitionist literature of the day, which during the 1850s abounded with discussions of slavery's retreat from the border states. Brown probably knew of the local situation.[9] He chose to attack Harpers Ferry because he wanted the weapons at the arsenal and believed its location would guarantee an almost unmolested retreat into the mountains.[10] Brown also expected more support than the slaves might provide, although he probably counted on the discontent of the local slave population (prompted by the prospect of removal to the Deep South), despite its decreasing numbers. One of the five blacks in his company, Dangerfield Newby, had a wife and children in bondage near Harpers Ferry who were scheduled for sale.[11]

So confident was Brown of his ultimate triumph, and so heedless of immediate difficulties, that he refused to tell the slaves in advance about his plans. But this does not mean that they remained ignorant of his movements. One of Brown's principal lieutenants, John E. Cook, resided in Harpers Ferry throughout the summer of 1859.[12] His responsibility was to gather intelligence; in various poses, he traveled widely in the area and visited a number of farmers and planters. At least a few slaves knew about the impending operation.[13] Tales of Cook's operations, as well as solid evidence that Brown himself had visited Harpers Ferry on more than one occasion during the summer of 1859, soon became matters of public discussion. This knowledge might have further unsettled Wise as well as confirmed to him that Brown's scheme was at least remotely sensible.

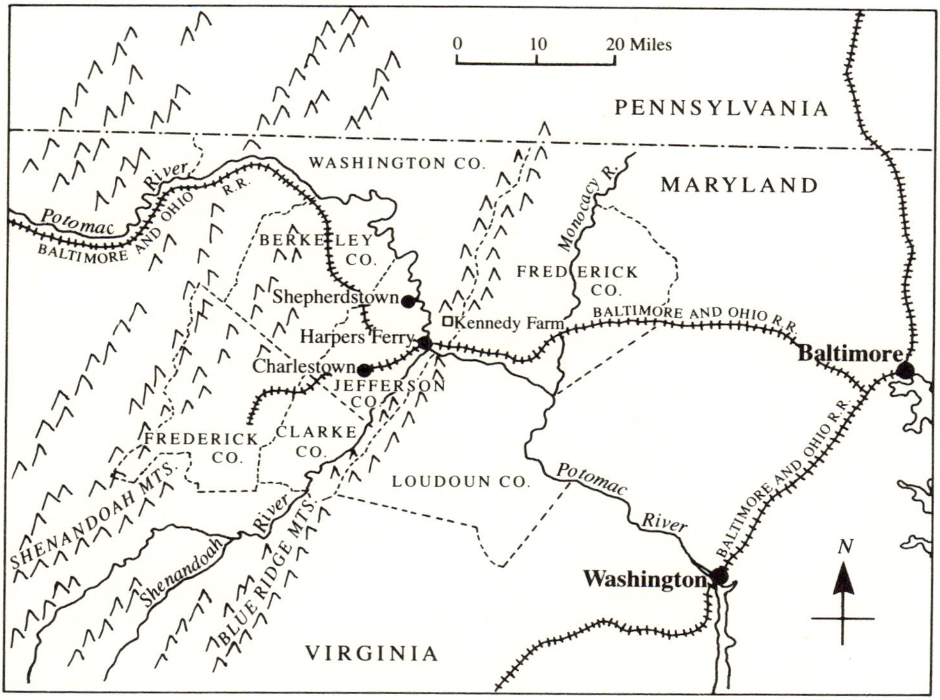

Harpers Ferry Region, 1859

Source: Stephen B. Oates, *To Purge This Land with Blood: A Biography of John Brown* (New York: Harper & Row, 1970), p. 277.

Having explored certain of Brown's intentions, it remains to comprehend a final body of evidence relating to his attack on the federal arsenal. It does not appear that he wanted to use the weapons there to supply the slaves. Brown did not believe that slaves possessed sufficient competence to use firearms effectively. He regarded the pikes he brought to the Ferry "as . . . cheap but effectual weapon[s] to place in the [hands] of entirely unskillful & unpracticed men."[14] He believed also that only with white leadership could the slaves successfully revolt.[15] Perhaps he intended to arm them with guns in the Appalachians, but the fact remains that in Harpers Ferry the slaves who joined him were, with only one exception, supplied exclusively with pikes.[16] "I would have armed the . . . blacks with the spears," he said in an interview shortly after his capture, "they not being sufficiently familiar with the other arms."[17] But he also seems to have feared the prospect of blacks with guns in their hands.[18] It was impossible to predict what they might do or whose leadership they might follow.

None of the many historians of Harpers Ferry has fully comprehended the significance of this point. Brown's conservative critics generally have been so mesmerized by the enormity of a slave insurrection that it has escaped them. Historians of more progressive political sympathies (such as Stephen B. Oates and Benjamin Quarles) have lost sight of its significance in deference to Brown's allegedly admirable radicalism. Surely at least a few slaves would have been discouraged at the thought of defending themselves only with pikes. Perhaps Abraham Lincoln was wiser than he knew when he remarked that Brown's plan was "so absurd that the slaves, with all their ignorance, saw plainly enough it could not succeed."[19]

What, finally, was Brown's aim in capturing the arsenal? He wished to strike terror into Virginians, of course, and to prepare the way for achieving other objectives outlined above. It seems a plausible conclusion, however, that he wanted the guns for the whites—the nonslaveholding whites—whom he expected to recruit.

Wise apparently did not realize that Brown expected to arm only whites with his captured weapons. He did believe, however, that the spears were intended exclusively for slaves. He also took pains to point out in Richmond, after returning from Harpers Ferry, that there were limits to Brown's willingness to trust slaves; the insurrection was to be led by white commanders.[20] Wise also sensed the significance of Brown's expectations of support from the nonslaveholding whites. It seems likely that an appreciation of these two factors centrally affected his response to Brown and helped convince him that Brown was a man of judgment as well as courage. Wise probably believed that Brown shared his view of an open-ended though deeply flawed and practically retarded potential for black development, which might someday be overcome. More important, the possible disaffection of the yeomen preoccupied him perennially. Brown admitted, in an interview following his capture during which Wise was present, that he hoped to overthrow the institution "with the aid or connivance of nonslaveholding whites."[21]

But why should this statement have either enhanced Wise's opinion of Brown or stimulated his fretfulness and anxiety? Because the people of Harpers Ferry, including many Northern-born workingmen, appeared either mesmerized with fright or uninterested in repelling the invaders. From 11:00 P.M. on 16 October, when Brown first appeared in town, until noon on the following day he confronted only desultory firing from local inhabitants. Wise found it difficult to believe and embarrassing to learn that few of his people were as heroic as the small group that overpowered them. By midafternoon on 17 October, Brown's men were surrounded and cut off by militia sent from Charlestown, Martinsburg, and Shepardstown in Virginia and from Baltimore and Frederick in Maryland. These troops, mostly nonslaveholders, showed some skill when first engaged at about midday but later their discipline collapsed. A substantial proportion of the militia (along with many of the townspeople) had become a disorganized, drunken, and cowering mob by the time that Colonel Robert E. Lee and the United States Marines captured Brown on Tuesday, 18 October.[22] Wise was appalled that Virginia troops had refused the honor of making the final assault. In a dramatic and inflammatory statement a few days later, he declared that he would have given his right arm "up to its shoulder" had Brown been captured by Virginians.[23]

Wise overstated the inefficiency and apprehension of the Harpers Ferry townspeople, perhaps an indication of his fear regarding the alleged disloyalty of those on Virginia's frontier. Some caution could have been expected from the citizens, of course, because Brown had captured a number of their friends during the first night of his invasion. Moreover, when they awoke the next morning the locals found themselves without many guns, although at midday they began firing irregularly with some weapons from a small cache established a few weeks earlier on the town heights because of a flood threat.[24] Their fire, which began shortly before noon (or about one hour before the first militia units arrived) killed or wounded several of Brown's associates and arguably helped to hem in his men and cut off their retreat,[25] although Brown's own mysterious indecisiveness probably contributed more to his refusal to evacuate Harpers Ferry.[26] The militia units only added to the sporadic and occasionally deadly fire that vexed and distracted Brown and his associates. They were also commanded efficiently enough to occupy, upon first arriving in the vicinity, the bridges over both the Potomac and Shenandoah rivers which afforded Brown his only potential means of escape. And, as Wise later admitted, the inadequate numbers and poor quality of the weapons available to the militia limited their effectiveness.[27] But evidence of extenuating circumstances does not ultimately undermine Wise's twin assertions: first, that a sizable number of Harpers Ferry townspeople appeared either sheepish and paralyzed or simply idled while the invaders proceeded with their work, and second, that the militia units declined to press the attack on Brown, even when presented with opportunities after several of his hostages had escaped. The disorderly and unreliable behavior of the militia and the carnival atmosphere that prevailed in some units evidently neutralized in Wise's thinking what was perhaps the border frontier's most impressive accomplishment during this crisis—the concentration of several hundred militiamen in Harpers Ferry within eighteen hours after Brown began his movement. Wise was not satisfied, however; there is, in my judgment, enough evidence to confirm his fears.

Wise's anxiety manifested itself repeatedly during the seven weeks between Brown's capture and execution. At a cost of some $250,000, he marched and countermarched thousands of troops around Harpers Ferry. This martial display confirmed abolitionist speculations about slavery's weakness, humiliated many thinking Southerners, and infuriated the extremists.[28] Wise superseded local militia commanders with pliable officers, eventually placing all forces assigned to guard duty in the area under the authority of Major General William B. Taliaferro, a Mexican War veteran and an old friend from Gloucester County. He demanded additional protection for the arsenal from President Buchanan. Just before Brown's execution, Wise again induced Buchanan to order Colonel Lee and 264 artillerists to the area.[29] As hundreds upon hundreds of letters began to pour in alternately urging clemency for Brown and threatening death and destruction for both Virginia and himself, Wise seemed obsessed with the condition of northwestern Virginia. "Information from every quarter leads to the conviction that there is an organized plan to harass our whole slave-border at every point," he advised Andrew Hunter, the chief prosecutor he appointed to try the cases of John Brown and his men: "*Day* is the *very* time to commit arson with the best chance agt. detection. No light shines, no smoke shows in daylight before the flame is off. . . . The rascal too escapes best by day; he sees best whether he is not seen, and best how to avoid persons pursuing. I tell you those Devils are trained in all the Indian arts of predatory war. They come, *one* by *one*, *two* by *two*, in *open* day, and make you stare that the thing be *attempted* as it was *done*."[30]

On 25 November, shortly after having arrived in Harpers Ferry to supervise final preparations for Brown's execution, Wise advised Buchanan that he had information "specific enough to be reliable, which convinced him that an attempt will be made to rescue the prisoners and if that fails, then to seize citizens of this State as hostages and victims in case of execution."[31]

Did Wise in fact possess reliable information? Was he engaged in an egomaniacal effort to improve his presidential chances? Had he, as several historians have all but concluded, lost control of his faculties? Several factors tend to confirm the accuracy of his perceptions and the reasonableness of his responses. First, we have only to examine the initial and wildly exaggerated reports of Brown's appearance at Harpers Ferry to understand the basis for the governor's fears and to see that others shared them. Most of the early telegraphic dispatches and newspaper reports talked of a slave uprising and gave out greatly inflated numbers. But many of the early reports suggested that the white mechanics at the Ferry were about to revolt because of wage difficulties. Certain contemporaries, such as J. W. Garrett, president of the Baltimore and Ohio Railroad, believed that slaves and white workingmen had allied themselves to capture the arsenal. In other words, some observers were predisposed to believe that the supposed uprising at Harpers Ferry was grounded in class interests.[32] Wise had access during the trials of Brown and his fellow insurgents to a "confession" prepared by John E. Cook. This document, in the language of Richard J. Hinton, suggests that "the laborers on the canal about the Ferry, and, indeed, generally the non-slaveholding white workmen of the neighborhood, took very little part in the fighting, and, while alarmed at tumult, were evidently somewhat disposed to feel kindly to the liberators . . . [Cook] was given coffee and food, as well as warned of the location of armed men and the danger of capture as he ran."[33] On 6 November Wise advised Andrew Hunter that a "secret agent" of the "State Executive" would soon visit Harpers Ferry, both "to trace the threads" of the "conspiracy into other states" and to "try to find out who is implicated in the locality about vou."[34] Again, in his lengthy and important letter to Hunter on 16 November, Wise directed him to "Watch Harper's Ferry people. Watch, I say and I *thought* watch when there."[35] It may be, therefore, that the governor intended that the troops stationed near Harpers Ferry would assist in controlling the citizens, as well as offering them protection and reassurance. He may also have recommended to the superintendent of the arsenal that detectives investigate the politics of his employees, which was done shortly after Brown's capture.[36] Wise's persistent sensitivity to any sign of disloyalty among the nonslaveholders surfaced when he ordered a search of a farm not far from Harpers Ferry belonging to Virginia abolitionist John C. Underwood, whom he feared would distribute a shipment of Hinton R. Helper's *Impending Crisis* that recently had been sent to him from Washington, D.C.[37] Wise's suspicions also led him to be mindful of the composition of the Old Dominion's militia when drawing up his final orders for Brown's execution. "Let no crowd be near enough to the prisoner to hear any speech he may attempt," he instructed General Taliaferro.[38] The apparent disloyalty of some of the local people along with a number of odd coincidences and information supplied by ordinarily steady individuals convinced Wise that the threat to Virginia's security was genuine.

Those historians who dismiss Wise's fulminations as hysterical also admit that Brown's followers were in fact intent on arranging a rescue. George Hoyt, one of the lawyers sent south to defend Brown and his fellow prisoners, proclaimed support for a conspiracy aimed at freeing them.[39] Brown refused to take part in any such conspiracy, but after his execution two of his associates with outside help nearly pulled off a successful jailbreak. Considerable anxiety existed along the Virginia border. But this reaction made sense. Even well-informed and intelligent observers grew jittery as nameless incendiaries and marauders burned barns and haystacks and occasionally shot up the houses of the local gentry.[40] Arsonists destroyed much of the worldly possessions of three jurymen who had convicted John Brown—a "doubtless accidental" development, according to Oswald G. Villard,[41] though Wise and Andrew Hunter could not have agreed. One of the western Virginia militiamen assigned to patrol duty advised a correspondent—at just the time when Wise indicated that he possessed reliable information about a planned rescue attempt—that unknown assailants had fired on his company's sentinels within two miles of Brown's jail cell in Charlestown. "There is no doubt," he continued, "but that spies and small detachments of men are prowling in the neighborhood, and will pick off our sentries if they can."[42]

The marauders have proven impossible to identify, although the prevailing view among both historians and contemporaries is that they were free blacks and slaves.[43] Wise had no way of knowing whether the slaves wanted revenge, or whether Northern intruders caused all the ruckus. Holding responsibility for protecting Virginia's shaky frontier and guarding Brown, he preferred to err on the side of excess. His later excuse for the martial extravaganza—that he wanted to prepare Virginia's troops for war and to inure them to camp life[44]—probably reflects an effort to respond to critics who charged that Wise incurred needless expense and shamed the slaveholders by responding to nonexistent threats.

Having suggested why Wise acted as he did during and after the attempted insurrection, and having also reflected on some problems peculiar to Brown's biography, one must ask why the governor chose to hang his antagonist, despite so many professions of respect. As a relatively decent man, whose personal history suggested a critical attitude toward slavery, Wise may not have been altogether anxious for an execution. He might have recommended a commutation of sentence, though persons convicted of treason against the Commonwealth could obtain a pardon only with the consent of the General Assembly declared by joint resolution.[45] Wise publicly but unsuccessfully requested that the assembly agree to commute to life imprisonment the death sentence of one of Brown's youngest associates, Edwin Coppic.[46] Although Wise sent a squadron of detectives into the North and Midwest to track Brown's co-conspirators, he called them off when Senator Mason announced that a congressional investigation would take place.[47] He also seemed anxious that Southerners such as himself, and not disunionist radicals, remain in charge and continue to press their appeals to conservatives in the North.[48] Did he have an option, however, beyond consenting to Brown's execution? The gravity of the crime seemed to preclude any commutation of sentence. But if Wise had possessed evidence of Brown's insanity, he could have stayed sentence until the General Assembly convened. If Brown were insane, according to Wise, no restrictions on the governor's pardoning power would have obtained.[49] After momentarily reflecting in November on the possibility of having Brown examined by the superintendent of the Western State Hospital, Wise allowed the execution. Wise could not believe that Brown was not responsible for his actions. His frequently repeated eulogies praising Brown's courage and fortitude were always proclaimed in the context of denying his insanity.[50]

Wise did acknowledge that sectional sympathy for Brown influenced his decision not to consider a pardon.[51] Much of the threatening or cajoling correspondence addressed to him held up the expediency of commuting Brown's sentence, whatever might be thought of his sanity. Allan Nevins also argues that he should have followed this course. If Wise's motives inclined him to search always for political advantage, as Nevins implies, then he might well have reprieved Brown until the assembly met and perhaps recommended incarceration for life. Such a gifted politician might have convinced his Virginia constituency of the expediency of this course and then reaped enormous political capital in the North. Yet Wise would still have been uncertain of Yankee support, besides risking the collapse of his hopes in the South. Nevins sees clearly enough that Wise had more to gain from hanging Brown than from reprieving him, even though Nevins's argument rests on the dubious assertion that Brown was insane. Yet a view that mechanically explains Wise's behavior as self-interested fails to appreciate the governor's genuine admiration for Brown, his preoccupation with Brown throughout the remainder of his days, and his real doubts about the wisdom of executing him.

Under the circumstances, therefore, what needs to be explained is the note the governor wrote to Dr. Francis T. Stribling of the Western State Hospital. It is dated 10 November 1859; the words "Countermanded upon reflection" appear on the back.[52] Wise composed it subsequent to the presentation at the trial of eighteen affidavits gathered by Brown's friends and relatives, purporting to demonstrate congenital insanity far back into his ancestry. In perhaps the most impressive passages in his biography, Stephen B. Oates undermines the authenticity of these documents,[53] but their existence may have had some influence on Wise. It is far more likely, however, that his decision was strongly affected by the numerous pleas for Brown's life from respectable Northerners. Wise had acted for many years with the Democratic party; he was no Deep South radical professing only disdain for Northern conservatives. Thus letters received before 10 November from his close friend, Mayor Fernando Wood of New York, and the textile magnate Amos Lawrence asking him to spare Brown probably had at least a momentary effect.[54] The suggestions of Brown's insanity and the pleas of Wise's Northern friends merely reinforced his own doubts about hanging a man of conscience whose reasonableness had impressed him. Brown had marginally challenged although he never overthrew the Virginia governor's values. In the end, however, Wise seems to have concluded that such a valorous and devoted man deserved the death he earned and for which he so obviously pined.

Wise never forgot Brown and consistently testified to his greatness.[55] In fact, when the Civil War began, Wise quickly formed a partisan command of his own—Wise's Legion—that sought to maintain by arms the hegemony over nonslaveholders that his political career had failed to preserve. The legion attempted to wage guerrilla war for slavery in western Virginia just as John Brown had waged guerrilla war against it, and it failed just as wretchedly.

In the long years that followed the war, Wise's admiration for Brown deepened. Indeed, before the war ended, resolutions from his brigade in the lines at Petersburg demonstrated his willingness to sacrifice slavery in order to preserve independence.[56] Like many other Southerners after 1865, he welcomed slavery's extinction.[57] It is dangerous to suggest that these postwar attitudes reflected Wise's perceptions before 1860. But an awareness of them compels us to ask if, in any sense, Wise agreed with Brown and therefore respected him because he believed that Brown was right in following his conscience and trying to destroy slavery.

Even if the answer is no, the question is not as ridiculous as it might first appear. Wise wanted no part in abolishing slavery in 1859, though he suspected that it had retarded Virginia's economic development. The evidence implies a nagging and occasionally immobilizing ambivalence on his part. These feelings, in my judgment, influenced his admiration for Brown. Brown seemed sure; ambivalence evidently had no part in his nature. He wanted freedom and would lose his life to obtain it. He seemed personally emancipated because his commitment surpassed and obliterated the guilt that might accrue from the killing of the innocent. His apparent certainties gave his life meaning.

But was Brown genuinely sure? It is here that Wise's perceptions confront the final problem about John Brown at Harpers Ferry. Neither the Virginia governor nor the vast majority of Brown scholars have understood, let alone resolved it. The problem is rooted in Brown's fatal indecisiveness and hesitation as his enemies closed on him and prevented his evacuation of Harpers Ferry. Why did he stay? Following his capture, Brown seized the initiative, proclaimed the purity of his motives, secured an eventual apotheosis, and convinced people such as Wise of his greatness. Before surrendering, however, Brown seemed unsure of himself and unable to come to terms with his mission. Wise and most others had little knowledge of Brown's peculiar hesitancy. Understandably, they were misled by the identity Brown forged for himself between the time of his capture and his execution.

From the hour Brown entered the Ferry, there is evidence of his divided mind about the insurrection he supposedly was leading. The principal manifestation of his attitude was his inability to make up his mind during the first night at Harpers Ferry and throughout the next day about whether to go or stay. As potential escape routes closed and the eventual outcome seemed certain, some followers begged him to retreat.[58] Others noted that he appeared shaken.[59] The peerless black historian, W. E. B. DuBois, suggested many years ago that Brown remained too long at the Ferry because he expected a wagonload of weapons to arrive from his Maryland headquarters. The wagon never arrived because (as DuBois asserts) the men sent from the Ferry for it lost heart and took flight. But why would Brown have waited for a wagon that was to bring weapons to an arsenal (the wagon contained both pikes and guns, but Brown had brought a share of the pikes with him when he entered the Ferry)? Moreover, DuBois's arguments do not integrate the evidence sufficiently. Why, in the midst of his revolution, did Brown allow a Baltimore and Ohio Railroad train to pass through Harpers Ferry after he had at first stopped it? He made this decision long before he expected additional arms to arrive from Maryland.[60] When the evidence is carefully considered, it appears that Brown could not act because in the midst of his life's great crisis, he became uncertain about the potential success and perhaps even the morality of what he was doing. He seemed unsure of himself, ambivalent about a slave uprising, and gravely unable to accept the potential consequences of what he had started.

For many years, Brown had reflected on the effects of his failure and death on the cause of freedom. His preoccupation with his own death in a just cause is so firmly established that there is no need to rely on any theoretical frameworks.[61] Instead of taking control after arriving at Harpers Ferry, he indicated an unwillingness to dominate events and succeed. Osborne Anderson, one of the few of Brown's men who survived, later wrote that Brown "was all activity, though I could not help thinking that at times he appeared somewhat puzzled."[62] He apologized, for example, to the conductor and passengers of the Baltimore and Ohio train that his men had stopped shortly after they entered the Ferry. "If you knew me," he said, "and understood my motives as well as I and others understand them, you would not blame me much."[63] He protected his white hostages, including slaveholders, because he did not want to harm them; later, he made this humane treatment the principal element in his trial defense. Finally, he admitted his sadness and uneasiness to his prisoners: "Gentlemen, if you knew my past history you would not blame me for being here. I went to Kansas, a peaceable man, and the pro-slavery people from Kentucky and Virginia hunted me down like a wolf. I lost one of my sons there."[64] Perhaps Brown wanted people to absolve him because he did not really desire to succeed.

Besides DuBois, only one other historian has had an adequate appreciation of the significance of Brown's hesitancy. Writing in 1889, Hermann von Holst asked why Brown stayed on at the Ferry against increasingly hopeless odds. With only a minimum of evidence at his disposal, Holst said the question was unanswerable. He suggested, however, that both the fear and the supposed impossibility of achieving success—the fear of a terrifying bloodbath and interracial war and the impossibility of triumphing over such long odds—mesmerized Brown.[65] I would agree and add that the incredible vision of what success might mean—in view of Brown's obvious aversion to the shedding of innocent blood and his doubts, however minimal, about black capacity and reliability—threw itself before him and gave him pause.

Nothing on this scale had ever been attempted on the American continent. Brown's previous history as a guerrilla fighter had not prepared him for the enterprise. Upon entering the Ferry, his men went to their appointed stations but thereafter received little support and almost no instruction from him. No one, and Wise least of all, ever questioned his courage and fortitude. But he seemed capable of leading only by example. His confusion developed long before the townspeople and the militia had rallied. Almost from the commencement of his insurrection, Brown drifted. He was uncertain about the sort of revolutionary he wanted to be. Perhaps he hoped merely to leave things to Providence. Such a decision would have made sense, especially because he had often reflected on the advantages to his cause of failure, as well as victory, at Harpers Ferry.[66]

Brown, of course, admitted his failure after his capture. Events over which he possessed no control precipitated his movement ahead of schedule, he said at one point.[67] He added that he was too lenient with his hostages and should have used them to aid his escape. Perhaps his most puzzling decision during the insurrection was to allow the Baltimore and Ohio train to pass, after stopping it for several hours. Brown said it was his greatest error because the passengers and trainmen quickly spread the alarm and prevented the "reinforcements" he expected from arriving before the Virginia militia and the federal troops.[68]

Why did he allow the conductor, Phelps, to take his train through? No one can know for certain, though Brown remarked to Phelps and his passengers: "If you knew knew my heart and history, you would not blame me."[69] Phelps, according to a newspaper report, "appealed to him in the strongest terms to allow him to pass with the train, saying he had women and children who were frightened nearly to death, and if he would let them pass they would do nothing to trouble him. Brown then said he could pass if he would hold his peace and say nothing along the route that anything was going on here, and he would go to the bridge himself and see that the train went through safely."[70] How could Brown possibly have done this? How could he have believed Phelps? Is it not sensible to suppose that Brown had never gained immunity from the fears and guilts of both his race and class and that having once destroyed innocent men in Kansas, he was not averse to being prevented from doing so again?

John Brown once remarked to Ralph Waldo Emerson that it was better that a whole generation of men, women, and children should pass away by violence than that slavery should endure. In Kansas he managed to live up to that injunction; at Harpers Ferry he could not. The Brown who survived at Black Jack and Pottowatomie Creek in 1856 was not the same man who materialized in Virginia three years later.

What he had gained from his experience was, in the end, an increased knowledge of self and his own limitations. He managed to transcend these feelings in the days before his death. He inspired enemies, such as Wise, to assist in the creation of his legend. Most important, he convinced the Virginia governor of his rationality. If Brown had been insane, he could have been dismissed. But because he was not, his crime of conscience could never be forgotten, especially by a man who shared some of Brown's values. Wise fought on resolutely through the war, overcoming certain of his doubts by iron determination. But whenever he reflected on Brown, he felt nostalgia over a missed opportunity and regret about a road not taken.

Chapter 12

Failed Hope and the Choice of War

When John Brown appeared at Harpers Ferry, Wise was busily embracing the program of the Deep South extremists and searching for ways to close the financial gap between himself and Tidewater Virginia's wealthy aristocrats. Brown did not divert him, but the conscience of a good slaveholder troubled him again. Only an awareness of what he had done and desired in the past allows us to comprehend why he pondered a pardon for Brown and requested one for a young follower of his. If Wise had been younger, he might have gone further.

Wise always believed that few exceeded his commitment to Virginia and the South during the secession crisis and the Civil War. Like many Southerners, he wished to be known as a man of peace who abided by the decision of his people and reluctantly took up arms. There was no ordinary reticence in him, however. He never wanted to argue the case for either secession or war because he thought each unprovable and therefore unwinnable. But if his decisions were thus hard ones, there was little chance of his forsaking the cause of Southern independence altogether, as Senators James H. Hammond of South Carolina and John Bell of Tennessee at least contemplated.[1] Wise's prevarications help to explain, in ways he never acknowledged, both the intensity of his commitment to political revolution and the wavering of his loyalty.

If Wise was not wholly committed to secession, neither did his decision result from his entanglement in the "relentless, horribly logical meshing of gears within" the political mechanism that "dictated an almost certain outcome" during the winter of 1860–61.[2] To be sure, Wise's maneuverability was diminished as a result of changes in the political structure. But as Barrington Moore, Jr., writes, "The uncertainty of all actors is one of the most significant and neglected aspects of historical crises, great and small."[3] Options remained open and potential outcomes appeared hazardous and unclear until very late. Secession startled and surprised him. It also provided an outlet for the accumulated rage and frustration that had become a part of the political drama. Violence, as it must, terminated thought and discussion. For Wise, it also provided a way to forget his feelings about men as disparate in condition as John Brown and William Henry Grey, which had shadowed him incessantly and blunted his enthusiasm for Southern revolution.

What Wise and many others wanted in 1860–61 was a way out. The choices confronting them made no sense. This was one reason why the choices they eventually made unleashed such powerful furies. They wanted to choose correctly because doing what was right—not merely what was required—mattered so much. Southern masters talked as much as anyone ever did about character, responsibility, and duty. Some chose defiantly, others hesitated, and most hoped that whatever they did would vindicate their honor and high-mindedness. The drama of choices made and deferred grew in intensity as imponderables and contingencies multiplied. Will the slaves rise? Will Lincoln fight or compromise? Will border states desert or remain loyal? Can the South win a war? What is it like to kill?[4]

Why desert the Union, Wise wrote late in 1860, for "the mere right of property in negroes?"[5] Yet he gave way. In fact, Wise and his eldest son regarded it as their prerogative to influence events in the Old Dominion and feared displacement by extremists in the midst of threatened revolutionary chaos. Eventually he felt compelled to neutralize his well-founded reputation for indecisiveness and inconsistency. He sanctioned violence even before Virginia had legitimately left the Union. It was his final response to those who regarded treason and renegadism as the gravamen of his political career. No one could thus impugn his honor, even as he transcended his father's dubious legacy from the Revolutionary era. He was never convinced, however, that he had done right. Could traitors come home to rest? The stigma of treason bore heavily during the secession crisis and influenced his peculiar proposals designed to resolve the conflict.

Once a critic of the established Southern order, Wise had become part of that order by 1860. As his commitment to reform waned, he shored up his claims as a benevolent patriarch. Because public life brought uncertain and irregular rewards, he sought greater financial security. Once achieved, however, it did not dominate him during the coming crises. He remained as mercurial, challenging, and contentious a character as ever.

With ever-growing wants, elegant tastes, and a sick wife, Wise needed an income at least equal to his gubernatorial salary, which ceased in December 1859. He thought himself too old for the law, except in "fancy cases." Indeed, he defended several accused murderers in a series of spectacular trials during the spring and summer of 1860 and managed either to secure acquittals or mild sentences.[6] His future, however, depended on "land and negroes." In 1858 he put Only on the market, perhaps because he could not conveniently purchase additional land adjacent to his own property. He might have rejected the option of purchasing another farm in Accomac because he could neither divide his slave force efficiently nor purchase a large number of additional Negroes. In September 1859, he sold the bulk of Only for $18,000, bringing him a $3,000 profit. Immensely pleased and buoyant with the sense of power and independence money can convey, he drew up a personal balance sheet for a friend. He planned to sell some additional small properties in Accomac for $4,000. These proceeds, together with stocks and other possessions, would give him a net worth of about $35,000, excluding his slaves. His debts came to about $7,000, leaving him the remainder to invest. He wanted to put about half in land and then buy a few more slaves while keeping about $5,000 as a margin. For the first time, Wise was a relatively wealthy man. Among other things, the money he and his blacks had earned now meant that he could afford to lose at politics.[7]

Accomac had once been the only place Wise had known intimately and the people there the only ones to have known him well. He felt most in command there. Now, however, his name and reputation would precede him wherever he went. The transition would be easier because he could anticipate a new community forming around himself. Many of those he most wanted to see were scattered elsewhere in Tidewater Virginia. Enthusiasm and anxiety to begin life afresh took hold of him.

To wield efficiently the larger slave force he desired, Wise required much more land. There was, however, an additional reason for leaving Accomac. His wife, he acknowledged, required a physician she could trust.[8] A semi-invalid from the time of their marriage, Mary Lyons Wise experienced irregular bleeding, inflammation of the breasts, and, it would seem, acute depression, in part the result of difficulties integrating herself into Wise's family. She found disciplining the children troublesome. Her symptoms indicate that she was experiencing menopause and that a fair amount of confusion and frustration intensified an already stressful situation. The doctor she evidently did not trust was Wise's son-in-law, Alexander Y. P. Garnett of Washington, D.C. Further tension resulted from long periods of sexual abstinence, which distracted Henry periodically, and a childless marriage, which possibly assaulted Mary's self-confidence and sense of purpose.[9] Henry's loyalty never diminished, however; in fact, his thoughtfulness and anxiety to provide for his wife and assuage her pervading sense of loneliness increased as her dependency mounted. During the war their love deepened. Imminent death and destruction drew them closer than ever and gave their relationship a profound, spiritual quality. Their need to share and the desire for intimate assurance, together with not a little guilt, steadied their marriage as they entered old age.[10]

Wise looked at one tract of 761 acres on the James River above Richmond but in the end purchased his crippled brother's 884-acre estate, Rolleston, in Princess Anne County, near Norfolk. John Cropper Wise sold this property—one of the largest in the county—to Henry for a little more than $19,000. The improved acreage amounted to only one-third of the land, but the place was extensively timbered and well watered by the east branch of the Elizabeth River. Notice of this transaction never appeared in the Princess Anne County Deed Books. John Cropper Wise continued to live at Rolleston. The arrangement the two brothers struck is thus unclear, but it is likely that John Cropper sold out to Henry at a low price to maintain his position as legal owner until paid the full amount. Perhaps he wanted to guarantee his support in sickness and old age.[11]

In the winter and spring of 1860 Wise threw himself into the construction of a new home, carriage house, and slave quarters at Rolleston. He also acquired three new slaves, giving him a total of twenty-one bondsmen. These were the most he ever owned and easily made him one of the preeminent slaveholders in Princess Anne. Evidence of the way Wise organized the work of his farm is skimpy. Tobacco predominated in Goochland County, where Wise had almost settled. Farmers in both Accomac and Princess Anne specialized in gardening, livestock, and grain. Most of the county's trade, Wise acknowledged during the secession convention, "except in negroes that are sold South, is with the North." The Norfolk merchants identified openly with Northern commercial interests in the late 1850s. The *Southern Argus*, Norfolk's Democratic newspaper and a traditional ally of Wise, gave up on direct Southern trade with Europe in 1858 and advocated that farmers in Norfolk's hinterland take up gardening for the Yankee market. How much Wise supported this movement is impossible to say, but the diversified nonstaple farming operations popular in the Norfolk area before and after the Civil War fulfilled his vision of a modernized Virginia.[12] However Wise marketed his crops, it seems that at Rolleston he continued at least one practice he had long maintained in Accomac: he used both white and black labor and in certain situations directed that they work more or less together. On the Eastern Shore, his tenant Thomas Snead had probably worked with his slave force. After reaching Rolleston, Wise retained an overseer, but he also hired several white craftsmen and laborers to aid him in construction, along with one man to operate the sawmill on his property. At least a few of these people stayed permanently.[13] Wise's highly diversified operations represented, I suspect, a hedge against the future. He wanted a farm that would integrate the best features of plantation agriculture while protecting himself, in some measure, against the possible eventuality of Yankee domination.

Once having projected the persona of a good slaveholder, Wise increasingly fitted his pretensions to reality. His livelihood and prosperity never depended exclusively on his slaves, but the likelihood of a greater relative dependence on them blurred the distinction between role and fact. Precisely at the time of national apocalypse, masterhood strengthened and confirmed him. He insisted that a heartfelt emotional bonding existed among himself, his slaves, and his white family. "Nobody shall ever disturb our patriarchal and happy home relations if I can help it," he wrote in 1859. "I will fight first—I will fight for them; and they, I know, will fight for me."[14] Unlike John Brown, he often predicted that slaves would fight the South's enemies. But like his antagonist, he believed they could act effectively only while serving under white officers.[15]

Aside from single males of recent purchase, Wise's slaves lived principally as members of two families. Although the evidence comes almost exclusively from him and his descendants, everything suggests that they were well treated and accorded some respect for their aspirations. When the Union army occupied Rolleston early in the Civil War, several of Wise's elderly slaves stayed behind. The family made no effort to evacuate them and regarded them as loyal. Of those shipped behind Confederate lines and distributed among the white family, however, at least three disappeared. One of them, Jim, was Wise's most trusted body servant. Another, Solomon, had been purchased in January 1860. Appalled by their action but grateful to those who remained loyal, Wise wrote his wife early in the war of his desire to shoot the absconders on sight. He also told her of a "dream that my negroes had my house and effects and showed signs of insulting" one of his daughters.[16]

Paternalism thus shattered easily—or did it? The preservation of Wise's black family became infinitely less important to him than the maintenance of his white family. The many premonitions of defeat and emancipation he experienced during the war culminated in his public proposal to grant the slaves freedom in return for Confederate independence. Afterward, an ever-deepening emotional chasm separated him not only from his own slaves but from blacks generally. They, in turn, cordially reciprocated. A number of Wise's bondsmen struggled furiously to retain control of his land after the war, as we shall see, but then, years later, Jim and several others did him and themselves the honor of attending his funeral.

The war demonstrated what Wise and most slaveholders knew all along: relations with a black family were inherently more unstable than those with a white family. Despite efforts to equalize priorities, only one of the two families deserved serious attention in the end. Though holding slaves increased one's income and self-esteem, the primary focus for Wise's sense of manliness was upon directing the lives of the whites around him. Insofar as the Republicans threatened slavery, they threatened Wise's ability to control his wife and children. Family was fundamental, but the intimate relationships with his women constituted the final and ultimate priority in his world.[17]

When women challenged him, as did Boston abolitionist Lydia Maria Child during Brown's incarceration, Wise reacted with sarcasm and disdain. Child wrote for permission to nurse Brown at Harpers Ferry. She suspected—with Emerson's insight—that even a slaveholding barbarian such as Wise might nurture sympathy "for the brave and suffering man." Despite this bold familiarity, Wise forwarded her request to the authorities at the Ferry. But he couched his response in language so threatening that she stayed in Massachusetts: "A few unenlightened and inconsiderate persons, fanatical in their modes of thought and action, to maintain justice and right, might molest you, or be disposed to do so; and this might suggest the imprudence of risking any experiment upon the peace of a society very much excited by crimes with whose chief author you seem to sympathize so much. . . . I could not permit an insult ever to woman in her walk of charity among us, though it be to one who whetted knives of butchery for our mothers, sisters, daughters, and babes."[18]

He repeatedly remarked that the crisis of the Union resembled a threatened marriage. In January 1860 he used almost the same language with which he had inflamed the Richmond masses in October 1856, when Frémont's victory loomed: "I know of but one thing worse than disunion—but one, and that is dishonor [applause]. I have said it, and I repeat a thousand times, it is with the Union of the States as it is with the union of matrimony—a good man, a good citizen, a good moralist, a good husband, a good father will bear anything, bear on, bear all, bear ever—all except one thing. The moment his honor is touched by a pin's point, he will burst the bonds of union, as the burning Wythes were bursted by the vigorous limbs of the yet unshorn Nazarite [Tremendous cheers]"[19] Honor was thus rooted in gender, and the metaphor was perfect, of course. Long-haired, eyes glaring intensely, scarcely controllable as he gathered himself for another overpowering outburst, Wise warned everyone of the day when the shackled Samsons of Virginia would unleash their pent-up fury.

Why did Wise identify the Union with marriage? He frequently referred to the Union as a sacred compact and suggested that in it reposed mankind's best hopes. For Wise, only intimate and personal relationships—rooted in their ambivalence and the instability of great passion, so easily whipped from love to hatred and back again—seemed an appropriate analogy to the amplitude of emotions that he experienced in this crisis.[20]

Wise identified Republican threats to the Union as effeminate, womanly assaults on the male Southern brotherhood that constituted the only genuine masculine force in the republic. "The *men* of the minority section are all needed," he wrote, "for the very women of the majority section are stimulating husbands, fathers, sons, brothers and all to *some spirit* in subduing us." One wonders about the suggestive power of this rhetoric among the nonslaveholders, given Wise's proven capacity to influence them. He thought most Northern politicians pliable and spineless. About many of them he was right, which helps to explain the resonating power of Republican calls for resistance among Northerners no longer willing to tolerate insults to their manhood. Wise's conviction about his Northern enemies sustained his hopes for avoiding war because he believed until the end that the Republicans would collapse. This attitude also explains his ridiculous posturing in the spring of 1861, when he predicted that Bowie knives alone would suffice to repel the Yankees. In the meantime, the best thing Wise could do for such creatures was to "rule 'em."[21] Tough and manly leadership in the style of Andrew Jackson might yet rebuke sectionalism. He stood proud among those who nostalgically invoked the legacy of the Old Hero. He offered, in a style provoking amazement, reprehensions, and even some acknowledgment of his pretensions, to take personal control of the Democratic party and lead it to a Union-saving victory in 1860.

The requirement that presidential candidates appeal to diverse constituencies highlighted the increasingly contradictory values

Wise wished to maintain. He yearned, for example, to preserve both the Union and slavery. He valued the leisure of the master class but, as his enemies Edmund Ruffin and Willoughby Newton suspected, he also fancied the bourgeois amenities of Yankee living. He wanted peace, fearing that war's devastation might shatter the bondings that held Virginia together, yet he advocated military preparedness following John Brown's raid. It is ironic that so brazen and volatile a character raised the specter of revolutionary violence far faster than many of the more methodical and dedicated Southern extremists. During the Harpers Ferry crisis, Wise publicly threatened to invade the free states in pursuit of escaping incendiaries or other malefactors sympathetic to Brown. When a stalemate occurred in the House of Representatives over the Speaker's election early in 1860, rumors circulated that Wise planned to seize the Capitol, but only after fighting had begun.[22] Having his choices narrowed to undesirable alternatives was insulting and dishonorable. It also trapped him into further inconsistencies which made his behavior appear even more eccentric and unpredictable and intensified his fury and frustration.

In his message to the General Assembly following Brown's raid, for example, Wise acknowledged that "present relations between the States cannot be permitted long to exist without abolishing slavery throughout the United States, or compelling us to defend it by force of arms." Edmund Ruffin thought this the best paper Wise ever produced. Only a few days later, however, speaking in Richmond to a group of Southern medical students who had withdrawn from Northern colleges as a consequence of Brown's raid, Wise took a different tack. He would never be driven from the Union, the governor proclaimed. He would fight, as had Andrew Jackson, for its preservation.

The most practical approach to the sectional crisis, he believed, lay in efforts to transcend, not to resolve it. He again suggested that the abolitionists' schemes made them the real traitors because their policies could only benefit Great Britain. Many people had argued that a war with the British might resolve the American crisis. Few of them, however, wore their hearts on their sleeves as did Wise. "It would be with an aching heart; it would be with a wild fever passion that I could be forced to strike against the bosom of my own countrymen of New England, New York, Pennsylvania or Ohio; but if I could only be relieved from that struggle I would gladly take the alternative of a war with England [Cheers]. My heart would leap to that alternative like a bridegroom going to his chamber, that that war could be brought about."[23]

"We suppose," commented the *Charleston Mercury*, "that there is but one man in the Southern country who could perpetuate such trashy nonsense." Beyond censuring Wise's Unionist dodges and distractions, the *Mercury* pointed out that fighting for the Union's preservation was the doctrine of the Black Republicans. Congressman Shelton Leake, an old enemy and Wise's defeated rival for the gubernatorial nomination in 1855, scorned his views from the floor of the House. South Carolina Congressman William Porcher Miles recalled that Leake "took the highest and firmest ground of State Sovereignty and the right of secession that has yet been taken on the floor." Miles then attempted an expostulatory coup de grace by pronouncing Wise's proposals both "*still born*" and an "abortion." But neither Leake nor disgusted representatives from the Deep South could dismiss the applause and popular enthusiasm Wise always inspired. How correct he was in a valedictory comment on his gubernatorial administration made near the close of his address to the medical students: "I have tried to demonstrate to any and all parties that at all events I am a Virginian."[24]

Still, the South Carolinians, at least the more moderate among them, persevered. Thinking that Virginia might finally wish to take the role to which tradition and precedence entitled her, South Carolina's legislature agreed on a mission to the Old Dominion. In mid-January 1860, the dignified and cautious Christopher G. Memminger arrived in Richmond as South Carolina's commissioner. He assured Virginians of the lower South's sympathy in the aftermath of John Brown's raid. Most important, he proposed a Southern conference either to create the unity necessary to launch a national effort to reconstruct the Union on Southern terms or to promote the likelihood of secession. Confident at first, Memminger was ultimately appalled at the political partisanship that prevented any action. The Whig remnant in the General Assembly—"a few men of signal ability and high character," as one legislator put it—along with a portion of the Democratic majority prevented assent to a Southern conference.[25]

In the midst of this maneuvering Wise rendered yet another account of his stewardship at a public dinner in January organized by members of the General Assembly to pay tribute to his gubernatorial administration. Farewell addresses always inspired him. In his speech, as Memminger described it, Wise appealed for a Southern conference. He told his listeners plainly that, if they declined, South Carolina, despairing of their assistance and repelled by their inconstancy, "would go on, act alone, and drag them along whether they would or not." Memminger called it "probably a true prophecy." The *Richmond Enquirer* endorsed Memminger's mission but inaccurately portrayed it as looking exclusively to the preservation of the Union. Once again, Wise appeared active and decisive, but only to defuse a crisis. The problem, of course, was that more extreme action had constantly to be legitimized to preserve the status quo. Such posturing infuriated a genuine revolutionary like Ruffin, who branded the former governor "a liar, a deceiver, a renegade, totally untrustworthy, except that, in all his changes, he will ever seek his own personal and political advancement." Ruffin's energies in old age were proverbial and frequently directed at restricting Wise's influence, but he had only limited success, as his continued exasperation demonstrates.[26]

Wise's shiftiness and evasions did not reflect an inability to perceive the options for Virginia and himself. Rather, he was plagued by his unwillingness to embrace any of the more likely alternatives. To espouse Whiggish submissionism was out of the question, yet his remarks at the January dinner deliberately rejected secession in the event of a Republican presidential victory later in the year. He continued to equivocate even after Lincoln's election. Almost a year before the Democratic National Convention scheduled for Charleston in the spring of 1860, he ruefully predicted a disintegration of the party because Senator Douglas would demand his own platform whereas the South could accept nothing less than the doctrine of congressional protection for slavery.[27] As Memminger perceived, Wise suspected that the initiative had already passed to South Carolina and the cotton states. Many of the secessionists accurately foresaw the future just as he did and planned fervently for the day when the lethargic and pampered Virginians would have to choose. Such a choice, Wise predicted, thrust upon the South amid conditions of revolutionary chaos, must irrevocably destroy its unity. It was also repulsive and enslaving to acknowledge that one's freedom and destiny lay in other hands.

What could be done? Many in Virginia and the South, particularly those whose economic stake in the slave system approximated Wise's, eventually found themselves defending secession. A collective withdrawal of assent to the Constitution seemed to them a logical and orderly response to continued assaults on their honor and interests. But this doctrine presented overwhelming constitutional, political, and personal difficulties for Wise. With Madison as his guide, he had always accepted secession as a last resort. But the problem with secessionist logic was its reversibility. Wise had spent much of his adult life wrestling with constitutional and legal problems. Despite occasional denials, he was never convinced that those favoring the maintenance of the Union could ever be compelled to recognize his right to secede. Madison saw the same problem.[28] So did numerous conservatives during the late 1850s. Virginia might secede, but there was no constitutional doctrine to prevent other states from stopping her. If Southerners brandished and bluffed, Republicans might back down. Maybe their spinelessness would tell in the end—though testing them would involve grave risks.

There is another dimension to this problem. In it we find Wise's response to both the South Carolinians and the Edmund Ruffins of the South, whatever their guise. Throughout the 1850s, the *Charleston Mercury* denied any necessary connection between secession and war. In utterly unprincipled fashion, it depicted peace and prosperity as the fruits of Southern independence. Wise frequently described the Republicans as unmanly, believed they could be bullied, and was shocked by Lincoln's decisiveness. But having witnessed John Brown's courage, he could never be sure. Elitists such as Ruffin, who agreed with the South Carolina radicals, concentrated on reaching only the intelligent and respectable. Ruffin never appreciated how his class had antagonized the nonslaveholders, especially in the upper South. He knew almost nothing about western Virginia. Wise held no particular brief for the yeomen, as we have seen, but he took them seriously. Ruffin dismissed all Northern charges that hostility existed between planters and nonslaveholders. Wise could scarcely afford such peace of mind.[29]

To contemplate a peaceful separation was irresponsible, he declared. And, befitting his pessimistic mood, he said little until the eve of the war about Southern victory. Instead, he conveyed the premonition of defeat in a noble though death-affirming enterprise. Rather than submitting to "the rotten and foeted dissolution of decay," he said early in 1860, let us experience "the healthy dissolution by arms, when the whizzing ball crushes through the brain, when the drawn sword severs the vitals, or the blazing faggot crisps the sinews."[30]

To risk this fate required a convincing rationale. The crisis of 1860–61 is often described as a crisis of loyalties, but it may as well be understood as a choice of treasons, particularly for men whose position restricted initiatives and constrained them to respond to events which they did not altogether control. Which should be renounced, one's state and family or the Union one had served and had hoped to renew? Traitors to Virginia were hanged, as John Brown had recently learned. Wise was an elected official who had sworn to uphold the federal Constitution, and the prospect of trampling it seemed unthinkable to him—particularly in view of the fear of treason to which his family's experience and his own career had sensitized him.

No one in the South wanted to admit to treason. Much discussion in the secession conventions involved efforts to evade this charge or affix it to one's enemies. With the secessionist mode of protest incapable of satisfying his need for justification, Wise had little choice but to preserve his position within the Union while arguing that this permitted ever more radical action. He eventually produced a remarkable doctrine called "fighting in the Union." Wise maintained his position until April 1861, although many contemporaries found his view dangerous, mystifying, or ridiculous. They reflected a series of timespun legalisms designed to confer legitimacy on an increasingly impossible position. Although Wise devised an original formulation, other Southern conservatives, such as Senator Hammond of South Carolina, also talked about eliminating New England and uniting the South for "a battle in the Union and for the Constitution." Hammond professed far more optimism than Wise about the South's future. But many of his extremist contemporaries, though discounting Hammond's views as irrelevant and incomprehensible, deeply feared their influence.[31]

Virginians had a special appreciation of the benefits conferred on them by the Union, as Wise and everyone else knew. To leave it meant giving up national symbols and sacrificing moral standing by appearing before the world as rebels. Whigs such as John Minor Botts taunted secessionists with their willingness to desert the national treasury in Washington and thereby alienate assets partly accumulated by Southerners.[32] Wise always heard Botts and responded directly: "If the last extremity must come—if separation must take place, I am for preparing first to take the *de facto* and *de jure* powers of the confederacy into our own hands, and not for leaving them in the hands of enemies who would endeavor to hang me for treason."[33] The former governor thus took ultimate recourse in the right of revolution, as had his grandfather. It was to be a revolutionary preservation of conservative government, however, instead of a movement to establish an independent confederacy. At the high tide of secessionist enthusiasm in Virginia in 1861, he sanctioned violence directed at precisely this objective.

Nevertheless, the "dissolution of decay" to which he referred had manifested itself in the "cancerous" free-soil invasion of Virginia. Botts, Hinton Helper, and John C. Underwood had done their work, he admitted. Not only were slaves being withdrawn to the interior, but Yankee capital spelled more difficulties for the future. In December 1859, he singled out Northern investment in the coal fields of Ritchie County as a particular irritant. But how could it be stopped? Difficulties seemed worse because he recommended fighting on in the very Union that had produced them. To follow Wise, as a Mississippian said in 1860, would be to "become hewers of wood and drawers of water to the North."[34] Wise could hope to deflect this criticism only by engaging and then trusting to the support of conservative Northern politicians (many of whom he did not know or had alienated), the immigrants, and Virginia's expatriate population. If their strength held, a reconstructed Union might somehow neutralize New England's influence or eliminate her altogether. If it withered, all maneuverability would end, secession would follow, and with it Virginia's prostration.

To avoid this prospect, Wise kept lengthening the number of intermediary steps required before he would assent to secession. One of his proposals seems especially perceptive because it responded to critics who insisted that a fight *within* the Union was by definition treasonous. Many of them maintained that only a solemn conventional renunciation of the Union, ratified by popular vote as the Constitution originally had been, could absolve obligations to the United States. Wise went instead to paragraph three, section ten, of the Constitution's first article: "No state shall, without the consent of Congress, lay any duty of Tonnage, keep Troops, or Ships of War in time of Peace, enter into any agreement or compact with another State, or with a foreign Power, or engage in War, unless actually invaded, or in such imminent danger as will not admit of delay." In the event of a grave national crisis such as the election of a Republican to the presidency, Virginia could thus exert a vast range of sovereign powers without deserting the Union. The constitutional resumption and exercise of these powers would presumably neutralize the arguments of those who believed "that to take up arms *in the Union* is to make Virginia guilty of the baseness of making every son of hers amenable to the crime of *Treason*."[35]

The Old Dominion, having assumed the posture of armed neutrality, as Wise later put it, might then mediate a compromise between sections. He explained in detail how this would occur, but he always rejected the idea of a conference of the border slave states that attracted so much support from conservatives during the Virginia convention of 1861. It made considerable sense to argue in defense of his theory that the Union belongs "to those who have kept, not those who have broken its convenants,"[36] meaning the slave stealers and those responsible for the enactment of personal liberty laws in the Northern states.

There were debatable assumptions underlying his doctrine of

"fighting in the Union," in addition to enormous practical difficulties in implementing it. One assumption was that he, the South, and Virginia occupied a morally and constitutionally impregnable position. For this to be true, the views he advocated in *Territorial Government and the Admission of New States to the Union*, for example, would have to command respect as unanswerable interpretations of the Constitution. More important, for Virginia to act as mediator, her politicians must command respect. What if Virginia had already lost her moral authority? What if people no longer deferred to the antiquated sensibilities of her leaders? Wise had no desire to confront these questions. Instead, the lure of the presidency drew him on in hopes that crucial decisions might yet be evaded and the Union preserved for the length of time it would take to remove the slaves and effect a national reconciliation.[37]

The distracting anxieties that the national crisis produced in him help to account for Wise's frantic pursuit of the presidency in the spring of 1860. They also explain the disappointment and mortification he experienced after his candidacy collapsed. He craved a lonely and heroic canvass, perhaps even as an independent candidate. Who can tell what might have happened if such a man had acquired endorsements enough to authorize a national canvass? More than twenty Southern newspapers supported his candidacy on the eve of the Democratic National Convention. Certainly the evidence that many Southern fire-eaters preferred Wise's nomination at the convention illustrates both their amenability to yet another Union-saving effort and the doubts and edginess they experienced about the success of their own movement.[38]

"I believe that I can count confidently from the start on North and South Carolina and Alabama and Tennessee," Wise advised Fernando Wood in January 1860. "If Va. is firm and united I will carry the South certainly, I think."[39] Hunter's adroit managers were never fooled. They planned a holding action through the Democratic state convention in February, followed by an aggressive effort to outfight Wise's supporters in conventions scheduled in each of Virginia's fifteen congressional districts. Each district meeting would select two delegates to the national convention in Charleston. An omen of Wise's subsequent misfortunes occurred in Berkeley County, where an early caucus appointed delegates to the district convention in Winchester. Here in the neighborhood of Harpers Ferry, and within the congressional district represented by Wise's ally, Charles James Faulkner, he received a resolution praising his gubernatorial administration but no presidential endorsement. Because Wise had both defended and insulted the citizens of Berkeley, such equivocal praise seemed appropriate.[40]

At the state convention in Richmond, Wise's friends pressed for an unprecedented confirmation of the former governor as Virginia's favorite son, but Hunter's skillful adviser, Lewis E. Harvie, threatened to bolt. Therefore, no preference was expressed, and the way was opened for a contest in the state at large. The result—a Hunter-controlled delegation to Charleston—was an astonishing upset. Even those who detested Wise acknowledged his immensely greater strength among the people. Although Hunter's lieutenants used the Lecompton issue, neither it, the Donnelly letter, nor the mystifications involved in "fighting in the Union" had disturbed Wise's hold on Virginia's popular imagination. What had happened?[41]

Hunter's supporters included the great majority of the state's legislators and almost all its elected federal politicians. Wise had embarrassed these people long enough. They wanted political vengeance. Time-honored usage sanctioned the rigging of local political meetings in Virginia. In some counties known to favor Wise overwhelmingly, Hunter's supporters prevented the convening of any caucus. The former governor could not be expected to triumph in a struggle that tested the strength of political organization. Cooperative effort frustrated him, and the advice of friends had only limited influence. "You can't offend me by friendly counsel," he had written Fernando Wood some months earlier, "but I am very apt to follow my own after all." Still, he should have won and would have if the results had been different in northwestern Virginia. The "listlessness and verdancy" of Wise's managers allowed the Kanawha, Wheeling, and Harpers Ferry districts to go for Hunter, according to the *Richmond Whig*. Unaccountably, State Auditor Jonathan M. Bennett and Lieutenant Governor William L. Jackson failed to rally Wise's forces. "I would have preferred the loss of my right arm to defeat to our side," Jackson wrote Bennett. Perhaps the impending oil boom in western Virginia and the Yankee money circulating in their neighborhoods lulled these politicos into overconfidence or distracted them altogether. At least one substantive issue harmed Wise's chances in this region, however. Federally sponsored protection for slavery in the territories—or anywhere else, one suspects—was a repulsive doctrine to most western Virginians, especially among Senator Douglas's supporters, who held some leverage in the northwest and would probably have favored a reaffirmation in Charleston of the 1856 national platform. They united with Hunter's friends to defeat Wise and thereby permitted the northwest to determine the fate of the Old Dominion.[42]

The loss of Virginia's confidence in the spring of 1860 was Wise's greatest defeat. Silence measured his pain. The man who bombarded press and public with defenses of himself and his views more frequently than perhaps any politician in America said and wrote nothing for public consumption from April to September of the most important year in the political history of the republic. In mid-June the *Richmond Enquirer* republished the former governor's speech from the public dinner given in his honor the previous January. No direct response from him appeared following the breakdown of the Democracy at Charleston, the failure to reunite it at Baltimore, and the twin candidacies of Douglas and John C. Breckinridge. He probably thought that his people deserved nothing. And yet, as the *Enquirer*'s unwearied efforts suggest, he never really accepted defeat and played all summer long with the notion of rejecting Breckinridge, abandoning the Democracy, and taking himself to the people. As politicians grew jittery about his intentions, one of Douglas's Virginia advisers reported rumors that Wise was undecided about his course and that he might even endorse the Little Giant.[43]

Douglas's bold and uncompromising speech late in August finally smoked out Wise. Douglas spoke for the Union throughout the South in 1860, but he was at his most unequivocal in Wise's own neighborhood. In response to two questions drawn up by William Lamb, editor of the *Southern Argus* and political friend of Wise, Douglas announced in Norfolk that Lincoln's election would not justify secession and if such were attempted, any president would be compelled to resist it. "In other words, I think the President of the United States, whoever he may be, should treat all attempts to break up the Union, by resistance to its laws, as Old Hickory treated the nullifiers in 1832."[44] It was as if Douglas were addressing Wise directly. Perhaps this was the only challenge that could have propelled him into speaking. Douglas, however, challenged on several levels at once. He received few votes in the Norfolk area and drew only about 9 percent of the popular vote in Virginia at large, but his speech called forth an impressive and frightening outburst of popular enthusiasm in Norfolk. Thus when Wise replied in late September, he acknowledged divisions among his friends—highlighted by Congressman John S. Millson's tilt to Douglas and his eventual public support of the Illinois senator.

Wise began his address by attributing his silence to the demands of his private affairs, but when had they ever muzzled him previously? He did his best for the South and tried to exact a measure of vengeance from his enemies, but in the end his speech was strange and opaque. *Territorial Government*, he admitted, may have denied him the presidency, but he claimed to accept the result with equanimity. If any thought his influence minimal, he would set the record straight: "I am fully and creditably informed that the publication of this treatise in the spring of 1859, gave origin both to Mr. Douglas's *Harpers* magazine exposition of Squatter Sovereignty, and to the resolutions of the Alabama State Democratic Convention, upon which the issue was finally joined . . . at Charleston and at Baltimore."[45] He added that had the South seen the light on the doctrine of protection, it would have remained united and controlled the Charleston Convention. He continued with another seemingly sterile review of constitutional law as it applied to the federal territories. It was not irrelevant; not only had Douglas elaborated and defended his own theories in Norfolk, but Wise's indecisiveness required him to operate necessarily within a web of legalism. There was now no substantive difference between Lincoln and Douglas, he declared. Each man would keep Southerners and slavery from the territories. Only the election of a Black Republican, however, justified a national crisis.[46]

In that event, disunion would probably follow although not to the South's advantage. If Southerners resisted, Republicans would manipulate the treason issue. If Southerners submitted, they were "degraded and undone." Perhaps the Republicans, who craved dominion above all else, might back down: "But the patriot," he remarked, "who now attempts to convince them that our people will manfully resist, incurs all the denunciation of disdain and treason—and this ties many a tongue." In almost his next breath, he pronounced Douglas's views on secession erroneous but again refused to specify clearly his own position. Nor did he address the issue of coercion directly, except to comment that if Virginia retreated, he would apply to some other Southern state and fight under its banner. It was a weak Southern reply to Douglas's powerful Unionist claims. Someone somewhere—perhaps in the lower South, although he never specified—might precipitate a crisis immediately following Lincoln's election because slave stealings and clamor for office among renegade Southerners suggested grave dangers in waiting for an "overt act." In the meantime, he repeated his favorite scheme by which Virginia might simultaneously resume elements of her sovereignty and remain in the Union. "I will not nullify, I will not secede," he declared, "but I will under sovereign State authority fight in the Union another revolutionary conflict for civil liberty, and a Union which will defend it." To reduce misunderstanding, he assured the timid: "I will wage no private war. I will take part in no unauthorized foray. I shall first await the action of my own sovereign State."[47]

A Good Southerner

The suspicions engendered by Douglas's appearance at Norfolk and elsewhere in Virginia were confirmed when the presidential balloting took place a few weeks after Wise's address. The former governor and most members of the Old Dominion's Democratic elite had heartily endorsed John C. Breckinridge's candidacy as a Union-saving measure. They thought a Breckinridge victory unlikely though possible and thus at least a long-shot gamble worth taking in hopes of achieving a reconstructed Constitution. Although Douglas obtained only a fraction of Virginia's popular vote, it was enough to deprive Breckinridge of the state. Lincoln obtained votes in Virginia, too, although Wise had reasons for focusing on Douglas's strength. For the first time during the antebellum period, Virginians rejected the Democracy in voting for a president. The state went narrowly for John Bell of Tennessee, candidate of the Whiggish Constitutional Union movement.

Elsewhere, prophecies were quickly verified. Lincoln's election seemed secure by late October. By mid-November, when South Carolinians held a state convention, the results were a foregone conclusion. Gloom, foreboding, and paralysis of will affected many conservatives, but for the people who lived through the experience and participated enthusiastically in it, time seemed shortened. Events tumbled one upon another. A springtime of hope and confidence settled on the South, despite the autumn season and its augury of death and decay. As with all revolutions, the momentum of forces beyond them uplifted men and women, propelled them to visions of bright destiny, and fueled their hatred and rage.

The intensity of this movement energized Wise as well, but the result considerably increased the frequency of his eccentric and contradictory responses. For example, he wrote Caleb Cushing in mid-October, urging him to make a final effort to instruct Northerners on Southern doctrine pertaining to federal territories. Yet he also acknowledged that the election results in Pennsylvania made his strategy irrelevant: "So is the nation gone—forever over to Black Republicanism. That breaks the charm of my life.—I am for Revolution—in earnest, to *blood and fire*. . . . I will not submit to Lincoln's election if I can get a single state to throw over me her aegis. It is war—I fight." Only two weeks later he wrote differently to the same correspondent: "Our politicians are far behind the masses in unanimity on the crisis. I will try faithfully to have 'em assume an attitude of defense—to fight first, but for the Constitution and the Union. They are willing to fight, and many are for disunion. I am not. I would hold federal gov't simply in abeyance until Black Rule is over."[48]

Meanwhile, more extreme preparatory action might bluff the Republicans, organize Virginia militarily, and satisfy the need to provide a specific, programmatic response to Lincoln's election. Wise therefore called a meeting in October in Princess Anne County, at which he presented a series of resolves modeled on the list of grievances in the Declaration of Independence. His program called for the establishment of groups of "Minute Men" in each magisterial district of the state, as well as committees of correspondence and finance. It looked like an attempt to create a carefully articulated system of institutions parallel to the ordinary processes of government and potentially useful as repositories of political legitimacy in the event of revolution.

Aside from certain rhetorical absurdities such as his charge that free-soilers were alone responsible for shackling the South with the Missouri Compromise, his indictment made sense. The free-soilers, after all, had depopulated entire areas of the border states of slaves. Lincoln and his associates had repudiated a Supreme Court decision. Republican convictions had already infected the federal judiciary, the party's influence controlled the House of Representatives, and the new apportionment following the census of 1860 would further dilute Southern political power. There was also much hostility toward Virginia among leading Republicans, as Wise perceived. A number of them argued that the Constitution permitted interdiction of the interstate slave trade as well as abolition of slavery "in the Districts, forts, arsenals, dockyards and other places ceded to the United States." All this might have led Wise to proclaim revolution, despite his inhibitions. Instead, he construed his movement as protecting "our own safety and honor as a people," defending "the Constitution of the United States," and saving "our rights in the Union."[49]

Aside from the understandable doubts halting him at the precipice, there was another problem with his indictment of Republicanism that might have prompted hesitation. Wise talked principally of the *prospective* changes that would follow from Republican rule. The only actual Republican "crime" he could specify was the nullification of the Fugitive Slave Act of 1850. Indignation at the personal liberty laws enacted by a number of Northern state legislatures commanded an impressive amount of attention during the secession crisis. This feeling manifested itself in the Deep South as well, which suggests more at stake than simply fugitive slaves, who of course were a far greater problem in the border states. Wise and others probably concentrated so much on this issue because, outside of Lincoln's election, the personal liberty laws represented one of the few Republican acts specifically designed to insult Southerners and assault their most important material interest.[50]

The lonely secessionist Edmund Ruffin knew what to expect from Wise. "I have studied his resolutions,—" he noted in his diary, "and cannot determine what he means—doubt whether he did not design so to envelop the subject in fog, as not to be understood, or to hereafter construe his resolutions as he may please, according to future events."[51] But Ruffin's opinion meant next to nothing in Virginia, as he fully appreciated. Instead, Unionists far more conservative than Wise retained imposing influence. The call to organize committees of safety in the Deep South rendered indispensable aid in radicalizing people. But in Virginia Wise's movement was finished within six weeks. The Bell and Douglas parties in Norfolk, who harmonized on little else during the fall of 1860, cooperated in a mass meeting whose purpose was to brand Wise's proposals as "treasonous" and aimed at usurping "the power of the people." One conservative orator suggested that if Minute Men ever visited his farm, their only object would be theft. When the former governor attempted a rebuttal a few nights later in Portsmouth, "a perfect storm of protest ensued" over his resolutions, and the meeting adjourned without voting on them. Resistance reached Wise's own neighborhood. A meeting in the third magisterial district in Princess Anne County expressed objections to the displacement of magistrates and militia by improperly constituted authority. Wise's friends accepted a resolution pledging that the committees of safety elected according to his proposals "shall do nothing in contravention of the constitution and laws of Virginia or the lawful authorities thereof, but shall assist the latter in all that shall tend to the safety and honor of the Commonwealth." This counterreaction proceeded amid an insurrectionary conspiracy among the slaves of Princess Anne County, which the authorities claimed to have uncovered just in time. As a further indication of the mood of Wise's region, a writer in the Whiggish *Norfolk and Portsmouth Herald* looked forward to the day when slaves "could be gotten rid of by gradual sales" and Virginia would join the free states.[52]

With his boldest initiative weakened, Wise could continue to regard himself as a principled man, ready for action but despairing about the future. "If ever, *now is the time*" for immediate action in the lower South, he advised his old Alabama friend, William F. Samford. "We see the end. Let us have the beginning. That beginning can't be made here. It must be made in the extreme South and at once," he added. He avowed his hope that Northern financial interests would "ground" the cotton states and rouse a militant consciousness. But even in the Deep South he never looked beyond organization. "Take no disunion stand, and make no unconstitutional movement," he publicly advised another correspondent. "Nobody South is going to be led into Revolution, and you and I wont shame men enough into resistance to be led into halters. I have thought so for years," he wrote Samford.[53]

Under the leadership of Wise's eldest son, the *Richmond Enquirer* also urged the cotton states to act and sustained the former governor's program of vigilance and preparedness. But O. J. Wise made sharper distinctions than his father. He expressed fewer qualms about the constitutionality of secession and more concern about Virginia's responsibility to stand with the Deep South instead of acting independently. "We must either have a vigorous, earnest war," he advised a Northern correspondent, "(which will certainly restore within a few months the guarantees of the constitution and the peace of the Union), or we must have abject submission on the part of the South, which will ensure a speedy revolution commencing in the border states, and resulting in a complete triumph of emancipationist sentiment and practice."[54] Both father and son endorsed the secession of the lower South, however, and pronounced against coercion. They also advocated a state convention, which the former governor had recommended in October during his speech in Princess Anne. Such a convention, Wise wrote in January, might unify the Old Dominion and present Northern conservatives with a final opportunity to act. It would also allow Virginia to stand as a "shield and bulwark" for the Southern states now out of the Union, in hopes of eventually inducing them to return—precisely the development that South Carolina's radicals and their associates were determined to prevent. With both the supporters of Wise and Senator Hunter determined on a convention, the opposition led by Governor Letcher relented. The convention met on 13 February 1861 with Wise in his seat as the representative of Princess Anne County.[55]

The election for seats in the convention on 4 February 1861 resulted in an overwhelming victory for the so-called conditional Unionists. The relief that followed among Southerners interested in quarantining South Carolina and the other seceded states, and among Northerners who perceived secession as a temporary infatuation, was decidedly premature. Most victors in the Virginia election recognized the right of secession and favored an immediate separation if either Buchanan or Lincoln should coerce the already seceded states. "Let not the Republicans misunderstand the result," wrote James Barbour, one of the leaders of the conditional Unionists and an acquaintance of both Seward and Douglas. "The vast majority of the 'Union' men elected are those like me who will make any personal sacrifice to preserve the Union but who will secede the first moment that the effort to obtain the constitutional amendments which our safety requires fails."[56] Estimates of the number of "precipitationists" elected ranged as low as 30 in the 152-member convention, although one careful observer indicated that as many as 50 delegates favored immediate secession. John R. Thompson, editor of the *Southern Literary Messenger*, counted 90 Unionists, 50 secessionists, and 12 doubtful.[57] Thompson's estimate and Barbour's conditions make Virginia's eventual decision more comprehensible.

Yet few contemporaries were certain of the outcome, and to most Virginians the future seemed murky and frightening. For the secessionists and those who wanted credit for associating with them, such as Wise, it was a truly miserable time. As the convention dragged on through March with nothing accomplished, the "disgrace" and "imbecility" imposed on the Old Dominion chafed all the more at the pride and tolerance of these men. Nor did they hold out any hope for the Washington Peace Conference, convened in February on Virginia's invitation and at the insistence of Governor Letcher. The Wises and men more extreme than they regarded Letcher as a traitor. Inevitably, frustration led to bold talk. The *Richmond Enquirer* openly advocated the seizure of Washington, assaults on federal forts and arsenals in Virginia, and prevention of Lincoln's inauguration by whatever means necessary.[58] The *Enquirer* frequently backed and filled, however. For example, it simultaneously called for a Southern convention, which might formulate a new Constitution and thus save the Union, and popularized revolutionary action.[59] Such threats bedeviled the Northern press and federal officials in Washington; several hundred troops were ordered into the capital to protect federal buildings and guarantee Lincoln's inauguration.[60] And when Republicans needed a prime villain and conspirator, they looked to Henry A. Wise.

Were they right? All during secession winter, Wise clung tenaciously to his doctrine of fighting in the Union, which was based upon his interpretation of the Constitution. It may have been consistent with this theory to view the national capital as the property of the South, as Wise did occasionally, but Lincoln's election and inauguration took place by constitutional prescription. They presented obstacles that Wise could barely argue around, let alone respond to with an attempted coup d'etat.[61] As a congressional investigation later determined, there was no conspiracy involving Wise—and probably none involving anyone else—to commandeer the government, at least before Lincoln's inauguration.[62] Both the *Enquirer* and the former governor backed down in February and denied ever contemplating an attack on Washington. It was far more in character for the Wises to bluff the Republicans in such a way as to offer encouragement for secessionists in Maryland and Virginia.[63]

Wise took far more seriously the federal presence at Harpers Ferry, Fortress Monroe, and the navy yard near Norfolk. From the time of the gag rule debates, he had feared the justifications offered by antislavery spokesmen for making free-soil enclaves out of these facilities. Late in December 1860, he called for the capture of the fortress, which was relatively defenseless against a land-based assault. It was located on a point of land near Hampton and guarded the western side of the entrance to Chesapeake Bay. At about the same time, a group of Virginians, probably including Wise, formed an organization that hoped to seize the fortress "without bloodshed." "They would have taken it," reported John C. Rutherfoord, "if they could have obtained the sanction of Governor Letcher, or even his assurance that, when taken, he would not return it to the Federal Government. But, unfortunately, Governor Letcher would not allow the blow to be struck."[64] As the fortress filled with troops and the possibility of its return to Virginia's control diminished, Wise's frustration with Letcher grew, prompting reports that the Virginia secessionists contemplated a coup within the Old Dominion. Alexander H. H. Stuart, an eminent Whig politician, feared that the state convention might change Virginia's "organic law" so as to "turn Gov. Letcher out of office and put Gov. Wise in his place."[65]

There was a lot of wind in this latter rumor, and it was not clear that Wise had ever sanctioned violence against federal facilities, although later he would. In the meantime, the former governor's growing willingness to accept violence probably depended in part on his son. Despite his own equivocations, O. J. Wise was consistently more extreme than his father.[66] In the end, he pledged himself to a plan providing for the toppling of Letcher and his replacement by a revolutionary regime. It was not merely that violence came more easily to the young. Sons in a rigidly patriarchal setting could, I suspect, most easily express their hostilities by claiming to be better at doing what their fathers advocated. Senator Hunter encountered a similar problem with his eldest son, as perhaps other Southerners did. The senator experienced much difficulty in explaining his refusal to sanction immediate secession as a consequence of Lincoln's election.[67] After a time, and with so many other critics attacking his views and calculating when he would sell out Virginia and the South, Wise may have sensed an erosion of trust in one of his most intimate relationships.

Unlike the cotton states, whose confederacy existed by the time Abraham Lincoln took the oath of office, Virginia and the other border slave states passed under the yoke of Republican rule. They did not do so quietly. Lincoln's inaugural message in March, which denied any constitutional sanctions for secession and implicitly countenanced coercion in order to preserve the Union, fragmented the conservative majority in the state convention. Wise and his associates trampled freely on the arguments of their enemies until, with only the loss of a few defectors, the majority restored its leverage days later. The long, set speeches recommenced, and the convention continued work on its principal business, the drafting of resolutions proposing constitutional amendments to end the crisis. Virginians seemed prepared to present these resolutions to nearly anyone who might agree to receive and consider them.

The actuality of Republican rule brought the dangers into sharp focus. Republicans did not have to foment slave insurrections for them to occur, as recent events in Princess Anne had demonstrated. Wise read and quoted to his auditors Wendell Phillips's call for an insurrection following John Brown's execution. John Quincy Adams's prediction that emancipation would follow any significant slave uprising, particularly one inspired by a war centered in the South, was as always on his mind. But taboos surrounding this subject restricted open discussion. The more modest Republican objectives seemed dangerous enough.[68]

During or shortly after the Christmas holidays of 1860, Wise read a Republican travelogue by the New England clergyman, educator, and popular historian, John Stevens Cabot Abbott. In the book, entitled *South and North*,[69] Abbott made scathing comments about Wise's threatening conduct following John Brown's raid, which probably drew Wise to the work in the first place. After the fashion of Hinton R. Helper, Abbott wrote of the "thriftlessness" and "desolation" afflicting the South. Despite his comment that slaveholders had "nothing to fear from the rising of the *blacks*" but "everything to fear from the rising of the whites," Abbott recommended no violence against the masters, as had Helper.[70] Nor did he advocate deportation of the blacks. Instead, emancipation and wage labor, together with a heavy dose of Christianity in hopes of inculcating middle-class morality, would make the South a paradise. He specifically endorsed a sharecropping system of agriculture. Abbott was confident that these enormous changes could occur peacefully for the same reasons Wise thought Abbott and other Republicans might be right. Abbott simply pointed to the Yankee investment and enterprise that had already disenthralled most of the border states, sent slavery into retreat, and thus confirmed the fondest hope of many principled Southerners. With slavery foreclosed from spreading into the federal territories and under assault in the upper South, its collapse was only a matter of time, Abbott confidently predicted. Moreover, he suggested that in the event of war the border slave states would adhere to the Union.[71] Wise took Abbott at his word. "You talk about slavery in the territories," he told the Virginia convention, "you talk about slavery in the District of Columbia—when its tenure in Virginia is doubtful."[72] "They mean to slough off the cotton states," he wrote of the Republicans in mid-March, "and keep the Border slave states in a Northern confederacy. They will draw off forces from the South and fill our forts with troops—our offices with retainers, and swerve and sway as with pacification and delay." Virginia did not have to fear a swift strike but rather the gradual withering of morale and an apathy and paralysis that Wise fought against in others as well as himself. The ultimate result could be the "mongrelization" of the Old Dominion and her dissolution as a proud commonwealth.[73]

A Republican administration, long continued in power, promised to displace Virginia's traditional ruling elite from office. So many old-line Whigs and moderates were available that Lincoln's only task would be to process the applications. Here was an issue about which Wise and Senator Hunter agreed. If Virginia remained in the Union, Hunter wrote in February, she would risk the growth of an abolition party at home, or a party based on class interests, or perhaps even a division of the state.[74] There is considerable though fragmentary evidence of discontent among the nonslaveholders of eastern Virginia. These vague hostilities had not yet been galvanized into class consciousness—although no one could tell what the future might bring.[75]

What Wise, Hunter, and their associates now feared most was a fragmenting of Virginia's elite, with some components deserting to the Republicans and others deserting the state altogether. As good elitists, they assumed automatically that those traitors who stayed would consolidate sufficient support to ensure their political impregnability. The Republicans clearly understood that disunity in Virginia provided them with an opportunity to build "an Emancipation interest."[76] Among the unreliable, John Minor Botts was, of course, the foremost. In March 1861 he did everything but nominate himself for office under the Republicans.[77] Equally disturbing to Wise was the prospect of Virginia's slaveholders abandoning her, enticed away by the temptations of Yankee money. "This national raid," Wise told the Virginia Convention, "is an agrarian rush upon lands as well as negroes." According to press reports, a number of Old Dominion planters were indeed migrating south, and some in the Tidewater were selling out to the Yankees.[78]

Despite his own prescience and private acknowledgments that separation was now "our *duty*," Wise provided only equivocal support for the secessionists until the eve of the firing on Fort Sumter.[79] When the twenty-one-man Committee on Federal Relations presented its report to the convention in mid-March, Wise introduced a minority report. Northerners would be required to acknowledge an amended Constitution that granted masters "temporary" rights of transit and sojourn with their slaves in the free states and forever forbade any discrimination against slavery either in the territories or the District of Columbia. If they did not respond by 1 October, Wise advocated Virginia's joining the Confederacy, although that decision for him represented no necessary commitment either to war or independence. At no time did the convention seriously consider Wise's report per se, though the strategy he favored of organizing for the anticipated spring elections had far greater appeal.[80]

Nor did anyone North or South take seriously an additional initiative he offered early in April. The convention sent a three-man delegation to Washington to ascertain Lincoln's intention regarding Fort Sumter. Wise refused membership on this committee because he desired untrammeled access to Lincoln. He volunteered but then withdrew a suggestion that he go as Virginia's single representative. In solitary conversation with that Republican "ignoramus," he might exploit the divisions within his cabinet or succeed in rousing the dormant conservatism in the North. If lower South politicians never trusted him, then Republicans caricatured him as an anachronism. It was ridiculous of Wise, according to Horace Greeley, to think that the entire North waited upon Virginia "as a supplicant." It seemed that his real policy looked toward the annexation of the United States to the "county of Accomac, so that the rest of the Union could enjoy such privileges as no schools or newspapers."[81]

Had Lincoln and his associates in the winter of 1860–61 accepted the Crittenden Compromise or the resolutions of the Washington Peace Conference, or had they evacuated Fort Sumter, the Virginia convention would likely have adjourned. The convention majority, until very late in its deliberations, desired an adjournment to a border states conference, which would meet later in 1861 and would presumably issue a series of demands, in hopes of mediating between the sections.[82] With moderates anxious to secure approval for their program, the sort of obstructionism for which Wise was temperamentally suited and intellectually predisposed became the order of the day for the minority. The limitations placed on debate during the last month before the firing on Fort Sumter meant that Wise, because of his parliamentary skills, usually acted as spokesman for the secessionist caucus and advanced its measures. No one else came close to spending so much time on the floor. Wise had lost some of his vigor and forcefulness, but feeble health and his sometimes incomprehensible proposals notwithstanding, the former governor was still a mesmerizing presence. Western delegates, in particular, believed that every radical plot and stratagem emanated from Wise.[83]

"If the people were ready I am ready to-day to go out of this house of bondage with the North, whose freedom is tyranny," he wrote Andrew Hunter, the prosecutor of John Brown, early in April. "But it is folly to tender naked Secession to Virginia and risk final defeat forever. We must train the popular head and heart. To do that I started the call of *Select* Convention with the sole end of thorough organization of a Resistance party for the spring elections. Once organized we will be ready to concert action for any emergency, mild, middle and extreme."[84] Wise, in other words, thought until late that the conservatives would succeed in adjourning the state convention. To place maximum pressure on them, invitations to the "Spontaneous People's Convention," signed by Wise and several others, requested the presence of reliable "friends of Southern Rights" in Richmond on 16 April. It was scarcely planned as a revolutionary conclave with the intent of delegitimizing and overthrowing the elected convention. About two hundred people showed up and were no doubt pleasantly surprised at the maelstrom into which they plunged. Conservatives had plenty of advance warning. News of the upcoming Spontaneous People's Convention had leaked to the press early in April.[85]

Momentum within the state convention shifted only gradually to the side of the radicals. Not only were there interminable delays but specific and vexing setbacks. The most ominous of these resulted from the growing militancy of a few northwestern Virginia delegates who were determined to redress grievances that dated back to the Constitutional Convention of 1850–51. Following the lead of certain state legislators, Waitman T. Willey of Morgantown proposed a system of ad valorem taxation embracing all property in the Commonwealth, including slaves. His plan would have ended the tax exemption of the roughly 240,000 slaves in Virginia aged eleven and under.[86] He acknowledged, however, that the class question was more significant as a *prospective* development; he also lamented the lack of aggressiveness among many western representatives.[87] Almost every westerner who pressed for tax reform expressed his devotion to Virginia in terms that fulfilled Wise's prophecies of a decade earlier. Several of them, such as Samuel Woods of Barbour and Alpheus F. Haymond of Marion, later fought for the Confederacy. Few joined the small group that rejected the right of secession on the floor of the convention.

However sincere the western delegates were in their protestations of loyalty, their program was unacceptable to Wise and the eastern representatives. The value of slaves depended on their worth in the Deep South. To tax them at this value would end slavery in Virginia.[88] A few easterners, led by Wise's friend Miers Fisher of Northampton County on the Eastern Shore, committed a gross tactical blunder in mid-March. They publicly offered to bribe the westerners with a reform of the state constitution in return for support in obtaining a secession ordinance.[89] Western delegates spurned this clumsy overture and responded with long-winded reflections upon the honor and manliness of their people. Trust was increasingly at a discount. Wise wanted to believe them but found it impossible to divine whether they meant to sell out Virginia, just as many observers suspected that he was himself prepared to sell out the South. The enabling legislation providing for the state convention was open-ended; it neither specified nor excluded the issues to be considered. Thus western representatives could argue that taxation and, indeed, many other subjects might legitimately come before the convention.[90] Wise announced his support for ad valorem taxation and maintained that he had perpetually favored it in principle, though neglecting to acknowledge that he had voted against it ten years earlier. Then he appropriately returned to the compromise of his fashioning: "Sir, if ever there was an understanding made, and of that understanding the Constitution itself is witness, it was that we were to let these questions alone until *Anno Domini* 1865." Even to raise the taxation issue constituted a breach of faith.[91]

In fact, Willey and his small group of supporters cared little for the convenants of a decade before. They wanted a new constitution that would not only extract money from slaveholders but provide for popular representation in the state senate and a new court system. Willey wanted a committee struck and a prompt report. On the eve of the bombardment of Fort Sumter, he accepted amendments that restricted the committee's inquiries exclusively to tax reform and provided for a report at the second session of the convention, which almost everyone thought would meet in the fall of 1861. The restrictive amendment originated with Franklin P. Turner, who represented the western counties of Jackson and Roane and later served as a captain in the Confederate army. The convention accepted it by a vote of 63 to 26 on the evening of 11 April. Wise left the floor a few minutes before the roll call and, with powerful constraints preventing him from voting either yea or nay, cast no ballot.[92]

At some point, however, he would have to make a choice. When Lewis E. Harvie moved a secession ordinance on 4 April, Wise voted for it, though avowedly in hopes of promoting a reconstruction of the Union. Harvie's motion lost, 88 to 45. Appalled at this margin, Wise suggested next day that moderates planned to "slough off the Southern States" and leave Virginia and her five hundred thousand slaves to the tender mercies of the Yankees. Powerless, the secessionists then charged their enemies with responsibility for determining Virginia's fate. It was thus left to Wise to berate them as rumors circulated that Lincoln's naval expedition to reprovision Fort Sumter had departed from Northern ports. Here his constitutional arguments, as well as events, outran his emotional commitment to the Union. He argued that state properties granted to the federal government as military reservations could be reclaimed when states resumed sovereignty. This meant that the continued federal presence in Forts Sumter and Pickens constituted coercion ipso facto. "If the time shall ever come," he remarked on 8 April, "and it will come—when you, too, must depart from the Union—the same question will then arise in respect to Fortress Monroe" because of its control over Chesapeake Bay.[93] Wise believed the Confederate authorities might open fire on Fort Sumter or on Fort Pickens in Florida. Until receiving confirmatory intelligence, he thought that Lincoln would evacuate Sumter.[94] Everything he had ever believed about the Republicans ill prepared him for the president's toughness and determination. Wise could assail the conservative schemes for consultation with Lincoln and for organizing a border states conference because he was convinced that disunion would come slowly, legally, and in the grave manner that Virginians loved, if indeed it occurred at all. He and such Whig leaders as Robert Y. Conrad and Robert E. Scott had all spun out the same sort of web. Not until Lincoln's call for seventy-five thousand troops in his proclamation of 15 April did Wise see clearly. "I don't believe it," he remarked, when first told about the proclamation. Informed that the Yankees would blockade Southern ports, he declared such action unconstitutional and "contrary to the laws of nations."[95]

By Friday, 12 April, as William W. Freehling put it, the "Virginia Unionists were on a collision course with the nation even if war had been avoided at Fort Sumter." During the balloting that day on the report of the Committee on Federal Relations, it had become clear that Virginia would accept nothing less than the Crittenden Compromise, which proposed a division between slavery and freedom of the federal territories at 36°30'. It had already been rejected by both houses of Congress, but Conrad, Scott, and their associates grimly pursued their fantasy of its reconsideration by a national or regional convention over the following weekend. Additional delays occurred when Letcher took time to verify Lincoln's requisition for troops and then delayed his response for a day—prompting Wise to question his patriotism on the floor of the convention.[96]

By the evening of 16 April no action had come from the convention, now securely locked away in secret session. Fort Sumter's commander had surrendered two days earlier. Crowds jammed the streets, conservative delegates risked insult and violence whenever they showed themselves publicly, and the Spontaneous People's Convention opened for business at Metropolitan Hall. Organization for the spring elections had lost its priority on the agenda. David Chalmers, a tobacco planter from Halifax County whom the convention quickly elected as its president, had already been conspiring with several leading Virginia secessionists who planned to kidnap Letcher and install a more pliant chief executive. Wise was not among this group, but his son was.[97] This development, plus impending anarchy and Lincoln's warning expressed in his proclamation to reclaim the forts and property which had been seized from the Union—with the direct threat to destabilize slavery this action represented, as Wise had suggested as far back as the gag rule debate—provided the final incentives required to nerve himself for action. Conservative representatives in the state convention feared an imminent revolution in eastern Virginia. That was exactly what Wise gave them.[98]

On 16 April, as its secret journals indicate, the Virginia convention was so immovable that only someone prepared to risk revolutionary violence could have controlled it. Despite the secession ordinance introduced by William B. Preston, the moderates remained in charge. Debate focused on their proposal for a spring ballot—with an option offered for secession (which might only be obtained from the convention, reconvened within thirty days of the voting) or a border states conference. Depressed and frustrated, and having endured yet another inconsequential meeting of the Committee on Federal Relations following the convention's adjournment, the former governor encountered an old friend and supporter as he walked dejectedly from the capitol. It was Captain John D. Imboden of Staunton, who commanded an artillery unit in the Virginia militia. Two years earlier Wise had obtained a pair of brass cannon from the federal authorities for Imboden's company, which had seen service during the Harpers Ferry crisis. The former governor had half jokingly told the captain that he could retain the guns, provided that whenever Wise called for them "you will obey the call, whether I be in or out of office, or the call be private or official."[99] The chance encounter triggered the memory of this conversation for both men. Imboden, a defeated candidate for the convention, wanted action, and Wise saw revolution like a gleaming crystal turning in the afternoon sun. He grasped it and thus, at nearly the final moment before his opportunity might dissolve, both rebuked his detractors and asserted his mastery over Virginia.

He told Imboden that he wanted the arsenal and armory at Harpers Ferry seized. He wanted some history of his own making to occur there. Both men quickly agreed to call several others together for a meeting that night in Wise's hotel rooms. Wise later drew the orders for Imboden and the other militia officers who joined him. They made arrangements with the railroad and telegraph companies. The plan called for approximately two thousand Virginians to assault Harpers Ferry the following afternoon. Wise also telegraphed Governor Francis Pickens of South Carolina and requested troops. Pickens refused because Letcher had made no call on him.[100] But for the Virginians on the evening of 16 April and for most of 17 April, during triumphal celebrations that marked passage of the secession ordinance, Wise was the only governor they wanted. Letcher had, in fact, been displaced, although not by the hothead members of the Spontaneous People's Convention, including Wise's own son. Furthermore, the conservatives who railed about Virginia's lack of preparation would now find their arguments answered.

Nor was that all. On the sixteenth Letcher had received two telegrams from a trusted and respectable source in Norfolk advising that United States naval forces were evacuating the Gosport Navy Yard and requesting authorization to obstruct their withdrawal. Letcher laid these reports before the convention but made no recommendation. Late that evening, after preparations for the assault on Harpers Ferry, Wise received a telegram from Norfolk: "The powder-magazine here can be taken, and the Yankee vessels can be captured and sunk, so as to obstruct the harbor. Shall we do it?" "Yes," responded the former governor. Letcher had no choice but to ratify this decision the next day and to sanction the attack on Harpers Ferry.[101] In the end, the United States garrisons at both Harpers Ferry and Gosport withdrew after destroying a substantial part of each facility. But the captured guns, ships, and manufacturing facilities later proved indispensable to the Confederacy. The naval base at Gosport was the American navy's largest. The secessionists of Norfolk honored Wise with a vote of thanks, which he cherished ever afterward as one of his most prized possessions.[102]

Wise waited for much of the convention's session the next day before rising to settle some old scores. Shortly before the vote on Preston's secession ordinance, which occurred on his motion, and with the moderates continuing their impassioned pleas for delay in order to preserve Virginia's unity, he rose to demonstrate what the times demanded. With a sense for the dramatic honed by nearly thirty years of public conflict, he drew a large horse pistol from his belt and laid it on the desk before him. He took a watch from his pocket "and with glaring eyes and bated breath declared that events were now transpiring which caused a hush to come over his soul; at such an hour, he said, Harpers Ferry and its armory were in possession of Virginia's soldiers; at another period the Federal navy yard and property at Norfolk were seized by troops of the State."[103] He then concentrated on Whiggish moderates such as John B. Baldwin and George Summers. The fury with which he shriveled these old opponents is lost in the obviously doctored text of the convention's proceedings. But one member who was present left a partial account: "The speaker was supernaturally excited. His features were as sharp and rigid as bronze. His hair stood off from his head, as if charged with electricity. Summers sat on the left of the chair, white and pale as the wall near him. It was the most powerful display of the sort I ever witnessed."[104]

Neither Baldwin nor Summers voted for the secession ordinance when the convention approved it, 88 to 55, a few minutes later. Along with most of the conservative leaders, however, they later signed it. Only 22 of the convention's 152 delegates refused to do so. Wise's verbal assaults on the western leaders seem a bit ill-advised in view of their strong support for the ordinance and the intensity of the western elite's later commitment to the Confederacy. Summers, in particular, never recovered from the thrashing he took and remained immobilized in Charleston some weeks later when Wise needed his support. But the lambasting of Baldwin and Summers, two men whose web he had spun as well as struggled in, signaled for Wise his final repudiation of all argument. No longer under any constraints, and having taken important initiatives to maintain his personal credibility amid the narrowing grooves that guided his fate, he embraced violence happily and eagerly, as if emancipated. On the evening of the seventeenth, he spoke at the Spontaneous People's Convention and "electrified the assembly, by a burst of eloquence, perhaps never surpassed by mortal orator." Should the Yankees seize his namesake (and scarcely favorite son), then a minister in Philadelphia, "it would not stay his hand." For those who doubted him, "he lamented the blindness which had prevented Virginia from seizing Washington before the Republican hordes got possession of it."[105] And there was always a special word of scorn and condescension for the westerners and for the nonslaveholders to whom he had devoted so much of his career. It was no longer time for concession and a feigned respect. It was now time for the killing.

Chapter 13

Steadfast to the Last

Wise's enthusiasm seemed boundless. He regained good health almost instantly. His age—he was approaching fifty-seven—mattered not. He bristled at the chance to confront his enemies and destroy them. This desire was behind his wild statements made to cheering crowds in Richmond that "it was not the improved *arm*, but the improved man" who would prevail. "Let brave men advance with flint locks and old-fashioned bayonets," he added, and they would see the Yankees run. "I rejoice in this war," he told another group of Richmonders who met to serenade President and Mrs. Davis early in June. "Who is there that now dares to put on sanctity to deprecate war, or the 'horrid glories of war?' None. Because it is a war of purification."[1] He returned promptly to Norfolk and assumed de facto command of the Confederate defenses.

But as always, memories and hopes shadowed him. Though its time had come, he hated the killing. Indeed, as far as I can determine, he never fired a shot. He experienced perpetual difficulty controlling his troops, brought kin together in his command to protect them, and acknowledged the collapse of slavery long before the war's end. Revolution nurtured some hopes but murdered others. Instead of preventing a fight, Virginia would now be the prize for contending armies. Thus he glanced over his shoulder even while embracing his own movement. On the evening of Virginia's secession, he told the Spontaneous People's Convention that its mode of redressing Virginia's grievances gnawed at him because he still "preferred fighting-in-the-Union."[2]

With the political structures that had so long restricted his alternatives momentarily fractured, his passion and excitement seemed transcendent. But this sense of freedom soon proved illusory. He would, after all, meet an "ordeal."[3] The compromises required by secession left little room for the expansive feelings of generosity that Wise cherished. Instead, a new and freshly enameled gloss of frustration added darker luster to Wise's fury and made the spring of 1861 a catharsis of hatred. Few fought harder during the war to come, few had so many critics to satisfy, and few despised their own comrades in arms, let alone the Yankees, as royally as did Wise.

From Norfolk, he fired a barrage of patronage requests—many of them in behalf of members of his family—at various state and Confederate authorities. He also called, as did countless other local commanders, for more troops and ordnance to protect his neighborhood. On 23 April he formally tendered his services to Letcher "in the highest military command you will confer on me."[4] Wise had some sense of his limitations and privately wrote that he wished not to "injure the state service by being put in any place which would be better filled by many better men." Never reticent about his ambitions, however, he immediately expressed his desire for "the responsibility . . . of commanding some line or other of the more important military operations." With the aid of "professional and technical men" he felt confident about exercising an independent command, preferably in the area around Norfolk. Concerned about harbor defense and a possible blockade, he also wrote General Robert E. Lee about the need to begin construction of ironclad ships immediately.[5] But Letcher had too many experienced people for whom to find appointments and for perfectly good reasons had never before reacted empathetically to Wise's claims.

Wise wanted something quickly, and the Confederate authorities were anxious to gratify him. In May, at the time of the ratification vote on Virginia's secession, Jefferson Davis offered him command of an expeditionary force designed to preserve the allegiance of the Kanawha Valley in western Virginia.[6] Immensely flattered, Wise accepted at once and was promised a commission as a brigadier general. He would eventually serve as senior brigadier in the army of the Confederate States—an embarrassment that caused him untold pain.

It would appear that in authorizing Wise's Legion Davis received full value. Almost the entire responsibility for its recruitment and provisioning devolved on Wise. The legion, which theoretically consisted of infantry, artillery, and cavalry units, also possessed a quasi-partisan status because its personnel were expected to arm themselves. Confederate authorities made it clear that little financial aid was available. Therefore, Wise frantically set to work contacting old friends, making speeches at county courthouses in lower Virginia, writing newspaper advertisements, and issuing proclamations inviting volunteers to join his command. He implored all recruits to bring such arms, clothing, and ammunition as they could. "Take a lesson from John Brown," he told a Richmond audience. "Manufacture your blades from old iron, even though it be the tires of your cart wheels. Get a piece of carriage spring, and grind and burnish it in the shape of a bowie knife, and put it to any sort of handle, so that it will be strong—ash, hickory, or oak. But, if possible, get a double barreled gun and a dozen rounds of buckshot, and go upon the battlefield with these."[7]

Only Wise's personal following, his reputation for savaging enemies, and his promise of early action could have produced the sizable contingent that marched with him into Charleston on 26 June. His command consisted of about twenty-eight hundred men, organized into two infantry regiments of about one thousand men each, with a scattering of additional companies for a third regiment and a few units of artillery and cavalry. A majority of his men came from Tidewater Virginia, principally from around Norfolk and the counties of Wise's old congressional district. But troops flocked to Wise from across the state. Lieutenant Obadiah Jennings Wise commanded the Richmond Light Infantry Blues, one of the few elite militia companies joining the legion. A number of other infantry and cavalry companies from the Richmond area enlisted. Several counties in southside Virginia sent companies to the legion, as did Albemarle County. In addition, perhaps one-fourth of Wise's troops came from counties west of the Blue Ridge.[8]

Wise's mission was to rally and defend the people of central western Virginia. No one could predict the character of his reception west of slave-dominated Greenbrier County. In Kanawha County, which surrounded Charleston, for example, the voters defeated the secession ordinance by a margin of more than three to one.[9]

Nonetheless, the political and social elite of central western Virginia remained loyal to the South. Prominent politicians, headed by George W. Summers, were Whiggish in outlook and thus found it the course of least resistance to go with their state. Summers himself, however, never joined either side actively and lifted not a finger to aid Wise. He and a few of his associates negotiated with both Union and Confederate authorities to keep all troops out of Charleston.[10] Local officials such as sheriffs and justices of the peace supported the Confederacy more aggressively, even in counties where Unionists dominated. Likewise, lawyers overwhelmingly sustained the Confederacy.[11] Officers in the state militia fully supported the ordinance, particularly if they came from old and native Virginia families. One of these, Colonel

Christopher Q. Tompkins, a slaveholder and highly visible aristocrat who lived near the strategically important Gauley Bridge at the head of the Kanawha Valley, had already organized portions of the state militia by the time Wise arrived in Charleston. But even Tompkins did not believe that the militia could be officially embodied given the political situation; his troops were all volunteers. Wise could thus count on an additional fifteen hundred men but only for local operations.

The general thus fared reasonably well after entering the valley, but his arrogance and disdain for western Virginians showed in unremitting complaints about the quality of the militia and the loyalties of the citizens. "We are treading on snakes while aiming at the enemy," he reported to Richmond. "The grass of the soil we are defending is full of copperhead traitors. . . . A spy is on every hill top, at every cabin, and from Charleston to Point Pleasant they swarm."[12] West Virginia's historians now understand the decade of the 1850s as a time of reconciliation. Most of the people who mattered in the valley were prepared to stay with Virginia, come what might, but in this crisis neither they nor Wise could convince many commoners to follow. It is likely that class-based resentments—directed against their own increasingly wealthy, powerful, and self-conscious local elites—aided in keeping the mountain people of central western Virginia neutral or inclined, if pressured, to repudiate the Confederacy. Also important would have been their understandable prejudices against slaves and slaveholders.[13]

Whatever the outlook in the Kanawha Valley, the situation appeared altogether hopeless in the counties along the northwestern rim of Virginia and bordering the Ohio River. Most of these districts were distinctly underpopulated relative to Ohio communities across the water. Governor William Dennison's vigorous dispatch of troops and supplies to the Ohio River towns demoralized secessionists even further.[14] Northern and foreign-born people reacted violently to the idea of secession. In one county a group of Welsh miners terrorized the secessionist minority until it was eventually eliminated. Preachers, especially those associated with the Northern and antislavery wing of the Methodist Episcopal church, lambasted secession.[15] Antislavery spokesmen protesting against tyranny and anarchy were not rare where Northern capital dominated, such as in the mining districts or in areas where petroleum had been discovered or was thought to exist.

The livelihood of the entire Kanawha Valley, as well as the northwestern counties, depended on the river trade. The salt and other mining operations carried on near Charleston required supplies from Cincinnati. In early May, long before Wise arrived at

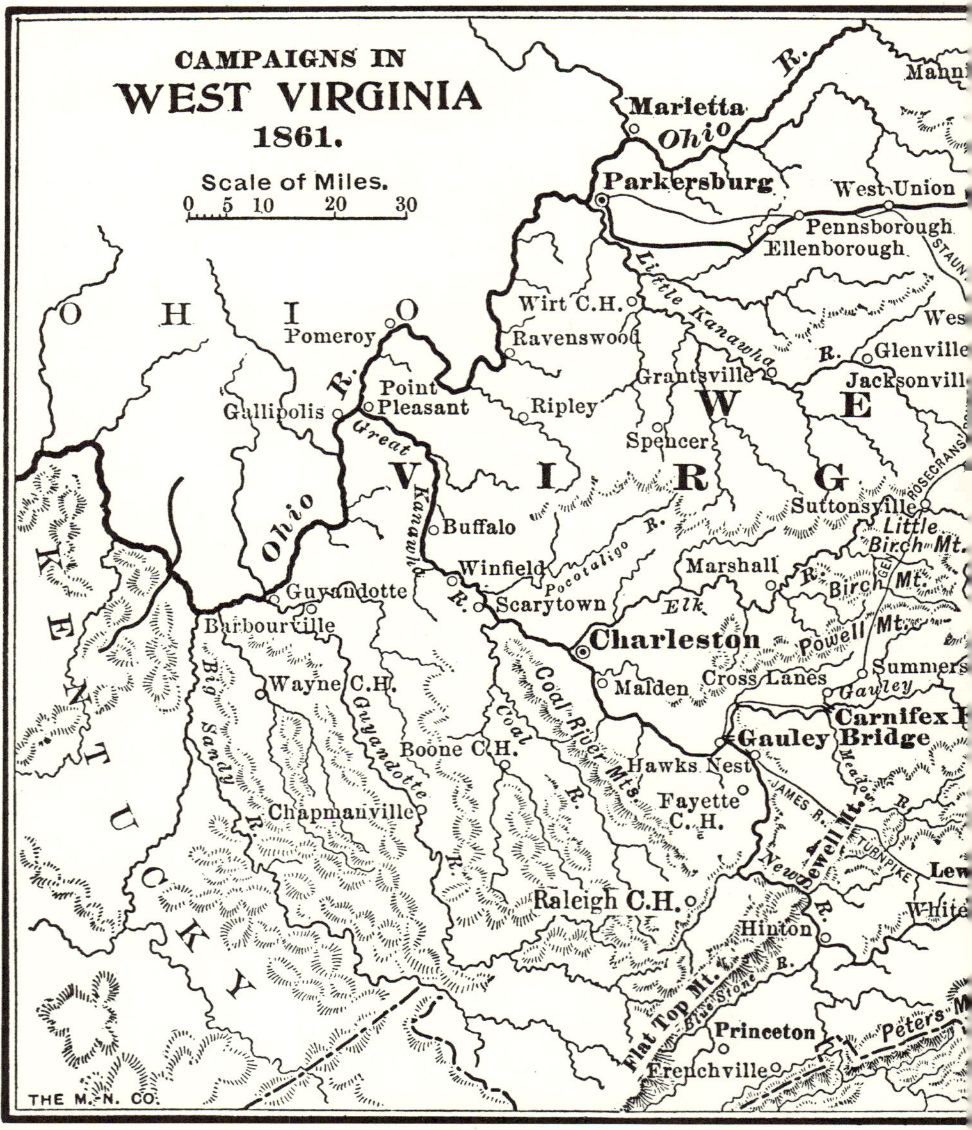

Campaigns in West Virginia, 1861

Source: Jacob Dolson Cox, *Military Reminiscences of the Civil War* (New York: Chas. Scribner's Sons, 1900), Vol. 1, April 1861–November 1863, p. 41.

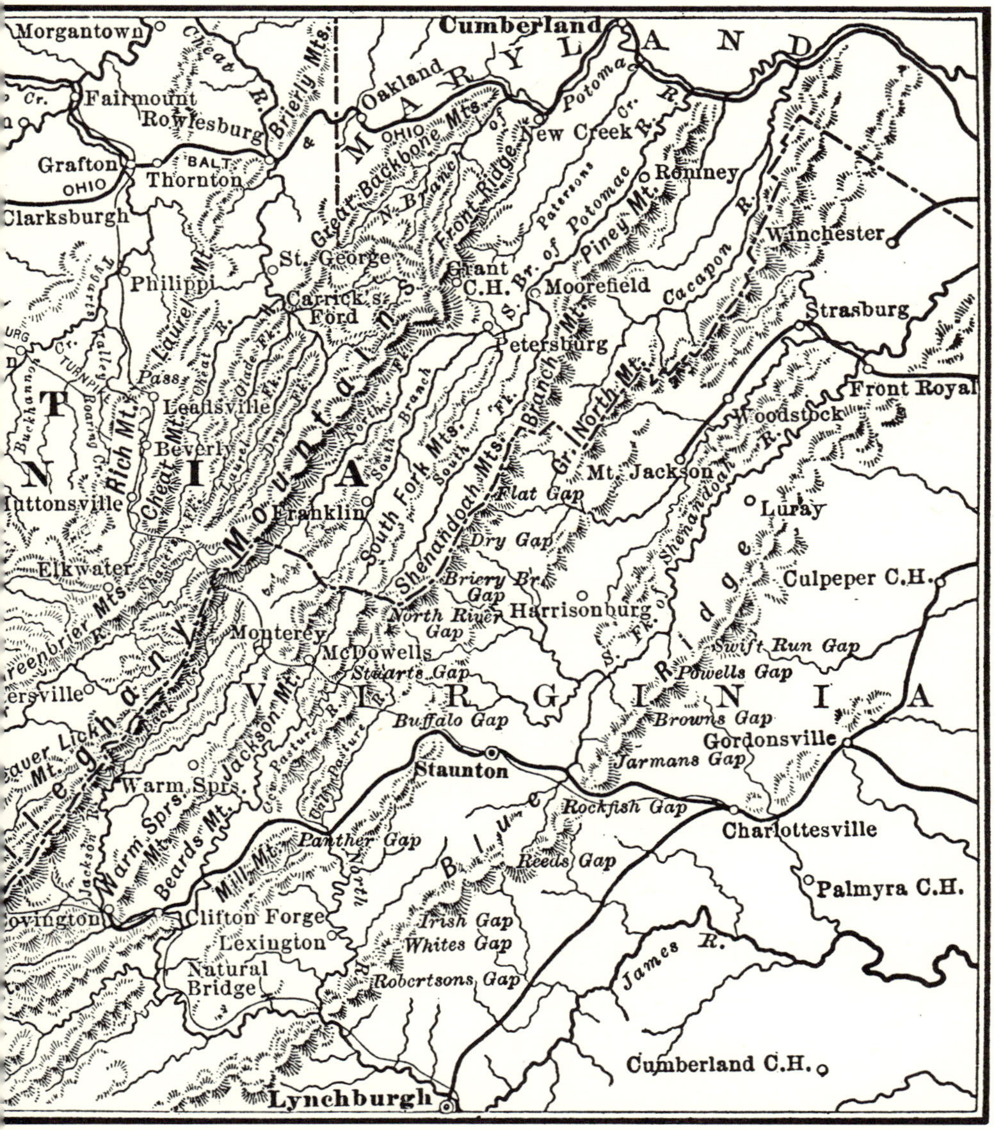
Morgantown
Cheat R.
Brierly Mts.
Cumberland
M A R Y L A N D
Oakland
Fairmount
Rowlesburg
BALT. & OHIO
Grafton
Thornton
Clarksburgh
Great Backbone Mts.
N. Branch of Potomac
New Creek R.
Potomac R.
Front Ridge
Romney
Patersons Cr.
S. Br. of Potomac
Piney Mt.
Cacapon R.
Winchester
St. George
Grant C.H.
Moorefield
Philippi
Laurel Mt.
Carrick's Ford
Petersburg
Strasburg
Tygarts Valley
TURNPIKE
Pass
Leadsville
Beverly
Rich Mt.
Cheat Mt.
Huttonsville
Buckhannon
Roaring Cr.
Glade Fk.
Dry Fk.
Laurel Fk.
Shavers Fk.
Front Royal
Woodstock
Mt. Jackson
North Mt.
Gr. North Mt.
Branch Mt.
Shenandoah Mts.
South Fork Mts.
South Branch
North Fk.
South Fk.
Franklin
Flat Gap
Dry Gap
Luray
Shenandoah R.
S. Fk. of Shenandoah
Elkwater
Greenbrier Mts.
Greenbrier R.
Briery Br. Gap
North River Gap
Harrisonburg
Culpeper C.H.
Monterey
McDowells
Staunton Gap
Stuarts Gap
Swift Run Gap
Powells Gap
Buffalo Gap
Browns Gap
Gordonsville
Jarmans Gap
Jackson Mt.
Beaver Lick Mt.
Allegheny Mountains
T N I A
V I R G I N I A
Cow Pasture R.
Calf Pasture R.
Staunton
Warm Sprs.
Warm Sprs. Mt.
Beards Mt.
Mill Mt.
Panther Gap
Rockfish Gap
Charlottesville
Blue Ridge
Reeds Gap
North R.
Palmyra C.H.
Covington
Clifton Forge
Jackson R.
Irish Gap
Whites Gap
Lexington
Natural Bridge
Robertsons Gap
James R.
Cumberland C.H.
Lynchburgh

Charleston, Lincoln's administration halted traffic on the Ohio River that was intended for insurgents. Without blasting powder, which could be procured only with difficulty from Richmond and with which Wise was not well supplied, the economy of the valley was jeopardized.[16] Relatively few of the capitalists and scarcely any of the laboring population rallied to his standard. Indeed, secession and continued loyalty to Virginia threatened to rupture the lives of these people. Instead of a decision to preserve the status quo, as it had been understood in eastern Virginia, secession in the Kanawha Valley appeared as a decisive and fearful assault on the status quo.

Wise appreciated the odds against him, but he could have handled the situation more diplomatically. His troops behaved with creditable restraint; there are few if any reports of their despoiling the countryside, despite their inadequate supplies. From the time he entered the valley, however, Wise interpreted his mission to "rally" the people as conferring authority on him to arrest, imprison, and threaten "traitors" to Virginia. His troops hauled in dozens of civilians, very few of whom were ever convicted of any offense. Most of them were later released,[17] causing the secessionist *Kanawha Valley Star* to gloat.[18] The *Star* was published in Charleston, and its paranoia is excusable. But Wise should have known better because these arrests clearly exasperated the people he wanted to conciliate. Although the other side took its share of hostages, Wise admitted to spending about one-half of his time prosecuting traitors. For the weaker force repeatedly to antagonize public opinion in western Virginia by arresting ordinary folk was counterproductive.

"None need be afraid that they will be held accountable for past opinions, votes, or acts under the delusions which have been practiced upon the Northwestern people," he wrote in a proclamation intended for distribution along the Ohio River, "if they will now return to their patriotic duty and acknowledge their allegiance to Virginia and her Confederate States as their true and loyal sovereigns."[19] Most people in this area, however, had good reason for staying away. Individuals among the western Virginians, such as Colonel Tompkins, became close friends of Wise, but he disliked them collectively just as in 1855. He withheld his trust and presumed them inferiors in every way.

Whatever his problems, Wise might have hung on indefinitely in the valley had it not been for matters over which he lacked control. By early July General George McClellan had perfected his plans to drive the Confederates from western Virginia. McClellan secured the Baltimore and Ohio Railroad to the north and rear of Wise's forces near Charleston after Union contingents drove Confederates south of the railroad. He then inflicted a serious defeat on them near Rich Mountain in mid-July, thereby opening an opportunity to penetrate the Shenandoah Valley and threaten Wise's communications. Had Wise remained in Charleston, McClellan might have cut him off. Had he moved north to meet McClellan, he would again have exposed his rear because Union forces under Brigadier General Jacob D. Cox had finally commenced their belated movement up the Kanawha Valley.

Cox got a late start because McClellan had commandeered several of his best-equipped regiments.[20] Moreover, McClellan seems to have delayed an advance up the Kanawha at the urging of George W. Summers and his associates.[21] The efforts of these moderates proved unavailing, although Unionist sympathizers in the Ohio River Valley feared the power of such Virginia conservatives and begged all spring for an advance by Federal troops.[22] Cox and his commanders warily advanced on Wise's positions. The former governor's reputation as a hangman carried him far during this war. One Union commander feared both the organized forces brought from eastern Virginia and the corps of "snake-hunters" Wise allegedly had recruited in the west.[23] Wise's troops performed capably in several minor skirmishes and then, on 16 July, they thrashed a twelve-hundred-man advance party of Cox's force. But with his command low on ammunition and threatened by the result at Rich Mountain some eighty miles to the northeast, Wise abandoned Charleston. His energy, dedication, and personal magnetism had not altogether failed him. Before beginning his retreat, Wise convinced most of Tompkins's militiamen to follow him, despite their intentions to serve only in the Kanawha Valley. Even though a number of them later deserted his command or resigned from it and returned to their homes, their action solidified Southern sympathy among the elite of the valley and gained the Confederacy many a fine soldier.[24] After a wearying eastward march of eight days, Wise brought his troops to White Sulphur Springs in Greenbrier County on 1 August. He expected to have time to rest and refit.

Wise behaved cautiously in the Kanawha Valley. He possessed physical courage in abundance, as subsequent events proved, but in his first command experience his main objective was to avoid defeat rather than to achieve victory. His legion was so scattered that when the retreat from Charleston began it was difficult to gather his troops and preserve their organization. He fretted about the possibilities of entrapment but probably thought it distasteful or even cowardly to plan for that contingency. When news came of the disaster at Rich Mountain, he reacted precipitously. In abandoning their camps, his troops neglected to gather equipment and showed signs of demoralization. The manner of his retreat, according to the Union commander, General Cox, demonstrated an intention to abandon the valley permanently. It did little good for Wise to rant about the "wholly disaffected and traitorous" region he had left. Important Confederate sympathizers in the area correctly regarded his retreat as a devastating political defeat for the South—something Wise could never acknowledge.[25]

By early August, strong Union detachments held the crucial mountain passes at Grafton in the northwest and also near Gauley Bridge, about forty-five miles to the west of Wise's camp. Wise had burned the bridge on his retreat (a mistake, he later confessed, caused by the inefficiency of his chief quartermaster[26]), but the Federals repaired it and their scouts had already crossed. Some observers believed that Wise should have ended his retreat at Gauley Bridge.[27] But with his command in poor condition he deemed it essential to move farther east; he possessed discretionary orders to retreat as far east as the terminus of the Virginia Central Railroad near Covington. The result of his movement, however, left the Federals in striking distance of Covington as well as various points on the Virginia and Tennessee Railroad, which lay to the southeast. Wise's orders were to protect the railroads if he failed to defeat the enemy and compel its retreat from the Kanawha Valley. So threatening had the many retreats and defeats inflicted on Southern armies become that in late July the Richmond authorities entrusted western Virginia to General Robert E. Lee, then commanding all of Virginia's forces.

After more than a week in White Sulphur Springs, Wise's command was still so disorganized that he did not know how many troops he had. All of them, in any case, had exhausted most of their supplies and ammunition. Tents were in short supply, and few men were sufficiently clothed. In chilly and rainy weather, typhoid fever struck hundreds. Irritable and quick-tempered, existing in miserable surroundings, and desperately desiring an opportunity to rest and refit, it is no wonder that Wise reacted furiously when a loathsome old enemy rode cockily into camp with twelve hundred well-equipped men, grandiosely announced his intention to reconquer the Kanawha Valley, and ordered him to follow. The Confederacy had enough problems in western Virginia without the feuding that flared between Wise and his onetime political ally, Brigadier General John B. Floyd.

Somehow the Richmond officials believed that Wise and Floyd

could maintain independent commands and yet operate in the same theater harmoniously. Floyd's commission as brigadier antedated Wise's, and he therefore acted as senior whenever their commands united. But Wise had recruited many more troops and put them into the field so rapidly that he felt indisposed to take direction from a Johnny-come-lately who put on superior airs. Not even Lee's formidable diplomatic talents could bring them together.

Shortly after arriving at Wise's camp Floyd reported its chaotic condition to Lee and Jefferson Davis.[28] Wise's reaction was a compound of the painful embarrassment he felt at the plight of his troops in the aftermath of a humiliating retreat and a studied arrogance at meeting a confident general who had not yet met the enemy or encountered the terrain. Floyd wanted to plunge immediately back into the Kanawha Valley. Wise refused, and Lee agreed. Wise argued that it would be better to compel the enemy to march east to meet them, rather than enduring the trek back into the Kanawha. Moreover, Wise pointed out that although there was little forage between White Sulphur Springs and the Gauley Bridge, excellent defensive positions existed in the wilderness areas east of the bridge. Wise had already been compelled to live off the country and did not relish moving through it again after once picking it over. Many of his troops lacked muskets, and most of them had not drawn their pay.[29]

The quarrel between Wise and Floyd went deep. Years before, when they had cooperated politically in Virginia, only love of lucre had united them. Floyd, if anything, was far less shy about tending to his own interests than Wise. He never became as wrought up or as self-deluding.[30] In Floyd, Wise saw the unprincipled and dishonest elements of his own character that he spent so much energy trying to repress. Floyd and the memory of their cooperation, which verified all the charges of crass opportunism that Virginia politicians had vainly attempted to answer for years, confronted Wise with the darker aspects of his own nature. The result was a fearful rage, directed not only at Floyd but at Wise's subordinates, followed by an intricate but ultimately unsuccessful effort to manipulate his way out of an impossible situation. To do so, Wise drafted a series of lawyerlike briefs under the guise of military communications. This strategy of asserting power over small matters in order to gain mastery in the larger sense, was a characteristic defensive device.

Wise's efforts to separate his troops from Floyd's and Floyd's designs on portions of Wise's command, together with the miseries their feuding brought the Confederates in western Virginia, have been ably recounted elsewhere.[31] Most of the problems that followed stemmed from the personal antagonism between the two men. Wise believed himself solely responsible for Floyd's cabinet appointment in Buchanan's administration. Had he not "made" Floyd, in the sense of providing his opportunity to serve the Confederacy in a visible capacity, despite Floyd's earlier service as governor of Virginia from 1849 to 1852? It was an enormous mortification to be commanded by such a man, especially one who evoked feelings of disgust, self-hatred, and self-pity. Moreover, Floyd's arrival reminded Wise of his own recent defeats. Never in the best of health, he grew sicker in camp, threw tantrums on the smallest pretext, cursed his officers and men, gave and countermanded orders, and generally appeared incapable of inspiring his demoralized troops.[32] Several of his officers considered openly defying his authority, and some members of Tompkins's command requested a transfer to Floyd's brigade.[33] These developments deeply mortified Wise. He carried a paternalistic outlook into the service and longed for a calm and secure environment in which, although perhaps not giving all the orders, he would be supreme. His closest kinsmen supported him through the crisis, but they were cause for pain and disappointment. His son and namesake had recently refused (citing the constraints of his "private affairs") the military chaplaincy Wise worked hard to obtain for him.[34]

Few choices presented themselves. Wise followed when Floyd commanded. Both of them marched westward toward the Kanawha on 20 August. Before long each had further infuriated the other. Floyd borrowed Wise's troops and supplies, communicated independently with Wise's officers, and avowed his desire to absorb the legion. Wise systematically disregarded Floyd's orders, insulted him to third parties, left no doubt about his feelings when they met personally, and afflicted Lee with requests to rectify the situation. Wise even asked his wife to have her brother intercede on his behalf with higher Confederate authorities. Lee talked about unity in the face of the enemy. "I feel," Wise replied, that "if we [he and Floyd] remain together, we will unite in more wars than one." Floyd promised to give Wise's troops away if anyone could provide him with three good regiments to replace them. Appalled by the conduct of both generals, Confederate sympathizers begged Jefferson Davis to remove one or both of them.[35] Even the immediate presence of the enemy failed to unite them.

Advancing near Gauley Bridge, they confronted Cox's Union troops and another force commanded by General William S. Rosecrans, which descended on them from the north. Wise and Floyd were split up over ten miles with the latter in position closer to

Rosecrans. Both expressed reservations about sending men or arms to the other because each seemed certain of an imminent Union assault. Various subordinate commanders shuttled troops back and forth constantly. At one point Floyd asked twice in the same day for a regiment and twice sent it back to Wise. For his part, Wise chafed to allow portions of his command to conduct partisan raiding expeditions down the Kanawha Valley rather than holding them under tight organization. Finally, on 10 September, Floyd beat back several attacks from Rosecrans's troops at Carnifex Ferry despite Wise's failure to reinforce him. Enraged by the insubordination of an inferior who cited his "sound military discretion" to disobey, Floyd fired off a letter to Jefferson Davis demanding Wise's transfer. An arrest and court-martial might have been the proper course, Floyd wrote, but this "would not have cured the evil, for he has around him a set of men extremely like himself."[36] Wise's renewed appeals to Lee did no good because Davis protected his opponent. In a private and unofficial letter that exposed his pathetic situation, Wise asked Davis to "send me anywhere, especially to General Lee, rather than let me remain under a sense of humiliation, by submitting to an unfriendly & unfair command. . . . If one head must order the defense here, let it be mine or his alone, and if I must be dependent upon a superior, let it be one who will make me & my men feel that our honor will be safe in our own camp as well as in the campaign."[37] A few days later, after both commands had retreated about ten miles east of Gauley Bridge, where, as usual, they bivouacked separately, Wise received orders to return immediately to Richmond. Earlier, he had indulged himself in speeches after the classical manner delivered to each of his regiments. He told them that they should expect Union attacks from all sides for successive days and that if any man desired safety he should step forward and go to Floyd's camp.[38] Because these assaults were yet expected, and because he was ordered to turn his entire command over to Floyd, Wise contemplated further disobedience. But Lee, who was present, counseled against it and eventually put him on the road to the Confederate capital.

For Henry A. Wise, the Civil War brought dark days too many to number. He lost his home, his slaves, and his fortune. He also lost his health and probably years from his life. His favorite son died in battle. And it all began with his loss of western Virginia, or at least a fair part of it. The Virginia General Assembly symbolically conceded the loss of the west in November 1861, when it proposed constitutional amendments rescinding many of the political reforms Wise had advocated during the antebellum period. In March 1862, however, voters defeated attempts to reduce the number of elected officials, to extend judges' terms of service, and to require the legislature to select the governor if no candidate achieved a popular majority. Perhaps Virginia was already divided and dismembered enough; a reactionary offensive by the General Assembly seemed both distasteful and dangerous.[39]

Through it all Wise displayed a remarkable toughness and resiliency. He outlasted, even in war, many of his critics. Jefferson Davis cashiered Floyd early in 1862 for abandoning Fort Donelson in Tennessee in the face of an enemy who eventually compelled capitulation of the remaining Confederate forces. Despite receiving a major general's commission in the militia from the Virginia General Assembly shortly thereafter, Floyd died in disgrace in 1863. Wise's political stature did him no disservice. Davis had to keep him, though Wise would participate in other disasters. Still, there was something unconquerable in him—perhaps a duty-bound sense of having to earn one's entitlement by living well with hard choices. "He was a grand old man," Walter H. Taylor, who served as Lee's adjutant, wrote many years later, "heroic in his courage and of inflexible will, knowing little of subordination, but ever ready to fight and steadfast to the last."[40] Wise was one revolutionary who had studied the consequences of treason. He had reason to feel the intense pressures created by the expectations of those who knew of his prewar vacillations. He would wait a long time for the chance to fight well in this war. It came at about the same time that he acknowledged slavery's doom.

Wise's body suffered nearly as much as his reputation. He remained severely ill in Richmond until mid-October 1861. After recovering, he discovered himself a general without a command and thereupon launched a furious letter-writing campaign aimed at getting his troops back. When recalled, he refused to communicate with Floyd but defiantly entrusted "the safety and honor of my Legion" to his "superior in every respect, General Robert E. Lee."[41] The unusually close personal relationship between the two men was, for Wise, rooted in family ties,[42] respect for Lee's professional accomplishments, and Lee's unequaled personal dignity and sense of fair play. Wise had honored these latter qualities in many others during his life. Confederate General P. G. T. Beauregard shared them to some extent and flattered Wise less subtly than Lee. Later in the war Beauregard managed to get the best out of Wise.

Lee probably aided Wise in securing another command, though the constant epistolary bombardment of the Confederate authorities may have helped by exhausting them into granting Wise's wishes. In a bulky apologia that masqueraded as a report on his operations in western Virginia, Wise all but acknowledged several catastrophes. "In each and every case," he wrote, they occurred "because of violations of my express orders." He defended his decision not to reinforce Floyd after he had crossed Gauley River at Carnifex Ferry by arguing that both of them might have been cut off. He then criticized Floyd's judgment in crossing the river, although praising his courage for retreating after withstanding several attacks from Rosecrans. He accurately perceived that Floyd hoped to destroy him.[43] Such bitterness and systematically insulting language directed toward a superior officer must have annoyed Jefferson Davis and the Confederate secretary of war, Judah P. Benjamin, but they dared not placate him with a significant command. They probably felt safe in assigning him to a district near his home (as he had originally desired) in which he would serve under an older and more traditional soldier who represented no threat to his vanity.

On 7 January 1862 Wise took command of the military district of northeastern North Carolina. General Benjamin Huger, headquartered at Norfolk, served as his immediate superior. Elements of Wise's Legion joined him in the east, but their transfer touched off an explosive and long-continuing feud between him and the War Department. Wise never struck a formal arrangement respecting the disposition of his troops before his departure from western Virginia. By an "understanding" with General Lee, and with Davis and Benjamin following his return to Richmond, "the Legion was to be restored to me, except the companies raised in Western Virginia for its defense who might elect to remain, and excepting one battery of light artillery." Six or eight companies stayed in western Virginia, but an equal number ended up mysteriously in South Carolina. Wise wanted them back, along with all of his scattered cavalry, the remaining artillery, and several additional companies of infantry he had recruited in western Virginia before leaving.[44] Benjamin tried to gratify him by forwarding two regiments of his legion from western Virginia—a formidable concession, in view of the demand this movement put on the Confederacy's already overtaxed transportation facilities. Wise also managed to gather up some of his cavalry and two or three light artillery companies. He then had, on paper, about twenty-three hundred troops, in addition to the three regiments of North Carolina troops already assigned to him. But it would take some weeks for all these forces to join him. The belief that he had been cheated out of a full regiment continued to fester.

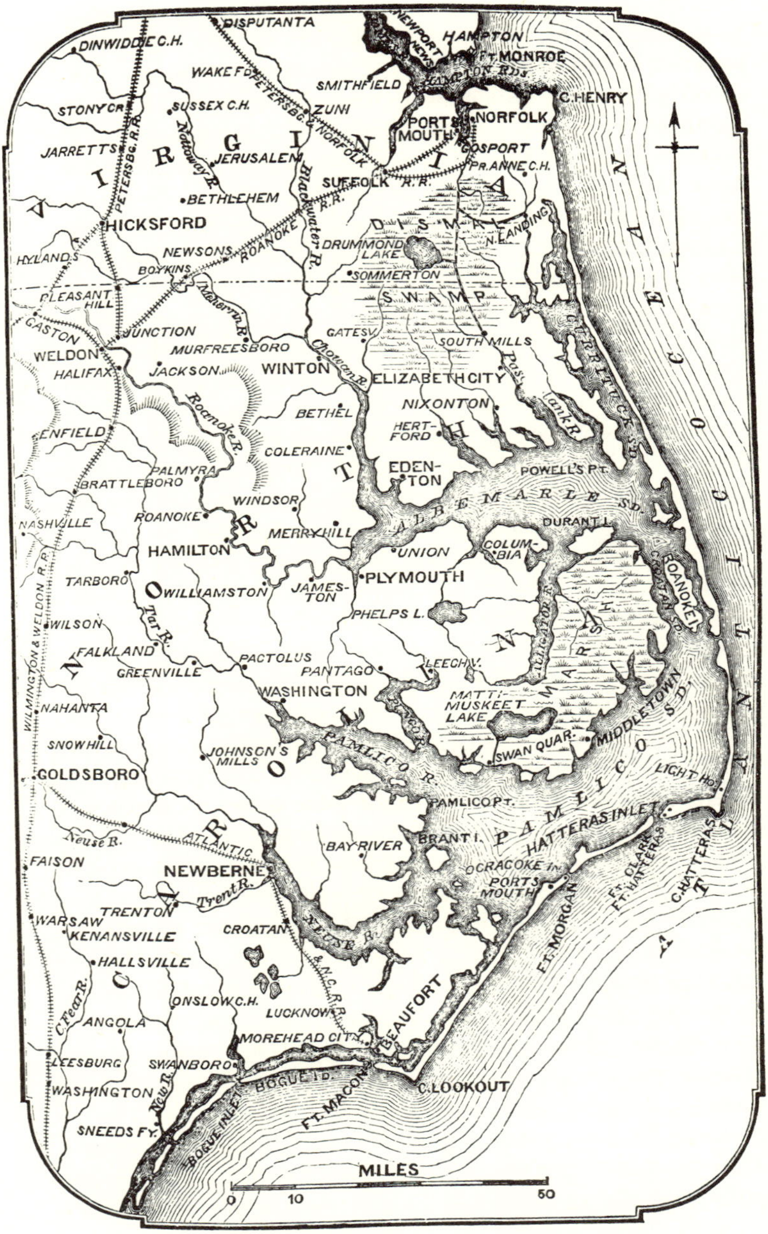

Pamlico and Albemarle Sounds

Source: John S. C. Abbott, *The History of the Great Civil War in America*. 2 vols. (Springfield, Mass.: Gurdon Bill and Co., 1867), Vol. 1, p. 200.

Even if he had possessed twice as many troops, the next disaster to befall him was probably unavoidable. On 29 August 1861 a powerful Federal flotilla rounded Cape Hatteras, off the North Carolina coast, compelled the surrender of the fort guarding the entrance to Pamlico Sound, and threatened to penetrate any of the North Carolina rivers or move directly north and assault Norfolk. After a lengthy interval, an additional Federal fleet of forty-two steamers and several sailing ships under General Ambrose Burnside reached Cape Hatteras on 17 January 1862.[45] Wise and everyone else in the Confederacy knew that this fleet's eventual objective was Roanoke Island, about eighty miles north of the cape and of incalculable importance for the defense of Norfolk and the northeastern North Carolina coast. Control of the island gave immediate access to Albemarle and Currituck sounds, eight rivers, four canals, two railroads, and more than four-fifths of Norfolk's supplies.[46] In the end, Roanoke Island became a tragedy exceeding in its miseries even what happened in western Virginia.

Shortly after taking charge, Wise inspected the island's defenses. He found few guns capable of resisting an enemy's fleet. Moreover, the principal ship channel had not been sufficiently obstructed to compel the Federals to come within range. There were "no teams for light artillery or for transportation, and no tools, axes, spades, shovels, or hoes for constructing breastworks." The North Carolina infantry on duty "were undrilled, unpaid, not sufficiently clothed and quartered, and were miserably armed with old flint muskets in bad order." In short, the island was a defenseless death trap. To his credit, Wise sensed the urgency of the situation. He immediately called for more men and matériel and attempted to impress the desperate situation and his own need for plenary power upon General Huger and Secretary of War Benjamin.[47] Men and supplies were so scarce as to compel reflection on what motives the Confederate high command could possibly have had in sending Wise and his men to an almost certain defeat. In the short run, of course, Benjamin had many defeats and the Confederacy's shortage of resources to think about. Huger offered nothing. His almost complete obliviousness to impending disaster indicates his gross incompetence.

When Burnside's fleet appeared off the island on 6 February, Wise lay immobilized by an acute attack of pleurisy. He issued such orders as he could but seemed powerless to do anything except send over to the island the only ten companies of the legion available. He remained bedridden at Nag's Head, half a mile east of the island. After an extended naval and artillery duel on 7 February in which the Confederates did no damage, Burnside landed about 7,500 troops. The next day Union forces turned the Confederate defenses and compelled the surrender of about 2,675 men, including more than 1,000 troops from Wise's Legion. Casualties were light on both sides, although Obadiah Jennings Wise suffered mortal wounds while commanding Confederate skirmishers.[48]

As Wise dragged himself to Currituck Court House, south of Norfolk, and rallied the remnants of his legion, sorrow and anger nearly overwhelmed him. In an effort to shift some of the enormity of his loss to other shoulders, he wrote that one cowardly regiment of North Carolina volunteers fled the battlefield. Colonel H. M. Shaw, commanding on Roanoke Island, had defied his orders to resist the enemy at the beaches, instead unaccountably retiring to his breastworks. The sly Yankees, Wise advised Jefferson Davis, had tricked his men at one point during the battle by advancing under cover of a white flag. He charged Huger with unconscionably diverting a portion of his artillery from the route he had selected, so that it never arrived, and also with failing to provide transportation for his infantry.[49] The military defeat was not his gravest loss, however. When the steamer bearing his son's body arrived at Currituck, he directed that the coffin be opened and bent over the body. Kissing his son's brow, he exclaimed, truly enough: "Oh, my brave boy, you have died for me, you have died for me."[50]

Wise continued to insist, in the weeks that followed, that guns, pile drivers, and labor were all available for use at Roanoke Island; they simply had not been forwarded with sufficient dispatch. Moreover, he argued that those of his troops who saw action behaved nobly and several times repulsed attacks by superior numbers. Fortunately for Wise, an investigating committee appointed by the Confederate Congress exonerated him and affixed responsibility for the disaster on General Huger and Secretary Benjamin. The latter resigned.[51] Though this was some solace, he required more, in view of the personal losses attendant on the Federal capture and occupation of Norfolk. Union troops soon took control of his estate, ransacked the house, and sent his correspondence to Boston, where it was examined for proof it might yield of Southern sympathizers living in the North. Many of his slaves stayed on the plantation, where they eventually became either employees or dependents of the Freedmen's Bureau. Wise moved his wife and the younger members of his family to a plantation in Goochland County, where they remained for most of the duration of the war.

What does a general do when his troops have lost two of the most important regions of his state to the enemy? Is he relieved of duty? Not if Congress has recently vindicated him. Might he be allowed to vegetate? Not if he were as vociferous as Wise. The former governor never seriously considered resigning, but by threatening resignation he exercised mild leverage on Confederate authorities. His first threat came in the immediate aftermath of Roanoke Island, when the War Department ordered him with only a portion of his command to Manassas, Virginia, to join General Joseph E. Johnston. He demanded additional time and an opportunity to reorganize his troops. Thereafter, it appeared that he might command a brigade of old men when Governor Letcher and Virginia Secretary of State George W. Munford contemplated calling out the second-class militia from Richmond for service under Wise. Letcher rescinded his order after Virginia's attorney general advised that this force could not legally be sent any distance from the city.[52]

By the late spring of 1862, Johnson had moved his headquarters from Manassas to cope with General McClellan's effort to assault Richmond from the east. McClellan's advance may have saved Wise, as had a second resignation threat that he sent Lee after the Richmond militia scheme failed to materialize. Lee helped him obtain a command in mid-May because Virginia needed every man and Wise's abilities as a recruiter were widely known. Thus two skeleton regiments from his legion arrived for him on the James River. But his original legion, with almost no artillery and cavalry, now more closely resembled a regular infantry brigade. For the most part it remained well to the rear.[53]

Confederate authorities, with Lee again perhaps the controlling influence, placed Wise's troops on the far right of their defenses during the subsequent engagements with McClellan. Johnston, who commanded until wounds forced him to give way to Lee, stated flatly that he no longer wanted Wise's brigade.[54] Galled because his services were neither trusted nor required, Wise grew increasingly restless and frustrated supervising garrison duty. His troops were posted about ten miles southeast of Richmond on the north bank of the James River, where they guarded the heavy batteries at Chaffin's Bluff. A portion of his brigade aided Major General Robert Rodes at Seven Pines on 30 May, though Wise was absent. Then, a month later, and after only an oral request from his commanding officer, General Theophilus Holmes, he moved his entire brigade near the front lines and attempted to take part in the abortive Confederate assault at Malvern Hill. For the greater part of the day his troops did nothing but countermarch, absorb a few shellings, and charge across fields only to find no Yankees on the other sides. Superior officers roundly criticized Wise for leaving his post and absorbing several casualties without orders. But it mattered little to a man desperate for achievement and vindication—especially against an old enemy such as McClellan—and who now in his solitary moments regarded himself as an exile in his own state.[55]

For the next sixteen months Wise remained at Chaffin's Bluff. His troops occupied themselves with tedious picket duty interrupted occasionally by a raid or foraging expedition into the no-man's-land between Richmond's outer defenses and Williamsburg. When McClellan evacuated his army from the peninsula later in the summer of 1862, Union forces continued to occupy the lower portion of it. In particular, they held a strong position at Fort Magruder immediately to the east of Williamsburg. Entrenched forces and powerful support from Union gunboats on the James River made a frontal assault potentially suicidal. Wise therefore settled down to exercise the functions of a military bureaucrat.

He began an incessant clamor for additional troops. Through these efforts and those of his recruiting officers, he gradually filled up the Forty-sixth and Twenty-sixth Virginia regiments of his brigade (the latter a well-commanded, well-drilled, and altogether superior unit). Large numbers of men in the Forty-sixth and Fifty-ninth Virginia regiments were captured at Roanoke Island, and many of them attempted to return to their homes in western Virginia following their exchange. Wise protested the War Department's decision to disband several companies of the Fifty-ninth while on parole. He also demanded restoration of several companies of the regiment that remained in western Virginia. The word must have fallen on fertile ground because by the fall of 1862 the Fifty-ninth approached full strength and he commanded 2,843 men, the highest number since his time in the Kanawha Valley.[56] His brigade again included artillery and cavalry detachments, though the troopers behaved like the dregs of the Confederate service. Portions of his cavalry were drunk and totally ineffective much of the time. Wise wanted the cavalry led by Colonel J. Lucius Davis, which had served in western Virginia, returned to him. But General J. E. B. Stuart liked Davis; Wise never again commanded him. Disappointments of this sort led him to moan that although he ranked as the senior brigadier general in the Confederate army (the War Department ranked him third) he had never enjoyed his proper command.[57]

Picketing and scouting duties took their toll on the brigade's morale. What Wise wanted was active service under General Lee. His mortification increased with the knowledge that some people referred to his unit as "the Life Insurance Company." During the summer of 1863, he probably took hope at news that General James Longstreet considered taking his men south for action. But Lee's principal lieutenant changed his mind when he learned that Wise's troops had not seen a major battle since Seven Pines. "I have been bereaved and wrecked and wronged," he wrote Nat Tyler, editor of the *Richmond Enquirer*, "but I try not to complain, and ask only to be allowed to serve and suffer as best I can."[58]

The intelligence operations required of Wise's troops aimed at more than keeping Union forces under surveillance. His men made special efforts to arrest Union sympathizers and aid Confederate families in withdrawing to friendly lines. Wise zealously endeavored to round up Confederate conscripts, free blacks, and fugitive slaves and to prevent suspicious blacks from either spying on his lines or escaping to Federal positions. He kept his men busy constructing fortifications and winter quarters. He never neglected to pay for equipment or supplies out of his own pocket if he could add to the men's comfort. He grew a large garden to help supply the brigade and ordered rawhides so that there would be no shortage of shoes.[59] He also maintained useful relations with many of his old constituents in lower Virginia, one of whom had given him his riding horse shortly after he had offered his services to the Confederacy. His command therefore ate and maintained itself reasonably well. But frustrations mounted. His irascibility provoked his officers, and he cursed them regularly in front of their troops.

If the number of desertions from his brigade is any guide, he experienced difficulty in disciplining his men.[60] More troops, including officers, deserted from the Fifty-ninth Regiment than from any other unit. Many had come from western Virginia. Others had "volunteered" from the Richmond prisons. But even his best regiment suffered. Several men from the Twenty-sixth deserted during Wise's stay at Chaffin's Bluff. Most of its enlistees lived in Tidewater counties abandoned to the Federals.[61] After his assistant adjutant general (whose drunkenness later prompted his suspension, although he subsequently returned to duty) expressed alarm late in November 1862, Wise acknowledged to superiors his dismay that desertions continued despite all precautions.[62] Also at this time, Wise assailed one cavalry commander, several of whose officers he had recently found hunting deer just a few days after a number of pickets were killed and the captain had protested his insufficiency of men.[63] Desertions and other disturbing incidents prompted Wise to request several courts-martial. They met only after considerable difficulty and inconvenience, however, because witnesses usually had to be detached from active service. Few were convened to deal with Wise's troops. There is also no evidence (and the record is rather full) that he ever ordered or approved the execution of any deserters, fugitive slaves, or accused spies. In fact, he typically asked clemency for deserters and apparently never recommended execution in his command for an infraction of discipline.[64]

Because he faced a powerful and entrenched enemy with troops whose quality may have been improving but of which he was suspicious, Wise's unwillingness to take military risks might be excused. After hearing of Lee's great victory at Fredericksburg in December 1862, for example, he advised one of his regimental commanders: "Now is the time to make a rapid demonstration. Do it if you dare."[65] But this tentative attitude ended early in April 1863. Wise received orders to raid down the peninsula as far as possible in support of General Longstreet's operations in southeastern Virginia.[66] This was the only large-scale action in which he participated during his time at Chaffin's Bluff. His cavalry drove off skirmishers from the Fifth Pennsylvania Cavalry—antagonists whom Wise despised, largely because he regarded them as ignorant Dutchmen—in front of Williamsburg, allowing him to occupy the city for several days. Meanwhile, elements of the Fifty-ninth Regiment under command of Colonel William B. Tabb circled behind Union lines and burned tens of thousands of dollars worth of property before escaping with small loss. The brigade carried off this raid handsomely but lacked the strength to occupy Williamsburg permanently. Wise gathered "all the plunder we could find and moved out the inhabitants and their effects," including several fugitive slaves whom his troops recaptured.[67]

Included in the plunder were hospital supplies from the Eastern State Hospital whose presence in Williamsburg once again produced a king-sized political problem for Wise, just as it had during his gubernatorial administration. Wise possessed insufficient resources to maintain the hospital, even had he retained control of Williamsburg.[68] To admit this lack, however, would have been to confess Virginia's weakness and inability to care for her own disadvantaged. This enforced dishonesty led him into strident condemnations of the Union authorities for neglecting the inmates of the asylum, for he fully realized that only they possessed adequate resources to operate it. After ordering out a Union army surgeon who was supervising operations, Wise attempted to convince a Virginia doctor to undertake its superintendency, hoping the Federals would turn him out.[69] Then after taunting his enemies for their unwillingness to leave Fort Magruder, Wise gradually withdrew his command late in April to Chaffin's Bluff.

Following his withdrawal, the Union commander protested Wise's raid, noted his inability to occupy the town, suggested that his tactics only discomfited the inmates at the asylum, and threatened to hang any townspeople who fired on Federal troops. Powerless in all other ways, Wise responded with his most blistering literary assault of the war, one reminiscent of his antebellum manifestos. He called Major General John A. Dix a liar and hypocrite for suggesting that United States forces permitted Williamsburg's citizens to pursue "their domestic avocations" in peace. He accused Dix's troops of cowardice and suggested that he might hang him like John Brown for treason against Virginia if captured. He alleged a number of crippling miseries suffered by Union armies as a result of his raids and grandiloquently maintained that they would continue. But they did not—could not, in view of the increasing strains on the Confederacy. General Dix returned Wise's letter as "fit neither to be written nor received."[70] By September 1863, Wise's brigade was on its way to South Carolina as one of Virginia's gifts to the besieged city of Charleston.

As befitted their reputation, Wise's troops were first placed in reserve. But the Confederates could afford only so much choosiness. Wise soon took control of a military district south of Charleston. Major General Arnold Elzey, his previous commander in Virginia, had handled Wise shrewdly and carefully, with an occasional flattering compliment that produced loyalty. General P. G. T. Beauregard did exactly the same in South Carolina, with similar results. Beauregard left nothing to Wise's imagination. He provided detailed orders on how the Virginian was to position his every man. Wise properly complained (but not very bitterly) that his artillery and cavalry were left behind in Virginia.

Some of the same problems endured, however. Although Wise assured Christian ministers that he paid considerable attention to religious instruction in his brigade, his troops repeatedly broke discipline. In December 1863, he reported that a contingent of his men desecrated several churches, tore private dwellings to pieces, and generally terrorized the people they were allegedly protecting. Personnel problems also persisted. Colonel Richard T. W. Duke of the Forty-sixth Regiment, who simultaneously served as the Commonwealth's attorney for Albemarle County in Virginia, resigned his commission in March 1864. Duke wanted either to return to

Charlottesville or to take the regiment back to Virginia. Duke attacked Wise's inefficiencies, complained about nepotism in the brigade, and protested Wise's interference when one of his nephews was charged with dereliction of duty. Wise called Duke a renegade and accused him of cowardice for communicating criticisms to high Confederate authorities only after his resignation, when he was not answerable to a military tribunal. Although at first reluctant to excuse Duke, Wise happily released him in the end. He threatened Beauregard with his own resignation should Duke have been allowed to depart with the Forty-sixth Regiment.[71]

Another inauspicious commencement plagued his command's military activity. In January 1864, his artillery fired about two hundred rounds at a Union gunboat off John's Island but failed to touch it. Meanwhile, Union troops sneaked behind a portion of the Twenty-sixth Regiment, killed a few men, and wounded several. Shortly thereafter, however, the brigade effectively repelled a Union assault. Despite Wise's failure to pursue the enemy—his artillery captain forgot to carry sufficient ammunition—Beauregard complimented him officially. In Lee's army no such action would have merited recognition, one of Wise's officers admitted. But for Wise, it was the first significant acknowledgment of his military services.[72]

Serving under Beauregard thus left him "contented," he wrote his wife. With time to spare, he puttered around a garden in an old frock coat talking indiscreetly with whoever approached. He transfixed his officers in the evening with stories about Clay and Webster, though he always began and ended with reminiscences of Andrew Jackson. He issued an extended series of regulations for his men, examined his officers' reports carefully, and attended to correspondence. Thoughts of old and new rivalries festered in this enervating environment. Lacking honor, he thought much of preserving it. Boredom was debilitating but not lethal. "I only seek to serve in this war," he wrote. "When it is over I desire only to have the means of subsistence."[73]

Amid the loneliness and disappointment, his wife, family and the consolations of religion dominated his thinking. He frequently took leave during the last year of the war to join his frail, sick wife in Goochland County, Virginia, an area threatened by marauders, bushwackers, and Union raiding parties. Indeed, Wise himself barely escaped when Colonel Ulric Dahlgren took his Federal cavalry through Goochland in May 1864, before meeting his death on the outskirts of Richmond. In his letters Wise cheered Mary, described their blessings, and directed his sons and other members of his family in providing for her comfort. Mary suffered so intensely from diarrhea and other ailments that she found opium a necessity. When fit, she used whatever influence her name commanded to forward hams, turkeys, and vegetables from her neighborhood to Henry's headquarters. Mary retained an oppressive sense of herself as a burden and continued to exasperate Wise, his paternalism notwithstanding, by her inability or unwillingness to make decisions. Afflicted at almost every turn by illness, dislocation, insecurity, and failure, Wise began attending religious services regularly early in 1864. He read the Scriptures and religious literature voraciously during the final eighteen months of the war. Occasionally—though always in the dead of night—a vision of peace with its fond and wonderful satisfactions calmed him. To inspire them, he described the vision for his family. He reveled in its serenity until wrenched back into reality by the horrors of a wretched war.[74]

Death threats spurred thoughts of preserving his immortality. These thoughts in turn led Wise to reflect on his remaining sons and his nephews for whose safety and honor he believed himself responsible. From four to eight members of his own family served, at various times, in his brigade, all as officers. Wise demanded as much preferment for them as he could obtain. During the war, he kept up as best he could on even the most minute details of family gossip. Whenever possible, he invited his youngest son, John Sergeant, his young nephews, and his grandchildren to his camp. Never uncritical, he found his son Richard "so impudent and insolent that I avoid talking to him." The nephews were "insufferably ignorant and lazy, selfish and conceited." Democratic in conferring his scorn, he hoped never to favor his kin in dispensing kindness and protection. "Your son does honour to you, Madam," he wrote one Virginian, "and I will take care of him & *all my boys*. The War has given me the large family of the camp, and the camp is now my household." It was, however, a house divided—buffeted by the storms and dissensions overwhelming the Confederacy itself.[75]

Camp life, like family and politics, was never as free from feuds and failures as he claimed. Given his age and lack of training, however, Wise's repeated pleas for justification both during and after the war made some sense. Not many of the political generals enjoyed the redemption he experienced at Petersburg, as we shall see. To those who reciprocated his benevolence, assented to his leadership, and confirmed his dignity during the war he returned unyielding loyalty ever after. Whatever it was in his power to provide—money, counsel, references, employment—

came merely for the asking. He wanted to protect his men as well as his family. But in the last year of the war dozens of his favorites died bravely. Except for Henry's invalid elder brother, every male member of the Wise family of Virginia aged sixteen and above served in the Confederate army. Of the nineteen who served, two were killed and ten wounded, including two crippled for life.[76]

Wise publicly articulated his private fears about the crushing of the Confederacy in the fall of 1863. Still he plodded on resolutely, indeed, enthusiastically. He invested at least $11,000 of his own money in Confederate bonds. With his land alienated, he gained between $15,000 and $25,000 in 1863 by selling his late son's share of the *Richmond Enquirer*.[77] A portion of these funds was apparently eaten up in the inflation that engulfed the Confederacy for no record exists of Wise purchasing any property or other hard assets during the war. Late in 1863, he composed an impressive paper on the inflation crisis in which he recommended stringent measures to encourage home manufactures in the South and demanded an end to inequitable taxation. This letter held a glimmer of the old defiance of the wealthy and privileged in which Wise had specialized before attaining considerable wealth himself.[78] With time heavy on his hands in South Carolina, he also prepared a paper on the governance of the army that reflected his growing and enforced interest in administrative affairs.[79]

Jefferson Davis visited Wise's camp in November 1863. For a time they tried to forget the discouraging progress of the war. They joked, exchanged horses, and did a little racing. But the goodwill was not to last. After Davis left, Wise sent him a playful note recalling their good fun that infuriated the Confederate president. Wise suggested in his note that if Davis did any more horse racing, he might have to be reported to his deacon. This joke was bad enough, but Wise added another, more serious matter. His son-in-law, Dr. A. Y. P. Garnett, served as Davis's personal physician. He had recently seen Mrs. Davis, who asked Garnett to send her love to his father-in-law. How fair it seemed, Garnett wrote, that Mrs. Davis should pass along her love to Wise, when the newspapers were full of reports that Jefferson Davis was kissing all the girls during his southern tour. Wise relished a chance to strip the president of his pretensions and included this reference in both his conversation with Davis (he talked about the president "smouching all the women in the South") and in his later note. Davis bristled at such "offensive familiarity" and demanded explanations from Wise and Garnett. Garnett felt compromised and then greatly relieved when he and Davis were reconciled a few days later. But Wise was at home in such a situation; indeed, he almost seemed to enjoy the controversy as a diversion from the war and his boredom. Calling Davis "a small, weak, little jaundiced bigot and vain pretender" in a letter to Garnett, he wrote the president one of his best sarcastic, point-by-point rebuttals. Evidently nothing came of the controversy, although Wise might have threatened Davis with a public airing of the story if the president had pushed matters further. But Wise added, for the benefit of his son-in-law, that as a private gentleman he believed himself "superior" to Davis. It was not, however, as private gentlemen that relations between them were maintained during the war. It is therefore little wonder that Wise continued with his brigade to idle away in South Carolina, despite his longing for vindication.[80]

His chance came at Petersburg in June 1864. As Grant's assaults brought him nearer to Richmond in the spring of 1864, the Confederate high command determined to move almost all of Beauregard's army north. Two regiments of Wise's brigade traveled to Florida, where they performed effectively in the Confederate victory at Olustee. His other two regiments were among the last to depart for Virginia, much to his regret. His officers and men inevitably reflected on this further evidence of how his command was so often mutilated, their general never trusted, and his brigade always denied "the post of honor."[81]

Wise literally fought his way into Petersburg. He traveled with his leading regiment, the Fifty-ninth Virginia, which detrained about forty miles southeast of Petersburg to defend a bridge on the Richmond and Danville Railroad. Greatly outnumbered by Federal cavalry, the regiment gave up the bridge, which was burned, but repelled several attacks and took a number of prisoners. Wise had reason to feel confident about his men, ably handled by Colonel Tabb.[82] Upon arriving at his new post in early May, he probably looked forward to offensive action. It came on 16 May, but with disappointing results. Under the direction of the newly appointed commander at Petersburg, Major General W. H. C. Whiting, Wise's brigade moved north of the city to attack Union forces near Port Walthall Junction. This maneuver was part of a general assault ordered by Beauregard in an effort to annihilate the Union army concentrated between Richmond and Petersburg. The attack failed, and Wise's troops were subjected to such confused and indecisive leadership that he charged his superior with drunkenness. Whiting's exhaustion, not intoxication, probably induced his ineffectiveness. He soon departed for North Carolina.

But the cloud over Wise continued. In view of the public criticism of Whiting and his peripheral involvement in a political tempest resulting from the alleged interest of the Confederate high command in defending Richmond with greater tenacity than Petersburg, he was detached from the greater part of his regiment.[83] On 1 June he took over at Petersburg as commander of the First Military District, Department of North Carolina and Southern Virginia. He was responsible for Virginia south of the Appomattox River. The command sounded imposing, although the intention may again have been to remove him from the field. Instead of a position in the rear, however, Petersburg within a week became the very center of the war and Wise found himself directing a battle for the first and only time in his life.

As the Union military leaders suffered disastrous casualties in front of Richmond in the spring of 1864, they gradually perceived the strategic importance of Petersburg. Through it passed most of the Confederate capital's supplies. Control of the city would probably compel the abandonment of Richmond. Before Grant shifted the larger part of his army south of the James River in mid-June to assault Petersburg directly, he ordered several efforts by advance columns of cavalry and infantry to take the city. These attacks, begun on 9 June, were made by veteran and well-supplied troops who far outnumbered the beleaguered city's defenders. Fortunately for the Confederates, almost all of these preliminary assaults were uncoordinated and led by overly cautious commanders.

Wise had barely a thousand men under his command on 9 June, including only the Forty-sixth Virginia Regiment from his own brigade. But several companies of veteran and highly mobile light artillery were in the city. He rallied the defenders, positioned his forces effectively, and shifted them around so rapidly that Union commanders grew confused about his numbers. Wise released wounded soldiers from hospitals and prisoners from jails. He drew them up in a thin line along the southern perimeter of the city. On his far right and directly south of the city's center he placed the Petersburg second-class militia, which though decimated during the day's fighting delayed the Union cavalry until reinforcements could arrive.

Brigadier General August V. Kautz commanded the Federal cavalry (numbering approximately thirteen hundred effectives), which attacked Wise's right. Kautz's objective was to smash the Confederate defenses and burn the bridges over the Appomattox, thereby isolating the city.[84] But artillery fire bothered his troops. The colonel commanding his lead regiment noted warily that "Wise in person" opposed him—indicating that some Federals had a higher opinion of Wise's abilities than most Confederates.[85]

Kautz worried about advancing too far into the city and being cut off by Confederate reinforcements such as Brigadier General James Dearing's cavalry, which assailed his force by midafternoon. Because Kautz arrived at his objective late, a planned and coordinated cavalry and infantry assault never took place. Major General Quincy H. Gillmore, at the head of the Union infantry on Kautz's right, delayed his advance awaiting the cavalry support he had expected much earlier. Gillmore never got his force, numbering perhaps five thousand, effectively engaged. His commanding officer cashiered him shortly thereafter.

Several days later, a similar action occurred. Again, the Confederates just managed to hold the city. By 15 June Wise had been reinforced with most of his own brigade, two other regiments, and several smaller units, so that he commanded about twenty-two hundred effectives.[86] He exposed himself continually, rallied stragglers, and again held out until the last possible moment. Although the Forty-sixth Virginia Regiment eventually gave way and broke under murderous Union assaults, both he and his men fought ferociously. Casualties were heavy; it was as if the entire brigade had waited through the war for an opportunity to prove itself. Once again, the hapless General Kautz led the Union cavalry on Wise's right. Though his force numbered twenty-five hundred men, they were at no time a serious threat. Artillery fire again distracted Kautz; he began withdrawing on the evening of 15 June at just the time when the Union infantry on Wise's left began its assault. Major General W. F. Smith, a daring and successful soldier, commanded this force of some ten thousand men. Smith probably had the city at his mercy, but he unaccountably delayed his principal attack until seven in the evening. Through the day, his forces gradually had gained control of portions of the Confederate outer defenses, even though resisted with "unflinching stubbornness" by Wise's troops. Beauregard, unable to get any reinforcements into the city until after dark, could only urge his forces "to hold on at all hazards." Perhaps Smith failed to realize the significance of Petersburg's railroads in the Confederate system of supply and defense; perhaps he waited too long for General Winfield Scott Hancock's II Corps, which joined him late in the afternoon. In any case, he paused unaccountably after his principal assault had swept the Southerners from nearly their entire line of defenses and had left the city before him as night fell. By morning, Wise and Beauregard had fixed another line of defense. The slaughter on both sides then began in earnest, though three days later the Confederacy still held the town and with the aid of Lee's just arriving army would be certain to maintain it.[87]

A humbler man and a commander less anxious for glory and revenge might have remained silent about the accomplishments at Petersburg. But true to form, Wise issued stirring congratulatory messages to his troops for driving "back the insolent foe from the approaches which their footsteps for the first time polluted." He then encouraged newspapers to publish these messages. He exaggerated the magnitude of his victory, especially by undercounting the numbers of his own troops and overestimating the enemy forces opposing him.[88] Indeed, he consistently exaggerated these matters in all his publications during and after the war. But Wise's urgency for recognition and respite from the slanders directed at him led him further. He forwarded to the Virginia secretary of state two Union battle flags captured on 16 June by Major General Bushrod R. Johnson's Tennesseans. Wise said nothing when the flags found their way to the offices of the *Richmond Examiner*, which printed an account of their capture on 20 June and credited them to his brigade. Johnson's protest then severely embarrassed him and probably soured relations between them when Wise a short time later found his brigade attached to Johnson's division.[89]

Even before the culmination of the fateful four-days battle for Petersburg from 15 to 18 June, Wise had left the field and resumed his responsibilities as commander First Military District, Department of North Carolina and Southern Virginia. Having played his part, he gave way to more senior officers. Considering Wise's irascible nature and spotty record, few superiors trusted him, despite his fine showing. He probably took a short leave before returning to duty. Little evidence remains from this period of his service, but his responsibilities seem to have been largely administrative. He operated from a private home in Petersburg, some distance from where his brigade served under Johnson in the trenches south of the city. He was absent on 30 June, when the Federals exploded a mine under a portion of the Confederate lines near its position. The brigade again took heavy casualties during the battle for the "Crater." It also participated in the successful Confederate counterattack led by Wise's good friend Brigadier General William Mahone, who preempted the sluggish and bewildered Johnson. Wise probably continued to designate the commanders of his brigade, who always were colonels of long service and intimate acquaintance from one of his regiments. Moreover, his blood relations on the brigade's staff kept him fully informed of its day-to-day operations.[90]

As the terrible winter of 1864–65 approached, senior Confederate officers such as Beauregard and Lee grew reluctant to require active service from someone of Wise's years and precarious health. Appalling accounts describe the environment of filth, vermin, and disease in which the Confederacy attempted to maintain the Army of Northern Virginia. Food was inadequate, often nonexistent. Shelter was primitive, weather frequently indescribable. Lee's army lost thousands to desertion; especially after Christmas 1864, many simply abandoned the lines and went home. And because the Confederates stood on the defensive, they were compelled constantly to guard their fortifications. Finally, those who subsisted under these conditions were in constant danger of death from sharpshooters who took their daily toll.

Determined not to evade the privations to which his troops were exposed, Wise petitioned for reassignment to his brigade and joined it just as the dead of winter approached. He and his kinsmen had narrowly defeated yet another conspiracy only a few weeks earlier. Several of his officers attempted to displace him with the brigade's senior colonel, J. Thomas Goode. But the majority rallied to his defense, composed appropriate resolutions, and requested that he rejoin the brigade. Thereafter, he speculated about resigning from the army so as to protect his family from some "great and final disaster." He decided against it because of the filial affection and loyalty of his troops.[91]

Wise remained with his brigade throughout most of January, February, and March of 1865, living in a so-called bombproof shelter slightly to the rear of the lines. Surely under these conditions he could see the end. Because only independence could avert vassalage to the Yankees, he enthusiastically endorsed one of the Confederacy's last ditch efforts to obtain an armistice. Along with a considerable number of regimental and brigade commanders in Lee's army, he forwarded a set of resolutions to Congress from his brigade indicating his willingness to give up slavery in return for Southern independence. The resolves reflected a speech he delivered before his troops. He hoped that they might convince the Congress to emancipate the slaves and thereby earn diplomatic recognition for the South from enough European powers to force its acceptance by Lincoln's government. Slavery in Virginia was dead and gone, he had told his men before the end of 1864. Because slaveholding had never been an obsession with him, he found it easy in the end to choose independence over slavery. About the justice of independence there were never any doubts. He would fight to the end, he told a cheering crowd in Richmond early in February. No matter how grim the outlook, no matter how tattered his troops, he would never surrender by his own consent and accept subjugation. Steadfastness came more easily once Wise had acknowledged slavery's collapse.[92]

Wise's defense at Petersburg had already prolonged the war. During the agonizing retreat to Appomattox he proved that he meant it when he said he would fight to the end. Late in March 1865, as the war's last campaign opened, his troops operated on the Confederate far right, as Lee attempted to prevent Grant's forces from cutting the railroads that had barely kept his forces alive in Petersburg during the winter. The brigade charged the enemy gallantly but fell back under punishing blows to the south bank of the Appomattox River. In detaching troops such as Wise's, Lee weakened his Petersburg lines. On 1 April, a sizable Confederate force operating to the west of Wise's brigade suffered a crushing defeat at Five Forks. On 2 April, Union troops massively assaulted the lines at Petersburg, breaching them on the west side of the city. With the Federals in their front and rear, Wise's forces and scattered other Confederate units escaped as best they could to the north bank of the Appomattox and joined Lee's retreat westward.

Wise and his officers performed superhumanly over the next week in merely keeping their command together. Finally, with a chance to fight in the army and very nearly under Lee's eye, Wise rallied his forces during the Confederate fiasco at Sayler's Creek and cut his way through the Union troops who had surrounded one-third of Lee's army. He also brought out several other straggling units from Johnson's division. His antagonist lost his head and fled momentarily during the action. Lee retaliated by giving Wise temporary command of these units, including personal supervision of Johnson. The grizzled old former governor relished this opportunity to participate in the humiliation of an enemy. Lee may even have wanted to promote Wise to major general in recognition of his effectiveness, but he never had the chance.[93]

At Appomattox, fewer than six hundred men from his brigade surrendered and accepted paroles. They were all that remained of the twenty-eight hundred who had come from South Carolina with him a year earlier. Wise knew the meaning of the surrender. His demeanor suggested how utterly crushed he was, as well as his continuing determination to convince victor and vanquished alike that he had fought the good fight. One Northern observer described him as "an old man, with spectacles and a short white beard, a stooping sickly figure with his legs tied round with gray blankets."[94] As the Virginia governor responsible for John Brown's execution, Wise commanded intense interest during the surrender ceremony. A few in Grant's army despised him and perhaps delighted in his predicament, but most were simply curious. How had this old general of a thousand consuming hatreds survived such a long and miserable war? Had it humbled his Virginia pride and compelled him to reflect on his foolhardy slogans of years earlier? In making no effort to repair his appearance, or even to remove the tobacco stains from his beard and clothing, Wise meant to proclaim his defiance. He bragged about the bravery of his troops to one Union commander. He also cursed his soldiers as he frequently did, although at Appomattox it seemed out of place. And he in turn was cursed by them. "Look at him," some of his men shouted, as he abused them for failing to dress their lines more rapidly. "He is brave enough now, but he never was so near the Yankees before in his life." He paced his horse back and forth restlessly and eccentrically engaged soldiers in conversation. He believed the South's lawyers remained supreme (doubtless reflecting on what he knew would now be his only means of obtaining a livelihood) because the Yankees stupidly failed to require all surrendered troops to sign their own paroles and instead took their assent more or less for granted. He also loudly descanted upon the irreversible hatreds nurtured by the war, the ruin of Virginia, and the homelessness of her people.[95]

A few humane Federals took pity on him. Two young Irish officers from New York, remembering his services during the Know-Nothing crusade, sought him out in a way that he never forgot. They cheered him and brought him food and a good pen knife, which Wise claimed was the only thing he needed because whittling was now a passion. General George G. Meade, who had married a sister of Wise's second wife, also made contact. Years earlier and in desperate straits himself, Meade had asked Wise for assistance in securing his reappointment to the army. Wise had aided Meade instrumentally and surely must now have reflected on the irony of having sustained the general who commanded the Union troops at Gettysburg. Concerned about the forlorn spectacle Wise presented, Meade put an ambulance and team at his disposal. Meade's wife took her sister's three children to Philadelphia for several months after the surrender of Lee's army.[96]

The former governor proceeded to Halifax County, where he visited his son and namesake, Reverend Henry A. Wise. Most of the female members of his family moved from Goochland County to a home in Richmond. Several months later, General Fitzhugh Lee finished his final report on operations during the retreat to Appomattox. Although memories of the war, defeat, and the emptiness of loss never left Wise's consciousness, Lee's language must have helped him endure and abide: "The past services of General Henry A. Wise, his antecedents in civil life, and his age, caused his bearing upon this most trying retreat to shine conspicuously forth. His unconquerable spirit was filled with as much earnestness and zeal in April, 1865, as when he first took up arms four years ago, and the freedom with which he exposed a long life laden with honors proved he was willing to sacrifice it, if it would conduce toward attaining the liberty of his country."[97]

Chapter 14

Confederate Past, Yankee Future

Few men ever gave more to a cause whose righteousness they doubted. Besides the blood sacrifices of his family, Wise lost perhaps $15,000 to 20,000 in direct donations to the Confederacy. This figure included Confederate bonds, forever worthless, and out-of-pocket expenses to equip himself and his troops. His farm was ransacked, his library pilfered. Friends and relatives kept him alive for several weeks after the surrender at Appomattox while he roamed Virginia attempting to determine where his best opportunities might lie. For some time, he occasionally accepted "loans" with no intention of repaying. He also benefited from public fund-raising activities undertaken in the South. Remembering his antebellum services, Catholics and Irish predominated in these efforts. In poor health throughout this period, he barely survived a cholera attack in the summer of 1866.[1]

His prospects were grim. Certainly no option of further fighting remained. At a public meeting in Halifax County late in April 1865, he counseled his listeners to accept defeat and rebuild their fortunes.[2] He would himself extract as much hope as possible from mournful circumstances. If he could reclaim his land in order to sell it—farming was now out of the question—and launch a law practice, his reputation might see him through. But hard times render good names precious and frail. Wise therefore insisted on proclaiming his achievements. Given his dubious record during the war, he could justify himself only by memorializing the Confederacy's accomplishments. In dozens of letters and addresses until his death in 1876, he glorified the Lost Cause, extolled the virtues of Confederate fighting men, and remembered the burdens borne by widows and orphans. Once merely a good Southerner, Wise now aspired to the part of best Southerner.

As always, he found it a goal impossible to attain. The Republicans later claimed his loyalty, for good reason, as we shall see. He simply protested too much, not only about the record of his brigade but about secession. Indignantly, he repudiated the charge of treason. Virginians had fought under the authority of their state, he declared at Alexandria early in 1866. Virginia's withdrawal from the Union legitimated his own resistance to federal authority. "The citizen is not responsible, the State alone can be, and the State can't be guilty of treason. I protest for myself and the dead, the glorious untarnished, Confederate dead, then, that we were no rebels, no traitors, and if I swear that they and I were in rebellion, I should put a foul blot upon the page of history as black as would be the spot of perjury on my own conscience!"[3] This view not only ignores his hesitations, it obliterates the memory of his failure to demonstrate the constitutional standing of secessionist doctrine. Moreover, Wise was in fact a revolutionary. He struck one of the first blows. But about the events of April 1861 he was notably and purposely silent after the war.[4]

If Wise refused to acknowledge his rebellion, he happily reiterated his prejudices against slavery and rejoiced in its extinction. "Slavery was a weakness, if not a wickedness—a wickedness because a weakness, to which I am not willing ever to expose my descendants, for fear of a humiliation like that to which I have been subjected." Emancipation came as a relief, the depth of which he alone knew. His contentment sharply delineated the limits of his paternalism. "I am now free of responsibility for [their] care and comfort, and, I repeat I am content," he told his Alexandria audience. "They are naturally lazy and unsteady at work," he remarked of the blacks, only two years following the collapse of a regime under which they had allegedly profited so much. Moreover, "they are the severest and most cruel taskmasters when invested with power." Emancipation, his own and theirs, thus seemed fraught with danger. "The dignity and status of our white race of men" was threatened by "the amalgamated and consolidated despotism of a new and mongrel republicanism."[5]

Small concessions when appropriate but unyielding resistance on all significant issues, using whatever leverage remained to his caste, remained his policy. "If negro equality and domination can be forced on us," he shrewdly remarked, "it can and must be forced upon the whites of the Northern States." Nor, of course, were these practical lessons, so aptly learned by Southern politicians then and since, his only counsel. Unyielding labor was now the lot of Virginians, particularly the young. Away with staple crops and plantations, he urged. The old vision of a commonwealth dominated by yeomen farmers and garden agriculture was reincarnated.[6] But how could it be effected? To many his plea for resistance seemed foolish because it invited continued Yankee occupation. To others, who sensed that his renewed calls for immigration were part of a supreme living fantasy in which he simply wrote the blacks and many former nonslaveholders out of his world, Virginia had been devastated enough. Further adventures were intolerable.

Wise talked, many listened, few followed. Power flowed away from him. Perhaps its absence heightened his eccentricities. Discoursing on the plants in his garden, reflecting on the Savior's divinity, riveting courtroom audiences with tales of Virginia's great men, consoling friends and family on the deaths of their beloved—all this was precisely what many Virginians craved. They conferred honor but withheld power. He suffered without it, found the disabling legislation that kept him from it infuriating, and doubted that any special entitlement would ever again be his. Meanwhile, the specter of destitution required him to seek control of his one tangible asset, now occupied, in part, by his former slaves.

Upon learning that he would not immediately suffer arrest and imprisonment, Wise sought to reclaim his property near Norfolk. He hired his old friend, former Congressman John Millson, to represent him before federal authorities. In a letter to General O. O. Howard, head of the Freedmen's Bureau, he claimed to have surrendered on condition that he be permitted "to return to his home and to remain there unmolested in all respects, as long as he obeyed the laws." The request was rejected on grounds that he had abandoned his home "in order that he might, to better advantage, engage in rebellion and civil war."[7] The bureau retained Rolleston nearly until it ceased operations late in 1868.

Henry, it turns out, was not the only Wise attempting to regain control of Rolleston. The unusual arrangement to purchase he made with his brother in 1859 now emerged to complicate matters. A bedridden invalid, John Cropper Wise remained on the estate throughout the war. Earlier in 1865, he had complained to federal authorities about his family's poverty. In the fall, however, and only after Henry's efforts were rejected, John Cropper Wise swore the required oath of allegiance to the United States and then forwarded to the Freedmen's Bureau copious documentation establishing himself as the legal owner of Rolleston. He also bombarded the bureau's agents with requests to cut wood, establish a grocery store, and repair the mill on the property. Bureau personnel interpreted these requests as efforts to regain legal ownership of the property and rejected them. Using alternately pleading and threatening language, John Cropper detailed his sufferings and complained that squatting blacks had stolen his stock and destroyed his fences. He went on to describe the plight of the poor freedmen, who were begging to establish labor contracts with him (as the bureau was urging them to do in 1865), but whom he could not gratify because title had not been returned to him. Bureau officials granted that John Cropper remained the legal owner, but they regarded the farm as the de facto property of Henry A. Wise, just as he did. Evidently, they obtained confidential information on the agreement Henry had made with his brother in 1859, and, in dismissing John Cropper Wise's claim, they asked why the general had recently applied for the restoration of his property if he was not the owner? In 1866, when John Cropper Wise died of articular rheumatism, Henry assumed his title. Having refused the Wises' claims, the bureau maintained at Rolleston a significant but flawed "experiment in liberty."[8]

As early as 1863, black "contrabands" occupied about fifty farms in Tidewater Virginia, including Wise's and former president John Tyler's. Several had already been assassinated. Among the hundreds of freedmen maintained on Wise's farm were twelve of his former slaves. The Freedmen's Bureau employed two of them, Joshua Phillips and William H. George, at $10 a month. A census completed sometime in 1866 suggests that Phillips was the head of a slave family formerly belonging to Wise. Most of his other slaves lived with the elderly George Douglas. Neither of these men, or any of the other slaves living on Wise's farm, seem to have acquired title to any of his property. Indeed, they owned nothing of any value. Adult males farmed eight-acre plots and divided the proceeds with the federal government. They worked under the eyes of a Freedmen's Bureau sublieutenant, who lived on the farm and reported to a superior officer in Norfolk.[9]

The American Missionary Association operated its only two schools in Princess Anne County on Wise's property. The young Yankee schoolmarms working under the auspices of the association created an impression in the area when they began in 1863 to teach the former governor's young slaves their letters.[10] Along with most freedmen in Tidewater Virginia and elsewhere, members of the Douglas and Phillips families seemed eager for instruction. They probably attended both the grammar and Sabbath schools; each met in Wise's former carriage house. The 1866 census designated the teenagers among Wise's former slaves as literate. Joshua Phillips may have learned how to read at the grammar school; the census also designates him as literate. If so, he was one of the few slave adults to have received instruction. Freedmen aged sixteen and under constituted almost the total enrollment.

Awestruck and envious of the elegance of Wise's home, the

Yankee teachers rode about in his carriage and inventoried all his possessions before they were shipped to Fortress Monroe; they also attempted to teach bourgeois habits to his former slaves. One of them reported that Wise's slaves "had no wish to see him back again; they spoke of him with little affection." Except for these ambivalent comments, reported by a presumably prejudiced source, there is no record of how the slaves viewed their former master. Nor is there any evidence of his having encountered them after the war. Wise visited Norfolk within weeks after surrendering at Appomattox, but federal officials prevented him from seeing Rolleston.[11]

Former slaves at Rolleston faced hard times. After mid-1865, the estate increasingly filled with dependent women, children, and the elderly, who turned it into a poor farm. This arrangement suited the convenience of the Freedmen's Bureau because the farm's function as an administrative headquarters probably made provisioning it relatively easy. There was considerable overcrowding and relatively little attention to farming the land. As late as November 1867, more than 250 people, most of them dependent on the bureau for subsistence, lived at Rolleston. Local bureau officials experienced continuing difficulty in attempting to dispose of these people to poor relief facilities in Princess Anne and elsewhere. Apparently because of the large numbers involved, these agents decided to resist restoration of the property to Wise. But the suffering and harassment endured by the freedmen led to an identity of interest among them. When the bureau agent in charge urged the young and able-bodied blacks to go elsewhere in Princess Anne and sign year-long contracts at the risk of having their huts pulled down, they resisted. This same agent later commented on the "harsh contrasts" demanded of blacks in the county and on how the whites in the area remained "vicious" and "unforgiving." By early 1868, the freedmen who remained had secured leases to portions of Wise's property and made it clear that they expected to gain title.[12] During the war, the Wises had happily left several slaves at Rolleston, regarding them as loyal and true. Others had evidently returned from their wartime dispersal. Now they wanted the land their toil had earned.

They failed. On 15 December 1868, just a few days before the bureau ended operations, Wise got Rolleston back. The educational facilities on the property, except for the Sabbath school, had closed several months earlier. Shortly afterward, Wise sold the entire estate for a little more than $26,000 to a New Yorker who had married one of his brother's daughters. He paid $7,000 of this sum to John Cropper Wise's widow as the unpaid balance of his original purchase price. The purchase price of $30 per acre was generous and undoubtedly reflected the kinship connection and the purchaser's admiration for the trials of a noble old Confederate. The Douglas and Phillips families shared in no bounty, however. They remained at Rolleston, probably as sharecroppers. As late as 1870 they owned no property of monetary value.[13]

For many months after Appomattox, Wise required permission from federal authorites to travel. At one point, several marauding Union cavalrymen divested him of most of his remaining possessions; he sought compensation, but the Quartermaster General's Office in Washington refused it.[14] He also encountered restrictions that prevented him from practicing law until 1866. Had he chosen to apply for a pardon, as did thousands of other former Confederates, his life would have been easier and simpler. But he refused amnesty altogether, despite pleas from members of his family.[15] Probably because it ran contrary to his interests, the old general regarded his defiant decision as his most important public act. It prevented, or at least substantially restricted, him from returning to public life, which was his fondest hope and ambition after the war.

President Andrew Johnson had issued a proclamation on 29 May 1865 offering amnesty to all those signing an oath to support the Constitution. As a high-ranking former Confederate and official of the Virginia and United States governments, Wise fell into one of the fourteen excepted classes whose members were required to make special application for individual pardon before filing the required oath. Johnson assured these Southerners that clemency would not be difficult to obtain. He would restore all property, except slaves, to those pardoned.

Taken together, three factors probably account for Wise's initial refusal to request a pardon. It is unlikely that he could ever have humbled himself sufficiently to make an abject appeal to Andrew Johnson, an acknowledged leader of the Southern yeomen. Johnson was precisely the sort of person Wise had both feared and despised for years.[16] Moreover, Wise had begun proceedings to reclaim his farm before he saw Johnson's proclamation. Under these circumstances, he may have thought an application crudely self-serving and dishonorable. Finally, Wise learned in midsummer of 1865 that an old antagonist, Federal District Judge John C. Underwood, was plotting retribution. Wise, Lee, and a host of other Virginians were indicted at Norfolk for treason. At Ulysses S. Grant's insistence, federal authorities later quashed the indictments.[17] But Wise grew uneasy when he heard that Lee had petitioned for pardon because this action might be construed as a confession of guilt and treason reflecting on the other Norfolk defendants. Wise therefore wrote Lee to urge a set of arguments against taking advantage of President Johnson's terms. "I have not applied for pardon," he advised, "because I was earnest and honest in my convictions that I was right and I am not yet convinced to the contrary and cannot admit therefore, under oath, either impliedly or expressly, that I was wrong, by the very fact of petitioning for pardon. Pardon implies, *ex vi termini*, guilt, crime—in this case the high crime of treason. I don't admit it and can't imply it by any act of mine. I was not a traitor to my country and cannot become a traitor to myself."[18] Lee responded perfunctorily. Ever superior and devotedly self-sacrificial, he had determined to request a pardon as an example for his men and the South. He thought it best to put the war behind as quickly as possible. Lee's commanding influence calmed the South generally, although nothing in "his career aroused so much antagonism," according to his celebrated biographer. Indeed, Lee eventually forwarded the proper amnesty oath, though unaccountably it was lost and not rediscovered until many years later.[19] Wise, on the contrary, remained unreconstructed and made a virtue out of consistency, to which he had seldom rendered slavish adherence.

Johnson's liberal approach produced some 13,500 pardons by September 1867. Before leaving office in 1869 he issued a general amnesty that fully restored ordinary civil and property rights to the Southern ruling class, Wise included. But the Fourteenth Amendment, ratified in 1868, prevented Wise from holding either state or federal office unless permitted by a two-thirds vote of Congress. He ached to have these liabilities removed, although he could never give his enemies the satisfaction of withdrawing his original pledge. They might relish, in any event, a chance to reject amnesty for the murderer of John Brown. But the refusal to take the risk left him helpless and despairing, repeating himself endlessly. He had become a crotchety old man—"a mere shadow of dried bones, firmly fastened together by cat gut," as one observer put it.[20] Why would he wish this humiliation?

The effort Wise made during and after the war to distance himself from the secessionists highlights his regret about the conflict. He constantly reiterated his interest in peace and emphasized the refusal of Virginia's secession convention to follow his advice. He said he had gone along "in full conviction that we could not succeed, and were likely to lose all."[21] Slavery compelled this result. Providence willed its destruction through war and the inevitability of Confederate defeat. "God knew that we could be torn away from our Black idol of Slavery only by fire and blood, and the drawn sword of the Destroying Angel of War. . . . I abide, therefore, the order of Providence, and ask pardon of God, and God only, in respect to slavery, and the war for its extinction."[22] After the war, Wise repeatedly condemned slavery as inefficient economically and bade it good riddance on that ground. But as he may have known better than most, slavery was also a moral wasteland. "We were obliged to fail, and we did fail," he remarked at a memorial service following Lee's death.[23]

Despite these reservations, he proclaimed to all who would listen that he did his "whole part at every post wherever put or trusted, from the first to the last," despite his age, sufferings, and losses. He was no traitor because his purpose was never "to secede from the Union" but "to fight all oppressors under the aegis of its Constitution . . . for the inalienable right of domestic, State, civil, self-government, and for my own liberty, guarded by the Constitution and laws!"[24] "I never fought under the Confederate flag," he said in 1866. "The Stars and Stripes were always my flag. I fought under the flag of Vir[ginia] and I never wore any buttons but the buttons of my own state."[25] In his heart, he claimed, he never left the Union. Thus he never joined the Confederacy.

To seek a pardon would therefore mean confronting the pain of acknowledging what he already knew to be true. He gave himself honestly to neither side. His commitments, though steadfast, never fully satisfied the demands of honor. Thus despite his overriding desire to influence public policy, Wise may well have doubted his right to do so. Speculation on such matters must, of course, be done with extreme caution. But it does seem plausible that Wise may never have wanted a pardon because he periodically thought himself undeserving and was perhaps fearful of rejection by former constituents should he be permitted to reenter public life.

A final influence on his decision comes, I suspect, from the example set in like circumstances by his great prewar antagonist, John Brown. There is no direct evidence, but one does not have to rely entirely on speculation. Brown was constantly on Wise's mind during and after the war. The general's former slaves and his neighbors reported to the Yankee schoolteachers on his farm how frequently he had discussed and praised Brown.[26] After Appomattox, he seems never to have lost an opportunity to invoke Brown's greatness.[27] Wise believed that Brown's effort to emancipate the slaves was noble, but what he most admired about the man was his firmness and steadiness. Brown possessed the courage of his convictions. He rejected efforts to secure clemency. So it was with

Wise, who seemed to associate Brown's example with his own refusal to appear penitent, contrite, or to seek forgiveness. "I could stand prouder on the gallows even," he wrote James L. Kemper, "than I could *on any condition of servile submission*."[28]

In the darkest days of war and reconstruction, Wise's primary fear was that some great catastrophe would destroy his white family and forever obliterate his name and memory. Other white Southerners experienced the same anxieties. Two potentialities provoked this terror: irrevocable alienation of land and revenge from the emancipated.[29] Afterward, Wise fought with all his remaining energy to guarantee for each of the young males in his clan as preferred a place as the postwar world could provide. Should the South ever rise, he wanted his family strategically situated in order to profit. Powerful and prominent as the Wises remain in our time, they have much to thank him for.

With the death of his brother and his sister Margaret in 1866, Henry became the only survivor of his generation. He most relied on his eldest surviving son, John Sergeant, whose conspicuous gallantry during the famous charge of the Virginia Military Institute's cadets at New Market in May 1864 endeared him ever afterward. Following John's graduation from law school at the University of Virginia in 1867, he and his father practiced law in partnership until Henry's death. Looking ahead, the general inquired carefully about the wealth and status of John's eventual bride.[30] Wise's second surviving son, Dr. Richard Alsop Wise, enjoyed a prominent medical and political career in Williamsburg. He married Mattie Peachy in 1870 and thus maintained the pattern of professional service and a socially appropriate marriage that structured the lives of the general's other sons. Wise's youngest son, Reverend Henry A. Wise, married into the well-to-do Haxall family before the war. But young Henry never satisfied his father. He served briefly as a chaplain in Wise's brigade during the war. Poor health then compelled him to decline a regular military chaplaincy. Futile efforts were made after the war to obtain for him the chaplaincy at the University of Virginia. Nursed by his father in his final illness, young Henry passed away in 1869 at age thirty-four. More than any of the other women in the general's family, Harriet Haxall Wise suffered unspeakably. Wearied by her husband's long final illness, she lost three of her children and her house and lived close to starvation the rest of her life.[31]

Wise's favorite daughter, Mary Garnett, survived the war, as did his daughter Anne, who lived in Goochland County. Their fortunes fared poorly, however. Anne's husband, Frederick Plumer Hobson, remained in bad health and experienced considerable difficulty in wringing a living out of his farm. Mary returned with her husband, Dr. Garnett, to Washington, D.C., but the doctor found it burdensome to reestablish his practice. Never reticent about offering advice, and now with the perfect excuse to do so, Wise suggested that the doctor resort to charging his patients small fees regularly. Professional men attempting to make a living amid blasted hopes had to be shrewd. Do not, he advised, try to collect large fees or extend long credit, both of which are resented.[32]

In the years after the war, Wise had nine grandchildren to think about, all but one of them born into the Hobson and Garnett families. In addition, the deaths of his sister Margaret and brother John left him with thirteen nieces and nephews. Wise took almost as much interest in these youngsters as he did in his own children. He not only enjoyed but genuinely relished the opportunity to advise his descendants, most of whom were male. He took a detailed interest in their reading and schoolwork. He wanted them to compete among each other for excellence and for his favor. Above all else, Virginians of the Wise lineage should cultivate a sense of honor. "Never fail, my son," he advised one of Mary Garnett's children, "to see fair play and to do justice as long as you live, even though you be kicked for it." The age demanded strength, toughness, and hard work, he wrote repeatedly. Whenever possible he drew on his own name and friends to create opportunity for the younger members of his family. No longer had he the power to dispense patronage, but it never demeaned him to claim it from others. He sought it aggressively for himself and his family, frequently mentioning the Wises' record of service and achievement established during the war.[33] His friendship and correspondence with a wealthy Ohioan, for example, led to a legal apprenticeship for one of his grandsons. This arrangement produced a lengthy homily in which he endeavored both to supply the youngster with a code of conduct and to conjure away some of his own demons:

> You must resolve instantly to *work, work, work* in earnest, patiently, slow, sure, carefully, without relaxation or let up. And to do that you must give up, without reserve, every luxurious indulgence. Touch, taste and handle no strong or malt drink or wine. . . . Leave off tobacco, both chewing and smoking. Give your leisure moments *to the most refined society of ladies*. . . . Learn *reticence* and the most circumspect prudence and punctilious politeness, and you will thus be enabled to keep your own counsel. . . .
>
> At the bar cultivate the persuasive, rather than the denunciatory. A

habit of invective impairs your own heart as well as your influence. Make friends, not enemies. . . .

Be always deferential to your Senior, especially Senior partner. If he is kind and generous to you, be reverential to him. Never show that you know or think you know more than he does.[34]

Steadfast in his duty to them, he merited his family's love and deference. Though the burdens splintered his nerves, he never broke. Until suffering a serious illness in 1874, he worked terribly hard. Crisscrossing eastern Virginia, he sought clients, tried cases, took depositions, and collected such debts as he could—whether paid in cash, credit, food, or favor. Like most older people, he relished opportunities to demonstrate his knowledge and expertise. One of these occurred in 1871, when the General Assembly enacted legislation providing for yet another effort to sort out Virginia's boundaries with Maryland, North Carolina, and Tennessee. It cost Governor Gilbert C. Walker some pride to appoint Wise to the joint commission on the Virginia-Maryland boundary because the old general had vilified him across the state for the previous two years. The work required extensive research and travel to interview residents along the border and to retrace the surveys completed during the previous history of the controversy. Wise confined his investigation almost exclusively to the Eastern Shore. His section of the voluminous report filed by Virginia's commissioners in 1874 easily outclassed the contributions of his two younger associates. But a panel of three arbitrators, in a split vote in 1877, awarded all the contested territory to Maryland, which retains it to this day. Virginia lost taxable property worth $50 million, Wise pointed out. But he had gained a generous stipend paid over three years, making the boundary commission probably his most lucrative enterprise of the postwar period.[35]

People who hired Wise always got more than their money's worth. He was unsurpassed, of course, in advising and protecting prewar acquaintances, political supporters, the widows of dear friends, soldiers in his brigade who professed loyalty to him, and those claiming a blood relationship with him, however distant. Defending their interests provoked nostalgic epiphanies. Perhaps fifteen minutes of his argument would address the merits of the case. Then he would go on to exhaustion recounting younger days in a particular county or village and describing the personalities and politics of the kinfolk of all those present in the courtroom. Wizened and brittle, he lived again amid the civilities of old Virginia. "A mental, moral, and physical phenomenon," one Northern observer described him, "for even now his faculties are as bright and quick, his eye as luminous, his gesticulation as spasmodic, his fluency and rapidity of thought and speech as perennial, and his manner as intense as when he led the Whig host in Congress and the nation and fought and won the victory over Know Nothingism so many years ago." These performances profoundly affected people who lacked hope. Audiences alternately laughed and cried. His clients typically swept to victory, although in a candid moment very late in life Wise acknowledged that younger lawyers knew more law than he did.[36]

Wise privately affected the same eccentric style. He gardened furiously while wearing a frock coat and black top hat and sometimes even carrying an umbrella. He frequently wore the same clothes on his daily trips to market in Richmond. He whittled wooden toys for his kin and cane tops for his friends. He looked, in other words, like a caricature of old Virginia in decline—a sort of John Randolph risen but not resurrected. He delivered advice incessantly on a wide variety of subjects. In late life, he pieced together his family's genealogy. "He could talk instinctively about any and everything," Judge George L. Christian reminisced. "He could tell the shoemaker how best to fix his last and thread, the carpenter how best to handle his plane and saw, and he actually told me how best to wear an artificial limb . . . his arguments were sometimes irrelevant, and as an illustration of this, I heard him discuss the divinity of the Savior, most interestingly, too, in the trial of a suit for breach of contract for the non-delivery of lumber."[37] As always, politics tempted his unceasing moralism above all else. He knew his enemies. His backward glances, sentimentalism, and evocations of old Virginia helped identify them. He also knew his friends but frequently hesitated in endorsing them unequivocally. To gain a cause lost required abandoning old ways.

The tradition of the Lost Cause required from history a vindication of the South's fighting prowess and assurances of sacrifice for a noble cause. Here Wise's tributes to the loyal and brave private soldiers of the Confederacy matched the zealousness with which he defended his own checkered military career. Vindication did not come unchallenged. Shortly after the war an acerbic Richmond newspaperman, Edward A. Pollard, published a book on Lee and his lieutenants that included a brief biography of Wise. Pollard credited Wise's courage and testified to how successfully he inspired his men. But Pollard also commented on Wise's love of paradox. He called it a "moral infirmity" and suggested that the old general suffered from an "afflicted intellect" and emerged from the war with only a minor reputation. In a letter to Pollard's publishers, Wise dismissed all specific reflections on his performance as beneath contempt and offered the judgment that Pollard was "*cursed* in the very heart and core of his *moral nature*." Mindful of history's judgments, Wise thereafter attended single-handedly to his reputation. He gave the dedicatory address at the Stonewall Jackson Cemetery in Winchester in 1867; he composed a personal apologia entitled "The Career of Wise's Brigade," which he delivered in Gloucester County at a reunion of his troops in 1870; he also reviewed the history of the Richmond Light Infantry Blues, once commanded by his lamented son, at the eighty-fifth anniversary of the company's founding in 1874. Wise's men never fought for "the inglorious privilege of owning slaves." Having fought instead for liberty and independence, they had enshrined themselves within an old and noble tradition.[38]

The testamentary power of the Lost Cause would be witnessed, he also suggested, by how effectively survivors attended to its most pathetic victims. Wise served for a time as president of the Southern Widows and Orphans Aid Association and gave his first major postwar address in January 1866 on behalf of Richmond's Female Orphan Asylum. To have lost a country, he said, was bad enough, but "none have a country, who have no home." "I too am a beggar," he added, doubtless reminding many Richmonders of their own condition. The "time ever comes to every orphan to know and feel, to those, even who never, in infancy, knew and felt a parent—that they have no father and mother. . . . And oh! how sadly old a child is suddenly made when it is made first to know and feel it is an orphan!" His own experience and empathy melded to promote whatever improvement his audience's tattered benevolence might afford. The plight of the orphans showed the result of the war at its worst and symbolized in the lives of some white Virginians what the fate of all might have been—indeed, still could be.[39]

Who were the enemies of the Confederate dead and their widows and orphans? None were more dangerous than Republicans and Virginia's half-million blacks, one would have supposed. Their cries for vengeance followed predictably from their liberation, however. What irritated and insulted Wise even more was the emergence from Reconstruction turbulence of a new political movement seeking Virginia's redemption. The so-called Conservatives masqueraded as political saviors. Their leadership of former Whigs and Know-Nothings, dissident Confederates, and capitalists on the prowl stamped them, in Wise's judgment, as traitors to the Virginia he loved. Wrongly, he charged that the Conservatives might inspire an unthinkable coalition between poor blacks and whites that Virginia politicians feared reflecting upon. But preventing this eventuality was precisely what the Conservatives intended.[40]

A Good Southerner

As the state most devastated by war and containing the largest number of freedmen, the Old Dominion held elements with a potential for social revolution. Few other Southern states exhibited a more radical or potentially stronger Republican party. Despite the suspicions and recriminations that divided its black and white leaders, they united sufficiently to write a new state constitution in 1868. This document enfranchised blacks, established a system of public education, set up a township form of local government, and granted a homestead exemption of $2,000 to every property holder, thereby protecting debtors from total dispossession at the hands of their creditors. It also disfranchised most Confederate sympathizers and mandated a host of other changes obnoxious to members of Virginia's ruling class, either former or aspiring. Armed with the new constitution—and never disarmed, their weapons a necessity in a state still organized for war—the blacks and their white allies sought ratification, Virginia's readmission to the Union, and election of their nominees for state office in 1868. Virginia's military governor sabotaged their timetable. General John H. Schofield postponed the election to give moderates an opportunity to organize. Wise had repeatedly gained access to Schofield and his predecessors, but his efforts to manipulate them proved redundant. With only one exception, all of Virginia's military governors mistrusted and shunned white Republicans and blacks. Instead, they preferred a rapid restoration to power of former Confederates and other "responsible" citizens.[41]

Seizing their opportunity, the Conservative inner circle—known as the Committee of Nine—traveled to Washington in January 1869. Speaking for capital and common sense, they offered Grant a compromise. If the president agreed to permit a separate vote on those provisions disfranchising masses of the former Confederacy's active supporters, Conservatives would support the remainder of the constitution. Grant accepted this arrangement but demanded, in addition, the withdrawal from the gubernatorial race of an extreme states'-rights ticket headed by Dr. Robert E. Withers, who planned a campaign devoted almost exclusively to racist virulence. After arduous effort, Conservative managers effected Withers's withdrawal. Voters then approved the constitution, rejected the disfranchising provisions, and elected the Conservative gubernatorial nominee over his Republican rival. They thus endorsed both black suffrage and an almost total political amnesty for whites. The Conservatives obtained home rule for

Virginia in 1870 and governed for a decade. Their twin policies of encouraging investment and alternately threatening or cajoling blacks kept them in power after Democrats had reasserted hegemony in most Southern states.[42]

Was Wise opposed to good money, from whatever source, finding its way to Virginia or to shackling blacks when necessary? Had he ever been? Yet the Conservatives drove him to distraction. Until his death, Wise believed these usurpers the bane of Virginia's politics. They were the wrong people, of course, members of a competing elite only once before victorious, in 1860, until now. It turned out that former Colonel Richard T. W. Duke, who had tried to steal Wise's Forty-sixth Virginia Regiment during the war, took a prominent part in the Albemarle County political meeting that in the view of some authorities inaugurated the Conservative movement.[43] Alexander H. H. Stuart, wheelhorse of the Whig and Know-Nothing parties, acted as Conservatism's spokesman and had published in December 1868 a manifesto of the movement's objectives. William T. Sutherlin of Danville, who offered Wise a small though nonrepayable loan a year earlier, served with Stuart on the Committee of Nine. Sutherlin was a genuine Southern Yankee—the sort easily fathomed by Wise—whose businesses had profited immensely during the war.[44] Shocked by the power and visibility of these men, and doubtless underestimating their adroitness, Wise reflected on how frequently he had pulverized them.

Mere jealousy made poor copy. And Wise was never a man of half-measures who preferred a one-column indictment when he could think of enough words to fill more. In a five-part essay published in late January 1869, he flailed the Conservatives on the Negro question. Let Virginia "take death rather than dishonor," he wrote. It was a "living lie," a "base hypocrisy," and a "disgrace to the Confederate living" to propose, as Stuart had done, to embrace "the Negro as our political equal." Wise made the telling point that Virginia should not proceed any more rapidly than the Northern states that had already rejected black suffrage. He supported Withers's gubernatorial candidacy. Moreover, Republican strength in Virginia gave his calls for unyielding resistance some credibility. The Conservatives asked what alternatives he offered. The choices were either the acceptance of the new constitution, with its universal male suffrage and other imperfections, or the maintenance of military government and an unstable climate for investment and economic recovery. Near universal amnesty offered considerable security that whites would not be overwhelmed. Virginians—particularly white Virginians—found it impossible to eat patience and defiance. After what amounted to nearly ten years of warfare they craved peace. Nonaction, suggested by Wise, former Senator Hunter, and a number of their impractical associates represented a political option devoid of hope.[45]

Moreover, the hostility Wise vented on the Conservatives seemed strange in view of their obvious agreements. Neither the Conservatives nor Wise wanted another war. They acknowledged slavery's extinction, while anathematizing Republicans. Some Conservatives may even have looked back more fondly on bygone days of masterhood than Wise. "For myself," he remarked, while fulminating against them, "I praise God for the war every day, notwithstanding its disasters and deaths, as a special providence indispensable to free men and my heirs from the weakness, if not the wickedness of African slavery."[46] Nonetheless, he contrasted their alleged spinelessness in accepting Republican terms for Virginia's reentry into the Union with his own refusal to accept amnesty. In mounting one of his classically convoluted constitutional arguments, he declared that Virginia had never left the Union, thus rendering all efforts at reconstruction illegal. Instead of a new constitution, the old one in which he maintained a proprietary interest was perfectly sound. This analysis ran directly counter to his previous postwar comments on Reconstruction, which had urged the legitimacy of secessionist doctrine to justify Confederates like himself who faced prosecution and confiscation. Now his arguments appeared to beg the question of what precisely Virginians had done between 1861 and 1865. If their state failed to break its connection with the Union, radical Republicans who insisted on doctrines of "state suicide" to justify dictatorial Reconstruction policies would find themselves outflanked and frustrated. But what about individual Virginians, whom Wise now left with the consolation that they fought as rebels? Defeated revolutionaries were traitors, as the critics of his 1861 doctrines had recognized. He now appeared to reaffirm those views, which in effect risked volunteering Virginians for the gallows. No wonder that most Virginians ignored his assaults on the Conservatives, as he later admitted.[47]

Despite the inconsistencies, opportunism, and efforts to put false distance between himself and the Conservatives, what remains worthy of note is Wise's instinctual reaction to them—his unalloyed fury and loathing. Noting that most Conservative leaders failed to enlist during the war, he questioned their manhood. By making peace on Republican terms, they acknowledged the South's guilt and bowed before the Yankees in emulation of their former slaves. "Submissionists" he called them—the famous epithet of 1861. Some of those once determined to sell out Virginia were at it again. Cowards and traitors, lovers of peace in time of war, even those willing to confess their errors—these were the men who needed conquering, the devils who required exorcising.[48]

The Conservatives' style of moderation represented Virginia's future, so that unyielding opposition to them stamped Wise as a reactionary. Although Wise, as always, could surprise, his personality and politics typically resonated with the interests of old Virginia. Scarcely a more congenial opportunity existed to serve those interests than in his association with the College of William and Mary. Burned during the war, the revitalized college self-consciously upheld the style and values of antebellum Virginia. Wise retained the seat he had held on the college's Board of Visitors since the 1840s. He spoke at the first postwar commencement in 1870. Consistent with his vision of self-sufficiency and small-scale agriculture, he urged the college's authorities to plow up the lawn and plant cowpeas on it.[49] Wanting to contribute something more substantial, and with no money to spare, he accepted an invitation to prepare a memoir of one of the college's most eminent graduates, John Tyler, who epitomized values it now wished to inculcate. Wise began work on *Seven Decades of the Union* in 1868; he finished it in 1871. The book's subtitle, *The Humanities and Maternalism, illustrated by a Memoir of John Tyler, with Reminiscences of Some of His Great Contemporaries. The Transition State of This Nation—Its Dangers and Their Remedy*, suggested its style of quaintness with a vengeance.

Certainly Wise discharged his primary obligation. *Seven Decades* is an anthem to lost causes, unpopular personalities, and lifestyles altogether gone or under fierce assault. Within this framework, many of its argumentative and illustrative sections are superbly done. Here are the anecdotes about Webster and Clay he had recounted for his alternately fascinated and bored troops during the war. The stories he told around those campfires started and ended with reflections on Andrew Jackson. So, too, did those in *Seven Decades*. He recapitulates Jackson's affirming confidence and the unforgettable pain caused by their separation. Tyler resisted Jackson as well, with more firmness and considerably less regret, one suspects.

Wise is true throughout to the only one of his older patrons with whom he never broke. Few men ever had such good reason to memorialize integrity and consistency. In one splendid polemical section, Wise points out that on grounds of frugality, genuine devotion to old republicanism, acquisition of territory, and extinction of Indian claims, as well as diplomatic productivity, Tyler's administration compared favorably with Jefferson's. Both together stood as hallmarks of states' rights now so fearsomely under assault by "consolidated despotism." Anticipating this theme's impact on Tidewater folk, he occasionally stretches artistic license. An example is the generous remembrance of former Senator Benjamin Watkins Leigh. Not only had Tyler disliked Leigh, but Wise as a young man thought him stuffy, effeminate, and an intolerant representative of the old Virginia he had wanted once and still burned to reform.[50]

It proved impossible, of course, for Wise to keep himself out of the text. Readers learn of his respectful dissent from Tyler's endorsement of nullification. They also find set against Tyler's approval of secession an extended defense of Wise's peculiar response to the crisis of 1861. Secessionist theory lacked constitutional standing, he argued, just as he simultaneously endeavored to convince the Conservatives that secession had never taken place. Had Virginians understood and accepted his doctrine of revolutionary opposition within the Union, a compromise would have avoided the war. One thus finds in the book a long series of regrets about missed opportunities and neglected advice.

Though the sections of constitutional argument lend a formalistic tone, Wise never loses touch with his readership. The anecdotes help, as does his preference for making Tyler and himself appear vulnerable. He wanted to write a book about how it felt to be an old Virginian—proud, generous, and good. More than his feelings show—literally himself, only thinly disguised. In describing the "reverence" characterizing Tyler as a young man, and how "his intercourse with the sages around him always struck him with awe and inspiration," Wise writes nostalgically of General Cropper and his own teachers. When he notes Tyler's "quick perception and great power of appropriating what he heard or read," he describes himself. In picturing the surveyor Hassler, whom Jefferson had invited to the United States, Wise pictures himself as a younger man: "An aquiline nose, thin and intellectual, and lips and chin which gave an expression of sweet manliness; a form erect and energetic; of an energetic nervousness, which made him unique and often grotesque; with a deep-set eye, sparkling, bright, and penetrating at a glance,—his appearance was attractively 'game'; and it did not falsify his heart; he was afraid of nothing; no intellectual puzzle, no physical obstruction or obstacle, no fear of man, could make him hesitate in his pursuit . . . after the truth."[51] That is Wise as he wanted to be remembered: manly, "dead game," a strange-looking but unforgettable creature on whom popular attention was always riveted.

Wise sought only a provincial audience. The Lippincott Company of Philadelphia printed a thousand copies for the first edition. The College of William and Mary probably subsidized the costs of publication, although all correspondence between Wise and his publishers is lost. Wise made no money but retained the stereotype plates. In decided contrast to the publicity accorded his memorial addresses on the Confederate living and dead and his political manifestos on all subjects from amnesty to usury, *Seven Decades* elicited little response. It was infrequently reviewed. Wise's postwar illnesses and narrow escapes from death provoked more attention. Most of the notable American historians of the late nineteenth and early twentieth centuries, with the exception of James Schouler and Hermann von Holst, used the work sparingly. But it had been a labor of love for Wise. He seemed immune to the neglect.[52]

Yet even before his death in 1876, times had changed. The exhaustion and cynicism of a failed Reconstruction created opportunities for a seemingly anachronistic work like *Seven Decades*. Perhaps the times favored books of mourning and recapitulation that highlighted missed opportunities. Wise anticipated a second printing aimed primarily at Northerners. It appeared in 1876, followed by a third printing in 1881.[53] Henry Adams's novel *Democracy*, published in 1880, suggested the attractiveness of good and decent Southerners amid the crassness and materialism of the Gilded Age political economy. After all, Wise preached the "humanities," by which he meant a revivification of the constitutional learning, legal thinking, and honorable living of antebellum Virginia in contradistinction to money-grubbing Republicanism. But the Virginia of *Seven Decades* is unpopulated by slaves. Thus it fitted the vogue of the mid-1870s, when Americans increasingly refused to hear or see blacks. This trend would continue through the immensely popular stories of Owen Wister, whose 1906 novel *The Virginian* suggested that high-minded Southerners were the best people to tame the wild West because they stood above the rampant commercialism that afflicted other Americans.

Certainly the appeal of *Seven Decades* was positive for one important authority, whose response may have instrumentally affected Wise's decision to press for a second printing. Thomas M. Cooley, a state judge and University of Michigan law professor, wrote Wise soon after the book appeared, praised it, and requested a list of his constitutional authorities. Wise's professed intent "to show the true Madisonian faith of State Rights in contrast with both Federalism—Absolutism in the Federal government and Calhounism, or South Carolina State rights—absolutism in the States" had found at least one influential reader perfectly positioned to appreciate it. Cooley was a conservative Republican interested in ending Reconstruction. He ranked as one of the foremost American constitutional authorities of the Gilded Age. His classic work *Constitutional Limitations* (1868) summarized his assault on state power and accentuated his respect for untrammeled property rights. He later led the judicial attack on the Fourteenth Amendment that in the end gutted its ability to protect blacks and enshrined it as a bulwark of corporate power. Cooley went no further, after the war, than rhetorical endorsements of equality of opportunity. He condemned as immoral all compensatory activity to aid the historically disadvantaged. Surprised and flattered by Cooley's interest, Wise referred him to a series of Virginia and Southern states'-rights theorists he had first read in his youth. A convert was won. But there were others because vast distances had never divided Wise from conservative Northerners. For many other Southerners, conciliating Yankees required abrupt shifts in attitude. Wise unceasingly sanctified the South, but he also promoted a future conforming to the hopes of the masters of capital he had always respected.[54]

Confederate ceremonials and rituals had their place, but no Yankee ever urged the gospel of work more intensely than Wise. No other option remained for indolent and improvident former masters. "No more fair hands," Wise proclaimed, just months after Appomattox. "No more lazy morning hours! No more cigars and juleps! No more card parties and club idleness!" In an 1867 speech at the dedication of the Stonewall Jackson Cemetery in Winchester, he memorialized the fidelity, constancy, and rigorous attention to work exemplified by the Confederate hero. He also begged young Virginians not to emigrate. They should, like him, abandon "guilt and remorse" and even beg bread before deserting the Old Dominion in her hour of need. Released from the bondage of slavery, they might finally realize an appropriate destiny by reducing Virginia's reliance on staple crop agriculture. This was an old vision whose time had come. Virginians must now cultivate "on a small scale none but the most improved lands, and these tilled to the square inch by the most able, intelligent, and skillful laborers, hired at a rate which close farming only can afford."[55] Antebellum Virginia had never permitted him the specificity in which he indulged himself in an 1867 address before the state's Horticultural and Pomological Society at Richmond:

The first change absolutely necessary to be made in agriculture, is, *From the Plantation to the Farming System*. . . . The plantation demanded . . . but little skill with rude hands to make the crude crops; habitually and ignorantly wasteful . . . monotonous in routine; worked by slaves, unskillful, unthrifty and costly, and not interested in success or profit; with no applied science or art beyond that of an uneducated overseer; and literally driving away from its sections, both from towns and country, "the strong man of America," the master mechanic . . . scattering and segregating and making sparse the white population of the country; utterly repelling the class of bold, working yeomanry, the proudest boast of any land and weakening the land for defensive war.[56]

The results of the war legitimized his rejected proposals of the 1850s. Only now, with slavery extinct, they might work. He urged members of the General Assembly to establish an agricultural college with the aid of federal monies. He remained devoted to his oyster tax and state insurance schemes. Renewed though doomed efforts to complete the James River and Kanawha Canal with the aid of French capital enlivened him.[57] With the power of the plantation interest broken, the commercial and manufacturing energies it had always opposed might now find liberation.

Despite old age and frail health, no one solicited immigrant capital and labor more aggressively that Wise. When Northern admirers—often drawn into contact by news of his personal financial distress—offered assistance, he never lost a chance to contrast Virginia's unlimited potential with the enslavement promoted by radical Republicans. He repeatedly advised a lawyer and businessman from Canton, Ohio, for example, of real estate available in Virginia. He offered to act as agent and importuned him to invest in the Old Dominion. He urged Northern correspondents to distribute his speeches and published letters. No distraction inhibited him from responding to Yankees. Politeness, punctuality, and an expressed fondness for the success of their private affairs were the hallmarks of his letters. Poor people could not afford bad manners, nor could they succumb to their abiding sense of loss and failure. "To work, and to know how to work well is the happiness of life," he wrote one Northerner. "Alas! I am so lazy and have to work *now* especially in such despair!"[58]

Nothing manifested so clearly the temptations of white Virginians to sink and surrender than the popularity of notions that sanctioned the repudiation of debt. "If we must accept the cancellation of the Confederate war debt," Wise said at Winchester in 1867, "let our enemies force it, never ourselves." After the Fourteenth Amendment's ratification doomed the Confederate debt,

Wise suggested that the federal government accept responsibility for Virginia's debt because it had obliterated old Virginia and established, by conquest, two new states in her place. Here in the early 1870s was yet another twist in Wise's convoluted and inconsistent arguments on Virginia's constitutional status after the war. Although his views commanded some support, no practical opportunity existed to enact them. Virginia was thus left with the choice after the war of either funding its full debt (and trusting the West Virginians to pay a third of it, which they never did) or repudiating it. Despite his fervent condemnations of the Conservatives, Wise never wavered from their policy of funding the debt, although he wanted to make people think of him as something of a dissenter. After all, his law practice depended on the sanctity of debt and contract, as did the reconstruction of his family's fortunes. Only in objecting strenuously to repeal of Virginia's usury laws—because high interest rates would cost Virginia farmers their lands—did Wise dissent from a program of unrestrained capitalism. A maverick at whatever he did, but with a Whig heritage, he happily sanctioned in Hamiltonian style a reconstituted national bank. He also favored the national resumption of specie payments. Such a program was altogether congenial to the Conservatives, it could be argued, or, more remarkably, approximating that of his Republican conquerers and oppressors.[59]

He got as close to them as he dared, despite his fear of the freedmen. But some Republicans were subject to flattery and manipulation. And if it seemed for a time that blacks could escape the control of good Southerners like himself, then it might be possible to write them out—to distance oneself from any need to reflect on their role in postbellum Virginia. When Wise talked about reforming Virginia's mangled agriculture, he listed agricultural education and the attraction of white immigrants as his top priorities. Like many other Virginians, he talked about recruiting peasants and yeomen from England, Europe, and the North. He urged Virginia landowners to "*advertize to select emigrants that you will gladly give to them one half your superfluous lands and help them build and fence that if they will come and settle the other half*." He advocated their settlement as families, with no barracks or gang labor. Schools and churches agreeable to their religion were a necessity. Subdividing their properties whenever possible would permit Virginians to build up "a solid Caucasian yeomanry" in place of "*negrodom*." Immigrant settlements would increase land values. "Intelligent, trained, self-sustaining laborers must be introduced," he remarked in 1867, "or our territory will be a waste and we must all go away to live." It was the antebellum Republican program of John C. Underwood that Wise now advocated, except that he envisioned its adoption by Virginians to retain substantial control of their own agriculture.[60]

Of the agricultural potential of Virginia's half-million freedmen he had almost nothing to say. Of their impudent deportment he spoke frequently. While Virginia awaited immigration and the benign effects of scientific agriculture, "the most intelligent and moral and industrious blacks" would have to do. He advocated settling them in families, as sharecroppers and tenants. But the conclusion seems unmistakable that he saw as a primary glory of truck gardening and small-scale agriculture its independence of both slaves and blacks.[61] Wise and other Virginians feared the departure of blacks—enticed north or south or simply taking advantage of their freedom to escape the Old Dominion—and thus campaigned hard for immigrants to replace them.[62] But Wise also embodied an older tradition that regarded their departure as a blessing, not a curse. Colonization, after all, had linked Jefferson and Lincoln. It had never lost its appeal for Wise. Indeed, the old general at his worst sounded remarkably like an exiled North Carolinian of the antebellum period. Blacks themselves, as much as their enslavement, constituted America's gravest problem, Hinton R. Helper had suggested. To eliminate both would realize the highest statesmanship. It would also best serve the interests of the Caucasian yeomanry for whom Helper and Wise claimed to speak.

An old enemy roused himself for yet another critical view of the former governor's proposals. With Edmund Ruffin gone—defiantly taking his own life in the spring of 1865—it was left to Willoughby Newton to expose Wise's fancies. Now president of the Virginia State Agricultural Society, Newton was more polite than in 1857 when he scorned Wise's educational proposals. But the same problems remained. Not even the "fascinating influence of Governor Wise's eloquence," Newton wrote, could disguise Virginia's sparse population. No efforts to attract immigrants—particularly the millions on whom Wise pinned his hopes—had ever succeeded or would succeed in the foreseeable future. "The Northern people affect to believe that we would assassinate them or burn their houses, if they settle among us," Newton advised. Meanwhile, the only practical approach to agricultural reform was mechanization. It should command whatever capital hard-pressed Virginia farmers could spare. It made little sense to reduce the size of agricultural holdings. Under no circumstances should Virginians give their lands away to just anyone, particularly in view of what their creditors might say.[63]

The immigration panacea, though popular throughout the

South, was doomed from the start. Exiting Virginians far outnumbered the few Yankees and foreigners attracted to the state during this period. Stabler and more sober-minded Virginians were left with the conclusion to which planter Thomas S. Watson had come: "The darkies have the long end of the pole for we can't supply their places that I know of."[64]

Thus Wise gave up a fantasy, only to replace it with recommendations bereft of paternalism. He repudiated all civil rights legislation because it potentially brought him into personal and disagreeable contact with freedmen. Only sexual admixture, with the threat it represented to the family, exceeded in its evil effects legislation that "might and could command and force men to sleep and dine and wine at the same hotels, ride in the same cars, sit at the same pews at church, mix and mingle together in the same public schools, and in a word *associate* with each other against their own wills to any extent or any degree." In late life, he successfully defended businessmen charged with violating federal civil rights statutes. The Fifteenth Amendment enfranchised blacks, but Wise calculated on their inability to use the ballot independently. Promoting civil rights or encouraging self-interested voting among the freedmen would also deter Virginia's recovery by discouraging immigrant capital and labor. He argued against integrated education on grounds that it would violate the interests of blacks by retaining whites in control of teaching and administration. This strategy allowed him to avoid the prescriptions of the Fifteenth Amendment that invalidated discrimination on grounds of "race, color, or previous condition of servitude." Then he returned to an old patron, Thomas R. Dew, and rendered a judgment harsher than any he seems to have entertained during the years of his experience as a good master: "For God Almighty has put His seal on that fixed fact, and human legislation cannot make 'the Leopard change his spots or the Ethiopian his color!' " Conceding anything less would now risk on a grand scale the miscegenation that had always threatened him most.[65]

These doctrines fed the prejudices of Virginia's Northern enemies but failed to scandalize those Republicans vulnerable to Reconstruction, Southern style. Like Wise, many white Southerners expected all along to give up as much as necessary but preserve essentials until they either wore down their enemies or co-opted them. One Republican demonstrating flexibility was John C. Underwood, who seemed anxious in 1865 to haul Wise and other Confederates before his court on charges of treason. In 1868 Underwood had chaired the Republican convention that wrote Virginia's new constitution. But frequent harassment of recalcitrant Virginians from the bench of his federal district court did not prevent him from praising Wise's eloquence as an advocate and expressing an admiration for him of many years' standing. Wise pleasantly reciprocated and thereafter legitimated Underwood's increasingly obvious efforts to transcend his reputation as a scoundrel and establish himself as a good Virginian. In 1872 the judge arranged for Wise to give one of his lectures on immigration as the key to Virginia's "material progress and improvement" in Alexandria under the auspices of the city council. Wise's frequent and predictable renunciations of slavery, which he pronounced at every opportunity, doubtless encouraged and sanctioned Underwood's professions of respect. They had always wanted a somewhat similar future for the Old Dominion. At the heart of the reconciliation between them was the firm conviction that Virginia could never permit any repudiation of debt or compromise on the obligations of contract.[66]

Underwood remained on his bench in 1870 when Wise risked his reputation and perhaps even his life by allying with blacks and Republicans. This reckless though highly principled gesture embodied more dramatically than any of his other postwar initiatives both his loathing for the Conservatives and his alignment with the party that would rule the future. When the Conservatives took power early in 1870, they enacted legislation permitting them to declare wholesale vacancies in various offices across the state, in one of which they installed, as the new mayor of Richmond, the publisher of the *Richmond Dispatch*, Henry K. Ellyson. This effort produced the so-called municipal war because Ellyson's appointment was resisted by the incumbent mayor, George Chahoon. Northern-born, Republican, and a Union army major, Chahoon fit one of the classic carpetbagger stereotypes. He called on both Wise and former Republican Governor H. H. Wells for counsel. Defying the odium and vituperation of most white Virginians, Wise joined Chahoon in the mayor's barricaded offices. With the aid of armed blacks, they resisted Ellyson's forces for two days until both sides agreed to let the courts settle the issue.

With his earlier arguments against the Conservatives either ignored or rejected as the ravings of a hopeless eccentric, Wise devised a powerful case on Chahoon's behalf. He argued that the act on which Ellyson's appointment rested was inconsistent with the so-called Underwood constitution of 1868 and therefore void. The only way Ellyson could have obtained the office was by election. Underwood's United States District Court heard the case first and issued an injunction against Ellyson, who now held de facto control of the mayor's powers. Underwood greeted Ellyson's defiance by mysteriously departing from Richmond—terrified for his life, the Conservatives charged. By processes never fully explained, the case was shifted out of the federal courts and referred to the Virginia Court of Appeals, where a unanimous decision in favor of Ellyson followed predictably.[67]

Wise was providentially absent from the scheduled rendering of the decision in the capitol on 27 April 1870. Just as the judges were filing in, the courtroom's gallery collapsed and broke through the floor. Fifty-eight persons died, dozens were injured, and the gloomy news spoiled what was to have been the glorious day of Richmond's return to home rule. His narrow escape terrified Wise's family. They feared his refusal of a conversion experience. Only a year earlier, afflicted by a particularly dreadful illness, Wise had promised if spared to "surrender himself to the will of God" and "lay down his life at the foot of the Cross." But he never knelt or bent. A few days after the capitol calamity, he spoke at the memorial service for the dead and injured. No Richmond newspaper published his remarks.[68]

Wise's support for Chahoon's Republicans—whether or not it involved a financial consideration, of which no record exists in any case—required as much moral and physical courage as any act of his illustrious public life. The Conservatives were deadly serious about redeeming Virginia. Despite their relatively temperate rhetoric, they used fair means and foul to achieve this objective. Chahoon and his supporters, for example, clearly outpolled the Ellyson forces in the election that followed the court decision. Indeed, it may have been Chahoon's confidence in this result that allowed him to accept with equanimity a decision rendered by the Virginia Court of Appeals. To defeat Chahoon, Conservative toughs bribed election officials, stole at least one ballot box from a precinct where his supporters dominated, and killed a man in broad daylight.[69]

Clever and manipulative he was, often either rash or cautious by design, but few people ever accused Wise of faint-heartedness in a crisis. The Chahoon incident marked a turning point. In 1872 Horace Greeley and other reform-minded Republicans gained control of the Democratic National Convention. Greeley himself emerged as the Democracy's presidential candidate, much to the disgust of Wise and many others. Supporting Greeley was impossible, Wise wrote, because it would force him "to consent" to his "own shame." He also denounced the Republicans in language as ripe as ever. But he clearly tilted toward Grant, much to the fascination of Northerners, because he sensed the possibilities of peace and reconciliation. So did most Republicans, of course, including one notable black Republican from Arkansas who once had known Wise well. At the Republican National Convention in Philadelphia, William Henry Grey became the first man of his race to address such a gathering. He, too, wanted reconciliation. "Let the dead past bury its dead," he remarked. Blacks wanted only opportunity, though they now required not only the suffrage but a new federal civil rights bill to guarantee even that. Lest anyone mistake his kindness for weakness, however, Grey permitted an allusion to topics he forbore from developing: "If I should go back to the primary history of my race in this country, I would open up, perhaps, to discussion things and circumstances that would make us blush, and the blood in our cheeks to tingle in view of the evidences of the shameful and horrible condition—such in its degradation as the American people have never thought of—from which we have just escaped."[70]

In 1873 Wise first announced himself as willing to accept a gubernatorial nomination from either the Conservatives or Republicans. He then planned to defeat the nominee of the other party, whoever it might be. In the end, he endorsed the Republican nominee because Virginia's material interests demanded it. Rumors abounded that he would seek a congressional seat as a Republican—a possibility forbidden to him because of his continuing refusal to seek amnesty. In fact, Wise's scarcely reticent pursuit of a gubernatorial nomination either rested on the contingency that he would seek amnesty or manifested the literal acting out of his fantasies. The General Amnesty Act of 1872 excluded former foreign ministers of the United States who had violated their oaths to uphold the Constitution and the Union. Wise might vote, but no federal or state office was open to him without a pardon. He thus remained unreconstructed whether he wished to acknowledge it or not.[71]

Notwithstanding his crude pronouncements on the race question and the occasional outbursts against the war's victors, he saw the future with as much clarity as he remembered the past. The Republicans themselves shifted ground. As they did, Wise sought whatever he could from them for his family, Virginia, and the South. In 1867, Massachusetts Senator Henry Wilson, who had once accused him of treason for his part in the Raleigh conference of 1856 and who evidently regarded slaveholders as little better than barbarians, arrived in Richmond and demanded nothing but hard work and no excuses from Virginia's freedmen. In 1874 Vice-President Wilson sent Wise the first volume of his *History of the Rise and Fall of the Slave Power*. With information supplied by

Wise himself, Wilson now accepted the former governor's actions at Raleigh as entirely conservative and Union saving. Sensing that Wilson was looking for more than a book review, Wise responded:

I do not concur in many of your conclusions, or in much of your coloring of statement, or in the grouping of facts in several instances, and cannot admit the fullness of the history; but I do accept your work as very valuable, as evidently an effort to be as just as you could be, and as a respectable and able *ex parte* production. It is enough for me to say:—that in the main result I am not only satisfied, but praise God that African Slavery is abolished. And again, I pray you to aid in restoring the rights of the States, and liberties of their white citizens. I am yet to read your work fully and critically.[72]

The old general's last public appearance confirmed his loyalties. He traveled to Washington in May 1876 to argue a contested election case before a committee of the House of Representatives. His client was James H. Platt, Jr., pure-blooded Republican carpetbagger born in Canada, educated in Vermont, and a surgeon in the Union army during the war. Three times elected to Congress from the Norfolk district after the war, he ran his last race against John Goode, Jr., who received support from both Democrats and Conservatives. Goode won a close election, partly because his friends had encouraged and financed an independent black candidate who drew strength away from Platt. Goode's forces intimidated voters, assaulted a few, and probably doctored the ballot boxes in York County. Platt's people shot up at least one village before the election and also mauled several people. It was a messy business and generated a bulky volume of evidence. Wise's last speech was as good and as effective as any he ever gave. People crowded to hear him, as always. Though "exceedingly feeble," as Goode recollected years later, and compelled to speak from his seat, he would occasionally "rise up and give utterance to a brilliant outburst, thus reminding one of a candle flickering in the socket and occasionally blazing up." He tried the case at his own speed, settling scores and perfecting the record. He condemned whiskey, blasted the Conservatives, praised Grant, and declared that, as governor, he should have hung Horace Greeley and pardoned John Brown. He won, too. The Committee on Elections ruled in Platt's favor, but the full House reversed it and permitted Goode to keep his seat.[73]

Having bowed out as a victor, Wise made no mistake about the political legacy he wished to bequeath. Both his sons later served as Republican congressmen from Virginia. The younger, Richard, represented a sizable portion of what had once been his father's district. The elder, John Sergeant, served only one term before enemies stole an election from him, just as James Platt's had done. So repulsive was Republicanism that old friends from the Confederate service, who once had named their children in John's honor, renamed them.[74] An exile from Virginia in later years, John found his fortune in New York among the rulers of the South.

Wise's was no ceremonial death. Wasted to a shadow by consumption, he lay immobile for the last several weeks of his life. "He has a violent awful cough," wrote John Sergeant, two days before the end, "& the most frightfully offensive expectorations I ever knew. His mouth and tongue are now terribly ulcerated which adds to the almost unbearable discomfort of his condition. Through it all his mind has remained clear and unclouded and while he lies a great portion of the time in a semi-sleeping state when he does rouse he is as rational as he ever was and more patient and composed than I ever knew him."[75] Thus he died hard but well satisfied and evincing all the toughness of his great antebellum adversary, John Brown, who showed America how to die.

The old general's precarious health throughout the postwar years had given him adequate warning. He repeatedly relived and recapitulated all his old battles and achievements. Writing *Seven Decades of the Union* was an important part of this process. He cemented what friendships he could, especially among old critics who, like himself, required solace. "What a boon it would be to you and me, and such like now," he wrote one former enemy from the period of Tyler's presidency, "if, as of old, the vulgar herd of men could allow really great men to think for them and save them the trouble and us the loss and cost of them trying to think for themselves."[76] Although he presumably visited with his friend, the rector of the Episcopal church, who presided at his funeral, no clergymen seem to have been present at his death. Wise made his own idiosyncratic Christian peace.

History's judgments were another matter because he had ample reason to seek vindication. During his abortive gubernatorial campaign in 1873, someone in the press dredged up the Graves-Cilley duel. Solely to preserve his reputation within his family, Wise prepared a justification of his role and sent it to a son-in-law. When former Senator George Jones of Iowa advised him two years later that the charge had surfaced again, he prepared a thirty-five-hundred word response. As always, he placed the responsibility on Clay. He permitted the notorious and fatal third shot, Wise insisted, only to save the honor of both principals because each had missed so badly in earlier fires as to call into question their reputations for manliness and honor. "I wish you to be possessed of my most secret and confidential statements," he closed to Jones. "You will outlive me, and I know you will defend me as yourself."[77]

Hope and regret lent a measure of integrity to Wise's death. It saddened him terribly a month before the end to miss the reunion of the first cavalry company he had recruited for the Confederate war. Gladly would he leave "this griddle of a town," he wrote. "I never expect to leave my room again until I am carried to my grave." Yet even while recalling it, he had already transcended the Confederacy. His family was preserved, poor but not destitute. He had taken Virginia through her worst crisis. Learning from the defeat he expected, unburdened of a boundless curse, she might rise again to claim her glory. "And I am sure of another thing," he wrote Robert Tyler in 1875. "I am spared for nothing else but to see my faith fulfilled—a *revulsion* which will change the cataract of our calamities like an Earthquake could [turn?] Niagara into a placid stream." It came less rapidly than he anticipated. But his program of economic development, racial control, and learning the lessons of his conquerers better than they themselves knew them prepared the South's rulers for the time when they would once again rule America. "There is but one true test of anything," he wrote to his son John shortly before the end, "and that is, is it right? If it isn't, turn right away from it." Having both accepted and defied this injunction, he had gained a measure of wisdom.[78]

In postwar Richmond only Lee's funeral evoked more emotion. Friends and enemies alike thought he deserved it. Remembering his crushing defeat of the Know-Nothings in 1855, Cardinal James Gibbons of Baltimore wrote the inscription on the floral tribute from the Catholics of Richmond. Amid the military processions, religious dignitaries, and civic officials were undoubtedly the curious and those searching for an emotional communion in the rituals of necrology so important among a defeated people. None were more curious than the several members of Wise's former black family whom the newspapers identified as attending the funeral. Included among them was James Turner—the Jim of the war years, who had once twisted Wise's trust to claim for himself a share of manhood and honor.[79] They kept their distance. In the end, perhaps they knew better than he the wisdom of decency and respect.

Abbreviations

Manuscripts

AAS	American Antiquarian Society, Worcester, Massachusetts
AU	Auburn University, Department of Archives, Auburn, Alabama
BECHC	Buffalo and Erie County Historical Society
BPL	Boston Public Library
BU	John Hay Library, Brown University, Providence, Rhode Island
CHS	Chicago Historical Society
CSmH	Henry E. Huntington Library, San Marino, California
DU	Duke University, William R. Perkins Library, Manuscripts Division
EI	Essex Institute, Salem, Massachusetts
ESHS	Eastern Shore Historical Society, Onancock, Virginia
EU	R. W. Woodruff Library for Advanced Studies, Emory University, Atlanta
HHS	Benjamin Perley Poore Papers, Haverhill Historical Society, Haverhill, Massachusetts
HSP	Historical Society of Pennsylvania
HU	Houghton Library, Harvard University
JDD	James Dorman Davidson Papers, McCormick Collection, State Historical Society of Wisconsin, Madison
JPL	John Janney Papers, in possession of Mr. Lucas Phillips, Leesburg, Virginia
KKCPL	McClung Historical Collection, Knoxville-Knox County Public Library, Knoxville, Tennessee
LC	Library of Congress, Manuscripts Division
LPL	John Letcher Papers, in possession of Brigadier General John Letcher, Lexington, Virginia
MaHS	Maryland Historical Society
MB	Boston Public Library, Manuscripts Division
MHS	Massachusetts Historical Society
NA	National Archives, Washington, D.C.
NHHS	New Hampshire Historical Society, Concord
NYHS	New York Historical Society
OHS	Ohio Historical Society, Columbus

RMC	Robert Muldrow Cooper Library, Clemson University
RRR	Rush Rhees Library, University of Rochester, Rochester, New York
SCL	South Caroliniana Library, University of South Carolina, Columbia
SHC	Southern Historical Collection, Wilson Library, the University of North Carolina at Chapel Hill
TSL	Tennessee State Library, Manuscripts Section
UC	University of Chicago Library
UM	Bentley Historical Library, University of Michigan, Ann Arbor
UVA	Alderman Library, University of Virginia, Charlottesville
VHS	Virginia Historical Society
VHS(oc)	Virginia Historical Society, old catalogue
VMI	Superintendent's Papers, Virginia Military Institute, Lexington, Virginia
VSL	Archives Branch, Virginia State Library, Richmond
WFP/VHS	Wise Family Papers, formerly in possession of John S. Wise, Charlottesville, Virginia, now in the Virginia Historical Society
WJC	Washington and Jefferson College Library, Washington, Pennsylvania
WM	Manuscripts Department, E. G. Swem Library, College of William and Mary
WVULM	West Virginia and Regional History Collection, West Virginia University Library, Morgantown

Journals and Documents

ACDB	Accomac County Deed Books, VSL
ACLB	Accomac County Land Books, VSL
ACOB	Accomac County Order Books, VSL
ACPPB	Accomac County Personal Property Books, VSL
ACWB	Accomac County Will Books, VSL
CG	*Congressional Globe* [abbreviation is followed by numbers designating both the Congress and session]
MHSP	*Massachusetts Historical Society Proceedings*
NNR	*Niles' National Register*
NYR	*New York Review of Books*
OR	*The War of the Rebellion: A Compilation of Official Records of the Union and Confederate Armies*
PACDB	Princess Anne County Deed Book, VSL

RDC	*Register of Debates in Congress* [abbreviation is followed by numbers designating both the Congress and session]
SHSP	*Southern Historical Society Papers*
SLM	*Southern Literary Messenger*
VMHB	*Virginia Magazine of History and Biography*

Notes

N.B. In all quotations I retained contemporary spelling but occasionally altered punctuation. Quotations from newspapers are from daily editions, unless otherwise noted by sw (semiweekly) or w (weekly). All Wise references that do not include initials are to Henry A. Wise.

Preface

1 Fischer, "Braided Narrative"; Benson, *Toward the Scientific Study of History*, pp. 225–333 and passim. I think Fischer mistakenly implies a lack of interest in power at pages 112–13, although he qualifies his view at page 121. Cf. Fox-Genovese and Genovese, "Political Crisis of Social History," and Foner, "Fragmentation of Scholarship."

2 On 20 February 1861, in the Virginia secession convention, Wise himself dropped the remark that may have inspired this search: "I have within the past week received no less than three letters from friends in Boston, informing me—to use their own language—of mysterious movements in the militia of Massachusetts" (*Proceedings*, ed. Reese, 1:119 [20 Feb. 1861]).

Chapter 1

1 Wise to James P. Hambleton, 13 Oct. 1855, Garnett Family Papers, VHS. Several months after his election as governor of Virginia in 1855, Wise wrote Hambleton a series of autobiographical letters that were used in preparing a volume commemorating his victory.

2 "An address to the voters for electors of President and Vice President of the United States, in the State of Virginia, with the American Republican ticket" [1800?], John Cropper Papers, VHS. For additional comments on Wise's public career, see Beeman, *Old Dominion*, pp. 189–90, 211–13, 233.

3 Wise, *Speech on the Basis Question*, Wise Papers, SHC, p. 19; Wise to Hambleton, 12 Oct. 1855, I, Garnett Family Papers, VHS (Wise wrote two letters to Hambleton on this date).

4 Jefferson's letter is in J. C. Wise, *Col. John Wise*, pp. 92–93.

5 The evidence of a rejected claim is in an affidavit, with endorse-

ments, from Levin Hyslop of Accomac County, 10 Feb. 1832, in the Rejected Revolutionary Claims File, VSL; on Toryism on the Eastern Shore, see Ambler, *Sectionalism in Virginia*, p. 25; J. C. Wise, *Col. John Wise*, pp. 89–91.

6 ACWB; B. H. Wise, *Life of Henry A. Wise*, p. 18; Brown, *Portrait Gallery*, p. 65; Wise to Brown, 20 Sept. 1843, Miscellaneous Manuscripts, KKCPL.

7 Brown, *Portrait Gallery*, p. 65.

8 Ibid.; ACLB, 1813.

9 B. H. Wise, "Memoir of General John Cropper," pp. 39, 42; B. H. Wise, *Life of Henry A. Wise*, p. 11; Wise to Hambleton, 9 Oct. 1855.

10 Wise to Hambleton, 12 Oct. 1855, I, Garnett Family Papers, VHS; Lewis W. Washington to Wise, 14 Apr. 1857, Letters Received, Governor's Office, Executive Department, VSL, Box 378; Hugh Blair Grigsby to Wise, 26 Oct. 1858, Hugh Blair Grigsby Papers, VHS.

11 Wise to Hambleton, 12 Oct. 1855, II, Garnett Family Papers, VHS; B. H. Wise, *Life of Henry A. Wise*, pp. 13–14.

12 Brown, *Portrait Gallery*, p. 66.

13 B. H. Wise, *Life of Henry A. Wise*, p. 13.

14 Jefferson, *Notes on the State of Virginia*, ed. Peden, pp. 162–63.

15 See, for example, *Richmond Enquirer*, 19 Apr. 1836, 7 Feb. 1837; Brown, *Portrait Gallery*, p. 67; B. H. Wise, *Life of Henry A. Wise*, pp. 13, 56–57.

16 B. H. Wise, *Life of Henry A. Wise*, p. 13. For contrasting modern views on these matters, see Genovese, *Political Economy of Slavery*, pp. 31–34; Genovese, *Roll, Jordan, Roll*, pp. 87–97; and Wyatt-Brown, *Southern Honor*, esp. chap. 6.

17 Wise to John Cropper, 5 May 1829, Barton H. Wise Papers, VHS(oc); Wise to Hambleton, 12 Oct. 1855, II, Garnett Family Papers, VHS.

18 Wise to Hambleton, 12 Oct. 1855, II, Garnett Family Papers, VHS; Wise to Alumni Committee of Washington College, 31 Jan. 1854, newspaper clipping, WJC.

19 Wise to Hambleton, 12 Oct. 1855, II, Garnett Family Papers, VHS.

20 B. H. Wise, *Life of Henry A. Wise*, p. 20.

21 Tucker, *Commentaries on the Laws of Virginia*, which dates the opening lecture "November, 1826."

22 Wise to Hambleton, 12 Oct. 1855, II, Garnett Family Papers, VHS.

23 Wise to Dr. John W. Cropper, 5 May 1829, Barton H. Wise Papers, VHS(oc).

24 Wise, *Seven Decades of the Union*, pp. 79–81; Wise to Hambleton, 12 Oct. 1855, II, Garnett Family Papers, VHS. I rely on Rogin's

Fathers and Children for the origins of Jackson's extraordinary need to assert his "fatherhood" and the potentially destructive effects this pathology produced. I believe that Wise had to assert his authority and independence yet required the approval and support of authority figures such as Jackson. He emulated Jackson's moods and manners and probably developed almost as great a capacity for self-deception as the Old Hero's. On the imperfections in Rogin's analysis, however, see Fox-Genovese, "Psychohistory versus Psychodeterminism."

25 Wise, *Seven Decades of the Union*, pp. 79–81.

26 Wise to Hambleton, 13 Oct. 1855, Garnett Family Papers, VHS; Wise to Robert Reed, 1 Oct. 1828, 9 May 1829, 13 Feb. 1830, WFP/VHS.

27 The 1829 ACPPB reveal that Tully R. Wise owned 9 slaves and 713 acres of land.

28 Brown, *Portrait Gallery*, p. 65.

29 Wise to Hambleton, 13 Oct. 1855, Garnett Family Papers, VHS.

30 Wise, *Seven Decades of the Union*, pp. 128–29, 131–32; *Richmond Enquirer*, 29 Mar. 1833. This issue of the *Enquirer* contains a critical review of the election address that Wise issued to his constituents before his campaign for Congress.

31 Brant, *James Madison*, p. 476.

32 In a letter addressed to Nicholas Trist, 15 February 1830, and widely circulated at the time, Madison vigorously denied both the legality and expediency of nullification. He mentioned several intermediary steps (for example, an appeal to the Supreme Court) that could possibly resolve South Carolina's grievances and prevent a dissolution of the Union. Madison also appeared to endorse, should the necessity arise, a convention of the states. This remedy remained a favorite of Wise's. See Hunt, ed., *Writings*, 9:351–58; Wise, *Seven Decades of the Union*, pp. 129–33.

33 Adkins, "Henry A. Wise in Sectional Politics," pp. 34–35; Wise to Hambleton, 15 Nov. 1855, Garnett Family Papers, VHS; B. H. Wise, *Life of Henry A. Wise*, pp. 39–41.

34 Wise to Hambleton, 13 Oct. 1855, Garnett Family Papers, VHS; Wise, *Seven Decades of the Union*, pp. 121–33. See also Wise's first speech delivered in the House of Representatives, 6 Feb. 1834, in *RDC*, 23, 1, 2668–82.

35 Risjord, *Old Republicans*, passim.

36 Ambler, *Sectionalism in Virginia*, p. 25; Fischer, *Revolution of American Conservatism*, pp. 211–12.

37 Wise to Hambleton, 13 Oct. 1855, Garnett Family Papers, VHS; Wise to Robert Reed, 1 Oct. 1828, WFP/VHS; *Richmond Enquirer*, 29 Mar. 1833.

38 *An Address to the Citizens of Accomac County, from the Jackson Correspondence Committee*, Henry A. Wise, Chairman, 27 Aug. 1832 (Snow Hill, Md., 1832?). For Wise's authorship, see an extract from his letter of 27 September 1840 in the *Richmond Whig and Public Advertizer* (hereafter *Richmond Whig*), 7 Oct. 1840.

39 *Address to the Citizens of Accomac County*; Thomas R. Joynes to Charles James Faulkner, 8 Sept. 1832, Faulkner Papers, WVULM.

40 *Richmond Enquirer*, 29 Mar. 1833.

41 "I, for one," Wise later remarked in the House, "once did think that the president would sanction such a charter. . . . On all proper occasions when using my feeble efforts to elect him, I confidently declared this belief to many of the people whom I represent" (quoted in Wilburn, *Biddle's Bank*, p. 132). Jackson equivocated sufficiently in his veto message of 10 July 1832 to justify this inference. See also Remini, *Andrew Jackson and the Bank War*, pp. 131–34.

42 Wise to Hambleton, 13 Oct. 1855, Garnett Family Papers, VHS.

43 The best account of this process is Wallace, "Changing Concepts of Party in the United States."

44 McCormick, *Second American Party System*, pp. 178–85.

45 The intensity of Southern suspicions of Van Buren's foppishness clearly suggests a sensitivity to feminine dominance. Several authorities believe that male members of the Southern middle and upper social strata thought very little of female capacity and regarded any independent women they encountered as fearful and threatening. Many of them were raised by both white and black women, although very few could have precisely duplicated Wise's experience. See, for example, Bartlett and Cambor, "History and Psychodynamics of Southern Womanhood."

46 Wise to Hambleton, 13 Oct. 1855, Garnett Family Papers, VHS.

47 Wise sold the last portions of his inheritance upon leaving for Nashville in 1828 (ACDB, 1827–28; ACLB, 1828–29).

48 ACPPB, 1833.

49 Throughout Wise's time in Congress, members of the House of Representatives earned $8 per day during the congressional session, plus a mileage allowance. The Pay and Mileage Books in Record Group 217, NA, show that Wise averaged annually about $1,500 in pay and allowances.

50 B. H. Wise, *Life of Henry A. Wise*, p. 38; Brown, *Portrait Gallery*, p. 67; J. Milton Emerson Journal, 9 Oct. 1841, DU. Cf., following p. 190, Sarah Peale's romanticized portrait of about 1840 with a more realistic, though flawed, version done some years earlier and attributed to John Gadsby Chapman.

Chapter 2

1 Wise to James H. Hambleton, 13 Oct. 1855, Garnett Family Papers, VHS.

2 *RDC*, 23, 1 (9 June 1834), 4427–29. The removal of the deposits cost Jackson considerable support within the Virginia General Assembly and throughout the state. See, for example, *NNR* 45 (25 Jan. 1834): 361.

3 Sellers, *James K. Polk, Jacksonian*, pp. 308–9; *United States Telegraph*, 11, 25 Jan., 26 Feb., 29 Mar. 1836; *NNR* 50 (9 Apr. 1836): 92; Wise to unknown, 2 Dec. 1846, Wise Papers, SHC.

4 Adams, ed., *Memoirs of John Quincy Adams*, 9:88 (6 Feb. 1834).

5 *RDC*, 23, 2 (16 Feb. 1835), 1399; Temin, *Jacksonian Economy*, pp. 59–68; Cooper, *The South and the Politics of Slavery*, pp. 54–58.

6 *RDC*, 23, 2 (16 Feb. 1835), 1398; Holst, *Constitutional and Political History*, 2:238. The *United States Telegraph*, 20–21 February 1835, picked up these passages and was mildly critical. This paper, edited by Duff Green and friendly to Calhoun's interests, soon became Wise's foremost public defender.

7 *NNR* 58 (18 Apr. 1840): 103; Wise, *Speech at Louisa Court House*.

8 *Richmond Enquirer*, 14 April 1833, gives partial returns for the Wise-Coke congressional contest. See also Beeman, *Old Dominion*, p. 232; unsigned communication from Powhatan County, in *Richmond Whig*, 26 May 1843; J. Milton Emerson Journal, 9 Oct. 1841, DU; B. H. Wise, *Life of Henry A. Wise*, p. 41.

9 McCormick, *Second American Party System*, p. 178. See also Wyatt-Brown, "Ideal Typology."

10 *Richmond Whig*, 9 May 1843.

11 Wise, "Farewell Address," *NNR* 66 (9 Mar. 1844): 25.

12 U.S. Congress, House of Representatives, Bill Books, Twenty-third through Twenty-eighth Congresses, RG 45, NA.

13 Sharp, *Jacksonians versus the Banks*, p. 247; Sutton, "Nostalgia, Pessimism, and Malaise."

14 *CG*, 25, 3, Appendix 39, 41. See also *RDC*, 25, 1 (27 Sept. 1837), 1036; *CG*, 26, 2, Appendix 298; B. H. Wise, *Life of Henry A. Wise*, p. 68. On the difficulty of adjusting to Virginia in the mid-nineteenth century, see Brugger, *Beverley Tucker*, and Dawidoff, *Education of John Randolph*.

15 Freehling, *Drift toward Dissolution*, p. 161; Truman, *Eastern Shore of Virginia*, pp. 173–75; Siegel, "Paternalist Thesis," p. 251; *Compendium of the Enumeration of the Inhabitants and Statistics of the United States*, pp. 154–55; Risjord, "Virginia Federalists," p. 496.

16 Wise to Anne E. Wise, 23 Jan. 1837, Wise Family Papers, VHS(oc);

Barnes, *Anti-Slavery Impulse*, p. 265; Adams, ed., *Memoirs of John Quincy Adams*, 9:393 (6 Oct. 1837); Anne E. Wise to Henry A. Wise, 11 Jan. 1836, Wise Family Papers, VHS(oc).

17 Torrence, ed., "From the Society's Collections," pp. 497, 503–5, 512–13.

18 Boorstin, *The Americans*, p. 214; Pearson and Hendricks, *Liquor and Anti-Liquor in Virginia*, p. 84; Nichols, *Franklin Pierce*, pp. 86–87; Wise to Robert C. Wright, 5 May 1848, Wise Papers, VSL.

19 Wise to Rev. Leonidas L. Smith, 4 Jan. 1838, Barton H. Wise Papers, VHS(oc).

20 Torrence, ed., "From the Society's Collections," p. 506.

21 Ibid., p. 513.

22 Anne E. Wise to Henry A. Wise, 21 Dec. [1835?], Wise Family Papers, VHS(oc).

23 Sarah to her mother, n.d. [1840?], Wise to Robert Reed, 1 Apr. 1840, and Wise to Sarah Sergeant, 21 May 1840, all in WFP/VHS.

24 Sarah S. Wise to Wise, 9 July 1843, WFP/VHS.

25 Wise to James H. Hambleton, 12 Oct. 1855, I, Garnett Family Papers, VHS.

26 Goldman and Young, eds., *United States Congressional Directories*, passim.

27 Wise to Mrs. Hugh L. White, 8 July 1838, White Papers, DU.

28 Cf. Moore, "Revolt against Jackson in Tennessee," p. 354, and Scott, ed., *Memoir*, p. 81n; Sellers, *James K. Polk, Jacksonian*, p. 282; *Washington Globe*, 31 July, 23 Sept. 1836.

29 Sellers, *James K. Polk, Jacksonian*, p. 265.

30 Wise to Nathaniel Beverley Tucker, 29 May 1841, in Tyler, ed., *Letters and Times*, 2:34.

31 Calhoun to Duff Green, 24 Jan. 1836, in Jameson, ed., "Correspondence of John C. Calhoun," p. 356; *Washington Globe*, 17 Feb., 9, 19 Apr., 28 May 1836.

32 *NNR* 52 (8 July 1837): 298.

33 *NNR* 51 (31 Dec. 1836): 285–86.

34 *Washington Globe*, 3, 5, 31 Jan. 1837; McFaul and Gatell, "The Outcast Insider," pp. 116–20, 124, 142; Sellers, *James K. Polk, Jacksonian*, p. 316.

35 Wise to Anne E. Wise, 28 Jan. 1837, Wise Family Papers, VHS(oc); Jackson's letter may conveniently be found in Bassett, ed., *Correspondence*, 5:452–55; *Washington Globe*, 3 Jan. 1837.

36 U.S. Congress, House of Representatives, *Report of the Select Committee on the Agent-Deposit Banks* and *Journal of the Select Committee to Investigate the Executive Departments*, 24, 2, Nos. 193, 194.

37 *RDC*, 24, 2 (4 Feb. 1837): 1575–77.

38 Sellers, *James K. Polk, Jacksonian*, pp. 315–17; *National Intelligencer*, 18 Feb. 1837.

39 Both the minority report Wise submitted with Peyton as a member of Garland's committee (attached to House Committee Report No. 193) and his personal contribution as chairman of his own committee (House Committee Report No. 194) stridently reviewed all the arguments against executive domination and interference, though supplying little evidence on alleged administration corruption. After Swartout's defalcation, however, the nine-man House investigatory committee elected on Wise's motion (and not appointed by the Speaker, as was typical) in January 1839 devastated the Jacksonians by revealing immense frauds, particularly in the customs houses and land offices, dating to the early 1830s. See White, *Jacksonians*, pp. 424–28; Wise, "Speech . . . on the . . . late defalcations," in *CG*, 25, 3, Appendix, 384–404.

Chapter 3

1 Cf. Freehling, *Prelude to Civil War*, p. 351, and Rable, "Slavery, Politics, and the South."

2 *RDC*, 24, 1 (15 Feb. 1836): 2533–35. Pinckney engaged in double-dealing on several levels. When Wise claimed on the floor that an "express pledge" was given him "that the ground would be taken in the report, that Congress had not the power to abolish slavery in the District of Columbia," Pinckney never denied it.

3 J. B. Lamar to Hammond, 27 Feb. 1836, J. W. Brevard to Hammond, 11 Mar. 1836, Hammond Papers, LC; *CG*, 25, 2 (20 Dec. 1837): 41.

4 McPherson, "Fight against the Gag Rule," p. 178.

5 *RDC*, 24, 1 (22 Dec. 1835): 2024–34.

6 *RDC*, 24, 1 (23 Dec. 1835): 2042–62, esp. 2049; Freehling, *Drift toward Dissolution*, pp. 141–42.

7 Slade conveniently ignored federal statutes that confirmed the power of Virginia and Maryland law in those sections of the district respectively ceded by them. See, for example, Peters, ed., *Public Statutes*, 2:103–8. See also Sunderland, *Anti-Slavery Manual*, pp. 91–92. I detect no Southern congressman making this argument at any point during the debates. The memorial Slade mentions is discussed in Green, *Secret City*, pp. 30–33.

8 *National Intelligencer*, 21 Dec. 1835.

9 *RDC*, 24, 1 (1 Feb. 1836): 2448–62, for Hammond's remarks; ibid.

(21 Jan. 1836): 2241–53, for Pickens's views.

10 *RDC*, 24, 1 (19 Jan. 1836): 2233, for comments of James Bouldin; ibid., 24, 2 (21 Dec. 1836): 1999, for John Patton's remark that the constitutional question represented "a mere abstraction"; *CG*, 24, 1, Appendix 18, for James Garland's remarks.

11 See the reports of the debates in Congress in *NNR* 53 and 54 (24 Feb., 14, 21 Apr. 1838).

12 *Richmond Whig*, 11 June 1841.

13 Barnes, *Anti-Slavery Impulse*, pp. 118–19; Wiltse, *John C. Calhoun*, 2: 396–97; Wise, *Speech at Louisa Court House*; Brown, "Missouri Crisis." For comments on how the national Whig party survived and even prospered, despite North-South divisions, see Holt, *Political Crisis*, pp. 28–31 and passim.

14 Rable's illuminating and helpful study, "Slavery, Politics, and the South," comes closer to recognizing this point than any other recent study. See also, on these issues generally, Cooper, *The South and the Politics of Slavery*.

15 Wise, *Speech at Louisa Court House*; White, *Robert Barnwell Rhett*, pp. 37–38. The continuing aggressiveness of Slade and Adams—far exceeding that of their Northern colleagues in the Senate—eventually convinced a majority in the House to approve nonreception.

16 Freehling's superb *Drift toward Dissolution* emphasizes the abolitionist consensus prevailing in Virginia during the 1830s. It supersedes Robert, *Road from Monticello*.

17 For Tucker's views in favor of gradual emancipation, see his *Commentaries on the Laws of Virginia*, 1:74–75. Wise heard these lectures during his time in Winchester. See also Wise to John Tyler, 26 Feb. 1841, John Murray Dunmore Papers, UVA, recommending the "incomparable" Tucker for a Supreme Court justiceship; Tucker to Thomas Walker Gilmer, 6 Jan. 1844 (excerpt), in Merk, *Slavery and the Annexation of Texas*, p. 267, for a reiteration of Tucker's abolitionist views.

18 Freehling, *Drift toward Dissolution*, passim; McDowell, *Speech, 21st January, 1832*; Goodloe, *Southern Platform*, pp. 45, 47, 49.

19 Adkins, "Henry A. Wise in Sectional Politics," p. 133.

20 There was evidently a desultory correspondence between Dew and Wise, but no letters are extant. See Wise to W. White, 17 Apr. 1836, Wise Correspondence, NYHS; Freehling, *Drift toward Dissolution*, pp. 206–8.

21 Wise's remarks appear in Slaughter, *Virginian History of African Colonization*, pp. 89–93. The draft from which I have quoted is in the C. E. French Papers, MHS.

22 See below, Chapters 6 and 9.

23 Wise to Rev. Nehemiah Adams, 22 Aug. 1854, in *New York Times*, 15 Sept. 1854.

24 I acknowledge here the aid of Tom Dillard, formerly editor of the *Pulaski County* (Arkansas) *Historical Review*, who assisted me in locating sources on Grey. The most useful are as follows: Obituary in *Freeman*, 2 Mar. 1889; Palmer, "Miscegenation as an Issue in the Arkansas Constitutional Convention of 1868," and an 1875 interview of Grey by H. H. Robinson, reprinted in the *Arkansas Gazette*, 21 Dec. 1958.

25 *Arkansas Gazette*, 21 Dec. 1958.

26 *Debates and Proceedings of the Convention Which Assembled at Little Rock, January 7, 1868*, p. 97. Grey advocated capital punishment for any white man "found cohabiting with a negro woman." The "purity of the blood has . . . been somewhat interfered with in this country," he remarked, an "intermixture" that had taken place illegitimately (quoted in Gutman, *Black Family*, p. 400).

27 Grey arrived in Helena in 1865. He operated a grocery and bakery store before launching a political career in Arkansas during Reconstruction. He held a number of state offices, both elective and appointed. In 1872 he seconded Grant's nomination at the Republican National Convention and thereby became the first black man ever to address such a gathering.

28 N. Woodward to Wise, 1860, Henry A. Wise Correspondence, AAS.

29 Vol. 1, p. 475, RG 21, Federal Records Center, Suitland, Maryland.

30 On the aid Wise provided individual free blacks, see Jackson, *Free Negro Labor*, p. 85; Wise to Mayor Snowden, 26 Feb. 1841, Additional Alexandria City Papers, UVA.

31 *National Intelligencer*, 27 Jan. 1842. See also the suggestive comments of George M. Fredrickson, in the introduction to his edition of Helper, *Impending Crisis*, and his *Black Image in the White Mind*, pp. 62, 66–68. In the longhand draft of his speech before the Colonization Society in 1838, Wise mentions the antagonism between eastern and western Virginia and links it to disagreements over the future of slavery. These sentiments never appeared in print.

32 Wise to Robert Reed, 22 July 1837, WFP/VHS; Wise to James P. Hambleton, 16 Oct. 1855, Garnett Family Papers, VHS.

33 See the two letters cited immediately above and B. H. Wise, *Life of Henry A. Wise*, pp. 70–71. I have accepted as "family tradition" a note (n.d., n.p.) suggesting a slave's responsibility for the second fire, which I found in the Wise Family Papers in Charlottesville before their transfer to the Virginia Historical Society. I have not located this note in the society's holdings. It was apparently dictated to John Sergeant Wise, great-grandson of my subject, by his father,

whose name was Henry A. Wise. Wise to Mary Lyons Wise, 22 Mar. 1864, WFP/VHS, refers directly to incendiaries having set both fires.

34 Wise to James Hambleton, 16 Oct. 1855, Garnett Family Papers, VHS.

35 Poore, *Perley's Reminiscences*, 1:208; Thomas Jefferson to John Wise, 12 Feb. 1799, in *VMHB* 12 (1904–5): 257–59; John Cropper to Washington Cropper, 28 Dec. 1816, Cropper Papers, VHS; Anne E. Wise to Wise, n.d., typescript [early 1835?], Wise Family Papers, VHS(oc).

36 *NNR* 50 (2 Apr. 1836): 76–78; Weld, *American Slavery As It Is*, p. 184; Wise, "To My Constituents," in *NNR* 54 (24 Mar. 1838): 52–54.

37 See, for example, *CG*, 25, 2 (1 June 1838): 422–23, for Wise acting as peacemaker between Tennessee Congressmen John Bell and Hopkins Turney; Wise to William L. Savage and Joseph Segar, 24 June 1838, in *NNR* 54 (18 Aug. 1838): 393–94, for his role in preventing a duel between them.

38 *Memoirs and Services of Three Generations*, p. 22; *National Intelligencer*, 16 Feb. 1838.

39 *Madisonian*, 30 Jan. 1838, 423; Wise, "To My Constituents," for the "misunderstanding" comment.

40 To James H. Hammond, 5 Mar. 1838, Hammond Papers, LC.

41 Webb's Public Letter, 28 Feb. 1838, in *NNR* 54 (10 Mar. 1838): 18.

42 Wise, "To My Constituents."

43 Ibid.

44 Joint Statement of George W. Jones and Wise, 26 Feb. 1838, *NNR* 54 (3 Mar. 1838): 6–7.

45 Hawthorne, "Biographical Sketch of Jonathan Cilley," p. 75.

46 *Memoirs and Services of Three Generations*, p. 40.

47 John L. O'Sullivan, in *Memoirs and Services of Three Generations*, p. 38; Spaulding, "Duelling in the District of Columbia," p. 188; *National Intelligencer*, 12, 15 May 1838; *Richmond Whig*, 6 Mar. 1838. U.S. Congress, House of Representatives, *Report of the Select Committee to Investigate the Death of Jonathan Cilley*, 24, 2, No. 825, attempts—unsuccessfully in my judgment—to deny that an issue of veracity was at stake.

48 Wise, "To My Constituents"; James N. Schaumberg to Wise, 26 Mar. 1842, Barton H. Wise Papers, VHS(oc).

49 Wise to O'Sullivan, n.d. [evidently early in 1842], Barton H. Wise Papers, VHS(oc).

50 Wise to Meade, 29 Apr. 1838, Henry A. Wise Papers, ESHS.

51 Wise to Graves, 25 Feb. 1842, in *National Intelligencer*, 28 Feb. 1842.

52 Thomas, *Weld*, pp. 205–6.

53 Adams to Charles F. Adams, 19 Mar. 1838, in *MHSP*, 2d ser., 12 (1898): 288–92; *CG*, 27, 2 (22 Jan. 1842): 163; Wise's remarks in the House, 26 Jan. 1842, in *National Intelligencer*, 27 Jan. 1842.

54 *National Intelligencer*, 27 Jan. 1842.

55 Ibid.; Stewart, *Joshua R. Giddings*, p. 72, which misses that Gilmer, not Wise, offered the resolution of censure; Wise to James P. Hambleton, 16 Oct. 1855, Garnett Family Papers, VHS.

56 Clay to Webb, 20 Jan. 1842, Henry Clay Collection, UVA; Clay to Graves, in *National Intelligencer*, 25 Feb. 1842; Graves to Wise, ibid., 22 Mar. 1842; Wise's "Statement," ibid., 28 Feb. 1842; Clay to Wise, ibid., 7 Mar. 1842.

57 "York" in *Madisonian*, 24 Mar. 1843; Adams, ed., *Memoirs of John Quincy Adams*, 10:407 (27 Jan. 1841), 11:101 (28 Feb. 1842).

58 Stewart, *Joshua R. Giddings*, p. 76.

59 Hambleton, *Biographical Sketch*, pp. 100–101.

Chapter 4

1 Wise to Charles James Faulkner, 18 Feb. 1838, Faulkner Papers, WVULM.

2 Van Buren to Andrew Jackson, 4 Mar. 1839, in Bassett, ed., *Correspondence*, 6:5–6; *CG*, 25, 3, Appendix 384–404; U.S. Congress, House of Representatives, *Report of the Committee of Investigation on the Subject of the Defalcations of Samuel Swartout and Others*, 25, 3, No. 313; Sellers, *James K. Polk, Jacksonian*, pp. 335–36.

3 Nathans, *Daniel Webster*, pp. 139–40; Scott, ed., *Memoir*, p. 380; Curtis, *Fox at Bay*, pp. 199–201; Holt, *Political Crisis*, pp. 32–34.

4 *Richmond Whig*, 7 July 1840; Wise to unknown, 2 Dec. 1846, Henry A. Wise Papers, SHC. One of Wise's more ignoble gestures in behalf of a potentially victorious coalition in 1840 was to permit a reconciliation between himself and Reuben Whitney. See Andrew Jackson to Francis P. Blair, 16 Jan. 1838, in Bassett, ed., *Correspondence*, 5:527.

5 Wise, in *RDC*, 25, 3 (13 Oct. 1837): 1631–81; ibid. (27 Sept. 1837), 1035; Wise, *Speech at Louisa Court House*; Holt, *Political Crisis*, p. 34.

6 Wise, *Speech at Louisa Court House*.

7 Wise to James Hambleton, 17 Oct. 1855, Garnett Family Papers, VHS; Wise to his constituents, in *National Intelligencer*, 24 Sept. 1842; *Richmond Whig*, 10 July 1840; Clay to Nathaniel Beverley

Tucker, 10 Oct. 1839, in Tyler, ed., *Letters and Times*, 1:601–2; Nathans, *Daniel Webster*, pp. 136–37; Dent, "Virginia Democratic Party," 1:271–72.

One problem with Wise's story is that White endorsed Clay for the presidency, albeit only in preference to Van Buren, in an 1838 speech in Knoxville, Tennessee. See Scott, ed., *Memoir*, p. 365. Another difficulty stems from Wise's own commitment, rendered sometime earlier, to support Clay.

8 Quoted in Gunderson, *Log-Cabin Campaign*, p. 198.

9 Wise to Robert Reed, 13 Jan. 1840, WFP/VHS.

10 25 Nov. 1840, Tyler, ed., *Letters and Times*, 3:84–85.

11 See, for example, the issues of 24 Nov. (reprinting the views of the *Globe*) and 1 Dec. 1840 (sw).

12 Tyler to Wise, 20 Dec. 1840, in Tyler, ed., *Letters and Times*, 3:86. See also Abel P. Upshur to Wise, 3 Jan. 1841, Atcheson L. Hench Collection, UVA.

13 Wise to John B. Coles et al., 5 Nov. 1841, in *Madisonian* (sw), 14 Dec. 1841.

14 *CG*, 26, 2, Appendix 286–302.

15 Wise to J. M. Mason, 29 May 1841, WFP/VHS; Wise's remarks in *CG*, 27, 3 (3 Mar. 1843): 399; Robert Charles Wickliffe to Wise, 28 Jan. 1843, Autograph File, HU.

16 *Richmond Whig*, 5, 12 Feb. 1841.

17 Wise, *Seven Decades of the Union*, p. 179.

18 Smith, *Annexation of Texas*, p. 103.

19 Wise to John Minor Botts, 1 Oct. 1841, in *National Intelligencer*, 7 Oct. 1841; Wise to Leslie Coombs, 29, 30 Dec. 1842, in Tyler, ed., *Letters and Times*, 3:106–8. In *CG*, 27, 3 (10 Jan. 1843): 147, Wise artfully accounts for his confusion about Tyler's intentions by saying that when the president in his inaugural address suggested that he would be following the advice of the "fathers of the Republican faith," Wise was unsure whether he meant Jefferson or Madison.

20 Stathis, "John Tyler's Presidential Succession"; Tyler to Caleb Cushing, 8 Oct. 1841, Caleb Cushing Papers, LC; *New York Tribune*, 5 Aug. 1841; William B. Campbell to David Campbell, 10 July 1842, Campbell Family Papers, DU. Cf. Wise to James Hambleton, 17 Oct. 1855, and Wise, *Seven Decades of the Union*, p. 182.

21 In 1842 Tyler reluctantly vetoed two tariff bills, but when the more important of them was overridden in the House, Wise and a few others absented themselves to assure its passage. See Edmund W. Hubard to R. T. Hubard, 16 July 1842, Hubard Family Papers, UVA. In a nine-column letter addressed to his constituents and published after the adjournment of Congress (*National Intelligencer*,

23 Sept. 1842), Wise maintained that an "accident" prevented him from voting.

22 Tyler to Nathaniel Beverley Tucker, 28 July 1841 (copy), Oliver P. Chitwood Papers, WVULM.

23 Wise to Nathaniel Beverley Tucker, 27 June 1841, WFP/VHS; Poage, *Henry Clay*, p. 60.

24 Nathans, *Daniel Webster*, pp. 173–79; Chitwood, *John Tyler*, p. 246; Brugger, *Beverley Tucker*, p. 142, for the comment on the veto message.

25 Wise to Nathaniel Beverley Tucker, 29 May 1841, in Tyler, ed., *Letters and Times*, 2:34. See also Wise to John B. Coles et al., 5 Nov. 1841, in *Madisonian* (sw), 14 Dec. 1841.

26 *New York Herald*, 25 June 1841.

27 Forney, *Anecdotes of Public Men*, 1:144.

28 Wise to John B. Coles et al., 5 Nov. 1841, in *Madisonian* (sw), 14 Dec. 1841.

29 Wise to Nathaniel Beverley Tucker, 29 May 1841, in Tyler, ed., *Letters and Times*, 2:34, for the quotation. See also Wise to James M. Mason, 29 May 1841, WFP/VHS; Poage, *Henry Clay*, p. 130; Brugger, *Beverley Tucker*, p. 139. See *Washington Globe*, 23 June 1841, and *Richmond Whig*, 18 Jan. 1842, for comments comparing Wise with Randolph.

30 Ruffin to Tyler, 29 June 1841, in Ruffin, *Diary*, ed. Scarborough, 1:614.

31 U.S. Congress, House of Representatives, *Report of the Minority of the Select Committee to Revise the Rules and Orders of the House*, 28, 1, No. 3, pp. 18–19. Wise wrote this report.

32 Thomas W. Gilmer to R. T. Hubard, 14 Feb. 1844, Hubard Family Papers, UVA; *Report of the Minority of the Select Committee to Revise the Rules and Orders of the House*, pp. 17–24.

33 Thomas H. Ellis to George W. Munford, 13 Aug. 1842, Munford-Ellis Family Papers, DU. On the heightened partisan loyalties of the 1840s, see Silbey, *Shrine of Party*, and Holt, *Political Crisis*.

34 Wise to John Y. Mason, 14 May 1845, Mason Family Papers, VHS; Cooper, *The South and the Politics of Slavery*, pp. 176–81; Bell to Thomas Ewing, 23 Oct. 1841, Ewing Papers, LC.

35 Quoted in Merk, *Slavery and the Annexation of Texas*, pp. 198–99. Unlike certain others among Tyler's Texas enthusiasts, such as Thomas W. Gilmer, Wise seems to have had no investments or other financial interest in Texas.

In later asserting that "slavery had been abolished" in Texas when he sought to purchase it from the Mexicans in 1825 during his presidency, Adams experienced a lapse of memory—one of the few to have afflicted him during a fabled public career. The Mexicans abolished slavery in 1829 but quickly thereafter annulled this decree so far as it applied to Texas. See Rives, *United States and Mexico*, 1:184–86; Barker, *Life of Stephen F. Austin*, pp. 202–11. Adams had earlier supported the acquisition of slave territory by the United States, as his biographer concedes. See Bemis, *John Quincy Adams and the Union*, pp. 363–69. Adams had thus sanctioned important precedents used relentlessly by annexationists. See, for example, *Richmond Whig*, 16 June, 4 July 1843.

36 Merk, *Slavery and the Annexation of Texas*, pp. 193, 197; Wise to Caleb Cushing (extracts), 6 Dec. 1845, Barton H. Wise Papers, VHS(oc). Walker's letter on annexation may conveniently be found in Merk, *Fruits of Propaganda*, pp. 221–52.

37 Merk, *Slavery and the Annexation of Texas*, p. 192n. Neither the *Congressional Globe* proper nor its Appendix contains any report of Wise's remarks. Wise had alluded to several of his themes in his 26 January 1842 philippic against Adams (*National Intelligencer*, 27 Jan. 1842), although he expanded considerably upon them here.

38 Speech in the House, 15 Apr. 1842, *NNR* 62 (30 Apr. 1842): 139. Wise's remarks were featured prominently in Adams, "Address to his Constituents of the Twelfth Congressional District of Massachusetts," in ibid. 63 (29 Oct. 1842), 136–40, and also in Adams et al., "Address to the People of the Free States of the Union," in ibid. 64 (13 May 1843): 173–75.

39 The evidence presented in the following works effectively overturns the benign view of British intentions defended by Frederick Merk and by Sidney Nathans, *Daniel Webster*, p. 122n, among others: Smith, *Annexation of Texas*, pp. 86–91, 116–18, 126, 150–53; Pletcher, *Diplomacy of Annexation*, p. 122; Ashbel Smith to Anson Jones, despatch 43, 31 July 1843, in Garrison, ed., "Diplomatic Correspondence of the Republic of Texas," p. 1117; Hansard's *Parliamentary Debates (Lords)*, 3d ser., 71, 18 Aug. 1843, for the comments of Lord Aberdeen, p. 918. Because there were only about twelve thousand slaves in Texas at this time, a scheme of compensated emancipation such as the British and certain Texans contemplated would have been inexpensive.

40 "Mr. Henry A. Wise and the Cilley Duel," *United States Magazine and Democratic Review* 10 (May 1842): 482–87. *CG*, 27, 3 (11 Mar. 1843): 313, for the comments of Meredith P. Gentry of Tennessee.

41 Mangum to Paul C. Cameron, 10 Feb. 1844, in Shanks, ed., *Papers of Willie P. Mangum*, 4:42.

42 Wise, *Seven Decades of the Union*, pp. 221–25. Cf. Sellers, *James K. Polk: Continentalist*, p. 56n, and Wiltse, *John C. Calhoun*, 3:161–63. I do not see the inconsistency alleged by Sellers between

Wise's account in *Seven Decades of the Union* and the letter he wrote Robert M. T. Hunter, 7 March 1844, Calhoun Papers, RMC. Nothing in McDuffie's letter of 5 March 1844 to Calhoun contradicts Wise's view. See Jameson, ed., "Correspondence of John C. Calhoun," p. 934. Tyler, ed., *Letters and Times*, 2:294, corroborates Wise's story.

43 Calhoun to James Buchanan, 24 Mar. 1845, Jameson, ed., "Correspondence of John C. Calhoun," p. 651; Buchanan to Calhoun, 9 Apr. 1845, Boucher and Brooks, eds., "Correspondence Addressed to John C. Calhoun, 1837–1849," p. 292.

44 *NNR* 66 (9 Mar. 1844): 25.

45 Ibid., pp. 24–26; Hudson, *Journalism in the United States*, p. 120.

46 *CG*, 28, 1 (21 Dec. 1843): 63; *Madisonian*, 22 Dec. 1843; Wise's and Holmes's remarks in the House, 1 Dec. 1843, in *New York Tribune*, 22 Dec. 1843; Joshua R. Giddings to his son, 24 Dec. 1843, Giddings Papers, OHS, which shows antislavery spokesmen exulting over what they interpreted as Wise's capitulation.

47 *Report of the Minority of the Select Committee to Revise the Rules and Orders of the House*, p. 20.

48 *CG*, 28, 1 (12 Jan. 1844): 141.

Chapter 5

1 Wise to James P. Hambleton, 17 Oct. 1855, Garnett Family Papers, VHS; B. H. Wise, *Life of Henry A. Wise*, pp. 116–17.

2 Calhoun to Wise, Despatches 4 and 10, 25 May 1844 and 20 Jan. 1845, RG 84, NA.

3 Soulsby, *Right of Search*, pp. 42–43; Wise to Hamilton Hamilton, 1 Dec. 1844, enclosed with Despatch 9 to John C. Calhoun, 14 Dec. 1844, RG 59, NA; George W. Gordon to James Buchanan, Consular Despatch 62, from Rio de Janeiro, 18 Sept. 1845, in ibid. See also Curtin, *Atlantic Slave Trade*, pp. 235–49.

4 Howard, *American Slavers*, p. 282.

5 Degler, *Neither Black nor White*, p. 52; Wise to Hamilton Hamilton, 1 Dec. 1844, enclosed with Despatch 9 to John C. Calhoun, 14 Dec. 1844, and Wise to Buchanan, Despatch 54, 9 Dec. 1846, both in RG 59, NA.

6 Howard, *American Slavers*, pp. 41–43; Booth, "United States African Squadron," pp. 99, 100–102, 105–7.

7 Cf. Brooks, *Yankee Traders*, pp. 194–95, 199, 205, 222, 259–61, 288–89.

8 Hill, *Diplomatic Relations*, pp. 122–24; Howard, *American Slavers*, p. 20; Bethell, *Abolition of the Brazilian Slave Trade*, pp. 189–90;

President's Message Transmitting Copies of Despatches from the American Minister at the Court of Brazil, Relative to the Slave Trade, 20 Feb. 1845, in House Executive Document 148, 28th Cong., 2d sess. (1844–45); Wise to Commander L. Rousseau, 15 Jan. 1846, enclosed with Despatch 40 to James Buchanan, 20 Feb. 1846, in RG 59, NA.

9 Howard, *American Slavers*, pp. 43–45; Bethell, *Abolition of the Brazilian Slave Trade*, pp. 309–41; Conrad, "Struggle for the Abolition of the Brazilian Slave Trade," pp. 304–58. Bethell and Conrad are persuasively critical of Howard's explanation at page 46.

10 Wise to Maxwell, Wright & Co., 9 Dec. 1844, enclosed with Wise to Calhoun, Despatch 9, 14 Dec. 1844, RG 59, NA.

11 Wise to Calhoun, Despatches 7, 1 Nov. 1844, and 9, 14 Dec. 1844, and Wise to Buchanan, Despatch 25, 31 July 1845, RG 59, NA; Gordon to Buchanan, 2 June 1845, Gordon Papers, LC.

12 Quaife, ed., *Diary of James K. Polk*, 1:458 (8 June 1846), 2:155 (25 Sept. 1846); Bancroft to Polk, 3 Feb. 1847, Bancroft Papers, MHS.

13 Calhoun to Thomas G. Clemson, 23 June 1845, in Jameson, ed., "Correspondence of John C. Calhoun," p. 665.

14 Wise to Mason, 5 Mar. 1844 and 14 May 1845 (for the quotation), Mason Family Papers, VHS. An implied sense of reciprocal obligation governed Wise in making this request; he had urged Mason's appointment to the cabinet on Tyler at the same time that he pressed for Calhoun's.

15 Wise to Maxwell, Wright & Co., 9 Dec. 1844, enclosed with Wise to Calhoun, Despatch 9, 14 Dec. 1844, RG 59, NA.

16 Wise to Robert Poulson, 15 Mar. 1846 (typescript), Grinnan Family Papers, UVA.

17 Wise to Buchanan, Despatch 16, 1 May 1845, RG 59; Wise to Poulson, 15 Mar. 1846 (typescript), Grinnan Family Papers, UVA.

18 Gordon to Buchanan, 18 Sept. 1845, Despatch 62, RG 59, NA.

19 *House Executive Documents*, 28, 2, No. 148; for a different view, which tends to emphasize English humanitarianism although dealing warily with motivational questions, see Bethell, *Abolition of the Brazilian Slave Trade*, passim.

20 Bethell, *Abolition of the Brazilian Slave Trade*, p. 283.

21 Hansard's *Parliamentary Debates (Commons)*, 3d ser., 77, 25 Feb. 1845, for the comments of Sir R. H. Inglis, pp. 1173–86, 26 Feb. 1845, for the comments of Lord John Russell, pp. 1242–47. See also Bethell, "Mixed Commissions," p. 89; Howard, *American Slavers*, p. 4; "East India Cotton," *Southern Quarterly Review* 1 (Apr. 1842): 446–93, esp. 450.

22 Wise to Hamilton Hamilton, 31 July 1846, enclosed with Wise to Buchanan, Despatch 50, 29 Sept. 1846, RG 59, NA. See also

Brooks, *Yankee Traders*, p. 113; Lloyd, *The Navy and the Slave Trade*, pp. 81–84. Wise did not specify any vessels that had delayed making seizures in order to gain pecuniary advantage; Lloyd points out that no one was ever able to do so.

23 Commander L. Rousseau to Wise, 1 Nov. 1846, Rousseau Papers, CHS; Wise to Buchanan, Despatches 53, 55, 62 (16 Nov. 1846, 27 Feb., 22 May 1847); McCormac, *James K. Polk*, p. 706; Wise to William H. D. C. Wright, 13 May 1847, Etting Papers, HSP.

24 Wise to R. M. T. Hunter, 12 May 1847, in Ambler, ed., "Correspondence of Robert M. T. Hunter," p. 9.

25 Margaret D. P. Wise to Wise, 29 May 1845, WFP/VHS; Wise to John Y. Mason, 14 May 1845, Mason Family Papers, VHS.

26 For Wise's role in supervising his brother's affairs, see the scattered notes and documents in the John W. Gillet Papers, VSL.

27 Wise to Robert Reed, 3 Mar. 1850, Henry A. Wise Papers, UVA.

28 ACOB, 1845–48 (Reel 105), p. 120, VSL; George W. P. Curtis to Wise, 15 Oct. 1850 (misdated 1820), Alexander William Armour Collection, LC.

29 Sally C. Parsons to Mrs. Frances Jones, 1 Jan. 1849, John Beauchamp Jones Papers, SHC; Sarah S. Wise to Wise, 14 Jan. and 5 Nov. 1849 (typescripts), Wise Family Papers, VHS(oc).

30 O. J. Wise to Wise, 12 Dec. 1847, and Wise to O. J. Wise, 18 Feb. 1848, WFP/VHS.

31 Wise to O. J. Wise, 18 Feb. 1848, WFP/VHS; O. J. Wise to Annie Wise, 24 July 1850 (typescript), Wise Family Papers, VHS(oc).

32 O. J. Wise to Annie Wise, 24 July 1850 (typescript), Wise Family Papers, VHS(oc); O. J. Wise to Mrs. Chapman, 6 Jan. 1855 (misdated 1854), WFP/VHS.

33 Sarah Wise to Wise, 5 Nov. 1843, and Margaret Sergeant to Sarah Wise, 13 Apr. 1846, in WFP/VHS; John Tyler to Caleb Cushing, n.d., but evidently from the winter of 1847–48, in Tyler, ed., *Letters and Times*, 2:459–60; *Richmond Whig*, 6 Mar. 1855, all of which deal with Wise's religiosity; J. S. Wise, *End of an Era*, pp. 38, 46. Henry's third son and namesake joined the Episcopal priesthood a few years later. See Chapter 7.

34 Census of 1850, Slave Schedules (Accomac County, Virginia), VSL. No farm records kept by the Wises are extant. It seems most unlikely that Wise's small pre-1844 slave force could have reproduced itself this extensively. Moreover, the explanation that they were "family inheritances" (affirmed by J. S. Wise, *End of an Era*, p. 37) seems vitiated by the debts and poverty then afflicting all branches of the Wise family.

There is much modern literature on male life cycles, some of which has alerted me to the usefulness of considering this period of

Wise's life as a moratorium from the political struggles that had energized him earlier, as they would do again during the 1850s. See, especially, Levinson et al., *Seasons of a Man's Life*; Erikson, "Reflections on Dr. Borg's Life Cycle"; Jung, "Stages of Life." But see also the reservations, particularly as they apply to Levinson's work, in Riley, "Aging, Social Change, and the Power of Ideas."

35 Wise, *Territorial Government*, p. 154; on Christian stewardship, see Faust, *Sacred Circle*, pp. 121–23.

36 See Chapter 12.

37 On this point, cf. Genovese, *Roll, Jordan, Roll*, pp. 4–7, 96–97, 146–49, and Gutman, *Black Family*, pp. 312–18. See also Anderson, "Aunt Jemima in Dialectics," p. 107, and Chapter 12.

38 Wise, *Speech on the Basis Question*, pp. 31, 36, Henry A. Wise Papers, SHC; Genovese, "Toward a Psychology of Slavery."

39 See Chapter 7.

40 22 Feb. 1848, Tucker-Coleman Papers, WM.

41 A. Y. P. Garnett to Muscoe Garnett, 5 Apr. 1848, William Garnett Chisolm Papers, VHS.

42 Gentry to Wise, 13 June 1848, Henry A. Wise Papers, UVA; *Union* (Washington, D.C.), 9 Aug. 1848.

43 To Robert Reed, 23 Mar. 1850, Henry A. Wise Papers, UVA.

44 To Richard J. Ayres, 9 Mar. 1850, in ibid.

45 Undated clipping from the *Snow Hill* (Md.) *Shield*, Henry A. Wise Papers, SHC. The crisis of the Union also commanded his attention, but seemingly in such a fashion as to permit him to preserve his own maneuverability in national politics. Early in 1849, John C. Calhoun circulated a Southern manifesto among members of Congress that threatened secession should the Wilmot Proviso become law. One of Calhoun's old enemies, Senator Thomas Hart Benton of Missouri, responded with a scathing indictment (in *National Intelligencer*, 21 June 1849), which came close to pronouncing Calhoun a traitor. Benton mentioned disapprovingly the proceedings of a political meeting in Accomac County, Virginia, evidently convened by people sympathetic to Calhoun's purposes. The Accomac resolves deplored the free-soil movement and suggested that a state convention "organized according to law" might "best settle the rule of conduct for the citizen" in the event of a national crisis. This convention would "inform its citizens and subjects whether they will be authorized to resist." I have found no other information on this meeting, but it would be difficult to suppose that such a gathering could take place in Accomac unknown to Wise and beyond his influence. Perhaps Wise had heard of Calhoun's displeasure with his conduct in Brazil. Because he later claimed a close relationship with the great Carolinian before his death in 1850, Wise may at this point have

effected a reconciliation in a subtle effort to preserve his self-respect. The decidedly equivocal resolves, Benton's own prejudiced construction notwithstanding, preview the problems Wise would experience in 1861, particularly with the issue of treason. He may well have written the resolves. His son-in-law, Dr. A. Y. P. Garnett, arranged for Senator Henry S. Foote of Mississippi to compose a letter addressed to Wise, which defended Calhoun and rebutted Benton's charges. See Foote's letter in the *Union* (Washington, D.C.), 24 June 1849; A. Y. P. Garnett to Muscoe Garnett, 29 June 1849 (typescript), William Garnett Chisolm Papers, VHS.

46 *Richmond Enquirer*, 16 Jan. 1850; Wise to Tucker, 14 May 1850, Tucker-Coleman Papers, WM; Tucker to James H. Hammond, 27 Jan. 1850, Hammond Papers, LC; Brugger, *Beverley Tucker*, p. 181.

47 *Speech Delivered at the Free School Celebration*; Dabney, "Education in Virginia"; "Education in the Southern and Western States"; J. H. Pendleton to Horace Mann, 17 Dec. 1849, and R. L. Lackey to Mann, 3 Feb. 1850, in Knight, ed., *Documentary History of Education*, 5:366–68. But cf., for warnings of Northern subversion, "On Public Education in Virginia."

48 Attendance, moreover, was optional, not compulsory, for free schools in all locations. The Constitutional Convention of 1850–51 made no changes. See Conway, *Free Schools in Virginia*.

Chapter 6

1 *Register of Debates and Proceedings*, 11 Feb. 1851, p. 209. During the convention, the reporter, W. G. Bishop, got embroiled with its members over his fees. Thus only a small number of these volumes were published, covering but a few weeks of the convention's deliberations. The best sources are the ninety-two convention supplements, issued periodically as inserts in the Richmond newspapers. Nearly complete files are available at the Virginia State Library and at the E. G. Swem Library, College of William and Mary.

2 For fuller commentary on the convention's historiography and political background, see Simpson, "Political Compromise and the Protection of Slavery."

3 Wise, *Speech on the Basis Question*, p. 36, Henry A. Wise Papers, SHC.

4 Convention Supplement 29, 7 Apr. 1851.

5 *Richmond Enquirer*, 4 Dec. 1849, 19 Apr. 1850. (All succeeding references to the *Enquirer* in this chapter, unless otherwise noted, are to the semiweekly edition.)

6 Chandler, *Representation in Virginia*, pp. 56–57; Eaton, "Henry A. Wise, A Liberal of the Old South," p. 489.

7 See Eaton's publications listed in the Bibliography.

8 Wise, *Speech on the Basis Question*, pp. 34–36, Henry A. Wise Papers, SHC; Shanks, "Conservative Constitutional Tendencies of the Virginia Secession Convention."

9 Wise began his address on the evening of 23 April and concluded on 28 April. No copy of it appeared in the convention supplements; the Henry A. Wise Papers, SHC, contain an incomplete version, forty pages long. See the comments on the unpopularity among most delegates of appeals to natural rights in Freehling, *Drift toward Dissolution*, p. 237.

10 Wise, *Speech on the Basis Question*, pp. 21, 31, and passim, Henry A. Wise Papers, SHC; Upshur, *Speech upon the . . . Basis of Representation*.

11 Wise, *Speech on the Basis Question*, pp. 7–12, Henry A. Wise Papers, SHC.

12 Ibid., pp. 11–12; Wheaton, *Discourse on St. Paul's Epistle to Philemon*; J. J. S. (Joseph J. Speed), *Letter from a Gentleman of Baltimore*.

13 Goode relied on Stringfellow's *A Brief Examination of Scripture Testimony on the Institution of Slavery* (pp. 25, 27 for the quotation), a series of newspaper articles first published collectively in pamphlet form in 1841. Years later, Stringfellow added a "Statistical View of Slavery," which appeared along with a retitled version of his first essay in the noted collection compiled by E. N. Elliott, *Cotton Is King* (1860). The closing sentence of the "Statistical View" suggests a slightly altered perspective, which curiously brings Stringfellow closer to Wise's outlook: "We cannot put an end to African slavery, if we would—and we ought not, if we could—until God opens a door to *make its termination a blessing, and not a curse*. When he does that, slavery in this Union will end."

At the time of Virginia's convention in Richmond, other prominent Southern opinion makers held sentiments similar to Wise's. The Rev. Dr. James H. Thornwell of Charleston, South Carolina, was perhaps the leading Presbyterian divine in the lower South. In *The Rights and the Duties of Masters* (1850), Thornwell denied the legitimacy of property in man and admitted that slavery was conceived in injustice though arguing for its maintenance as the least of evils. Aware, like Wise, of the South's moral isolation, Thornwell suggested that this liability might be overcome if all realized the nature of the worldwide struggle between "the friends of order and regulated freedom" and the jacobins, communists, and socialists.

Thornwell believed, with Wise, that slaves retained their "moral freedom"; nothing in their status could divest them of their humanity. Although Thornwell, unlike Wise, never postulated a Southern abandonment of slavery before the coming of the millennium, there was nonetheless a "soft" side to his commitment. Thornwell's Christianity and his knowledge of the South's international isolation shaped his views. Jack P. Maddex underestimates these aspects of Thornwell's thinking in "Proslavery Millennialism." Cf. Loveland, *Southern Evangelicals*, p. 207. In his *Speech Delivered in the Southern Convention* at Nashville, in 1850, Nathaniel Beverley Tucker argued for a dissolution of the Union but advocated gradual emancipation in the aftermath. He proposed establishing a large free black colony in Haiti, populated by Southern expatriates, who would eventually (in accord with the notions of Wise and many others) civilize and Christianize Africa. This theme in Tucker's address, and his uncertainties about slavery's future, are missed in Brugger's *Beverley Tucker*.

For a contemporary though far less qualified view of these matters, largely at variance with the authors just cited, see Ruffin, *Address to the Virginia State Agricultural Society*.

14 *Richmond Examiner*, 27 May 1851; Convention Supplement 44, 15 May 1851.

15 *Richmond Examiner*, 27 May 1851; Convention Supplement 44, 15 May 1851. Among the eight or nine delegates from eastern Virginia responsible for the compromise, partisan political allegiance was unimportant. Some were Democrats, for example, but other crucial votes came from Whigs.

16 Muscoe Garnett to his mother, 12 May 1851, William Garnett Chisolm Papers, VHS; Richard I. Cocke to Charles Ellis, 10 June 1851, Munford-Ellis Family Papers, DU; Convention Supplement 48, 20 May 1851.

17 Convention Supplement 77, 3, 5 July 1851.

18 The petition, bearing 248 signatures, was originally directed to the Virginia General Assembly. It predicted that unless the assembly enacted legislation "securing to the white man the exclusive privilege of the mechanic arts," the day "is not far distant, when the mechanics and nonslaveholders, generally, will demand the total expulsion of the negros from our state." The petitioners made it clear that they opposed the employment of both slaves and free blacks as mechanics. They complained that "negro mechanics had retarded the prosperity, enterprise, and progress of the state by driving out native Virginians to other states" and asked that a tax be imposed on the blacks sufficient "to render their employment unprofitable"

(Legislative Petitions, Portsmouth, Norfolk County, 25 Feb. 1851, VSL). See also Jackson, *Free Negro Labor and Property Holding in Virginia*, p. 67.

19 Convention Supplement 80, 9 July 1851; *Richmond Enquirer*, 7 Mar., 18 Apr. 1851. On the value of Virginia slaves in 1850, see Goldin, *Urban Slavery*, pp. 72–73. Of Virginia's 472,528 slaves in 1850, 146,414 were aged nine and under. The census of population was broken down into five-year segments, so it is possible to estimate that about 26,500 slaves were aged ten and eleven. Thus the convention exempted from taxation approximately 173,000 slaves (U.S. Census Office, *Seventh Census of the United States*, pp. 242–46).

20 Convention Supplement 80, 9 July 1851. One representative indicated later that the convention's committee on suffrage had rejected the idea of making payment of the capitation tax a prerequisite for the ballot. Instead, the committee and later the convention accepted a two-year residence requirement in lieu of a taxpaying qualification (Convention Supplement 83, 16 July 1851).

21 *Richmond Enquirer*, 28 May 1850; Richard I. Cocke to Charles Ellis, 10 June 1851, Munford-Ellis Family Papers, DU; *Richmond Examiner*, 18 Feb. 1851.

22 Ruffner, *Address to the People of West Virginia.*

Chapter 7

1 Convention Supplement 33, 18 Apr. 1851.

2 *Richmond Enquirer*, 16 Jan. 1850.

3 Nathaniel Beverley Tucker to James H. Hammond, 8 Feb. 1850, Tucker Papers, DU.

4 Tucker to Hammond, 13 Mar. 1847, 29 Dec. 1849, and 15 Mar. 1851 (typescripts), Tucker Papers, DU; Hammond to William Gilmore Simms, 16 June 1850, Hammond Papers, LC; Muscoe Garnett to his mother, 29 Mar. 1852, and 21 Jan. 1857, William Garnett Chisolm Papers, VHS.

5 Muscoe Garnett to his mother, 11 Jan. 1858, William Garnett Chisolm Papers, VHS.

6 Holt, *Political Crisis*, pp. 226–57.

7 *Richmond Whig*, 18 Feb. 1851; Alexander H. H. Stuart to Gideon Camden, 23 Mar. 1851, Camden Papers, WVULM; John Minor Botts to Stuart, 30 Nov. 1851, Stuart Papers, UVA.

8 *Richmond Examiner*, 18 Feb. 1851; *Richmond Enquirer*, 18 Feb. 1851; Willis P. Bocock to R. M. T. Hunter, 13 Feb. 1851, in Ambler, ed., "Correspondence of Robert M. T. Hunter," pp. 124–26; Wise to

Buchanan, 20 Feb. 1851, Buchanan Papers, HSP. See also Nevins, *Ordeal of the Union*, 1:367.

9 Brown, "Missouri Crisis"; *Richmond Examiner*, 18 Feb. 1851.

10 Wise to Buchanan, 8 July 1851 and 3 Mar. 1852, Buchanan Papers, HSP; Buchanan to Wise, 18 Mar., 10 May, 9 June, and 1 Dec. 1852, WFP/VHS.

11 Wise to Buchanan, 8 June 1851, Buchanan Papers, HSP. Klein's *President James Buchanan* details the many difficulties Buchanan experienced in gaining advantage over his Democratic rivals in Pennsylvania.

12 Wise to Cushing, 24 Apr. and 29 May 1853, Caleb Cushing Papers, LC.

13 Wise to Buchanan, 11 June 1853, Buchanan Papers, HSP.

14 Muscoe Garnett to W. H. Trescot, May 1851, cited in Shanks, *Secession Movement in Virginia*, p. 39; Wise to Buchanan, 20 Apr. 1851, Buchanan Papers, HSP.

15 U.S. Census Office, *Seventh Census of the United States, Slave Schedules*, Accomac County, Virginia; *Productions of Agriculture*, Accomac County; *Free Inhabitants*, Accomac County; O. J. Wise to Wise, 13 Mar. [1852], and Wise to Mary Lyons Wise, 25 Sept. 1858, in WFP/VHS; Wise to James Lyons, 6 Nov. 1856, Brock Collection, CSmH.

16 Brugger, *Beverley Tucker*, p. 34.

17 See the memoir of Wise by Col. Thos. S. Hudson in the *Crisfield* (Md.) *Times*, 28 Sept. 1912, and Wise to Mary Lyons Wise, 29 Sept. 1854, both in WFP/VHS; ACOB (microfilm), VSL; Robert Taylor Wilson to Alexander Garrett (?), 15 Apr. 1852 (incomplete fragment), Garrett Papers, UVA; Order Book 43, 1851–57, pp. 58–60, Northampton County Court, and Common Law Order Book 2, 1852–74, Northampton County Superior Court, p. 88, courtesy of Virginia Williams, deputy clerk of Northampton County. There are scattered items relating to Wise's law practice in the WFP/VHS, but no systematic records, such as fee or account books, are extant.

18 Hunter, *Memoir of Robert M. T. Hunter*, pp. 25–29, 31, 79–80.

19 Muscoe Garnett to Hunter, 5 Aug. 1850, Hunter Papers, UVA; Francis Mallory to Garnett, 2 Dec. 1856, William Garnett Chisolm Papers, VHS.

20 Foote, *Casket of Reminiscences*, p. 370.

21 Hunter to Wise, 12 and 14 Jan. 1853, WFP/VHS; Wise to P. R. George, 13 and 15 Jan. 1852, John Hatch George Collection, NHHS.

22 Wise to George Booker, 12 Dec. 1852, WFP/VHS; Wise to Hunter, 13 and 15 Jan. 1853, Hunter Papers, UVA; Wise to Robert Tyler, 5 Apr. 1853, in Tyler, ed., *Letters and Times*, 2:504–5.

23 Booker to Hunter, 7 June 1852, in Ambler, ed., "Correspondence of Robert M. T. Hunter," pp. 144–45.

24 Seddon to Hunter, 18 Jan. 1851 (misdated 1852), in ibid., pp. 131–32.

25 Wise to James Hambleton, 17 Oct. 1855, Garnett Family Papers, VHS.

26 Wise to Mary Lyons, 19 Sept. 1853, WFP/VHS.

27 Mary Lyons to Wise, 25 Aug. 1853, Wise to Mary Lyons, 10 Apr. 1853, in ibid.

28 Wise to O. J. Wise, 14 Feb. 1848, WFP/VHS.

29 Wise to Col. Francis H. Smith, 13 and 20 Mar. 1852, Superintendent's Papers, VMI; Wise to William F. Samford, 2 Dec. 1858, Samford-Wise Papers, AU; Wise to O. J. Wise, 20 Apr. 1851, and to Mary Lyons Wise, 1 Apr. 1860, in WFP/VHS.

30 Wise to Mary Lyons Wise, 8 Oct. 1855, WFP/VHS.

31 Wise to Mary Lyons Wise, 18 Jan. 1855, WFP/VHS; Mary Lyons Wise to James Lyons, 6 Dec. 1857, Brock Collection, CSmH.

32 Wise, *Argument of the Hon. Henry A. Wise and William Selden*; Wise to Mary Lyons Wise, 5 Feb., 7 and 9 June 1854, WFP/VHS; Wise to Cushing, 4 Dec. 1854, Cushing Papers, LC.

33 Quoted in Brown, "Missouri Crisis," p. 60.

34 Quoted in Rawley, *Race and Politics*, pp. 39–40.

35 *Richmond Enquirer*, 10, 11 Mar., 3 Oct. 1854. Nor did the *Enquirer* expect slavery to expand into Kansas. It argued only for "the recognition of a principle" (quoted in Craven, *Coming of the Civil War*, p. 352).

36 Wise to Kidwell, 21 July 1854. This letter also appeared in the *Washington Union*, 29 July, and the *New York Times*, 1 August. Millson's remarks on the Kansas-Nebraska Bill appeared in the *Richmond Enquirer*, 30 March 1854. Other Southern representatives in Congress objected to the Badger proviso on grounds that it would nullify much of the prospective advantage accruing to their region from the repeal of the Missouri Compromise. But no one else, so far as I can tell, made such an issue of it.

37 The original longhand version of Wise's letter to Kidwell is in the Henry A. Wise Papers, DU. The last, excised sentence reads as follows: "Please show this to Mr. Hunter & Gen'l Millson & to Virginia Congressman Thomas S. Bocock & any other members you choose & do with it what you please." Senator Hunter himself may have crossed out this passage. Unless I am mistaken, the words "Yrs. truly, Henry A. Wise," written above the excised passage, are in Hunter's handwriting. It is therefore probable that Hunter edited Wise's letter for publication.

38 Goode's speech of 19 May 1854 is found in *CG*, 33, 1, Appendix,

903–8. See also the speeches of Charles James Faulkner, 10 Apr. 1854, in ibid., 482–88, and John S. Caskie, 19 May 1854, in ibid., 1141–45.

39 Several twentieth-century observers have pointed out that the views of Millson, Wise, and others on the existence of slavery in the Louisiana Purchase rested ultimately on the unconstitutional premise that treaties take precedence over laws of Congress. But their arguments typically depend, in part, on Supreme Court decisions rendered late in the nineteenth century. See, for example, Fehrenbacher, *Dred Scott Case*, pp. 402, 411, and citations.

Millson argued that it was intolerable to contemplate settlers in the territorial condition legislating at all on the subject of slavery. He thus placed little faith in the clause of the act providing that all such legislation should be "subject only to the Constitution." Southern Democrats consistently based their support for the act on this language, which they said provided both themselves and the courts with continuing opportunity to vindicate their constitutional doctrines relating to slavery's mobility in the territories. Millson's argument is difficult to fathom because he scorns Southerners such as Badger who specifically disavowed their interest in legislating slavery into the territories but never demanded congressional protection. Millson later supported the Lecompton Constitution. But his record at the end of the decade—Douglas elector in 1860 and vigorous opponent of secession—raises doubts about his commitment to extremism in 1854.

40 Wise to William F. Samford, 6 Aug. 1857, Samford-Wise Papers, AU; Nevins, *Ordeal of the Union*, 2:135–38, esp. 136.

41 Wise to Adams, 22 Aug. 1854, in *Washington Union*, 13 Sept. 1854; *Enquirer*, 19 Sept., 2 Oct. 1854; *New York Times*, 15 Sept., 30 Oct. 1854. See also Wise to the editor of the *Union*, 5 Oct. 1854, Wise Correspondence, NYHS. Adams expressed surprise and annoyance at having initially received Wise's letter in manuscript without any intimation that it was written for publication. In a note appearing in the *Union*, 26 September 1854, Adams also revealed Wise's failure to obtain consent before publishing his original letter with its queries.

42 The sources for the two previous paragraphs are Adams, *South-Side View*, pp. 45–47, 89, 97–99, 118, 142, 152–57, 180–87.

43 *New York Times*, 15 Sept., 30 Oct. 1854, for the quotation from the review by "X."

44 Wise acknowledged in the Adams letter a knowledge of the views of Dr. Daniel Drake of Cincinnati, a pioneer medical educator and practitioner in the Ohio Valley for whom ethnography was a principal ancillary interest. Drake's avowals of black inferiority and his

attempted scientific demonstrations fit perfectly with much of the extremely conservative variant of American racialist thought that gained credibility during the 1850s, according to Fredrickson, *Black Image*, pp. 71–96. Drake probably influenced Wise's ruminations on the lethal effects of northern climates on blacks. Drake also proposed that free states refuse entry to all blacks, under all circumstances (thus incidentally resolving the fugitive slave crisis). Wise turned this proposal to his own purposes by opposing, after 1854, all efforts to encourage the migration of Virginia's free blacks to the North. Drake agreed with Wise that colonization was the answer for Southerners; he thus calculated on an end to slavery. But in yet another verification of Alexis de Tocqueville's classic hypothesis on the locus of racialism in areas free of slavery, Drake—and perhaps Adams as well—appeared to maintain a more pessimistic view of black capacity than did Wise. See *Dr. Daniel Drake's Letters on Slavery to Dr. John C. Warren*; Virginia, General Assembly, 1857–58, *Governor's Message III*.

45 For another Southern authority who experienced this difficulty, see Thornwell, *State of the Country*, pp. 17–18.

46 Quoted, but not dated, in DuBois, *Black Reconstruction*, p. 5.

47 Bernstein, "Southern Politics and Attempts to Reopen the African Slave Trade," pp. 16–17. See also Takaki, "Movement to Reopen the African Slave Trade in South Carolina," p. 38. Spratt edited the *Charleston Standard*.

48 Diary of John Coles Rutherfoord, 16 July 1857, Rutherfoord Family Papers, VHS.

49 Takaki, *Pro-Slavery Crusade*, p. 131.

Chapter 8

1 *Richmond Examiner*, 8, 29 Aug. 1854; Wolff, "The Slaveocracy and the Homestead Problem of 1854"; Holt, *Political Crisis*, pp. 140–41.

2 *Richmond Enquirer* extra, 8 Mar. 1855. This Know-Nothing ritual and constitution is probably the same one supplied to Wise at the beginning of his canvass by Governor Lybrook of Illinois. The *Richmond Penny Post*, avowed organ of Virginia Know-Nothingism, never denied its authenticity (Hambleton, *Biographical Sketch*, pp. 46–47).

3 Lipset and Raab, *Politics of Unreason*, pp. 55–59; Turner, "The 1855 Gubernatorial Campaign in Virginia," p. 27; Rice, "Know-Nothing Party in Virginia."

4 Hambleton, *Biographical Sketch*, pp. 7–27. Sometime later, the

Fredricksburg Herald (quoted in *Richmond Whig*, 7 May 1858) revealed that Wise plagiarized about a page and a half of his highly effective rhetoric from William Hazlitt's noted study of the Elizabethan theater. Cf. Wise's letter in Hambleton, *Biographical Sketch*, pp. 20–21, and Hazlitt, *Lectures on the Dramatic Literature of the Age of Elizabeth*, pp. 9–10. Wise had cited Hazlitt, with appropriate credit, in his letter to Rev. Nehemiah Adams.

The Know-Nothings attempted several replies to Wise's letter, all of which he ignored. One of the more important efforts to rebut his views, in An American, *The Sons of the Sires*, pp. 183–223, reiterated the usual Know-Nothing arguments about the threat immigration represented for the American character and institutions. It also contained a particularly virulent assault on the "Romanish imperium" in America. But such replies were pallid and dull when compared to the energy and conviction with which Wise attacked the movement. See also Bryce, *An Address to the People of Accomac and Northampton Counties*; Rayner, *Reply to the Manifesto of Hon. Henry A. Wise*.

5 Muscoe Garnett to his mother, 7, 18 Feb. 1856, William Garnett Chisolm Papers, VHS; Wise to Hunter, 11 Aug. 1855, Hunter Papers, UVA; James Seddon to Hunter, 3 Dec. 1855, in Ambler, ed., "Correspondence of Robert M. T. Hunter," pp. 172–74.

6 The best account of the convention's deliberations appeared in the *Richmond Dispatch*, reprinted in the *Richmond Examiner*, 5 Dec. 1854.

7 *New York Herald*, quoted in *Richmond Whig*, 19 Jan. 1855; Boney, *John Letcher*, pp. 61–62; *Richmond Whig*, 20 Mar., 1 May 1855; *Richmond Penny Post*, 6, 22 Mar., 11 Apr. 1855; R. M. T. Hunter to George Booker, 25 Apr. 1855, Booker Papers, DU.

8 *Richmond Whig*, 13 Mar. 1855; *Richmond Penny Post*, 21 Mar. 1855; *Alexandria Gazette*, 1 May 1855.

9 *Richmond Whig*, 12 Jan., 13 Mar. 1855, and many other issues during this period.

10 S. L. Stuart to William M. Burwell, 13 Nov. 1854, Burwell Papers, LC; Overdyke, *Know-Nothing Party in the South*, pp. 36, 42–43.

11 *Whig*, 20 Mar. 1855.

12 *Savannah Republican*, 19 Mar. 1855; Alexander H. H. Stuart to Millard Fillmore, 1 Jan. 1855, Fillmore Papers, BECHC.

13 Hambleton, *Biographical Sketch*, prints Flournoy's letter at p. 170.

14 *Richmond Enquirer*, 2 Apr. 1855.

15 Ibid., 29, 30 Mar., 10 Apr. 1855.

16 *Jackson Semi-Weekly Mississippian*, 13 Apr. 1855; Flournoy, *Address, Delivered at the Second Annual Exhibition of the Union Agricultural Society of Virginia and North Carolina*.

17 J. D. Imboden et al., to Flournoy, 22 Mar. 1855, Imboden Papers, UVA; John M. Bott's remarks, reported in *Richmond Enquirer*, 12 June 1855.

18 Forney, *Anecdotes of Public Men*, 1:135; Beach, "Example of Political Oratory in 1855."

19 *Richmond Penny Post*, 13 Feb. 1855.

20 Hambleton, *Biographical Sketch*, pp. 105–6.

21 Ibid., p. 115.

22 *Charleston Mercury*, 27 Mar. 1855; *Jackson Semi-Weekly Mississippian*, 22 May 1855, quoting the *Enquirer*; Wise to George W. Jones, 27 July 1855 (typescript), WFP/VHS. The slaves had secret, fraternal associations of their own, at least in Richmond, as Wise later acknowledged in Virginia, General Assembly, 1859–60, *Governor's Message II*. For evidence on the existence and functions of these societies see O'Brien, "Factory, Church, and Community," p. 535, as well as his forthcoming study from the University of Illinois Press. See also the Diary of John Coles Rutherfoord, 16 July 1857, Rutherfoord Family Papers, VHS.

23 Wise quoted in *Richmond Whig*, 27 Apr. 1855; Hambleton, *Biographical Sketch*, p. 95.

24 Hunter to Wise, 8 Feb. 1855, Barton H. Wise Papers, VHS(oc); *Piedmont Whig*, quoted in *Richmond Penny Post*, 5 Feb. 1855; McFarland, "Extension of Democracy in Virginia," pp. 23–24.

25 Wise to Mary Lyons Wise, 14, 23 Mar. 1855, WFP/VHS.

26 Wise to Jonathan M. Bennett, 2 Feb. 1855, Bennett Papers, WVULM.

27 Four-fifths of the thirty counties in southwestern Virginia reported an increase in slaves between 1850 and 1860, although white population in the area generally increased at a faster rate (U.S. Census Office, *Seventh Census of the United States: 1850*, pp. 242–44; *Population of the United States in 1860*, pp. 500–503).

28 John Coles Rutherfoord to James L. Kemper, 24 June 1855, Kemper Papers, UVA. See also *Richmond Enquirer*, 5 June 1855, for a letter from Charlotte County, Virginia, which appeared originally in the *Daily American Organ* (Washington, D.C.); John Coles Rutherfoord Diary, 22 Apr. 1855, Rutherfoord Papers, VHS. Because of the *viva voce* ballot, no one's partisan allegiance was a secret on election day. By penetrating the lodges, Democratic informants aimed at preventing members of their party from voting for the Know-Nothings and then claiming that it was a spur-of-the-moment decision that did not represent an endorsement of nativist principles.

Some Whig and Know-Nothing election post-mortems admitted that an unknown number of Democrats had probably infiltrated the new order's lodges for the purpose of keeping it under surveillance. See *Washington American Organ*, 28 May 1855, quoted in *New York Herald*, 30 May 1855; *Alexandria Gazette*, 28 May 1855. Wise's opponents usually and foolishly blamed their defeat, however, on the immigrant and Catholic vote in Virginia. See ibid.; *Richmond Whig*, 5 June 1855; and W. E. Cunningham to Daniel Ullman, 30 May 1855, Ullman Papers, NYHS.

29 Hunter roused himself for an effective address in Petersburg, which Wise understandably found insulting because it did not mention his name. The senator appeared in response to an appeal from one of his advisers, Lewis E. Harvie, who suggested that "it would be well to give the canvass in Virginia a somewhat less personal cast than it has been made to appear" (Harvie to Hunter, 5 Mar. 1855, in Ambler, ed., "Correspondence of Robert M. T. Hunter," pp. 161–62). See also Wise to James L. Kemper, 23 July 1857, Kemper Papers, UVA. Hambleton prints Hunter's speech in *Biographical Sketch*, pp. 70–93.

30 Wise to Senator George W. Jones, of Iowa, 29 June, 27 July 1856 (typescripts), WFP/VHS; Wise to Henry Augustus Wise, 11 Sept. 1855, Wise Papers, LC; Hudson, *Journalism in the United States*, p. 249; Wise to John Y. Mason, 20 Apr. 1856, Mason Papers, VHS. My views on Wise's conscious efforts to imitate Jackson have been reinforced by two letters written by William H. Richardson to James Lawson Kemper, 18 Apr. and 20 May 1856, Kemper Papers, UVA.

31 *New York Herald*, 9 Jan. 1857; Robert Tyler to Wise, 9 Sept. 1857, Tyler Family Papers, WM.

32 A seminal essay on American culture in the 1850s is Higham, *From Boundlessness to Consolidation*. See also Forgie, *Patricide in the House Divided*, pp. 159–241; Douglas, *Feminization of American Culture*, p. 307; and Chapter 9, below.

33 23 Aug. 1855, in Hambleton, *Biographical Sketch*, pp. 437–39.

34 Wise to George W. Munford, 13, 17 Aug. 1855, Dreer Collection, HSP; Wise to the Boston Committee, 5 Oct. 1855, in Hambleton, *Biographical Sketch*, pp. 439–40.

35 Chalmers, "Fernando Wood and Tammany Hall"; Wood to Wise, 29 Oct. 1855, Benjamin Perley Poore Papers, HHS.

36 DeBow, *Statistical View of the United States*, p. 114; Forgie, *Patricide in the House Divided*, p. 233.

37 Wise to Hunter, 11 Aug. 1855, Hunter Papers, UVA.

38 *Whig* (sw), 29 Feb. 1856.

39 A Virginian, *The Life and Death of Sam, in Virginia*, pp. 107–8, 112, 155–56, 165–66, and 222 for the final quotation; *Richmond Enquirer*, 28 June 1856. In his *Bibliography of Virginia*, Earl G.

Swem attributes the book to Wise. No one else does. Almost all other sources attribute it to an otherwise unidentified William Gardner.

"Christian politics" for Wise represented the efforts of Northern, antislavery, and nativist preachers to meddle improperly in public affairs "instead of humbly letting the carnal kingdom alone and preaching singly Christ crucified." The phrase comes, in all probability, from Clarke, *Rendition of Anthony Burns*. Slavery's ascendancy over freedom, in Clarke's view, dated from the annexation of Texas. He named Wise as having "proclaimed in Congress" that annexation's purpose was "avowedly to prevent the abolition of slavery and to strengthen the Slave Power."

40 That same day the governor's son-in-law, Dr. A. Y. P. Garnett of Washington, advised him that scarcely anyone in the capital took his presidential ambitions seriously (Henry A. Wise Papers, EI).

41 *Richmond Enquirer*, 24 Apr. 1856.

42 Ibid., 11 Mar. 1856.

43 Ibid., 14, 15 Mar. 1856; Wise to Kemper, 23 July 1856, Kemper Papers, UVA. See also Jones, "Forgotten Virginian," p. 182.

44 *Richmond Enquirer*, 18 June 1859.

45 Wise to Buchanan, 26 June and 6 July 1856, Buchanan Papers, HSP.

46 Buchanan to Wise, 28 June 1856 (copy), ibid.

47 Wise to Munford, 3 Oct. 1855, Munford-Ellis Family Papers, DU.

48 *Richmond Enquirer*, 17 June 1856.

49 Wise to Nehemiah Adams, 22 Aug. 1854, in *Washington Union*, 13 Sept. 1854; Wise, *Territorial Government*, p. 135. The California gold mines, incidentally, are north of the line 36° 30′. I have no way of knowing whether Wise realized this. See *New York Tribune*, 14 July 1856. The *Richmond Whig*, 22 Aug. 1856, printed a letter to Isaac Butts, editor of the *Rochester Union*, from Wise, 28 July 1856. I have quoted its editorial comment.

50 Governor Wise's remarks at Corinthian Hall, in Richmond, 20 Sept. 1856, in *Richmond Enquirer*, 2 Oct. 1856.

51 Wise to Robert Tyler, 9 Oct. 1856, in Tyler, ed., *Letters and Times*, 2:533; *Richmond Enquirer*, 2, 7 Oct. 1856; Foner, *Free Soil*, p. 123.

52 Wise to George Booker, 21 Oct. 1855, in *National Era*, 22 Nov. 1855; Wise to an unidentified correspondent, 9 Oct. 1856, Society Collection, HSP; *Richmond Enquirer*, 8 July 1856.

53 Seward, *Dangers of Extending Slavery*; Foner, *Free Soil*, pp. 119–23, 207–9.

54 Wise to Henry Augustus Wise, 13 July 1856, Wise Papers, LC. For details of Frémont's illegitimate birth, see Nevins, *Frémont*, pp. 6–8.

55 Wise to Henry Augustus Wise, 6 Oct., 11 Sept. 1855, and 13 July,

16 Sept. 1856, Wise Papers, LC; *Richmond Enquirer*, 28 June, 26 Aug., 13 Sept. 1856.

56 For Botts's solicitation of a federal appointment from the Republicans five years later, see below, Chapter 12. The *Raleigh Evening Standard*, 28 September 1856, and the Virginia correspondent of the *New York Herald*, 28 September 1856, both speculate on Botts's desire to enter Frémont's cabinet.

57 Neither the Whig nor Democratic presses in Virginia printed Botts's two major campaign speeches, probably because they found them so distasteful and embarrassing. Full versions of them appeared in the *New York Herald*, 14 September, 6 October 1856. See also Botts, *Speech at Powhatan Court House, 1850*, and *Nebraska Question*. For Botts's continuing devotion to Whig doctrine, see his letter to Henry C. Carey, 7 June 1858, Simon Gratz Autograph Collection, HSP.

58 Botts to Anna Carroll, 31 July 1859, Carroll Papers, MaHS.

59 *New York Herald*, 16 Sept. 1856; *New York Evening Post*, 15 Sept. 1856, quoted in *Richmond Examiner*, 19 Sept. 1856.

60 See, for example, the vilifying reviews of Botts's course in *Richmond Enquirer*, 8, 11, and 15 Mar. 1859.

61 *Richmond Enquirer*, 2 Oct. 1856.

62 Wise to Robert Tyler, 9 Oct. 1856, in Tyler, ed., *Letters and Times*, 2:533; Wise, *Address before the Virginia Mechanics Institute*.

63 *Salem* (Mass.) *Register*, quoted in *New York Herald*, 19 Nov. 1856.

64 Augustus Mahoney et al. to Wise, 22 Dec. 1856, Letters Received, Governor's Office, Executive Department, Archives Branch, VSL, Box 375; J. R. Micou to Wise, 23 Dec. 1856, in ibid.; Wise to "Any Commandant of a regiment of the First brigade of the Second division of Virginia militia," 23 Dec. 1856, in ibid.

65 Eaton, "Henry A. Wise and the Virginia Fire-eaters," p. 511; Wise to Henry Augustus Wise, 29 Sept. 1856, Wise Papers, LC; Nicolay and Hay, *Abraham Lincoln*, 2:300.

66 Wilson, *Speech on the Territorial Slave Code*; *National Era*, 31 Mar. 1859.

67 *New Orleans Delta*, printed in *Charleston Mercury*, 25 Sept. 1856; *Mercury*, 8 Oct. 1856; Wise's remarks at Corinthian Hall, in Richmond, 20 Sept. 1856, in *Richmond Enquirer*, 2 Oct. 1856.

68 Wise to Governor Thomas W. Ligon, of Maryland, 15 Sept. 1856, in B. H. Wise, *Life of Henry A. Wise*, p. 209.

69 Wickliffe to Wise, 9 Oct. 1856 (copy), Breckinridge Family Papers, vol. 189, LC. See also John C. Breckinridge to John B. Breckinridge, 10, 21 Oct. 1856, in ibid.

70 Eaton, "Henry A. Wise and the Virginia Fire-eaters," p. 511; *National Era*, 9 Oct. 1856.

71 *Whig* quoted in *Raleigh Register* (w), 22 Oct. 1856.

72 Wise to C. H. K. Taylor et al., Oct. 1856, in *North Carolina Evening Standard* (sw), 29 Oct. 1856.

73 Wise to Tyler, 9 Oct. 1856, in Tyler, ed., *Letters and Times*, 2:533; Wise to Tyler, 15 Aug. 1856, Henry A. Wise Papers, DU; *Letter from Governor Wise to the Editors of the Richmond Enquirer*, cited in Eaton, "Henry A. Wise and the Virginia Fire-eaters," p. 504.

74 *Raleigh Register* (w), 8 Nov. 1856; Wise to Waddy Thompson, 21 Oct. 1856, Thompson Letters, EU.

75 Wise to John Tyler, 16 Oct. 1856, WFP/VHS.

76 Wise to Meade, 5 June 1856, Henry A. Wise Papers, VHS; Wise to Robert Tyler, 6 July 1856, in Tyler, ed., *Letters and Times*, 2:530. Wise's post–Civil War account emphasizes his conservative purposes. It appears in Wilson, *History of the Rise and Fall of the Slave Power*, 2:520–21.

77 Wise to Waddy Thompson, 21 Oct. 1856, Thompson Letters, EU.

78 Bragg to Wise, 25 Oct. 1856, Henry A. Wise Papers, DU; Wise to Robert Tyler, 18 Oct. 1856, in Tyler, ed., *Letters and Times*, 2:533–34; *Richmond Enquirer*, 10 Nov. 1856; *Richmond Whig*, 28 Oct. and 7 Nov. 1856.

79 Buchanan to Wise, 5 Nov. 1853, WFP/VHS; Wise to Buchanan, 30 Nov. 1856, Buchanan Papers, HSP.

80 Wise to George Booker, 11 Mar. 1857, WFP/VHS; Floyd to Wise, 24 Dec. 1856, A. H. Joline Collection, CSmH.

81 *Herald*, 8, 12 Dec. 1856; Letcher to J. D. Dorman, 10, 21 Dec. 1856, Letcher Papers, UVA.

82 Pryor to Hunter, 14 Dec. 1856, Hunter Papers, UVA; Letcher to J. D. Dorman, 10 Dec. 1856, Letcher Papers, UVA; Wise to Buchanan, 1 Aug. 1856, Buchanan Papers, HSP; Tucker to Wise, 29 Nov. 1856, Letters Received, Governor's Office, Executive Department, Archives Branch, VSL, Box 376.

Chapter 9

1 For recent analyses of economic growth in Virginia during the late antebellum period, see Goldfield, *Urban Growth*, pp. 1–138, and Siegel, "New South in the Old."

2 *New York Tribune*, 13 May 1854. For repeated abolitionist charges that Virginia was a giant slave-breeding farm, see the files of the *National Era* and the *National Anti-Slavery Standard* for the 1850s.

3 *New York Tribune*, 29 Aug. 1854.

4 Although they do not use the term, it is apparent that Virginians of

extremist sympathies such as Edmund Ruffin and Willoughby Newton regarded Wise in this fashion.

5 Helper, *Impending Crisis of the South*, pp. 96–109, and quoting Wise at pp. 13–14, 90–91, 102; Olmsted, *Journey in the Seaboard Slave States*, esp. pp. 290–97; Shortreed, "Anti-Slavery Radicals," p. 70, for the quotation from Wilson.

6 Clay, *Speech before the Young Men's Republican Central Union*; *New York Herald*, 11 Apr. 1857.

7 Virginia, General Assembly, *Governor's Communication on the Subject of the Erection of Monuments on Independence Square, in Philadelphia*.

8 Wise, "Oration, at Lexington, 4th July, 1856." On the important "sentimental center" of American political culture during the 1850s, see Forgie, *Patricide in the House Divided*, pp. 159–99. Forgie identifies Edward Everett, the Massachusetts highbrow and vice-presidential nominee on the Constitutional Union ticket in 1860, as the key figure in the national campaign to rekindle patriotism by recalling the achievements of the Founding Fathers—Washington especially. Everett and Wise kept abreast of each other's efforts through an intermediary. See the letters between the governor and his cousin, Captain Henry Augustus Wise of the United States Navy, in Wise Papers, LC.

Wise believed that cold, calculating, and passionless politicians could never hope to tap Americans' latent though profound loyalty to the Union because its evocation depended on a proper emotional climate. In emphasizing Washington's passions, Wise encouraged public men to expose their emotions—as he did, of course. His efforts ran counter to the efforts of many of the antipolitical publicists analyzed by Forgie. Wise envisioned men such as himself tapping the longing for comfort and assurance that characterized so much of American culture in the 1850s. His own experience had confirmed the power and mesmerizing force of these needs. He feared granting women, such as Harriet Beecher Stowe, suzerainty in the emotional sphere.

9 Wise, "Oration, at Lexington, 4th July, 1856," pp. 13, 17. Part of this "Christian politics" movement manifested itself, according to Wise, in the effort to make a day of thanksgiving a national holiday. He derisively refused to countenance this project. See Wise to Sarah J. Hale, 24 Sept. 1856, Executive Letter Book, 1848–56, VSL.

10 *Richmond Whig*, 7 Nov. 1856.

11 Wise to George W. Munford, 21 Aug. 1858, Letters Received, Governor's Office, Executive Department, Archives Branch, VSL, Box 388; Wise to Leonidas Baugh, 13 Oct. 1858, Executive Letter

Book, 1856–58, VSL; Wise to Angus W. McDonald, 18, 20 Sept. 1858, in ibid.; Wise to L. V. Buckholtz, 28 Mar. 1859 (draft), Letters Received, Governor's Office, Executive Department, Archives Branch, VSL, Box 394. For Wise's reflections on Richmond's undignified political environment, see the John Coles Rutherfoord Diary, 24 Nov. 1857, Rutherfoord Papers, VHS.

12 Wise, "Address at the Inauguration of the Equestrian Statue of George Washington."

13 *World the Slaveholders Made*, p. 204.

14 Fitzhugh, "Disunion within the Union"; Freehling, *Drift toward Dissolution*, p. 249; Fitzhugh to Wise, Mar. 1857, Wise Correspondence, NYHS.

15 George M. McFarland, "Extension of Democracy in Virginia," pp. 25–26; Goldfield, "Triumph of Politics over Society," pp. 90–91.

16 *Richmond Whig*, 25 Dec. 1856.

17 See William H. Richardson to James L. Kemper, 4 June 1858, Kemper Papers, UVA, for Wise's appointment of a man who had been dismissed from the Virginia Military Institute as a visitor to that institution; William K. Heiskell to Kemper, 4 Aug. 1858, in ibid., on the bad characters and Know-Nothing sympathies of several people Wise appointed to resurvey the Virginia-Tennessee boundary; Wise to James K. Bruce, 12 July 1857, in ibid., justifying the appointment of a Know-Nothing as colonel of cavalry in the state militia.

18 William B. Shephard to Edmund W. Hubard, 15 Feb. 1858, Hubard Family Papers, SHC; Muscoe Garnett to his mother, 11 Jan. 1858, William Garnett Chisolm Papers, VHS. See also Ruffin, *Diary*, ed. Scarborough, 1:144 (11 Jan. 1858), and McFarland, "Extension of Democracy in Virginia," p. 25.

19 "Report of the Committee on Finance," in *Richmond Enquirer*, 20, 21 Feb. 1856, written by Muscoe Garnett; Rutherfoord, *Speech . . . 1st March 1859*; "N," in *Richmond Whig*, 11 Mar. 1856; Ratchford, *American State Debts*, p. 127; Hambleton, *Biographical Sketch*, p. 95; "The Wealth, Resources, and Hopes of Virginia," pp. 65–66.

20 Neely, "Development of Virginia Taxation," pp. 399–409.

21 Dunaway, *History of the James River and Kanawha Company*.

22 R. H. Bolling to Edmund W. Hubard, 9 Mar. 1851, Hubard Family Papers, SHC; Virginia, General Assembly, *Report of the Chairman and Minority of the Committee of Finance*, signed by John Seddon; Diary of John Coles Rutherfoord, 25 Mar. 1858, Rutherfoord Papers, VHS; *Richmond Whig*, 25 Dec. 1855, 11 Apr. 1856; *Richmond Examiner* (w), 25 Jan. 1856, and 29 Jan. 1858.

23 McFarland, "Extension of Democracy in Virginia," p. 10; Rice, *Life*

of Jonathan M. Bennett, pp. 85–88; Virginia, General Assembly, 1857–58, *Governor's Message I*.

24 For an excellent discussion of the debt question in Reconstruction Virginia, see Maddex, *Virginia Conservatives*, pp. 95–99, 233–75, and passim.

25 "The Wealth, Resources," p. 68.

26 *Enquirer*, 16 Mar. 1858.

27 "The Wealth, Resources," p. 59.

28 Wise, "Address . . . to Dedicate the Stonewall Cemetery," in *Richmond Enquirer*, 4 Jan. 1867. I have not located these instructions. In this speech, however, Wise referred to preparing Preston's "letters of credence"—perhaps Virginia's "only imprimature of a foreign embassy"—in which he "set forth the causes which had made Virginia both unmanufacturing and uncommercial." At one "fell swoop," he added, "this cause of obstruction has been swept away. Slavery has ceased . . . and negroes are no longer operatives."

29 "The Wealth, Resources," p. 62; "Objections to Col. Cocke's Proposed Donation to the University of Virginia," p. 6. The unsigned, sarcastic reference to Wise's language probably came from Edmund Ruffin.

30 Wise's remarks quoted by Willoughby Newton, in the *South*, 1 Dec. 1857.

31 "The Wealth, Resources," p. 66.

32 Wise to George Booker, 26 Nov. 1856, Booker Papers, DU; Ruffin, *Slavery and Free Labor Described and Compared*, p. 17.

33 Wise, *Speech on the Basis Question*, p. 31, Henry A. Wise Papers, SHC; Dew, *Review of the Debate in the Virginia Legislature of 1831 and 1832*, p. 70; *Dr. Daniel Drake's Letters on Slavery to Dr. John C. Warren*, p. 15; Adams, *South-Side View*, pp. 89–91; Smith, *Lectures on the Philosophy and Practice of Slavery*, p. 233.

34 Freehling, *Drift toward Dissolution*, pp. 206–8.

35 Eli Thayer to Jonathan Bennett, 7 Apr. 1857, in *New York Herald*, 11 Apr. 1857.

36 See also Ruffin, *African Colonization Unveiled*. A good measure of the continuing popularity of African colonization in Virginia might be the number of "proslavery" theorists who regarded it as not only the preferred but as the inevitable solution. Dr. William A. Smith, the Reverend Thornton Stringfellow, and Professor Albert Taylor Bledsoe all fell into this category.

37 Genovese, *Political Economy of Slavery*, pp. 138–39; Goldfield, *Urban Growth*, pp. 118–19; Dew, "Disciplining Slave Iron Workers in the South"; Goldin, *Urban Slavery*, p. 86.

38 Virginia, General Assembly, 1859–60; *Governor's Message II*, p. 29. See also Engerman, "Marxist Economic Studies of the Slave

South," pp. 157, 164; Dodd and Dodd, *Historical Statistics of the South*, p. 58.

39 The best estimate is that 67,398 native whites aged ten or older in 1860 left Virginia during the 1850s. See Lang, "Effects of Net Interregional Migration on Agricultural Income Growth," p. 48. See also Goldfield, *Urban Growth*, p. 121; *Richmond Morning News*, in *National Era*, 25 Aug. 1859.

40 Goldfield, *Urban Growth*, pp. 234–35, 240–41, 251, 258, and passim; Wise to Kader Biggs, 26 Sept. 1858, in *Richmond Enquirer*, 12 Oct. 1850 (sw); Fields, "Agricultural Population of Virginia," pp. 52, 81–84; Pred, *Urban Growth*, pp. 115–16, 120–21, 167; "Virginia Statistics"; Willoughby Newton to Messrs. Boulware & Co., 28 July 1857, in *South*, 4 Aug. 1857; *DeBow's Review* 24 (June 1858): 573; *Richmond Examiner*, 12 Mar. 1861; Bateman and Weiss, *Deplorable Scarcity*.

41 *Richmond Examiner*, 12 Mar. 1861; *Cincinnati Enquirer*, quoted in *Wheeling Intelligencer*, 5 June 1857; Weston, *Progress of Slavery in the United States*, p. 118; *Correspondence between Lydia Maria Child, and Gov. Wise and Mrs. Mason, of Virginia*.

I would like to acknowledge the indispensable aid of Stanley L. Engerman and Jim Irwin of the University of Rochester in preparing the following calculations. Their procedure involved taking Richard Sutch's estimate of slave exiles from Virginia during the 1850s (67,716) and Michael Tadman's reckoning for the number sold (about 60 percent). How much income did they represent? Engerman and Irwin then calculated average profits from selling slaves of various ages, based on an average price for prime male field hands of $1,500 over the decade and using the age distribution tables supplied by Tadman. This figure is a bit high but probably by not more than $100, as indicated in Tadman's price data for prime males sold at Richmond in his doctoral dissertation, "Speculators and Slaves," p. 362. The estimate for the decade 1850–60, having taken account of costs to masters and the slightly lower prices commanded on the average by females, was $42,514,000 (in 1860 dollars). For 1860, then, the income obtained from sales by Virginians approximated $4,250,000. I must acknowledge that *this figure is distinctly an upper bound estimate*. For contrast, I rely on Irwin's research, which suggests the following 1860 incomes from various crops and livestock: cattle, $7.56 million; hogs, $14.47 million; wheat, $11.45 million; corn, $3.16 million; tobacco, $10.65 million. See Sutch, "Breeding of Slaves for Sale," Appendix, and Tadman, "Slave Trading in the Old South," p. 218.

In light of these findings, the figures in Goldfield, *Urban Growth*, p. 121, seem considerably exaggerated, as do Ruffin's in

"Effects of High Prices of Slaves," p. 655.

What profits derived from the intrastate slave trade is, of course, another matter, as is the impact of these profits on agricultural improvements and diversification. My suspicion is that during the 1850s profits from the intrastate trade were very substantial.

42 *Richmond Whig*, 25 Mar. 1856; Wise to James Lawson Kemper, 19 May 1856, Kemper Papers, UVA, requesting Kemper to assume "paternity" of the Oyster Fundum in the House of Delegates. Kemper later declined, and Delegate James Paxton of Rockbridge agreed to introduce the measure. As a further indication of the obstacles Wise faced, a front-page advertisement from the *Richmond Enquirer*, 4 January 1858, shows that George W. Munford, secretary of the Commonwealth, and Thomas H. Ellis, president of the James River and Kanawha Company, both served on the board of the New York Life Insurance Company's Richmond agency.

43 *Wheeling Intelligencer*, 10 Mar. 1858; *Richmond Enquirer*, 17 Mar., 21 July, 23 July (sw), 10 Dec. 1858. In the latter issue, see O. J. Wise's remarks in the state Democratic convention. See also Rice, *Life of Jonathan Bennett*, p. 73; Virginia, General Assembly, *Report of the Chairman and Minority of the Committee of Finance*, in which Arthur I. Boreman, an important northwestern Virginia legislator, joins the eastern Virginians in opposition to appropriations for internal improvements; *Petersburg Press*, quoted in *National Era*, 8 Mar. 1860.

44 Underwood to the editor of the *New York Tribune*, 20 Apr. 1857; Underwood to the editor of the *New York Times*, n.d., but early in 1857, both in the Underwood Scrapbook, Underwood Papers, LC; Underwood to the editor, 28 May 1857, in *Wheeling Intelligencer*, 3 June 1857. Underwood scored Wise's correspondence with the French capitalists as tending to permit Virginia only an exchange of masters.

45 Underwood to Eli Thayer, 7 Feb. and 4 June 1857, Eli Thayer Papers, BU; undated clipping from *Albany Evening Journal*, in ibid.

46 Hickin, "John C. Underwood"; Rice, "Eli Thayer and the Friendly Invasion"; Underwood to Thayer, 4 June 1857, Thayer Papers, BU. Underwood to William H. Seward, 26 Jan. 1858, Seward Papers, RRR, appends a list of some thirty-seven Virginians to whom Seward is requested to send documents. Most were residents of Fauquier, a wealthy northern Virginia county in the piedmont. Included in this group was Robert E. Scott, leader of the mixed-basis forces in 1850–51 and later a prominent conservative in the secession convention, and James Strother, an influential Whig member of the House of Delegates.

47 B. H. Wise, *Life of Henry A. Wise*, pp. 211–13.

48 Rice, "Eli Thayer and the Friendly Invasion," p. 587.

49 *Richmond Examiner*, quoted in *National Era*, 14 May 1857; *South*, 18 Aug. 1857.

50 J. F. Hoffman to Underwood, 10 Feb. 1858, and Underwood to Bennett, 6 Apr., 1 May 1858, Bennett Papers, WVULM; Underwood to Gideon D. Camden, 18 Aug. 1851, Camden Papers, WVULM; Camden to Underwood, 28 Dec. 1858, Underwood Papers, LC. See also *Wheeling Intelligencer*, 2 June, 3 Dec. 1857, and 1 Feb. 1858.

51 Smith, "Antebellum Attempts," pp. 201–3; *Southern Argus*, in *New York Herald*, 10 Mar. 1857, Eli Thayer Papers, BU; Rollin Sanford to Thayer, 7 Apr. 1857, in ibid; *Norfolk Herald*, 9 May 1857, in *National Era*, 21 May 1857.

52 *New York Tribune*, 13 May 1854, 7 Feb. 1861. See also *New York Herald*, 11 Apr. 1857; Lowe, "Republicans, Rebellion and Reconstruction," p. 40; and several letters written by and about Virginians ready to sell out in the Eli Thayer Papers, BU.

53 *New York Herald*, quoted in *New York Evening Post*, 3 May 1857, clipping in the Eli Thayer Papers, BU. See also Fields, "Agricultural Population of Virginia," p. 197, and Goldfield, "Triumph of Politics over Society," p. 35, for the comment that in the 1850s Virginia slavery was "losing its grip both statistically and psychologically."

54 "The Eli Thayer Invasion," pp. 303–6.

55 This paragraph is based on a series of interviews between Seddon and John Coles Rutherfoord, reported in Rutherfoord's Diary, 25 Dec. 1856, 17 June and 21 Nov. 1857, and 31 Mar. 1858, Rutherfoord Papers, VHS. See also Seddon to William Patterson Smith, 24 Feb. 1859, Smith Papers, DU. For the complementary views of Edmund Ruffin, see Takaki, *Pro-Slavery Crusade*, p. 37. A later extension of Seddon's views is in the frequently cited letter from John Coles Rutherfoord to William C. Rives, 11 Apr. 1860, Rives Papers, LC.

56 See Bruce's comments in the *South*, 15 Mar. 1858; Rutherfoord's views in his "Speech . . . on the Bill, Authorizing a Loan to the Orange and Alexandria Railroad Company"; *South*, quoted in *National Era*, 30 Apr. 1857; for comments on how the prolongation of a General Assembly session resulted in "shameless" appropriations for internal improvements, see Rutherfoord, Diary, 25 Mar. 1858, Rutherfoord Papers, VHS.

57 See the comments of Francis H. Pierpont in *Fairmont True Virginian*, 8 Nov. 1856; *National Era*, 8 Mar. 1860.

58 Wise to Robert Whitehead, 18 Nov. 1858 (draft), Letters Received, Governor's Office, Executive Department, Archives Branch, VSL,

Box 394; Jones, "Forgotten Virginian," pp. 205–6; Richardson to Kemper, 11 Apr. 1860, Kemper Papers, UVA.

59 Virginia, General Assembly, 1857–58, *Governor's Message III*. See also the correspondence between Wise and Thomas H. Ellis, president of the James River and Kanawha Company, in Letters Received, Governor's Office, Executive Department, Archives Branch, VSL, Boxes 387 and 393 (1858 and 1859); Joseph C. Spalding to J. M. Bennett, 13 Nov. 1858, Bennett Papers, WVULM.

60 Winston to Wise, 28 Sept. 1857, in Virginia, General Assembly, 1857–58, Document 1, Appendix, 135; Wise to Winston, 10 Oct. 1856, in Executive Letter Book, 1856–60, VSL; *Richmond Enquirer*, 18 Apr. 1858.

61 Ruffin, *Diary*, ed. Scarborough, 1:294–95 (23 Mar. 1859); *Richmond Enquirer* (sw), 4, 11 Jan. 1859, responding to criticism of Wise in the *Lynchburg Republican*; Berlin, *Slaves without Masters*, p. 324.

62 To Henry Augustus Wise, 9 Oct. 1855, Wise Papers, LC; Maddex, *Virginia Conservatives*, pp. 18–19.

63 *New York Tribune*, 13 May 1854; *Wheeling Intelligencer*, 5 Feb. 1858; Goldfield, "Triumph of Politics over Society," p. 74. I would estimate that in the late 1850s the number of white functional illiterates in Virginia exceeded one-fifth of the adult population.

64 Virginia, General Assembly, 1857–58, *Governor's Message III*; *Richmond Enquirer*, 27 Aug. 1857.

65 Wise to Dr. William A. Smith, 9 Dec. 1856, Executive Letter Books, VSL; Virginia, General Assembly, 1857–58, *Governor's Message III*; *Richmond Enquirer*, 26 Feb. 1858.

66 "Delta," in the *Richmond Enquirer*, 7 August 1856, applauds and encourages Wise's shift in focus to the concerns of the middle class. For a self-consciously middle-class effort to promote educational reform, see *The Memorial of Sundry Citizens of the County of Halifax to the Virginia Legislature, Praying for the Establishment of Free Schools in the State*, Southern Pamphlet Collection, University of North Carolina Library, Chapel Hill. It praised the New England system of education as a conservatizing and civilizing force. The memorialists asked state authorities to compel local jurisdictions to establish public schools and argued that good schools would attract immigrants to the state and prevent too many people from leaving rural areas.

67 Wise to Dr. William A. Smith, 9 Dec. 1856, Executive Letter Books, VSL.

68 Wise to Smith, 3 Jan. 1857, Executive Letter Books, VSL; Smith

to Wise, 29 Dec. 1856, 12 Jan. and 26 May 1857 (for the quotation), in Letters Received, Governor's Office, Executive Department, Archives Branch, VSL, Box 383; Mathews, *Slavery and Methodism*, passim.

69 Wise to Smith, 3 Jan. 1857, Executive Letter Books, VSL. The Reverend Robert Ryland, president of Richmond College, agreed substantially with Smith. See his *American Union*.

70 *Lectures on the Philosophy and Practice of Slavery*, p. 17, as quoted in Donald, "Pro-Slavery Argument Reconsidered," p. 9.

71 *Lectures on the Philosophy and Practice of Slavery*, pp. 57–58, 150, 182, 187, 195, 223, 233, 247, 266–70, 315–16.

72 Newton to Wise, 19 Nov. 1857, in *South*, 1 Dec. 1857. See *Richmond Examiner* (sw), 1 Sept. 1857.

73 *Virginia and the Union*, pp. 10–11, 15–16, 20, 28.

Chapter 10

1 Harvie to Hunter, 11 Feb. 1857 (copy), Hunter Papers, UVA. Pryor received but $5,000 of the $10,000 originally promised him; his financial difficulties were later to prove fatal to his enterprise (John Seddon to John Letcher, 31 Aug. 1858, LPL).

2 *South*, 7 Apr. 1857.

3 Wise to George Booker, 10 May 1857, Booker Papers, DU; Diary of John Coles Rutherfoord, 11 July 1857, Rutherfoord Papers, VHS.

4 Wise to George W. Munford, 8 Aug. 1857, Munford-Ellis Family Papers, DU.

5 Wise to Richard K. Crallé, 7 Feb. 1857, Crallé Papers, LC; Wise to George Booker, 11 Mar. 1857, WFP/VHS.

6 Edward DeLeon to Hunter, 19 May 1858, Hunter Papers, VSL; John Seddon to Muscoe Garnett, 5 July 1856, William Garnett Chisolm Papers, VHS.

7 John Coles Rutherfoord Diary, 16 July 1857, Rutherfoord Papers, VHS; Wise to Patrick Henry Aylett, 23 July 1854 (copy), Aylett Family Papers, VHS; Wise to Richard K. Crallé, 7 Feb. 1857, Crallé Papers, LC. I located no letters between Wise and Calhoun other than their official correspondence.

8 To R. M. T. Hunter, 15 Sept. 1857, in Ambler, ed., "Correspondence of Robert M. T. Hunter," pp. 227–29.

9 Nevins, *Emergence of Lincoln*, 1:144–46; Shenton, *Robert John Walker*.

10 U.S. Congress, House of Representatives, *Report of the Select Committee on Alleged Corruptions*, 36, 1, no. 648, pp. 108–9 (hereafter cited as *Covode Investigation*).

11 Walker to Buchanan, 26 Mar. 1857, Eldridge Collection, CSmH.

12 Nevins, *Emergence of Lincoln*, 1:151, 161–62; *Covode Investigation*, p. 106.

13 Nevins, *Emergence of Lincoln*, 1:151; Shenton, *Robert John Walker*, p. 155.

14 Nevins, *Emergence of Lincoln*, 1:166; Shenton, *Robert John Walker*, pp. 165–66; Thornton, *Politics and Power*, pp. 360–63.

15 Rawley, *Race and Politics*, pp. 208–9, 215–16. Stephens to Thomas W. Thomas, 29 Feb. 1856 and 16 Jan. 1857, Stephens Papers, DU; Abele, *Alexander H. Stephens*, pp. 163–64.

16 Ruffin, *Diary*, ed. Scarborough, 1:180 (23 Apr. 1858).

17 To William F. Samford, 6 Aug. 1857, Samford-Wise Papers, AU.

18 Wise to George W. Munford, 8 Aug. 1857, Munford-Ellis Family Papers, DU; *Richmond Enquirer*, 19 Sept., 9 Oct. 1857.

19 Hunter to Shelton F. Leake, 16 Oct. 1857, and Hunter to Samuel J. Walker et al., 28 Oct. 1857, in Ambler, ed., "Correspondence of Robert M. T. Hunter," pp. 237–41, 245–50.

20 *South*, 12 Jan. 1858.

21 Wise to editor of *Richmond Enquirer*, 16 Nov. 1857, in *Enquirer*, 17 Nov.

22 Nichols, *Disruption of American Democracy*, p. 127, points out that the results of the Lecompton convention's deliberations were known in the East between 15 and 17 November. Telegraphic dispatches announcing the outcome were printed in the *Richmond Enquirer* of 17 November; they had presumably arrived the afternoon or evening of the previous day. Wise's letter was written on that same day—16 November.

23 Fehrenbacher, *Dred Scott*, p. 465. Rawley, *Race and Politics*, at pages 237–38, offers a good critique of Buchanan's biographer, Phillip S. Klein, who argued that the president had accepted the Lecompton Constitution principally because of his "legalistic" mind. For another review, decidedly sympathetic to Buchanan, see Meerse, "Presidential Leadership." An important letter from Supreme Court Justice Peter V. Daniel to John M. Daniel, 13 April 1858, Brock Collection, Box 82, CSmH, states that Buchanan originally favored the submission of the Lecompton Constitution to the people of Kansas. But Daniel claims that he convinced the president otherwise, on grounds that it would constitute an improper intervention by the federal government in territorial affairs.

24 Wise to Isaac Butts, 28 July 1856, in *Richmond Whig*, 21 Aug. 1856.

25 Printed in Wise, *Lecompton Question*.

26 O. J. Wise to Buchanan, 17 Dec. 1857, Buchanan Papers, HSP; Nevins, *Emergence of Lincoln*, 1:232–33.

27 Wise to Douglas, 14 Jan. 1858, Box 8, Folder 12, Douglas Papers, UC. Wise referred here to the abortive efforts of William W. Walker and his associates to colonize Central America (Wise to Tyler, 17 Jan. 1858, Henry A. Wise Papers, VHS).

28 Dusinberre, *Civil War Issues in Philadelphia*, pp. 11, 30, 80; Potter, *Lincoln and His Party*, pp. 316–18 and passim; Wise's remarks at Corinthian Hall, in Richmond, 20 Sept. 1856, in *Richmond Enquirer*, 2 Oct. 1856.

29 Wise to David Hubbard, 3 Mar. 1859, George Washington Campbell Papers, LC. See also Wise, *Territorial Government*, p. 110.

30 *New York Herald*, 14 Jan. 1858; *New York Times*, quoted in *South*, 11 Jan. 1858.

31 *New York Herald*, 10 Jan. 1858.

32 Fernando Wood to Wise, 5 Jan. 1857, Benjamin Perley Poore Papers, HHS.

33 Smith's remarks in *CG*, 35, 1 (26 Mar. 1858), 1372.

34 See, for example, the speech of Representative Thomas S. Bocock, in *Richmond Enquirer*, 26 Mar. 1858.

35 Ruffin, *Diary*, ed. Scarborough, 1:138, 149 (18 Dec. 1857, 22 Jan. 1858); Toombs to W. W. Burwell, 20 Nov. 1857, in Phillips, ed., "Correspondence of Toombs, Stephens, and Cobb," pp. 425–27; Rhett to Edmund Ruffin, 5 Apr. 1860, Ruffin Papers, VHS.

36 *National Era*, 31 Mar. 1859; *New York Times*, quoted in *South*, 11 Jan. 1858.

37 *New York Times*, quoted in *South*, 11 Jan. 1858.

38 Tyler to Buchanan, 12 Jan. 1858, Buchanan Papers, HSP.

39 Stephens to Thomas W. Thomas, 18 Dec. 1857, Stephens Papers, LC; Thomas to Stephens, 21 Jan. and 7 Feb. 1858, in Phillips, ed., "Correspondence of Toombs, Stephens, and Cobb," pp. 428–29.

40 Quoted in *New York Herald*, 19 Jan. 1858; Porter to James H. Hammond, 30 Jan. 1858, and Hammond to I. W. Hayne, 17 Sept. 1860, both in Hammond Papers, LC.

41 *New York Times*, quoted in *South*, 11 Jan. 1858.

42 *South*, 12 Jan. 1858. See also the *Washington* (D.C.) *Union*, quoted in *South*, 16 Feb. 1858, for an editorial contrasting the views of Wise and Douglas on Lecompton.

43 *Charleston Mercury*, quoted in *South*, 12 Jan. 1858.

44 Wise to the Philadelphia Anti-Lecompton Meeting, 6 Feb. 1858, in Wise, *Lecompton Question*. Wise inserted the italics.

45 Ibid.

46 Ibid.; Meerse, "Presidential Leadership," 312, for the quotation. Meerse contends that Buchanan recognized that freedom would triumph eventually in Kansas, that he never endorsed Lecompton unequivocally, and that he sought only a fair expression of opinion

by the properly qualified voters of Kansas. Yet this defense does not absolve Buchanan of his lies. The president expressed his commitment to the principle of submitting the constitution to the people yet endorsed a proslavery instrument on which there had been no expression of public opinion. Cf. Meerse, passim, and Potter, *Impending Crisis*, pp. 312–13, for a close commentary on the president's inconsistencies. Meerse was nearer the mark in an earlier publication, when he described the dispute between Douglas (and Wise, I would say) and Buchanan as grounded in "ideology and principle." See his "Origins of the Buchanan-Douglas Feud Reconsidered," p. 174.

47 Wise to Robert Tyler, 11 Jan. 1858, in Auchampaugh, *Robert Tyler*, pp. 227–28.

48 Wise to Tyler, 17 Jan. 1858, Henry A. Wise Papers, VHS; Wise to Tyler, 20 Mar. 1858, Wise Correspondence, NYHS; William J. Robertson to Muscoe Garnett, 23 Jan. 1858, William Garnett Chisolm Papers, VHS.

49 To William Sergeant, Wise Correspondence, NYHS. The shortsightedness of many Southern politicians in 1858, and also the temptations presented by another prospective slave state and the pressures exerted on them to obtain it, are illustrated by the convolutions of Senator James H. Hammond of South Carolina. "I now say Lecompton or separation," Hammond wrote his friend William Gilmore Simms on 7 February (Hammond Papers, LC). And yet by the fall he represented himself as having been opposed to Lecompton all along and contrived an argument to avow that in losing Kansas the South had lost nothing. See Hammond, *Speech delivered at Barnwell Court House, October 29, 1858*.

50 The resulting compromise, the English bill, offered Kansans the opportunity of choosing either statehood and slavery or continued territorial status and freedom. On 2 August they chose the latter.

51 *Enquirer*, 14 May and 13 July 1858. The *Enquirer's* endorsement of the Lecompton Constitution obviously influenced the efforts of the Wises to secure a measure of direct editorial control over the paper.

52 Wise to Fernando Wood, 14 Oct. 1858 (copy), WFP/VHS; Wise to Buchanan, 16 Jan. 1858, Buchanan Papers, HSP.

53 Wise to Buchanan, 12 Oct. 1858, Buchanan Papers, HSP; Milton, *Eve of Conflict*, p. 308; William R. Ritchie to R. T. Hubard, 14 Dec. 1858, Hubard Family Papers, UVA.

54 Wise to David Hubbard, 3 Jan. 1859, George Washington Campbell Papers, LC, suggested that the Pacific railroad advocated by Buchanan remained obnoxious to Virginia, probably because of lingering hopes that the James River canal and railroad would someday be completed.

55 Wise to the Central Committee of the Democratic party of Illinois, 13 Oct. 1858, in Wise, *Lecompton Question*; Wise to Douglas, 12 Nov. 1858, Box 20, Folder 18, Douglas Papers, UC.

56 Wise to William F. Samford, 3 Nov. 1858, Samford-Wise Papers, AU.

57 To William F. Samford, 6 Aug. 1857, in ibid.

58 Cited in *Fairmont True Virginian*, 1 May 1858.

59 Cited in *Richmond Whig*, 30 July 1858. The *Herald's* correspondent had interviewed many of the Southern luminaries vacationing at the Virginia springs in Greenbrier county.

60 On Douglas's 1855 visit to Virginia, see Johannsen, *Stephen A. Douglas*, p. 478. Douglas's Senate speech of 3 March 1854 in defense of the Kansas-Nebraska Act is included in Hambleton, *Biographical Sketch*, pp. 365–409.

61 19 Nov. 1858, John Floyd Papers, WVULM.

62 S. Bassett French to Douglas, 5 May 1860, Box 32, Folder 4, Douglas Papers, UC.

63 On Douglas, see the incisive comments in Forgie, *Patricide in the House Divided*. See also Johannsen, *Stephen A. Douglas*, pp. 240, 297.

64 Fehrenbacher, *Dred Scott*, pp. 379, 492–94.

65 Fehrenbacher, *Prelude to Greatness*, p. 139n. For a vigorous defense of Douglas, see the *Enquirer* of 22 June 1858.

66 "Letter of Governor Wise to the Central Committee of the Democratic Party of Illinois," 13 Oct. 1858, in Wise, *Lecompton Question*. Typically, the *Enquirer* took a harder line than Wise, as in its issue of 11 November 1858.

67 Wise to William F. Samford, 3 Nov. 1858, Samford-Wise Papers, AU.

68 20 Oct. 1858, Clement Claiborne Clay Papers, DU.

69 Wise to William F. Samford, 3 Nov. 1858, Samford-Wise Papers, AU.

70 J. Withers Clay to Clement Claiborne Clay, 30 Mar. 1860, Clay Papers, DU.

71 Yancey to T. J. Orme, 24 May 1858, in *Richmond Enquirer*, 11 June 1858.

72 *Enquirer*, 9 June, 26 Aug., 3 Sept. (sw), 28 Sept. (sw), 26 Oct., and 24 Dec. (sw) 1858.

73 25 Mar. 1858, for the quotation, and 4 June 1858. Cf. ibid., 22 July and 1 Aug. 1858.

74 Ibid., 26–29 Dec. 1858.

75 Wise to David Hubbard, 3 Mar. 1859, George Washington Campbell Papers, LC; Wise to Udolpho Wolfe et al., 15 July 1859, in *Richmond Enquirer*, 2 Aug. 1859.

76 *Whig* (sw), 12 Feb. 1858.

77 Wise to J. Y. Mason, 20 Apr. 1856, Mason Papers, VHS; Ruffin, *Diary*, ed. Scarborough, 1:329–30 (16 Aug. 1859); William B. Campbell to David Campbell, 19 Dec. 1858, Campbell Family Papers, DU.

78 See the correspondence and commentary published in *Richmond Whig* (sw), 26 Jan. 1858.

79 Ibid., 16 Feb. 1858.

80 R. M. T. Hunter to Letcher, 22 Aug. 1858, LPL; *Richmond Whig* (sw), 20 Aug. and 26 Nov. 1858.

81 Clemens to Letcher, 14 and 24 Aug. 1858, LPL. See Brockenbrough's card in *Richmond Whig* (sw), 22 Nov. 1858.

82 *Richmond Whig* (sw), 28 Sept. and 19, 23, 26 Nov. 1858; O. J. Wise to Wise, 10 Oct. 1858, Dreer Collection, HSP.

83 Wise to William F. Samford, 3 Nov. 1858, Samford-Wise Papers, AU.

84 David Campbell to William B. Campbell, 18 Dec. 1856, Campbell Family Papers, DU; William Gilmore Simms to James Henry Hammond, 28 Jan. 1858, and John Belton O'Neall to Hammond, 17 Mar. 1860, Hammond Papers, LC; *Richmond Whig* (sw), 7 Oct. 1859; Jones, "Forgotten Virginian," p. 164n; *Charleston Mercury*, 5 Jan. 1860; John Bachman to Edmund Ruffin, 18 Jan. 1860, in Channing, *Crisis of Fear*, p. 120.

85 Wise to Samford, 17 Nov. 1858, Samford-Wise Papers, AU.

86 Nevins, in *Emergence of Lincoln*, comments (1:415–18) on Wise's commitment to a congressional slave code for the territories but never mentions *Territorial Government*. Nor do any of the other major political historians. There is a brief and uncritical notice in Shanks, *Secession Movement in Virginia*, p. 63.

87 Wise to "My Dear Sir," 9 Mar. 1859, Henry A. Wise Papers, VHS.

88 Ibid.; Wood to Wise, 13 Mar. 1859, Henry A. Wise Papers, VSL; *Richmond Enquirer*, 31 Mar. 1859. For blistering critiques of Wise and the *Enquirer*, see *National Era*, 31 Mar., 23 June 1859. On these matters generally, see Fehrenbacher, *Dred Scott*, pp. 506–13.

89 Fehrenbacher, *Dred Scott*, p. 87; Bestor, "State Sovereignty and Slavery," pp. 153–55.

90 Wise, *Territorial Government*, p. 78.

91 Ibid., pp. 14, 18–19, 149; Fehrenbacher, *Dred Scott*, esp. pp. 380–81.

92 "Governor Wise's Speech at Norfolk," 27 Sept. 1860, in *Southern Argus*, 12 Oct. 1860; *Richmond Enquirer*, 27 May 1858 and 12 May 1860, in Crenshaw, *Slave States*, pp. 49–50.

93 Wise, *Territorial Government*, pp. 150, 153, 154, for the quotations in the previous two paragraphs.

94 Ibid., pp. 155–56.

95 Ibid., p. 156; Wise to Udolpho Wolfe et al., 15 July 1859, in *Richmond Enquirer*, 1 Aug. 1859.

96 Wise to C. H. K. Taylor et al., in *North Carolina Evening Standard* (sw), 29 Oct. 1856; Wise to John Beauchamp Jones, 18 Aug. 1859, Jones Papers, SHC.

97 Finkelman, *Imperfect Union*, pp. 296–97.

98 Wise to Johnson, 16 Mar. 1857, Executive Letter Books, VSL; Charles O'Conor to Letcher, 14 Apr. 1860, Letters Received, Governor's Office, Executive Department, Archives Branch, VSL, Box 409; Reverdy Johnson to Letcher, 16 Apr. 1860, in ibid.

99 Wise, *Territorial Government*, p. 154; see also p. 110.

100 Ibid., pp. 110, 154 (for the quotation). See also Wise to Udolpho Wolfe et al., 15 July 1859, in *Richmond Enquirer*, 1 Aug. 1859. I mean here to enter a respectful dissent to the findings in Finkelman, *Imperfect Union*, which makes the Lemmon case a centerpiece in a Southern offensive to compel "a judicial nationalization of slavery" (p. 283). Finkelman formulates a plausible hypothesis and adduces a fair bit of evidence to show that Lincoln and other Republicans may have had good reason to fear a revival of slave law in the North. But why did Virginia fail to appeal the decision in *Lemmon*? Alas, neither Finkelman nor I has an answer.

101 *New York Daily News*, 9 May 1859; *Richmond Enquirer*, 4, 5 July, in the *New York Times* 11, 21 July 1859; *Concord* (New Hampshire) *Democratic Standard*, 2 July 1859 (clipping in Henry A. Wise Papers, SHC); *Richmond Whig*, 8 July 1859.

102 *New York Herald*, 30 May 1859; Wise to Udolpho Wolfe et al., 15 July 1859, in *Richmond Enquirer*, 1 Aug. 1859; Forgie, *Patricide in the House Divided*, pp. 159–99.

103 *Wheeling Intelligencer*, 5 Feb. 1858; *Wheeling Argus*, in the *Richmond Enquirer*, 21 June 1859; *Fairmont True Virginian*, 13 Aug. 1859.

104 *Enquirer*, 18 June 1859.

105 *Richmond Whig* (sw), 8, 22 July 1859; *Richmond Enquirer*, 18 June 1859, 2 Aug. 1859; John Coles Rutherfoord Diary, 11 July 1859, Rutherfoord Papers, VHS; Wise to Wood, 12 July 1859, Brock Collection, Box 35, CSmH.

106 *Richmond Enquirer*, 9, 26 Aug. 1859.

107 *Richmond Whig* (sw), 11 Aug. 1859.

108 *Richmond Enquirer*, 16, 25 Aug. 1859.

109 Wise to Wood, 10 Sept. 1859, Henry A. Wise Papers, VSL; Wise to John Beauchamp Jones, 18 Aug. 1859, Jones Papers, SHC.

110 O. J. Wise to Harper and Bros., 21 Sept. 1859, in Douglas, *Letters*,

ed. Johannsen, pp. 449–50n; *Richmond Enquirer*, quoted in *National Era*, 22 Sept. 1859.

Chapter 11

1 Far fewer people are critical of Brown's operations at Harpers Ferry than react with loathing to the notorious massacre of five unarmed proslavery sympathizers at Pottawatomie Creek in 1856. Brown was directly responsible for this incident, as his own guilt-ridden later evasions about it suggest. Most commentators, I suspect, have had greater difficulty accepting Brown's violence on the Pottawatomie because it seemed more indiscriminate than at Harpers Ferry (the Virginians appeared less innocent) and less noble in design because no direct effort at emancipation was involved. The best of Brown's modern biographers, Stephen B. Oates, published his *To Purge This Land with Blood* in 1970. Though masking his biases throughout, Oates is sympathetic to the means Brown chose to assault slavery in Virginia and enters a plea that his Kansas activities should be understood in the context of the indiscriminate violence usually associated with guerrilla warfare. See *NYR* 16 (22 Apr. 1971): 60.

But Oates completely misses what we might call Brown's "inner drama." *To Purge This Land with Blood* serves admirably at providing a reasonably objective view of Brown's public career and therefore intelligently corrects the vast body of partisan literature. But Oates's book, like Richard O. Boyer's *The Legend of John Brown*, is unsatisfactory on questions of motivation. Boyer argues that the violence of mid-nineteen-century America led inevitably to a prophetic avenger like Brown; Oates maintains that a rigidly Calvinist upbringing produced the Kansas and Virginia revolutionary. But how many people grew up in this fashion? The problem with these arguments from "context," as Willie Lee Rose writes in "Killing for Freedom," is that they cannot address John Brown as easily as they can account for "other revolutionaries" like him. Yet there was only one Brown.

A slightly different version of this chapter appeared as "John Brown and Governor Wise: A New Perspective on Harpers Ferry," in *Biography: An Interdisciplinary Quarterly* 1 (Fall 1978): 15–38. © Copyright 1978 by the Biographical Research Center.

2 Quoted in McDonald, "Emerson and John Brown," pp. 385–86.

3 Oates, *To Purge*, p. 303.

4 *Richmond Enquirer*, 25 Oct. 1859.

5 Correspondence of *Baltimore American*, in *New York Tribune*, 24 Nov. 1859.

6 Brown to Andrew Hunter, 22 Nov. 1859, in U.S. Congress, Senate, *Report of the Select Committee to Inquire into the Late Invasion . . . at Harpers Ferry*, 36, 1, No. 278, pp. 67–68 of the testimony (hereinafter cited as the *Mason Committee Report*); Rose, "Killing for Freedom," p. 16.

7 Hambleton, *Biographical Sketch*, pp. 94–115.

8 *Richmond Enquirer*, 25 Oct. 1859; see also, on these issues generally, Freehling, "The Boyd Revolution, Virginia, and the Coming of Civil War"; *Richmond Enquirer*, 27 Oct. 1859; Abbott, "Yankee Farmers in Northern Virginia," pp. 55–56; Hickin, "Gentle Agitator."

9 Whitman, "Re-evaluating John Brown's Raid," p. 56; *Shepherdstown Register*, 22 Oct. 1859; *Mason Committee Report*, p. 66 of the testimony.

10 Whitman, "Re-evaluating John Brown's Raid," p. 61; *New York Tribune*, 20 Oct. 1859.

11 Quarles, *Allies for Freedom*, pp. 86–87.

12 Cook arrived in Harpers Ferry on 5 June 1858. He took several odd jobs in the area. In April 1859 he married a local girl and continued to work as a lock tender on the Chesapeake and Ohio Canal. See Villard, *John Brown*, pp. 344, 408. Villard reports at page 408 that Brown cautioned his loquacious subordinate not to reveal his plans to the slaves. At no other point, it seems to me, does Brown's celebrated unrealism and willingness to take the slaves for granted show more to his disadvantage. It is likely, however, that Cook had already established contact with the slaves. Wise declared that he had, and a report in the *New York Herald* named a slaveholder who lived some fifteen to twenty miles from Harpers Ferry and who confirmed that Cook had talked with his slaves. See the *Richmond Enquirer*, 25 Oct., 3, 24 Nov. 1859, and the *Mason Committee Report*, p. 63 of the testimony. W. W. Throckmorton affirms in the *Shepherdstown Register*, 5 November 1859, that Cook conferred with a slave named Charles Williams before the attempted insurrection (Williams sympathized openly with Brown during his movement and fled following his capture). Senator James M. Mason's letter in the *Enquirer*, 27 October 1859, maintaining that Cook imputed no information about Brown's plans to anyone living in Harpers Ferry, might be dismissed as self-serving and aimed at exonerating the locals as well as calming the frazzled nerves of Virginians generally.

13 Quarles is therefore in error in *Allies for Freedom*, p. 104. In his confession, John E. Cook mentions that, mindful of Brown's in-

structions, he held only one conversation with slaves in the area before the attempted insurrection. Even this admission is striking, it seems to me, in view of Cook's obvious efforts to save his own neck. The confession was itself part of a carefully orchestrated effort by his friends and family to obtain mercy. Undoubtedly, few slaves knew of Brown's movements in advance. One member of his company, Osborne P. Anderson, put the figure at 150 during an 1870 interview. See Hinton, *John Brown and His Men*, pp. 272–73, and 700–714 for the confession.

14 Oates, *To Purge*, p. 216.

15 This seems a proper inference in view of Brown's behavior in Kansas and elsewhere. It is also implicit in Brown's essay "Sambo's Mistakes," composed in the late 1840s, and in his "Words of Advice" to the United States League of Gileadites, written in 1851 in Springfield, Massachusetts. Both documents are reprinted in Hinton, *John Brown and His Men*, pp. 585–92. At page 260, Hinton quotes Brown's daughter Annie on the same point, but I believe her views require independent corroboration.

16 *Richmond Enquirer*, 31 Oct. 1859. According to Osborne P. Anderson, one of Brown's men who escaped from the Ferry, a member of their party supplied a slave with a shotgun taken from Col. Lewis Washington, who was one of Brown's white hostages. In his *Voice from Harpers Ferry*, pages 37–38, Anderson alleges that the slave in question shot and killed a Harpers Ferry citizen.

17 *Baltimore Sun*, 20 Oct. 1859. Hinton, in *John Brown and His Men*, page 260, quotes Annie Brown as saying that it was her father's intention to arm the slaves. Boyer, in *The Legend of John Brown*, page 371, quotes Frederick Douglass to the same effect. Both made their statements many years after Brown's death. Brown may have planned eventually to arm the slaves, but at the Ferry, such was not the case.

The only other evidence I have found to the contrary comes from Nevins, *Emergence of Lincoln*, 2:92: "Armistead Ball, master machinist at the Ferry, and one of Brown's prisoners, testified that Brown had said he was determined to seize the arms of the government to enable the slaves to defend themselves, and had called on him and others to deliver up the government stores." But Nevins does not provide a citation. And in his testimony before the Mason Committee (the only place where Ball could have "testified," as far as I know), Ball said nothing of the kind.

18 *Shepherdstown Register*, 22 Oct. 1859.

19 Quoted in Woodward, "John Brown's Private War," in *Burden of Southern History*, p. 45. In his brilliant and cynical indictment of Brown's vanity and unwillingness to communicate his purposes to

the slaves beforehand, David M. Potter points out for whom the pikes were intended. But Potter does not realize that some slaves knew in advance about Brown's proposed insurrection. He is also too busy flailing at Brown's stupidity to comprehend entirely his motives for attacking the arsenal. Finally, Potter says that Brown delayed fatally at Harpers Ferry because he expected more slaves to join him. More complex motives than that influenced Brown's uncharacteristic hesitancy once he entered the Ferry, as I shall argue below. See Potter, *The South and the Sectional Conflict*, pp. 201–18.

20 *Richmond Enquirer*, 25 Oct. 1859. Five of Brown's twenty-one compatriots at Harpers Ferry were free blacks, who would presumably have exercised some command responsibility had his insurrection materialized. But Brown all along had maintained a much higher opinion of free blacks than of slaves.

21 Eby, "Last Hours of the John Brown Raid," p. 177; *Mason Committee Report*, Testimony of Andrew Hunter, p. 61; *New York Times*, 20 Oct. 1859.

22 Villard, *John Brown*, pp. 464–65; *Mason Committee Report*, pp. 7–8 of the testimony; Oates, *To Purge*, pp. 295–97; *Shepherdstown Register*, 29 Oct. 1859.

23 *Richmond Enquirer*, 25 Oct. 1859; *New York Times*, 21 Oct. 1859; *Shepherdstown Register*, 29 Oct. 1859. For the anger prompted by this remark, see Col. Robert W. Baylor to Wise, 4 Nov. 1859, John Brown Papers, LC. Baylor commanded the Virginia militia during the insurrection. Col. Robert E. Lee's official report commends the militia for its "promptness," "alacrity," and "zeal," although not for its bravery. The original, dated 19 October 1859, is found in Record Group 94, Records of the Adjutant General's Office, Letters Received Relating to John Brown's Raid at Harpers Ferry, NA. It is more conveniently available in the *Mason Committee Report*, pp. 40–43. Lee discreetly omitted from his report his suggestion that the militia make the final assault; not so, his biographer. See Freeman, *R. E. Lee*, 1:398.

24 Barry, *Strange Story of Harpers Ferry*, pp. 64–65, 71; Moore, ed., "John Brown's Raid at Harpers Ferry," p. 389; *Mason Committee Report*, pp. 25–26.

25 *New York Tribune*, 19 Oct. 1859; *Baltimore Sun*, 22 Oct. 1859. See also, for the reports of the militia commanders at Harpers Ferry, the *Richmond Enquirer*, 28 Oct. 1859.

26 Oates, *To Purge*, p. 293.

27 *Baltimore Sun*, 3 Nov. 1859.

28 Hunter, "John Brown's Raid," p. 190; Holst, *Constitutional and Political History*, 7:42–43, for comments of the *Charleston Mer-*

cury; John Coles Rutherfoord Diary, 24 Nov. 1859, Rutherfoord Papers, VHS.

29 Villard, *John Brown*, p. 523; Wise to Buchanan, 24 Oct. 1859, RG 94, Records of the Adjutant General's Office, Letters Received Relating to John Brown's Raid at Harpers Ferry, NA.

30 Wise to Hunter, 16 Nov. 1859, in *MHSP*, 41 (1907–8): 93–94.

31 Villard, *John Brown*, p. 523.

32 *New York Tribune*, 18 Oct. 1859; *Baltimore Sun*, 22 Oct. 1859; Garrett to John B. Floyd, 17 Oct. 1859 (telegram), RG 94, Records of the Adjutant General's Office, Letters Received Relating to John Brown's Raid at Harpers Ferry, NA.

33 Hinton, *John Brown and His Men*, pp. 298, 700–714. I do not see what motives Cook could have had for falsifying this information.

34 *MHSP* 41 (1907–8): 94.

35 Ibid., 93–94.

36 A. M. Barbour to A. R. Boteler, 30 Dec. 1859, Boteler Papers, DU.

37 Wise to Captain John Scott, 17 Nov. 1859, John Hay Papers, LC. Boteler was the congressman from the Harpers Ferry area. He advised Wise that a package of Helper's books had been sent from New York to Underwood, who was then staying at Willard's Hotel in Washington. Boteler at first stopped delivery on the books. Then, after consulting with the rest of the Virginia delegation, he decided to permit delivery but hired a detective to observe Underwood's movements.

38 Villard, *John Brown*, pp. 522–23.

39 Ibid., pp. 484–85, 511–14; Nevins, *Emergence of Lincoln*, 2:91–93, 95. See also Edelstein, *Strange Enthusiasm*, pp. 227, 229–30, 234, 236.

40 Andrew Hunter to Wise, 10 Nov. 1859, Executive Papers (John Brown), Box 11, VSL; *Richmond Enquirer*, 19 Nov. 1859; Robert Y. Conrad to his wife, 27 Nov. 1859, Holmes Conrad Papers, VHS; John Caperton to his mother, 21 Nov. 1859, William Gaston Caperton Papers, WVULM; see also Hunter, "John Brown's Raid," p. 179; J. W. Garrett to James Buchanan, 26 Oct. 1859 (telegram) and to John B. Floyd, 26 Oct. 1859 (telegram), RG 94, Records of the Adjutant General's Office, Letters Received Relating to John Brown's Raid at Harpers Ferry, NA; *Shepherdstown Register*, 29 Oct., 19 Nov. 1859.

41 Villard, *John Brown*, p. 520.

42 C. T. Bruen to Jonathan M. Bennett, 23 Nov. 1859, Bennett Papers, WVULM.

43 DuBois, *John Brown*, p. 354; Quarles, *Allies for Freedom*, pp. 107–8.

44 Wise to George Booker, 3 Dec. 1859, WFP/VHS.

45 *Shepherdstown Register*, 12 Nov. 1859. A few historians have suggested that Andrew Hunter, who prosecuted Brown, decided to charge him with treason as well as murder and inciting insurrection because Virginia's constitution prevented a governor from granting executive clemency to convicted traitors. Although this hypothesis, if true, might strengthen my view of Wise's attitudes, not a shred of evidence has been advanced in support of it. See Filler, *Crusade against Slavery*, pp. 272–73; Goldfield, "Triumph of Politics over Society," p. 91.

46 Villard, *John Brown*, p. 570; John Coles Rutherfoord Diary, 12 Dec. 1859, Rutherfoord Papers, VHS.

47 On Wise's use of various spies, see J. Lucius Davis to Wise, 28 Oct. 1859, Executive Papers (John Brown), Box 10, VSL; Alexander Jones to Wise, 31 Oct. 1859, in ibid., Box 14; C. Camp to Wise, 25 Nov. 1859, in ibid. The governor reflected on turning over at least one of Brown's associates to the federal authorities, but local opposition in the Harpers Ferry area and the news that Senator Mason would head an investigation evidently dissuaded him. See Mason to Wise, 15 Dec. 1859, in Flournoy, Palmer, and McRae, eds., *Calendar of Virginia State Papers*, 9:93–94; Wise to Andrew Hunter, 18 Dec. 1859 (typescript), John Brown Papers, MHS; *Charlestown Independent Democrat*, 8 Nov. 1859.

48 Wise to John B. Jones, 26 Oct. 1859, Jones Papers, SHC.

49 Governor's Message I, in *Richmond Enquirer*, 6 Dec. 1859.

50 As in ibid., for example.

51 Ibid.

52 John Brown Papers, LC.

53 Oates, *To Purge*, pp. 329–34; see also "Notes and Documents: 'Sir, This Is Not the End of It,' " ed. Draughon.

54 Villard, *John Brown*, pp. 502–3; Nevins, *Emergence of Lincoln*, 2:91–93.

55 John Sergeant Wise to O. G. Villard, 11 June 1908, WFP/VHS; Josiah Quincy, quoted in *MHSP*, 41 (1907–8): 326; Swint, ed., *Dear Ones at Home*, pp. 79–80.

56 *Resolutions of Wise's Brigade*.

57 B. H. Wise, *Life of Henry A. Wise*, pp. 378, 385, 398–99, 412–13.

58 Oates, *To Purge*, p. 293.

59 Anderson, *Voice from Harpers Ferry*, p. 36.

60 DuBois, *John Brown*, pp. 312–19. DuBois never confronts Brown's decision to permit the train to pass. The great majority of Brown's biographers either ignore altogether his fateful choice not to evacuate the Ferry on the morning of 17 October, or they retreat to Oates's characterization of this decision as "mysterious," or they advance

explanations too cursory or incredible to require refutation. The resources of the armory and arsenal dwarfed Brown's arms cache at his rented farm in Maryland. The Harpers Ferry installation could produce approximately ten thousand stand of arms per year. See Oates, *To Purge*, pp. 275–76, 289.

61 Nevins, *Emergence of Lincoln*, 2:84.

62 Anderson, *Voice from Harpers Ferry*, p. 36.

63 Shepherdstown Register, 29 Oct. 1859.

64 Nevins, *Emergence of Lincoln*, 1:82. See also Hamilton, "John Brown in Canada," pp. 133–34.

65 See Holst's superb (and typically overlooked) discussion in *John Brown*, pp. 120–30.

66 For the crucial point on Brown anticipating his own failure, see Oates, *To Purge*, p. 289. On Brown's trust of the Almighty, see ibid., p. 287.

67 This allegation is probably true. Quarles, *Allies for Freedom*, pp. 82–83, has reasonably firm evidence that Brown struck about ten days earlier than he had planned; see also *Baltimore Sun*, 20 Oct. 1859. With his customary acuteness, DuBois made the same point long ago, though with much thinner evidence. See *John Brown*, pp. 304–7.

68 *Baltimore Sun*, 20 Oct. 1859; *Shepherdstown Register*, 22 Oct. 1859; *New York Tribune*, 20 Oct. 1859.

69 *Shepherdstown Register*, 29 Oct. 1859. This statement is separately attributed to Brown by the same source, cited here and in n. 63.

70 Ibid., 5 Nov. 1859.

Chapter 12

1 McDonnell, "Struggle against Suicide"; Currie, "Death of John Bell."

2 Thornton, *Politics and Power*, p. 449.

3 *Injustice*, p. 114.

4 I mean here to express my reservations about Thornton's defiant and disturbing *Politics and Power*. Thornton's analysis exposes how threats to freedom and equality could incite a slaveholding society, which above all others knew the value of independence. With a degree of unanimity unappreciated by most historians, white Alabamians rose to defend their rights following Lincoln's election. Consistent with his theory that Alabamians were only slightly affected by national affairs, Thornton sees secession following from perceptions of an internal crisis that the state's extremist leadership turned brilliantly to their advantage. Crises of this magnitude had

long brewed in Alabama, traceable ultimately to the nature of Jacksonian Democracy. Thornton also claims that "the institutional and intellectual structure which effectively impelled Alabamians into secession was operative, *mutatis mutandis*," in most other states North as well as South (pp. xxi, 458). Holt, *Political Crisis*, represents an effort to extend Thornton's ideas on secession to the "rest of the South" (p. 279).

I suspect, first, that state and local concerns failed to dominate Alabamians' perceptions as much as Thornton argues. Given slavery's importance in Alabama (only Virginia, Georgia, and Mississippi had more slaves in 1860), national political and judicial decisions exerted a potentially decisive influence. Cf. Wright, *Political Economy*, p. 125n.

Second, the degree of unity Thornton posits in Alabama was not replicated in Virginia—to say the least. In part, this resulted from an equivalency in Virginia—indeed, an exact identity—between decisions taken for secession and war. As the closing date in his title suggests, Thornton typically prefers to keep the issues of secession and war analytically distinct, which aids his elegant argument for unity. Yet the ornate metaphor he uses to describe a united Alabama in 1860—drawn from the commentaries of Caesar, who proudly recounts how his troops plunged into surf of uncertain depth in order to assault British troops defending the shore before them—is explicitly martial.

The problem is that despite the enthusiasms of 1861, the South fragmented quickly as the war commenced in earnest. Even before the fighting, significant dissent appeared in Alabama and elsewhere. See Escott, *After Secession*, pp. 26, 39; McDonnell, "Struggle against Suicide," pp. 109n., 112; and Hahn, "Roots of Southern Populism," pp. 157–63. In Virginia, divisions already present deepened instantly and soon took on institutional form, partly because the enactment of the secession ordinance represented a declaration of war. It was, indeed, preceded by an act of war that Wise initiated. The disunity existing all along in the South and manifest after the outbreak of war implies an environment of mistrust, fear, and rage. See the remarkable exposition of these feelings, which also portrays slaves and antisecession whites as important actors in Alabama, in J. J. Hooper to J. deB. Hooper, 25 Dec. 1860, J. DeB. Hooper Papers, SHC. See also Septimus D. Cabiness to Governor A. B. Moore, 29 Oct. 1860, in *Alabama Historical Quarterly* 23 (1961): 6–9.

To some extent, Southerners may well have thought of themselves as a band of brothers, just as Caesar's men did. But they also despised one another, as the subsequent history of the Confederate war demonstrates. A more apt classical parallel than Caesar's commentaries exists in Thucydides. Secession took place in an atmosphere, I suspect, dominated by partisan hatreds and moral chaos much like that prevailing in Corcyra after the outbreak of the Peloponnesian War. As Thucydides put it: "To fit in with the change of events, words, too, had to change their usual meanings. What used to be described as a thoughtless act of aggression was now regarded as the courage one would expect to find in a party member; to think of the future and wait was merely another way of saying one was a coward; any idea of moderation was just an attempt to disguise one's unmanly character; ability to understand a question from all sides meant that one was totally unfitted for action. Fanatical enthusiasm was the mark of a real man, and to plot against an enemy behind his back was perfectly legitimate self-defence. Anyone who held violent opinions could always be trusted, and anyone who objected to them became a suspect. To plot successfully was a sign of intelligence, but it was still cleverer to see that a plot was hatching" (*Peloponnesian War*, trans. and ed. Warner, p. 209).

Given this environment, it is not surprising that secessionists—or those, such as Wise, drawn ultimately to disunion—boldly reflected on coercion and then acted accordingly. Most were slaveholders, after all. On these themes, see Channing, *Crisis of Fear*, p. 282; Johnson, "New Look at the Popular Vote for Delegates to the Georgia Secession Convention"; Barney, *Secessionist Impulse*, pp. 169–78, 212–18; Wise in *Richmond Enquirer*, 17 Nov. 1857, for his statement that "the masses never did make a revolution, never can and never will. A devoted and self-sacrificing few must ever take the initiative and lead the first movements of resistance."

Finally, I suspect that acts of coercion unify far less than Thornton may believe, just as democracy is far healthier than he allows. If the Civil War was only "the catastrophe of Jacksonian America, the denouement of the Jacksonian drama" (p. xxi), then politicians like Wise would probably have found a way out. Few Southerners were more conscious of the national interest in reconciliation, few embodied a more Jacksonian fear of disrupting the Union, few so much appreciated and thus feared the incisiveness of the abolitionists, and few had sought as aggressively to confer on the South the benefits of Yankee living.

5 Quoted in Ambler, *Francis H. Pierpont*, p. 73.

6 One of his clients, Tully Lilliston of Accomac, may well have breathed easier after receiving a sentence of twelve years in the state penitentiary. The charge was murder in the first degree; he acknowledged having convinced a woman that she should confess to his crime. See ACOB, 1857–66, pp. 203–8, 258.

7 Wise to Mary Lyons Wise, 2 Sept. 1858, WFP/VHS; Wise to

George Booker, 5 Oct. 1859, Booker Papers, DU. Only thus sold at $41 an acre, far above the $24 an acre average value of land in Accomac in 1860. See Pressly and Scofield, *Farm Real Estate Values*, p. 42. After arduous searching, I found no evidence on Wise's investments.

8 Wise to George Booker, 5 Oct. 1859, Booker Papers, DU; Wise to J. S. Gillet, 23 Aug. 1859, WFP/VHS.

9 Wise to Mary Lyons Wise, 18 Jan., 6 Feb., 23 Apr. 1855, WFP/VHS; Reitz, *Menopause*, p. 31 and passim.

10 Wise to Mary Lyons Wise, 11, 18 Apr. 1855, 9 Feb. 1864, WFP/VHS.

11 PACDB, No. 49, p. 22 (which records the post–Civil War sale of Rolleston but has no information on its prewar sale to Henry); William H. Parker to Wise, 25 Nov. 1862, WFP/VHS. Wise paid approximately $21, which exceeds by 50 percent the average value of an acre in Princess Anne in 1860. See Pressly and Scofield, *Farm Real Estate Values*, p. 43. One gets a sense of the profitable arrangement Wise made from the Princess Anne County Federal Census of Population, 1860, microfilm reel 103, VSL, which records the value of his real estate at $32,000, though this may have included a couple of small parcels he retained in Accomac.

12 Wise to Mary Lyons Wise, 8, 11 Jan. 1860, WFP/VHS; Goldfield, *Urban Growth*, p. 246; Gray, *History of Agriculture*, 2:922; *Proceedings*, ed. Reese, 3:613 (12 Apr. 1861).

13 Wise to Mary Lyons Wise, 17 May 1860, and John S. Wise to Henry A. Wise, 5 Apr. 1863, both in WFP/VHS. Princess Anne County Federal Census of Population, 1860, VSL.

14 Wise, *Territorial Government*, p. 154.

15 Wise to Rev. Nehemiah Adams, 22 Aug. 1854, in *New York Times*, 15 Sept. 1854; Governor Wise's speech at Corinthian Hall, in Richmond, 20 September 1856, in *Richmond Enquirer*, 2 Oct. 1856; Wise's speech at a Richmond dinner, 26 Jan. 1860, in *Richmond Enquirer*, 31 Jan. 1860.

16 Wise to Mary Lyons Wise, 8 Jan. 1860 and 17 July 1862 (for the quotation), and Richard A. Wise to Henry A. Wise, 7 May 1862, all in WFP/VHS. On 31 March 1862, Wise advised his wife to sell "old Carnifex." This is the only such extant instruction from him. I know nothing of the circumstances, but I do not believe that Carnifex was one of Wise's Rolleston slaves. For Jim's escape, see J. S. Wise, *End of an Era*, pp. 206–9.

17 On these issues, see Gay, "Tangled Skein of Romanticism and Violence in the Old South"; Johnson, "Planters and Patriarchy"; Wyatt-Brown, "Ideal Typology."

18 *Correspondence between Lydia Maria Child and Gov. Wise*, p. 5.

19 *Richmond Enquirer*, 2 Oct. 1856.

20 I have two additional thoughts. "Union" might have had a literal rather than a metaphorical meaning. The physical meant much to Wise. He had suffered interference enough with his efforts to achieve "Union." It was important for him to serve notice that he would tolerate only so much. Finally, he might have intended to warn people other than Republicans. How much force was there in Mary Lyons Wise, after all? Did she typically reserve herself, only to express an independent judgment on the greatest issue of the day? Was the Union something else about which they had "agreed to disagree"?

21 Wise to Waddy Thompson, 21 Oct. 1856, Thompson Letters, EU; Wise to Robert M. T. Hunter, 11 Aug. 1855, Hunter Papers, UVA.

22 Salmon P. Chase to Wise, 1 Dec. 1859 (copy), John Brown Papers, CHS; Fehrenbacher, *Dred Scott*, p. 528.

23 Wise's Message, in *Richmond Enquirer*, 6 Dec. 1859; Ruffin, *Diary*, ed. Scarborough, 1:385 (24 Dec. 1859); *Enquirer*, 24 Dec. 1859, for Wise's remarks to the medical students. Wise's notions about resolving the sectional crisis by a war with Great Britain were at least as old as his 1842 speech on Texas annexation. Seward was probably the most prominent Republican statesman who thought along the same lines in 1860–61.

24 *Mercury*, 5 Jan. 1860; *National Era*, 12 Jan. 1860; Miles to Christopher G. Memminger, 10 Jan. 1860, Memminger Papers, SHC.

25 Channing, *Crisis of Fear*, pp. 102, 112–20; John Coles Rutherfoord Diary, 13 Jan. 1860, Rutherfoord Papers, VHS.

26 Memminger to William Porcher Miles, 30 Jan. 1860, Miles Papers, SHC; *Enquirer*, 2 Jan. and 1 Feb. 1860; Ruffin, *Diary*, ed. Scarborough, 1:405–6 (23 Feb. 1860).

27 Wise to Fernando Wood, 6 July 1859, Brock Collection, Box 35, CSmH.

28 Madison's 1832 letter to Nicholas Trist, quoted by John S. Carlile, in *Proceedings*, ed. Reese, 1:481 (7 Mar. 1861); Gov. Wise's Speech at Norfolk, 27 Sept. 1860, in *Richmond Enquirer*, 12 Oct. 1860.

29 Ruffin, *Diary*, ed. Scarborough, 1:373 (4 Dec. 1859), 408 (1 Mar. 1860).

30 *Richmond Enquirer*, 31 Jan. 1860.

31 Hammond to Col. M. C. M. Hammond, 23 July 1859, and to William G. Simms, 23 Oct. 1860, Hammond Papers, LC; McDonnell, "Struggle against Suicide." See also above, Chapter 5, n. 45.

32 *The Past, the Present, and The Future of Our Country*.

33 This passage and much of what follows in the next several paragraphs come from Wise's speech to a Richmond dinner, *Richmond Enquirer*, 31 Jan. 1860.

34 Powhatan Ellis to Charles Ellis, Jr., 25 Dec. 1860, Munford-Ellis Family Papers, DU. Earlier in the year, Powhatan Ellis had praised Wise as a man of firmness and decision (to Charles Ellis, Jr., 27 Feb. 1860, in ibid.).

35 James E. B. Stuart to John Overton Steger, 23 Mar. 1861, Miscellaneous Personal Papers, UVA. Wise first alluded to this doctrine in his gubernatorial message on John Brown. Criticism increased his emotional and intellectual commitment to it.

36 Wise's public letter to an unidentified correspondent from Columbia, S.C., in Ambler, *Francis H. Pierpont*, p. 73. This letter appeared, among other places, in the *Wellsburg Herald*, 21 and 28 Dec. 1860, the *Southern Argus*, 15 Dec. 1860, and the *Philadelphia Public Ledger*, 17 Dec. 1860.

37 Wise, *Seven Decades of the Union*, p. 278.

38 Thornton, *Politics and Power*, p. 383. See also Johnson, *Toward a Patriarchal Republic*, pp. 28–78.

39 20 Jan. 1860, Henry A. Wise Papers, VSL.

40 *New York Tribune*, 24 Nov. 1859; *Charlestown Independent Democrat*, 29 Nov. 1859.

41 *Richmond Enquirer*, 28 Feb. 1860; *Richmond Whig*, 20 Mar. 1860, for the quotation; Goode, *Recollections of a Lifetime*, pp. 34–35.

42 Wise to Wood, 10 Sept. 1859, Henry A. Wise Papers, VSL; *Richmond Whig*, 20 Mar. 1860; Jackson to Bennett, 25 Mar. 1860, Bennett Papers, WVULM; *Richmond Enquirer*, 7 Apr. 1860; *Fairmont True Virginian*, 17 May 1860; Crenshaw, *Slave States*, pp. 139–41.

43 *Enquirer*, 16 June 1860; John M. Savage to Douglas, 21 July 1860, Box 34, Folder 42, Douglas Papers, UC.

44 *Southern Argus*, 27 Aug. 1860.

45 Ibid., 12 Oct. 1860; *Richmond Whig*, 28 Sept. and 19 Oct. 1860; Nevins, *Emergence of Lincoln*, 2:293–94.

46 The Whig press typically made this point. See *National Era*, 22 Sept. 1859.

47 Gov. Wise's Speech at Norfolk, 27 Sept. 1860, in *Richmond Enquirer*, 12 Oct. 1860. See also ibid., 10 July 1860, in Dumond, ed., *Southern Editorials*, pp. 140–42.

48 13, 26 Oct. 1860, Cushing Papers, LC.

49 *Southern Argus*, 26 Oct. 1860. Wise avoided claiming that the Republicans obtained control of the House in 1860. They had not, as Holt points out in *Political Crisis*, p. 220.

50 Thornton, *Politics and Power*, p. 448, for his comment that histori-

ans have underestimated the significance of the personal liberty laws as a talking point for the secessionists, although the reasons he advances for their importance are different than mine.

51 Ruffin, *Diary*, ed. Scarborough, 1:491 (11 Nov. 1860). Crenshaw is thus in error at page 126 of *The Slave States* in classifying both Wise and Ruffin as advocates of extreme measures.

52 *Richmond Whig*, 6 Nov. 1860; *Southern Argus*, 2, 3, 21 Nov. and 18 Dec. 1860; *Alexandria Gazette and Public Advertiser*, 8 Nov. 1860; Goldfield, "Triumph of Politics over Society," p. 61, for the quotation; Shanks, *Secession Movement in Virginia*, p. 125.

53 To Samford, 21 Oct. 1860, Samford-Wise Papers, SHC; Wise to Rufus Dolbear, 21 Oct. 1860, copied from *New Orleans Delta* in *Richmond Enquirer*, 27 Nov. 1860; Wise to C. B. Harrison et al., 1 Sept. 1860, in *Philadelphia Public Ledger*, 17 Dec. 1860.

54 To Henry J. Randall, 16 Nov. 1860, Henry A. Wise Correspondence, NYHS.

55 Wise to R. D. Wade et al., 31 Dec. 1860, in *Richmond Enquirer* (sw), 8 Jan. 1861; *Southern Argus*, 11 Dec. 1860; White, *Robert Barnwell Rhett*, pp. 199, 203; Barney, *Road to Secession*, p. 196.

56 Barbour to Stephen A. Douglas, 6 Feb. 1861, Box 37, Folder 27, Douglas Papers, UC. For a similar estimate, see William C. Rives's letter cited in Eaton, *History of the Southern Confederacy*, p. 39. The conservative tone of the convention owed much to the revival of Virginia Whiggery during the 4 February balloting. Alexander H. H. Stuart, Robert E. Scott, and Timothy Rives, who had all played active roles in John Bell's successful presidential movement in Virginia the previous fall, were elected to the convention. Because the Virginia General Assembly was scheduled to meet simultaneously with the convention, it appears that many members of the assembly declined to seek seats in it. Only seven members of the assembly—an increasingly radical body in early 1861—were elected to the convention.

57 The printed list of delegates, with Thompson's markings, is in the John R. Thompson Papers, UVA. He marked Wise as doubtful.

58 *Alexandria Gazette and Public Advertiser*, 28 Dec. 1860 and 24 Jan. 1861, on the editorial policy of the *Enquirer*, noted in Boxes 18 and 14, respectively, Frank M. Anderson Papers, LC.

59 Ibid., 4 Jan. 1861, Box 14.

60 *New York Herald*, 2, 22 Dec. 1860, 3, 8, 15 Jan. 1861; *New York Tribune*, 10, 15 Jan. 1861; Joseph Holt to James Buchanan, 18, 20 Feb. 1861, Buchanan Papers, HSP; F. W. [?] Ruffin to Edmund Ruffin, 2 Feb. 1861, Ruffin Papers, VHS. See also Gunderson, *Old Gentlemen's Convention*, p. 7.

61 Wise to George Booker, 20 Jan. 1861, Booker Papers, DU.

62 U.S. Congress, House of Representatives, *Report of the Select House Committee of Five*, 36, 2; *New York Tribune*, 28 Jan. 1861; Diary of Thomas Bragg, 1, 12 Feb. 1861, Bragg Papers, SHC.

63 *Richmond Enquirer*, 1 Feb. 1861; Wise to various Philadelphia gentlemen, 4 Feb. 1861, in ibid., 12 Feb. 1861. See also Wise's denial on 15 Feb. 1861, in *Proceedings*, ed. Reese, 1:30–36.

64 John Coles Rutherfoord Diary, 5 Jan. 1861, Rutherfoord Papers, VHS.

65 M. G. Harman to John D. Imboden, 10 Feb. 1861, Imboden Papers, UVA. Wise disavowed this charge and engaged in a colloquy with Stuart on 15 February 1861, in *Proceedings*, ed. Reese, 1:30–36.

66 Wilson, *History of the Rise and Fall of the Slave Power*, 3:164–65, on O. J. Wise's radicalism versus his father's caution.

67 R. M. T. Hunter to his son, 22 Nov. 1860, Hunter Papers, UVA.

68 Wise's speech to a Richmond dinner, *Richmond Enquirer*, 31 Jan. 1860, and Wise to R. D. Wade et al., 31 Dec. 1860, in ibid. (sw), 8 Jan. 1861; *Proceedings*, ed. Reese, 3:704 (13 Apr. 1861).

69 Wise to George Booker, 14 Jan. 1861, Booker Papers, DU; Abbott, *South and North*.

70 Abbott, *South and North*, pp. 130, 285.

71 Ibid., pp. 55–56, 72, 106, 179–85, 215, 314.

72 Quoted in Freehling, "Editorial Revolution," p. 69; see also John Smith Preston to Francis Pickens, 17 February 1861, Preston Papers, *SCL*.

73 Wise to John H. McCue, 14 Mar. 1861, Perry-Martin-McCue Papers, UVA; Wise to R. D. Wade et al., 31 Dec. 1860, in *Richmond Enquirer* (sw), 8 Jan. 1861. The despoliation of Virginia's slave system and the threat of a similar development reaching further into the South preoccupied many speakers in the state convention. See Freehling, "Editorial Revolution."

74 Hunter to George Booker, 8 Feb. 1861, Booker Papers, DU. On Lincoln's ability to recruit Virginians, see John Rutherfoord to A. H. Rutherfoord, 19 Dec. 1860, Rutherfoord Papers, DU; John Randolph Tucker to James L. Kemper, 19 Nov. 1860, Kemper Papers, UVA; Garnett, *Speech on the State of the Union*; *Richmond Enquirer*, 10 July and 16 Nov. 1860; O. J. Wise to Henry A. Randall, 16 Nov. 1860, Henry A. Wise Papers, NYHS. See also the remarks of James P. Holcombe, in *Proceedings*, ed. Reese, 2:92 (20 Mar. 1861).

75 W. H. J'Anson to Edmund Ruffin, 28 Nov. 1860, Ruffin Papers, VHS, on "the unreliability of the poorer class of nonslaveholders"; Peter W. Adams to John Letcher, 10 Jan. 1861, Letters Received, Governor's Office, Executive Department, Archives Branch, VSL, Box 417, on the presence of an abolitionist blacksmith in Farming-

ton; *Richmond Examiner*, 4 Aug. 1860, for a Douglas rally in Richmond whose working-class listeners were told that they would have no place in a Southern slaveholding confederation, cited in Crenshaw, *Slave States*, p. 144; John Coles Rutherfoord Diary, 21 Nov. 1859, Rutherfoord Papers, VHS, for comments on the unsoundness of the nonslaveholders; ibid., 23 Jan. 1861, for a report on a "rowdy and disorderly" meeting of workingmen in Richmond at which both Wise and Botts were denied a hearing; Crenshaw, "Psychological Background," p. 271, for additional evidence of abolitionism in eastern Virginia.

76 William H. Seward to John C. Underwood, 20 Nov. 1858, quoted in Smith, "Antebellum Attempts," p. 212.

77 Botts to Edward Bates, 27 Mar. 1861, RG 60, Attorney General's Papers, Letters Received, Virginia, 1814–70, I, NA. Botts commented: "*Especially is it of first importance* that all secession postmasters and Mail Agents should be removed at once. I have reason to know that the foulest practices are of daily occurrence." For other Virginians interested in taking office under the Republicans, see John C. Underwood to Archibald Campbell, 21 Jan. 1859, Archibald Campbell Papers, WVULM, and R. G. Banks to Stephen A. Douglas, 8 Mar. 1861, Box 38, Folder 14, Douglas Papers, UC.

78 *Proceedings*, ed. Reese, 1:45 (16 Feb. 1861); *Richmond Dispatch* reprinted in *Charleston Mercury*, 28 Feb. 1861; *Dispatch*, 13 Apr. 1861; Colin Clarke, of Gloucester County, to Mrs. John Manning, 27 Mar. 1861, Williams-Chesnut-Manning Collection, SCL, for which I am indebted to William W. Freehling. Clarke was deeply disturbed by the demands put forward by western Virginians in the state convention for changes in the tax system. "I cannot pay ad valorem tax on my negro's," he wrote, "I will set them free first. The value of our negros are not what they are *here* but what they are worth in the South. *You* may afford to pay an ad valorem tax, we *cannot*. . . . The whole County is in motion. R. P. Jones, Posey Pope and Mr. Curtis have already written to an agent in New York offering their lands to the Yankees. Fielding Taylor, Nicolson, Backhouse etc. etc. have determined to leave and I must."

79 Wise to J. H. McCue, 14 Mar. 1861, Perry-Martin-McCue Papers, UVA.

80 Richard S. Ellis, Jr., to Charles Ellis, 13 Apr. 1861, Munford-Ellis Family Papers, DU.

81 *Journals and Papers of the Virginia State Convention of 1861*, 1:145–46 (29 Mar.); *Proceedings*, ed. Reese, 3:359–60, 363; *New York Tribune*, 14 Mar. 1861.

82 Letters in JDD, JPL, and Robert Y. Conrad Papers, VHS, all demonstrate that moderates remained in control of the convention until

very late. See also Crofts, "Union Party of 1861 and the Secession Crisis."

83 Ephraim B. Hall to Francis H. Pierpont, 15 Feb. and 22 Mar. 1861, Pierpont Papers, WVULM; Samuel McD. Moore to James D. Davidson, 29 Mar. 1861, in Greenawalt, ed., "Unionists in Rockbridge County," p. 93.

84 2 Apr. 1861, in *MHSP*, 3d ser., 45 (1912): 248.

85 On preparations for this convention, see Shanks, *Secession Movement in Virginia*, p. 202; on the number in attendance, see Ruffin, *Diary*, ed. Scarborough, 2:569 (7 Feb. 1863). Henry G. Latham to George W. Bagby, 26 Mar. 1861, and, for the quotation, F. J. Barnes to Bagby, 30 Mar. 1861, both in the Bagby Family Papers, VHS.

86 See the remarks of Willey on 16 March and of Samuel Woods (a confirmed secessionist and friend of Wise's) on 19 March, in *Proceedings*, ed. Reese, 1:766; 2:51. See also the speech of Mr. Hoffman, of Harrison, "On the Proposition to Exempt from Taxation Young Animals," in *Richmond Enquirer*, 2 Apr. 1860. For additional comments on western grievances, see Lowe, "Republicans, Rebellion, and Reconstruction," pp. 5–7. The westerners' proposals for reform are ignored in Shanks, *Secession Movement in Virginia*.

87 Willey to Francis Pierpont, 26 Mar. 1861, Pierpont Papers, WVULM.

88 *Proceedings*, ed. Reese, 2:17 (18 Mar.); Colin Clarke to Mrs. John Manning, 27 Mar. 1861, Williams-Chesnut-Manning Collection, SCL.

89 See the debate on 18 March, in *Proceedings*, ed. Reese, 2:10–25.

90 Remarks of Ephraim B. Hall, 22 Mar. 1861, in ibid., 2:160–65.

91 Wise, 10 Apr. 1861, in ibid., 3:514; *Richmond Examiner* (sw), 19 Mar. 1861.

92 Willey's remarks, 10 Apr. 1861, in *Proceedings*, ed. Reese, 3:510; Willey's remarks and the relevant roll calls, 11 Apr. 1861, in ibid., 3:525, 590, 601. Details on the public lives of the delegates may be found in Gaines, ed., *Biographical Register of Members of the Virginia State Convention of 1861*.

93 *Proceedings*, ed. Reese, 3:186 (5 Apr.), 309 (8 Apr. 1861).

94 Ibid., p. 308.

95 Jones, *Rebel War Clerk's Diary*, ed. Swiggett, 2:25–26 (22 Apr. 1861).

96 Freehling, "Editorial Revolution," p. 67; *Proceedings*, ed. Reese, 4:28 (16 Apr.).

97 I rely here on the post-facto but detailed and authoritative account in Ruffin, *Diary*, ed. Scarborough, 2:568–71 (7 Feb. 1863).

98 See Wise's comment on the proclamation in *Proceedings*, ed. Reese, 3:759 (15 Apr. 1861); Bear, ed., "Henry A. Wise and the

Campaign of 1873," p. 326; James B. Dorman to James D. Davidson, 16 Apr. 1861, JDD.

99 *Journals and Papers of the Virginia State Convention of 1861*, 1:159–61 (16 Apr.); Siviter, *Recollections of War and Peace*, pp. 224–25.

100 Besides the account in Siviter, *Recollections of War and Peace*, pp. 226–29, see B. H. Wise, *Life of Henry A. Wise*, pp. 274–77; Pickens to Wise (telegram), 17 Apr., Letters Received, Governor's Office, Executive Department, Archives Branch, VSL, Box 421; *New York Tribune*, 17 Apr. 1861.

101 *Proceedings*, ed. Reese, 4:37 (16 Apr. 1861); B. H. Wise, *Life of Henry A. Wise*, p. 277.

102 William H. Parker to Wise, 7 June 1874, WFP/VHS.

103 Hagans, *Brief Sketch of the Erection and Formation of the State of West Virginia*, p. 28.

104 Quoted in B. H. Wise, *Life of Henry A. Wise*, p. 280.

105 Jones, *Rebel War Clerk's Diary*, ed. Swiggett, p. 23 (17 Apr. 1861). On the day Virginia seceded Wise urged Letcher to persuade the Confederate authorities to assault Washington, D.C.—a plan evidently rejected after Senator Mason had advised of its foolhardiness. Wise to Letcher (telegram), 21 Apr. 1861, Mason to Letcher (telegram), 21 Apr. 1861, in Letters Received, Governor's Office, Executive Department, Archives Branch, VSL, Box 422.

Chapter 13

1 Quoted in McWhiney, "Who Whipped Whom?" p. 12, and Lockard, "Unfortunate Military Career of Henry A. Wise," p. 41.

2 Jones, *Rebel War Clerk's Diary*, ed. Swiggett, p. 23 (17 Apr. 1861). "Then was the time," Wise wrote after the war, "for a mediatorial armed neutrality on the part of this State, to say to the North, 'Hold Back!' and to the South, 'give up' their slaves in order that their masters may remain free!" (*Seven Decades of the Union*, p. 278).

3 Jones, *Rebel War Clerk's Diary*, ed. Swiggett, p. 23 (17 Apr. 1861).

4 Telegram, Letters Received, Governor's Office, Executive Department, Archives Branch, VSL, Box 423.

5 Wise to Francis H. Smith, 7 May 1861, Superintendent's Papers, VMI. After the war, in his book *Seven Decades of the Union*, Wise wrote that during his congressional service on the Naval Affairs Committee in the House, Commodore James Barron exhibited before the committee his model of an ironclad war vessel, for which he desired approval. Though the ship was never built, Wise wrote that when the war started he advised General Lee early in May of the

existence of Barron's model. He also stated that the idea for the Confederate States ship *Virginia* (more familiarly known as the *Merrimac*) originated from his proposal. Lee laid Wise's letter before high Confederate officials. It is possible that Secretary of the Navy Stephen R. Mallory saw it. Early in June 1861, Mallory asked officers in his department to design an ironclad. There is no evidence, however, that either he or they followed Wise's advice and worked from Barron's model. See B. H. Wise, *Life of Henry A. Wise*, pp. 316–17; Barton H. Wise to John Mercer Brooke, 18 June 1896, and 28 Mar. 1898, John Mercer Brooke Papers, SHC; Brooke, "The Virginia or Merrimac," pp. 3–34; Porter, *Record of Events in Norfolk County*.

6 Wise to Letcher, 26 May 1861, Letters Received, Governor's Office, Executive Department, Archives Branch, VSL, Box 432.

7 Wise to "The Citizen Soldiers of Virginia," 5 May 1861, C. E. French Papers, MHS; *Kanawha Valley Star*, 4 June 1861; Samuel Cooper to Wise, 6 June 1861, in *OR*, 1st ser., 2:909; Wise to Lt.Col. Charles Ellis Munford, 12 June 1861, Munford-Ellis Family Papers, DU; Lockard, "Unfortunate Military Career of Henry A. Wise," p. 41. Of the ten legions that served in the provisional army of the Confederate States, Wise's was the only one supplied by Virginia (Wallace, *Guide to Virginia Military Organizations*, p. 201).

8 Lockard, "Unfortunate Military Career of Henry A. Wise"; Wallace, *Guide to Virginia Military Organizations*, passim; see also, among many possible examples, H. W. Adams to Wise, 1 Aug. 1861, Eldridge Collection, CSmH.

9 Curry, *House Divided*, p. 142.

10 McClellan to Col. E. D. Townsend (telegram), 1 June 1861, RG 108, NA; Summers to John Letcher, 3 May 1861, and Letcher to Summers, 10 May 1861, "Gov. Letcher's Official Correspondence," *SHSP* 1 (1876): 456–58; George S. Patton to Christopher A. Tompkins, 9 June 1861, Tompkins Family Papers, VHS.

11 Daniel Polsley to Gen. George B. McClellan, 3 June 1861, McClellan Papers, LC; C. B. Hall to McClellan, 24 June 1861, in ibid.; J. J. M. McGinnis to Letcher, 1 May 1861, Letters Received, Governor's Office, Executive Department, Archives Branch, VSL, Box 427.

12 Wise to Gen. Robert E. Lee, 17 July 1861, in *OR*, 1st ser., 2:291.

13 Williams, "New Dominion and the Old," p. 341 and passim; Williams, *West Virginia*, p. 46. For a remarkable recent study that suggests the power of similar influences in determining the loyalties of North Carolina mountain Unionists, see Paludan, *Victims*.

14 James M. H. Beale to Letcher, 29 Apr. 1861, James Hutchinson to Letcher, n.d. (ca. 1 May 1861), and other Letters Received,

Governor's Office, Executive Department, Archives Branch, VSL, Boxes 425, 427; Curry, "McClellan's Western Virginia Campaign of 1861," pp. 87–88.

15 James Hutchinson to Letcher, 1 May 1861, Letters Received, Governor's Office, Executive Department, Archives Branch, VSL, Box 427; William Thompson to Letcher, 3 June 1861, in ibid.; L. S. Burnaugh to Letcher, 5 June 1861, in ibid., Box 434; Curry, *House Divided*, p. 25.

16 James M. Laidly to Letcher, 13 May 1861, Letters Received, Governor's Office, Executive Department, Archives Branch, VSL, Box 432. Results of the 23 May referendum on the secession ordinance are suggestive of general trends, but I have not wanted to rely overly on these results in view of Carl Degler's comments on the intimidation that took place on election day. See *The Other South*, pp. 166–67.

17 Shoen, ed., "Pryce Lewis, Spy for the Union," pp. 28–29; unsigned and incomplete letter (typescript), dated at Charleston, 8 Sept. 1861, complaining of Wise's treatment of J. H. Gosham, in Francis Pierpont Papers, WVULM, Box 1; *OR*, 2d ser., 2:1384–85.

18 2 July 1861.

19 6 July 1861, in the Civil War Scrapbook, Roy Bird Cook Collection, WVULM; Wise to Mary Lyons Wise, 4 July 1861, WFP/VHS.

20 Cox to McClellan, 1 July 1861, McClellan Papers, LC.

21 McClellan to Col. E. D. Townsend (telegram), 1 June 1861, RG 108, NA.

22 "Fellow Citizens" to McClellan, 3 June 1861, Daniel Polsley to McClellan, 3 June 1861, Simeon Rush to McClellan, 4 June 1861, all in McClellan Papers, LC.

23 E. B. Tyler to McClellan, 8 July 1861, and W. J. Smith to McClellan, 10 July 1861, in ibid.

24 Unsigned and undated typescript entitled "Explanation of Why the Kanawha Valley veered toward the South," evidently written by Francis Pierpont, in Pierpont Papers, WVULM, Box 2.

25 Cox to W. S. Rosecrans, 7 Aug. 1861, in *OR*, 1st ser., 51 (pt. 1):440; Wise to Mary Lyons Wise, 23 July 1861, WFP/VHS.

26 Wise to Lee, 1 Aug. 1861, *OR*, 1st ser., 5:766.

27 "Record of the Revolution," undated (early 1862?) and unsigned memoir, probably written by Christopher Q. Tompkins, Tompkins Papers, VHS.

28 Floyd to Lee, 12 Aug. 1861, Lee Papers, VHS; Floyd to Davis, 4 Aug. 1861, *OR*, 1st ser., 51 (pt. 2):213–14.

29 Wise to Samuel Cooper, 31 July 1861, in Wise's Letters Sent, RG 109, chap. 2, vol. 318, NA.

30 See Floyd to Wise, 24 Dec. 1856, Brock Collection, CSmH.

31 I regard the "Record of the Revolution," cited in note 27, as perhaps the finest contemporary memoir dealing with military and political affairs in western Virginia. See also Cox, "McClellan in West Virginia"; Lockard, "Unfortunate Military Career of Henry A. Wise"; Curry, *House Divided*; Freeman, *R. E. Lee*, 1:579–94.

32 Robert Coles to John C. Rutherfoord, 17 Aug. 1861, Rutherfoord Papers, VHS; John Z. H. Scott Memoir, VHS.

33 Wise to Christopher Q. Tompkins, 18 Aug. 1861, Tompkins Papers, VHS; Same to same, 29 Aug. 1861, Barton H. Wise Papers, VHS; Wise to Mary Lyons Wise, 8 Aug. 1861, WFP/VHS.

34 Wise to Col. Francis H. Smith, 7 May 1861, Superintendent's Papers, VMI; Henry A. Wise (his son) to Governor John Letcher, 24 June 1861, Letters Received, Governor's Office, Executive Department, Archives Branch, VSL, Box 436. On 8 July 1861, WFP/VHS, Wise wrote his wife that he never felt so much like a father as before an anticipated action.

35 Lockard, "Unfortunate Military Career of Henry A. Wise," p. 49; Floyd to Leroy P. Walker, 23 Aug. 1861, *OR*, 1st ser., 5:799; Mason Mathews et al., to Jefferson Davis, 19 Sept. 1861, ibid., pp. 864–65; Wise to Mary Lyons Wise, 13 Aug. 1861, WFP/VHS.

36 Floyd to Davis, *OR*, 1st ser., 51 (pt. 2):296. The volume, Correspondence between Generals John B. Floyd and H. A. Wise, July–September, 1861, RG 109, chap. 2, vol. 232, NA, includes all of their exchanges, not only those printed in the *OR*.

37 28 Aug. 1861, Wise Papers, HU.

38 *Richmond Examiner*, 30 Sept. 1861; *Richmond Dispatch*, 1 Oct. 1861.

39 Maddex, *Virginia Conservatives*, p. 23; Shanks, "Conservative Constitutional Tendencies of the Virginia Secession Convention."

40 Taylor, *General Lee*, p. 34.

41 General Orders 106, 25 Sept. 1861, *OR*, 1st ser., 51 (pt. 2):313.

42 Wise had family ties by marriage with the Custis family, from which Lee's wife had come. Years earlier, a sister of Wise's father married into the Custis clan. Wise knew George Washington Parke Custis, the father of Lee's wife, very well and probably had met Lee long before the war. See above, Chapter 5, n. 28.

43 To Judah P. Benjamin, 26 Oct. 1861, *OR*, 1st ser., 5:150–65.

44 To Benjamin, 22 Mar. 1862, *OR*, 4th ser., 1:1015–16.

45 See General Richard C. Gatlin's report, 1 Oct. 1862, *OR*, 1st ser., 4:576.

46 B. H. Wise, *Life of Henry A. Wise*, p. 305.

47 See Wise's voluminous report on operations at Roanoke Island, 21 Feb. 1862, *OR*, 1st ser., 9:122–65.

48 See Wise's report, and James I. Robertson, Jr., "Roanoke Island Expedition," pp. 321–46.

49 Wise's report, and Wise to Jefferson Davis, 13 Feb. 1862, Wise, Letters Sent, RG 109, chap. 2, vol. 318, NA.

50 Quoted in Nevins, *War for the Union*, 2:41n.

51 Wise to Congressman B. S. Gaither, chairman of the committee, 14, 15 Mar. 1862, in Wise, Letters Sent, RG 109, chap. 2, vol. 318, NA; the committee's report is in *OR*, 1st ser., 9:183–91. See also Eaton, *History of the Southern Confederacy*, p. 60.

52 Munford to Gen. William H. Richardson, 23 Apr. 1862, Munford to Wise, 29 Apr. 1862, in Flournoy, ed., *Calendar of Virginia State Papers*, 2:210.

53 Wise to Lee, 29 Apr. 1862, in Wise, Letters Sent, RG 109, chap. 2, vol. 319, NA; Lee to Wise, 30 Apr. 1862, Lee Papers, CHS; Lee to Wise, 7 May 1862, WFP/VHS.

54 Wise to George W. Randolph, 24 Apr. 1862, in Henry A. Wise Combined Service Record, NA.

55 Fleet and Fuller, eds., *Green Mount*, pp. 129–30, 144–46.

56 See Wise's report, 22 Nov. 1862, as well as Wise to George W. Randolph, 12 Sept. 1862, and to Gen. G. W. Smith, 6 Oct. 1862, all in Wise, Letters Sent, RG 109, chap. 2, vol. 319, NA.

57 Wise to Lee, 8 June 1862, Stuart Collection, CSmH; Wise to Gen. James Longstreet, 31 July 1862, in Wise, Letters Sent, RG 109, chap. 2, vol. 319, NA; Col. William Barksdale Tabb to Wise, 18 Feb. 1863, Tabb Letterbook 2, VHS; Wise to Gen. Arnold Elzey, 16 Apr. 1863, *OR*, 1st ser., 18:994.

58 Younger, ed., *Inside the Confederate Government*, p. 102; Freeman, *Lee's Lieutenants*, 3:223–24; Wise to Nat Tyler, 20 Jan. 1863, Box 36, Brock Collection, CSmH.

59 Wise to Col. W. B. Ball, 27 Oct. 1862, in Wise, Letters Sent, RG 109, chap. 2, vol. 319, NA; to Gen. G. W. Smith, 1 Nov. 1862, in ibid.; Harmon, ed., "Letters of Luther Rice Mills," p. 293. Mills served as a lieutenant in Wise's brigade and had a low opinion of his commanding general.

60 Fleet and Fuller, eds., *Green Mount*, pp. 184–85, 280.

61 Robertson and McMurry, eds., *Rank and File*, pp. 115–16; Wise to Gen. John H. Winder, 4 Nov. 1862, in Wise, Letters Sent, RG 109, chap. 2, vol. 319, NA.

62 Pearce to Gen. Samuel W. Melton, 30 Nov. 1862, in Wise, Letters Sent, RG 109, chap. 2, vol. 319, NA; Wise to Gen. Arnold Elzey, 24 Dec. 1862, in ibid., vol. 320; Wise to Pearce, 10 May 1863, in ibid.; Pearce to Capt. E. W. Clapp, 11 Aug. 1863, in ibid., vol. 321.

63 Wise to McKissick, 3 Dec. 1862, in ibid., vol. 320; McKissick to

Wise, 25 Nov. 1862, Eldridge Collection, CSmH.

64 Wise to Gen. P. G. T. Beauregard, 24 Mar. 1864, in Wise, Letters Sent, RG 109, chap. 2, vol. 322, NA. At least two men in his brigade were executed for desertion, however. See RG 109, entry 69, General Order 24, Department of North Carolina and Southern Virginia, NA; Maj. John R. Bagby to his wife, 18 Mar. 1864, Bagby Family Papers, UVA.

65 Wise to Lt. Col. J. C. Councill, 14 Dec. 1862, *OR*, 1st ser., 18:800–801.

66 Wise, "Career of Wise's Brigade," p. 4.

67 Dain, *Disordered Minds*, p. 178.

68 Wise to Gen. Arnold Elzey, 11 Apr. 1863, in Wise, Letters Sent, RG 109, chap. 1, vol. 320, NA.

69 Wise to William Martin, 19 Apr. 1863, Brock Collection, CSmH. The denouement occurred later, when Talbot Sweeney, to whom Wise had given the keys to the institution, undertook to run it without pay. Sweeney was the only Virginia officer of the asylum remaining in the area. He hired several of its former employees and remained in charge until early 1864, aided indispensably by the resources of the United States.

70 Dix to Wise, 28 Apr. 1863, *OR*, 1st ser., 18:664–65; Wise to Dix, 12 May 1863, Eldridge Collection, Box 65, CSmH.

71 Wise to Captain Schultz, 29 Dec. 1863 and to Rev. F. G. Packett, 9 Feb. 1864; unsigned memo, 23 Jan. 1864, Wise to Gen. Thomas Jordan, 18 Feb. 1864, and to Gen. Samuel Cooper, 14 Apr. 1864, all in Wise, Letters Sent, RG 109, chap. 2, vol. 322, NA.

72 On Wise's success at John's Island, see his report, 13 Feb. 1864, *OR*, 1st ser., 35 (pt. 1):144–48, with Beauregard's endorsement dated 17 Feb. But see also Capt. Edward L. Parker to Capt. J. H. Pearce, 23 Feb. 1864, ibid., p. 610; Harmon, ed., "Letters of Luther Rice Mills," p. 295; Maj. John R. Bagby to his wife, 18 Feb. 1864, Bagby Family Papers, VHS.

73 Wise to his wife, 20 Sept. 1863, Henry A. Wise Papers, VHS; Wise to Nat Tyler, 20 Jan. 1863, Brock Collection, CSmH; Maj. John R. Bagby to his wife, 24 Oct. 1863, Bagby Family Papers, VHS.

74 B. H. Wise, *Life of Henry A. Wise*, pp. 331–32. See also the large number of letters exchanged between Henry and Mary Lyons Wise in WFP/VHS, especially Henry's letter of 13 and 14 November 1864 for his vision of peace.

75 Wise to William B. Preston, 30 Apr. 1862, Preston Family Papers, VHS; Richard A. Wise to Mary Lyons Wise, 16 Aug. 1864, Wise to Mary Lyons Wise, 17 July 1862 and 24 Apr. 1864, all in WFP/VHS; Fleet and Fuller, eds., *Green Mount*, p. 302n.

76 Fleet, ed., *Green Mount after the War*, pp. 14, 17, 27; Wise to John

Gadsby Chapman, 13 June 1872, Conrad Wise Chapman Papers, VHS; B. H. Wise, *Life of Henry A. Wise*, pp. 339–340n; J. C. Wise, *Col. John Wise*, p. 187.

77 Wise, *Currency Question*; Receipt from the Confederate States government dated January 1863, in Barton H. Wise Papers, ESHS; Wise to Tyler, 20 Jan. 1863, and to Willie Lyons, 30 Jan. 1863, both in Brock Collection, Box 36, CSmH.

78 Wise, *Currency Question*.

79 Wise, *Letter from Gen. Wise addressed to the Virginia delegation to the Confederate Congress*. Wise urged that no reorganization of the army take place by elections because they destroyed discipline. Instead, he demanded reform of the quartermaster, commissary, and medical departments. He also indicated his support for the views of many other officers who urged such reforms as an end to favoritism in granting leaves and furloughs, a pay increase, and the prohibition of paid substitutes.

80 This discussion is based on the exchange of correspondence among Wise, Garnett, and Davis in November 1863 in the Garnett-Wise Family Papers, SHC. For the "smouching" remark, see Wise to Mary Lyons Wise, 7 Nov. 1863, WFP/VHS.

81 Fleet and Fuller, eds., *Green Mount*, pp. 322, 359; Maj. John R. Bagby to his wife, 25 Mar. 1864, Bagby Family Papers, UVA.

82 Tabb's report, *OR*, 1st ser., 36 (pt. 2):362–64; Dr. J. H. Claiborne to his wife, 14 May 1864, Claiborne Papers, UVA.

83 Freeman, *Lee's Lieutenants*, 3:471–95; Wise to Gen. D. H. Hill, 31 May 1864, *OR*, 1st ser., 36 (pt. 3):859–60, for Wise's conviction, shared by Beauregard, that General Braxton Bragg had indicated his willingness under certain contingencies to advocate the evacuation of Petersburg as early as 16 May. This would, of course, have threatened the Confederate hold on Richmond. As Freeman writes, the entire affair was probably founded on misunderstanding.

84 Kautz Diary and typescript, "Reminiscences of the Civil War," Kautz Papers, LC.

85 Col. Samuel Spear to Gen. Q. A. Gillmore, 18 June 1864, *OR*, 1st ser., 36 (pt. 2):313.

86 I rely here more on the estimate in Livermore, "Failure to Take Petersburg," p. 65, than on Wise, "Career of Wise's Brigade." Livermore points out that Wise received cavalry reinforcements during the day numbering about one thousand troops. Wise's 18 June 1864 letter to his wife reports that he had 2,013 men available on 15 June. On that day and the next, he lost as casualties or captured nine out of the twelve officers above the rank of captain in his brigade.

87 Beauregard, "Four Days of Battle at Petersburg," p. 540, for the quotations. See also Livermore, "Failure to Take Petersburg"; W.

Gordon McCabe, "Defence of Petersburg," pp. 266–68; Bernard, comp. and ed., *War Talks of Confederate Veterans*.

88 *OR*, 1st ser., 36 (pt. 2):316–17; *Richmond Enquirer* clipping in Henry A. Wise Papers, SHC.

89 See Johnson's report of 22 June 1864 and Wise's endorsement in *OR*, 1st ser., 40 (pt. 1):769–71; Cummings, *Yankee Quaker*, pp. 291–92.

90 Harmon, ed., "Letters of Luther Rice Mills," p. 305; Fleet and Fuller, eds., *Green Mount*, p. 350; *OR*, 1st ser., 35 (pt. 1):551.

91 "Resolution of the Officers of the 34th and 46th Regiments" (n.d., but obviously late 1864), WFP/VHS; Wise to Mary E. Garnett, 12 Jan. 1865, Garnett-Wise Family Papers, SHC. In his biography of his grandfather, Barton H. Wise mentions none of these challenges to his authority.

92 *Resolutions of Wise's Brigade*, 1 Feb. 1865, Brock Collection, CSmH; Fleet and Fuller, eds., *Green Mount*, p. 349; John A. Jordan to Mary Ann Jordan, 12 Feb. 1865, Jordan Papers, DU. So far as I have learned, Wise never advocated emancipation in return for service in the Confederate army. On the contrary, he suggested that more slaves be put to work on fortifications and railroads. See letter to his wife, 21 Jan. 1865, WFP/VHS.

93 B. H. Wise, *Life of Henry A. Wise*, p. 366; John Sergeant Wise to Barton H. Wise, 27 Apr. 1898, WFP/VHS.

94 Figures on the numbers of Confederates, by unit, who surrendered with Lee's army may be found in R. A. Brock, "Appomattox Roster"; Schaaf, *Sunset of the Confederacy*, p. 130.

95 Chamberlain, *Passing of the Armies*, pp. 266–69; Cauble, *Proceedings*, p. 165, for the quotation.

96 B. H. Wise, *Life of Henry A. Wise*, pp. 367–69; Meade, *Life and Letters*, 1:17; Meade to Wise, 9 Nov. 1853, George G. Meade Papers, CHS; Meade to Wise, 8 June 1869, WFP/VHS; Campbell, "John Sergeant Wise," p. 13.

97 B. H. Wise, *Life of Henry A. Wise*, pp. 365–66.

Chapter 14

1 Wise to William T. Sutherlin, 27 Apr. 1867, Sutherlin Papers, SHC; clipping from a Memphis newspaper, headed "Resolutions of the Irish Literary Associations of Memphis, A Fund to be Raised to secure him a home," in Henry A. Wise Papers, SHC; Wise to John Loague of the Irish Literary Society of Memphis, 20 Nov. 1868, in *New York Times*, 24 Dec. 1868; Wise to "My Dear Children," 18

May 1865, and to Mary E. Wise, 30 May 1865, in WFP/VHS; Christian, *Richmond*, p. 279.

2 Abbott, ed., "A Southerner Views the South, 1865," pp. 478–79.

3 Wise, "Speech Delivered on July 13, 1866, at Norfolk," in *Richmond Enquirer*, 9 Aug. 1866.

4 See, for example, Wise, *Seven Decades of the Union*, p. 279.

5 Wise in *Richmond Enquirer*, 9 Aug. 1866; Litwack, *Been in the Storm So Long*, p. 196; Wise in *New York Times*, 25 Aug. 1867.

6 Wise, "Address to Dedicate the Stonewall Cemetery."

7 B. H. Wise, *Life of Henry A. Wise*, pp. 373–74; *New York Times*, 31 July 1865.

8 This paragraph is based on a sizable packet of letters and affidavits dealing with John Cropper Wise's claim in Virginia, Assistant Commissioner of the Freedmen's Bureau, Letters Received, RG 105, Box 45, NA, and on John Cropper Wise to General Gordon, 30 May 1865, RG 109, Union Provost Marshal's Files, microcopy 416, NA.

9 Gerteis, *From Contraband to Freedman*, p. 37; Testimony of F. W. Bird before the American Freedmen's Inquiry Commission, RG 94, Letters Received by the Adjutant General's Office, 1861–70, microcopy 619, Roll 200, NA; Census Returns of Colored Population of Princess Anne County, Virginia, RG 105, vol. 403, NA; Swint, *Northern Teacher*, p. 62.

10 Swint, ed., *Dear Ones at Home*, p. 50n.

11 Ibid., p. 79; Wise to an unidentified correspondent, 15 Nov. 1870, newspaper clipping, WFP/VHS; Siviter, *Recollections of War and Peace*, p. 218.

12 William P. Austin to Morton Havens, 21 July 1866; Havens to Gen. Orlando Brown, 25 Feb., 31 Dec. 1867, all in Virginia, Assistant Commissioner of the Freedmen's Bureau, Letters Received, RG 105, Box 45, NA; James N. Croft to Brevet Major [?], 26 Feb. 1868, and to Gen. Orlando Brown, 29 Feb. 1868, in ibid., vol. 477.

13 Receipt for Rolleston, 15 Dec. 1868, signed by Wise, in ibid., Reel 229; PACDB, p. 22, for the sale; J. C. Wise, *Col. John Wise*, p. 22; 1870 Federal Census of Population, M-1074, NA. Land values in Princess Anne remained stable at $14 per acre between 1860 and 1870. See Pressly and Scofield, eds., *Farm Real Estate Values*, p. 43.

14 Gen. Alfred H. Terry to Wise, 1 Sept. 1865, and Gen. James A. Blue to Wise, 28 July 1866, in Barton H. Wise Collection, ESHS.

15 Ellen Wise Mayo to Wise, 25 Sept. 1865, WFP/VHS.

16 Wise later referred to Johnson as a "Sans Culotte" who "stood over" cringing Virginians "like an overseer with a whip in his hand." See Wise to the Republican party of the Third Congressional District of

Virginia, 14 Sept. 1874, Barton H. Wise Papers, VHS(oc).

17 Dorris, *Pardon and Amnesty under Lincoln and Johnson*, pp. 120–21.

18 B. H. Wise, *Life of Henry A. Wise*, p. 376.

19 Freeman, *Lee*, 4:205; Parker, "Why Was Lee Not Pardoned?"

20 Stampp, *Era of Reconstruction*, p. 68; "Olla Podrida" for the quotation.

21 Bear, ed., "Henry A. Wise and the Campaign of 1873," pp. 325–26.

22 Ibid.; Wise in *Richmond Enquirer*, 9 Aug. 1866.

23 Wise in *Richmond Enquirer*, 4 Jan. 1867; Jones, *Army of Northern Virginia Memorial Volume*, p. 31, for the quotation; extracts of a letter from Wise to Gen. U. S. Grant, in *New York Times*, 10 Sept. 1865. Many observers responded to Wise with befuddlement or mistrust, just as they always had. Cf. *New York Times*, 11 Sept. 1865; Strong, *Diary*, ed. Nevins and Thomas, 4:33–34 (11 Sept. 1865); *Tuscaloosa Independent Monitor*, quoted in Trelease, *White Terror*, p. 253.

24 From a letter, 13 Nov. 1870, in a newspaper clipping, WFP/VHS.

25 Swint, ed., *Dear Ones at Home*, p. 211.

26 Ibid., pp. 79, 211.

27 Ambler, *Francis H. Pierpont*, pp. 323–24; Siviter, *Recollections of War and Peace*, p. 219.

28 Bear, ed., "Henry A. Wise and the Campaign of 1873," p. 326.

29 Wise in *New York Times*, 11 Aug., 17 Oct. 1867; B. H. Wise, *Life of Henry A. Wise*, p. 392. See also John H. Gilmer to William T. Sutherlin, 27 Mar. 1867, Sutherlin Papers, SHC; Carter, "Anatomy of Fear," pp. 354–55n; Gay, "Tangled Skein of Romanticism," pp. 133–70; Roark, *Masters without Slaves*, pp. 160, 194.

30 John Sergeant Wise to Henry A. Wise, 1 Mar. 1863, WFP/VHS; Henry A. Wise to Gen. Francis H. Smith, 12 July 1863, Superintendent's Papers, VMI; Henry A. Wise to Mary E. Garnett, 21 Feb. and 18 Oct. 1867, Garnett-Wise Family Papers, SHC.

31 Harriet Haxall Wise to Mary Lyons Wise, 28 Aug. 1868, WFP/VHS.

32 Wise to Mary Garnett, 21 Feb. 1867, Garnett-Wise Family Papers, SHC.

33 Wise to J. Harvie Lacy, 5 May 1868, WFP/VHS.

34 Wise to Henry Wise Garnett, 11 May 1870, Garnett-Wise Family Papers, VHS.

35 *Report and Journal of Proceedings of the Joint Commissioners to Adjust the Boundary Line*; *Opinions and Award of Arbitrators on the Maryland and Virginia Boundary Line*; *Richmond Enquirer and Examiner*, 13 Mar. 1873. Virginia, General Assembly, *Senate Jour-*

nal, 16 March 1874, reports that Wise earned $3,329.24 for his services and expenses as a member of the boundary commission.

36 Reminiscences of Colonel Thomas S. Hudson in the *Crisfield* (Md.) *Times*, 28 Sept. 1912, clipping in WFP/VHS; Wise to John H. Gillet, 21 Aug. 1875, in ibid.; "Olla Podrida" for the quotation.

37 B. H. Wise, *Life of Henry A. Wise*, pp. 416–17; Wise, "Tribute to Hon. James Murray Mason"; Wise to the Republican party of the Third Congressional District of Virginia, 14 Sept. 1874, Barton H. Wise Papers, VHS(oc); Christian, "Reminiscences of Some of the Dead," pp. 20–21, for the quotation. In his eulogy on Mason, Wise wrote that while in the Senate he was never distinguished by any great speech or measure, but an asterisk in the version published in the Southern Historical Society Papers denotes that Mason authored the Fugitive Slave Act of 1850.

38 Pollard, *Lee and His Lieutenants*, pp. 558–70; Wise to Messrs. E. B. Treat & Co., 8 Oct. 1867 (typescript), Barton H. Wise Papers, VHS(oc); *New York Times*, 2 Nov. 1867; Wise, "Career of Wise's Brigade"; Wise, *Speech of General H. A. Wise, War Roll, Roll of Honorary Members, and Present Roll of the Company* [Richmond Light Infantry Blues].

39 Wise in *Richmond Enquirer*, 9 Aug. 1866; Wise in *New York Times*, 25 Aug. 1867; Bradley T. Johnson to Wise, 22 May 1869, Miscellaneous Manuscripts, MaHS; Wise, "Address in Behalf of the Female Orphan Asylum of Richmond, 30 January 1866," clipping, WFP/VHS, for the quotations.

40 Maddex, *Virginia Conservatives*, pp. 46–66; Perman, *Reunion without Compromise*, pp. 277–93.

41 Schofield, *Forty-Six Years in the Army*, pp. 394–405; Alderson, "Influence of Military Rule and the Freedmen's Bureau on Reconstruction in Virginia," pp. 210–13; H. H. Wells to Schofield, 17 Feb. 1869, Schofield Papers, LC; B. H. Wise, *Life of Henry A. Wise*, p. 381; Siviter, *Recollections of War and Peace*, p. 185.

42 Maddex, *Virginia Conservatives*, pp. 46–85; Withers, *Autobiography of an Octogenerian*, pp. 273–75.

43 Alderson, "Influence of Military Rule and the Freedmen's Bureau on Reconstruction in Virginia," p. 179; Lowe, "Republicanism, Rebellion and Reconstruction," p. 269.

44 Siegel, "New South in the Old," pp. 219–30, 242–44, 250.

45 Wise's letters on "The New Movement," addressed to R. R. Collier of Petersburg, appeared in the *Richmond Enquirer and Examiner*, 19–23 Jan. 1869; clipping from the *Virginian Pilot and Norfolk Landmark*, 20 Aug. 1933, WFP/VHS, for the quotation; Maddex, *Virginia Conservatives*, pp. 72–73; B. H. Wise, *Life of Henry A.*

Wise, p. 396; Jonathan Worth to William A. Graham, 9 Mar. 1867, William A. Graham Typescripts, SHC.

46 Wise, in *Richmond Enquirer and Examiner*, 23 Jan. 1869.

47 See, esp., Wise in ibid., 20 Jan. 1869. See also Bear, ed., "Henry A. Wise and the Campaign of 1873," p. 330.

48 Bear, ed., "Henry A. Wise and the Campaign of 1873," pp. 328–30; Wise to the Republican party of the Third Congressional District, 14 Sept. 1874, Barton H. Wise Papers, VHS(oc).

49 Tyler, "Virginia Principles"; Maddex, *Virginia Conservatives*, p. 217.

50 Wise, *Seven Decades of the Union*, pp. 139–45, 230–32.

51 Ibid., pp. 32, 47.

52 Wise to Robert Tyler, 19 July 1875, Tyler Papers, LC; Wise to an unidentified correspondent, 28 Oct.?, Wise Papers, LC; Charles W. Lindsay, president of J. B. Lippincott Company of Canada, to the author, 7 July 1978. Even the Richmond newspapers carried only brief and cursory reviews. For examples of newspaper comment on Wise's illnesses, see *Newark* (N.J.) *Daily Advertizer*, 31 Jan. 1874, *New York Tribune*, 9 Mar. 1874.

Holst, Schouler, McMaster, and Rhodes all wrote with a Northern bias and manifested very little respect for Wise. Rhodes, whose history of the United States commenced in 1850, cited *Seven Decades of the Union* only once. He tended to accept the plausibility of Wise's recruitment of John C. Calhoun for Tyler's cabinet. In writing his multivolume social history of antebellum America, McMaster appears never to have consulted *Seven Decades*. Holst despised Wise throughout his *Constitutional and Political History of the United States*. Nonetheless, in volume 2 he accepted Wise's version of politics during the Tyler administration with evangelistic fidelity. In volume 4 of his *History of the United States of America under the Constitution*, Schouler cited *Seven Decades* more extensively than any of these other authorities, though usually with biting sarcasm. Schouler failed, for example, to understand how Tyler's son—Lyon G. Tyler, who spent a lifetime at the College of William and Mary glorifying his father's memory—could have relied so much on *Seven Decades* without realizing Wise's anxiety to promote his own views and influence at the expense of the former president's (4:373n.).

53 Perhaps the wheel had begun to turn even earlier. The *New York Times* in a very brief review of *Seven Decades* praised Wise's "understated" defense of states-rights but censured his "grandiloquent" style (26 Jan. 1872).

54 Wise to Cooley, 5 Feb. 1872, Cooley Papers, UM; Paludan, *Covenant with Death*, pp. 249, 265–73.

55 Wagstaff, "Call Your Old Master—'Master,' " p. 334; *Richmond Enquirer*, 4 Jan. 1867.

56 16 Oct. 1867, in *Southern Planter*, n.s., 1 (Nov. 1867):579. For certain of Wise's practical proposals, relating to swine raising, see his 1870 letters to Benjamin Stoddert Ewell, president of the College of William and Mary, Ewell Papers, WM.

57 Wise to William T. Sutherlin, 8 Apr. 1867, Sutherlin Papers, SHC; Bear, ed., "Henry A. Wise and the Campaign of 1873," pp. 336–37; Wise to Thomas H. Ellis, 18 Mar. 1866, Henry A. Wise Papers, UVA; *Richmond Enquirer*, 4 Jan. 1867; Wise, *Address before the Literary Societies of Roanoke College*.

58 See the correspondence between Wise and Lewis Schaefer in the Barton H. Wise Papers, VHS(oc); Wise to Nahum Capen, 9 Feb. 1868, Wise Papers, DU, for the quotation.

59 *Richmond Enquirer*, 4 Jan. 1867; Wise to Nathaniel B. Meade, 6 Jan. 1867, in *Richmond Enquirer*, 9 Jan. 1867; Maddex, *Virginia Conservatives*, pp. 233–55; Wise to Daniel M. Barringer, 20 Mar. 1872, Barringer Papers, SHC; Bear, ed., "Henry A. Wise and the Campaign of 1873," p. 334. Virginia's 1868 constitution raised the legal rate of interest to 12 percent from the 6 percent advocated by Wise.

60 *Richmond Enquirer*, 4 Jan. 1867; Wise to William T. Sutherlin, 8 Apr. 1867, Sutherlin Papers, SHC; Wise to H. Bolton, 26 Nov. 1867, Miscellaneous Papers, VHS; Maddex, *Virginia Conservatives*, p. 37.

61 Wise, "Address before the Virginia Horticultural and Pomological Society," p. 598.

62 "Address of Major William T. Sutherlin Delivered before the Mechanics Association of Danville," 11 Mar. 1867, in *Richmond Enquirer*, 8 Apr. 1867; *Richmond Whig* (sw), 8 Mar. 1870.

63 "Gov. Wise's Address," *Southern Planter*, n.s., 1 (Dec. 1867): 678, 682.

64 Maddex, *Virginia Conservatives*, pp. 178–83; Roark, *Masters without Slaves*, p. 153.

65 Wise to George W. Jones, 7 Oct. 1872, Barton H. Wise Papers, VHS(oc); Wise to William J. Adelott, in *Maryland School Journal* 2 (May 1876):369–71; Bear, ed., "Henry A. Wise and the Campaign of 1873," p. 333.

66 Perman, *Reunion without Compromise*; Wise to Underwood, 19 Mar. 1872, Underwood Papers, LC; undated newspaper clippings in John C. Underwood Scrapbook, pp. 223, 227, Underwood Papers, LC.

67 For evidence on the preceding two paragraphs, see *Richmond Whig* (sw), 18 Mar., 12, 30 Apr. 1870; Christian, *Capitol Disaster*; Mad-

dex, *Virginia Conservatives*, pp. 88–90; Chesson, *Richmond after the War*, pp. 112–14; undated newspaper clippings, John C. Underwood Scrapbook, pp. 245, 247, Underwood Papers, LC.

68 Christian, *Capitol Disaster*; Anne J. W. Hobson to Wise, 28 Apr. 1870, WFP/VHS.

69 See the comments by Virginia Representative James H. Platt, in *CG*, 42, 2, Appendix 197 (6 Apr. 1872).

70 *New York Times*, 1 July 1872; Wise to Col. John Mosby, 15 June 1872, in ibid., 2 July 1872; Speech of Mr. William H. Grey of Arkansas in *Proceedings of the National Union Republican Convention*, p. 19 (5 June 1872).

71 *New York Times*, 25 July, 19 Sept. 1873; Wise to James Barron Hope, 29 May 1873, in *Norfolk Virginian*, 5 June 1873; Dorris, *Pardon and Amnesty*, p. 376; Rawley, "General Amnesty Act of 1872."

72 Foner, "Thaddeus Stevens, Confiscation and Reconstruction," p. 179; Wise to Wilson, 6 July 1874, Henry Alexander Wise Papers, VHS, for the quotation.

73 Goode, *Recollections of a Lifetime*, p. 109; *New York Times*, 5 May 1876; U.S. Congress, House of Representatives, *Papers in the Matter of James H. Platt, Jr., vs. John Goode, Jr.*, 44, 1, no. 65, pp. 1–55.

74 Fleet, ed., *Green Mount after the War*, p. 190n.

75 John Sergeant Wise to John James Henry Wise, 10 Sept. 1876, WFP/VHS.

76 Wise to Edward W. Hubard, 13 Sept. 1872, Hubard Family Papers, SHC.

77 Wise to Dr. A. Y. P. Garnett, 27 Jan. 1873, Garnett-Wise Family Papers, SHC; Wise to Jones, 7 Oct. 1875 (typescript), Barton H. Wise Papers, VHS(oc).

78 Wise to Lt. S. H. Bowman, 20 July 1876, in *New York Times*, 15 Aug. 1876; Wise to Tyler, 19 July 1875, Tyler Papers, LC; B. H. Wise, *Life of Henry A. Wise*, p. 422. On the themes of integrity and wisdom in old age, see the classic essay by Erikson, "Reflections on Dr. Borg's Life Cycle."

79 Undated clipping, Henry A. Wise Papers, SHC.

Bibliography

For their courtesy in permitting use of private collections which they control, I thank Brig. Gen John Letcher (USMC Ret.), of Lexington, Virginia, John Letcher Papers, and Mr. Lucas Phillips, of Leesburg, Virginia, John Janney Papers.

Primary Sources

Manuscripts

American Antiquarian Society, Worcester, Massachusetts
  Henry Alexander Wise Correspondence
Auburn University, Department of Archives, Auburn, Alabama
  Samford-Wise Papers
John Hay Library, Brown University, Providence, Rhode Island
  Eli Thayer Papers
Buffalo and Erie County Historical Society
  Millard Fillmore Papers (microfilm)
Chicago Historical Society
  John Brown Papers
  Robert E. Lee Papers
  George G. Meade Papers
  Rousseau Papers
University of Chicago Library
  Stephen A. Douglas Papers
Robert Muldrow Cooper Library, Clemson University, Clemson, South Carolina
  John C. Calhoun Papers
Manuscript Department, Duke University Library, Durham, North Carolina
  Angus R. Blakey Papers
  George Booker Papers
  Alexander Robinson Boteler Papers
  James Buchanan Papers
  William Henry Lytton Earle Bulwer, Baron Dalling, and Bulwer Papers
  Campbell Family Papers

Clement Claiborne Clay Papers
John Esten Cooke Papers
James D. Davidson Papers
Jubal Anderson Early Papers
J. Milton Emerson Journal
Charles J. Faulkner, Jr., Papers
John B. Floyd Papers
Tazewell M. Howard Papers
John A. Jordan Papers
John Letcher Papers
Munford-Ellis Family Papers
James N. Riddle Papers
Hanson A. Risley Papers
John Rutherfoord Letters and Papers
Langhorne Scruggs Papers
William Patterson Smith Papers
Alexander Hamilton Stephens Papers
Nathaniel Beverley Tucker Papers
Hugh Lawson White Papers
Henry Alexander Wise Papers

Eastern Shore Historical Society, Onancock, Virginia
Barton H. Wise Papers
Henry Alexander Wise Papers

R. W. Woodruff Library for Advanced Studies, Emory University, Atlanta
Waddy Thompson Letters

Essex Institute, Salem, Massachusetts
Henry Alexander Wise Papers

Houghton Library, Harvard University, Cambridge, Massachusetts
Autograph File
Henry Alexander Wise Papers

Haverhill Historical Society, Haverhill, Massachusetts
Benjamin Perley Poore Papers

Henry E. Huntington Library, San Marino, California
Brock Collection
Eldridge Collection
Harbeck Collection
A. H. Joline Collection
James Ewell Brown Stuart Collection
Henry Alexander Wise Papers

Knoxville–Knox County Public Library, Knoxville, Tennessee
Miscellaneous Manuscripts, McClung Historical Collection

Library of Congress, Manuscripts Division, Washington, D.C.
Frank M. Anderson Papers

Alexander William Armour Collection
John Bell Papers
Breckinridge Family Papers
John Brown Papers
William M. Burwell Papers
Campbell-Preston-Floyd Papers
George Washington Campbell Papers
Jonathan Cilley Papers
Henry Clay Papers
D. H. Conrad Papers
Richard K. Crallé Papers
John J. Crittenden Papers
Caleb Cushing Papers
Jefferson Davis Papers
Stephen A. Douglas Papers
Jubal Early Papers
Thomas Ewing Papers
John Forney Papers
Douglas Southall Freeman Papers
Galloway-Markoe-Marcy Papers
George W. Gordon Papers
James Henry Hammond Papers (microfilm)
John Hay Papers
Reverdy Johnson Papers
August V. Kautz Papers
William L. Marcy Papers
George B. McClellan Papers (microfilm)
Franklin Pierce Papers
William Cabell Rives Papers
Edmund Ruffin Diary
George N. Sanders Papers
Schofield Papers
A. R. Shepherd Papers
Alexander H. Stephens Papers
Alexander H. H. Stuart Papers
John Tyler Papers
John C. Underwood Papers and Scrapbook
Henry Alexander Wise Papers

Maryland Historical Society, Baltimore
Anna Ella Carroll Papers, Ms. 1224
Civil War Collection, Ms. 1860
William H. DeCourcy Wright Papers, Ms. 1467

Massachusetts Historical Society, Boston
Bancroft Papers

John Brown Papers
C. E. French Papers
Andrew Hunter Papers
Miscellaneous Personal Papers
Michigan Historical Collections, Bentley Historical Library, University of Michigan
Thomas M. Cooley Papers
National Archives, Washington, D.C.
RG 45: U.S. Congress, House of Representatives, Bill Books
RG 59: Henry A. Wise Despatches, Brazil, 17 February 1844 to 3 November 1847 (microfilm)
RG 60: Attorney General's Papers, Letters Received, Virginia, 1814–70. Vol. 1
RG 84: Records of the Foreign Service Posts of the Department of State
RG 94: Records of the Adjutant General's Office
American Freedmen's Inquiry Commission Records, microcopy 619, Roll 200
Letters Received Relating to John Brown's Raid at Harpers Ferry
RG 105: Bureau of Refugees, Freedmen, and Abandoned Lands
Census Returns of Colored Population of Princess Anne County, Virginia, Vol. 403
Virginia, Assistant Commissioner of the Freedmen's Bureau, Letters Received, Reel 229, Box 45, Vol. 477
RG 108: Records of the Headquarters of the Army, 1821–1903
Entry 25, Telegrams Received, February 1861 to March 1862
RG 109: Union Provost Marshal's Files, microcopy 416
War Department Collection of Confederate Records
Civil War Records of Henry A. Wise
Letters Sent, 1861–64, Chap. 2, Vols. 318–22
Special Orders Issued, 1861–64, Chap. 2, Vols. 323–24
Miscellaneous Record Book, 1861–63, Chap. 2, Vol. 325
Correspondence between Generals John B. Floyd and H. A. Wise, July–September 1861, Chap. 2, Vol. 232
RG 217: Pay and Mileage Books
Henry A. Wise, Combined Service Record
Federal Census of Population, Slave Schedules, and Census of Agriculture, Accomac and Princess Anne Counties, Virginia, 1840–70 (microfilm)
Federal Records Center, Suitland, Maryland
RG 21: Manumission and Emancipation Record for the District of Columbia, 6 vols.
New Hampshire Historical Society, Concord
John Hatch George Collection

New York Historical Society, New York
Daniel Ullman Papers
Henry Alexander Wise Correspondence
Southern Historical Collection, Wilson Library, University of North Carolina at Chapel Hill
Daniel Moreau Barringer Papers
Leonidas Baugh Papers
Thomas Bragg Papers
John Mercer Brooke Papers
Garnett-Wise Family Papers (microfilm)
William A. Graham Typescripts
J. DeB. Hooper Papers
Hubard Family Papers
John Beauchamp Jones Papers
Christopher G. Memminger Papers
William Porcher Miles Papers
Kenneth Rayner Papers
Abraham Rencher Papers
William Thomas Sutherlin Papers
Littleton Waller Tazewell Papers
Tucker-Randolph Family Papers
White-Wellford-Taliaferro-Marshall Family Papers
L. N. Whittle Papers
Henry A. Wise Papers (microfilm)
Ohio Historical Society, Columbus
Joshua R. Giddings Papers
Special Collections, Penfield Library, State University of New York, Oswego
Millard Fillmore Papers
Historical Society of Pennsylvania, Philadelphia
James Buchanan Papers
Dreer Collection, including the John Brown volume
Etting Papers
Simon Gratz Autograph Collection
Society Collection
Rush Rhees Library, University of Rochester, Rochester, New York
William H. Seward Papers
South Caroliniana Library, University of South Carolina, Columbia
Williams-Chesnut-Manning Collection
John Smith Preston Papers
Manuscripts Section, Tennessee State Library, Nashville
John P. Heiss Papers
Virginia Historical Society, Richmond
Aylett Family Papers (Mss 1AY445b)

Bagby Family Papers (Mss 1B1463b)
Conrad Wise Chapman Papers (Mss 2C3663b)
William Garnett Chisolm Papers (Mss 1C4485a)(typescript)
Holmes Conrad Papers (Mss 1C7637a)
Robert Y. Conrad Papers (Mss 1C7638a)
John Cropper Papers (Mss 1C8835a)
Garnett Family Papers (Mss 1G1875a)
Hugh Blair Grigsby Papers (Mss 1G8782b)
Robert Edward Lee Papers (Mss 3L515676)
Mason Family Papers, 1805–86 (Mss 1M3816a)
Miscellaneous Personal Papers
Preston Family Papers (Mss P9267d703)
Edmund Ruffin Papers (Mss 1R8385a)
Rutherfoord Family Papers (Mss 1R93376)
John Z. H. Scott Memoir (Mss 2Sco843al)(copy of a copy)
William Barksdale Tabb Letterbooks (Mss 5:2T1127:1–2)
Tompkins Family Papers (Mss 1T5996)
Barton H. Wise Papers (old catalog)
Henry Alexander Wise Papers, 1858–74 (Mss 2W7544c)
John Cropper Wise Papers (Mss 2W7545b)
Wise Family Papers, formerly in possession of John Sergeant Wise
Wise Family Papers (old catalog)(typescript)

Virginia Military Institute Archives, Lexington
Superintendent's Papers

Archives Branch, Virginia State Library, Richmond
Accomac County Deed Books (microfilm), Land and Personal Property Books, Order Books and Will Books (microfilm)
Campbell-Brown Collection (Accession 20799)
Executive Letter Books, 1848–61 (microfilm)
Executive Papers (John Brown, 1859)
Legislative Petitions, Portsmouth, Norfolk County
Letters Received, Governor's Office, Executive Department, 1860–61 (John Letcher)
Letters Received, Governor's Office, Executive Department, 1856–59 (Henry A. Wise)
Federal Census of Population (microfilm), Slave Schedules, and Census of Agriculture, Accomac and Princess Anne Counties, Virginia, 1840–60
John S. Gillet Papers (Accession 22407)
Robert Mercer Taliaferro Hunter Papers (Accession 25064)
James Lawson Kemper Papers (Accession 24692)
George Wythe Munford Papers (Accession 21731)
Princess Anne County Deed Book (microfilm)

Rejected Revolutionary Claims File
Henry Alexander Wise Papers (Accession 24724)
University of Virginia Library, Charlottesville
Additional Alexandria City Papers (#7146, -a)
Bagby Family Papers (microfilm)(#4445)
James Barbour Papers (#1486)
Baugh Family Papers (#9308)
Dr. John Herbert Claiborne Letters (#3633)
Henry Clay Collection (#5694)
John Cropper Papers (#6711)
John Murray Dunmore Papers, 1776–1846 (#7879)
Garnett Family Papers (#38-45)
Garrett Family Papers (#9974, 9974a)
Grinnan Family Papers (#49, 2118)
Atcheson L. Hench Collection (#6435)
Hubard Family Papers, 1749–1951 (#8039, -a, -b)
Robert Mercer Taliaferro Hunter Papers, 1826–60 (#6662)
John Daniel Imboden Papers (#38-23)
James Lawson Kemper Papers (#4098)
John Letcher Papers (#6687)(microfilm)
John B. Minor Papers, 1843–92 (#3114)
Miscellaneous Personal Papers, 1808–81 (#6394)
Perry-Martin-McCue Papers (#6806, -a, -b)
Alexander Hugh Holmes Stuart Papers (#345)
Taliaferro Family Papers (#4370, -a, -b)(microfilm)
John R. Thompson Papers (#38-705)
Washington and Jefferson College Library, Washington, Pennsylvania
Miscellaneous Papers
West Virginia and Regional History Collection, West Virginia University Library, Morgantown
Jonathan M. Bennett Papers
Gideon D. Camden Papers
Archibald Campbell Papers
John Floyd Papers
William Gaston Caperton Papers
Oliver P. Chitwood Papers
Roy Bird Cook Collection, including the Civil War Scrapbook
Charles James Faulkner Papers
Francis H. Pierpont Papers
Waitman T. Willey Papers
Manuscripts Department, E. G. Swem Library, College of William and Mary, Williamsburg, Virginia
Benjamin Stoddert Ewell Papers

Tucker-Coleman Papers
Tyler Family Papers
State Historical Society of Wisconsin, Madison
James D. Davidson Papers, McCormick Collection (including typescripts)

Public Documents

Compendium of the Enumeration of the Inhabitants and Statistics of the United States . . . from the Returns of the Sixth Census. Washington, D.C.: U.S. Government Printing Office, 1841.

Debates and Proceedings of the Convention Which Assembled at Little Rock, January 7, 1868, under the Provisions of the Act of Congress of March 2nd, 1867, and the Acts of March 23 and July 19, 1867, Supplementary Thereto, to Form a Constitution for the State of Arkansas. Little Rock, 1868.

Flournoy, Henry W., Wm. P. Palmer, and Sherwin McRae, eds. *A Calendar of Virginia State Papers and Other Manuscripts . . . Preserved in the Capital at Richmond*. 11 vols. Richmond: Virginia State Library, 1875–93.

Journal of the Acts and Proceedings of a General Convention of the State of Virginia, Assembled at Richmond, on Wednesday, the Thirteenth Day of February, Eighteen Hundred and Sixty-One. Richmond: Wyatt M. Elliott, 1861.

Journals and Papers of the Virginia State Convention of 1861. 3 vols. Richmond: Wyatt M. Elliott, 1861.

The Memorial of Sundry Citizens of the County of Halifax to the Virginia Legislature, Praying for the Establishment of Free Schools in the State. Richmond: Macfarlane and Fergusson, 1854.

Opinions and Award of Arbitrators on the Maryland and Virginia Boundary Line. Washington, D.C.: McGill and Witherow, 1877[?].

Peters, Richard, ed. *The Public Statutes at Large of the United States of America from the Organization of the Government in 1789, to March 3, 1845*. Vol. 2. Boston: Little, Brown, 1862.

Proceedings of the National Union Republican Convention Held at Philadelphia, June 5 & 6, 1872. Reported by Francis H. Smith. Washington, D.C.: Gibson Brothers, 1872.

Proceedings of the Virginia State Convention of 1861, February 13–May 1. Edited by George H. Reese. 4 vols. Richmond: Virginia State Library, 1965.

Register of Debates and Proceedings of the Virginia Reform Convention. W. G. Bishop, reporter. Richmond: R. H. Gallaher, 1851.

*Report and Journal of Proceedings of the Joint Commissioners to Adjust *the Boundary Line of the States of Maryland and Virginia*. Annapolis: Wm. T. Iglehart & Co., 1874.

U.S. Census Office. *Population of the United States in 1860; Compiled from the Original Returns of the Eighth Census*. Washington, D.C.: U.S. Government Printing Office, 1864.

———. *The Seventh Census of the United States*. Washington, D.C.: U.S. Government Printing Office, 1853.

U.S. Congress. House of Representatives. *Journal of the Select Committee to Investigate the Executive Departments*. 24th Cong., 2d sess., no. 194, 1837.

———. *Papers in the Matter of James H. Platt, Jr., vs. John Goode, Jr.*. 27 January 1876. 44th Cong., 1st sess., Miscellaneous Document 65, 1876.

———. *Report of the Committee of Investigation on the Subject of the Defalcation of Samuel Swartout and Others, and the Correctness of the Returns of Collectors and Receivers of the Public Money*. 25th Cong., 3d sess., no. 313, 1839.

———. *Report of the Minority of the Select Committee to Revise the Rules and Orders of the House*, 27 January 1844. 28th Cong., 1st sess., no. 3, 1844.

———. *Report of the Select Committee on the Agent-Deposit Banks, 1 March 1837*. 24th Cong., 2d sess., no. 193, 1837.

———. *Report of the Select Committee on Alleged Corruptions, 16 June 1860*. [The Covode Investigation.] 36th Cong., 1st sess., no. 648, 1860.

———. *Report of the Select Committee Appointed to Investigate the Causes Which Led to the Death of the Hon. Jonathan Cilley, 21 April 1838*. 25th Cong., 2d sess., no. 825, 1838.

———. *Report of the Select Committee of Five, on the Alleged Hostile Organization against the Government within the District of Columbia, 14 February 1861*. 36th Cong., 2d sess., no. 79, 1861.

———. Senate. *Executive Documents*. 4 vols. Vol. 4, no. 28. 30th Cong., 1st sess., 1848.

———. *Report of the Select Committee Appointed to Inquire into the Late Invasion and Seizure of the Public Property at Harper's Ferry, 15 June 1860*. [The Mason Committee Report.] 36th Cong., 1st sess., no. 278, 1860.

Virginia. General Assembly. *Acts, 1855–1861*.

———. *Governor's Communication on the Subject of the Erection of Monuments on Independence Square, in Philadelphia*. House Document 42, 1855–56.

———. *Governor's Messages I, II, and III*. House Document 1, 1857–58.

———. *Governor's Messages I and II*. House Document 1, 1859–60.

______. *Report of the Chairman and Minority of the Committee of Finance of the House of Delegates of Virginia.* House Document 62, 1857–58.

______. *Senate Journal*, 1872–74. Richmond, 1872–74.

The War of the Rebellion: A Compilation of Official Records of the Union and Confederate Armies. 70 vols. Washington, D.C.: U.S. Government Printing Office, 1880–1901.

Published Correspondence and Speeches, Contemporary Articles, Reminiscences, Books, and Diaries

Abbot, Martin, ed. "A Southerner Views the South, 1865: Letters of Harvey M. Watterson." *Virginia Magazine of History and Biography* 68 (1960): 478–89.

Abbott, John Stevens Cabot. *South and North; or, Impressions Received during a Trip to Cuba and the South.* New York: Abbey & Abbot, 1860.

Adams, Charles F., ed. *Memoirs of John Quincy Adams, Comprising Portions of His Diary from 1795 to 1848.* 12 vols. Vols. 7–12. Philadelphia: Lippincott, 1874–77.

Adams, Nehemiah. *A South-Side View of Slavery; or, Three Months at the South, in 1854.* Boston: T. R. Marvin and B. B. Mussey & Co., 1854.

An Address to the Citizens of Accomac County, from the Jackson Correspondence Committee. Henry A. Wise, Chairman. 27 August 1832. Snow Hill, Md.: [1832?].

Ambler, Charles H., ed. "Correspondence of Robert M. T. Hunter, 1826–1876." *Annual Report of the American Historical Association for the Year 1916.* 2 vols. Vol. 1. Washington, D.C.: U.S. Government Printing Office, 1916.

An American. *The Sons of the Sires; A History of the Rise, Progress, and Destiny of the American Party, and Its Probable Influence on the Next Presidential Election, to Which Is Added a Review of the Letter of the Hon. Henry A. Wise, against the Know-Nothings.* Philadelphia: Lippincott, Grambo & Co., 1855.

Anderson, Osborne P. *A Voice from Harpers Ferry.* 1861. Reprint. Freeport, N.Y.: Books for Libraries Press, 1972.

Bartlett, David V. G. *Presidential Candidates: Containing Sketches, Biographical, Personal, and Political of Prominent Candidates for the Presidency in 1860.* New York: A. B. Burdick, 1959.

Bassett, John Spencer, ed. *The Correspondence of Andrew Jackson.* 6

vols. Washington, D.C.: Carnegie Institution of Washington, 1926–31.

Beach, Mrs. Arthur G. "An Example of Political Oratory in 1855." *Ohio Archaeological and Historical Quarterly* 39 (1930): 673–82.

Bear, James A., Jr., ed. "Henry A. Wise and the Campaigns of 1873: Some Letters from the Pages of James Lawson Kemper." *Virginia Magazine of History and Biography* 62 (1954): 320–42.

Boney, F. N. "Governor Letcher's Candid Correspondence." *Civil War History* 10 (1964): 167–80.

Botts, John M. *The Great Rebellion: Its Recent History, Rise, Progress, and Disastrous Failure. The Political Life of the Author Vindicated.* New York: Harper and Bros., 1866.

———. *The Nebraska Question.* Washington, D.C.: J. T. & L. Towers, 1854.

———. *Speech at Powhatan Court House, Virginia, June 15, 1850.* [Richmond ? 1850].

———. *To the Whole Whig Party of the United States.* Washington, D.C.: J. & G. S. Gideon, 1848.

———. *Union or Disunion: The Union Cannot and Shall Not Be Dissolved, Mr. Lincoln Not an Abolitionist.* [Lynchburg, Va.? 1860].

Boucher, Chauncey S., and Robert P. Brooks, eds. "Correspondence Addressed to John C. Calhoun, 1837–1849." *Annual Report of the American Historical Association for the Year 1929.* 2 vols. Vol. 2. Washington, D.C.: U.S. Government Printing Office, 1930.

Boyett, Gene W., ed. "A Letter from Archibald Yell to Henry A. Wise, July 12, 1841." *Arkansas Historical Quarterly* 32 (Winter 1973): 336–41.

Brown, William H. *A Portrait Gallery of Distinguished American Citizens.* Hartford, Conn.: E. B. & E. C. Kellogg, 1845.

Bryce, J. C. *An Address, to the People of Accomac and Northampton Counties, in Reply to the Letter of Hon. Henry A. Wise, on Know Nothingism.* [Snow Hill, Md., 1855].

Christian, George L. *The Capitol Disaster: A Chapter of Reconstruction in Virginia.* Richmond: Richmond Press, n.d. [1915?].

———. "Reminiscences of Some of the Dead of the Bench and Bar of Richmond." *Virginia Law Register* 14 (1909): 1–53.

Clarke, James Freeman. *The Rendition of Anthony Burns: Its Causes and Consequences, A Discourse on Christian Politics.* Boston: Crosby, Nichols, & Co., 1854.

Clay, Cassius M. *Speech before the Young Men's Republican Central Union of New York, 24 October 1856.* [New York? 1856?].

Colton, Calvin, ed. *The Private Correspondence of Henry Clay.* New York: A. S. Barnes and Co., 1855.

Conway, Moncure Daniel. *Free Schools in Virginia: A Plea of Education, Virtue, and Thrift, vs. Ignorance, Violence, and Poverty*. Fredricksburg, Va., 1850.

Correspondence between Lydia Maria Child, and Gov. Wise and Mrs. Mason, of Virginia. Anti-Slavery Tracts 1, New Series. New York: American Anti-Slavery Society, 1860.

Dabney, G. E. "Education in Virginia." *Southern Literary Messenger* 7 (1841): 631–37.

DeBow, James D. B. *The Interest in Slavery of the Southern Non-slaveholders*. Charleston, S.C.: Presses of Evans & Cogswell, 1860.

———. *Statistical View of the United States*. Washington, D.C.: U.S. Government Printing Office, 1854.

Dew, Thomas R. *Review of the Debate in the Virginia Legislature of 1831 and 1832*. 1832. Reprint. Westport, Conn.: Negro Universities Press, 1970.

Douglas, Stephen A. *Letters*. Edited by Robert W. Johannsen. Urbana: University of Illinois Press, 1961.

Dr. Daniel Drake's Letters on Slavery to Dr. John C. Warren, of Boston, Reprinted from the National Intelligencer, April 3, 5, and 7, 1851, with an Intro. by Emmet Field Hornine. New York: Schuman's, 1940.

Drew, Thomas, ed. *The John Brown Invasion: An Authentic History of the Harper's Ferry Tragedy*. Boston: James Campbell, 1860.

Dumond, Dwight, ed. *Southern Editorials on Secession*. New York: Century Co., 1931.

Eby, Cecil D., ed. "The Last Hours of the John Brown Raid: The Narrative of David H. Strother." *Virginia Magazine of History and Biography* 73 (1965): 169–77.

"Education in the Southern and Western States." *Southern Literary Messenger* 11 (1845): 603–7.

"The Eli Thayer Invasion," *Southern Planter* 17 (May 1857): 303–6.

Elliott, E. N., comp. *Cotton Is King, and Pro-Slavery Arguments: Comprising the Writings of Hammond, Harper, Christy, Stringfellow, Hodge, Bledsoe, and Cartwright on This Important Subject*. 1860. Reprint. New York: Negro Universities Press, 1968.

Fitzhugh, George. *Cannibals All! or, Slaves without Masters*. Edited by C. Vann Woodward. Cambridge, Mass.: Harvard University Press, 1960.

———. "Disunion within the Union." *DeBow's Review* 28 (January 1860): 1–7.

———. *Sociology for the South, or the Failure of Free Society*. Richmond: A. Morris, 1854.

Fleet, Betsy, ed. *Green Mount after the War: The Correspondence of Maria Louise Wacker Fleet and Her Family, 1865–1900*. Charlottesville: University Press of Virginia, 1978.

Fleet, Betsy, and J. D. P. Fuller, eds. *Green Mount: A Virginia Plantation Family during the Civil War: Being the Journal of Benjamin Robert Fleet and Letters of His Family*. Lexington: University Press of Kentucky, 1962.

Flournoy, Thomas S. *Address, Delivered at the Second Annual Exhibition of the Union Agricultural Society of Virginia and North Carolina, 25 October 1855*. Petersburg, Va.: Lewellen & Marks, 1855.

Foote, Henry S. *A Casket of Reminiscences*. Washington, D.C.: Chronicle Publishing Company, 1874.

Forney, John. *Anecdotes of Public Men*. 2 vols. New York: Harper and Brothers, 1873–81.

Garnett, Muscoe R. H. *Speech on the State of the Union: House of Representatives, 16 January 1861*. Washington, D.C.: McGill & Witherow, 1861.

———. *The Union, Past and Future: How It Works, and How to Save It*. Charleston, S.C.: Walker and James, 1850.

Garrison, George P., ed. "Diplomatic Correspondence of the Republic of Texas." *Annual Report of the American Historical Association for the Year 1908*. 2 vols. Vol. 2. Washington, D.C.: U.S. Government Printing Office, 1908.

Goode, John. *Recollections of a Lifetime*. New York: Neale Publishing Co., 1906.

Goodloe, Daniel R. *The Southern Platform: or, Manual of Southern Sentiment on the Subject of Slavery*. Boston: John P. Jennett Co., 1858.

"Gov. Letcher's Official Correspondence." *Southern Historical Society Papers* 1 (1876): 455–62.

Greenawalt, Bruce S., ed. "Unionists in Rockbridge County: The Correspondence of James Dorman Davidson." *Virginia Magazine of History and Biography* 73 (1965): 78–102.

Hambleton, James P., ed. *A Biographical Sketch of Henry A. Wise, with a History of the Political Campaign in Virginia in 1855*. Richmond: J. W. Randolph, 1856.

Hammond, James H. *Speech Delivered at Barnwell Court House, October 29, 1858*. Charleston, S.C.: Walker Evans, 1858.

Harmon, George D., ed. "Letters of Luther Rice Mills—A Confederate Soldier." *North Carolina Historical Review* 4 (1927): 285–310.

Hawthorne, Nathaniel. "Biographical Sketch of Jonathan Cilley." *United States Magazine and Democratic Review* 3 (September 1838): 69–76.

Hazlitt, William. *Lectures on the Dramatic Literature of the Age of Elizabeth*. New York: Wiley and Putnam, 1845.

Helper, Hinton R. *The Impending Crisis of the South: How to Meet It*. Edited by George M. Fredrickson. Cambridge, Mass.: Harvard University Press, 1968.

Hinton, Richard J. *John Brown and His Men*. 1894. Reprint. New York: Arno Press, 1968.
Hunt, Gaillard, ed. *The Writings of James Madison, Comprising His Public Papers and His Private Correspondence, Including Numerous Letters and Documents Now for the First Time Printed*. 9 vols. New York: G. P. Putnam's Sons, 1900–1910.
Hunter, Martha T. *A Memoir of Robert M. T. Hunter*. Washington, D.C.: Neale Publishing Co., 1903.
Hunter, Robert M. T. *Address before the Democratic Association of Richmond, October 1, 1852*. Richmond: Ritchies and Dunnavant, 1852.
Hunton, Eppa. *Autobiography*. Richmond: William Byrd Press, 1933.
Jameson, J. Franklin, ed. "Correspondence of John C. Calhoun." *Annual Report of the American Historical Association for the Year 1889*. 2 vols. Vol. 2. Washington, D.C.: U.S. Government Printing Office, 1900.
Jefferson, Thomas. *Notes on the State of Virginia*. Edited with introduction and notes by William Peden. Chapel Hill: University of North Carolina Press, 1955.
"John Brown's Raid at Harper's Ferry: An Eyewitness Account by Charles White." Edited by Rayburn S. Moore. *Virginia Magazine of History and Biography* 67 (1959): 387–95.
Jones, John B. *A Rebel War Clerk's Diary at the Confederate States Capital*. Edited by Howard Swiggett. 2 vols. New York: Old Hickory Bookshop, 1935.
Knight, Edgar W., ed. *A Documentary History of Education in the South before 1860*. 5 vols. Chapel Hill: University of North Carolina Press, 1949–53.
The Life and Death of Sam in Virginia. By a Virginian. Richmond: Published for the Author, A. Morris [attributed by some to Henry A. Wise, by others to William Gardner].
The Life, Trial & Execution of Captain John Brown, Known as "Old Brown of Ossawatomie," with a Full Account of the Attempted Insurrection at Harper's Ferry. New York: Robert M. Dewitt, 1860.
McDowell, James, Jr. *Speech of James McDowell, Jr., of Rockbridge, upon the "Slave Question," Delivered in the House of Delegates of Virginia, on Saturday, the 21st, January, 1832*. Charlottesville, 1832.
Meade, George. *The Life and Letters of George Gordon Meade*. 2 vols. New York: Charles Scribner's Sons, 1913.
Memoirs and Services of Three Generations [of the Cilley Family]. Rockland, Me.: Courier Gazette, 1909.
"Mr. Henry A. Wise and the Cilley Duel." *United States Magazine and Democratic Review* 10 (May 1842): 482–87.

Nevins, Allan, ed. *The Diary of Philip Hone, 1828–1851*. 2 vols. New York: Dodd, Mead, 1936.

Newton, Willoughby. *Virginia and the Union: An Address, before the Literary Societies of the Virginia Military Institute*. Richmond: Macfarlane and Fergusson, 1858.

"Notes and Documents: 'Sir, This Is Not the End of It': The Mobile *Register* Interviews John Brown." Edited by Ralph Brown Draughon, Jr. *Alabama Review* 27 (1974): 152–55.

"Objections to Col. Cocke's Proposed Donation to the University of Virginia." *Southern Planter* 18 (1858): 3–6.

"Olla Podrida Our Jumble of Sense and Nonsense." *Nineteenth Century* 1 (November 1869): 492.

Olmsted, Frederick Law. *A Journey in the Seaboard Slaves States, with Remarks on Their Economy*. New York: Dix and Edwards, 1856.

"On Public Education in Virginia." *Southern Literary Messenger* 13 (1847): 685–89.

Opinions of Hon. Henry A. Wise, upon the Conduct and Character of James K. Polk, as Speaker of the House of Representatives, with other "Democratic" Illustrations. [Washington, D.C.?, 1844?].

The Past, the Present, and the Future of our Country: Interesting and Important Correspondence between Opposition Members of the Legislature of Virginia and Hon. John M. Botts, January 17, 1860. Richmond: Whig Book and Job Office, 1860.

Phillips, Ulrich B., ed. "The Correspondence of Robert Toombs, Alexander H. Stephens, and Howell Cobb." *Annual Report of the American Historical Association for the Year 1911*. 2 vols. Vol. 2. Washington, D.C.: U.S. Government Printing Office, 1913.

Pollard, Edward. *Lee and His Lieutenants: Comprising the Early Life, Public Services, and Campaigns of General Robert E. Lee and His Companions in Arms, with a Record of Their Campaigns and Heroic Deeds*. New York: E. B. Treat & Co., 1867.

Poore, Benjamin Perley. *Perley's Reminiscences of Sixty Years in the National Metropolis*. 2 vols. Philadelphia: Hubbard Brothers, 1886.

Prentiss, George L., ed. *A Memoir of S. S. Prentiss*. 2 vols. New York: Scribners, 1879.

Pryor, Mrs. Roger A. *My Day: Reminiscences of a Long Life*. New York: Macmillan, 1909.

Quaife, Milo M., ed. *The Diary of James K. Polk during His Presidency, 1845 to 1849*. 4 vols. Chicago: Published for the Chicago Historical Society by A. C. McClurg & Co., 1910.

Rayner, Kenneth. *Reply to the Manifesto of Hon. Henry A. Wise*. Washington, D.C.: American Organ Office, 1855.

Resolutions of Wise's Brigade. 1 February 1865. [n.d., n.p.]

Robertson, James I. "The Roanoke Island Expedition: Observations of a Massachusetts Soldier." *Civil War History* 12 (1966): 321–46.

Ross, Alexander M. *Memoirs of a Reformer, 1832–1892*. Toronto: Hunter, Rose & Co., 1893.

Ruffin, Edmund. *Address to the Virginia State Agricultural Society, on the Effects of Domestic Slavery on the Manners, Habits and Welfare of the Agricultural Population of the Southern States, and the Slavery of Class to Class in the Northern States, 16 December 1852*. Richmond: P. D. Bernard, 1853.

———. *African Colonization Unveiled*. Washington, D.C.: Lemuel Towers, 1859.

———. *The Diary of Edmund Ruffin*. Edited by William Kauffman Scarborough. 2 vols. Vol. 1, *Toward Independence*. Vol. 2, *The Years of Hope*. Library of Southern Civilization. Baton Rouge: Louisiana State University Press, 1972, 1976.

———. "The Effects of High Prices of Slaves." *DeBow's Review* 25 (June 1859): 647–57.

———. *The Political Economy of Slavery; or, The Institution Considered in Regard to Its Influence on Public Wealth and the General Welfare*. Washington, D.C.: Lemuel Towers, 1860.

———. *Slavery and Free Labor Described and Compared*. N.p. [1860?].

Ruffner, Henry. *Address to the People of West Virginia: Shewing that Slavery Is Injurious to the Public Welfare, and That It May be Gradually Abolished, without Detriment to the Rights and Interests of Slaveholders*. Lexington, Va.: R. C. Noel, 1847.

Rutherfoord, John Coles. *Speech Delivered in the House of Delegates of Virginia, 1st March 1858, on the Bill, Authorizing a Loan to the Orange and Alexandria Railroad Company*. [Richmond, 1858].

———. *Speech on the Removal from the Commonwealth of the Free Colored Population, February 18, 1853*. Richmond: Ritchies and Dunnavant, 1853.

Ryland, Robert. *The American Union: An Address Delivered before the Alumni Association of the Columbian College, D.C., June 23, 1857*. Richmond: H. K. Ellyson, 1857.

Sabine, Lorenzo. *Notes on Duels & Dueling, Alphabetically Arranged, with a Preliminary Historical Essay*. Boston: Crosby, Nichols, & Company, 1855.

Schofield, John M. *Forty-Six Years in the Army*. New York: Century Co., 1897.

Scott, Nancy N., ed. *A Memoir of Hugh Lawson White, with Selections from his Speeches and Correspondence*. Philadelphia: J. B. Lippincott, and Co., 1856.

Seward, William Henry. *The Dangers of Extending Slavery, and the*

Contest and the Crisis. Washington, D.C.: Republican Association, 1856.

Shanks, Henry T., ed. *The Papers of Willie P. Mangum*. 4 vols. Raleigh: North Carolina State Historical Commission, 1955.

Slaughter, Phillip G. *The Virginian History of African Colonization*. Richmond: Macfarlane and Fergusson, 1855.

Smith, W. A. *Lectures on the Philosophy and Practice of Slavery, as Exhibited in the Institution of Domestic Slavery in the United States, with the Duties of Masters to Slaves*. Edited by Thomas O. Summers. Nashville: Stevenson and Evans, 1856.

J.J.S. [Joseph J. Speed]. *A Letter from a Gentleman of Baltimore, to His Friend in the State of New York, on the Subject of Slavery*. Baltimore: Sherwood & Co., 1841.

Stringfellow, Thornton. *A Brief Examination of Scripture Testimony on the Institution of Slavery, in an Essay, First Published in the Religious Herald and Republished by Request, with Remarks on a Review of the Essay*. Richmond: Office of the Religious Herald, 1841.

Strong, George Templeton. *Diary*. Edited by Allan Nevins and Milton Halsey Thomas. 4 vols. New York: Macmillan, 1952.

Strother, David H. "The Late Invasion at Harper's Ferry." *Harper's Weekly* 3 (5 November 1859): 712–14.

Sunderland, Laroy. *Anti-Slavery Manual, Containing a Collection of Facts and Arguments on American Slavery*. 1834. Reprint. New York: Negro Universities Press, 1969.

Sutherlin, William T. "Address Delivered before the Mechanics Association of Danville." 11 March 1867. *Richmond Enquirer*, 8 April 1867.

Swint, Henry L., ed. *Dear Ones at Home: Letters from Contraband Camps*. Nashville: Vanderbilt University Press, 1966.

Taylor, Walter H. *General Lee: His Campaigns in Virginia, 1861–1865, with Personal Reminiscences*. Brooklyn: Braunworth & Co., 1906.

Thornwell, James H. *The Rights and Duties of Masters: A Sermon Preached at the Dedication of a Church, Erected in Charleston, S.C., for the Benefit and Instruction of the Coloured Population*. Charleston, S.C.: Walker and James, 1850.

———. *The State of the Country: An Article Republished from the Southern Presbyterian Review*. Columbia, S.C.: Southern Guardian Steam-Power Press, 1861.

Thucydides. *The Peloponnesian War*. Translated and edited by Rex Warner. Baltimore: Penguin Books, 1954.

Torrence, Clayton, ed. "From the Society's Collections: Letters of Mrs. Ann (Jennings) Wise to Her Husband, Henry A. Wise." *Virginia Magazine of History and Biography* 58 (1950): 492–515.

Tucker, Henry St. George. *Commentaries on the Laws of Virginia, Comprising the Substance of a Course of Lectures Delivered to the Win-*

chester Law School. 2 vols. Winchester, Va.: At the Office of the Winchester Republican, 1836–37.

Tucker, Nathaniel Beverley. *Prescience: A Speech Delivered in the Southern Convention, Nashville, April 13, 1850*. Richmond: West and Johnson, 1862.

Upshur, Abel P. *Speech upon the Subject of the Basis of Representation*. N.p., n.d. [1830].

"Virginia Statistics." *Southern Planter* 17 (1857): 486–87.

Walmsley, James E., ed. "The Change of Secession Sentiment in Virginia." *American Historical Review* 31 (1925–26): 82–101.

"The Wealth, Resources, and Hopes of Virginia [Excerpts from the letter of Gov. Wise to E. Lacouture]." *DeBow's Review* 23 (July 1857): 58–70.

Weld, Theodore Dwight. *American Slavery As It Is: Testimony of a Thousand Witnesses*. New York: American Anti-Slavery Society, 1839.

Weston, George Melville. *The Progress of Slavery in the United States*. Washington, D.C.: Published by the Author, 1857.

Wheaton, N. S. *A Discourse on St. Paul's Epistle to Philemon; Exhibiting the Duty of Citizens of the Northern States in Regard to the Institution of Slavery; Delivered in Christ Church, Hartford; December 22, 1850*. Hartford, Conn.: Case, Tiffany and Company, 1851.

Wilson, Henry. *Speech on the Territorial Slave Code, January 25, 1860*. N.p. [1860?].

Wilson, John Lyde. *The Code of Honor; or, Rules for the Government of Principals and Seconds in Duelling*. Charleston, S.C.: James Phynney, 1858.

Wise, Henry A. "Address at the Inauguration of the Equestrian Statue of George Washington, February 22, 1858." *Southern Literary Messenger* 26 (April 1858): 242–44.

———. *Address before the Literary Societies of Roanoke College, Salem, Virginia, June 17, 1873*. Baltimore: J. D. Ehlers & Co., 1873.

———. "Address before the Virginia Horticultural and Pomological Society at Its First Exhibition at Richmond, October 16, 1867." *Southern Planter*, n.s., 1 (November 1867): 577–604.

———. *Address before the Virginia Mechanics Institute*. Richmond: Ritchies and Dunnavant, 1857.

———. "Address in Behalf of the Female Orphan Asylum of Richmond." January 30, 1866. Newspaper clipping, WFP/VHS.

———. "Address Prepared for the Memorial Association at Winchester, Va., to Dedicate the Stonewall Cemetary." *Richmond Enquirer*, 4 January 1867.

———. *Argument of the Hon. Henry A. Wise and William Selden, Esq., in Favor of the Payment of the East Florida Claims Arising from the*

Ninth Article of the Treaty of 1819 between the United States and Spain. Washington, D.C.: W. H. Moore, 1853.

———. "The Career of Wise's Brigade, 1861–5: An Address Delivered by General Henry A. Wise, near Cappahoosic, Gloucester County, Virginia, about 1870." *Southern Historical Society Papers* 25 (1897): 1–22.

———. *The Currency Question: Letter of Gen. Henry A. Wise to Hon. J. E. Holmes, of South Carolina, November 11, 1863*. [Charleston, S.C.?, 1863].

———. *The Lecompton Question: Gov. Wise's Tammany, Philadelphia and Illinois Letters, Together with Letters to Charles W. Russell, Esq., by a Virginia Democrat*. [Richmond, 1858].

———. *Letter from Gen. Wise Addressed to the Virginia Delegation to the Confederate Congress . . . Recommending Certain Regulations for the Army, January 3, 1864*. [Richmond, 1864?].

———. "Oration, at Lexington, 4th July, 1856." *Southern Literary Messenger* 23 (July 1856): 1–19.

———. *Seven Decades of the Union: The Humanities and Materialism, Illustrated by a Memoir of John Tyler, with Reminiscences of Some of His Great Contemporaries. The Transition State of This Nation—Its Dangers and Their Remedy*. Philadelphia: Lippincott, 1872.

———. *Speech at Louisa Court House, November 16, 1839*. Richmond: John S. Gallaher, 1839.

———. *Speech Delivered at the Free School Celebration in the County of Northampton, July 4, 1850*. Baltimore: Bull and Tuttle, 1850.

———. "Speech Delivered on July 13, 1866, at Norfolk, on the Subject of Rebuilding and Repairing the Churches of the South, Dilapidated by the War." *Richmond Enquirer*, 9 August 1866.

———. *Speech of Gen. H. A. Wise, War Roll, Roll of Honorary Members, and Present Roll of the Company* [The Richmond Light Infantry Blues]. Richmond: Clemmitt & Jones, 1874.

———. *Speech on the Basis Question, Delivered in the Virginia Reform Convention, on Wednesday, Thursday, Friday, Saturday, Monday, April 23, 24, 25, 26, and 28, 1851* [incomplete]. Richmond: R. H. Gallaher, 1851. Henry A. Wise Papers, SHC.

———. *Territorial Government and the Admission of New States into the Union*. Richmond, 1859.

———. "A Tribute to the Hon. James Murray Mason." *Southern Historical Society Papers* 25 (1897): 1–22.

Wise, John Sergeant. *The End of an Era*. Boston: Houghton, Mifflin and Co., 1900.

———. *Recollections of Thirteen Presidents*. New York: Doubleday, Page & Co., 1906.

Withers, Robert Enoch. *Autobiography of an Octogenarian*. Roanoke, Va.: Stone Printing and Mfg. Co. Press, 1907.
Younger, Edward, Jr., ed. *Inside the Confederate Government: The Diary of Robert Garlick Hill Kean*. New York: Morrow, 1957.

Newspapers

Abingdon (Va.) *Democrat*, 1856
Alexandria (Va.) *Gazette and Public Advertizer*, 1855, 1860
Arkansas Gazette (Little Rock), 1958
Baltimore Sun, 1859
Charleston (S.C.) *Mercury* (daily and semiweekly), 1855, 1856, 1860–61
Charlestown (Va.) *Independent Democrat* (weekly), 1859
Clarksburg (Va.) *Register*, 1856–68
Fairmont (Va.) *True Virginian*, 1856–58
Freeman: A National Colored Weekly Newspaper (Indianapolis), 1888
Jackson Semi-Weekly Mississippian, 1855
Kanawha (Va.) *Valley Star*, 1861
Madisonian (daily and semiweekly, Washington, D.C.), 1841–44
Nashville (Tenn.) *Republican*, 1836
National Anti-Slavery Standard (weekly, New York), 1856–60
National Era (weekly, Washington, D.C.), 1855–60
National Intelligencer (Washington, D.C.), 1836–42, 1859
Newark (N.J.) *Daily Advertizer*, 1874
New York Herald, 1855–61
New York Times, 1852, 1854, 1859–61, 1865–76
New York Tribune, 1843, 1854, 1856, 1857, 1859–61, 1874
Niles National Register (weekly, Baltimore), 1834–48
North Carolina Evening Standard (semiweekly), 1856
Philadelphia (Pa.) *Public Ledger*, 1860
Raleigh (N.C.) *Register* (weekly), 1856
Richmond (Va.) *Dispatch*, 1861
Richmond (Va.) *Enquirer* (daily and semiweekly), 1833–61
Richmond (Va.) *Enquirer and Examiner*, 1873
Richmond (Va.) *Examiner* (daily and semiweekly), 1851, 1854–56, 1861
Richmond (Va.) *Penny Post*, 1855
Richmond (Va.) *Whig* (daily, weekly, and semiweekly), 1835–44, 1850–51, 1855–61, 1870
Savannah (Ga.) *Republican*, 1855
Shepherdstown (Va.) *Register* (weekly) 1859–60
South (Richmond), 1857–58
Southern Argus (Norfolk,Va.), 1855, 1860–61

Union (Washington, D.C.), 1848
United States Telegraph (Washington, D.C.), 1835–36
Washington (D.C.) *Globe*, 1835–42
Wellsburg (Va.) *Herald* (weekly), 1860
Wheeling (Va.) *Intelligencer*, 1857–59

Secondary Sources

Books and Articles

Abbott, Richard H. "Yankee Farmers in Northern Virginia, 1840–1860." *Virginia Magazine of History and Biography* 76 (1968): 56–66.

Abel, Annie H., and Frank J. Klingberg, *A Side-Light on Anglo-American Relations, 1839–1858*. Lancaster, Pa.: Lancaster Press, for the Association for the Study of Negro Life and History, Inc., 1927.

Abele, Rudolph von. *Alexander H. Stephens: A Biography*. 1946. Reprint. Westport, Conn.: Negro Universities Press, 1971.

Ambler, Charles H. *Francis H. Pierpont: Union War Governor of Virginia and Father of West Virginia*. Chapel Hill: University of North Carolina Press, 1937.

———. *Sectionalism in Virginia from 1776–1861*. 1910. Reprint. New York: Russell and Russell, 1964.

———. *Thomas Ritchie: A Study in Virginia Politics*. Richmond: Bell Book and Stationery Co., 1913.

Anderson, James D. "Aunt Jemima in Dialectics: Genovese on Slave Culture." *Journal of Negro History* 61 (1976): 99–114.

Auchampaugh, Philip G. *James Buchanan and His Cabinet on the Eve of Secession*. 1926. Reprint. Boston: J. S. Canner, 1965.

———. *Robert Tyler: Southern Rights Champion, 1847–1866: A Documentary Study Chiefly of Antebellum Politics*. Duluth, Minn.: H. Stein, 1934.

Barker, Eugene C. *The Life of Stephen F. Austin*. Austin: Texas State Historical Society, 1949.

Barnes, Gilbert Hobbs. *The Anti-Slavery Impulse, 1830–1844*. New York: D. Appleton-Century, 1930.

Barney, William L. *The Road to Secession: A New Perspective on the Old South*. New York: Praeger, 1972.

———. *The Secessionist Impulse: Alabama and Mississippi in 1860*. Princeton: Princeton University Press, 1974.

Barry, Joseph. *The Strange Story of Harpers Ferry with Legends of the Surrounding Country*. Martinsburg, W.Va.: Thompson Brothers, 1903.

Bartlett, Irving H., and C. Glenn Cambor. "The History and Psychodynamics of Southern Womanhood." *Women's Studies* 2 (1974): 9–24.

Bateman, Fred, and Thomas Weiss. *A Deplorable Scarcity: The Failure of Industrialization in the Slave Economy*. Chapel Hill: University of North Carolina Press, 1981.

Bean, William G. "An Aspect of Know-Nothingism—The Immigrant and Slavery." *South Atlantic Quarterly* 23 (1924): 319–34.

______. "John Letcher and the Slavery Issue in Virginia's Gubernatorial Contest of 1858–1859." *Journal of Southern History* 20 (1954): 22–49.

______. "The Ruffner Pamphlet of 1847: An Anti-Slavery Aspect of Virginia Sectionalism." *Virginia Magazine of History and Biography* 61 (1953): 260–82.

Beauregard, P. G. T. "Four Days of the Battle at Petersburg." In *Battles and Leaders of the Civil War*, edited by Robert Underwood Johnson and Clarence Clough Buel. 4 vols. 4:540–44. 1887–88. Reprint. New York: Thomas Yoseloff, 1956.

Beeman, Richard R. *The Old Dominion and the New Nation, 1788–1801*. Lexington: University Press of Kentucky, 1972.

Bemis, Samuel F. *John Quincy Adams and the Union*. New York: Knopf, 1956.

Benson, Lee. *Toward the Scientific Study of History: Selected Essays*. Philadelphia: J. B. Lippincott, 1972.

Berlin, Ira. *Slaves without Masters: The Free Negro in the Antebellum South*. New York: Pantheon, 1974.

Bernard, George S., comp. and ed. *War Talks of Confederate Veterans*. Petersburg, Va.: Fenn & Owen, 1892.

Bernstein, Barton J. "Southern Politics and Attempts to Reopen the African Slave Trade." *Journal of Negro History* 51 (1966): 16–35.

Bestor, Arthur. "State Sovereignty and Slavery: A Reinterpretation of Proslavery Constitutional Doctrine, 1846–1860." *Journal of the Illinois State Historical Society* 44 (1961): 117–80.

Bethell, Leslie. *The Abolition of the Brazilian Slave Trade: Britain, Brazil and the Slave Trade Question, 1807–1869*. Cambridge, Eng.: Cambridge University Press, 1970.

______. "The Mixed Commissions for the Suppression of the Transatlantic Slave Trade in the Nineteenth Century." *Journal of African History* 7 (1966): 79–93.

Boney, F. N. *John Letcher of Virginia: The Story of Virginia's Civil War Governor*. University, Ala.: University of Alabama Press, 1966.

Boorstin, Daniel J. *The Americans: The National Experience*. New York: Random House, 1965.

Booth, Alan R. "The United States African Squadron, 1843–1861." In

Boston University Papers in African History, edited by Jeffrey Butler, 1:77–117. Boston: Boston University Press, 1964.

Boyer, Richard O. *The Legend of John Brown: A Biography and a History*. New York: Knopf, 1973.

Brant, Irving. *James Madison: Commander in Chief, 1812–1836*. Indianapolis: Bobbs-Merrill, 1961.

Brock, R. A. "The Appomattox Roster: A List of the Paroles of the Army of Northern Virginia Issued at Appomattox Court House on April 9, 1865." *Southern Historical Society Papers* 15 (1887): 1–487.

Brooke, John Mercer. "The Virginia or Merrimac." *Southern Historical Society Papers* 19 (1891): 3–34.

Brooks, George E., Jr. *Yankee Traders, Old Coasters, and African Middlemen: A History of American Legitimate Trade with West Africa in the Nineteenth Century*. Brookline, Mass.: Boston University Press, 1970.

Brown, Richard H. "The Missouri Crisis, Slavery and the Politics of Jacksonianism." *South Atlantic Quarterly* 65 (1966): 55–72.

Brugger, Robert J. *Beverley Tucker: Heart over Head in the Old South*. Baltimore: Johns Hopkins University Press, 1978.

Carter, Dan T. "The Anatomy of Fear: The Christmas Day Insurrection Scare of 1865." *Journal of Southern History* 42 (1976): 345–64.

Cauble, Frank P. *The Proceedings Connected with the Surrender of the Army of Northern Virginia, April, 1865*. Appomattox Court House National Historical Park, 1962. Revised 1975.

Chalmers, Leonard. "Fernando Wood and Tammany Hall: The First Phase." *New York Historical Society Quarterly* 52 (October 1978): 379–402.

Chamberlain, Joshua L. *The Passing of the Armies: An Account of the Final Campaign of the Army of the Potomac, Based upon Personal Reminiscences of the Fifth Army Corps*. New York: G. P. Putnam's Sons, 1915.

Chandler, Julian A. C. *Representation in Virginia*. Baltimore: Johns Hopkins University Press, 1896.

Channing, Steven A. *Crisis of Fear: Secession in South Carolina*. New York: Charles Scribner's Sons, 1970.

Chesson, Michael B. *Richmond after the War, 1865–1890*. Richmond: Virginia State Library, 1981.

Chitwood, Oliver Perry. *John Tyler: Champion of the Old South*. 1939. Reprint. New York: Russell and Russell, 1964.

Christian, William Asbury. *Richmond: Her Past and Present*. Richmond: L. H. Jenkins, 1912.

Cole, Arthur Charles. *The Whig Party in the South*. 1913. Reprint. Gloucester, Mass.: Peter Smith, 1962.

Cooper, William J., Jr. *The South and the Politics of Slavery, 1828–1856*. Baton Rouge: Louisiana State University Press, 1978.

Cox, Jacob D. "McClellan in West Virginia." In *Battles and Leaders of the Civil War*, edited by Robert Underwood Johnson and Clarence Clough Buel. 4 vols. 1:126–48. 1887–88. Reprint. New York: Thomas Yoseloff, 1956.

______. *Military Reminiscences of the Civil War*. 2 vols. New York: Charles Scribner's Sons, 1900.

Craven, Avery. *The Coming of the Civil War*. 2d ed. rev. Chicago: University of Chicago Press, 1957.

______. *Soil Exhaustion as a Factor in the Agricultural History of Virginia and Maryland, 1606–1860*. Urbana: University of Illinois Press, 1926.

Crenshaw, Ollinger. "The Psychological Background of the Election of 1860 in the South." *North Carolina Historical Review* 19 (1942): 260–79.

______. *The Slave States in the Presidential Election of 1860*. 1945. Reprint. Gloucester, Mass.: Peter Smith, 1969.

______. "The Speakership Contest of 1859–1860: John Sherman's Election a Cause of Disruption." *Mississippi Valley Historical Review* 29 (December 1942): 323–38.

Crofts, Daniel W. "The Union Party of 1860 and the Secession Crisis." *Perspectives in American History* 11 (1977–78): 327–78.

Crouthamel, James L. *James Watson Webb: A Biography*. Middletown, Conn.: Wesleyan University Press, 1969.

Cummings, Charles M. *Yankee Quaker, Confederate General: The Curious Career of Bushrod Rust Johnson*. Rutherford, N.J.: Fairleigh Dickinson University Press, 1971.

Curry, Richard O. *A House Divided: A Study of Statehood Politics and the Copperhead Movement in West Virginia*. Pittsburgh: University of Pittsburgh Press, 1964.

______. "McClellan's Western Virginia Campaign of 1861." *Ohio History* 71 (1962): 83–96.

Curtin, Philip D. *The Atlantic Slave Trade: A Census*. Madison: University of Wisconsin Press, 1969.

Curtis, James C. *The Fox at Bay: Martin Van Buren and the Presidency, 1837–1841*. Lexington: University Press of Kentucky, 1970.

Dain, Norman. *Disordered Minds: The First Century of Eastern State Hospital in Williamsburg, Virginia, 1766–1866*. Williamsburg: Colonial Williamsburg Foundation, Distributed by the University Press of Virginia, 1970.

Dawidoff, Robert. *The Education of John Randolph*. New York: Norton, 1979.

Degler, Carl N. *Neither Black nor White: Slavery and Race Relations in Brazil and the United States*. New York: Macmillan, 1971.

———. *The Other South: Southern Dissenters in the Nineteenth Century*. New York: Harper & Row, 1974.

Dew, Charles B. "Disciplining Slave Iron Workers in the South: Coercion, Conciliation, and Accommodation." *American Historical Review* 79 (April 1974): 393–418.

———. "Who Won the Secession Election in Louisiana?" *Journal of Southern History* 36 (1970): 18–32.

Dilthey, Wilhelm. *Pattern and Meaning in History: Thoughts on History and Society*. Edited by H. P. Rickman. New York: Harper Torchbooks, 1962.

Dodd, Donald S., and Wynelle S. Dodd. *Historical Statistics of the South, 1790–1970*. University, Ala.: University of Alabama Press, 1973.

Donald, David. "The Pro-Slavery Argument Reconsidered." *Journal of Southern History* 37 (1971): 3–18.

Dorris, Jonathan Truman. *Pardon and Amnesty under Lincoln and Johnson: The Restoration of the Confederates to Their Rights and Privileges, 1861–1868*. Chapel Hill: University of North Carolina Press, 1953.

Douglas, Ann. *The Feminization of American Culture*. New York: Knopf, 1977.

DuBois, W. E. Burghardt. *Black Reconstruction: An Essay toward a History of the Part Which Black Folk Played in the Attempt to Reconstruct Democracy in America, 1860–1880*. New York: Harcourt, Brace, 1935.

———. *John Brown*. Philadelphia: G. W. Jacobs and Co., 1909.

DuBose, John Witherspoon. *The Life and Times of William Lowndes Yancey*. 2 vols. 1892. Reprint. New York: Peter Smith, 1942.

Dumond, Dwight L. *The Secession Movement, 1860–1861*. New York: Macmillan, 1931.

Dunaway, Wayland F. *History of the James River and Kanawha Company*. New York: Columbia University Press, 1922.

Dusinberre, William. *Civil War Issues in Philadelphia, 1856–1865*. Philadelphia: University of Pennsylvania Press, 1965.

Eaton, Clement. *The Freedom of Thought Struggle in the Old South*. Revised and enlarged edition. New York: Harper & Row, 1964.

———. "Henry A. Wise: A Liberal of the Old South." *Journal of Southern History* 7 (1941): 482–94.

———. "Henry A. Wise and the Virginia Fire Eaters of 1856." *Mississippi Valley Historical Review* 21 (1934–35): 495–512.

———. "Henry A. Wise: A Study in Virginia Leadership, 1850–1861."

West Virginia History 3 (1942): 187–204.

———. *A History of the Southern Confederacy*. New York: Free Press, 1954.

———. *The Mind of the South*. Baton Rouge: Louisiana State University Press, 1964.

Edelstein, Tilden G. *Strange Enthusiasm: A Life of Thomas Wentworth Higginson*. Studies in American Negro Life, edited by August Meier. New York: Atheneum, 1970.

Engerman, Stanley L. "Marxist Economic Studies of the Slave South." *Marxist Perspectives* 1 (Spring 1978): 148–64.

Erikson, Erik H. "Identity and the Life Cycle." In David Rapaport, ed., *Psychological Issues* 1 (1959): 3–171.

———. "Reflections on Dr. Borg's Life Cycle." *Daedalus* 105 (Spring 1976): 1–28.

Escott, Paul. *After Secession: Jefferson Davis and the Failure of Confederate Nationalism*. Baton Rouge: Louisiana State University Press, 1978.

Faust, Drew Gilpin. *A Sacred Circle: The Dilemma of the Intellectual in the Old South, 1840–1860*. Baltimore: Johns Hopkins University Press, 1977.

Fehrenbacher, Don E. *The Dred Scott Case: Its Significance in American Law and Politics*. New York: Oxford University Press, 1978.

———. *Prelude to Greatness: Lincoln in the 1850's*. Stanford: Stanford University Press, 1962.

Filler, Louis. *The Crusade against Slavery, 1830–1860*. New York: Harper & Row, 1960.

Finkelman, Paul. *An Imperfect Union: Slavery, Federalism and Comity*. Chapel Hill: University of North Carolina Press, 1981.

Fischer, David Hackett. "The Braided Narrative: Substance and Form in Social History." In *The Literature of Fact: Selected Papers from the English Institute*, edited with a foreword by Angus Fletcher, pp. 109–33. New York: Columbia University Press, 1976.

———. *The Revolution of American Conservatism: The Federalist Party in the Age of Jeffersonian Democracy*. New York: Harpers, 1965.

Foner, Eric. "The Fragmentation of Scholarship: History in Crisis." *Commonweal* 108 (18 December 1981): 723–26.

———. *Free Soil, Free Labor, Free Men: The Ideology of the Republican Party before the Civil War*. New York: Oxford University Press, 1970.

———. "Thaddeus Stevens, Confiscation and Reconstruction." In *The Hofstadter Aegis: A Memorial*, edited by Stanley Elkins and Eric McKitrick, pp. 154–83. New York: Knopf, 1974.

———. "Yes, Va., There Was a Civil War." *New York Times*, 14 September 1980.

Forgie, George B. *Patricide in the House Divided: A Psychological Inter-*

pretation of Lincoln and His Age. New York: Norton, 1979.

Fox-Genovese, Elizabeth. "Psychohistory versus Psychodeterminism: The Case of Rogin's Jackson." *Reviews in American History* 3 (December 1975): 407–18.

Fox-Genovese, Elizabeth, and Eugene Genovese. "The Political Crisis of Social History: A Marxian Perspective." *Journal of Social History* 10 (1976–77): 205–20.

Fredrickson, George M. *The Black Image in the White Mind: The Debate on Afro-American Character and Destiny, 1817–1914*. New York: Harper & Row, 1971.

———. "A Man But Not a Brother: Abraham Lincoln and Racial Equality." *Journal of Southern History* 41 (1975): 39–58.

Freehling, Alison Goodyear. *Drift toward Dissolution: The Virginia Slavery Debate of 1831–1832*. Baton Rouge: Louisiana State University Press, 1982.

Freehling, William W. "The Editorial Revolution, Virginia, and the Coming of the Civil War." *Civil War History* 16 (1970): 64–72.

———. "The Founding Fathers and Slavery." *American Historical Review* 77 (February 1972): 81–93.

———. *Prelude to Civil War: The Nullification Controversy in South Carolina, 1816–1836*. New York: Harper & Row, 1966.

Freeman, Douglas S. *Lee's Lieutenants: A Study in Command*. 3 vols. New York: Charles Scribner's Sons, 1942–46.

———. *R. E. Lee: A Biography*. 4 vols. New York: Charles Scribner's Sons, 1934–35.

Gaines, William H., Jr., ed. *Biographical Register of Members of the Virginia State Convention of 1861, First Session*. Richmond: Virginia State Library, 1969.

Gatell, Frank Otto. "Spoils of the Bank War: Political Bias in the Selection of Pet Banks." *American Historical Review* 70 (October 1969): 35–58.

Genovese, Eugene D. *The Political Economy of Slavery: Studies in the Economy and Society of the Slave South*. New York: Pantheon, 1965.

———. *Roll, Jordan, Roll: The World the Slaves Made*. New York: Pantheon, 1974.

———. "Toward a Psychology of Slavery: An Assessment of the Contribution of *The Slave Community*," in *Revisiting Blassingame's The Slave Community: The Scholars Respond*, edited by Al-Tony Gilmore, pp. 27–41. Westport, Conn.: Greenwood Press, 1978.

———. *The World the Slaveholders Made: Two Essays in Interpretation*. New York: Pantheon, 1969.

Gerteis, Lewis S. *From Contraband to Freedman: Federal Policy toward Southern Blacks, 1861–1865*. Westport, Conn.: Greenwood Press, 1973.

Goldfield, David R. *Urban Growth in the Age of Sectionalism: Virginia, 1847–1861*. Baton Rouge: Louisiana State University Press, 1977.

______. "Urban-Rural Relations in the Old South: The Example of Virginia." *Journal of Urban History* 2 (1976): 146–68.

Goldin, Claudia Dale. *Urban Slavery in the American South, 1820–1860*. Chicago: University of Chicago Press, 1976.

Goldman, Perry M., and James S. Young, eds. *The United States Congressional Directories, 1789–1840*. New York: Columbia University Press, 1973.

Goodrich, Carter. "The Virginia System of Mixed Enterprise: A Study of State Planning of Internal Improvements." *Political Science Quarterly* 64 (1949): 355–87.

Graebner, Norman A., ed. *Politics and the Crisis of 1860*. Urbana: University of Illinois Press, 1961.

Gray, Lewis C. *History of Agriculture in the Southern United States to 1860*. 2 vols. Washington, D.C.: Carnegie Institution, 1933.

Green, Constance McLaughlin. *The Secret City: A History of Race Relations in the Nation's Capital*. Princeton: Princeton University Press, 1967.

Gunderson, Robert G. *The Log-Cabin Campaign*. Lexington: University Press of Kentucky, 1957.

______. *Old Gentlemen's Convention: The Washington Peace Conference of 1861*. Madison: University of Wisconsin Press, 1961.

Gutman, Herbert G. *The Black Family in Slavery and Freedom, 1750–1925*. New York: Pantheon, 1976.

Hagans, John Marshall. *Brief Sketch of the Erection and Formation of the State of West Virginia from the Territory of Virginia*. Charleston, W.Va.: Poulter Printing Co., 1891.

Hall, Granville D. *The Rending of Virginia, A History*. Chicago: Mayer and Miller, 1902.

Hamilton, James Cleland. "John Brown in Canada." *Canadian Magazine* 4 (December 1894): 119–40.

Hickin, Patricia. "Gentle Agitator: Samuel M. Janney and the Antislavery Movement in Virginia, 1842–1851." *Journal of Southern History* 37 (1971): 159–90.

______. "John C. Underwood and the Anti-Slavery Movement in Virginia, 1847–1860." *Virginia Magazine of History and Biography* 73 (1965): 165–68.

Higham, John. *From Boundlessness to Consolidation: The Transformation of American Culture, 1848–1860*. Ann Arbor: William L. Clements Library, 1969.

Hill, Lawrence F. *Diplomatic Relations between the United States and Brazil*. 1932. Reprint. New York: Kraus Reprint, 1969.

Hinton, Richard. *John Brown and His Men*. 1894. Reprint. New York: Arno Press, 1968.

Holst, Hermann von. *The Constitutional and Political History of the United States*. 8 vols. Chicago: Callaghan and Company, 1876–92.

———. *John Brown*. Edited by Frank Preston Stearns. Boston: Cupples and Hurd, 1889.

Holt, Michael F. *The Political Crisis of the 1850's*. New York: John Wiley and Sons, 1978.

Howard, Warren S. *American Slavers and the Federal Law, 1837–1862*. Berkeley: University of California Press, 1963.

Hudson, Frederic, *Journalism in the United States from 1690 to 1872*. New York: Harper and Brothers, 1873.

Hunter, Andrew. "John Brown's Raid." *Southern History Association Publications* 1 (1897): 165–95.

Jackson, Luther P. *Free Negro Labor and Property Holding in Virginia, 1830–1860*. Studies in American Negro Life, edited by August Meier. 1942. Reprint. New York: Atheneum, 1969.

Jenkins, William S. *Proslavery Thought in the Old South*. 1935. Reprint. Gloucester, Mass.: Peter Smith, 1960.

Johannsen, Robert W. *Stephen A. Douglas*. New York: Oxford University Press, 1973.

Johnson, Michael P. "A New Look at the Popular Vote for Delegates to the Georgia Secession Convention." *Georgia Historical Quarterly* 56 (1972): 259–75.

———. "Planters and Patriarchy: Charleston, 1800–1860." *Journal of Southern History* 46 (1980): 45–73.

———. *Toward a Patriarchal Republic: The Secession of Georgia*. Baton Rouge: Louisiana State University Press, 1977.

Johnston, F. *Memorials of Old Virginia Clerks*. Lynchburg, Va.: J. P. Bell & Co., 1888.

Jones, Rev. J. William, comp. *Army of Northern Virginia Memorial Volume*. 1880. Reprint. Dayton, Ohio: Morningside Bookshop, 1976.

Jung, Carl G. "The Stages of Life." In *Collected Works*, edited by Sir Herbert Read et al., translated by R. F. C. Hall. 18 vols. 8:387–403. London: Routledge & Kegan Paul, 1953–77.

Klein, Philip S. *President James Buchanan*. University Park: Pennsylvania State University Press, 1962.

Knoles, George Harmon, ed. *The Crisis of the Union, 1860–1861*. Baton Rouge: Louisiana State University Press, 1965.

Latner, Richard B. "A New Look at Jacksonian Politics." *Journal of American History* 51 (March 1975): 943–69.

Levinson, Daniel J., et al. *The Seasons of a Man's Life*. New York: Knopf, 1978.

Lipset, Seymour M., and Earl Raab. *The Politics of Unreason: Right Wing Extremism in America, 1790–1970*. New York: Harper & Row, 1970.

Litwack, Leon F. *Been in the Storm So Long: The Aftermath of Slavery*. New York: Knopf, 1979.

Livermore, Thomas L. "The Failure to Take Petersburg, June 15, 1864." *Papers of the Military Historical Society of Massachusetts* 5 (1906): 35–73.

Lloyd, Christopher. *The Navy and the Slave Trade: The Suppression of the African Slave Trade in the Nineteenth Century*. London: Longmans, Green, 1949.

Lockard, E. Kidd. "The Unfortunate Military Career of Henry A. Wise in Western Virginia." *West Virginia History* 31 (1969): 40–54.

Loveland, Anne C. *Southern Evangelicals and the Social Order, 1800–1860*. Baton Rouge: Louisiana State University Press, 1980.

Maddex, Jack P., Jr. "Proslavery Millennialism: Social Eschatology in Antebellum Southern Calvinism." *American Quarterly* 31 (1979): 46–62.

———. *The Virginia Conservatives, 1867–1879: A Study in Reconstruction Politics*. Chapel Hill: University of North Carolina Press, 1970.

Maddox, William Arthur. *The Free School Idea in Virginia before the Civil War: A Phase of Political and Social Evolution*. New York: Teachers College, Columbia University, 1918.

Mathews, Donald G. *Slavery and Methodism: A Chapter in American Morality, 1780–1845*. Princeton: Princeton University Press, 1965.

McCabe, W. Gordon. "Defence of Petersburg." *Southern Historical Society Papers* 2 (1876): 257–306.

McCormac, Eugene Irving. *James K. Polk, A Political Biography*. Berkeley: University of California Press, 1922.

McCormick, Richard P. *The Second American Party System: Party Formation in the Jacksonian Era*. Chapel Hill: University of North Carolina Press, 1966.

McDonald, John J. "Emerson and John Brown." *New England Quarterly* 44 (1971): 377–96.

McDonnell, Lawrence T. "Struggle against Suicide: James Henry Hammond and the Secession of South Carolina." *Southern Studies* 22 (1983): 109–37.

McFaul, John M. *The Politics of Jacksonian Finance*. Ithaca: Cornell University Press, 1972.

McFaul, John M., and Frank Otto Gatell. "The Outcast Insider: Reuben M. Whitney and the Bank War." *Pennsylvania Magazine of History and Biography* 91 (1967): 115–44.

McGregor, James C. *The Disruption of Virginia*. New York: Macmillan, 1922.

McMaster, John Bach. *A History of the People of the United States, from the Revolution to the Civil War*. 8 vols. New York: D. Appleton and Co., 1884–1926.

McPherson, James M. "The Fight against the Gag Rule: Joshua Leavitt and Antislavery Insurgency in the Whig Party, 1839–1842." *Journal of Negro History* 48 (1963): 177–95.

McWhiney, Grady. "Who Whipped Whom? Confederate Defeat Re-examined." *Civil War History* 11 (1965): 5–26.

Meerse, David E. "Origins of the Buchanan-Douglas Feud Reconsidered." *Journal of the Illinois State Historical Society* 67 (1974): 154–74.

———. "Presidential Leadership, Suffrage Qualifications, and Kansas in 1857." *Civil War History* 24 (1978): 293–313.

Merk, Frederick. *Fruits of Propaganda in the Tyler Administration*. Cambridge, Mass.: Harvard University Press, 1971.

———. *Slavery and the Annexation of Texas*. New York: Knopf, 1972.

Milhous, Phil. "A Footnote to John Brown's Raid." *Virginia Magazine of History and Biography* 67 (1959): 396–98.

Milton, George Fort. *The Eve of Conflict: Stephen A. Douglas and the Needless War*. Boston: Houghton Mifflin, 1934.

Moore, Barrington, Jr. *Injustice: The Social Bases of Obedience and Revolt*. New York: M. E. Sharpe, 1978.

Moore, Powell. "The Revolt against Jackson in Tennessee, 1835–1836." *Journal of Southern History* 2 (1936): 335–57.

Munford, Beverly Bland. *Virginia's Attitude toward Slavery and Secession*. New York: Longmans, Green, 1909.

Nathans, Sidney. *Daniel Webster and Jacksonian Democracy*. Baltimore: Johns Hopkins University Press, 1973.

Nevins, Allan. *The Emergence of Lincoln*. 2 vols. New York: Charles Scribner's Sons, 1950.

———. *Frémont, Pathmarker of the West*. New York: Harper and Bros., 1939.

———. *Ordeal of the Union*. 2 vols. New York: Charles Scribner's Sons, 1947.

———. *The War for the Union*. 4 vols. New York: Charles Scribner's Sons, 1959–69. Vol. 1, *The Improvised War, 1861–1862*. 1959.

Nichols, Roy F. *The Democratic Machine, 1850–1854*. 1923. Reprint. New York: AMS Press, 1967.

———. *The Disruption of American Democracy*. New York: Macmillan, 1948.

———. *Franklin Pierce: Young Hickory of the Granite Hills*. 1931. Reprint. Philadelphia: University of Pennsylvania Press, 1958.

Nicolay, John G., and John Hay. *Abraham Lincoln: A History*. 10 vols. New York: Century Company, 1890.

Oates, Stephen B. *To Purge This Land with Blood: A Biography of John Brown*. New York: Harper & Row, 1970.

O'Brien, John T. "Factory, Church, and Community: Blacks in Antebellum Richmond." *Journal of Southern History* 54 (1978): 509–36.

Overdyke, W. Darrell. *The Know-Nothing Party in the South*. Baton Rouge: Louisiana State University Press, 1950.

Palmer, Paul C. "Miscegenation as an Issue in the Arkansas Constitutional Convention of 1868." *Arkansas Historical Quarterly* 24 (1965): 99–119.

Paludan, Phillip Shaw. *A Covenant with Death: The Constitution, Law, and Equality in the Civil War Era*. Urbana: University of Illinois Press, 1975.

———. *Victims: A True Story of the Civil War*. Knoxville: University of Tennessee Press, 1981.

Parker, Elmer Oris. "Why Was Lee Not Pardoned?" *Prologue* 2 (1970): 181.

Patterson, A. W. *The Code Duello with Special Reference to the State of Virginia*. Richmond: Richmond Press, Inc., 1927.

Pearson, C. C., and J. Edwin Hendricks. *Liquor and Anti-Liquor in Virginia, 1619–1919*. Durham: Duke University Press, 1967.

Perman, Michael. *Reunion without Compromise: The South and Reconstruction, 1865–1868*. Cambridge, Eng.: Cambridge University Press, 1973.

Pletcher, David M. *The Diplomacy of Annexation: Texas, Oregon, and the Mexican War*. Columbia: University of Missouri Press, 1973.

Poage, George Rawlings. *Henry Clay and the Whig Party*. 1936. Reprint. Gloucester, Mass.: Peter Smith, 1965.

Pole, J. R. *Political Representation in England and the Origins of the American Republic*. New York: St. Martin's Press, 1966.

Porter, John W. H. *A Record of Events in Norfolk County, Virginia, from April 19, 1861, to May 10, 1862, with a History of the Soldiers and Sailors of Norfolk County, Norfolk City and Portsmouth Who Served in the Confederate States Army or Navy*. Portsmouth, Va.: W. A. Fiske, 1892.

Potter, David M. *The Impending Crisis, 1848–1861*. Completed and edited by Don E. Fehrenbacher. New York: Harper & Row, 1976.

———. *Lincoln and His Party in the Secession Crisis*. 2d ed. New Haven, Conn.: Yale University Press, 1962.

———. *The South and the Sectional Conflict*. Baton Rouge: Louisiana State University Press, 1968.

Pred, Allan. *Urban Growth and City-Systems in the United States, 1840–1860*. Cambridge, Mass.: Harvard University Press, 1980.

Pressly, Thomas J., and William H. Scofield. *Farm Real Estate Values in the United States by Counties, 1850–1959*. Seattle: University of Washington Press, 1965.

Quarles, Benjamin. *Allies for Freedom: Blacks and John Brown*. New York: Oxford University Press, 1974.

Rable, George. "Slavery, Politics, and the South: The Gag Rule as a Case Study." *Capital Studies* 3 (1975): 69–87.

Ratchford, B. U. *American State Debts*. Durham: Duke University Press, 1941.

Rawley, James A. "The General Amnesty Act of 1872: A Note." *Mississippi Valley Historical Review* 47 (1960–61): 480–84.

———. *Race and Politics: "Bleeding Kansas" and the Coming of the Civil War*. Philadelphia: Lippincott, 1969.

Reitz, Rosetta. *Menopause: A Positive Approach*. New York: Penguin, 1979.

Remini, Robert V. *Andrew Jackson*. New York: Twayne, 1966.

———. *Andrew Jackson and the Bank War: A Study in the Growth of Presidential Power*. New York: Norton, 1967.

Rhodes, James Ford. *History of the United States from the Compromise of 1850 to the Final Restoration of Home Rule at the South in 1877*. 8 vols. New York: Macmillan Co., 1913–19.

Rice, Harvey Mitchell. *The Life of Jonathan M. Bennett: A Study of the Virginias in Transition*. Chapel Hill: University of North Carolina Press, 1943.

Rice, Otis K. "Coal Mining in the Kanawha Valley to 1861: A View of Industrialization in the Old South." *Journal of Southern History* 31 (1965): 393–416.

———. "Eli Thayer and the Friendly Invasion of Virginia." *Journal of Southern History* 37 (1971): 575–96.

Rice, Philip M. "The Know-Nothing Party in Virginia, 1854–1856." *Virginia Magazine of History and Biography* 55 (1947): 61–75, 159–67.

Riley, Matilda White. "Aging, Social Change, and the Power of Ideas." *Daedalus* 107 (Fall 1978): 39–52.

Risjord, Norman. *The Old Republicans: Southern Conservatism in the Age of Jefferson*. New York: Columbia University Press, 1965.

———. "The Virginia Federalists." *Journal of Southern History* 3 (1967): 486–517.

Rives, George L. *The United States and Mexico, 1821–1848*. 2 vols. New York: Charles Scribner's Sons, 1913.

Roark, James L. *Masters without Slaves: Southern Planters in the Civil War and Reconstruction*. New York: Norton, 1977.

Robert, Joseph Clarke. *The Road from Monticello: A Study of the Virginia Slavery Debate of 1832*. Durham: Duke University Press, 1941.

Robertson, Alexander F. *Alexander H. H. Stuart, 1807–1891, A Biography*. Richmond: William Byrd Press, 1925.

Robertson, James I., Jr., and Richard M. McMurry, eds. *Rank and File: Civil War Essays in Honor of Bell Irvin Wiley*. San Rafael, Calif.: Presidio Press, 1976.

Rogin, Michael Paul. *Fathers and Children: Andrew Jackson and the Subjugation of the American Indian*. New York: Knopf, 1975.

Rose, Willie Lee. "Killing for Freedom." *New York Review of Books* 15 (3 December 1970): 12–19.

Scarborough, William Kauffman. *The Overseer: Plantation Management in the Old South*. Baton Rouge: Louisiana State University Press, 1966.

Schaaf, Morris. *Sunset of the Confederacy*. Boston: J. W. Luce and Company, 1912.

Schouler, James. *History of the United States of America under the Constitution*. 5 vols. New York: Dodd, Mead, 1880–91.

Schultz, Harold. *Nationalism and Sectionalism in South Carolina, 1852–1860: A Study of the Movement for Southern Independence*. Durham: Duke University Press, 1950.

Seager, Robert II. *And Tyler, too: A Biography of John and Julia Gardner Tyler*. New York: McGraw-Hill, 1963.

Sellers, Charles G., Jr. *James K. Polk, Continentalist, 1843–1846*. Princeton: Princeton University Press, 1966.

———. *James K. Polk, Jacksonian, 1795–1843*. Princeton: Princeton University Press, 1957.

Shanks, Henry T. "Conservative Constitutional Tendencies of the Virginia Secession Convention." In *Essays in Southern History Presented to Joseph Gregoire de Roulhac Hamilton, Ph.D., LL.D., by His Former Students at the University of North Carolina*, edited by Fletcher M. Green, pp. 28–48. Chapel Hill: University of North Carolina Press, 1949.

———. *The Secession Movement in Virginia, 1847–1861*. Richmond: Garrett and Massie, 1934.

Sharp, James R. *The Jacksonians versus the Banks: Politics in the States after the Panic of 1837*. New York: Columbia University Press, 1970.

Shenton, James P. *Robert John Walker: A Politician from Jackson to Lincoln*. New York: Columbia University Press, 1961.

Shoen, Harriet H., ed. "Pryce Lewis, Spy for the Union: Operations in Western Virginia, June–July, 1861." *Davis and Elkins Historical Magazine* 2 (1949): 22–30.

Shortreed, Margaret. "The Antislavery Radicals: From Crusade to Revolution, 1840–1868." *Past and Present* 16 (1959): 65–87.

Siegel, Fred. "The Paternalist Thesis: Virginia as a Test Case." *Civil War History* 25 (September 1979): 246–61.

Silbey, Joel H. *The Shrine of Party: Congressional Voting Behavior, 1841–1852*. Pittsburgh: University of Pittsburgh Press, 1967.

Simpson, Craig. "Political Compromise and the Protection of Slavery: Henry A. Wise and the Virginia Constitutional Convention of 1850–51." *Virginia Magazine of History and Biography* 83 (1975): 387–405.

Siviter, Anna (Pierpont). *Recollections of War and Peace, 1861–1868*. Edited by Charles H. Ambler. New York: G. P. Putnam's Sons, 1938.

Smith, George Winston. "Antebellum Attempts of Northern Business Interests to 'Redeem' the Upper South." *Journal of Southern History* 11 (1945): 177–213.

Smith, Justin H. *The Annexation of Texas*. 1911. Reprint. New York: AMS Press, 1971.

Soulsby, Hugh G. *The Right of Search and the Slave Trade in Anglo-American Relations, 1814–1862*. Baltimore: Johns Hopkins University Press, 1933.

Spaulding, Myra K. "Duelling in the District of Columbia." *Records of the Columbia Historical Society* 29 (1928): 117–210.

Stampp, Kenneth M. *The Era of Reconstruction, 1865–1877*. New York: Knopf, 1965.

———. *The Peculiar Institution: Slavery in the Antebellum South*. New York: Knopf, 1956.

Stathis, Stephen W. "John Tyler's Presidential Succession: A Reappraisal." *Prologue* 8 (Winter 1976): 223–36.

Stenberg, Richard R. "An Unnoted Factor in the Buchanan-Douglas Feud." *Journal of the Illinois State Historical Society* 25 (1932–33): 276–84.

Stephenson, George N. *The Political History of the Public Lands, from 1840 to 1862: From Pre-emption to Homestead*. Boston: Little, Brown, 1917.

Stewart, James Brewer. *Joshua R. Giddings and the Tactics of Radical Politics*. Cleveland: Case–Western Reserve University Press, 1970.

Stone, Charles P. "Washington on the Eve of War." In *Battles and Leaders of the Civil War*, edited by Robert Underwood Johnson and Clarence Clough Buel. 4 vols. 1:7–25. 1887–88. Reprint. New York: Thomas Yoseloff, 1956.

Sutch, Richard. "The Breeding of Slaves for Sale and the Westward Expansion of Slavery, 1850–1860." In *Race and Slavery in the Western Hemisphere: Quantitative Studies*, edited by Stanley L. Engerman and Eugene D. Genovese, pp. 173–210. Princeton: Princeton University Press, 1975.

Sutton, Robert P. "Nostalgia, Pessimism, and Malaise: The Doomed Aristocrat in Late Jeffersonian Virginia." *Virginia Magazine of History and Biography* 76 (1968): 41–55.

Sweig, Donald M. "Reassessing the Human Dimension of the Interstate Slave Trade." *Prologue* 12 (Spring 1980): 5–21.

Swem, Earl Gregg. *A Bibliography of Virginia*. 5 vols. Richmond: D. Bottom, 1916–55.

Swint, Henry Lee. *The Northern Teacher in the South, 1862–1870*. 1941. Reprint. New York: Octagon Books, 1967.

Sydnor, Charles S. "The Southerners and the Laws." *Journal of Southern History* 6 (February 1940): 3–23.

Tadman, Michael. "Slave Trading in the Old South: An Estimate of the Extent of the Inter-Regional Slave Trade." *Journal of American Studies* 13 (1979): 195–220.

Takaki, Ronald T. "The Movement to Reopen the African Slave Trade in South Carolina." *South Carolina Historical Magazine* 39 (1965): 38–54.

———. *A Pro-Slavery Crusade: The Agitation to Reopen the African Slave Trade*. New York: Free Press, 1971.

Temin, Peter. *The Jacksonian Economy*. New York: Norton, 1971.

Thomas, Benjamin P. *Theodore Weld: Crusader for Freedom*. New Brunswick, N.J.: Rutgers University Press, 1950.

Thornton, J. Mills, III. *Politics and Power in a Slave Society: Alabama, 1800–1860*. Baton Rouge: Louisiana State University Press, 1978.

Trelease, Allen. *White Terror: The Ku Klux Klan Conspiracy and Southern Reconstruction*. New York: Harper & Row, 1971.

Turman, Nora Miller. *The Eastern Shore of Virginia, 1603–1964*. Onancock, Va.: Eastern Shore News, Inc., 1964.

Tyler, Lyon G. "Virginia Principles." *Tyler's Quarterly* 9 (January 1928): 167–83.

———, ed. *Letters and Times of the Tylers*. 3 vols. Richmond and Williamsburg: Whittet and Shepperson, 1884–96.

Villard, Oswald G. *John Brown, 1800–1859: A Biography Fifty Years After*. 1909. Reprint. Gloucester, Mass.: Peter Smith, 1965.

Wagstaff, Thomas. "Call Your Old Master—'Master': Southern Political Leaders and Negro Labor during Presidential Reconstruction." *Labor History* 10 (1969): 323–45.

Wallace, Lee A., Jr. *A Guide to Virginia Military Organizations, 1861–1865*. Richmond: Virginia Civil War Commission, 1964.

Wallace, Michael. "Changing Concepts of Party in the United States: New York, 1815–1828." *American Historical Review* 74 (December 1968): 453–91.

White, Laura A. *Robert Barnwell Rhett: Father of Secession*. New York: Century Co., Published for the American Historical Association, 1931.

White, Leonard. *The Jacksonians: A Study in Administrative History, 1829–1861*. New York: Macmillan, 1954.

Whitman, Karen. "Re-evaluating John Brown's Raid at Harpers Ferry." *West Virginia History* 34 (October 1972): 46–84.

Wiecek, William W. *The Sources of Antislavery Constitutionalism in America, 1760–1848*. Ithaca: Cornell University Press, 1977.

Wilburn, Jean Alexander. *Biddle's Bank: The Crucial Years*. New York: Columbia University Press, 1967.

Willey, Waitman P. *An Inside View of the Formation of the State of West Virginia, with Character Sketches of the Pioneers in That Movement*. Wheeling: News Publishing Co., 1901.

Williams, Jack K. *Dueling in the Old South: Vignettes of Social History*. College Station: Texas A & M University Press, 1980.

Williams, John A. "The New Dominion and the Old: Antebellum and Statehood Politics as the Background of West Virginia's 'Bourbon Democracy.'" *West Virginia History* 33 (1972): 317–407.

———. *West Virginia: A Bicentennial History*. New York: Norton, 1976.

Wilson, Henry. *History of the Rise and Fall of the Slave Power in America*. 3 vols. 1872–77. Reprint. New York: Negro Universities Press, 1969.

Wiltse, Charles M. *John Calhoun*. 3 vols. Indianapolis: Bobbs-Merrill Co., 1944–51.

Wise, Barton H. *The Life of Henry A. Wise, 1806–1876*. New York: Macmillan, 1899.

———. "Memoir of General John Cropper of Accomac County, Virginia." [Richmond], 1892.

Wise, Jennings Cropper. *Col. John Wise of England (1617–1695) and America: His Ancestors and Descendants*. Richmond: Bell Book and Stationery Co., 1918.

Wolff, Gerald. "The Slavocracy and the Homestead Problem of 1854." *Agricultural History* 40 (1966): 101–11.

Woodward, C. Vann. *American Counterpoint: Slavery and Racism in the North-South Dialogue*. Boston: Little, Brown and Co., 1971.

———. *The Burden of Southern History*. Rev. ed. Baton Rouge: Louisiana State University Press, 1968.

Wooster, Ralph A. *The Secession Conventions of the South*. Princeton: Princeton University Press, 1962.

Wright, Gavin. *The Political Economy of the Cotton South: Households, Markets, and Wealth in the Nineteenth Century*. New York: Norton, 1978.

Wyatt-Brown, Bertram. "The Ideal Typology and Antebellum Southern History: A Testing of a New Approach." *Societas* 5 (Winter 1975): 1–29.

———. *Lewis Tappan and the Evangelical War against Slavery*. Cleveland: Case–Western Reserve University Press, 1969.

———. *Southern Honor: Ethics and Behavior in the Old South*. New

York: Oxford University Press, 1982.
Yonge, J. E. Davis. "Henry A. Wise and the Presidency." *Quarterly Periodical of the Florida Historical Society* 13 (October 1934): 65–81.

Unpublished Materials

Adkins, Edwin P. "Henry A. Wise in Sectional Politics, 1833–1860." Ph.D. dissertation, Ohio State University, 1948.
Alderson, William. "The Influence of Military Rule and the Freedmen's Bureau on Reconstruction in Virginia, 1865–1870." Ph.D. dissertation, Vanderbilt University, 1952.
Campbell, Otho Carlino. "John Sergeant Wise: A Case Study in Conservative-Readjuster Politics in Virginia, 1869–1889." Ph.D. dissertation, University of Virginia, 1979.
Conrad, Robert Edgar. "The Struggle for the Abolition of the Brazilian Slave Trade, 1808–1853." Ph.D. dissertation, Columbia University, 1967.
Currie, Gordon. "The Death of John Bell, April 23, 1861." Unpublished paper, University of Western Ontario, 1979.
Dent, Lynwood, Jr. "The Virginia Democratic Party, 1824–1847." 2 vols. Ph.D. dissertation, Louisiana State University, 1974.
Dillard, Tom. "Three Important Black Leaders in Phillips County History." Unpublished paper, Little Rock, Arkansas, 1978.
Fields, Emmett B. "The Agricultural Population of Virginia, 1850–1860." Ph.D. dissertation, Vanderbilt University, 1953.
Freeman, Douglas S. "The Attitude of Political Parties in Virginia towards Slavery and Secession, 1846–1861." Ph.D. dissertation, Johns Hopkins University, 1908.
Gaines, Francis P., Jr. "The Virginia Constitutional Convention of 1850–1851: A Study in Sectionalism." Ph.D. dissertation, University of Virginia, 1950.
Gay, Dorothy Ann. "The Tangled Skein of Romanticism and Violence in the Old South: The Southern Response to Abolitionism and Feminism, 1830–1861." Ph.D. dissertation, University of North Carolina, 1975.
Goldfield, David R. "The Triumph of Politics over Society: Virginia, 1851–1861." Ph.D. dissertation, University of Maryland, 1970.
Hahn, Steven H. "The Roots of Southern Populism: Yeoman Farmers and the Transformation of Georgia's Upper Piedmont, 1850–1890." Ph.D. dissertation, Yale University, 1979.
Hickin, Patricia. "Antislavery in Virginia, 1831–1861." Ph.D. dissertation, University of Virginia, 1968.
Jones, Robert R. "Forgotten Virginian: The Early Life and Career of

James Lawson Kemper, 1823–1865." M.A. thesis, University of Virginia, 1961.

Lang, Edith Mae. "The Effects of Net Interregional Migration on Agricultural Income Growth: The United States, 1850–60." Ph.D. dissertation, University of Rochester, 1971.

Lowe, Richard Grady. "Republicans, Rebellion and Reconstruction: The Republican Party in Virginia, 1856–1870." Ph.D. dissertation, University of Virginia, 1968.

McFarland, George M. "The Extension of Democracy in Virginia, 1850–1895." Ph.D. dissertation, Princeton University, 1934.

Neely, Frederick Tilden. "The Development of Virginia Taxation, 1725 to 1860." Ph.D. dissertation, University of Virginia, 1956.

Rice, Phillip M. "Internal Improvements in Virginia, 1775–1860." Ph.D. dissertation, University of North Carolina, 1948.

Siegel, Fred F. "A New South in the Old: Sotweed and Soil in the Development of Danville, Virginia." Ph.D. dissertation, University of Pittsburgh, 1978.

Simpson, Craig. "Henry A. Wise in Antebellum Politics, 1850–1861." Ph.D. dissertation, Stanford University, 1973.

Tadman, Michael. "Speculators and Slaves in the Old South: A Study of the American Domestic Slave Trade, 1820–1860." Ph.D. dissertation, University of Hull, 1977.

Turner, Charles W. "The Virginia Railroads, 1828–1860." Ph.D. dissertation, University of Minnesota, 1948.

Turner, John R. "The 1855 Gubernatorial Campaign in Virginia." M.A. thesis, University of Virginia, 1966.

Index